Motives for Writing

MOTIVES FOR WRITING

SECOND EDITION

ROBERT KEITH MILLER
University of St. Thomas

SUZANNE S. WEBB
Texas Woman's University

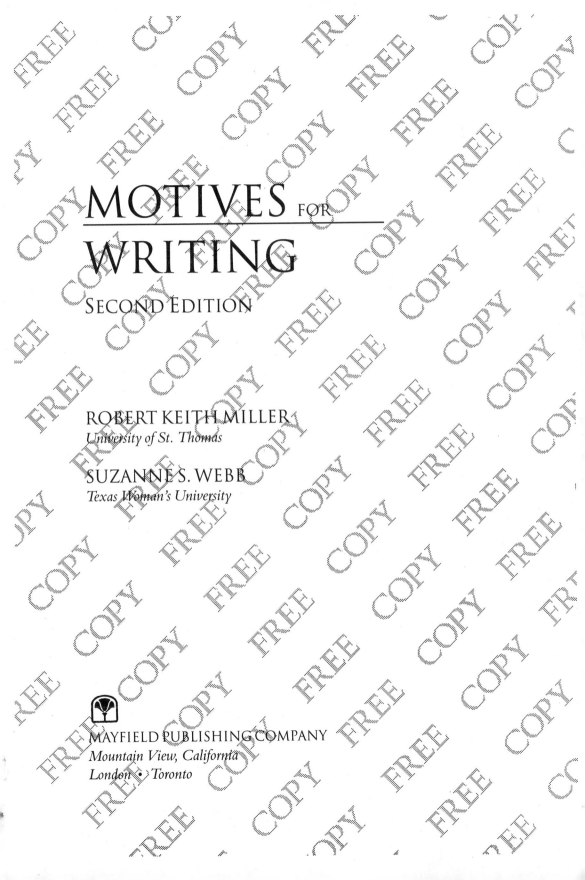

MAYFIELD PUBLISHING COMPANY
Mountain View, California
London • Toronto

LIBRARY OF CONGRESS CATALOGING-IN-PUBLICATION DATA

Motives for writing / [compiled by] Robert Keith Miller, Suzanne Webb.
    — 2nd ed.
        p.   cm.
    ISBN 1-55934-468-7
    1. College readers.   2. English language—Rhetoric.   I. Miller,
Robert Keith   II. Webb, Suzanne S.
    PE1417.M65   1994
    808'.0427—dc20   94-30498
                                                                    CIP

Manufactured in the United States of America
10 9 8 7 6 5 4 3 2 1

Mayfield Publishing Company
1280 Villa Street
Mountain View, California 94041

Sponsoring editor, Thomas V. Broadbent; *production editor,* Merlyn Holmes;
copyeditor, Carol Beal; *text designer,* David Bullen; *cover designer,* Donna Davis;
cover art, Gary Overacre; *manufacturing manager,* Aimee Rutter. The text was set
in 11/12 Bembo by Thompson Type and printed on 45# Restorecote Satin by
The Maple-Vail Book Manufacturing Group.

*Text and photo credits appear on page 549, which constitutes a continuation of the
copyright page.*

PREFACE

The second edition of this book continues to reflect our belief that helping students to discover and fulfill their motives for writing will help them to write well. As its title suggests, *Motives for Writing* emphasizes the importance of the writer's purpose—the reason for composing and the ends that process should achieve. In focusing upon purpose, we have been influenced by the work of such theorists as James Britton, James Kinneavy, and James Moffett, all of whom have shown that understanding the aims of discourse can contribute to better communication. We believe that an emphasis upon these aims can help students to develop the active minds that are essential for making sense of the world and conveying that sense to others.

Each of these aims—or motives, as we call them—is the subject of one of the introductions that we provide for Chapters 1–10. Our introduction for the book as a whole, "Writing for Your Life," places the aims within the context of other elements of the rhetorical situation, such as audience and occasion, and discusses strategies for invention, arrangement, and revision so that students will be better prepared to accomplish their aims.

All of the introductions are designed to provide both instructors and students with flexibility. We frequently remind writers that the aims of discourse can be pursued by different means, and as we discuss different methods of planning and drafting we encourage writers to choose the methods that work best for them. The entire book reflects our awareness that not only do different writers work well in different ways but the same writer may work well by using different approaches at different times. We have seen in our own classrooms that providing students with choices can enable them to overcome the difficulties writers encounter.

Because of the importance we attach to flexibility, we have not tied the book to the work of any single theorist. However, because we believe that the pentad of Kenneth Burke provides a useful means for helping students both to read and to write, we have drawn upon it at several points. Its presence is most noticeable in the headnotes that precede the selections in Chapters 1–10. Rather than write headnotes devoted to biographical and bibliographical information about the authors, we have used these notes to orient students to concerns of special importance in the selections that follow.

The selections themselves have been chosen to illustrate the various motives for writing and to provide examples of different writing styles and patterns of arrangement. Of the seventy-two selections, thirty-four are new in the second edition. Our selection of pieces has resulted in a second edition even more diverse than the first in terms of race, class, gender, and sexual orientation. We have also included a number of familiar pieces both because they have proven records as classroom favorites and because we wanted to spare instructors the necessity of undertaking an entirely new class preparation. Maya Angelou, Joan Didion, Annie Dillard, Mark Twain, Martin Luther King, Jr., Lewis Thomas, and Susan Glaspell are just a few of the authors represented by well-known works. Although the readings vary in length—with the longer, more challenging selections concentrated in the second half of the book—they all address issues that are likely to inspire good class discussion, and we have provided an alternative table of contents grouping selections on related topics for readers interested in pursuing a particular subject or theme.

To facilitate class discussion, every selection has its own apparatus. Although some of the Questions for Discussion are designed simply to gauge reading comprehension, most raise concerns that invite readers to think about what they have read and to formulate their own responses. Every reading is also followed by two Suggestions for Writing. Individual readers may well identify other questions and suggestions; we did not attempt to exhaust the possibilities of any piece. Our goal was simply to encourage thoughtful responses to reading, and we recognize that such responses, when encouraged, can take any number of directions.

Most chapters begin with short, readily accessible readings and conclude with more demanding pieces. And the motives themselves have been arranged according to the degree of difficulty inexperienced writers are likely to have with them. Instructors familiar with the first edition will find that we have changed the order in which we present the motives. Responding to the experience of instructors who used the first edition, we now have the two exploratory chapters ("Writing to Explore the Self" and "Writing to Explore an Idea") grouped together. We also moved our two chapters on exposition to an earlier position in the book and extensively revised the introductions to these chapters, now called "Writing to Report Information" and "Writing to Interpret Information," to clarify how these motives differ.

If you examine our new sequence of chapters, you will find that we begin with such writer-oriented motives as "Writing to Record a Memory" and "Writing to Explore the Self," move on to such topic-oriented motives as "Writing to Report Information" and "Writing to Interpret Information," and conclude with such reader-oriented motives as "Writing to Amuse Others" and "Writing to Persuade Others." But because every chapter is self-contained, the various motives can be studied in any sequence that seems appropriate for a specific class—just as the readings within any chapter can be read in a sequence determined by individual interests or needs.

A word here about the rhetorical modes: We teach that writing seldom involves conforming to a fixed pattern, that a single piece usually involves several modes, and that no mode is limited to any one motive. In other words, we present the modes as means that writers employ when pursuing different aims, but we do not present them as models to which writers should make their thoughts conform. We believe that instruction based upon fixed patterns of arrangement can turn writing into an academic exercise that bears little relation to the way writers write in the world beyond the classroom. Patterns such as definition, classification, and comparison are more likely to grow out of the act of writing than to be imposed at the outset as a framework to which invention must be subordinate. We recognize, however, that teachers of composition must be prepared to help students organize their thoughts, and the modes can be useful for this type of instruction. The Index by Rhetorical Strategy (Mode) beginning on page 549 is designed to be helpful in this regard. Our book thus encourages students not only to concern themselves with the modes when doing so might be useful but at the same time to recognize that arrangement is simply one of the writer's tools and not an end in itself.

In completing this edition of *Motives for Writing,* we are indebted to colleagues and friends with whom we have discussed our work. Mary Rose O'Reilley, Lon Otto, Joan Piorkowski, and Erika Scheurer all provided good counsel. Kimberly Allison wrote the instructor's manual—*Teaching Motives for Writing,* Second Edition, and also worked tirelessly to help us select new readings and secure permission to reprint the pieces we selected. We continue to be grateful to our friend Sally Reagan Ebest, who wrote the instructor's manual for the first edition and who remains very much a part of both the book and the manual. We also thank John Blodgett of the Congressional Research Service for his timely help. Merlyn Holmes, our production editor; Carol Beal, our manuscript editor; Jeanne Schreiber, Mayfield's art director; and Pamela Trainer, permissions editor, all provided much appreciated support. We also want to thank those instructors who told us, directly or indirectly, about their experience with the first edition. Finally, to Tom Broadbent, our editor, we both join in special thanks for the generosity with which he gave us friendship, advice, and attention to detail.

CONTENTS

> One of our best nature writers recalls Death Valley as a place that reveals "the unutterable beauty, terror, and strangeness of everything we think we know."

who feels the consequences of her education, the weight of her possibilities. . . ."

A flaming moth, caught within a candle's wax, illuminates a writer's night.

Believing that science is an adventure within a "wilderness of mystery," a leading medical educator explores why so many science classes are boring.

Focusing on *sodai gomi,* "bulky garbage," Fallows explores an aspect of Japanese culture that he witnessed when living in Japan.

By exploring a troubling word, and drawing upon memories of her own childhood, Naylor comes to a better understanding of her African-American heritage.

Visiting an exhibit of medieval torture instruments near where she goes for a massage prompts Rose to explore the relationship between pleasure and pain.

By describing a series of scenes most tourists would overlook, Orwell leads readers to reflect upon racism and exploitation.

Selzer explores what a visit to a slaughterhouse reveals about our relationship with animals.

After spending a week eating different kinds of dog food, the author reports what she learned about taste.

A reporter for the *New York Times* summarizes the life and career of a much-admired actress.

With powerful images, a Jesuit priest proclaims God's presence in the natural world.

In this one-act play, Glaspell offers evidence by which an audience can judge who is guilty of a farmer's murder and why it occurred.

READINGS ARRANGED BY SUBJECT AND THEME

Nature

Science and Technology

Sports

Motives for Writing

Introduction

Writing for Your Life

Writing can change your life. It can help you to deepen your understanding of yourself as well as to achieve the goals you set for yourself. It can help you to make sense of the information that assaults you daily and to present ideas so that others will take you seriously. And it can broaden your world by enabling you to communicate effectively with people you have never met.

Despite the tremendous advantages of writing well, many people persuade themselves that they can never learn to write because they believe that writing is a talent they were denied at birth. People who think in these terms are unlikely to write well, because they lack the motivation to take their writing seriously. It is true that some people learn to write more easily than others because they have a certain aptitude for it or because they have been encouraged by parents, friends, or good teachers. But to a large extent writing is a skill that can be learned by anyone who is willing to take the trouble. Believe that you will fail, and you are likely to fail. Believe that you can succeed, and you will have begun to succeed. It will certainly take time and effort to write successfully, for writing involves hard work; but you will find that this investment will pay rich dividends.

You probably know more about writing than you realize, but you may not know how to use that knowledge to accomplish the full range of writing you need to do. You may have been discouraged by assignments that seemed silly and pointless. If so, you probably wondered "Why?" and, when you finished, "So what?" What you sensed was that real writing is done for a real purpose. Someone has a motive for writing—a motive that is stronger than simply wanting to complete an assignment. There are, as you will see, many motives for writing. Whatever the specific motive may be, however, writers write because they understand that writing is a way to satisfy a purpose that is important to them.

This book takes the position that successful writing begins with having a motive for writing and understanding how that motive can be fulfilled. The ten chapters that follow this introduction discuss a number of these motives and show how various writers have realized them: to record a memory, to explore the self, to explore an idea, to report information, to interpret information, to evaluate something, to amuse others, to move others, and to persuade others. The final chapter emphasizes writing to understand reading, but the entire book assumes that reading is intimately connected to writing. Recognizing, through reading, the motives of other writers can help you to discover your own sense of what you hope to accomplish when you write and to understand the principles likely to help you succeed.

THE RHETORICAL SITUATION

Any act of writing involves five elements that together form what is called the rhetorical situation:

- Author
- Audience
- Purpose
- Topic
- Occasion

As writers pursue different motives, they emphasize certain elements of the rhetorical situation over others. Recording a memory and exploring the self focus mainly on satisfying the needs of the writer. Amusing, moving, and persuading others focus mainly on eliciting an appropriate response from the audience. Although reporting and interpreting information, evaluating something, and writing about reading certainly satisfy the writer's needs and require the writer to think about the reader's needs, they all focus in varying degrees on the subject matter or topic. Whatever your emphasis, though, you can seldom lose sight of any of these elements of the rhetorical situation for long.

Author

Some writers do their best work in the early morning, others at night. Some need a quiet place, and others write happily with music playing and friends wandering around the room. In short, different writers write best in different environments. To the extent that your time and circumstances permit, you should choose the environment that allows you to be most productive.

Although writers have different habits and write in different ways, good writers all have at least one common characteristic: They are active readers. As readers, they are constantly acquiring new information; much of it they may never use, but some of it will help them to write. To put it simply: The more you know, the more you have to say, and the easier it is to discover ideas for writing.

But good writers are also readers in another sense: They are critical readers of their own work. When they write—and especially when they revise—they consider their work not only from their own point of view (by asking, for example, "Have I said what I wanted to say?") but also from the point of view of readers (by asking, for example, "Is this point clear?"). Such writers understand that writing is a form of communication—usually a transaction between people.

One way of thinking about the variety of possible transactions between writers and readers is to envision them on a scale ranging from the personal and private at one end to the impersonal and public at the other, with additional motives brought into play as you move from the private toward the public. This is not to say that any one type of writing is necessarily better than another, just different. Successful writing calls upon the writer's ability to analyze the rhetorical situation and make appropriate adjustments.

Audience

Having a good sense of audience is one of the most important factors in writing well. Inexperienced writers often write as if they did not really expect anyone else to read what they have written. There are, without question, times when writers write solely for their own benefit, putting on paper words they have no intention of sharing with others; but most writing involves communicating with other people. The "others" with whom we communicate can range from a single individual, whom we may or may not know, to a large group that includes people we have never even met. When addressing an unfamiliar audience, beware of being ethnocentric—of assuming that your nation or your state is at the center of human affairs. Realize that readers from other regions may not be receptive to your ideas. And don't make the mistake of thinking that all your readers are exactly like you. In a large audience they may come from different socioeconomic groups, from different ethnic groups, and from different geographic regions. About half of them are probably of a different gender. Your readers may also differ in ways that are not readily apparent. A large audience—or even a small audience—can include readers who differ in religious faith, political affiliation, or sexual orientation. As a general rule, your writing will benefit if you are aware of how readers differ, for this awareness can help you to avoid questionable generalizations and language that has the potential to exclude or offend.

You can see how audiences differ if you think about a time that you wrote an essay explaining something to your fellow students but also had to turn it in to your English teacher. You might have used different language or different examples if you had not been going to turn it in to the teacher. For instance, your friends and your teacher need to know different things, and your friends may need their information more urgently than your teacher does. You will need to decide carefully how much information to give each audience, what order to put it in, and what to leave out.

Whoever these "others" may be, however, they are your readers; you must be concerned that they are well disposed to what you have to say and that they understand your meaning. One strategy for reaching these readers is to identify with them as much as possible—to become as much like them as you can, to put yourself in their shoes, to see through their eyes. Identifying with readers in this way requires imagination. To some extent, of course, you always imaginatively construct your audience, even when writing for a particular person you believe you know well—your English teacher, for instance. Because there is much about that audience you do not know, you must create an imaginary image of it to some extent. If you present yourself as a credible and well-intentioned writer, your readers are likely to be willing to join this imaginative creation and play whatever role is required of them.

At this point, we offer two principles that are useful in most rhetorical situations.

1. Whoever your readers may be, recognize their values and needs and do not rely too much on their patience and cooperation. If readers find that they have to work unnecessarily hard, or if they feel that a writer is underestimating their knowledge or their intelligence, they will often stop reading, even if they believe that the material is important.

2. Try to imagine more than one type of audience. If you dwell too much on a particular audience, especially one that has power and expertise, you may end up feeling intimidated. In such circumstances you may benefit from constructing another audience in your mind, an audience with which you feel comfortable. Doing so can help you to draft the first (and often most difficult) version of the work at hand, and you can always make adjustments for other readers as you revise.

Purpose

A writer's *purpose* is essentially the same as a writer's *motive;* both terms are used to describe what a writer hopes to accomplish. The benefit to a writer of having a clear sense of purpose is obvious. You are much more likely to accomplish your objective if you know what it is. When you are reading other people's writing, a good way to understand purpose is to ask yourself why a writer chose to approach a topic one way rather than another. For example, when reading a humorous essay, you might immediately recognize that the writer's motive was to amuse, but you might be able to enrich your understanding of the essay by considering why someone would want to be amusing on the topic this writer chose.

We have already identified a number of motives for writing, each of which will be discussed individually in the chapters that follow this general introduction. Keep in mind, however, that writing often reveals an interplay among various motives. For example, although the primary purpose of an argument may be to persuade readers to accept some belief or undertake some action, an argument might easily include paragraphs devoted to informing, amusing, or moving readers. Having more than one purpose is fine as long as one purpose does not conflict with another in the same work. An a general rule, however, you should try to make one purpose prevail within any one work, for this will help make the work unified and coherent.

Topic

Although the terms *subject* and *topic* are often used interchangeably, a distinction can be made between them. *Subject* is often used to describe the general area that a writer has considered; *topic* identifies the specific part of that subject that the writer has discussed. Writers often begin with a subject and then narrow it down to a topic suitable for the work (and audience) they have in mind. If you are interested in writing about the Second World War, you could not hope to discuss more than a small part of this subject in an essay of three or four pages. The subject contains many possible topics, and you might decide to write about the attack on Pearl Harbor or the firebombing of Tokyo—both of which topics might be narrowed even further. Decisions about how much to include depend on whom you are writing for and why as well as upon the length appropriate for the occasion.

By narrowing a subject to a specific topic, you focus attention on something that you want your readers to see in detail. To use an analogy: If you are watching a football game from a seat high up in a large stadium, you have a very large field of view, much of which is totally irrelevant to the game—thousands of spectators, the curve of the bleachers, the pitch of the ramps, and so on. Unless you find some way to narrow that field of view, you are going to be distracted by these irrelevancies, and you will not be able to get a clear view of exactly what is happening on the field. A pair of binoculars will help immensely, for you can train them on the players, and the binoculars will magnify the images of the players so that you can see more details of each play. However, you have to adjust the focus of the binoculars to see the players clearly. Just as you have too large a field of view from the top of the stadium, you may target too large an area to write about at first; and, as you proceed, you may discover that you are most interested in a much smaller part of it. Thus, just as you would at the ball game, you must shut out some details and focus on others.

Finally, a good topic will lead to your saying something worth saying. Some topics have been written about so extensively that you may find it difficult to communicate something that your readers do not already know. A writer with an original topic, or a topic about which something new can be said, has a head start on maintaining the interest of readers. Because choosing a topic is such an important part of writing well, we will offer additional advice on how to do it later in this introduction.

Occasion

Writing is also influenced by the particular event or circumstance that prompted it—what is called the *occasion* for writing. Writing an essay in class, for example, may be very different from writing an essay out of class to be turned in next week—even though the author, audience, purpose, and topic have remained the same. Or suppose you want to write a letter to a friend. If you are a thoughtful writer, your tone will reflect what you know of your friend's state of mind even though the basic elements of the rhetorical situation have remained the same: A light letter full of jokes might not be appropriate if you knew your friend had just sustained a serious loss. A sense of occasion helps writers to satisfy these conventions.

In summary, let's look at all the elements of the rhetorical situation in the context of academic writing. Your purpose is in part determined by your assignment. However, your thoughtful response to that assignment, your care in making sure that you satisfy your instructor's expectations, and your clear sense of what you want to accomplish regarding that assignment are the means for fulfilling that purpose. The audience and the occasion determine your topic, as well as how you choose to present yourself— serious or humorous, confident or timid, and so on. For instance, your political science instructor might expect you to demonstrate an objective rather than a partisan attitude in a report summing up the results of a recent session of Congress. The nature of the assignment will influence not only your purpose but also your vocabulary and tone. Your physics instructor, for example, might wonder if you knew what you were talking about if you substituted the word *doughnut* for the technical physics term *torus* in a report on fusion reaction; *doughnut* is the wrong level of language for this occasion, even though it can mean *torus* and might be used in an informal conversation between physicists. Moreover, writing a formal paper in the sciences often requires a pattern of organization that is inappropriate for writing in the humanities. Thus, a paper reporting the results of research in psychology might begin with a summary (or abstract) and then move on to separate sections devoted to research methods, results, and implications. Although each of these examples involves the expectations of certain readers (the audience), these expectations have in turn been shaped by the conventions of different disciplines.

THE WRITING PROCESS

How do writers go about meeting the demands we have just discussed? The answer is that there are about as many ways as there are writers; everyone has his or her own process. Generally speaking, however, every successful writing process includes planning, drafting, revising, and editing, even though the writer may sometimes be engaged in all of these activities at once. That is, there is no predetermined order in which these activities must occur, no obligation to complete one activity before beginning another. When we write, we loop back and forth over our own mental tracks time and again, rethinking, rearranging, restating, researching. We may not complete one loop before we're off in another direction with another loop. And we don't necessarily begin at the beginning; sometimes, we finish at the beginning. Writing, in short, is a fairly chaotic process. Still, we do know some things about it.

Writers need something to write about, and finding a topic is often the most difficult part of the writing process. Writing often goes best when we can write about something we are vitally interested in and know a good deal about; sometimes, however, we are required to write on a subject dictated by someone else or by circumstances. In that case the preliminary work becomes deciding what to say about that subject. Regardless of whether we have chosen the subject or had it imposed on us, however, we have to plan what to include and what to leave out. We also must settle on the order of presenting our material. Some of this work may go on informally while we are actually doing other things, but some of it is more deliberately structured, as in the lists we may make to be sure we don't forget important points.

Once we have an idea of what we want to write about, we may begin *drafting,* writing it down. Here is where the "looping back" (or recursive) nature of the writing process is most readily apparent. We may draft several pages to discover what we want to say and then throw out all but two or three sentences. Or if we are more confident of what we mean to say, we may draft several pages before we are interrupted; then when we come back to the writing, we may start out by revising what we have written, or we may find ourselves starting over—but we'll save the writing we're not using because it may be useful later. We may also draft a part of the writing we feel most comfortable about first to warm up our brains in an effort to hit our intellectual stride for the more difficult parts. It doesn't matter if the piece of writing we do first will come near the end. We'll put it where it belongs when we have a clearer vision of the shape of what we are saying.

When we've developed all of these pieces of writing, we can weave them together—a process we may have begun earlier. If we begin to see gaps that we have to fill with new writing, we're doing part of our job as writers. And if we haven't already done so, we have to find a way to begin and a way to conclude. We may have been revising all along, reshaping sentences that disappoint us as soon as we see them and rearranging paragraphs when we are only midway through our initial draft. But when we can see the whole composition, we can move into a different kind of *revising*, testing everything we say against what we have already said or what comes later, seeking the greatest possible clarity and coherence.

Unlike revising, which often generates new writing, *editing* is primarily devoted to polishing what we have already written. When editing, we look for ways to tighten our prose, eliminating wordy constructions or unnecessary repetition. We also check our grammar, punctuation, and spelling. Many writers treat editing as the final stage of their writing process; they recognize that there is no point in perfecting material that they may eliminate during revision. Others find comfort in fixing errors when they are briefly stymied at an earlier point of their process (instead of stopping work altogether), but their work is also likely to benefit from additional editing when they reach the end of their writing process.

Although there's no real order to the parts of the writing process, obviously we can't revise what never was written; and we've stopped all the other parts of the process when we do final proofreading. It is therefore within the boundaries defined by finding a topic and proofreading the final copy that the writing process occurs.

Finding a Topic

So how do we know what we want to write about? Conventional wisdom tells new writers, "Write what you know," "Write about what you enjoy"—sound advice, but not terribly practical if you're not sure what you know and why what you know could interest other readers.

For most of us a choice of subject is seldom entirely free, and for everyone the subject for writing derives directly from the rhetorical situation. In this way college writing is not really very different from writing on the job. In college writing the choice of a subject is conditioned by the courses in which the writer is enrolled—by the academic discipline as well as by the dictates of the professor. In the working world the subject for writing depends on the constraints of employment—the employer's attitudes and requirements. Insofar as we have choices, we are well advised to follow our interests, keeping in mind that our topic should be appropriate for our purpose and our audience.

Consider the full rhetorical situation in which you are writing: Precisely what do you hope to accomplish, and what information do you need to do it? Ask yourself who will read your writing, bearing in mind that your audience may be larger than it seems: You might write a memo to your boss, but your boss may decide to distribute it to other people in the company. Remember also the occasion for writing: You may have a topic you want to bring to the attention of your boss, but the time isn't right. You may have to wait for a more opportune occasion. In the meantime you have to find something else to say.

CHAOTIC PROCESSES Ways of exploring a subject fall rather naturally into two groups: chaotic processes and structured processes. Among the chaotic processes for exploring subjects are those that rely on the subconscious knowledge we all have. They are time-tested techniques for encouraging that kind of knowledge to surface so that we can impose order on it. Depending upon your inclination and your topic, two of these techniques—*brainstorming* and *freewriting*—may be interchangeable; the other technique, *mapping,* places ideas in spatial relationships to each other. You may already be familiar with these methods; if they have worked for you in the past, by all means continue to use them. If you've never tried them, you may find them useful. But if they don't work for you, try something else, perhaps some of the structured processes described later.

Brainstorming A time-honored way to increase creativity and productivity is to get a small group of people together for unstructured discussion—a process called brainstorming; but it can also be used successfully by one person looking for ideas about a subject. It involves listing everything that occurs to you (or that others say) about the idea as fast as possible in a limited period of time. You can do it over and over, checking your list at the end of each spurt of intensive thinking.

To try it out, get a pen or pencil and a sheet of paper. Set your alarm clock or the oven timer for fifteen or twenty minutes. Concentrate on your subject. Ask yourself what you know about it and jot down your answers. As ideas come crowding to the surface, write as fast as you can to jot them down. Don't worry about spelling or sequence or anything except putting ideas on paper. And don't worry about whether your answers seem worthwhile. You can evaluate them later. The point is to get as many thoughts as you can on paper. If you keep your mind working, a good idea may come only after a dozen that you'll later reject. Stop when the alarm goes off and take a few minutes to look over your jottings. Mark ideas you find useful or interesting. (Colored markers ease the task of grouping those that seem to go together.) If you think you still don't have enough to go on, you can brainstorm again, perhaps focusing on one of the ideas you wrote down or taking a new direction; but give yourself a rest between sessions.

Freewriting Like brainstorming, freewriting is done nonstop, it occurs intensely for a short period of time, and it is done without worrying about audience. Although freewriting will produce much that is unusable, it can also produce much that will be surprisingly important, attesting to the notion that our subconscious minds contain enormous amounts of valuable information. Freewriting is a way to get some use out of this information, and it may very well give us a focus for the rest of our work on the subject. Sometimes, when we find an approach to a subject through brainstorming, freewriting unlocks a wealth of ideas to pursue.

Some writers like to think informally about an idea before they put pen to paper; others like to simply begin and see whatever comes out. Both approaches are okay. When you begin writing, don't worry if you can't think of something to write. Just write anything; it doesn't matter what it is or whether it makes sense. Don't stop for any reason: to figure out how to spell a word, to choose between two terms, or for any other reason. Don't worry if you find yourself straying from your guide sentence at the top of the page. The new direction may be useful. When your buzzer sounds, stop writing and look at what you have. If you find a good idea, you may be able to develop it into a part of your finished work or even into an entire draft.

Mapping Mapping (sometimes called *clustering* or *webbing*) is a way of visually analyzing the parts of a subject. Write the subject in the middle of your paper and circle it. From the edges of the circle, draw lines radiating outward to nodes labeled to represent the main parts of the subject. Repeat this process for each of those nodes until you have exhausted all the information you have. You will notice that some parts generate several levels, whereas others do not, and that the interrelationships between parts of the idea are easy to see in this kind of graphic chart. Consider the illustration on page 11, but note that no two maps look alike.

Brainstorming, freewriting, and mapping can be used together to bring some order to the chaotic information that surfaces from the unconscious. Try pulling some of the related ideas that surfaced during a brief brainstorming session into a single statement and jotting that statement at the top of your freewriting paper. When you are through freewriting, look at what you have produced and try to map related ideas. This activity will focus your efforts to find the vein of gold in the ton of sludge.

STRUCTURED PROCESSES Structured processes are conscious ways to encourage thinking along specific lines. People have been successful with these techniques for centuries. In classical times Aristotle provided thirty-two ways to get below the surface of a subject. They are called *topoi,* the word from which *topic* has been derived. In our own century the philosopher Kenneth Burke offered an alternative way to explore a subject by using five elements called the *pentad.* A related method, *journalists' questions,*

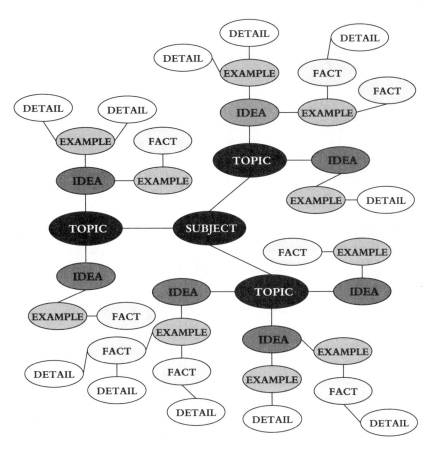

FIGURE 1. Mapping

lists six aspects of a subject; and *varying perspectives,* a highly systematic approach, offers at least nine ways to view a subject.

Classical Topics It is often useful to look at a subject from the perspectives originally developed by Aristotle to help people generate ideas. Aristotle proposed that questions can be asked to define what something is and others to compare and contrast it with other things. Still other questions help in examining the relationships that are possible: cause, antecedent, contraries, contradictions. Questions about circumstances explore matters of possibility and factuality. And questions about testimony—authority, statistics, maxims, law, examples—can help writers support their points.

Originally designed as ways to discover proofs in persuasive writing, Aristotle's topics provided a foundation for the work of many other rhetoricians and have played an important role in education for more than two thousand years. One of the advantages of the topics is that they remind us to consider both the general qualities and particular features of any given subject. At least one of Aristotle's questions should always be appropriate, whatever we want to write about. The answers we provide help us to decide what we want or need to say.

Aristotle identified thirty-two topics, and few people are able to keep them all in mind. But without memorizing a long list of topics, you can still benefit from classical rhetoric by asking yourself a series of questions when preparing to write. These questions can help you not only to generate ideas when you feel stymied but also to narrow and focus a subject so that you can choose an appropriate topic.

- Should I provide an *example* of what I mean?
- Should I *divide* this subject into parts, discuss each separately, or focus upon a single part?
- Can I *classify* this subject by putting it within categories?
- Would it be useful to *narrate,* or provide a short story?
- Would it be appropriate to see this subject as a *process* and explain how it takes place?
- Should I explain what *caused* this subject or what its *effects* will be?
- Should I *define* what I mean?
- Should I *describe* the features of my subject?
- Should I *compare* my subject to something similar or *contrast* it with something with which it might be confused?

Providing the answers to these questions has led some people to think that writing needs to be organized along the lines that the topics suggest. You may have already studied a book that taught you how to write a "description" or a "definition." Such assignments have a certain value, but it is much like the value that practicing scales has for a musician. Outside of classes in composition, a writer is unlikely to wake up some morning and decide, "Today, I am going to write an essay of comparison and contrast." Writers are much more likely to begin with a motive or a topic and then decide upon a plan that best suits what they want to say. When you use classical topics or questions derived from them, think of them as a way to get started rather than as a pattern of organization that you are bound to follow.

Pentad   Kenneth Burke believed that neither reading nor writing can be passive. Burke's pentad explains how this active response takes place. We'll be discussing it here as an aid to thinking about reading and writing and will draw upon it elsewhere to help you understand the reading selections in the chapters that follow.

Burke defines five elements that are always present to some degree in a piece of writing:

Scene
Purpose
Act
Agent
Agency

For instance, a writer may concentrate attention on a particular locale in a particular moment in time; these are a part of what Burke calls *scene.*

Similarly, a writer may choose to emphasize a *purpose,* that is, a motive, rationale, or reason; a goal, aim, or objective; an intention or design; a mission or cause. And, of course, the writer may choose to focus on an event, an *act,* which may involve examining something that happens but may also include delving into the meaning of the event. Sometimes, a writer chooses to spotlight an *agent,* which may be a person but may also be a force or a power or a catalyst for producing an event. The other element the writer may examine is *agency,* which can be described as an instrument that causes something, the mechanism or vehicle by which something is accomplished.

But even if a writer has emphasized one element of the pentad, you should be able to find the others if you look for them. Burke's own analogy may help you to understand how the various elements of the pentad are related to one another. He compared them to the five fingers on a hand—separate, but ultimately joined. Tracing down one finger should help you make a path to another. We can, of course, cross our fingers or clench them together. Similarly, we can consider any element of the pentad in combination with any other to establish a relationship (what Burke called a *ratio*) among the elements. And these relationships expand meaning. For instance, an act can be examined in its relationship to the scene, the agent, the agency, and the purpose; just as the scene can be examined in relationship to act, agent, agency, and purpose; and so on. These expanded perspectives from which to view the subject matter are useful to writers as well as readers. They help us to understand more fully and more clearly what we mean to say as well as what some other writer meant us to know. Two examples illustrate how this method works. The first shows that the method is especially useful when we apply it to drama (hence the method is called *dramatistic*), and the second shows how suggestive it can be when we think about any subject.

This book includes a play called *Trifles,* in which the scene is a farmhouse, the act is a murder, and the agency is a piece of rope. When we consider the act in terms of the scene, we learn the agent and the agent's purpose—who killed the victim and why. An examination of the scene alone tells us that the farmhouse is old, cold, messy, and deserted. Examining the scene in the light of the act reveals much about the killer's motivation—what kind of a husband the victim was, that the couple had no children, and a number of other facts that lead us to decide who committed the murder.

For the second example, suppose the subject is hot weather. We can examine what people do and how they feel in hot weather, when and where hot weather occurs and what the world looks like when it is hot, what causes hot weather, how hot weather develops, and what purpose it serves. And as Burke argued, we will discover the most if we view each of these parts of the pentad in relation to every other part (the ratios).

This dramatistic method has been used to analyze all kinds of subjects and to reveal how the elements of which a subject is composed relate to each other. For example, what happens when we see the act in relation to the scene? In our example about hot weather, we can look at what people do (act) in certain cultures (scene) when it is hot. Or we can examine how people respond to hot weather in the South and in the North or how we lived with hot weather before air-conditioning.

If you think about the pentad in this way, your understanding of an event changes as you combine and recombine the elements. This leads also to the idea Burke later advanced that the pentad is enriched and expanded by considering the combinations in the context of social concerns and economic processes. When we do that, we gain a new perspective on what we see. For instance, keeping the effects of rural isolation in mind when reading *Trifles* reveals that economic forces created a brutal and insensitive husband who emotionally abused his wife for years—an understanding that can lead us to see that neither agent nor agency in this play is as simple as it first appears.

How, then, can the pentad help you as a writer? If you use it as a tool to analyze what others have written, you discover that you have much to say about that piece. But you can also use it as a means for writing something entirely on your own. Burke himself described dramatism as "a generating principle." Suppose that you have been asked to write about a significant personal experience. Once you have identified that experience (or act, in Burke's terms), you have to decide where to begin your essay, how much to include, and what points to emphasize. In one case the pentad might lead you to discover the importance of scene, and much of the essay you write will then focus on how the scene contributed to the act. In another instance you may realize that you want to emphasize the means through which an act was done or the agents who committed that act.

Journalists' Questions Journalists' questions are similar to Burke's pentad, but they do not incorporate the relationships to the same extent. They look only at *who* did *what* to whom, *when* and *where*, and *why* and *how*. Here is the first sentence of a news story from the business section of the *Dallas Times Herald* for January 30, 1991:

Last week California-based Intel Corp. sold an early model of its new parallel-processing supercomputer to an arm of the Mitsubishi group, scoring a major American coup in a key high-tech field that the Japanese government has targeted for world domination.

Notice how much information the reader is given in this first sentence: who, what, when, where, and why. The only vital piece of information the reader is not given in this lead is *how* the event occurred, information that will follow shortly. The rest of the news story was devoted to developing and expanding the information given in this sentence.

- *Who:* "Intel Corp." We want to know more about Intel. What kinds of products does it make? Is it big or small? New or old?
- *What:* "sold an early model of its new parallel-processing supercomputer to an arm of the Mitsubishi group." Is this new supertechnology? What's a supercomputer? Why is it newsworthy to have sold this to a Japanese company?
- *When:* "last week." Exactly when did this sale happen? Had it been planned for a long time?
- *Where:* "California-based." We're interested in this story because it tells us that an American company made an important sale. But can we assume that Intel is American-owned simply because it is based in California?
- *Why:* "scoring a major American coup in a key high-tech field that the Japanese government has targeted for world domination." Now we know why the story is news. An American company has broken into a difficult overseas market.
- *How:* is presented in the next sentence of the article: "By successfully marketing its iPSC-860 supercomputer. . . ."

These questions work well for exploring almost any kind of subject; and by answering each of them, you can discover interesting material for writing. Although not all the questions will be suitable for every subject, this method almost always gives you something to say.

Varying Perspectives Another way to explore a subject is based on the particle-wave-field theory of physics. Scientists and other people who are most comfortable with empirical information often find this technique more helpful than the less structured ones. It involves thinking of a subject as something in a stable state (static), as something that changes through time and space (dynamic), and as something that exists in relationship to other things (relational). Within each of these contexts this method also involves seeing a subject as a single entity, as a member of a group or class, and as part of a larger system. Thus, a single rose (static, single entity), say, is part of a class of objects called plants (static, class). Plants are part of a larger system of biology (static, system). That single rose might change over time from a bud (single, static) to a full-blown blossom, to a husk, and finally to a berry-like object (single, dynamic) containing seeds. Those seeds are part of the seasonal cycle of renewal (single, relational). We can thus construct a matrix that gives us nine different perspectives from which to examine a rose.

Dealing with Writer's Block

It is easy to get sidetracked in your writing at this point. You may even talk yourself into a case of writer's block. You know what you are going to write about and you know what the main points are, but you just can't seem to begin writing. There's that awful piece of blank paper staring back at you. How do you overcome writer's block? Many of the techniques useful for exploring ideas are also useful for getting over this snag, but you should consider, too, whether you are trying to write in a setting conducive for doing good work. You may be tensing up simply because you are trying to work in the wrong place or in the wrong clothes.

Make yourself as comfortable as you can, but don't get so comfortable that you will fall asleep. (Going to sleep is a particularly insidious way of avoiding writing.) Fish out your favorite sweatshirt, loosen your belt, clear your desk, sharpen your pencils and arrange your pens or start your word processor, provide yourself with a stack of paper or some fresh disks, arrange the lighting, set a snack nearby, and sit down. Take up your pen or pencil, or place your fingers on the keys, and begin to freewrite. At this point it doesn't matter what you write. You are just breaking through your block.

As soon as your ideas are flowing freely, you can begin to be more conscious of what you are saying and how the pieces are going together. Perhaps the piece you are working on isn't very congenial just at the moment. So change it; start on something else. You don't have to begin at the beginning. You can begin with something that will flow easily for you, and you can fit it into the whole later on. This method has been called *chunking.* Writers begin with a piece of writing they feel comfortable working on and develop that piece as far as it needs to go. Then they set it aside and take up another piece, sometimes at the same sitting, sometimes not. When all the pieces have been written, writers fit the pieces into a whole, linking them with appropriate transitional material and providing introductions and conclusions.

If you are particularly susceptible to writer's block, it may be a good idea to do what Ernest Hemingway used to do and end each writing session at a point where you feel sure you know what will come next. That way you can pick up quickly where you left off. Other things you can do to stave off writer's block include talking into a cassette recorder and then transcribing what you have dictated, rereading or retyping on your typewriter or word processor material you have already written, writing on the backs of old drafts so that you don't really have a blank sheet of paper, writing on small pieces of paper so as not to be intimidated by a large one, writing letters to friends to exercise your writing muscles, writing in a journal, or using a "magic" pen or pencil—one that has already written a number of completed compositions or one that feels especially good in the hand. If none of these techniques helps, try anything you think will help. Exercise: Ride your bicycle, go for a walk, wash dishes, shovel snow, or do some other physical task that requires little concentration, during which a good idea may come to mind if you keep your mind receptive. You will come back to writing refreshed. If that doesn't seem fruitful, put the idea of writing aside for the time being; go to a movie, watch television for an hour, read a couple of chapters of a novel. But be alert for ways you may be fooling yourself out of, rather than into, writing. If you find a way to overcome a block, remember it and use it whenever you need it, much as baseball players wear lucky socks or eat certain meals before games.

As you write more and more, you will acquire a variety of techniques that will help you get over future writing blocks. Some writers keep files of interesting material they find while reading for leisure, just as they do when they are actually researching. Others keep a journal in which they record ideas and perceptions that may be useful in the future. When you feel like writing, you can go to this material to find a subject to explore, and you can consult it to help you when you are stuck.

Planning

How can you arrange your ideas into an effective sequence? Some writers find it helpful to make an outline or to list the order in which they will present their main points. Others prefer going wherever the writing takes them. Even when they prepare an outline, they wind up not following it. There is nothing intrinsically wrong with that; writing is, after all, one of the best ways to learn, and you will generally wind up with something that can be reworked into a worthwhile piece of prose. Writing often takes its own shape as you do it, and plans developed beforehand go out the window. That's all right, too. Planning and drafting can occur over and over until you feel that you have said exactly what you intended. The point is that some kind of plan needs to be evident in the writing when it is completed, whether or not the plan was there from the beginning.

Some writers work one way on one project and a different way on the next. The important thing to understand about planning is that your plans are not contracts. They can easily be changed. In fact, most writing plans do change during drafting and revision. So there's no single, correct way to plan that will work every time you write. Any plan that works for you is the correct plan for that writing activity. With that in mind, let's look at a number of different methods.

DISCOVERY DRAFTS Your creative juices are flowing and the pieces of information are crowding each other to get out onto paper. It's all right to go ahead and let them flow; write them down as fast as you can. Writers frequently begin with only a general idea of what they want to discuss, and they simply let the ideas flow naturally until they have figured out what point or points they really want to make. If you write without any kind of formal plan, letting your ideas on a specific topic flow and take shape as you set them down, you are producing a discovery draft, an extended piece of freewriting in which you try to stick to a topic. For this kind of draft the end is usually signaled by the discovery of the point you want your essay to make or of unexpected material to support that point.

The important thing to remember is that the discovery draft is only a beginning, a way to let ideas find their own shape, and that ultimately you will have to identify the most effective plan inherent in the draft and reshape it with this plan in mind. In other words, a discovery draft can help you to define the main point of the paper you are planning and generate related material, making it easier for you to then write a draft that is more focused and orderly or to arrange your ideas into a plan that will guide your next draft.

OUTLINES There are several kinds of outlines, each of which might suit a different kind of project or a different kind of writer. Some outlines are exceedingly detailed, presenting almost as much information as the completed project will. Other outlines are very sketchy, offering only a general road map of where to go next. The kind you need depends on a combination of your working habits, your style, and your project. But if you find that your readers frequently comment that they can't follow what you're writing about, you probably need to make your outline a little more detailed. Or when you finish drafting, you may need to outline your draft meticulously and compare the "before" outline with the "after" outline. At the least you will see where you need to revise heavily, and you may even be able to chart where the revision should go. Conversely, if your readers tell you that your writing is boring and mechanical, you need to loosen up some. Making your outline a little less formal may be one way to go about it.

Lists and Jottings The most informal kind of outline is a list you jot down on a scrap of paper or keep in your head. It may be as informal as listing two or three points you don't want to forget. Such a list for a paper on hunting elephants for ivory, say, may look like this:

Health hazards
Economic consequences
Poaching
U.S. trade policy
Popularity of ivory in Asia
Endangered species
Effects on other animals

Nothing is indicated about other points you may plan to include, nor is anything noted about the order the points will appear in, although you can easily add numbers once you decide upon the sequence you think will be best. Furthermore, as your plan evolves, you may find that some items on your list are not appropriate; if so, just ignore them. This kind of outline is for you only, and you don't need to worry about making it more comprehensive if it does the job for you. Many students find this kind of outline helpful in taking essay examinations because it is brief enough to occupy a very small space and it doesn't take much time to produce. But it can be suitable for other occasions as well.

Here is a somewhat more detailed list for the same writing project.

1. Place in endangered species lists
    Reasons, locations
2. Place in environmental chain
    Above and below in food chain
    Relationship to other animals
    Meaning for humans
3. Who hunts ivory
    Licensed hunters, poachers
4. Human impact
    Physical dangers of elephant hunting:
        From elephants
        From authorities
    Health hazards:
        Food-related—rotting meat, malnutrition
        Ivory-related—elephant anthrax

Formal Outlines A formal outline for the same paper would indicate the relationships between main points and details more clearly than a list.

Thesis: Hunting elephants for ivory has two negative effects: It causes environmental damage, and it is dangerous to humans.

I. Environmental effects
    A. Endangered species
        1. Reasons
        2. Locations
    B. Place in environmental chain
        1. Relationship of elephant to other animals
            a. Effect on food chain
            b. Maintenance of grasslands
        2. Importance of elephant for humans
II. Human impact
    A. Physical dangers of elephant hunting

1. Unpredictability of elephants
2. Crackdown by governments on poachers
B. Health hazards
    1. Carcasses left to rot
    2. Elephant anthrax
        a. Conditions for infecting humans
        b. Locations of the disease

Notice that the formal outline is a graphic representation of the paper and that it shows balance and completeness. For this reason, some people insist that if there is an item 1, there must be an item 2, or if there is an item A, an item B must follow. Actually, there is no hard-and-fast rule, but common sense suggests that if there is only an item 1, say, either the writer has not pursued the subject far enough or the main heading and subheading can be combined. For example, if there were only a human disease issue and no consideration of geography in point 2 under "Health hazards," the idea should be expressed as "2. Elephant anthrax dangerous to humans."

Beginning with uppercase roman numerals, a formal topic outline relies upon indented uppercase letters of the alphabet, Arabic numbers, lowercase letters, Arabic numbers in parentheses, and so on to reflect various levels of relationships. Each topic should be grammatically parallel with other topics on the same level.

Any topic outline can easily be turned into a sentence outline by stating all points as sentences. A sentence outline has the advantage of helping writers be specific. For instance, a sentence outline for our example may have the item "B. Elephant hunting poses health hazards."

Formal outlines can be developed as plans for writing, as tools for revision, or as guides for readers. Most writers need flexibility in the plans they make to guide their writing, because the human mind often develops new insights during drafting. If you do make a formal outline before you write, review it when drafting to see whether you have lost sight of any points you had intended to make and if you are satisfied with the direction your writing has taken. But don't let your outline become a straitjacket.

NUTSHELLS, ABSTRACTS, AND CAPSULES   Another way to bring some order to writing is to use a summary paragraph (sometimes called a nutshell, abstract, or capsule). Consider this paragraph, for example:

> Under the microscope we can see that blood is composed of a watery fluid called plasma, in which certain formed elements are suspended. The formed elements are different types of cells—red blood cells, white blood cells and platelets. —*Louis Faugeres Bishop*

It is easy to imagine how we could use this paragraph as a nutshell for organizing a paper that would follow. The first group of paragraphs following this one could describe red blood cells, what they look like, how they are made, what their parts are; the next group of paragraphs might offer the same kind of information about white blood cells; and the final paragraphs would describe platelets. That is, indeed, how Bishop developed this piece of writing, and the technique works well for some situations.

Classic Oration The classic pattern for presenting information was in full use at least two thousand years ago, and that pattern continues to be useful today, especially in writing to persuade. People who gathered to listen to the great orators of classical times generally knew that right after they had been exhorted to pay attention, they would get background information on the subject, which would be followed by a clear statement of what issues would be addressed and what position the speaker would take. Then they could expect information that would confirm the speaker's point and would refute the opposing viewpoint. And finally, they usually expected a summary of what had been said and sometimes even a call to act upon it. (A variation in the sequence could draw attention to a particular part of the oration and thereby divert attention from another part.) In other words, classic oration had the following outline.

- *Introduction:* Inform the audience of the goal and gain their attention and confidence.
- *Statement of issues, facts, or circumstances:* Give the relevant background information and description of present conditions.
- *Proof of the case:* Select and arrange the material collected during the exploring and planning stages.
- *Refutation of opposing viewpoints:* State the objections and any complications; then show why these points should not trouble the audience.
- *Conclusion:* Sum up, highlight important points, point out future directions, and give a call to action.

Originally developed for oral presentations, this sequence became well established because nearly everyone used the same pattern or some variation of it—thus making it easy for listeners to follow the speech. And if the sequence varied, the listeners could depend upon their experience to know which part they were listening to. Even today, we often expect written presentations to follow the same pattern or some variation of it.

Drafting

Drafting means writing a preliminary version of a work that you will later revise. That is, it means getting your ideas on paper (or screen) so that you can work with them. If you think of drafting as "writing the paper," you put yourself at risk. Thinking in these terms can lead to writer's block by making drafting seem excessively important. And if you think *drafting* means "writing," you may be less likely to appraise your work critically before preparing another version of it. Drafting is simply one of the stages of the writing process, and experienced writers usually compose more than one draft of what they write.

Unlike planning and revision—both of which can be undertaken at various times throughout a busy day—drafting usually requires a block of uninterrupted time. If you have twenty minutes free between classes, you can brainstorm or refine a paragraph or two that are already drafted. But when you are ready to write the first draft of a paper, you should plan to set aside at least two or three hours when you can give undivided attention to this work. You may finish your draft much sooner, but knowing that you have a few hours at this point in the writing process will help you to avoid feeling tense. Providing yourself with adequate time for drafting can also protect you from being forced to stop prematurely just as your ideas have started to flow.

You may be thinking by now, "Don't these people know how busy I am? Where can I ever find two or three hours to draft a paper?" The answer is that busy people can usually find time to do the things that they genuinely want or need to do—even if it means getting up earlier, staying up later, or putting another activity aside. But no one expects you to invest an afternoon in everything you draft. The strategy we are recommending is for writing that matters to you. And as you become a more experienced writer, you may find that you need less time for drafting. Because experienced writers expect to revise their work, they often draft quickly—aware that they are only composing a preliminary version of their work.

Recognizing that writing a good introduction can be difficult, some writers draft by beginning in the middle and compose an introduction only after they have drafted several pages. But some writers draft most comfortably after they have composed an introduction that pleases them, and there are even some writers who need to write a good title before they can draft with any ease. Such writers like the sense of direction that they obtain from a title or an introduction, for a good title or introduction often reveals a writer's thesis. Follow the procedure that seems best suited to you.

Drafting should normally lead to identifying a main point or thesis. A thesis is usually stated early in a piece of writing, probably in the first paragraph or two (or the first chapter of a book), and is repeated at some point later. Because writers continue to think about ideas as they write, the thesis with which a writer begins may not be the thesis that governs the completed work, though. In other words, writers often begin drafting with a main point in mind, only to find that the thesis has changed as the essay has unfolded. Don't be alarmed if you think your thesis is changing or if you cannot identify a clear thesis in your draft; clarifying your thesis is something you can take care of later.

Neither writing nor reading would be much fun if all writers had to work the same way. Although classical rhetoric emphasized the need to follow predetermined patterns, modern rhetorical theory has given writers much more freedom. Thus, writers may state the main point early in an essay and restate it in the conclusion, or they may engage the attention of the reader by experimenting with introductions that seem at first unrelated to the topic. Moreover, writers are not always bound to a single main point. Sometimes, particularly in a long piece, a writer will develop two or more main points. And when pursuing some motives, a writer may not have a thesis as that concept is usually understood. When writing to explore an idea, for example, a writer may unify the work by a search for meaning rather than by a central idea that can be stated in a sentence or two. (For an example of this kind of writing, see "How to Build a Slaughterhouse" in Chapter 3.)

You should recognize, however, that writing without either a thesis or a clearly defined goal can leave readers feeling confused. When you read a piece that seems pointless, you may feel that you missed something. As a reader, you may be willing to go back and reread; but as a writer, you should recognize that some readers are not going to take that trouble. So if you are writing without a thesis, be sure to consider the expectations of your audience. You should also consider your motive for writing: Writing to explore the self may not need a thesis, but writing for other motives, such as writing to persuade, will. In short, ask yourself whether you are following a strategy suitable for your rhetorical situation.

By itself, even a well-crafted thesis statement will not suffice to make your readers feel comfortable trying to understand what you have to say. People resist taking in new information unless you can link it to information they already know. You can link information in two ways: by repetition—focusing on one idea and going back to it repeatedly—and by association—linking new information to an idea established previously.

The following paragraph by David Groff shows how a writer uses repetition.

> **Imagine** for yourself the immense relief, the knot of tension sliced through the light-headed desire to hug the doctor and laugh. But
> **imagine** also the doctor's pronouncement, his optimistic droning about prolonged longevity and further T-cell tests, the spit in the stomach forming a big sickening ball, the disbelief, the thousands of self-steelings.
> **Imagine** that different sort of light-headedness.

Groff repeats *imagine* at the beginning of each sentence. He does not tell us about the kind of laughter that the release of tension brings. Nor does he tell us about how we steel ourselves to bad news. He does return again and again to "imagining." This focused development gives the reader a sense of coherence and has the advantage of allowing the writer to explore an idea thoroughly.

If the foregoing technique allows you to develop an idea in depth, the one that follows allows you to introduce a number of related ideas. The paragraph by Edward Abbey proceeds by association, each idea linked to the one before.

> We consider the dunes, the sea of sand. Around the edges of the dunes grow clumps of arrowweed tall as corn shocks, scattered creosote shrubs bleached out and still, a few shaggy mesquite trees. These plants can hardly be said to have conquered the valley, but they have in some way made a truce—or found a point of equilibrium in a ferocious, inaudible struggle between life and entropy. A bitter war indeed: The creosote bush secretes a poison in its roots that kills any other plant, even its own offspring, attempting to secure a place too near; in this way the individual creosote preserves a perimeter of open space and a monopoly of local moisture sufficient for survival. —*Edward Abbey, "Death Valley"*

Notice that the subject of sentence 2, *dunes,* links to *dunes* in the predicate of sentence 1. The subject of sentence 3 (*plants*) links to the series of plant names in the predicate of sentence 2. The next sentence begins a focused development in this long paragraph: Each sentence will focus upon the war these plants fight. Such a chain of associations allows a writer to introduce a variety of information.

Revising

Revising distinguishes writing from speaking: Revision affords the writer a second (or third, or tenth) chance to get the meaning right. Donald Murray, a professional writer and writing teacher, explains that he always produces a "zero draft," a draft that is even rougher than a first draft. Then he feels he can get down to the business of writing as he reshapes those rough ideas into the first of many drafts. Many writers feel, as Murray does, that they aren't writing when they are drafting; they are only writing when they are revising.

Good writers can often be distinguished from poor writers by their attitude toward revision. Good writers don't expect to have gotten it right the first time. Poor writers assume that they have. As we have seen, writing is a dynamic and unpredictable process: It doesn't begin with planning and then proceed systematically through drafting, revising, editing, and proofing. Each of these activities can occur or recur at any moment during the production of a finished piece of prose. You may even get an idea that you want to include in your paper just as you are typing the final word of the final draft. If that happens, don't be discouraged; and above all, don't throw that good idea away. Just work it into your paper and produce another final copy. Conversely, you may know from the very first moment you set pencil to paper what the final words of your piece will be. Go ahead, write them down. Let them stay there throughout your whole effort as a beacon to aim toward. There's no right or wrong way to go about writing; if a technique works for you, then go ahead and use it.

Revising involves considerably more than fixing up the spelling and punctuation before you pass your writing on to a reader. It is easier to understand what revising is if we break the word into its parts: *re-* meaning "again" and *vising* meaning "seeing." Revising is seeing again, taking another look. Even though writers often do some revising as they draft, revision is most productive when something written days or weeks ago can be viewed with "new" eyes, almost as another person would see it. (Days and weeks are desirable incubation periods for writing, but writers do not always have that luxury. It is often possible, however, to let writing incubate is overnight.) When you revise in this way, if you are alert and keep your audience in mind, you will notice parts that are unclear, inaccurately phrased, carelessly organized, inadequately explained.

Think of revision as reentering the writing on at least three different levels to see what works and what might need changing: appraising the content, checking the organization, and refining the style. On the first, or deepest, level you can look at whether you have conveyed the proper meaning, done what you promised the reader you would do, provided enough support, focused clearly enough on your main point. You can use several techniques to reenter and review your writing at this level. One good way to see whether you have said what you intended is to read your manuscript aloud, pretending to be your audience. If it helps, try to read your writing as if you were the person you most admire. You may immediately see where you have gone astray. You can also do the same exercise pretending that you have just received the manuscript in the mail.

Another technique is to try to answer the following questions.

- Have I stressed the important issues?
- Have I made sure my point is clear?
- Have I dealt fairly with my audience?
- Did I promise anything that I could not deliver?
- Have I accounted for any objections that might be raised?
- Has my attitude been appropriate? That is, have I been condescending or arrogant?
- Have I apologized too much?
- Have I been overly familiar or friendly?

Revision at this level is not merely a way to fix problems that you can see on the page. It is also a way to identify where you need to say more. Play the audience role again, this time looking for what is *not* said. Are there any points that have not been made that should have been? Would an example make a point clearer? Are there any unexplored consequences or loose ends? Is anything taken for granted that readers may not understand?

When you have answered these questions as well as you can, you are ready to move on to a closer examination of structure, considering the unity of each paragraph and the organization of your essay as a whole. You may have already cut some sentences that didn't seem to fit and decided to move others to different paragraphs. But since your first level of revision may have led to major changes, including the addition of new material, you should now focus upon your essay's structure.

Look at each paragraph to see whether it is truly coherent and unified. In a *coherent paragraph* each sentence picks up a word or concept from the preceding sentence. In a *unified paragraph* all the sentences relate to a single idea. Do you need to combine any paragraphs? Split others? Shift them around? Have you provided transitions so that each paragraph seems to follow from the paragraph that precedes it? Do you need to delete irrelevant information? Do these changes require you to make any others?

Pay particular attention to the first and last paragraphs, which receive extra emphasis. Readers have certain expectations of these paragraphs. A good introductory paragraph will capture the attention of readers and provide them with a sense of where the essay is going. A good concluding paragraph will draw the essay together.

Although writers sometimes begin by drafting a strong introduction or conclusion, they may find that these paragraphs no longer fit the essay they have written. You can't be altogether sure what you are introducing until you have written what you want to introduce. And revision could also lead you to decide that you have begun before the beginning or ended after the ending. For instance, you may get off to a slow start and write a paragraph or two that adds little to the paper; in this case you may find that the second or third paragraph provides the best beginning. Similarly, you may sometimes ramble on a bit after you have said what you needed to say; in this case the conclusion of your essay may be buried somewhere before the point where you stopped writing.

If you discover that you need to write a new introduction, you could try starting with a nutshell paragraph that states the major points the following paragraphs will discuss. But for variety, try beginning with an anecdote, example, quotation, unusual detail, or statement of the problem you hope to resolve. If you find that you need a conclusion, you can restate or summarize your major points. But this strategy often works best for long essays during which readers might lose sight of an idea. Repeating key points may be unnecessary within a short essay, and it may leave some readers feeling as if you doubt their intelligence. When trying to write an effective conclusion, you can often benefit from asking yourself, "Why have I told you all this?" or, as a reader might put it, "So what?" Thinking along these lines may lead you to take one last step that will make the significance of your paper clear. Another effective strategy is to repeat an element found in the introduction, thus framing the essay with two paragraphs that seem related to each other. You can also try either rephrasing your thesis or asking your readers to undertake an action that the essay seems to invite.

After studying the structure of your work as a whole, you should then check to see whether individual sentences can be improved. Here are a few basic points to bear in mind.

- Vary the length of your sentences. If too many sentences are short, your writing will be choppy. If too many of your sentences are long, your readers may grow tired and impatient. A mixture of lengths usually works best; but note that short sentences are more emphatic than long ones, so use short sentences to make key points.
- Vary the structure of your sentences. If too many sentences follow a pattern of subject-verb-object, your writing may seem monotonous. Try beginning with an adverb, a phrase, or a subordinate clause. Check the rhythm of your sentences by reading them aloud and listening carefully to how they sound.
- If your sentences are often described as "too long," your problem may be wordiness. Wordiness refers to redundancy, padding, and unnecessary clutter. Look for unnecessary repetition. See also whether you can reduce wordiness by eliminating qualifiers and intensifiers such as *rather, very*, and *quite*. Look for such phrases as *in the event that, on the part of, it seems to me that, as a matter of fact, in view of, the point that I am trying to make* and see whether you can phrase them more precisely or delete them.
- Use the active voice, which means making the grammatical subject of a sentence the same as the doer of the action: I *broke your bowl* (active), as opposed to *Your bowl was broken by me* (passive). Note that the passive voice is wordier and also allows a writer to duck responsibility, reducing clarity: *Your bowl was broken.* As a general rule, use the passive voice only if the receiver of an action is more important than the doer or if the doer is unknown.
- Rework your sentences so that the verb reflects an action rather than a state of existence. For instance, write *Eating rich desserts makes you fat* instead of *Getting fat is often the result of eating rich desserts.* In general, avoid using an abstract subject with a linking verb and an abstract complement. Instead of saying *Overeating is a leading cause of weight gain,* say *Overeating makes you fat.*
- Make sure that elements that should be parallel are parallel. That is, use the same pattern and the same grammatical forms to express words, phrases, and clauses that have the same function and importance. For example: I have learned how much water I am using whenever I *wash my car, water my lawn,* or *take a shower.*
- Check your sentences for clichés and jargon. Clichés are those tired expressions that show up in your paper without your ever thinking about them, such as *in today's society, at the crack of dawn,* or *hitting the books.* Jargon is language that is specific to a particular group or field. If you find yourself writing about *font managers* and *scalable outlines,* for example, you had better be sure that your audience consists only of computer experts; other readers would be grateful for simpler language.

Soliciting help from well-disposed, thoughtful readers can help you gain a new perspective on what you have written. You can begin to recognize your own developing maturity as a writer when you are able not only to accept and profit from constructive criticism but also to seek it out. When you think you are finished, or after you have made several revision cycles through your writing, get a friend to read your draft aloud and listen for any weak spots. Then, ask your friend to read through it again and point out any weaknesses he or she notices. Professional writers seldom rely only upon their own judgment. They test what they have written by having others read it—family, friends, other authors, professional editors—to determine whether the writing communicates what the writer intended to say. And very often, these early readers make suggestions that help the writer produce a more effective text.

Try to make your own early readers understand that you are not just looking for praise. Be frank with them about anything that concerns you and direct their attention specifically to those points of concern, but also be open to comment on things you have not considered. And when you yourself review someone's writing, don't think it is a kindness *not* to criticize things you think need attention. Tactful, constructive criticism is always appropriate; personal attacks never are. Because writing is so intimately bound up with who we are, we all feel that we put ourselves at risk when we show our writing to others. From its earliest flowering as the private, interior, and highly specific expression of the young child, communication becomes increasingly public and increasingly general until it reaches the impersonal and distant stage most often represented by academic discourse. As we learn to risk showing our writing to others, we mature as writers but we never really lose the fear that someone may think us fools or idiots when we show them our writing. Cynthia Ozick refers to this feeling of risk when she says that writing is "an act of courage." And Barbara Mellix, in an essay in this book, says, "Each experience of writing was like standing naked and revealing my imperfection, my 'otherness.'" So it is understandable if a writer feels hurt or defensive when his or her writing has elicited something other than a totally favorable response. Writing is intensely personal. We offer the world a part of ourselves, and we don't want to be rejected. But it is important to overcome undue sensitivity if you want to write well. Be honest with others and encourage others to be honest with you. You may find yourself wincing every now and again when criticism is directed at your work, and you may get some unhappy looks when you offer criticism to others. But pleasure in a job well done ultimately outweighs any aches along the way.

Editing

When you believe that you have said what you want to say the way you want to say it, you are ready to edit your paper. Check your grammar.

Make sure that each sentence is complete. Check each subject–verb pair to make sure that they agree. Correct dangling modifiers and shifts in tense, person, or tone. Look for instances of mixed metaphors and faulty predication. Make sure that all your pronouns clearly refer to their antecedents.

Pay attention to spelling, mechanics, and punctuation. If you are using a word processor, this is the time to run your spelling checker. But don't expect a computer program to identify every problem. If you used *there* when you needed *their,* or mistyped *fro* (as in *to and fro*) instead of *for,* your spelling checker is unlikely to notice. Be careful about the final appearance of your paper. First impressions are just as important in writing as they are in social relationships. But don't confuse good typing with good writing. A beautifully printed essay on thick, expensive paper may be a pleasure to see and to hold. What ultimately matters, however, is what you have written and how well you have written it. Consider the presentation of your final draft as a symbol rather than a disguise. It should look good because it is good.

Finally, don't be overwhelmed by the advice in this introductory section or elsewhere in this book. Remember that no one is expecting you to become a perfect writer by the end of the semester. Writing well is a lifelong challenge. The immediate challenge, the one confronting you in the weeks ahead, is to understand the principles that can help you to become the best writer you can be. Although these principles can be studied in the abstract, they are best understood through examples and through practice. If you want to write well, you must be prepared to write often and to appraise your work critically. You must also be prepared to read often and to think critically about what you read. The essays, stories, and poems collected in this book offer you an opportunity to exercise your reading and thinking skills; and they will introduce you to authors and topics that you may want to read more of in the future.

1

Writing to Record a Memory

The wish to record a memory is one of the most common motives inspiring people to write. In her memoir *An American Childhood* Annie Dillard records how her own motive for writing can be traced to a wish to rescue the beauty of experience from the destructiveness of change. Describing an early ideal, she writes:

> As a life's work, I would remember everything—everything, against loss. I would go through life like a plankton net. I would trap and keep every teacher's funny remark, every face on the street, every microscopic alga's sway, every scrap of overhead cloud. . . .
>
> Some days I felt an urgent responsibility to each change of light outside the sunporch windows. Who would remember any of it, any of this our time, and the wind thrashing the buckeye limbs outside? Somebody had to do it, somebody had to hang on to the days with teeth and fists, or the whole show had been in vain.

Dillard's youthful ideal is impossible to fulfill. Some algae will sway unseen, and some changes of light will pass unnoticed while we're talking on the telephone. But even if it is impossible to remember *everything,* Dillard understands a basic truth about writing: Writers need to have memories, and memories need to be preserved from loss. ,

In addition to inspiring memoirs and journals, this motive can also prompt something as simple as a list. To remember passing thoughts, we scribble "Call George" or "Buy milk" on whatever paper is close at hand. In doing so, we demonstrate a fundamental connection between the written word and how we conduct our lives: By writing things down, no matter how small or insignificant, we can bring order to experience.

KEEPING A JOURNAL

Like the lists we make to organize our days, a journal is written for ourselves. The difference, of course, is that a journal allows us to record in detail whatever we have in mind—what happened, for example, when we called George (or why we decided to postpone that call, since George is starting to get on our nerves). Many writers find this kind of writing highly satisfying. Because we write journals for ourselves, we can write whatever we want without worrying about grammar, style, or what someone else might think of us. And we can also dispense with much of the background information we would have to include for other readers. So don't allow any concerns about audience to interfere with the free flow of your ideas in your journal; you are writing for the audience you know best of all: yourself. While recording our memories, we may sometimes have other motives as well—writing to explore our feelings, for example, or evaluate an experience. But the initial impulse that leads most people to keep a journal is the need to record memories before they become lost beneath the ever-growing accumulation of experience as each day slips into the next.

Strictly speaking, the difference between a journal and a diary is that a diary is simply a record of what happens every day, whereas a journal includes reflections and observations. Some diaries offer little more than weather reports, meals eaten, and bedtimes. Journals, on the other hand, often pass over the surface details of life and focus instead upon how the writer reacts to experience: A journal is less likely to note what the writer ate for breakfast than to record how the writer responded to a novel, a sunset, or a quarrel. To put it simply, journals are often more personal and more reflective than diaries. But the distinction between the two should not be overemphasized. When writing to record memories, writers often move back and forth between entries that list events and those that explore their significance.

Keeping some type of daily record of your life—whatever you choose to call it—offers a number of advantages. By making writing a normal part of every day, you can protect yourself from the anxiety some people feel when they are forced to write. As a general rule, the more writing you do, the more natural it seems to write. Another advantage is that you can explore experience that you would be reluctant to discuss with anyone, believing it to be too trivial, too personal, or too confusing for sharing with others. A final advantage is that a written record of your life can jog your memory when you undertake other types of writing. No matter how much experience a writer may have, it is not unusual to feel, at times, that there's "nothing to write about." Most people know much more than they realize, and reviewing the entries in a journal can often help writers recall events and ideas that they had somehow lost sight of—thus generating topics for further writing.

But you should not let the prospect of some future advantage obscure the immediate benefits of keeping a written record of your life. If you feel as if you are writing for posterity or are obliged to be sensitive and profound whenever you write in your journal, you may very well deprive yourself of the principal pleasure of writing to record a memory: the freedom to write what you choose. You will profit the most from this writing experience if you are willing to devote some time to it, but time will vary from day to day. On some days you may have a lot to say; on others you may not. The main thing is to write something every day without worrying about a specific quota—and to feel free to let the words come tumbling out whenever you have something in particular on your mind.

Journal writing can be a form of freewriting, with one sentence leading to another that you had not anticipated when you began to write. When you are writing for yourself in this way, some entries will be stronger than others. But it would be a mistake to try to edit yourself as you write, attempting to write a consistent series of well-crafted passages, each of the same length. Don't worry about grammar or punctuation or spelling; even professional writers may make mistakes when writing primarily for themselves. And don't worry about wandering off the point. Although you will not want even your journal writing to be point-*less,* the point can be anything you want it to be, for you are your own audience.

Writing of this sort is analogous to snapshots. If you like to take pictures of the people you know and the places you've been, you've probably taken some that you like very much and others that didn't turn out the way you expected. On most rolls of film there are pictures that are similar to other pictures—and perhaps a few in which someone has been caught in an awkward position. You might not consider entering any of these pictures in a photography contest, but the pictures have value for you because of the associations you bring to them. "Oh, look at the food on Scott's plate!" you might exclaim. "Wasn't that the day he ate so much that he got sick?" If you asked strangers to look at the same picture (and the other seventy-one shots you took at the family picnic), they probably wouldn't enjoy them as much as you do. Except for those exceptional photographs that are works of art, most pictures have value because they are visual records of memory. By looking at them, we can recover part of our past.

Writing our memories down on paper offers the same advantage. As writers, you shouldn't be afraid to waste film. People who manage to make a single roll of film last three years (convinced that they see nothing worth photographing or determined to wait for the perfect shot) may find that the film is spoiled by the time it gets out of the camera. Experienced photographers snap lots of pictures, in part because they know that some will not turn out, but also in part because an unplanned shot can sometimes prove to be the best on the roll. Think along these lines when you are writing in your journal: The more you write, the more likely you are to produce something that will one day give you great pleasure to reread. As for the shots that don't turn out, take comfort in the knowledge that no one else has to see them.

Although it is the work of a professional writer and has been edited for publication, Edward Abbey's "Death Valley" illustrates how recording memories in a journal helps a writer preserve details that might otherwise be lost. Within his first three paragraphs Abbey records the altitude (4,317 feet) from which he descended into Death Valley and the temperature (114 degrees) he found there at ten o'clock on a June morning. It's hard to remember specific numbers, and these details are useful enough as far as they go. But the record of a trip that limited itself to numbers would not take anyone far into the experience of that trip. Memory, like understanding, is clearest when we see what we are looking at and when we can give names to what we see. Because Abbey was a trained observer of the natural world, he records the vegetation he sees—arrowweed, creosote shrubs, and mesquite trees. He also notes that creosote bushes secrete a poison that kills other plants. When writing to record your own memories, realize that although it is better to describe a *creosote* bush when you see it than to settle for the obvious and general "There weren't many trees around," the first step is to see the bush. You will have more memories to record if you keep your eyes and ears open.

If you are observant, you will note things that other people miss. These unexpected details are often the most interesting for both writers and readers. Consider what happens to Abbey when he stops at a gas station for a cold drink:

> Sipping cold drinks, we watch through the window a number of desert sparrows crawl in and out of the grills on the front of the parked automobiles. The birds are eating tourists—bugs and butterflies encountered elsewhere and smashed, baked, annealed to the car radiators. Like the bears of Yellowstone, the Indians of Arizona, and roadside businessmen everywhere, these birds have learned to make a good thing off passing trade. Certainly they provide a useful service; it's a long hot climb out of here in any direction and a clean radiator is essential.

Where an inexperienced writer might have only noted, "Stopped for a soda," Abbey records a glimpse of birds eating bugs, and that in turn leads him to reflect upon the relationship between the natural world and the people who drive through it. Think how much is conveyed because Abbey remembered these birds: We learn that there are birds in Death Valley, what kind of birds they are, how difficult it must be for them to survive, and how nature seems able to accommodate at least some of the incursions of humans. As readers, we can be pleased that Abbey took the trouble to record that memory in his journal, for it is precisely the sort of small but illuminating moment that most people would either fail to note or fail to remember.

As this excerpt from "Death Valley" suggests, journal writing often involves a combination of narration and description. The anecdote about the birds is a story told within a few sentences. As in any narrative, we find all the elements of Kenneth Burke's pentad (pp. 12–14): The *scene* is a gas station/store in Death Valley, the *act* is the eating of bugs, the *agents* are the birds, the *agency* is the cars that have brought the insects into the Valley, and the *purpose* is survival. But if we can see all this happening, it is because of Abbey's descriptive detail. The bugs aren't simply somewhere outside the window; they are "smashed, baked, annealed to the car radiators." The birds must be small if they can crawl in and out of the grills to reach the radiators, and, as already noted, they must be hungry if they are willing to go to the trouble. There are only two additional details that we might ask for. What kind of a cold drink was Abbey sipping? (Was it a beer or a Diet Pepsi?) And whom does that "we" include?

You will find additional information on narration and description later in this introduction. For the moment, it is enough to make these observations.

- Narration and description go together naturally when we write to record a memory.
- Details are essential for making memories come alive upon the page.
- Writers select the details they report and do not have the responsibility of reporting everything they see and do.

Even in a journal, when you are writing only for yourself, you don't have to tell what you were drinking if you don't feel like it.

WRITING A MEMOIR

Journal writing focuses on the writer; memoir (from *memoria*, Latin for "memory") usually focuses on a writer's experiences with a person, place, or event. While both journal writing and memoir writing thus have an autobiographical dimension to them, memoir writing directs the writer's attention outward rather than inward. Moreover, unlike diary writing or journal writing, memoir is a type of public writing designed to communicate memories to others.

A memoir can emphasize and illuminate certain things and gloss over or eliminate others entirely. Essayists usually focus upon something specific, because they are working on a small canvas. In "Taking the Test," for example, David Groff confines himself to remembering his test for AIDS and what it was like to wait for the results. There are probably many stories he could tell from his life before that test, but Groff wisely recognized that there is a limit to how much he could cover in a short essay. Other writers summarize an overall situation and then dramatize it with a close-up or two. At the heart of "Finishing School" is the moment when Maya Angelou deliberately breaks some dishes. But before Angelou narrates that specific afternoon in an Arkansas kitchen, she builds up to it by providing readers with necessary background information.

Both of these writers made good strategic decisions. Groff could safely assume that most readers today would understand why taking an AIDS test would be stressful. He doesn't need to provide information on AIDS or discuss his sexual history in detail. On the other hand, without some background, readers would probably have trouble understanding why someone would deliberately break an employer's favorite dishes. What you should note about both examples, however, is that close-ups are usually more dramatic—make more of an impact—than overviews.

When writing an essay of your own, try to make the focus specific, and include background information only to the extent that it is necessary for your audience to understand what you want the heart of your essay to convey. That is, look for ways to link your essay to your readers' experience. Are you writing for readers who come from the same part of the country as you do? Are they about your own age? Do they have similar family backgrounds? If so, you can depend on those shared experiences to provide background for your essay without having to refer to them directly, but you also need to keep your readers' interest by giving them something new, something different from their own histories. And if your readers are different from you, consider what similarities you might point up so that you can take advantage of Kenneth Burke's idea of identification between writer and reader.

As an essay like Marilyn Schiel's "Levi's" suggests, a writer with a well-chosen focus can say a lot within a few pages. In this case the focus is on a pair of used jeans. Most people would think, "What could be simpler than that?" And inexperienced writers might not even consider writing on such an apparently simple topic because they have convinced themselves that writers need extraordinary material in order to be interesting. But interest is something the writer creates. Some writers are capable of making the extraordinary seem boring; others help us to see what is wonderful about the ordinary. In Schiel's hands the memory of a pair of jeans becomes a vehicle for understanding the author's life. We can see what she was like, what her brother was like, and what her mother was like. We also come away understanding something of what it meant to grow up in the 1950s.

Although the essay includes some narration (girl wants jeans, girl is denied jeans, girl gets jeans), the focus is on an object rather than an event, so description prevails. By the time we finish Schiel's essay, we learn about triple-roll cuffs with sidewalk burns, real pockets marked with metal rivets, and a difficult-to-manage button fly. Details combine to re-create through words a specific pair of jeans. As you search among your own memories for a writing topic, you might try thinking of something that you once felt privileged to possess and then try writing about it so that other people can understand why it mattered to you.

Recording one memory can sometimes lead to another. When this happens, you should feel free to tie one memory to another. Some forms of writing (like writing a journal or writing to explore oneself) can become voyages of discovery that take us far away from where we began. A short memoir, however, does not afford room for every memory that occurs to you. If you find yourself wanting to move from one memory to another, ask yourself if they are closely related or if you are being lured away from your original focus by material that might best be saved for another writing occasion. (If they are not closely related, you might jot the extra one in your journal or idea book to use another time.)

Two of the essays in this chapter demonstrate how writers can include more than one memory without losing their focus. Geoffrey Norman's "Gators" moves between the recent and distant past. In this essay Norman begins by narrating his experience with an alligator "a couple dozen years ago" and then moves on to record a recent experience with alligators. The transition between these memories occurs midway through the essay, when the author observes, "I had not seen one for years until the other day." Although Norman does not come out and tell us what motivated him to write about alligators, it is likely that his experience "the other day" triggered the earlier memory with which the essay began. The essay as a whole is unified—but not just because both of the stories it includes are about alligators. In this case an older memory provides the background for understanding a recent memory. In "Life with Father" Itabari Njeri shares memories of her father, a brilliant philosopher and teacher who abused his wife and alienated himself from his daughter, who simultaneously admired and hated him. By writing, Njeri tries to understand not only her father but also her own responses to him, as a child and as an adult. Thirty years separate the two kinds of responses, which are naturally related by Njeri's consistent focus upon her father.

When we are writing a memoir about our experiences with another person, a place, or an event, we may begin to wonder how that experience affected us, changed us, made us who we are today. Njeri's essay illustrates how writing about memories of another person can lead a writer to reflect upon her relationship with that person and gain insight into her own life. For as we noted earlier, there is an autobiographical component to memoir even though the focus is primarily outward rather than inward. When a writer's primary purpose is to better understand herself, another kind of writing emerges: writing to explore the self, the subject of Chapter 2.

The sequence of the events remembered in "Gators" is chronological, which means that events are presented in the order in which they occurred. When writing about his mother in "The Contest," Michael Dorris also arranges his material chronologically. This is the easiest and most common way of recording a memory of events, but variation is often possible. In "Life with Father," for example, Njeri includes references to the present in the midst of her memories of the distant past. This is one variation on the straightforward approach of "Gators," and Maya Angelou's essay presents another. Angelou begins with the memory of a recent conversation that leads her back to the older memory that is the focus of "Finishing School." In an essay of your own you might begin in the middle of a story—if the middle provides an opening that would attract the attention of readers— and then go back to the start before finishing with the conclusion.

There is no single method of organization that works all the time. But there are two principles that you should try to keep in mind when planning how to share a memory with readers.

1. Remember to give readers a clear indication of where your memories are located in time.
2. Whether you are writing chronologically or moving backward and forward in time for dramatic effect, try to save a strong scene for the ending so that your essay does not trail off after reaching an early climax.

Dorris begins his essay by establishing that he was two and his mother was in her late thirties when they moved to Louisville. He is nine during the first memory upon which he focuses and a year or two older in the second. Groff makes it clear that only a few days pass between taking the test and getting the results; but he also makes clear that those few days represent an eternity. And Angelou lets us know that she is recalling events that happened when she was ten.

A memoir can easily end with what is simply the final event of the story—as when Angelou concludes with the dramatic moment when she breaks some valued dishes or Shiel ends with her mother's change of attitude about clothing. This strategy works best when you are recalling a memory that has a clear ending built right into it. At other times you may end with a paragraph or two reflecting upon the significance of what you have remembered. This does not mean tacking some kind of moral onto the end of the story, but it does mean giving readers an additional clue about why you found this memory worth writing about. Groff, Njeri, and Norman all conclude by offering a brief comment upon the memories they have recorded.

As should be clear by now, writing a memoir is different from recording memories in a journal. Because memoir is aimed at an audience beyond the writer, it must be more focused and shaped than journal writing. Although you can include anything in a journal (and the more the better), you need to be selective about what to include in a memoir. Whether you are emphasizing an event, a person, a place, or an object from your past, you must try to convey a sense of why this memory is significant. In many memoirs this significance is achieved through a conflict between the writer and the writer's world. Angelou is in conflict with her employer, Schiel with her mother, Njeri with her father, and Groff with her own fear. Conflict not only heightens the reader's sense of "What's going to happen?" but also shows the writer being tested—and how that test is met may be significant. In some cases conflict may be only implied, and it need not necessarily involve the writer directly. In "Gators," for example, Norman suggests a conflict between alligators and encroaching civilization. In another memoir—such as the memory of a wonderful restaurant that no longer exists—the conflict may simply be between the present and the past.

Do not think that a memoir must be deeply personal. Some of the best examine life at a distance. If you watch television talk shows, you may get the misguided impression that memoir must deal with sexual abuse, dysfunctional families, or chemical dependency. An inexperienced writer who attempts to discuss such intimate material may subsequently regret what she or he has revealed to others. Remember that an evocative memoir can be written about nothing more intimate than a pair of Levi's or a broken dish. You are the best judge of what is significant to you, and you are ultimately responsible for what you decide to share with others. The challenge of memoir is to convey significant experience—be it large or small—without embarrassing yourself or your readers.

DEATH VALLEY

Edward Abbey

> *Death Valley is considered one of the most inhospitable places on earth, but this selection comes from a work called* The Journey Home—*a title that suggests the author found satisfaction of some sort in visiting this place. Edward Abbey was a professional writer who wrote many works about the American West. Look for clues that indicate how Abbey felt about Death Valley. Learn what you can about this place, and consider why it was important to Abbey.*

SUMMERTIME

From Daylight Pass at 4,317 feet we descend through Boundary Canyon and Hell's Gate into the inferno at sea level and below. Below, below . . . beneath a sea, not of brine, but of heat, of shimmering simmering waves of light and a wind as hot and fierce as a dragon's breath.

The glare is stunning. Yet also exciting, even exhilarating—a world of light. The air seems not clear like glass but colored, a transparent, tinted medium, golden toward the sun, smoke-blue in the shadows. The colors come, it appears, not simply from the background, but are actually present in the air itself—a vigintillion microscopic particles of dust reflecting the sky, the sand, the iron hills.

On a day in June at ten o'clock in the morning the thermometer reads 114 degrees. Later in the day it will become hotter. But with humidity close to zero such heat is not immediately unpleasant or even uncomfortable. Like the dazzling air, the heat is at first somehow intoxicating—one feels that grace and euphoria that come with just the right ration of Old Grandad, with the perfect allowance of music. Sunlight is magic. Later will come. . . . Yes, out of the car and standing hatless under the sun, you begin to feel the menace in this arid atmosphere, the malignancy within that silent hurricane of fire.

We consider the dunes, the sea of sand. Around the edges of the dunes grow clumps of arrowweed tall as corn shocks, scattered creosote shrubs bleached out and still, a few shaggy mesquite trees. These plants can hardly be said to have conquered the valley, but they have in some way made a truce—or found a point of equilibrium in a ferocious, inaudible struggle between life and entropy. A bitter war indeed: The creosote bush secretes a poison in its roots that kills any other plant, even its own offspring, attempting to secure a place too near; in this way the individual creosote preserves a perimeter of open space and a monopoly of local moisture sufficient for survival.

We drive on to the gas station and store at Stovepipe Wells, where a few humans huddle inside beneath the blast of a cold-air blower. Like other

5

mammals of the valley, the human inhabitants can endure its summer only by burrowing deep or by constructing an artificial environment—not adaptation but insulation, insularity.

Sipping cold drinks, we watch through the window a number of desert sparrows crawl in and out of the grills on the front of the parked automobiles. The birds are eating tourists—bugs and butterflies encountered elsewhere and smashed, baked, annealed to the car radiators. Like the bears of Yellowstone, the Indians of Arizona, and roadside businessmen everywhere, these birds have learned to make a good thing off passing trade. Certainly they provide a useful service; it's a long hot climb out of here in any direction and a clean radiator is essential.

The Indians of Death Valley were cleverest of all. When summer came they left, went up into the mountains, and stayed there until it was reasonable to return—an idea too subtle in its simplicity for the white man of today to grasp. But we too are Indians—gypsies anyhow—and won't be back until September.

FURNACE CREEK, SEPTEMBER 17. Again the alarming descent. It seemed much too hot in the barren hills a mile above this awful sinkhole, this graben (for Death Valley is not, properly understood, a valley at all), this collapsed and superheated trench of mud, salt, gravel, and sand. Much too hot—but we felt obliged to come back once more.

A hard place to love, Death Valley. An ugly place, bitter as alkali and rough, harsh, unyielding as iron. Here they separate the desert rats from the mice, the hard-rock prospectors from the mere rock hounds.

Cactus for example. There is none at all on the floor of the valley. Too *10* dry or too brackish or maybe too hot. Only up on the alluvial fans and in the side canyons 1,000 feet above sea level do we find the first stunted and scrubby specimens of cholla and prickly pear and the pink-thorned cottontop—poor relation of the barrel cactus.

At first glance, speeding by car through this valley that is not a valley, one might think there was scarcely any plant life at all. Between oases you will be impressed chiefly by the vast salt beds and the immense alluvial fans of gravel that look as hostile to life as the fabled seas of the moon.

And yet there is life out there, life of a sparse but varied sort—salt grass and pickleweed on the flats, far-spaced clumps of creosote, saltbush, desert holly, brittlebush, and prickly poppy on the fans. Not much of anything, but a little of each. And in the area as a whole, including the surrounding mountains up to the 11,000-foot summit of Telescope Peak, the botanists count a total of 900 to 1,000 different species, ranging from microscopic forms of algae in the salt pools to limber pine and the ancient bristlecone pine on the peaks.

But the first impression remains a just one. Despite variety, most of the surface of Death Valley is dead. Dead, dead, deathly—a land of jagged salt pillars, crackling and tortured crusts of mud, sunburnt gravel bars the color of rust, rocks and boulders of metallic blue naked even of lichen. Death Valley is Gravel Gulch.

TELESCOPE PEAK, OCTOBER 22. To escape the heat for a while, we spend the weekend up in the Panamints. (Summer still baking the world down below, far below, where swirls of mud, salt, and salt-laden streams lie motionless under a lake of heat, glowing in lovely and poisonous shades of auburn, saffron, crimson, sulfurous yellow, dust-tinged tones of white on white.)

Surely this is the most sterile of North American deserts. No matter how high we climb it seems impossible to leave behind the influence of aridity and anti-life. At 7,000 feet in this latitude we should be entering a forest of yellow pine, with grassy meadows and freshwater brooks. We are farther north than Santa Fe or Flagstaff. Instead there are only the endless barren hills, conventional in form, covered in little but shattered stone. A dull monotonous terrain, dun-colored, supporting a few types of shrubs and small, scattered junipers.

From 7,000 to 9,000 feet we pass through a belt of more junipers and a fair growth of pinyon pines. Along the trail to Telescope Peak—at 10,000 feet—appear thin stands of limber pine and the short, massive, all-enduring bristlecone pine, more ancient than the Book of Genesis. Timberline.

There is no forest here. And fifty or sixty airline miles to the west stands the reason why—the Sierra Nevada Range blocking off the sea winds and almost all the moisture. We stand in the rain shadow of that still higher wall.

I walk past three wild burros. Descendants of lost and abandoned prospectors' stock, they range everywhere in the Panamints, multiplying freely, endangering the survival of the native bighorn sheep by trespassing on the latter's forage, befouling their springs. But the feral burros have their charm too. They stand about 100 feet from the trail watching me go by. They are quite unafraid, and merely blink their heavy eyelashes like movie starlets when I halt to stare at them. However they are certainly not tame. Advance toward them and they trot off briskly.

The bray of the donkey is well known. But these little beasts can make another sound even more startling because so unexpected. Hiking up some arid canyon in the Panamints, through what appears to be totally lifeless terrain, you suddenly hear a noise like a huge dry cough behind your shoulder. You spring ten feet forward before daring to look around. And see nothing, nothing at all, until you hear a second cough and scan the hillsides and discover far above a little gray or black burro looking down at you, waiting for you to get the hell out of its territory.

I stand by the cairn on the summit of Telescope Peak, looking out on a cold, windy, and barren world. Rugged peaks fall off southward into the haze of the Mojave Desert; on the west is Panamint Valley, the Argus Range, more mountains, more valleys, and finally the Sierras, crowned with snow; to the north and northwest the Inyo and White mountains; below lies Death

Valley—the chemical desert—and east of it the Black Mountains, the Funeral Mountains, the Amargosa Valley and farther mountains, wave after wave of wrinkled ridges standing up from the oceanic desert sea until vision gives out somewhere beyond the curving rim of the world's edge. A smudge hangs on the eastern horizon, suggesting the presence of Death Valley's counterpart and complement, the only city within 100 miles: Las Vegas: Glitter Gulch West.

ECHO CANYON, NOVEMBER 30. A hard place to love. Impossible? No, there were a few—the prospectors, the single-blanket, jackass prospectors who wandered these funeral wastes for a century dreaming of what? Sudden wealth? Not likely. Not Shorty Borden, for example, who invested eight months of his life in building by hand a nine-mile road to his lead and silver diggings in Hanaupah Canyon. Then discovered that even with a road it would still cost him more to transport his ore to the nearest smelter than the ore itself was worth.

Echo Canyon. We are deep into the intricacies of the Funeral Mountains. Named not simply for their proximity to Death Valley, but also for shape and coloration: lifeless escarpments of smoldering red bordered in charcoal, the crags and ridges and defiles edged in black and purple. A primeval chaos of faulted, uplifted, warped, and folded dolomites, limestones, fanglomerates of mud, sand, and gravel. Vulcanism as well: vesiculated andesite, walls embellished with elegant mosaics of rose and yellow quartz. Fool's gold—pyrite—glittering in the black sand, micaceous shales glinting under back light, veins of pegmatite zigzagging and intersecting like an undeciphered script across the face of a cliff: the writing on the wall: "God Was Here." Shallow caves, holes in the rock, a natural arch, and the canyon floor littered with boulders, deep in coarse gravel.

Nowhere in Echo Canyon can I find the slightest visible trace of water. Nevertheless, it must be present under the surface, at least in intermittent or minute amounts, for here and there stand living things. They look dead but are actually dormant, waiting for the resurrection of the rain. I mean the saltbush, the desert fir, the bladderweed, a sprinkling of cottontop cactus, the isolated creosote bush. Waiting.

You may see a few lizards. In sandy places are the hoofprints of bighorn sheep, where they've passed through on their way from the high parts of the range to the springs near Furnace Creek. Sit quite still in one spot for an hour and you might see a small gray bird fly close to look you over. This is the bird that lives in Echo Canyon.

The echoes are good. At certain locations, on a still day, one clear 25 shout will create a series of overlapping echoes that goes on and on toward so fine a diminuendo that the human ear cannot perceive the final vibrations.

Tramp far enough up Echo Canyon and you come to a ghost town, the ruins of a mining camp—one of many in Death Valley. Deep shafts, a tipple, a rolling mill largely intact, several cabins—one with its inside walls papered with pages from the *Literary Digest*. Half buried in drifted sand is a rusted model-T Ford without roof or motor, a child's tricycle, a broken shovel.

Returning through twilight, I descend the narrow gorge between flood-polished walls of bluish andesite—the stem of the wineglass. I walk down the center of an amphitheater of somber cliffs riddled with grottoes, huge eyesockets in a stony skull, where bats hang upside down in the shadows waiting for night.

Through the opening of the canyon I can see the icy heights of Telescope Peak shining under the cloud-reflected light of one more sunset. Scarlet clouds in a green sky. A weird glow pervades the air through which I walk; it vibrates on the canyon walls, revealing to me all at once a vision of the earth's slow agony, the convulsive grinding violence of a hundred thousand years. Of a million years. I write metaphorically, out of necessity. And yet it seems impossible to believe that these mountains, old as anything on the surface of the planet, do not partake in some dim way of the sentience of living tissue. Genealogies: From these rocks struck once by lightning gushed springs that turned to blood, flesh, life. Impossible miracle. And I am struck once again by the unutterable beauty, terror, and strangeness of everything we think we know.

Questions for Discussion

1. Abbey describes Death Valley as a "hard place to love." How would you characterize his attitude toward this place?
2. What role do human beings play in Death Valley? What is the implication of comparing people to "other mammals" and describing bugs as "tourists"?
3. According to Abbey, Las Vegas is the "counterpart and complement" of Death Valley. What do you think he means by this? What could a growing American city, famous for gambling casinos, have in common with "the most sterile of North American deserts"?
4. In paragraph 28 Abbey claims, "I write metaphorically, out of necessity." A metaphor is a comparison between unlike things that does not use either *like* or *as*. An example is describing grottoes as "huge eye-sockets in a stoney skull." Identify at least three other metaphors in this work, and be prepared to discuss why Abbey found it necessary to use them.
5. Although "Death Valley" is set up like a journal and may have originated as a journal, Abbey almost certainly revised his original notes before publishing them. His language is polished, there are no loose ends, and the longer work from which this selection has been excerpted even includes a footnote at one point. In writing what could be described as an essay, why do you think Abbey chose to build his work from a series of journallike entries? What advantage is there to this form? Are there any disadvantages?

Suggestions for Writing

1. Experiment with keeping a written record of your life, varying entries between those that record events and those that record thoughts and feelings. Try to write at least a hundred words a day.
2. Try to discover beauty where someone else might miss it. Visit a specific spot at least twice, preferably at different times of day or under different weather conditions. Record details and impressions in a journal, and draw upon these entries to write a description that reveals a clear point of view.

LEVI'S

Marilyn Schiel

In "Levi's" Marilyn Schiel paints a picture of the past that focuses on a pair of blue jeans. Think about how the clothes people wear help determine what acts they perform—what they can and cannot do. As you read, ask yourself why the Levi's were so important to Schiel. What would they enable her to do? If you have seen reruns of such TV series as "Leave It to Beaver" or "Father Knows Best," you have some knowledge of American values in the fifties and early sixties. Draw upon what you know of that era so that you can locate Schiel's memoir within a context of time and place.

They weren't boot cut, or spiked leg, or 501. They weren't stone washed, or acid bleached, or ice black. They weren't Guess, or Zena, or Jordache. They were just blue jeans—old, worn Levi's.

My ten-year-old brother wore blue jeans. I wore slacks. In summer, cotton pastel pants with embroidered bunnies or ducks. In winter, grey-corduroys with girl-pink flannel lining. I wanted to wear blue jeans.

As a five-year-old I didn't understand the difference between cause and coincidence. My brother's jeans meant he could wander his two-wheel bike blocks from home after school; he could, with a crew of blue-jeaned boys, build a tree house in the oak in the vacant lot next door; he could carry a BB gun all the way to the cemetery to shoot at squirrels. I had to be content triking my embroidered bunnies up and down the driveway; I had to settle for building domino houses on the living room floor; I could shoot only caps at imaginary black-hatted cowboys in the basement. I wanted to wear blue jeans.

But little girls in my 1950 world didn't wear blue jeans. Big girls didn't wear them either. Big girls didn't even wear pastel cotton slacks or winter corduroys. At least my mother, the big girl I knew best, didn't. When the family gathered for breakfast, seven days a week sharp at 7:30, Mom was already in uniform, a shirtwaist dress garnished with a colored, beaded necklace that matched clip-on earrings. By the 1960s June Cleaver may have been an anachronism, but in the early 1950s she lived at my house.

Mothers stayed home. Unlike dads, mothers didn't work. Mothers made the beds, cooked the meals, cleaned the house, baked the cookies, tended the garden, canned the vegetables, squeezed the clothes through the wringer-washer, hung washed clothes to dry on lines strung through the basement, ironed everything—including sheets and towels—scrubbed the floors while kneeling on pink rubber pads, walked seven blocks pulling an empty Red-flyer wagon to buy groceries, struggled seven blocks home with a week's worth of carefully budgeted supplies, and picked out the clothes their children would wear. My brother got blue jeans. I got embroidered bunnies.

Then, in 1953, my world changed. Elvis took us all to Heartbreak Hotel; Eisenhower brought us home from Korea; and my mother went to work. The hardware store Dad bought pulled Mom from the home to the business. Her transition from the breadbaker to a breadwinner taught my mother that women, big or little, didn't have to wear embroidered bunnies anymore.

The change was more evolutionary than revolutionary. She still wore the housewife uniform—but now she wore it to work. She still did the laundry, but now with an automatic washing machine and electric dryer. We still ate breakfast together at 7:30, but now cereal and milk replaced eggs and bacon. The ironing went out every Tuesday night to a house on the hill behind the railroad tracks and came back folded every Wednesday evening. And as a businesswoman, my mother discovered that sometimes function was more important than fashion, at least for little girls.

Those old, worn Levi's of my brother's met the expectations of the advertisements. They survived an entire season of his hard wear and, unlike most of his clothes, were outgrown before worn out. And as mother used to say about anything that might be salvaged for use, "These old pants still have a little life left in them."

Not only did they have some life left in them, but they were going to give that life to me. A year earlier they would have been boxed with other we-don't-want-them-anymore clothes for the "naked children" of some foreign country I'd never heard of or, if the postage wasn't too expensive, shipped off to my poor cousins in South Dakota. With her newfound economic acumen and with her slowly evolving awareness of a woman's place, my mother looked at those blue jeans differently than she would have the year before. Maybe she looked at me a little differently, too.

"Marilyn, come here," she called from my brother's room. That in itself tripped anticipation. Now that Bob was approaching adolescence, his room held the mystery earned of secrecy. The door to his room was open; my mother leaned over the bed folding and sorting boy-clothes. Shirts in one stack, pants in another, worn to see-through-thin garments in still a third pile. But smoothed out full length along the edge of Bob's bed were a pair of old, worn Levi's.

"Here, try these on." She held them up against my seven-year-old middle. "I think these will fit you if you roll up the legs."

And fit they did, more like a gunnysack than a glove, but they were blue jeans and they were my brother's—and they were now mine. Cinched tightly with an Indian-beaded belt scrounged from my brother's dresser, the chamois-soft denim bunched in unplanned pleats at my waist. No more sissy elastic for me. Triple-roll cuffs still scuffed the ground by my shoe heels when I walked—my excuse for the swaggering steps those Levi's induced. After a time sidewalk burns frayed the bottom edge, finally denoting my singular ownership. Metal rivets marked the pockets and seam overlaps. Gone were the telltale girl-white overstitching outlines. And those pockets.

10

Real pockets. Not that patch pocket pretend stuff of girl-pants, but deep inside pockets of white, soft, gather-in-my-fist material that could be pulled inside out in search of the disappeared dime.

But those Levi's marked more than my move from little-girl clothes to big-brother clothes. Indeed, they were the only hand-me-downs ever handed down. Instead, those old ratty pants marked my move to freedom, freedom from the conventional girl-stuff my mother had so carefully fostered only one year earlier. Maybe my mother—who was learning the difference between roofing nails and wood screws, who was learning to mix paint in the vise-gripping shake-machine bolted to the floor in the back room of the hardware store, who would later teach me to cut glass, make keys, and clean Surge milk pumpers—wanted me to know what she was learning about women's work and men's work. I don't know. I just know that those Levi's—old, worn, with a difficult-to-manage button fly—meant the world to me, at least the limited world offered by my neighborhood.

The next summer I got my first two-wheeled bike, a full-size, blue, fat-tire Schwinn off the store's showroom floor. It was mother who convinced Dad that I didn't need training wheels. "If you want her to learn to ride, put her on it and let her ride." Oh, I dented the fenders some that summer and suffered some scars from the inescapable tip-overs, but I learned to ride as well as the boys. And by the end of the summer, Mom was packing peanut butter sandwiches for me to take on fishing expeditions down at the Chippewa River below the railroad trestle.

Along with the traditional dolls and play cookware, Christmas Eve   *15* brought chemistry kits and carpenter tools. Even my brother acknowledged my newfound worldliness. Better than any gift were the after-school hours spent helping him rebuild an old auto engine in the basement. I didn't do much, but watching him work and occasionally fetching wrenches taught me where pistons went and what they did, and that my big brother didn't mind having me around.

By junior high, I had my own .22. Our family Sundays in the fall found three of us in the woods searching the squirrel. My brother elected to hunt a more dangerous game, senior high school girls. Dad wore that goofy brown billed hat with cold-weather earflaps; I wore wool side-zipping slacks from the juniors department at Daytons, topped by a crew-neck matching sweater—style in a seventh-grade girl mattered even in the woods; Mom wore a turtleneck under one of Dad's wool shirt-jacs pulled out to hang over her blue jeans—old, worn Levi's.

Questions for Discussion

1. How does Schiel characterize her mother in this piece? What causes her mother to change? Does Schiel approve of this change?
2. Why did Schiel want to wear jeans when she was a little girl? What details in this essay help you to understand her point of view?

3. The first three sentences in this essay begin with the same two words, and the fourth provides only a minor variation. What is the effect of paragraph 1? Do you note any other examples of repetition in this essay? What does repetition contribute to the essay as a whole?
4. Consider the third sentence in paragraph 5. What is the effect of conveying so much information within a single sentence?
5. In the last glimpse of herself that she provides here, Schiel remembers wearing a pair of slacks from a fashionable department store rather than the jeans that once meant so much to her. What is this meant to show?

Suggestions for Writing

1. Remember a favorite possession of yours when you were young. Write about that item in enough detail for readers to understand why it mattered to you.
2. Write about a time when you were denied the chance to do something because other people considered it unsuitable for your gender.

THE CONTEST

Michael Dorris

> *In the following essay Michael Dorris writes about his mother by focusing upon two different memories of her in action. As you read, consider what her acts have in common and what they reveal about her. Be alert for details that convey the sense of a specific person, in a specific situation, at a specific moment in time.*

After my father, an army lieutenant, passed away at the end of World War II, my mother and I returned to Louisville to live with my grandmother and aunt. I was two; my mother was in her late thirties—a good ten years younger than my current age. A widow after less than five years as a wife—most of them spent away from my father, who was overseas—she must have been lonely and confused, but I never heard her complain or question the sharp turn in her future. With a small monthly stipend from my father's military pension and social security to supplement my aunt's income, my mother ran the house and devoted herself to the perfection of my childhood. To this day, she and my aunt continue to share that same house.

Before her marriage, according to the snips of stories I've heard and to the evidence of the family photo album, my mother had been famous in her circle as a free spirit. She swam at midnight in the Ohio River, spent her vacations from Colgate Palmolive as a passenger on United Fruit Company boats in the Caribbean, even once sang on a local radio show with Dale Evans. In the snapshots from her early twenties, my mother often has flowers tucked in her long, curly black hair, or sports off-the-shoulder blouses.

Early on my mother had taught herself to sew—she needed a wardrobe for the fun she intended to have, and there wasn't much money during the Depression for store-bought clothes. In my favorite picture of her, she had glamorized a cloth coat with epaulets cut from an old carpet. She has a bold look in her eye, is interested to see what comes next.

I first noticed this side of my mother when I was nine years old. A friend of my aunt's, Henry Lea, had a job as assistant stage manager at the Memorial Auditorium, the theater where touring out-of-town plays were presented. One January day he called to offer my mother and me free tickets to see a matinee of *The Dark Is Light Enough*, starring Katharine Cornell and my mother's favorite actor, Tyrone Power. I was happy to go—this was, after all, an unusual event—but my anticipation paled beside my mother's.

She took a long time to get ready, and when she appeared she looked   5 beautiful, perfumed and made-up, transformed in my eyes into a movie star herself. The last thing she did before we departed was to write a few words on a piece of paper, stare at it for a moment, make a change or two, then slip it into her purse. When I asked for an explanation, she would only say mysteriously, "Just in case."

I don't recall much of the play—its drama was far over my head—but I can tell you that my mother sat at attention the whole time, her back straight, her full concentration on the rhythm of the lines, the flow of the action on the stage. During intermission we stayed in our seats, didn't talk much and read the program. Once or twice my mother checked the paper in her purse but refused to let me see the words.

There were curtain calls, many of them, yet we didn't leave when the house lights went up.

"A surprise," my mother whispered. "Henry is going to sneak us in backstage." Her voice was nervous, tense, and she seemed less thrilled than terrified by the prospect. I followed her to a small door near the orchestra pit, and our friend met the knock.

"You'll have to be quick," Henry warned us. "He's exhausted. I'll put you in wardrobe, and he'll drop in for a minute to say hello."

We waited in a room filled with wonderful costumes in brilliant colors, *10* drawers overflowing with masks and capes, the props from many productions stacked upon every surface. But instead of exclaiming at each new thing I pointed out, my mother dug once again into her purse and found the now familiar paper. She was still looking at it, whispering to herself. When we heard someone at the door, she quickly crumbled it in her fist and stuffed it into her coat pocket.

Tyrone Power was the first famous person I ever met, and what I remember about him were his eyelashes, which were unnaturally long. I shook hands when we were introduced, but I hung my head, tongue-tied with shyness, incapable of uttering a sound.

"Ty," Henry said next. "I want you to meet my friend Mary Besy."

My mother stepped forward without hesitation, flashed a brilliant smile.

"Oh, Mr. Power." She spoke smoothly, confidently, each syllable enunciated distinct and clear. "We missed you every moment you were offstage."

It was just the right thing. Tyrone Power smiled back—that was the *15* other thing he had besides eyelashes: teeth—and stayed for a few minutes longer than I think he'd planned.

It must have been a year or two later when my mother heard about a competition run by the local Singer sewing machine shop. Each contestant paid a fee to enroll in an advanced class during which she would design and construct something called an "afternoon dress." Eventually there would be a fashion show, with judges, and the grand prize was a trip to Florida for two, all expenses paid.

The tuition put a strain on our finances, but my mother had confidence that it was a gamble worth taking. Every Tuesday night for three months she went to her course, discussed the intricacies of basting and pleating and tucks with other women, and returned with ideas that she translated into sketches. She took me along when she shopped for the right material, examining each flat bolt with an eye toward the cloth's hang and texture.

On the big night, however, my mother wouldn't let anyone accompany her to the actual event. She had made a blue linen sundress—for Florida, she had assured us—with a matching ivory bolero jacket. She even dyed a pair of shoes and covered a hat frame to match. My aunt contributed her good white gloves, and my grandmother came up with a pair of earrings to complete the ensemble. My mother got a permanent that afternoon, dressed early, and stood during supper so as not to wrinkle. We all applauded when she did a last twirl before walking out the door alone.

My mother has suffered many disappointments, big and small, in her life, and borne them all bravely, but that night was a triumph. She arrived home at nine o'clock with a velveteen crown, a plastic scepter and a certificate worth two airplane tickets, four days at the Belmar Hotel, a cabana by the pool and a welcome dinner that included shrimp cocktails.

I recall very well that trip thirty-five years ago—for I was my mother's *20* chosen companion, the chief beneficiary, as always, of her labor. She made me a plaid sports coat, a new pair of long pants, bought me a clip-on bow tie, and that first night in the tropics we sat together near the pool, listening until long past my usual bedtime as the hotel band played the music of my mother's youth. She was wearing the linen dress, of course, and her hair was blowing in the ocean breeze. Her eyes were closed, and she was smiling, singing the words to herself.

Questions for Discussion

1. Dorris claims that his mother was "a free spirit" before her marriage. How free does she seem by the time she enters the sewing contest?
2. When this essay was first published, it was paired with another memoir under the title "What My Mother Taught Me." Dorris does not directly state what his mother taught him, but judging from the way she is presented in this piece, what do you think he learned from her?
3. When Dorris wrote this memoir, he was ten years older than his mother was when she won the sewing contest he describes. In recording this memory, does he succeed in conveying a sense of what the experience meant to him as a child?
4. Dorris claims that his mother "devoted herself to the perfection of my childhood." Do you see any details in this piece suggesting that she had other goals of her own?
5. Dorris first mentions his mother's sewing in paragraph 3, but he then moves on to remember a trip to the theater before focusing upon the sewing contest that provides him with his title. How do these two memories relate to one another? How would the essay change if Dorris reversed the order in which he records them?

6. Consider this essay's title. Does it refer only to the sewing contest, or does it have a larger meaning?

Suggestions for Writing

1. Think of the various people you know best, and then write about the one who seems the most adventurous, the person most likely to swim the Ohio River at midnight. Focus your essay on one or two memories that show this person in action.
2. Write about a time you competed for a prize or for recognition. Try to make readers understand why this competition mattered to you at that point in your life.

FINISHING SCHOOL

Maya Angelou

> *As you read this chapter from Angelou's first volume of autobiography,* I
> Know Why the Caged Bird Sings, *think about the relationship between
> the setting, a small Southern town during the 1930s, and the events that
> happened there to a ten-year-old African-American girl—Angelou herself. At
> a time when many people questioned the value of higher education for women,
> young women were sometimes sent to "finishing schools"; their brothers went
> to college. Finishing schools offered a limited curriculum that emphasized such
> skills as giving parties and writing thank-you notes. Angelou's finishing school
> is the kitchen of a middle-class white woman who takes her social position
> seriously. Think about what Angelou learned when working there, and ask
> yourself if these lessons are still being taught today.*

Recently a white woman from Texas, who would quickly describe
herself as a liberal, asked me about my hometown. When I told her that in
Stamps my grandmother had owned the only Negro general merchandise
store since the turn of the century, she exclaimed, "Why, you were a debu-
tante." Ridiculous and even ludicrous. But Negro girls in small Southern
towns, whether poverty-stricken or just munching along on a few of life's
necessities, were given as extensive and irrelevant preparations for adult-
hood as rich white girls shown in magazines. Admittedly the training was
not the same. While white girls learned to waltz and sit gracefully with a
tea cup balanced on their knees, we were lagging behind, learning the mid-
Victorian values with very little money to indulge them. (Come and see
Edna Lomax spending the money she made picking cotton on five balls of
ecru tatting thread. Her fingers are bound to snag the work and she'll have
to repeat the stitches time and time again. But she knows that when she
buys the thread.)

We were required to embroider and I had trunkfuls of colorful dish-
towels, pillowcases, runners and handkerchiefs to my credit. I mastered the
art of crocheting and tatting, and there was a lifetime's supply of dainty
doilies that would never be used in sacheted dresser drawers. It went without
saying that all girls could iron and wash, but the finer touches around the
home, like setting a table with real silver, baking roasts and cooking vegetables without meat, had to be learned elsewhere. Usually at the source of
those habits. During my tenth year, a white woman's kitchen became my
finishing school.

Mrs. Viola Cullinan was a plump woman who lived in a three-
bedroom house somewhere behind the post office. She was singularly unattractive until she smiled, and then the lines around her eyes and mouth
which made her look perpetually dirty disappeared, and her face looked like

the mask of an impish elf. She usually rested her smile until late afternoon when her women friends dropped in and Miss Glory, the cook, served them cold drinks on the closed-in porch.

The exactness of her house was inhuman. This glass went here and only here. That cup had its place and it was an act of impudent rebellion to place it anywhere else. At twelve o'clock the table was set. At 12:15 Mrs. Cullinan sat down to dinner (whether her husband had arrived or not). At 12:16 Miss Glory brought out the food.

It took me a week to learn the difference between a salad plate, a bread   5
plate and a dessert plate.

Mrs. Cullinan kept up the tradition of her wealthy parents. She was from Virginia. Miss Glory, who was a descendant of slaves that had worked for the Cullinans, told me her history. She had married beneath her (according to Miss Glory). Her husband's family hadn't had their money very long and what they had "didn't 'mount to much."

As ugly as she was, I thought privately, she was lucky to get a husband above or beneath her station. But Miss Glory wouldn't let me say a thing against her mistress. She was very patient with me, however, over the housework. She explained the dishware, silverware and servants' bells. The large round bowl in which soup was served wasn't a soup bowl, it was a tureen. There were goblets, sherbet glasses, ice-cream glasses, wine glasses, green glass coffee cups with matching saucers, and water glasses. I had a glass to drink from, and it sat with Miss Glory's on a separate shelf from the others. Soup spoons, gravy boat, butter knives, salad forks and carving platter were additions to my vocabulary and in fact almost represented a new language. I was fascinated with the novelty, with the fluttering Mrs. Cullinan and her Alice-in-Wonderland house.

Her husband remains, in my memory, undefined. I lumped him with all the other white men that I had ever seen and tried not to see.

On our way home one evening, Miss Glory told me that Mrs. Cullinan couldn't have children. She said that she was too delicate-boned. It was hard to imagine bones at all under those layers of fat. Miss Glory went on to say that the doctor had taken out all her lady organs. I reasoned that a pig's organs included the lungs, heart and liver, so if Mrs. Cullinan was walking around without those essentials, it explained why she drank alcohol out of unmarked bottles. She was keeping herself embalmed.

When I spoke to Bailey° about it, he agreed that I was right, but he   10
also informed me that Mr. Cullinan had two daughters by a colored lady and that I knew them very well. He added that the girls were the spitting image of their father. I was unable to remember what he looked like, although I had just left him a few hours before, but I thought of the Coleman girls. They were very light-skinned and certainly didn't look very much like their mother (no one ever mentioned Mr. Coleman).

Bailey: Identified earlier in the work from which this selection is excerpted, Bailey is the author's brother.

My pity for Mrs. Cullinan preceded me the next morning like the Cheshire cat's smile. Those girls, who could have been her daughters, were beautiful. They didn't have to straighten their hair. Even when they were caught in the rain, their braids still hung down straight like tamed snakes. Their mouths were pouty little cupid's bows. Mrs. Cullinan didn't know what she missed. Or maybe she did. Poor Mrs. Cullinan.

For weeks after, I arrived early, left late and tried very hard to make up for her barrenness. If she had had her own children, she wouldn't have had to ask me to run a thousand errands from her back door to the back door of her friends. Poor old Mrs. Cullinan.

Then one evening Miss Glory told me to serve the ladies on the porch. After I set the tray down and turned toward the kitchen, one of the women asked, "What's your name, girl?" It was the speckled-faced one. Mrs. Cullinan said, "She doesn't talk much. Her name's Margaret."

"Is she dumb?"

"No. As I understand it, she can talk when she wants to but she's   *15* usually quiet as a little mouse. Aren't you, Margaret?"

I smiled at her. Poor thing. No organs and couldn't even pronounce my name correctly.

"She's a sweet little thing, though."

"Well, that may be, but the name's too long. I'd never bother myself. I'd call her Mary if I was you."

I fumed into the kitchen. That horrible woman would never have the chance to call me Mary because if I was starving I'd never work for her. I decided I wouldn't pee on her if her heart was on fire. Giggles drifted in off the porch and into Miss Glory's pots. I wondered what they could be laughing about.

Whitefolks were so strange. Could they be talking about me? Every-   *20* body knew that they stuck together better than the Negroes did. It was possible that Mrs. Cullinan had friends in St. Louis who heard about a girl from Stamps being in court and wrote to her. Maybe she knew about Mr. Freeman.°

My lunch was in my mouth a second time and I went outside and relieved myself on the bed of four-o'clocks. Miss Glory thought I might be coming down with something and told me to go on home, that Momma would give me some herb tea, and she'd explain to her mistress.

I realized how foolish I was being before I reached the pond. Of course Mrs. Cullinan didn't know. Otherwise she wouldn't have given me the two nice dresses that Momma cut down, and she certainly wouldn't have called me a "sweet little thing." My stomach felt fine, and I didn't mention anything to Momma.

That evening I decided to write a poem on being white, fat, old and

---

Mr. Freeman: He had sexually abused the author during an earlier scene set in St. Louis, and she testified against him in court.

without children. It was going to be a tragic ballad. I would have to watch her carefully to capture the essence of her loneliness and pain.

The very next day, she called me by the wrong name. Miss Glory and I were washing up the lunch dishes when Mrs. Cullinan came to the doorway. "Mary?"

Miss Glory asked, "Who?" 25

Mrs. Cullinan, sagging a little, knew and I knew. "I want Mary to go down to Mrs. Randall's and take her some soup. She's not been feeling well for a few days."

Miss Glory's face was a wonder to see. "You mean Margaret, ma'am. Her name's Margaret."

"That's too long. She's Mary from now on. Heat that soup from last night and put it in the china tureen and, Mary, I want you to carry it carefully."

Every person I knew had a hellish horror of being "called out of his name." It was a dangerous practice to call a Negro anything that could be loosely construed as insulting because of the centuries of their having been called niggers, jigs, dinges, blackbirds, crows, boots and spooks.

Miss Glory had a fleeting second of feeling sorry for me. Then as she 30 handed me the hot tureen she said, "Don't mind, don't pay that no mind. Sticks and stones may break your bones, but words . . . You know, I been working for her for twenty years."

She held the back door open for me. "Twenty years. I wasn't much older than you. My name used to be Hallelujah. That's what Ma named me, but my mistress give me 'Glory,' and it stuck. I likes it better too."

I was in the little path that ran behind the houses when Miss Glory shouted, "It's shorter too."

For a few seconds it was a tossup over whether I would laugh (imagine being named Hallelujah) or cry (imagine letting some white woman rename you for her convenience). My anger saved me from either outburst. I had to quit the job, but the problem was going to be how to do it. Momma wouldn't allow me to quit for just any reason.

"She's a peach. That woman is a real peach." Mrs. Randall's maid was talking as she took the soup from me, and I wondered what her name used to be and what she answered to now.

For a week I looked into Mrs. Cullinan's face as she called me Mary. 35 She ignored my coming late and leaving early. Miss Glory was a little annoyed because I had begun to leave egg yolk on the dishes and wasn't putting much heart in polishing the silver. I hoped that she would complain to our boss, but she didn't.

Then Bailey solved my dilemma. He had me describe the contents of the cupboard and the particular plates she liked best. Her favorite piece was a casserole shaped like a fish and the green glass coffee cups. I kept his instructions in mind, so on the next day when Miss Glory was hanging out clothes and I had again been told to serve the old biddies on the porch, I dropped the empty serving tray. When I heard Mrs. Cullinan scream, "Mary!" I picked up the casserole and two of the green glass cups in readiness. As she rounded the kitchen door I let them fall on the tiled floor.

I could never absolutely describe to Bailey what happened next, because each time I got to the part where she fell on the floor and screwed up her ugly face to cry, we burst out laughing. She actually wobbled around on the floor and picked up shards of the cups and cried, "Oh, Momma. Oh, dear Gawd. It's Momma's china from Virginia. Oh, Momma, I sorry."

Miss Glory came running in from the yard and the women from the porch crowded around. Miss Glory was almost as broken up as her mistress. "You mean to say she broke our Virginia dishes? What we gone do?"

Mrs. Cullinan cried louder, "That clumsy nigger. Clumsy little black nigger."

Old speckled-face leaned down and asked, "Who did it, Viola? Was it Mary? Who did it?" 40

Everything was happening so fast I can't remember whether her action preceded her words, but I know that Mrs. Cullinan said, "Her name's Margaret, goddamn it, her name's Margaret." And she threw a wedge of the broken plate at me. It could have been the hysteria which put her aim off, but the flying crockery caught Miss Glory right over her ear and she started screaming.

I left the front door wide open so all the neighbors could hear.

Mrs. Cullinan was right about one thing. My name wasn't Mary.

Questions for Discussion

1. Why does Mrs. Cullinan call the author Mary when her name is Margaret? Why did Angelou resent this (even she herself eventually changed her name)?
2. In a house stocked with so many glasses, why did Angelou and Miss Glory have their own drinking glasses on a separate shelf?
3. According to Angelou, Mrs. Cullinan's kitchen became her "finishing school." What exactly did she learn there?
4. Although Miss Glory is patient with Angelou and even sticks up for her at one point, she ultimately sides with Mrs. Cullinan. What is Miss Glory's function in this narrative? How is she different from Angelou?
5. When this work is reprinted in anthologies, editors usually omit the line "I decided that I wouldn't pee on her if her heart was on fire." Now that you have read this selection as originally published, consider the effect of omitting paragraph 19. Which version do you prefer and why?

Suggestions for Writing

1. Have you ever been the victim of an unkind employer or been trapped in a relationship that seemed difficult to break? Write about a time when you felt frustrated enough to drop dishes on the floor.

2. Narrative often involves a "turning point"—a point when a character changes in some fundamental way. Such a change can be caused by almost anything. But whether the cause is something big or something small, it seems significant within the narrative. Write an essay that will show a turning point in your own life.

GATORS

Geoffrey Norman

> *As you read the following essay, bear in mind that time is part of any scene:*
> *A place can seem different at different times of the year, and some places change*
> *as time passes. "Gators" take place in Florida, but the scene shifts from Florida*
> *in the 1950s to Florida in 1980, when this essay was first published. Consider*
> *why this shifting scene is important. As you read about Norman's experience*
> *with alligators, it might help you to know that they were on the endangered-*
> *species list when he wrote.*

One of my jobs a couple dozen years ago was to haul the garbage from our family's summer place. It was good training for a boy. It taught me humility and reminded me to wash my hands. And though the job had its disciplinary aspect, it was just about the only chore I looked forward to. Because of the alligator.

The summer house was on a beach so remote that we had no electricity. There was no garbage pickup, either, so at first we buried the stuff. The boys in the family were reminded to dig deep holes for the garbage, meaning six feet, at least—deep enough to decently bury a dead man, which was one of the few things we never actually put in those holes.

Ours was a big house and a big family, and there was a lot of garbage. We caught and cleaned all our own seafood, so there were fish heads and shrimp shells by the pound. We also buried all the road kills, which were frequent, probably because the blacktop was new and the animals had not yet learned to fear it. Every day there was a dead possum, armadillo, or snake to dispose of. Burying those bodies and all that garbage became the grimmest part of my day—worse, even, than baths or bedtime or Sunday school.

Then, about three hundred yards from the house, we discovered the slough and the gator. The slough was a depression full of dark water, lily pads, cattails, and frogs. It was perhaps as big as a football field. One day an alligator appeared there.

It was not a large gator like those ten- or twelve-footers you see in   *5*
dirty concrete pits at the cheap Florida roadside attractions. But it was not a toy or a pet, either. This was a mature alligator, six or seven feet long. At first, we tried out its appetite on a few simple things: leftover fish, stale bread, overripe fruit. Whatever we offered, it ate greedily, which may be the only way an alligator ever eats. Then we made it tougher, tossing the gator crab scraps and dead raccoons, watermelon rinds and coffee grounds. Suddenly there were no more tedious pits and smelly funerals; when we boys were called on to take out the garbage, it was an adventure. Now we gladly took the short walk to the slough, hoping all the way that the gator would be in sight once we got there. About half the time, it would be out where we could get a good look.

It was something I never got over. Although I did not fear the alligator with a trembling, cold-fleshed fear, I knew when I saw it that I was looking at the *other*. This was a creature governed by the oldest, most irreducible urges, and they seemed almost visible on him. No other creature so clearly displays its origins and, in some fashion, its essence. An alligator is not mean; it is merely primitive.

We all understood that, even though we were just boys, and we watched the gator through three or four summers without ever trying to touch it or feed it with our hands or wrestle with it. We respected that alligator and appreciated the job it did.

One night, as the cold-blooded gator lay on the road enjoying the residual warmth of the blacktop, a carful of drunks came along. They stopped their car, got out, and beat the alligator to death with tire irons. Then they sped off in the night, whooping it up. They were called rednecks then, and that was their style. We heard the whole thing, but there wasn't enough time to get to the road and stop it.

The next morning, we buried the alligator and went back to burying the garbage. We watched the slough to see if another gator would move in and claim the vacant turf. When that didn't happen, I thought about going back to the swamp and catching a small one, which was easy and safe enough to do if you used a snare or a net. I never caught one for the slough, though. There was no need. Electricity came to town. The road was improved. We got a telephone. And somebody started hauling garbage.

As civilization arrived, the alligators disappeared. Soon a golf course   10
was built on the black-water lake they used to inhabit, and I could not have found one to transplant even if I'd wanted to.

The problem, of course, was not just local, and the alligator made the endangered-species list several years ago. Women—and some men, no doubt—liked alligator-skin belts, boots, and bags so much that it was possible to make a living by killing them and selling the hides. What the Army Corps and the developers had started, fashion and the poachers threatened to finish.

The alligators' turnaround since that time has made national news. Protection and strict controls on interstate shipment of gator hides have worked: the animals have come back strong. Every so often, one will eat a poodle or take up residence in the water hazard on the sixteenth hole. Fish-and-game people are then called out to lasso the uncomprehending reptile and move it to an out-of-the-way place. There is even some limited commerce again in the skins. At least one entrepreneur is ranching alligators, just as though they were cattle or mink. Not long ago, someone in Florida was killed by an alligator in what I suspect must have been a well-deserved attack.

But to survive is not necessarily to thrive, and although the gator is back from the jaws of extinction, I had not seen one for years until the other day. I was coming home with my daughter from a prosaic errand, driving along the old winding blacktop instead of on the straight new highway. It was late in the afternoon. The earth glistened from a thunderstorm that had built up all day and had then climaxed in a wild discharge of lightning and sheets of driving rain. Now the air was cool, and the low country had come to life.

The road ran through a flat, desolate marsh, where blackbirds darted across meaty cattail pods. Seven bobwhite chicks marched behind their mother like nervous recruits. A water moccasin lay dead in the road where an automobile tire had flattened it. I remembered a time when I had watched an alligator devour a big moccasin. The snake had struck repeatedly and futilely at the gator's head, but mere fangs had no chance against that hide. The alligator swallowed the snake with primitive nonchalance, swam back to a clear stretch of bank, crawled out of the pond, and disappeared in the saw grass.

In the midst of recalling that scene, I noticed a characteristic profile— nose, then eyes—and a slight disturbance on the surface of the water above a massive body. There was an alligator in the drainage pond just off the shoulder of the road. I stopped the car and walked to the water's edge with my daughter, who had never seen an alligator except in books. I pointed to the low profile, not really expecting her to appreciate it for what it was. It looked like a log. They always do.   15

The gator turned. I expected it to dive and swim away. Instead, it swam right for us, stopping when it reached the water's edge, its snout less than a yard from our feet. My daughter was delighted and slightly concerned. She held my hand tightly and willingly. We had nothing to feed the gator except a piece of bubble gum that the bank clerk had given us. I unwrapped it and tossed it to the gator, which took it down with a single swallow.

We told that story for a day or two, then returned, with my wife and a bag of marshmallows, to the little pond. When we walked to the bank, the gator swam over to meet us. We threw marshmallows, but they were ignored. Instead of eating, the alligator hissed at us, the air making a rattling sound as it escaped the gator's throat. My daughter was frightened. We put the marshmallows down and stood there. The alligator looked up at us with vacant eyes and a reptilian grin, like a captured creature trapped in some zoo. I felt terrible for all of us.

Then my daughter pointed and said, "Another one."

I looked, and, indeed, another gator had materialized about thirty feet from the bank. This one was about five feet long, a little smaller than the one that lay unblinking at our feet.

I threw a marshmallow, and it landed four feet from the alligator's nose.   20 The large mouth opened in what looked like an exaggerated yawn. The marshmallow disappeared. For my daughter's amusement I threw half a dozen more of them at the cruising gator, feeling worse all the time.

Then the alligator at our feet slid back into the water and swam for the middle of the pond. We assumed that he was after marshmallows and, for some reason, would not eat them at the bank. We watched as the two alligators glided closer together, graceful and silent. Then the larger alligator attacked. It was deliberate and swift. There was no damage, only a sudden noisy swirl of dark water and a splashy retreat by the smaller alligator. The first gator then returned to his station at our feet and hissed at us rudely.

"What was that all about?" my wife asked.

"No telling," I said.

In a few minutes, the second alligator reappeared. The marshmallows must have been irresistible. I threw a few more out on the surface of the pond, where they were snapped up. Then the gator at our feet backed off the bank, swam effortlessly to the middle of the pond, and attacked again.

"I don't get it," my wife said. . . .

"I don't know," I said. I felt much better, though.

25

That night, we decided that the first gator must have been a nesting female and the second a transient male. The first had come to warn us off and to defend her nest. The second was hungry and couldn't pass up easy food. The first did not approve of the invasion of her nest. It was a plausible theory, though I did not try to verify it by locating the nest. Happy as I was to see an alligator after all those years, I knew that if I had stepped into the pond or reached too close with one of those marshmallows, the primeval imperative would have taken over, and that gator would have taken off my arm.

Questions for Discussion

1. Norman claims that he never got over his boyhood experience with an alligator. What did the alligator represent for him?
2. Much of paragraph 3 is devoted to road kills. What connection is there between these dead animals and the alligators that are the focus of this essay?
3. Norman reports that he was "feeling worse all the time" when feeding marshmallows to the alligator. After watching another alligator attack, he reports that he felt much better. Why did he have these responses?
4. In paragraphs 11 and 12, Norman departs from recording memories to offer background information on the status of alligators. Are these paragraphs worth including, or do they distract attention from the memories that come before and after them?
5. Is there anything admirable about the alligators described in this essay? Why should anyone care that alligators have been rescued from what Norman aptly calls "the jaws of extinction"?

Suggestions for Writing

1. Norman remembers a chore that became an adventure. Write about one of your own childhood chores if you can remember a time when performing that chore was especially interesting or difficult.

2. Write about some aspect of your childhood that has been lost or endangered by "civilization." Describe an environment that now seems at risk, and show what has caused it to change.

TAKING THE TEST

David Groff

As its title suggests, the focus of this essay is on an act: taking a test. The test in question is the test for HIV-positive antibodies that indicate infection with the AIDS virus. The author takes the test because he is gay and considers himself at risk. As you read, try to imagine what it would be like to wait for your test results if you knew that you might have been exposed to AIDS. Think about why Groff chose to write about this experience and then publish what he wrote.

The time had come for me to take the Test, as we gay men call it. "The Test" is part of our succinct new vocabulary of non-words—PCP, DDI, KS, DHPG, CMV, AZT—all representing either opportunistic infections or treatments for that acronym looming in so many of our lives: AIDS. For years I had wondered which non-word might ambush me and which series of non-words could prolong my life. Now I sat on an examining table, my left hand a fist, as the doctor's latexed fingers drew my purple blood into a vial. For years—practically ever since the HIV antibody test had been released in 1985—I had avoided this moment, avoided knowing whether or not I was antibody-positive and therefore more likely to develop immunosuppression, which could lead to AIDS. Along with my friends, I could justify avoiding the Test. It seemed better to be surprised by AIDS than to live paralyzed by a prospect I was powerless to alter.

That isn't true anymore. Or, as my doctor put it, "Two years ago, if you took the Test and you were positive, all I could do would be to send you to a shrink. Now if you're positive, we still send you to a shrink—but we can intervene."

My rational self agreed with my doctor. If I was positive and if my level of helper cells was suppressed, I could go on AZT, the very toxic drug that seems to counter the virus in some people and that remains the only antiviral approved by the government for widespread and standard use. But watching my blood enter the vial still panicked me. I had made the first of a series of decisions that could change forever how I lived my life—if not how long my life might be.

The doctor withdrew the needle, capped the vial, and labeled the tube. On a little form he checked off half the risk groups listed: gay or bisexual male, sexual partner of persons at risk, and "other." He scrawled something on an envelope and shoved the vial and form inside. Then he explained where to drop it off, told me a bad joke, bandaged my arm, patted it, and left.

Minutes later I was on the subway from my doctor's office on the Upper East Side, heading down to the Department of Public Health at *5*

Twenty-sixth and First Avenue. They would test the blood not confiden-
tially but anonymously—I was identified only by number—and in two
weeks I would visit my doctor again to find out the results face to face.

The vial balanced on top of the papers in my shoulder bag. I imagined
the blood rolling out and smashing onto the floor amid the evening rush-
hour commuters. I imagined them leaping back, wondering—just as I wondered—whether the blood was infected. I almost wanted the vial to crash
and break; then I wouldn't have to deliver it and I would never know. Even
though I intended to keep private the fact of my taking the Test, a part of
me wanted to appall the commuters—just as I was appalled.

It was after hours, and the lobby to the building was deserted. I asked
the guard where Room 102 was, feeling obvious, feeling infected. With a
nearly imperceptible and perhaps contemptuous nod he directed me the
right way. My question, and my situation, were ordinary for him.

Room 102 was a refrigerator in a closet. I had expected a bustling
clinic of white-coated lab technicians testing the city's blood day and night.
Inside the refrigerator, envelopes with vials of blood lay on the trays, each
one labeled with a series of medical abbreviations unfamiliar to me. There
were hundreds of vials. I laid my blood in gently among them and thought
for a long moment before I shut the refrigerator door and left.

When I turned around I found a woman in front of me, tall, dressed
in sleek black, her hair hidden under a black scarf and her face dead white.
She was holding an envelope identical to mine. I met her blue eyes for an
instant and then we both looked away. I made my way around her, speculating a little on what brought her here—marriage, prospective pregnancy,
a boyfriend, a tragedy. For a moment we were a two-person community of
the worried well, eyes averted just like regular New Yorkers. Someone knew
my secret; someone knew hers.

When I got outside, the city was beautiful, even this unphotogenic   *10*
section of First Avenue. The gray lines of buildings and sky seemed like a
riot of subtle colors, the horns and headlights a vigorous party. I felt acutely
aware of my possibly infected body, how it took up space, how the muscles
worked in my legs and how, as a result, I moved. I wouldn't be moving
forever, I knew that; someday I would be still. I turned around and saw the
woman in black hurrying the opposite way. I wondered if she felt about her
body the way I felt about mine.

For the next two weeks I ate bacon cheeseburgers almost daily, a series
of last meals. Every time the phone rang, at home or at the office, I felt an
electric anxiety. My doctor had promised he would not call, but I kept
hoping he'd break our agreement and phone to say I was negative. That way
I could sleep at night. He didn't call.

I grew more obsessed daily. Even though for hours at a time I'd forget to anticipate my test results, my fear would ambush me like a bowel-
loosening punch in the gut. I told myself that I wouldn't die the very day
the doctor told me the bad news. My HIV-positive friends, and those who

had been diagnosed with AIDS, were still alive—mostly. They'd coped. I'd cope too. Cold comfort.

I'd wake up in the middle of the night trying to remember the details of every sexual experience I'd ever had, however minimal the risk of infection might have been. I went so far as to get up at 2 A.M. and scour the phone book to locate those men I'd lost contact with. One name was absent. That was unnerving, because I knew he had been listed and that he owned his apartment and thus wasn't likely to leave New York. Probably he was just unlisted now. But I lay awake the rest of the night wondering if Peter was still alive.

Two weeks later, my body feeling oddly light, as if I could still sense the ounce of blood I'd lost, I was sitting on that same examining table, hearing my doctor's low voice from the next room. He was running late. I told myself I'd know how to react, but I knew I wouldn't. I let my eyes focus on a bad watercolor above the sink: a beached sailboat lying coyly on its side in the sand. The pastels were fey but they seemed brilliant to me.

The door opened and my doctor's face appeared, sweaty at the end of the workday, as bemused as usual. *15*

Forgive me, but I will not tell you what my doctor told me.

Imagine for yourself the immense relief, the knot of tension sliced through, the light-headed desire to hug the doctor and laugh. But imagine also the doctor's pronouncement, his optimistic droning about prolonged longevity and further T-cell tests, the spit in the stomach forming a big sickening ball, the disbelief, the thousands of self-steelings. Imagine that different sort of light-headedness.

My antibody status does not matter to you. Certainly it matters—with absolute enormity—to me. But what I'd like you to remember is the blood on the subway, the click of the refrigerator door, the woman in black so elegant and uneasy, First Avenue at gritty, gorgeous dusk, the brilliance of that bad art in the examining room, the pores of the doctor's face—all of them declaring, by their very existence: As long and as well as you can, live, live.

Questions for Discussion

1. AIDS is not restricted to gay men, and Groff could have written about being tested for this disease without revealing his sexual orientation. But he makes this revelation in the opening sentence of his essay, and repeats it in paragraphs 4 and 13. What do you think motivated this candor? How would the essay change if the author did not disclose his sexual preference?
2. What does the fantasy in paragraph 6 reveal about Groff's state of mind?
3. In his conclusion Groff writes that he wants us to remember the woman in black. What is her role in the essay?

4. Why does Groff find the city beautiful after he leaves the Department of Public Health? Did the city change or did Groff?

5. Consider Groff's decision to withhold the results of his AIDS test. How would the essay change if you knew he had tested either positive or negative?

Suggestions for Writing

1. Recall situations in which you suffered from anxiety waiting for the results of a medical test, a job interview, an examination at school—or any other time when news of your future seemed only a phone call away. Focus upon one specific memory and write about it so that others can understand how you felt.

2. Write about a time when you did something against your will because you believed this action was necessary.

LIFE WITH FATHER

Itabari Njeri

> *The following memoir is set in a Harlem apartment during the mid-1960s—a time when African-Americans were struggling for civil rights. The scene thus includes not only the apartment but also the era in which the author was growing up. As you read this account of family conflict, think about how racial prejudice in the world beyond the apartment can help to account for the personal conflicts that happened within it.*

Daddy wore boxer shorts when he worked; that's all. He'd sit for hours reading and writing at a long, rectangular table covered with neat stacks of *I. F. Stone's Weekly, The Nation, The New Republic,* and the handwritten pages of his book in progress, *The Tolono Station and Beyond.* A Mott's applesauce jar filled with Teacher's scotch was a constant, and his own forerunner of today's wine coolers was the ever-present chaser: ginger ale and Manischewitz Concord grape wine in a tall, green iced-tea glass.

As he sat there, his beer belly weighing down the waistband of his shorts, I'd watch. I don't know if he ever saw me. I hid from him at right angles. From the bend of the hallway, at the end of a long, dark, L-shaped corridor in our Harlem apartment, it was at least thirty feet to the living room where my father worked, framed by the doorway. I sat cross-legged on the cold linoleum floor and inspected his seated, six-foot-plus figure through a telescope formed by my forefinger and thumb: bare feet in thonged sandals, long hairy legs that rose toward the notorious shorts (I hated those shorts, wouldn't bring my girlfriends home because of those shorts), breasts that could fill a B cup, and a long neck on which a balding head rested. Viewed in isolation, I thought perhaps I'd see him clearer, know him better.

Daddy was a philosopher, a Marxist historian, an exceptional teacher, and a fine tenor. He had a good enough voice to be as great a concert artist as John McCormack, one of his favorites. The obstacles to that career couldn't have been much greater than the ones he actually overcame.

The state of Georgia, where my father grew up, established its version of the literacy test in 1908, the year he was born. If you substituted Georgia for Mississippi in the story that Lerone Bennett Jr. relates in *Before the Mayflower: A History of Black America,* the main character could easily have been my father: A black teacher, a graduate of Eton and Harvard, presents himself to a Mississippi registrar. The teacher is told to read the state constitution and several books. He does. The registrar produces a passage in Greek, which the teacher reads. Then another in Latin. Then other passages in French, German, and Spanish, all of which the teacher reads. The registrar finally holds up a page of Chinese characters and asks: "What does this mean?" The teacher replies: "It means you don't want me to vote."

Apocryphal, perhaps, but the tale exemplified enough collective ex-   5
perience that I heard my father tell virtually the same story about a former
Morehouse College classmate to a buddy over the phone one afternoon. At
the punchline, he fell into a fit of laughter, chuckling hard into a balled fist
he held at his mouth. Finally, he said, "Fred, I'll have to call you back," then
fell back on the bed, in his boxer shorts, laughing at the ceiling.

He claimed he burst out laughing like this once in a class at Harvard.
A law professor, discussing some constitutional issue in class, singled out my
father and said, "In this matter, regarding men of your race—"

"Which race is that?" my father boomed, cutting him off, "the 50 yard
or the 100?" But it seemed to me he always related that particular tale with
a sneer on his lips.

He'd been at Harvard studying law on a postdoctoral scholarship from
1942 to 1943. After receiving his Ph.D. in philosophy from the University
of Toronto ten years earlier, he had headed toward the dust bowls others
were escaping in the mid-1930s and became the editor of a black newspaper,
the *Oklahoma Eagle,* in Tulsa. He eventually returned to academia and by
1949 was the head of the philosophy department at Morgan State University
in Baltimore. That's where he met my mother, a nurse many years his junior.

My mother—who commits nothing to paper, speaks of the past cryp-
tically, and believes all unpleasantries are best kept under a rug—once leaked
the fact that she and my father took me to a parade in Brooklyn when I was
about three. We were standing near the arch at Grand Army Plaza when he
suddenly hauled off and punched her in the mouth, with me in her arms.
My mother, a very gentle and naive woman, said the whole thing left her in
a state of shock. My father had never been violent before.

They separated, and I seldom saw my father again until my parents   10
reunited when I was seven. We moved into my father's six-room apartment
on 129th Street, between Convent Avenue and St. Nicholas Terrace. It was
certainly far more spacious than the apartment I'd lived in with my mother
on St. James Place in Brooklyn. The immediate neighborhood was an
attractive, hilly section of Harlem, just a few blocks from City College.
All things considered, I hated it. More precisely, I hated my father, so I
hated it all.

Because of his past leftist political affiliations, Daddy had lost his government and university jobs. Now, out of necessity but also desire, he decided to devote his time to teaching younger people. He wanted to reach
them at a stage in their lives when he felt he could make a difference. He
joined the faculty of a Jersey City high school and began teaching journal-
ism, history, and English. He also taught English at night to foreign-born
students at City College. His students, I came to learn, loved him; his daughter found it hard to. I made the mistake of calling him Pop—once. He said,
"Don't ever call me that again. If you don't like calling me Daddy, you can
call me Dr. Moreland."

Once, my mother deserted me, leaving me alone with him. She went to Atlanta for several weeks with my baby brother to tend my ailing Grandma Hattie, my father's mother. Since I hadn't known this man most of my seven years on the planet, and didn't like him much now that I did, I asked him if I could stay around the corner with a family friend, Aunt Pearl. "If she asks you to stay, fine. But don't ask her," he told me. Naturally I asked her.

When he asked me if I had asked her, I hesitated. But I was not a child inclined to lie. So I said, "I don't want to lie. I asked her." I got a beating for that, a brutal beating with a belt that left welts and bruises on my legs for months.

My father felt children should be hit for any infraction. Further, they should be seen and not heard, speak only when spoken to, etc. From the day he hit me, the latter became my philosophy, too. I never consciously decided to stop speaking to my father, but for the next ten years, I rarely initiated a conversation with him. Later he would tell me, "You were a very strange child."

But if I would not accept him as a father, my curiosity would not let   *15* me deny him as a teacher. One day, a question about the nature of truth compelled a thaw in my emotional cold war—nothing less could have. Truth changes, a classmate in the seventh grade had insisted that day. It is constant, I argued, and went to my father for confirmation.

People's perceptions change, I explained. New information debunks the lies of the past, but the truth was always there. And I told my father what I had told my mostly white classmates in a Bronx junior high school at the height of the civil rights movement: Black people were always human beings worthy of the same rights other Americans enjoyed, but it took hundreds of years of a slave system that dehumanized the master as well as the slave and a social revolution before most white Americans would accept that truth.

My father turned from his worktable, took off his glasses, with their broken right temple piece, and released a long and resonant "Yesssss." And then he spoke to me of a rational cosmos and what Lincoln had to do with Plato. When our philosophical discussion ended, we each went to our separate corners.

My father had a beaten, black upright piano in the parlor, badly out of tune. But its bench was a treasure of ancient sheet music: Vincent Youman's "Through the Years," with a picture of Gladys Swarthout on the frayed cover. And I loved the chord changes to "Spring Is Here."

I ventured from the sanctuary of my blue-walled room one summer afternoon, walking down the long hallway toward the kitchen, then stopped abruptly. I heard my father in the kitchen several feet away; he was making an ice-cream soda, something as forbidden to him as alcohol since he was a diabetic. I heard the clink of a metal spoon against a glass as he sang, "For I lately took a notion for to cross the briny ocean, and I'm off to Philadelphia in the morning." It was an Irish folk song made famous by John McCormack. I backed up. Too late. He danced across the kitchen threshold in his boxer shorts, stopped when he spotted me in the shadows, then shook his head. He smiled, lifted one leg and both arms in a Jackie Gleason "and away we go" motion, then slid off.

Minutes later he called me. "Jill the Pill, you know this song!" I knew   20 all the songs and wrote down the words to "Moon River" for him. Then he asked me to sing it. I was always ready to sing, even for my father.

He sat on the edge of his bed with the lyrics in his hand as I sang. When I finished the phrase "We're after the same rainbow's end, waitin' round the bend, my huckleberry friend," my daddy looked at me and said what others would tell me years later but with far less poetry: "My girl, you have the celestial vibration." And then he asked me to sing it again and told me it was "wonderful." Then I left him.

For days, maybe weeks, a tense calm would reign in the apartment. Then, without warning, the hall would fill with harsh voices. My father stood in the narrow, shadowy space hitting my mother. "Put it down," he yelled. "Put it down or I'll . . ."

My mother had picked up a lamp in a lame effort to ward off his blows. His shouting had awakened me. I'd been sick in bed with the flu and a high fever. When he saw me open my bedroom door he yelled, "Get back in your room." I did, my body overtaken by tremors and the image of my mother branded on my eyeballs. I swore that I would never let anyone do that to me or to anyone else I had the power to help. I had no power to help my mother. It was an oath with terrible consequences, one I'd have to disavow to permit myself the vulnerability of being human.

I know my father's fury was fueled by his sense of insignificance. He felt himself to be an intellectual giant boxed in by mental midgets. Unlike Ralph Ellison, Paul Robeson, or Richard Wright°—all contemporaries and acquaintances of my father's—he was never acknowledged by the dominant culture whose recognition he sought. He could be found, Ellison once told me, pontificating in Harlem barbershops, elucidating the dialogues of Plato for a captive audience of draped men, held prone, each with a straight-edge razor pressed against his cheek.

My father's unreconciled identities—the classic schizophrenia of being   25 black and an American, the contradictions of internalizing whole the cultural values of a society that sees you, when it sees you at all, as life in one of its lower forms—stoked his alcoholism. And since my father at once critiqued the society that denied him and longed for its approbation, he lived with the pain-filled consciousness of one who knows he is a joke. I think

---

Ralph Ellison: American novelist (1914–1994) best known for *Invisible Man* (1952). *Paul Robeson:* American singer, actor, and political activist (1898–1976). *Richard Wright:* American writer (1908–1960), best known for *Native Son* (1940).

sometimes he laughed the hardest, so often did I stumble upon him alone, chuckling into his balled fist at some silent, invisible comedian.

When his drunken rages ended, he slept for days, spread out on the bed wearing only his boxer shorts. I watched him on those days, too, daring to come closer, safe with the knowledge that Morpheus° held him. I examined his face, wondering who he was and why he was. As I watched, he'd lift his head off the pillow, then fall back muttering: "Truth and justice will prevail."

Questions for Discussion

1. Njeri opens her essay with a vivid description of her father sitting in his underpants and drinking scotch out of an applesauce jar. What do the details in this opening reveal, and how do they prepare for the essay that follows?
2. What makes Daddy laugh in paragraphs 4–6? Is the laughter good-humored?
3. Njeri records that she hated Daddy and "would not accept him as a father." Does she succeed in making this response understandable to you as a reader? What personal factors kept the two in "separate corners"?
4. Consider Njeri's discussion of the family violence she witnessed and experienced as a child. What does she understand now that she is an adult?
5. Does Njeri seem at all reconciled with the past she is recalling? Were you led to feel any sympathy for her father?
6. How do you interpret the concluding line, "'Truth and justice will prevail'"? What does this belief say about Njeri's father? Does it have any additional significance for writers of memoir?

Suggestions for Writing

1. Njeri's father tells her. "You were a very strange child." Think about times when your behavior seemed strange to others, even though it made perfect sense to you. Write about one such time so that readers can understand what the people around you failed to grasp at the time.
2. When she was in junior high school, Njeri believed, "Perceptions change. . . . New information debunks the lies of the past, but the truth was always there." Write about a person toward whom your own perceptions have changed as you have grown more mature. Describe that person as you initially saw him or her, and then record what you have since come to understand.

Morpheus: In Greek mythology, one of the children of Sleep.

2

Writing to Explore the Self

Self-discovery is one of the most rewarding activities we can engage in, because understanding who we are can help us to lead the lives we want to have. Although there are some similarities between writing to explore the self and writing to record a memory, the emphasis is different. All of the writers in this chapter make use of memories to some extent, but for them remembering is a means to an end rather than an end in itself. Moreover, when you write to explore the self, you can look not only to your past but also to your present and your future; meditate upon your feelings and your hopes; examine your relationships to the people around you; and investigate aspects of your social, cultural, and racial heritage of which you have no direct memory. The writers in this chapter follow many of these avenues as they seek a deeper knowledge and understanding of themselves.

Most people spend some time trying to figure out reasons for things they have done or felt. For instance, suppose that you normally conduct yourself sedately in public; but one evening, feeling particularly joyous and full of zest for living, you begin to tap dance down the street and swing around lampposts—as Gene Kelly did in the movie classic *Singing in the Rain.* The next day, you are probably going to wonder not only who saw you do it but also, more significantly, why you did it. Attempting to answer such questions can motivate writing to explore yourself—or, more accurately, a part of yourself, for there are many sides to what is commonly called the "self."

The answer to the first question, "Who saw you swing on the lamp-post?" may lead to the kind of writing in which you make discoveries about yourself by seeing yourself through the eyes of others. Scott Russell Sanders gives us an example when he speculates about another customer in the restaurant he is leaving:

> She might figure me for a carpenter, noticing my beard, the scraggly hair down over my collar, my banged-up hands, my patched jeans, my flannel shirt the color of the biscuits I just ate, my clodhopper boots. Or maybe she'll guess mechanic, maybe garbageman, electrician, janitor, maybe even farmer.

In another kind of writing for self-discovery we look inside ourselves, asking why we feel the way we feel, think what we think, and do what we do. For example, Steven Barboza, when telling the story of his religious conversion, comes to the following insight: "And I hadn't rejected Christianity so much as embraced Islam. Malcolm X's struggle—and Mom's death—had been Allah's instruments for my conversion."

You might also write an essay by looking outside yourself to consider how something (or someone) has helped make you the person you have become or led you to do something that you might not otherwise have done. For instance, Barbara Mellix writes about how other people influenced her use of language. You might also look for parallels between what you see in the world around you and how you perceive yourself. Cynthia Ozick, for example, comes to a richer understanding of her quest for excellence by describing her mother's character and contrasting it with her own. And Annie Dillard engages in self-discovery by meditating on the death of a moth at a time when she was unsure of her purpose in life.

You may have already experienced using writing to explore your purpose in life, or you may have convinced yourself long ago that writing about your inner life was something that you wanted to avoid. The extent to which people are motivated to write about themselves varies from one individual to another and can change from one time of life to another. But all should agree that self-discovery is not to be confused with self-indulgence or self-obsession. Writing to explore the self requires time, effort, and discipline. Seldom do we know during or immediately after an experience what its implications will be or why we acted in a particular way. It is the distance in time that enables Julia Alvarez, for instance, to comment upon the ironic reversal in her life between the time when she was a child who feared having a stepmother and her present status as a stepmother. Distance is essential. Writing about a current romance may allow you to vent your feelings, but it is unlikely to lead you to significant self-knowledge. You might, however, write successfully about a former romance if you have the distance necessary for understanding it and the discipline to present it with restraint. Writing for self-discovery relies upon thought and reflection more than emotion and confession. Thinking can be difficult when your heart is full.

Your motive for such thinking and writing is to discover something about yourself rather than to report something you knew before you began to write. Insight will be generated by the act of writing. Do not suppose, however, that writing to explore yourself means finding a truth that is conveniently stored somewhere in your head, some magic key that makes sense of everything. Self-discovery always leads to new perceptions. You will be constructing self-knowledge as you proceed.

For some ideas on how to get started you can look at the beginnings of the essays in this chapter. For example, Sanders tells us he was inspired by a newspaper report that Indiana leads the nation in fat; Joan Didion was motivated to write by rereading her notebook. Perhaps your own reading—of a newspaper, magazine, novel, or an essay in this chapter—will prompt you to reflections that inspire writing. Or you may get your inspiration from a film, play, television program, or your favorite compact disc.

Conversations, too, may lead to essays of self-discovery. If you've ever said something you later regretted, or played a conversation over again in your mind, you may have the beginnings of an essay. Mellix, for example, begins her essay with words she spoke to her daughter and later found puzzling. Or talking to a friend about some event that has left you feeling uneasy may lead to a good essay. When you talk, you may discover that you had more to say than you had realized, and the give and take of conversation may lead to a clearer understanding of what you are talking about. Consider writing to explore the self as a way to continue such a conversation—or even to initiate it.

Another possibility is to explore the significance of behavior with which you are content. For instance, if you enjoy getting up earlier than most people, you might explore how early rising affects you. This is the approach that Didion takes when she explores why she enjoys keeping a notebook. Alternatively, you might write about a habit you would like to change. Have your friends complained that you always interrupt them? You might want to explore that behavior to see when you began it, why you do it, and what it says about you.

Search through your memories to see whether you can find experiences that have made you the way you are. Perhaps you can pull them together to show, for instance, the development of an interest in art or the ways travel made you more tolerant of other people's customs. Or you might explore why you have lost interest in something that once mattered to you or have grown away from a person with whom you were once close.

As you prepare to write your own essay of self-discovery, remember that you can achieve a unique perspective on yourself. No one else can know exactly what you know. What you discover and how much you tell is your choice, though. Take some risks, but don't feel that you have to confess all. What ultimately matters is the degree of insight that you achieve through writing, not the degree of intimacy with which you report your personal life. As Didion's essay shows, a thoughtful writer can discover important things about herself when writing about why she writes. Another writer could address much more personal material without reaching a better understanding of herself. To a large extent, the topic matters less than what you do with it.

ON KEEPING A NOTEBOOK

Joan Didion

Although she has written both novels and screenplays, Joan Didion is best known for personal essays. "On Keeping a Notebook" comes from Slouching Towards Bethlehem, *the 1966 collection that won her a national audience. This essay is built around a series of brief passages that Didion quotes from a notebook she had kept several years earlier and is now trying to decipher. "I have already lost touch with a couple of people I used to be," she writes. One way of approaching her essay is to read it as Didion's attempt to renew acquaintance with the person she once was. As you read it, try to understand what the author is saying about herself.*

"'That woman Estelle,'" the note reads, "'is partly the reason why George Sharp and I are separated today.' *Dirty crepe-de-Chine wrapper, hotel bar, Wilmington RR, 9:45 A.M. August Monday morning.*"

Since the note is in my notebook, it presumably has some meaning to me. I study it for a long while. At first I have only the most general notion of what I was doing on an August Monday morning in the bar of the hotel across from the Pennsylvania Railroad station in Wilmington, Delaware (waiting for a train? missing one? 1960? 1961? why Wilmington?), but I do remember being there. The woman in the dirty crepe-de-Chine wrapper had come down from her room for a beer, and the bartender had heard before the reason why George Sharp and she were separated today. "Sure," he said, and went on mopping the floor. "You told me." At the other end of the bar is a girl. She is talking, pointedly, not to the man beside her but to a cat lying in the triangle of sunlight cast through the open door. She is wearing a plaid silk dress from Peck & Peck, and the hem is coming down.

Here is what it is: the girl has been on the Eastern Shore, and now she is going back to the city, leaving the man beside her, and all she can see ahead are the viscous summer sidewalks and the 3 A.M. long-distance calls that will make her lie awake and then sleep drugged through all the steaming mornings left in August (1960? 1961?). Because she must go directly from the train to lunch in New York, she wishes that she had a safety pin for the hem of the plaid silk dress, and she also wishes that she could forget about the hem and the lunch and stay in the cool bar that smells of disinfectant and malt and make friends with the woman in the crepe-de-Chine wrapper. She is afflicted by a little self-pity, and she wants to compare Estelles. That is what that was all about.

Why did I write it down? In order to remember, of course, but exactly what was it I wanted to remember? How much of it actually happened? Did any of it? Why do I keep a notebook at all? It is easy to deceive oneself on all those scores. The impulse to write things down is a peculiarly compulsive one, inexplicable to those who do not share it, useful only accidentally, only secondarily, in the way that any compulsion tries to justify itself. I suppose that it begins or does not begin in the cradle. Although I have felt compelled to write things down since I was five years old, I doubt that my daughter ever will, for she is a singularly blessed and accepting child, delighted with life exactly as life presents itself to her, unafraid to go to sleep and unafraid to wake up. Keepers of private notebooks are a different breed altogether, lonely and resistant rearrangers of things, anxious malcontents, children afflicted apparently at birth with some presentiment of loss.

My first notebook was a Big Five tablet, given to me by my mother   5
with the sensible suggestion that I stop whining and learn to amuse myself by writing down my thoughts. She returned the tablet to me a few years ago; the first entry is an account of a woman who believed herself to be freezing to death in the Arctic night, only to find, when day broke, that she had stumbled onto the Sahara Desert, where she would die of the heat before lunch. I have no idea what turn of a five-year-old's mind could have prompted so insistently "ironic" and exotic a story, but it does reveal a certain predilection for the extreme which has dogged me into adult life; perhaps if I were analytically inclined I would find it a truer story than any I might have told about Donald Johnson's birthday party or the day my cousin Brenda put Kitty Litter in the aquarium.

So the point of my keeping a notebook has never been, nor is it now, to have an accurate factual record of what I have been doing or thinking. That would be a different impulse entirely, an instinct for reality which I sometimes envy but do not possess. At no point have I ever been able successfully to keep a diary; my approach to daily life ranges from the grossly negligent to the merely absent, and on those few occasions when I have tried dutifully to record a day's events, boredom has so overcome me that the results are mysterious at best. What is this business about "shopping, typing piece, dinner with E, depressed"? Shopping for what? Typing what piece? Who is E? Was this "E" depressed, or was I depressed? Who cares?

In fact I have abandoned altogether that kind of pointless entry; instead I tell what some would call lies. "That's simply not true," the members of my family frequently tell me when they come up against my memory of a shared event. "The party was *not* for you, the spider was *not* a black widow, *it wasn't that way at all.*" Very likely they are right, for not only have I always had trouble distinguishing between what happened and what merely might have happened, but I remain unconvinced that the distinction, for my purposes, matters. The cracked crab that I recall having for lunch the day my father came home from Detroit in 1945 must certainly be embroidery, worked into the day's pattern to lend verisimilitude; I was ten years old and would not now remember the cracked crab. The day's events did not turn on cracked crab. And yet it is precisely that fictitious crab that makes me see the afternoon all over again, a home movie run all too often, the father bearing gifts, the child weeping, an exercise in family love and guilt. Or that is what it was to me. Similarly, perhaps it never did snow that August in Vermont; perhaps there never were flurries in the night wind, and maybe no one else felt the ground hardening and summer already dead even as we pretended to bask in it, but that was how it felt to me, and it might as well have snowed, could have snowed, did snow.

How it felt to me: that is getting closer to the truth about a notebook. I sometimes delude myself about why I keep a notebook, imagine that some thrifty virtue derives from preserving everything observed. See enough and write it down, I tell myself, and then some morning when the world seems drained of wonder, some day when I am only going through the motions of doing what I am supposed to do, which is write—on that bankrupt morning I will simply open my notebook and there it will all be, a forgotten account with accumulated interest, paid passage back to the world out there: dialogue overheard in hotels and elevators and at the hat-check counter in Pavillon (one middle-aged man shows his hat check to another and says, "That's my old football number"); impressions of Bettina Aptheker and Benjamin Sonnenberg and Teddy ("Mr. Acapulco") Stauffer; careful *aperçus*° about tennis bums and failed fashion models and Greek shipping heiresses, one of whom taught me a significant lesson (a lesson I could have learned from F. Scott Fitzgerald, but perhaps we all must meet the very rich for ourselves) by asking, when I arrived to interview her in her orchid-filled sitting room on the second day of a paralyzing New York blizzard, whether it was snowing outside.

I imagine, in other words, that the notebook is about other people. But of course it is not. I have no real business with what one stranger said to another at the hat-check counter in Pavillon; in fact I suspect that the line "That's my old football number" touched not my own imagination at all, but merely some memory of something once read, probably "The Eighty-Yard Run." Nor is my concern with a woman in a dirty crepe-de-Chine wrapper in a Wilmington bar. My stake is always, of course, in the unmentioned girl in the plaid silk dress. *Remember what it was to be me:* that is always the point.

It is a difficult point to admit. We are brought up in the ethic that   10
others, any others, all others, are by definition more interesting than ourselves; taught to be diffident, just this side of self-effacing. ("You're the least important person in the room and don't forget it," Jessica Mitford's governess would hiss in her ear on the advent of any social occasion; I copied that into my notebook because it is only recently that I have been able to enter a room without hearing some such phrase in my inner ear.) Only the very young and the very old may recount their dreams at breakfast, dwell upon self, interrupt with memories of beach games and favorite Liberty lawn

aperçus: French for "sketches."

dresses and the rainbow trout in a creek near Colorado Springs. The rest of us are expected, rightly, to affect absorption in other people's favorite dresses, other people's trout.

And so we do. But our notebooks give us away, for however dutifully we record what we see around us, the common denominator of all we see is always, transparently, shamelessly, the implacable "I." We are not talking here about the kind of notebook that is patently for public consumption, a structural conceit for binding together a series of graceful *pensées;*° we are talking about something private, about bits of the mind's string too short to use, an indiscriminate and erratic assemblage with meaning only for its maker.

And sometimes even the maker has difficulty with the meaning. There does not seem to be, for example, any point in my knowing for the rest of my life that, during 1964, 720 tons of soot fell on every square mile of New York City, yet there it is in my notebook, labeled "FACT." Nor do I really need to remember that Ambrose Bierce liked to spell Leland Stanford's name "£eland $tanford" or that "smart women almost always wear black in Cuba," a fashion hint without much potential for practical application. And does not the relevance of these notes seem marginal at best?:

> In the basement museum of the Inyo County Courthouse in Independence, California, sign pinned to a mandarin coat: "This MANDARIN COAT was often worn by Mrs. Minnie S. Brooks when giving lectures on her TEAPOT COLLECTION."

> Redhead getting out of car in front of Beverly Wilshire Hotel, chinchilla stole, Vuitton bags with tags reading:

> > MRS LOU FOX
> > HOTEL SAHARA
> > VEGAS

Well, perhaps not entirely marginal. As a matter of fact, Mrs. Minnie S. Brooks and her MANDARIN COAT pull me back into my own childhood, for although I never knew Mrs. Brooks and did not visit Inyo County until I was thirty, I grew up in just such a world, in houses cluttered with Indian relics and bits of gold ore and ambergris and the souvenirs my Aunt Mercy Farnsworth brought back from the Orient. It is a long way from that world to Mrs. Lou Fox's world, where we all live now, and is it not just as well to remember that? Might not Mrs. Minnie S. Brooks help me to remember what I am? Might not Mrs. Lou Fox help me to remember what I am not?

But sometimes the point is harder to discern. What exactly did I have in mind when I noted down that it cost the father of someone I know $650 a month to light the place on the Hudson in which he lived before the Crash? What use was I planning to make of this line by Jimmy Hoffa: "I

---

pensées: French for "thoughts or reflections."

may have my faults, but being wrong ain't one of them"? And although I think it interesting to know where the girls who travel with the Syndicate have their hair done when they find themselves on the West Coast, will I ever make suitable use of it? Might I not be better off just passing it on to John O'Hara?° What is a recipe for sauerkraut doing in my notebook? What kind of magpie keeps this notebook? *"He was born the night the Titanic went down."* That seems a nice enough line, and I even recall who said it, but is it not really a better line in life than it could ever be in fiction?

But of course that is exactly it: not that I should ever use the line, but 15 that I should remember the woman who said it and the afternoon I heard it. We were on her terrace by the sea, and we were finishing the wine left from lunch, trying to get what sun there was, a California winter sun. The woman whose husband was born the night the *Titanic* went down wanted to rent her house, wanted to go back to her children in Paris. I remember wishing that I could afford the house, which cost $1,000 a month. "Some-day you will," she said lazily. "Someday it all comes." There in the sun on her terrace it seemed easy to believe in someday, but later I had a low-grade afternoon hangover and ran over a black snake on the way to the supermar-ket and was flooded with inexplicable fear when I heard the checkout clerk explaining to the man ahead of me why she was finally divorcing her hus-band. "He left me no choice," she said over and over as she punched the register. "He has a little seven-month-old baby by her, he left me no choice." I would like to believe that my dread then was for the human condition, but of course it was for me, because I wanted a baby and did not then have one and because I wanted to own the house that cost $1,000 a month to rent and because I had a hangover.

It all comes back. Perhaps it is difficult to see the value in having one's self back in that kind of mood, but I do see it; I think we are well advised to keep on nodding terms with the people we used to be, whether we find them attractive company or not. Otherwise they turn up unannounced and surprise us, come hammering on the mind's door at 4 A.M. of a bad night and demand to know who deserted them, who betrayed them, who is going to make amends. We forget all too soon the things we thought we could never forget. We forget the loves and the betrayals alike, forget what we whispered and what we screamed, forget who we were. I have already lost touch with a couple of people I used to be; one of them, a seventeen-year-old, presents little threat, although it would be of some interest to me to know again what it feels like to sit on a river levee drinking vodka-and-orange-juice and listening to Les Paul and Mary Ford and their echoes sing "How High the Moon" on the car radio. (You see I still have the scenes, but I no longer perceive myself among those present, no longer could even improvise the dialogue.) The other one, a twenty-three-year-old, bothers me more. She was always a good deal of trouble, and I suspect she will

John O'Hara: American novelist (1905–1970).

reappear when I least want to see her, skirts too long, shy to the point of aggravation, always the injured party, full of recriminations and little hurts and stories I do not want to hear again, at once saddening me and angering me with her vulnerability and ignorance, an apparition all the more insistent for being so long banished.

It is a good idea, then, to keep in touch, and I suppose that keeping in touch is what notebooks are all about. And we are all on our own when it comes to keeping those lines open to ourselves: your notebook will never help me, nor mine you. *"So what's new in the whiskey business?"* What could that possibly mean to you? To me it means a blonde in a Pucci bathing suit sitting with a couple of fat men by the pool at the Beverly Hills Hotel. Another man approaches, and they all regard one another in silence for a while. "So what's new in the whiskey business?" one of the fat men finally says by way of welcome, and the blonde stands up, arches one foot and dips it in the pool, looking all the while at the cabaña where Baby Pignatari is talking on the telephone. That is all there is to that, except that several years later I saw the blonde coming out of Saks Fifth Avenue in New York with her California complexion and a voluminous mink coat. In the harsh wind that day she looked old and irrevocably tired to me, and even the skins in the mink coat were not worked the way they were doing them that year, not the way she would have wanted them done, and there is the point of the story. For a while after that I did not like to look in the mirror, and my eyes would skim the newspapers and pick out only the deaths, the cancer victims, the premature coronaries, the suicides, and I stopped riding the Lexington Avenue IRT because I noticed for the first time that all the strangers I had seen for years—the man with the seeing-eye dog, the spinster who read the classified pages every day, the fat girl who always got off with me at Grand Central—looked older than they once had.

It all comes back. Even that recipe for sauerkraut: even that brings it back. I was on Fire Island when I first made that sauerkraut, and it was raining, and we drank a lot of bourbon and ate the sauerkraut and went to bed at ten, and I listened to the rain and the Atlantic and felt safe. I made the sauerkraut again last night and it did not make me feel any safer, but that is, as they say, another story.

Questions for Discussion

1. Consider the questions with which paragraph 4 begins. Where else does Didion ask questions? Why does she raise questions instead of simply giving answers?
2. According to Didion, how does keeping a notebook differ from keeping a diary? Why isn't she interested in keeping a diary? What use is a notebook to her?
3. Why does Didion find it difficult to admit her motive in keeping a notebook?

4. What is the "significant lesson" that Didion learns when she interviews a Greek shipping heiress?

5. In paragraph 13 Didion contrasts two entries about women. How does Mrs. Minnie S. Brooks differ from Mrs. Lou Fox? Why does Didion find them worth remembering?

6. How does Didion present herself in this essay? What have you learned about her?

Suggestions for Writing

1. For a period of at least a week, keep both a diary and a notebook. Consider which type of journal you find the most satisfying. Write an essay in which you contrast these two exercises and reveal your preference.

2. Didion believes, "we are well advised to keep on nodding terms with the people we used to be, whether we find them attractive company or not." Study a journal, letter, or essay that you wrote when you were younger. Consider how you sounded then and whether you now find yourself different in any way from the person who wrote what you have just reread. Have you lost a quality that you once valued or overcome a limitation that you now find irritating? Define an aspect of yourself that makes for attractive or unattractive company.

MY CONVERSION

Steven Barboza

"My Conversion" describes a change in religious faith from Catholicism to Islam. Rather than presenting this conversion as a single, isolated act, Steven Barboza describes it as an "odyssey"—which implies a long voyage of discovery. As you read his essay, look for what Barboza discovers about his spiritual needs and how these needs have been shaped by his experience as an African-American in a racially divided society.

My abandonment of Roman Catholicism was spawned by a premature death, my mother's at age 49, on the day before my 22d birthday. I prayed like crazy for God to spare her, and when He did not, I established a new line of communication. I called God Allah and prayed with my palms cupped (to catch blessings) and my eyes wide open (to keep Allah's creations in sight).

Given the irony and absurdity of events in racially torn Boston, where I lived, Islam was a godsend. A few months after my mother's death, whites assaulted a black man in front of Boston City Hall, using as one weapon a flagpole with an American flag attached. With that attack and my mother's death, a lifetime of frustrations reached the breaking point.

My odyssey 20 years ago was not unlike that of hundreds of thousands of blacks in the United States. The journey became my jihad—literally "struggle"—waged not for political power or economic enfranchisement, but for control over my own soul.

Then as now, in the Roxburys and Harlems across America, only liquor stores outnumbered churches in vying for blacks' attention, and in my opinion, both stupefied millions of black Americans.

Islam, as I was familiar with it, seemed the perfect way to fight back. 5 As a religion, it offered clear-cut guidelines for living; as a social movement, it stood for a pride born of culture and discipline.

Before my mom died, I had dipped into Malcolm X's autobiography. After she passed, I plunged into it. Malcolm had undergone a metamorphosis: from hoodlum to cleaned-up spokesman for the Nation of Islam and finally a convert to orthodox Islam, and through his own transformation he had shown that change, even from the most miserable beginnings, was possible.

Of course, Malcolm's life and mine were very different. He had discovered Islam in prison. I discovered it in college. He was the spokesman for a black theocratic visionary. I held down a midlevel white-collar job in a Fortune 500 company. Still, I felt a kinship with Malcolm and the Black Muslims. The color of our skin made us all cargo in a sinking ship, and Islam beckoned like a life preserver.

Two decades ago in Boston and New York, however, there were few orthodox mosques. In black neighborhoods, one institution, the Nation of

Islam, dominated in the teaching of Islam, or, rather, a homegrown version
of it. Many blacks who converted took to the Nation's teachings—its ad-
monitions to self-love and racial solidarity; its belief in productivity and
entrepreneurship. And with equal ardor, they also took to the Nation's other
teachings—its racial chauvinism, and belief that white people were genetically inferior, intrinsically evil "blue-eyed devils" who had been created to
practice "tricknology" against blacks.

Using the twin motivators of myth and pride, Elijah Muhammad°
built the Nation into one of the largest black economic and religious organizations America had seen. It claimed a heavyweight boxing champion the
whole world adored, Muhammad Ali. Its women looked like angels in their
veils, crisp jackets and ankle-length skirts; its men cut no-nonsense yet gallant figures in their smart dark suits and trademark bow ties.

But sitting in the Nation's Roxbury temple was like being on a jury   10
listening to a closing argument. The defendants (in absentia): white folks.
The prosecutor: a dapper minister who practically spat, saying whites were
so utterly devilish that their religion was grotesquely symbolized by a "symbol of death and destruction"—the crucifix. The charge: perpetrating das-
tardly deeds on blacks "in the name of Christianity." The verdict: guilty.

I barely lasted my one visit. To me, demonizing the "enemy" as the
Nation did hardly seemed the best way to learn to "love thyself." Anyway, I
abhorred the idea of colorizing God, or limiting godly attributes to one
race. And though Elijah deserved credit for redeeming legions of blacks
from dope and crime when all else, including Christianity, had failed them,
I didn't believe that earned him the title of Allah's "messenger."

So I moved to New York and became an orthodox Muslim in the
manner all converts do: I declared before Muslim witnesses my belief in
Allah and my faith that the Prophet Muhammad of Arabia was His very last
messenger. I entered a Sunni mosque and prostrated myself on rugs beside
people of all ethnicities.

Here was what I deemed a truer Islam—the orthodoxy to which
Malcolm had switched, the one most of Elijah's followers opted for when
the Nation of Islam waned after his death, the Islam to which most of
America's 135,000 annual converts, 80 to 90 percent of them black, belong.

Questions, however, persisted. For example: Why didn't we blame
Arabs for their ancestors' role in slave trading the way we blamed white
Americans and Europeans? One answer is that mistreatment of slaves is
specifically prohibited by Islamic law, and the vast majority of Muslims living
during the slave trade era observed that law. The children of female slaves
and free men would assume the social status of the father, unlike the children
of American slave owners. And while the children of two slaves remained
slaves, Islamic law encouraged manumission.

And why did so many black Americans revere the Middle East as if   15
it were their homeland? On a plane to Senegal, sitting next to a black

Elijah Muhammad: African-American leader (1897–1970).

American wearing a traditional Arab robe, I got an inkling of the answer. The man was headed to meet an imam, his spiritual leader, a black African Muslim. I later met other black Americans who had spent years in Africa studying Islam. Through research, I found that up to 35 percent of enslaved blacks brought to the New World were Muslim. In converting, many black Americans may have been simply returning to the religion of their fore-fathers.

Over the years, I have come to understand what should have been obvious long ago—that Jesus had not forsaken my mother. She died because God had willed it, regardless of what form my prayers took.

And I hadn't rejected Christianity so much as embraced Islam. Malcolm X's struggle—and Mom's death—had been Allah's instruments for my conversion. After all, Allah, it is said, makes Muslims by whatever means He sees fit.

Questions for Discussion

1. Barboza begins this essay by claiming that his conversion to Islam was prompted by his mother's death. As he explores further, do other causes emerge?
2. Consider Barboza's definition of *jihad* in paragraph 3. What do you think it means to struggle for control of your soul? With whom or what would you have to struggle?
3. Why was Barboza inspired by the life of Malcolm X? How did their situations differ? In what sense were they similar?
4. Paragraph 7 ends with Barboza comparing himself to "cargo in a sinking ship." What are the implications of this metaphor? Does it have particular meaning for African-Americans?
5. Why did Barboza become disillusioned with the Nation of Islam? Why do you think he devoted four paragraphs to a faith he did not embrace?
6. In his conclusion Barboza writes, "And I hadn't rejected Christianity so much as embraced Islam." What distinction is he making here, and why is it useful for him to make it?

Suggestions for Writing

1. Barboza writes about why Islam appeals to African-Americans. If you have a religious faith, explore its cultural significance. Aside from the religious beliefs they hold, do people in your faith come from similar backgrounds or live similar lives? If so, how has religion helped to define the common culture you have identified?
2. Although *conversion* is usually associated with a change of religious faith, there are many other ways we can choose to change our lives. Write about the most serious change you can imagine making in your own life, exploring what this change would cost and what it might yield.

GRUB

Scott Russell Sanders

The following essay includes many details about the author and a café where he goes for breakfast. Look for connections between the scene and Scott Russell Sanders himself so that you can understand what he is doing there—and what he learns about himself by reflecting upon his meal. If you are surprised that a writer could discover something about himself by considering why he eats "slithery eggs and gummy toast," ask yourself if what you eat and where you eat it says anything about who you are.

The morning paper informs me that, once again, Indiana leads the nation in fat. The announcement from the Centers for Disease Control puts it less bluntly, declaring that in 1989 our state had the highest percentage of overweight residents. But it comes down to the same thing: on a globe where hunger is the rule, surfeit the exception, Indiana is first in fat.

I read this news on Saturday morning at a booth in Ladyman's Cafe, a one-story box of pine and brick wedged between the Christian Science Reading Room and Bloomington Shoe Repair, half a block from the town square. It is a tick after 6 A.M. My fellow breakfasters include a company of polo-shirted Gideons clutching Bibles, a housepainter whose white trousers are speckled with the colors of past jobs, two mechanics in overalls with "Lee" and "Roy" stitched on their breast pockets, three elderly couples exchanging the glazed stares of insomniacs, and a young woman in fringed leather vest and sunglasses who is browsing through a copy of *Cosmopolitan*. Except for the young woman and me, everyone here is a solid contributor to Indiana's lead in fat. And I could easily add my weight to the crowd, needing only to give in for a few weeks to my clamorous appetite.

I check my belt, which is buckled at the fourth notch. Thirty-two inches and holding. But there are signs of wear on the third and second and first notches, tokens of earlier expansions.

The lone waitress bustles to my booth. "Whatcha need, hon?" Her permed hair is a mat of curls the color of pearls. Stout as a stevedore, purple under the eyes, puckered in the mouth, she is that indefinite age my grandmother remained for the last twenty years of her long life.

"What's good today?" I ask her.   5

"It's all good, same as every day." She tugs a pencil from her perm, drums ringed fingers on the order pad. Miles to go before she sleeps. "So what'll it be, sugar?"

I glance at the smudgy list on the chalkboard over the counter. Tempted by the biscuits with sausage gravy, by the triple stack of hotcakes slathered in butter, by the twin pork chops with hash browns, by the coconut cream pie and glazed doughnuts, I content myself with a cheese omelet and toast.

"Back in two shakes," says the waitress. When she charges away, a violet bow swings into view among her curls, the cheeriest thing I have seen so far this morning.

I buy breakfast only when I'm on the road or feeling sorry for myself. Today—abandoned for the weekend by my wife and kids, an inch of water in my basement from last night's rain, the car hitting on three cylinders—I'm feeling sorry for myself. I pick Ladyman's not for the food, which is indifferent, but for the atmosphere, which is tacky in a timeless way. It reminds me of the truck stops and railroad-car diners and jukebox cafés where my father would stop on our fishing trips thirty years ago. The oilcloth that covers the scratched Formica of the table is riddled with burns. The seat of my booth has lost its stuffing, broken down by a succession of hefty eaters. The walls, sheathed in vinyl for easy scrubbing, are hung with fifty-dollar oil paintings of covered bridges, pastures, and tree-lined creeks. The floor's scuffed linoleum reveals the ghostly print of deeper layers, material for some future archaeologist of cafés. Ceiling fans turn overhead, stirring with each lazy spin the odor of tobacco and coffee and grease.

There is nothing on the menu of Ladyman's that was not on the menus   *10* I remember from those childhood fishing trips. But I can no longer order from it with a child's obliviousness What can I eat without pangs of unease, knowing better? Not the eggs, high in cholesterol, not the hash browns, fried in oil, not the fatty sausage or bacon or ham, not the salty pancakes made with white flour or the saltier biscuits and gravy, not the lemon meringue pies in the glass case, not the doughnuts glistering with sugar, not the butter, not the whole milk.

Sipping coffee (another danger) and waiting for my consolatory breakfast, I read the fine print in the article on obesity. I learn that only thirty-two states took part in the study. Why did the other eighteen refuse? Are they embarrassed? Are they afraid their images would suffer, afraid that tourists, knowing the truth, would cross their borders without risking a meal? I learn that Indiana is actually tied for first place with Wisconsin, at 25.7 percent overweight, so we share the honors. For Wisconsin, you think of dairies, arctic winters, hibernation. But Indiana? We're leaders in popcorn. Our hot and humid summers punish even the skinny, and torture the plump. Why us? There's no comment from the Indiana Health Commissioner. This gentleman, Mr. Woodrow Myers, Jr. (who is now on his way to perform the same office in New York City), weighed over three hundred pounds at the time of his appointment. He lost more than a hundred pounds in an effort to set a healthy example, but has since gained most of it back. He doesn't have much room to talk.

My platter arrives, the waitress urging, "Eat up, hon," before she hustles away. The omelet has been made with processed cheese, anemic and slithery. The toast is of white bread that clots on my tongue. The strawberry jelly is the color and consistency of gum erasers. My mother reared me to eat whatever was put in front of me, and so I eat. Dabbing jelly from my beard with a paper napkin as thin as the pages of the Gideons' Bibles, I look around. At six-thirty this Saturday morning, every seat is occupied. Why are we all here? Why are we wolfing down this dull, this dangerous, this terrible grub?

It's not for lack of alternatives. Bloomington is ringed by the usual necklace of fast food shops. Or you could walk from Ladyman's to restaurants that serve breakfast in half a dozen languages. Just five doors away, at the Uptown Cafe, you could dine on croissants and espresso and quiche.

So why are we here in these swaybacked booths eating poorly cooked food that is bad for us? The answer, I suspect, would help to explain why so many of us are so much bigger than we ought to be. I sniff, and the aroma of grease and peppery sausage, frying eggs and boiling coffee, jerks me back into the kitchen of my grandparents' farm. I see my grandmother, barefoot and bulky, mixing biscuit dough with her blunt fingers. Then I realize that everything Ladyman's serves she would have served. This is farm food, loaded with enough sugar and fat to power a body through a slogging day of work, food you could fix out of your own garden and chicken coop and pigpen, food prepared without spices or sauces, cooked the quickest way, as a woman with chores to do and a passel of mouths to feed would cook it.

"Hot up that coffee, hon?" the waitress asks.   15

"Please, ma'am," I say, as though answering my grandmother. On those fishing trips, my father stopped at places like Ladyman's because there he could eat the vittles he knew from childhood, no-nonsense grub he never got at home from his wife, a city woman who had studied nutrition, and who had learned her cuisine from a Bostonian mother and a Middle Eastern father. I stop at places like Ladyman's because I am the grandson of farmers, the son of a farm boy. If I went from booth to booth, interviewing the customers, most likely I would find hay and hogs in each person's background, maybe one generation back, maybe two. My sophisticated friends would not eat here for love or money. They will eat peasant food only if it comes from other countries—hummus and pita, fried rice and prawns, liver pâté, tortellini, tortillas, tortes. Never black-eyed peas, never grits, never short ribs or hush puppies or shoofly pie. This is farm food, and we who sit here and shovel it down are bound to farming by memory or imagination.

With the seasoning of memory, the slithery eggs and gummy toast and rubbery jam taste better. I lick my platter clean.

Barely slowing down as she cruises past, the waitress refills my coffee once more, the oil-slicked brew jostling in the glass pot. "Need anything else, sugar?"

My nostalgic tongue wins out over my judgment, leading me to say, "Could I get some biscuits and honey?"

"You sure can."   20

The biscuits arrive steaming hot. I pitch in. When I worked on farms as a boy, loading hay bales onto wagons and forking silage to cows, shoveling manure out of horse barns, digging postholes and pulling barbed wire, I could eat the pork chops and half a dozen eggs my neighbors fed me for breakfast, eat corn bread and sugar in a quart of milk for dessert at lunch, eat ham steaks and mashed potatoes and three kinds of pie for supper, eat a bowl of hand-cranked ice cream topped with maple syrup at bedtime, and stay skinny as a junkyard dog. Not so any longer. Not so for any of us. Eat like a farmer while living like an insurance salesman, an accountant, a beautician, or a truck driver, and you're going to get fat in a hurry. While true farmers have always stored their food in root cellars and silos, in smoke shacks and on canning shelves, we carry our larders with us on haunches and ribs.

The Gideons file out, Bibles under their arms, bellies over their belts.

With the last of my biscuits I mop up the honey, thinking of the path the wheat traveled from Midwestern fields to my plate, thinking of the clover distilled into honey, of grass become butter, the patient industry of cows and bees and the keepers of cows and bees. Few of us still work on the land, even here in Indiana. Few of us raise big families, few of us look after herds of animals, few of us bend our backs all day, few of us build or plow or bake or churn. Secretaries of Agriculture tell us that only four percent of our population feeds the other ninety-six percent. I have known and admired enough farmers to find that a gloomy statistic.

I am stuffed. I rise, stretch, shuffle toward the case register. The woman in the fringed vest looks up from her *Cosmopolitan* as I pass her booth. She might figure me for a carpenter, noticing my beard, the scraggly hair down over my collar, my banged-up hands, my patched jeans, my flannel shirt the color of the biscuits I just ate, my clodhopper boots. Or maybe she'll guess mechanic, maybe garbageman, electrician, janitor, maybe even farmer.

I pluck a toothpick from a box near the cash register and idly chew on it while the waitress makes change. "You hurry back," she calls after me.   *25*

"I will, ma'am," I tell her.

On the sidewalk out front of Ladyman's, I throw my toothpick in a green trash barrel that is stenciled with the motto "Fight Dirty." I start the car, wincing at the sound of three cylinders clapping. I remember yesterday's rainwater shimmering in the basement, remember the house empty of my family, who are away frolicking with relatives. Before letting out the clutch, I let out my belt a notch, to accommodate those biscuits. Thirty-three inches. One inch closer to the ranks of the fat. I decide to split some wood this morning, turn the compost from the right-hand bin to the left, lay up stones along the edge of the wildflower bed, sweat hard enough to work up an appetite for lunch.

Questions for Discussion

1. Why is Sanders eating breakfast in a restaurant? Why has he chosen Ladyman's when he could be dining on "croissants and espresso and quiche"?

2. Why is it that Sanders hesitates to eat food that he enjoys? How has his life changed since he was a young man?
3. The essay begins with what turns out to be an exaggeration about Indiana. Why do you think Sanders waits for several paragraphs before reporting more about the study first cited in paragraph 1?
4. What role does the waitress play in this essay? How does she help Sanders enjoy a bad meal?
5. Consider the description of himself that Sanders provides in paragraphs 3 and 24. Why is it misleading? What is the woman reading *Cosmopolitan* unlikely to realize?

Suggestions for Writing

1. Are there any foods that you enjoy even though you know they are not good for you? Of all the things you eat, is there any food that you are most likely to eat when you are alone? Write an essay about eating that will reveal something about yourself.
2. Visit a place that reminds you of your past. Write a description of it that will make readers understand what you see and feel when you visit there.

HOLD THE MAYONNAISE

Julia Alvarez

> *In the following essay Julia Alvarez reflects upon her experience as a Latina stepmother to two blond teenagers who represent a way of life that she found alien as a child. As you read, think about how this essay reveals a conflict between different cultures. Think also about whether the relationships explored here lead to understanding anything about what people need to do when learning to live together as a family.*

"If I die first and Papi ever gets remarried," Mami used to tease when we were kids, "don't you accept a new woman in my house. Make her life impossible, you hear?" My sisters and I nodded obediently, and a filial shudder would go through us. We were Catholics, so of course, the only kind of remarriage we could imagine had to involve our mother's death.

We were also Dominicans, recently arrived in Jamaica, Queens, in the early 60's, before waves of other Latin Americans began arriving. So, when we imagined who exactly my father might possibly ever think of remarrying, only American women came to mind. It would be bad enough having a *madrastra,* but a "stepmother." . . .

All I could think of was that she would make me eat mayonnaise, a food I identified with the United States and which I detested. Mami understood, of course, that I wasn't used to that kind of food. Even a madrastra, accustomed to our rice and beans and tostones and pollo frito, would understand. But an American stepmother would think it was normal to put mayonnaise on food, and if she were at all strict and a little mean, which all stepmothers, of course, were, she would make me eat potato salad and such. I had plenty of my own reasons to make a potential stepmother's life impossible. When I nodded obediently with my sisters, I was imagining not just something foreign in our house, but in our refrigerator.

So it's strange now, almost 35 years later, to find myself a Latina stepmother of my husband's two tall, strapping, blond, mayonnaise-eating daughters. To be honest, neither of them is a real aficionado of the condiment, but it's a fair thing to add to a bowl of tuna fish or diced potatoes. Their American food, I think of it, and when they head to their mother's or off to school, I push the jar back in the refrigerator behind their chocolate pudding and several open cans of Diet Coke.

What I can't push as successfully out of sight are my own immigrant   5
childhood fears of having a *gringa* stepmother with foreign tastes in our house. Except now, I am the foreign stepmother in a gringa household. I've wondered what my husband's two daughters think of this stranger in their family. It must be doubly strange for them that I am from another culture.

Of course, there are mitigating circumstances—my husband's two daughters were teen-agers when we married, older, more mature, able to understand differences. They had also traveled when they were children with their father, an eye doctor, who worked on short-term international projects with various eye foundations. But still, it's one thing to visit a foreign country, another altogether to find it brought home—a real bear plopped down in a Goldilocks house.

Sometimes, a whole extended family of bears. My warm, loud Latino family came up for the wedding: my *tia* from Santo Domingo; three dramatic, enthusiastic sisters and their families; my papi, with a thick accent I could tell the girls found it hard to understand; and my mami, who had her eye trained on my soon-to-be stepdaughters for any sign that they were about to make my life impossible. "How are they behaving themselves?" she asked me, as if they were 7 and 3, not 19 and 16. "They're wonderful girls," I replied, already feeling protective of them.

I looked around for the girls in the meadow in front of the house we were building, where we were holding the outdoor wedding ceremony and party. The oldest hung out with a group of her own friends. The younger one whizzed in briefly for the ceremony, then left again before the congratulations started up. There was not much mixing with me and mine. What was there for them to celebrate on a day so full of confusion and effort?

On my side, being the newcomer in someone else's territory is a role I'm used to. I can tap into that struggling English speaker, that skinny, dark-haired, olive-skinned girl in a sixth grade of mostly blond and blue-eyed giants. Those tall, freckled boys would push me around in the playground. "Go back to where you came from!" "*No comprendo!*" I'd reply, though of course there was no misunderstanding the fierce looks on their faces.

Even now, my first response to a scowl is that old pulling away. (My husband calls it "checking out.") I remember times early on in the marriage when the girls would be with us, and I'd get out of school and drive around doing errands, killing time, until my husband, their father, would be leaving work. I am not proud of my fears, but I understand—as the lingo goes—where they come from. *10*

And I understand, more than I'd like to sometimes, my stepdaughters' pain. But with me, they need never fear that I'll usurp a mother's place. No one has ever come up and held their faces and then addressed me, "They look just like you." If anything, strangers to the remarriage are probably playing Mr. Potato Head in their minds, trying to figure out how my foreign features and my husband's fair Nebraskan features got put together into these two tall, blond girls. "My husband's daughters," I kept introducing them.

Once, when one of them visited my class and I introduced her as such, two students asked me why. "I'd be so hurt if my stepmom introduced me that way," the young man said. That night I told my stepdaughter what my students had said. She scowled at me and agreed. "It's so weird how you call me Papa's daughter. Like you don't want to be related to me or something."

"I didn't want to presume," I explained. "So it's O.K. if I call you my stepdaughter?"

"That's what I am," she said. Relieved, I took it for a teensy inch of acceptance. The takings are small in this stepworld, I've discovered. Sort of like being a minority. It feels as if all the goodies have gone somewhere else.

Day to day, I guess I follow my papi's advice. When we first came, he   15 would talk to his children about how to make it in our new country. "Just do your work and put in your heart, and they will accept you!" In this age of remaining true to your roots, of keeping your Spanish, of fighting from inside your culture, that assimilationist approach is highly suspect. My Latino students—who don't want to be called Hispanics anymore—would ditch me as faculty adviser if I came up with that play-nice message.

But in a stepfamily where everyone is starting a new life together, it isn't bad advice. Like a potluck supper, an American concept my mami never took to. ("Why invite people to your house and then ask them to bring the food?") You put what you've got together with what everyone else brought and see what comes out of the pot. The luck part is if everyone brings something you like. No potato salad, no deviled eggs, no little party sandwiches with you know what in them.

Questions for Discussion

1. The author's father and husband appear only briefly in this memoir, which begins with an imagined conflict between women and moves on to reflect upon an uneasy relationship between the author and her step-daughters. Why do you think Alvarez chose to focus upon relationships with other women?

2. Alvarez reflects, "I've wondered what my husband's daughters think of this stranger in their family. It must be doubly strange for them that I am from another culture." Do you agree that coming from a different culture can complicate integration into a new family? And why do you think Alvarez wondered about what the daughters felt? What would keep her from asking them directly?

3. Writing about her experience as a stepmother, Alvarez observes, "The takings are small in this stepworld, I've discovered. Sort of like being a minority. It feels as if all the goodies have gone somewhere else." What kind of "goodies" is she missing?

4. Alvarez recalls that she used to avoid being home alone with her step-daughters and then states, "I am not proud of my fears, but I understand . . . where they come from." What has she come to understand about herself?

5. This essay opens and concludes with reflections on mayonnaise— "American food"—which Alvarez dislikes. What does Alvarez accomplish by focusing attention on potato salad, deviled eggs, and the jar of mayonnaise she pushes to the back of the refrigerator? What is the relationship between food and family?

Suggestions for Writing

1. Write about a time when you were a stranger in someone else's territory. Explore why you felt out of place and whether or not you wanted to be accepted.
2. Study the food in your refrigerator, paying particular attention to whatever has been pushed to the back. What do the contents of your refrigerator say about who you are?

THE SEAM OF THE SNAIL

Cynthia Ozick

> *Struggling with the perfectionism that causes her to move at a snail's pace, Cynthia Ozick explores how she differs from her lavish, energetic, and somewhat haphazard mother. As you read "The Seam of the Snail," notice the mother's many accomplishments and the price that Ozick pays for living her own life differently. Consider whether the act of writing helps Ozick to reconcile mixed feelings about both her mother and herself.*

In my Depression childhood, whenever I had a new dress, my cousin Sarah would get suspicious. The nicer the dress was, and especially the more expensive it looked, the more suspicious she would get. Finally she would lift the hem and check the seams. This was to see if the dress had been bought or if my mother had sewed it. Sarah could always tell. My mother's sewing had elegant outsides, but there was something catch-as-catch-can about the insides. Sarah's sewing, by contrast, was as impeccably finished inside as out; not one stray thread dangled.

My uncle Jake built meticulous grandfather clocks out of rosewood; he was a perfectionist, and sent to England for the clockworks. My mother built serviceable radiator covers and a serviceable cabinet, with hinged doors, for the pantry. She built a pair of bookcases for the living room. Once, after I was grown and in a house of my own, she fixed the sewer pipe. She painted ceilings, and also landscapes; she reupholstered chairs. One summer she planted a whole yard of tall corn. She thought herself capable of doing anything, and did everything she imagined. But nothing was perfect. There was always some clear flaw, never visible head-on. You had to look underneath, where the seams were. The corn thrived, though not in rows. The stalks elbowed one another like gossips in a dense little village.

"Miss Brrrrooobaker," my mother used to mock, rolling her Russian *r*'s, whenever I crossed a *t* she had left uncrossed, or corrected a word she had misspelled, or became impatient with a *v* that had tangled itself up with a *w* in her speech. ("*Vv*entriloquist," I would say. "*Vv*entriloquist," she would obediently repeat. And the next time it would come out "wiolinist.") Miss Brubaker was my high school English teacher, and my mother invoked her name as an emblem of raging finical obsession. "Miss Brrrrooobaker," my mother's voice hoots at me down the years, as I go on casting and recasting sentences in a tiny handwriting on monomaniacally uniform paper. The loops of my mother's handwriting—it was the Palmer Method—were as big as soup bowls, spilling generous splashy ebullience. She could pull off, at five minutes' notice, a satisfying dinner for ten concocted out of nothing more than originality and panache. But the napkin would be folded a little off center, and the spoon might be on the wrong side of the knife.

She was an optimist who ignored trifles; for her, God was not in the details but in the intent. And all these culinary and agricultural efflorescences were extracurricular, accomplished in the crevices and niches of a fourteen-hour business day. When she scribbled out her family memoirs, in heaps of dog-eared notebooks, or on the backs of old bills, or on the margins of last year's calendar, I would resist typing them; in the speed of the chase she often omitted words like "the," "and," "will." The same flashing and bountiful hand fashioned and fired ceramic pots, and painted brilliant autumn views and vases of imaginary flowers and ferns, and decorated ordinary Woolworth platters with lavish enameled gardens. But bits of the painted petals would chip away.

Lavish: my mother was as lavish as nature. She woke early and saturated the hours with work and inventiveness, and read late into the night. She was all profusion, abundance, fabrication. Angry at her children, she would run after us whirling the cord of the electric iron, like a lasso or a whip; but she never caught us. When, in seventh grade, I was afraid of failing the Music Appreciation final exam because I could not tell the difference between "To a Wild Rose" and "Barcarole," she got the idea of sending me to school with a gauze sling rigged up on my writing arm, and an explanatory note that was purest fiction. But the sling kept slipping off. My mother gave advice like mad—she boiled over with so much passion for the predicaments of strangers that they turned into permanent cronies. She told intimate stories about people I had never heard of.

Despite the gargantuan Palmer loops (or possibly because of them), I   5
have always known that my mother's was a life of—intricately abashing word!—excellence: insofar as excellence means ripe generosity. She burgeoned, she proliferated; she was endlessly leafy and flowering. She wore red hats, and called herself a gypsy. In her girlhood she marched with the suffragettes and for Margaret Sanger and called herself a Red. She made me laugh, she was so varied: like a tree on which lemons, pomegranates, and prickly pears absurdly all hang together. She had the comedy of prodigality.

My own way is a thousand times more confined. I am a pinched perfectionist, the ultimate fruition of Miss Brubaker; I attend to crabbed minutiae and am self-trammeled through taking pains. I am a kind of human snail, locked in and condemned by my own nature. The ancients believed that the moist track left by the snail as it crept was the snail's own essence, depleting its body little by little; the farther the snail toiled, the smaller it became, until it finally rubbed itself out. That is how perfectionists are. Say to us Excellence, and we will show you how we use up our substance and wear ourselves away, while making scarcely any progress at all. The fact that I am an exacting perfectionist in a narrow strait only, and nowhere else, is hardly to the point, since nothing matters to me so much as a comely and muscular sentence. It is my narrow strait, this snail's road; the track of the sentence I am writing now; and when I have eked out the wet substance, ink or blood, that is its mark, I will begin the next sentence. Only in treading out sentences am I perfectionist; but then there is nothing else I know how to do, or take much interest in. I miter every pair of abutting sentences as scrupulously as Uncle Jake fitted one strip of rosewood against another. My mother's worldly and bountiful hand has escaped me. The sentence I am writing is my cabin and my shell, compact, self-sufficient. It is the burnished horizon—a merciless planet where flawlessness is the single standard, where even the inmost seams, however hidden from a laxer eye, must meet perfection. Here "excellence" is not strewn casually from a tipped cornucopia, here disorder does not account for charm, here trifles rule like tyrants.

I measure my life in sentences pressed out, line by line, like the lustrous ooze on the underside of the snail, the snail's secret open seam, its wound, leaking attar. My mother was too mettlesome to feel the force of a comma. She scorned minutiae. She measured her life according to what poured from the horn of plenty, which was her own seamless, ample, cascading, elastic, suspectible, inexact heart. My narrower heart rides between the tiny twin horns of the snail, dwindling as it goes.

And out of this thinnest thread, this ink-wet line of words, must rise a visionary fog, a mist, a smoke, forging cities, histories, sorrows, quagmires, entanglements, lives of sinners, even the life of my furnace-hearted mother: so much wilderness, waywardness, plenitude on the head of the precise and impeccable snail, between the horns. (Ah, if this could be!)

Questions for Discussion

1. Ozick writes that her mother's life embodied "excellence" in the sense of "ripe generosity." What do you think she means by this? What kind of excellence does Ozick herself pursue?
2. What do you think Ozick means when she writes that for her mother "God was not in the details but in the intent"?
3. If Ozick believes that perfectionists "use up our substance and wear ourselves away, while making scarcely any progress at all," why do you think she continues to be a kind of human snail?
4. What does Ozick hope to accomplish in her writing? Judging from this essay, how well do you think she is succeeding?
5. Consider the final sentence of this essay. Why is it parenthetical, and what does it reveal about the author?

Suggestions for Writing

1. What is your own definition of excellence, and how are you most likely to achieve it? Are you more concerned with doing something perfectly or managing to get a lot of things done reasonably well? Write an essay describing how you function when you are doing an activity that deeply matters to you.

2. Write an essay contrasting yourself with a friend or relative who has characteristics that you admire and wish you could emulate. Explore how you would have to change and whether this change is possible.

FROM OUTSIDE, IN

Barbara Mellix

Barbara Mellix teaches writing at the University of Pittsburgh. By recounting events in her own life, she shows how language is a means to an end—an agency that can be used for different acts. As you read the following essay, notice how Mellix uses narrative to convey the person she once was and the person she became by learning how to write. When trying to understand how Mellix has changed, consider what she means by her title.

Two years ago, when I started writing this paper, trying to bring order out of chaos, my ten-year-old daughter was suffering from an acute attack of boredom. She drifted in and out of the room complaining that she had nothing to do, no one to "be with" because none of her friends were at home. Patiently I explained that I was working on something special and needed peace and quiet, and I suggested that she paint, read, or work with her computer. None of these interested her. Finally, she pulled up a chair to my desk and watched me, now and then heaving long, loud sighs. After two or three minutes (nine or ten sighs), I lost my patience. "Looka here, Allie," I said, "you too old for this kinda carryin' on. I done told you this is important. You wronger than dirt to be in here haggin' me like this and you know it. Now git on outta here and leave me off before I put my foot all the way down."

I was at home, alone with my family, and my daughter understood that this way of speaking was appropriate in that context. She knew, as a matter of fact, that it was almost inevitable; when I get angry at home, I speak some of my finest, most cherished black English. Had I been speaking to my daughter in this manner in certain other environments, she would have been shocked and probably worried that I had taken leave of my sense of propriety.

Like my children, I grew up speaking what I considered two distinctly different languages—black English and standard English (or as I thought of them then, the ordinary everyday speech of "country" coloreds and "proper" English)—and in the process of acquiring these languages, I developed an understanding of when, where, and how to use them. But unlike my children, I grew up in a world that was primarily black. My friends, neighbors, minister, teachers—almost everybody I associated with every day—were black. And we spoke to one another in our own special language: *That sho is a pretty dress you got on. If she don' soon leave me off I'm gon tell her head a mess. I was so mad I could'a pissed a blue nail. He all the time trying to low-rate somebody. Ain't that just about the nastiest thing you ever set ears on?*

Then there were the "others," the "proper" blacks, transplanted relatives and one-time friends who came home from the city for weddings, funerals, and vacations. And the whites. To these we spoke standard English. "Ain't?" my mother would yell at me when I used the term in the presence of "others." "You *know* better than that." And I would hang my head in shame and say the "proper" word.

I remember one summer sitting in my grandmother's house in Gree-   *5* leyville, South Carolina, when it was full of the chatter of city relatives who were home on vacation. My parents sat quietly, only now and then volunteering a comment or answering a question. My mother's face took on a strained expression when she spoke. I could see that she was being careful to say just the right words in just the right way. Her voice sounded thick, muffled. And when she finished speaking, she would lapse into silence, her proper smile on her face. My father was more articulate, more aggressive. He spoke quickly, his words sharp and clear. But he held his proud head higher, a signal that he, too, was uncomfortable. My sisters and brothers and I stared at our aunts, uncles, and cousins, speaking only when prompted. Even then, we hesitated, formed our sentences in our minds, then spoke softly, shyly.

My parents looked small and anxious during those occasions, and I waited impatiently for our leave-taking when we would mock our relatives the moment we were out of their hearing. "Reeely," we would say to one another, flexing our wrists and rolling our eyes, "how dooo you stan' this heat? Chile, it just too hy*ooo*-mid for words." Our relatives had made us feel "country," and this was our way of regaining pride in ourselves while getting a little revenge in the bargain. The words bubbled in our throats and rolled across our tongues, a balming.

As a child I felt this same doubleness in uptown Greeleyville where the whites lived. "Ain't that a pretty dress you're wearing!" Toby, the town policeman, said to me one day when I was fifteen. "Thank you very much," I replied, my voice barely audible in my own ears. The words felt wrong in my mouth, rigid, foreign. It was not that I had never spoken that phrase before—it was common in black English, too—but I was extremely conscious that this was an occasion for proper English. I had taken out my English and put it on as I did my church clothes, and I felt as if I were wearing my Sunday best in the middle of the week. It did not matter that Toby had not spoken grammatically correct English. He was white and could speak as he wished. I had something to prove. Toby did not.

Speaking standard English to whites was our way of demonstrating that we knew their language and could use it. Speaking it to standard-English-speaking blacks was our way of showing them that we, as well as they, could "put on airs." But when we spoke standard English, we acknowledged (to ourselves and to others—but primarily to ourselves) that our customary way of speaking was inferior. We felt foolish, embarrassed, somehow diminished because we were ashamed to be our real selves. We were reserved, shy in the presence of those who owned and/or spoke *the* language.

My parents never set aside time to drill us in standard English. Their forms of instruction were less formal. When my father was feeling particularly expansive, he would regale us with tales of his exploits in the outside world. In almost flawless English, complete with dialogue and flavored with gestures and embellishment, he told us about his attempt to get a haircut at a white barbershop; his refusal to acknowledge one of the town merchants until the man addressed him as "Mister"; the time he refused to step off the sidewalk uptown to let some whites pass; his airplane trip to New York City (to visit a sick relative) during which the stewardesses and porters—recognizing that he was a "gentleman"—addressed him as "Sir." I did not realize then—nor, I think, did my father—that he was teaching us, among other things, standard English and the relationship between language and power.

My mother's approach was different. Often, when one of us said, "I'm gon wash off my feet," she would say, "And what will you walk on if you wash them off?" Everyone would laugh at the victim of my mother's "proper" mood. But it was different when one of us children was in a proper mood. "You think you are so superior," I said to my oldest sister one day when we were arguing and she was winning. "Superior!" my sister mocked. "You mean I'm acting 'biggidy'?" My sisters and brothers sniggered, then joined in teasing me. Finally, my mother said, "Leave your sister alone. There's nothing wrong with using proper English." There was a half-smile on her face. I had gotten "uppity," had "put on airs" for no good reason. I was at home, alone with the family, and I hadn't been prompted by one of my mother's proper moods. But there was also a proud light in my mother's eyes; her children were learning English very well.

Not until years later, as a college student, did I begin to understand our ambivalence toward English, our scorn of it, our need to master it, to own and be owned by it—an ambivalence that extended to the public-school classroom. In our school, where there were no whites, my teachers taught standard English but used black English to do it. When my grammar-school teachers wanted us to write, for example, they usually said something like, "I want y'all to write five sentences that make a statement. Anybody git done before the rest can color." It was probably almost those exact words that led me to write these sentences in 1953 when I was in the second grade:

> The white clouds are pretty.
> There are only 15 people in our room.
> We will go to gym.
> We have a new poster.
> We may go out doors.

Second grade came after "Little First" and "Big First," so by then I knew

10

the implied rules that accompanied all writing assignments. Writing was an occasion for proper English. I was not to write in the way we spoke to one another: The white clouds pretty; There ain't but 15 people in our room; We going to gym; We got a new poster; We can go out in the yard. Rather I was to use the language of "other"; clouds *are*, there *are*, we *will*, we *have*, we *may*.

My sentences were short, rigid, perfunctory, like the letters my mother wrote to relatives:

> *Dear Papa,*
> How are you? How is Mattie? Fine I hope. We are fine. We will come to see you Sunday. Cousin Ned will give us a ride.
> > Love,
> > Daughter

The language was not ours. It was something from outside us, something we used for special occasions.

But my coloring on the other side of that second-grade paper is different. I drew three hearts and a sun. The sun has a smiling face that radiates and envelopes everything it touches And although the sun and its world are enclosed in a circle, the colors I used—red, blue, green, purple, orange, yellow, black—indicate that I was less restricted with drawing and coloring than I was with writing standard English. My valentines were not just red. My sun was not just a yellow ball in the sky.

By the time I reached the twelfth grade, speaking and writing standard English had taken on new importance. Each year, about half of the newly graduated seniors of our school moved to large cities—particularly in the North—to live with relatives and find work. Our English teacher constantly corrected our grammar: "Not 'ain't,' but 'isn't'." We seldom wrote papers, and even those few were usually plot summaries of short stories. When our teacher returned the papers, she usually lectured on the importance of using standard English: "I *am*; you *are*; he, she, or it *is*," she would say, writing on the chalkboard as she spoke. "How you gon git a job talking about 'I is,' or 'I isn't' or 'I ain't'?"

In Pittsburgh, where I moved after graduation, I watched my aunt and uncle—who had always spoken standard English when in Greeleyville—switch from black English to standard English to a mixture of the two, according to where they were or who they were with. At home and with certain close relatives, friends, and neighbors, they spoke black English. With those less close, they spoke a mixture. In public and with strangers, they generally spoke standard English. 15

In time, I learned to speak standard English with ease and to switch smoothly from black to standard or a mixture, and back again. But no matter where I was, no matter what the situation or occasion, I continued to write as I had in school:

Dear Mommie,
How are you? How is everybody else? Fine I hope. I am fine. So are
Aunt and Uncle. Tell everybody I said hello. I will write again soon.
Love,
Barbara

At work, at a health insurance company, I learned to write letters to customers. I studied form letters and letters written by co-workers, memorizing
the phrases and the ways in which they were used. I dictated:

Thank you for your letter of January 5. We have made the changes in
your coverage you requested. Your new premium will be $150 every
three months. We are pleased to have been of service to you.

In a sense, I was proud of the letters I wrote for the company: they were
proof of my ability to survive in the city, the outside world—an indication
of my growing mastery of English. But they also indicate that writing was
still mechanical for me, something that didn't require much thought.

Reading also became a more significant part of my life during those
early years in Pittsburgh. I had always liked reading, but now I devoted more
and more of my spare time to it. I read romances, mysteries, popular novels.
Looking back, I realize that the books I liked best were simple, unambiguous: good versus bad and right versus wrong with right rewarded and wrong
punished, mysteries unraveled and all set right in the end. It was how I
remembered life in Greeleyville.

Of course I was romanticizing. Life in Greeleyville had not been so
very uncomplicated. Back there I had been—first as a child, then as a young
woman with limited experience in the outside world—living in a relatively
closed-in society. But there were implicit and explicit principles that guided
our way of life and shaped our relationships with one another and the people
outside—principles that a newcomer would find elusive and baffling. In
Pittsburgh, I had matured, become more experienced: I had worked at three
different jobs, associated with a wider range of people, married, had children. This new environment with different prescripts for living required
that I speak standard English much of the time, and slowly, imperceptibly, I
had ceased seeing a sharp distinction between myself and "others." Reading
romances and mysteries, characterized by dichotomy, was a way of shying
away from change, from the person I was becoming.

But that other part of me—that part which took great pride in my
ability to hold a job writing business letters—was increasingly drawn to the
new developments in my life and the attending possibilities, opportunities
for even greater change. If I could write letters for a nationally known
business, could I not also do something better, more challenging, more
important? Could I not, perhaps, go to college and become a school
teacher? For years, afraid and a little embarrassed, I did no more than imagine this different me, this possible me. But sixteen years after coming north,

when my youngest daughter entered kindergarten, I found myself unable—
or unwilling—to resist the lure of possibility. I enrolled in my first college
course: Basic Writing, at the University of Pittsburgh.

For the first time in my life, I was required to write extensively about   *20*
myself. Using the most formal English at my command, I wrote these sentences near the beginning of the term:

> One of my duties as a homemaker is simply picking up after others. A
> day seldom passes that I don't search for a mislaid toy, book, or gym
> shoe, etc. I change the Ty-D-Bol, fight "ring around the collar," and
> keep our laundry smelling "April fresh." Occasionally, I settle argu-
> ments between my children and suggest things to do when they're
> bored. Taking telephone messages for my oldest daughter is my newest
> (and sometimes most aggravating) chore. Hanging the toilet paper roll
> is my most insignificant.

My concern was to use "appropriate" language, to sound as if I belonged in
a college classroom. But I felt separate from the language—as if it did not
and could not belong to me. I couldn't think and feel genuinely in that
language, couldn't make it express what I thought and felt about being a
housewife. A part of me resented, among other things, being judged by such
things as the appearance of my family's laundry and toilet bowl, but in that
language I could only imagine and write about a conventional housewife.

For the most part, the remainder of the term was a period of adjustment, a time of trying to find my bearings as a student in a college composition class, to learn to shut out my black English whenever I composed,
and to prevent it from creeping into my formulations; a time for trying to
grasp the language of the classroom and reproduce it in my prose; for trying
to talk about myself in that language, reach others through it. Each experience of writing was like standing naked and revealing my imperfection, my
"otherness." And each new assignment was another chance to make myself
over in language, reshape myself, make myself "better" in my rapidly changing image of a student in a college composition class.

But writing became increasingly unmanageable as the term pro-
gressed, and by the end of the semester, my sentences sounded like this:

> My excitement was soon dampened, however, by what seemed like a
> small voice in the back of my head saying that I should be careful with
> my long awaited opportunity. I felt frustrated and this seemed to make
> it difficult to concentrate.

There is a poverty of language in these sentences. By this point, I knew that
the clichéd language of my Housewife essay was unacceptable, and I generally recognized trite expressions. At the same time, I hadn't yet mastered the
language of the classroom, hadn't yet come to see it as belonging to me.
Most notable is the lifelessness of the prose, the apparent absence of a person
behind the words. I wanted those sentences—and the rest of the essay—to

convey the anguish of yearning to, at once, become something more and yet remain the same. I had the sensation of being split in two, part of me going into a future the other part didn't believe possible. As that person, the student writer at that moment, I was essentially mute. I could not—in the process of composing—use the language of the old me, yet I couldn't imagine myself in the language of "others."

I found this particularly discouraging because at midsemester I had been writing in a much different way. Note the language of this introduction to an essay I had written then, near the middle of the term:

> Pain is a constant companion to the people in "Footwork." Their jobs are physically damaging. Employers are insensitive to their feelings and in many cases add to their problems. The general public wounds them further by treating them with disgrace because of what they do for a living. Although the workers are as diverse as they are similar, there is a definite link between them. They suffer a great deal of abuse.

The voice here is stronger, more confident, appropriating terms like "physically damaging," "wounds them further," "insensitive," "diverse"—terms I couldn't have imagined using when writing about my own experience—and shaping them into sentences like, "Although the workers are as diverse as they are similar, there is a definite link between them." And there is the sense of a personality behind the prose, someone who sympathizes with the workers: "The general public wounds them further by treating them with disgrace because of what they do for a living."

What caused these differences? I was, I believed, explaining other people's thoughts and feelings, and I was free to move about in the language of "others" so long as I was speaking *of* others. I was unaware that I was transforming into my best classroom language my own thoughts and feelings about people whose experiences and ways of speaking were in many ways similar to mine.

The following year, unable to turn back or to let go of what had become something of an obsession with language (and hoping to catch and hold the sense of control that had eluded me in Basic Writing), I enrolled in a research writing course. I spent most of the term learning how to prepare for and write a research paper. I chose sex education as my subject and spent hours in libraries, searching for information, reading, taking notes. Then (not without messiness and often-demoralizing frustration) I organized my information into categories, wrote a thesis statement, and composed my paper—a series of paraphrases and quotations spaced between carefully constructed transitions. The process and results felt artificial, but as I would later come to realize I was passing through a necessary stage. My sentences sounded like this:

> This reserve becomes understandable with examination of who the abusers are. In an overwhelming number of cases, they are people the

25

victims know and trust. Family members, relatives, neighbors and close family friends commit seventy-five percent of all reported sex crimes against children, and parents, parent substitutes and relatives are the offenders in thirty to eighty percent of all reported cases.[12] While assault by strangers does occur, it is less common, and is usually a single episode.[13] But abuse by family members, relatives and acquaintances may continue for an extended period of time. In cases of incest, for example, children are abused repeatedly for an average of eight years.[14] In such cases, "the use of physical force is rarely necessary because of the child's trusting, dependent relationship with the offender. The child's cooperation is often facilitated by the adult's position of dominance, an offer of material goods, a threat of physical violence, or a misrepresentation of moral standards."[15]

The completed paper gave me a sense of profound satisfaction, and I read it often after my professor returned it. I know now that what I was pleased with was the language I used and the professional voice it helped me maintain. "Use better words," my teacher snapped at me one day after reading the notes I'd begun accumulating from my research, and slowly I began taking on the language of my sources. In my next set of notes, I used the word "vacillating"; my professor applauded. And by the time I composed the final draft, I felt at ease with terms like "overwhelming number of cases," "single episode," and "reserve," and I shaped them into sentences similar to those of my "expert" sources.

If I were writing the paper today, I would of course do some things differently. Rather than open with an anecdote—as my teacher suggested—I would begin simply with a quotation that caught my interest as I was researching my paper (and which I scribbled, without its source, in the margin of my notebook): "Truth does not do so much good in the world as the semblance of truth does evil." The quotation felt right because it captured what was for me the central idea of my essay—an idea that emerged gradually during the making of my paper—and expressed it in a way I would like to have said it. The anecdote, a hypothetical situation I invented to conform to the information in the paper, felt forced and insincere because it represented—to a great degree—my teacher's understanding of the essay, *her* idea of what in it was most significant. Improving upon my previous experiences with writing, I was beginning to think and feel in the language I used, to find my own voices in it, to sense that how one speaks influences how one means. But I was not yet secure enough, comfortable enough with the language to trust my intuition.

Now that I know that to seek knowledge, freedom, and autonomy means always to be in the concentrated process of becoming—always to be venturing into new territory, feeling one's way at first, then getting one's balance, negotiating, accommodating, discovering one's self in ways that previously defined "others"—I sometimes get tired. And I ask myself why I keep on participating in this highbrow form of violence, this slamming against perplexity. But there is no real futility in the question, no hint of that part of the old me who stood outside standard English, hugging to herself a disabling mistrust of a language she thought could not represent a person with her history and experience. Rather, the question represents a person who feels the consequence of her education, the weight of her possibilities as a teacher and writer and human being, a voice in society. And I would not change that person, would not give back the good burden that accompanies my growing expertise, my increasing power to shape myself in language and share that self with "others."

"To speak," says Frantz Fanon, "means to be in a position to use a certain syntax, to grasp the morphology of this or that language, but it means above all to assume a culture, to support the weight of a civilization."* To write means to do the same, but in a more profound sense. However, Fanon also says that to achieve mastery means to "get" in a position of power, to "grasp," to "assume." This, I have learned—both as a student and subsequently as a teacher—can involve tremendous emotional and psychological conflict for those attempting to master academic discourse. Although as a beginning student writer I had a fairly good grasp of ordinary spoken English and was proficient at what Labov calls "code-switching" (and what John Baugh in *Black Street Speech* terms "style shifting"), when I came face to face with the demands of academic writing, I grew increasingly self-conscious, constantly aware of my status as a black and a speaker of one of the many black English vernaculars—a traditional outsider. For the first time, I experienced my sense of doubleness as something menacing, a built-in enemy. Whenever I turned inward for salvation, the balm so available during my childhood, I found instead this new fragmentation which spoke to me in many voices. It was the voice of my desire to prosper, but at the same time it spoke of what I had relinquished and could not regain: a safe way of being, a state of powerlessness which exempted me from responsibility for who I was and might be. And it accused me of betrayal, of turning away from blackness. To recover balance, I had to take on the language of the academy, the language of "others." And to do that, I had to learn to imagine myself a part of the culture of that language, and therefore someone free to manage that language, to take liberties with it. Writing and rewriting, practicing, experimenting, I came to comprehend more fully the generative power of language. I discovered—with the help of some especially sensitive teachers—that through writing one can continually bring new selves into being, each with new responsibilities and difficulties, but also with new possibilities. Remarkable power, indeed. I write and continually give birth to myself.

Questions for Discussion

1. Is there a difference between standard English and proper English?

Black Skin, White Masks (1952; rpt. New York: Grove Press, 1967), pp. 17–18.

2. How does context determine the language that Mellix uses? In what sort of "other environments" would she be reluctant to use the language she grew up speaking?

3. How does Mellix feel about black English? Does she think it is inferior to the language she learned in school? What obstacles did she have to overcome in learning to speak and write in a public voice?

4. In paragraph 9 Mellix realizes something that she did not realize as a child. What does she mean when she writes that her father had tried to teach her "the relationship between language and power"?

5. What does Mellix mean by "the generative power of language"? How can writing lead someone to "continually bring new selves into being"?

Suggestions for Writing

1. What would happen if you always spoke the same way, regardless of what you were speaking about, where you were speaking, and whom you were speaking to? Write an essay that shows you using language in different ways depending upon context.

2. Mellix reports that her first experiences with college writing made her feel "like standing naked and revealing my imperfection." Write an essay about how you feel when you show your writing to someone else.

THE DEATH OF A MOTH: TRANSFIGURATION IN A CANDLE FLAME

Annie Dillard

You will find that this essay can be divided into three sections. If the divisions startle you at first, think about how the various parts of the essay fit together. And as you read, keep the essay's subtitle in mind: "Transfiguration in a Candle Flame." Transfiguration means "a change in form or appearance, especially a spiritual change." Dillard includes so many details that you should have little difficulty seeing the death of a moth, but understanding the significance of that death will be more challenging. The subtitle provides a clue. Ask yourself what it refers to, and look for similarities between Dillard and the moth. What could an insect have in common with an author whose nonfiction has been awarded a Pulitzer Prize?

I live alone with two cats, who sleep on my legs. There is a yellow one, and a black one whose name is Small. In the morning I joke to the black one. Do you remember last night? Do you remember? I throw them both out before breakfast, so I can eat.

There is a spider, too, in the bathroom, of uncertain lineage, bulbous at the abdomen and drab, whose six-inch mess of web works, works somehow, works miraculously, to keep her alive and me amazed. The web is in a corner behind the toilet, connecting tile wall to tile wall. The house is new, the bathroom immaculate, save for the spider, her web, and the sixteen or so corpses she's tossed to the floor.

The corpses appear to be mostly sow bugs, those little armadillo creatures who live to travel flat out in houses, and die round. In addition to sow-bug husks, hollow and sipped empty of color, there are what seem to be two or three wingless moth bodies, one new flake of earwig, and three spider carcasses crinkled and clenched.

I wonder on what fool's errand an earwig, or a moth, or a sow bug, would visit that clean corner of the house behind the toilet; I have not noticed any blind parades of sow bugs blundering into corners. Yet they do hazard there, at a rate of more than one a week, and the spider thrives. Yesterday she was working on the earwig, mouth on gut; today he's on the floor. It must take a certain genius to throw things away from there, to find a straight line through that sticky tangle to the floor.

Today the earwig shines darkly, and gleams, what there is of him: a dorsal curve of thorax and abdomen, and a smooth pair of pincers by which I knew his name. Next week, if the other bodies are any indication, he'll be shrunk and gray, webbed to the floor with dust. The sow bugs beside him are curled and empty, fragile, a breath away from brittle fluff. The spiders lie on their sides, translucent and ragged, their legs drying in knots. The

5

moths stagger against each other, headless, in a confusion of arcing strips of chitin like peeling varnish, like a jumble of buttresses for cathedral vaults, like nothing resembling moths, so that I would hesitate to call them moths, except that I have had some experience with the figure Moth reduced to a nub.

Two summers ago I was camped alone in the Blue Ridge Mountains of Virginia. I had hauled myself and gear up there to read, among other things, *The Day on Fire*, by James Ullman, a novel about Rimbaud° that had made me want to be a writer when I was sixteen; I was hoping it would do it again. So I read every day sitting under a tree by my tent, while warblers sang in the leaves overhead and bristle worms trailed their inches over the twiggy dirt at my feet; and I read every night by candlelight, while barred owls called in the forest and pale moths seeking mates massed round my head in the clearing, where my light made a ring.

Moths kept flying into the candle. They would hiss and recoil, reeling upside down in the shadows among my cooking pans. Or they would singe their wings and fall, and their hot wings, as if melted, would stick to the first thing they touched—a pan, a lid, a spoon—so that the snagged moths could struggle only in tiny arcs, unable to flutter free. These I could release by a quick flip with a stick; in the morning I would find my cooking stuff decorated with torn flecks of moth wings, ghostly triangles of shiny dust here and there on the aluminum. So I read, and boiled water, and replenished candles, and read on.

One night a moth flew into the candle, was caught, burnt dry, and held. I must have been staring at the candle, or maybe I looked up where a shadow crossed my page; at any rate, I saw it all. A golden female moth, a biggish one with a two-inch wingspread, flapped into the fire, dropped abdomen into the wet wax, stuck, flamed, and frazzled in a second. Her moving wings ignited like tissue paper, like angels' wings, enlarging the circle of light in the clearing and creating out of the darkness the sudden blue sleeves of my sweater, the green leaves of jewelweed by my side, the ragged red trunk of a pine; at once the light contracted again and the moth's wings vanished in a fine, foul smoke. At the same time, her six legs clawed, curled, blackened, and ceased, disappearing utterly. And her head jerked in spasms, making a spattering noise; her antennae crisped and burnt away and her heaving mouthparts cracked like pistol fire. When it was all over, her head was, so far as I could determine, gone, gone the long way of her wings and legs. Her head was a hole lost to time. All that was left was the glowing horn shell of her abdomen and thorax—a fraying, partially collapsed gold tube jammed upright in the candle's round pool.

And then this moth-essence, this spectacular skeleton, began to act as a wick. She kept burning. The wax rose in the moth's body from her soaking

Rimbaud: Arthur Rimbaud (1854–1891), a French poet.

abdomen to her thorax to the shattered hole where her head should have been, and widened into flame, a saffron-yellow flame that robed her to the ground like an immolating monk. That candle had two wicks, two winding flames of identical light, side by side. The moth's head was fire. She burned for two hours, until I blew her out.

She burned for two hours without changing, without swaying or kneeling—only glowing within, like a building fire glimpsed through silhouetted walls, like a hollow saint, like a flame-faced virgin gone to God, while I read by her light, kindled, while Rimbaud in Paris burnt out his brain in a thousand poems, while night pooled wetly at my feet. *10*

So. That is why I think those hollow shreds on the bathroom floor are moths. I believe I know what moths look like, in any state.

I have three candles here on the table which I disentangle from the plants and light when visitors come. The cats avoid them, although Small's tail caught fire once; I rubbed it out before she noticed. I don't mind living alone. I like eating alone and reading. I don't mind sleeping alone. The only time I mind being alone is when something is funny; then when I am laughing at something funny, I wish someone were around. Sometimes I think it is pretty funny that I sleep alone.

Questions for Discussion

1. As the title reveals, this essay is about the death of a moth. Yet it begins and ends with paragraphs focused upon how the author lives and sleeps alone with two cats. How do these paragraphs relate to the story of the moth that flew into the candle?
2. In paragraph 1 Dillard jokes with one of her cats. "Do you remember last night?" she asks. Can you explain this joke—and why it is appropriate for the essay?
3. Why did Dillard go camping in Virginia? What does her reading reveal about her?
4. Consider the reference to "angels' wings" in paragraph 8. What does it imply about the moth? Are there any other religious references within the essay?
5. Dillard reports that the moth that burns for two hours was a female, and paragraphs 8–10 include several references to "she" and "her." How would the essay change if Dillard wrote about a male moth?
6. According to Dillard, "I believe I know what moths look like, in any state." Do you believe her? Why do you think this might be worth knowing?

Suggestions for Writing

1. Study the behavior of an animal that you can observe firsthand. Consider whether it reminds you of yourself in any way. Write a description of the

animal's behavior that will accurately report the details of what you have seen and, if possible, suggest a parallel with human behavior.

2. Experiment with writing by composing a narrative essay framed, like Dillard's, with paragraphs that seem unrelated to your main story but that are nevertheless related to that story on some level.

3

Writing to Explore an Idea

These days, there always seems to be more to do than there is time to do it in. Efficiency, we are told, is a virtue. "Just do it," an advertisement for running shoes proclaims; and indeed, we always seem to be running, one way or another. In writing, too, we are often urged to be efficient: Put the thesis first so that your reader can quickly find the main points; pare down to the leanest language you can produce; get to the point. Efficiency *is* important. We wouldn't ever get anything done without some of it. But efficiency, carried to an extreme, would deny us the opportunity to contemplate, to reflect, and to play with alternatives.

Before you pursue other motives for writing—such as writing to interpret, evaluate, or persuade—you may benefit from writing to explore ideas. If you deprive yourself of the opportunity to play with ideas before you commit yourself to proving a point, you may become stuck in predictable patterns and conventional thoughts.

The purpose of exploring ideas is to discover rather than to assert. Consider how Lewis Thomas, a distinguished physician and hospital administrator, explores what science education could be like in the future.

117

But maybe, just maybe, a new set of courses dealing systematically with ignorance in science will take hold. The scientists might discover in it a new and subversive technique for catching the attention of students driven by curiosity, delighted and surprised to learn that science is . . . an "endless frontier." The humanists, for their part, might take considerable satisfaction in watching their scientific colleagues confess openly to not knowing everything about everything. And the poets, on whose shoulders the future rests, might, late nights, thinking things over, begin to see some meanings that elude the rest of us.

Although there is a persuasive dimension to this passage, Thomas has not committed himself to making a sustained argument. He is, instead, conveying a sense of thinking aloud. Note that he uses *might* three times and *maybe* twice. He does not pause to explain why the future rests upon the shoulders of poets; he leaves readers to reflect upon that thought for themselves. And rather than dwelling upon facts, he seems to delight in the idea that scientists do not know everything.

If you think things over late at night, like the poets Thomas imagines, you may have already felt that your mind was freely ranging, stopping here and there on an interesting point or image, and moving on to something else. This kind of thinking is usually unstructured, but lack of formal structure does not make it pointless. Associating one idea with another may take you far from where you began—and on a bad day it may take you nowhere—but if you persevere, you should find that thinking will usually take you some place worth being.

For example, suppose that riding down the highway, you notice a gnarled tree far away in a field. Wondering why the tree is so gnarled can lead you to ponder the forces that may have caused the tree to grow crooked. But as you think about the tree, you realize that it is beautiful because of what you initially perceived as a flaw, and that realization could lead you to further reflections. If you have been trying to straighten every irregularity in your life and landscape your world with carefully pruned trees all neatly aligned, the discovery of a different aesthetic can transform the way you want to live.

Richard Selzer engages in this kind of thinking when he meditates on his visit to a slaughterhouse. The visit reminds him of Yale, where he will judge architectural designs for a model slaughterhouse; that idea in turn leads him to another: a vision of animals being treated with dignity and ceremony. The essay does not have a thesis, but it is unified by the spirit of inquiry and Selzer's strong voice as a writer.

As Selzer's essay demonstrates, exploration gives writers the advantage of flexibility so that they can experiment with forms, adopting strategies that work for them and avoiding a predetermined pattern that dictates what must happen in any given paragraph. In this respect exploration honors a motive especially associated with essays. The word *essay* comes from *essayer,*

French for "to try." By providing an opportunity to try and test ideas—instead of proving points that are already known—essays that explore ideas operate within a distinguished rhetorical tradition that can be traced back to such writers as Michel Montaigne and Francis Bacon.

Of the various essays in this chapter, you may find the form of George Orwell's "Marrakech" the most unusual. Orwell is writing what is called an essay of *montage*—from the term used in photography to describe a rapid sequence of related short scenes, or the process of making one picture by closely arranging many. When experimenting with this form, a writer composes a series of separate scenes and arranges them in a meaningful pattern without providing transitions between them. These scenes are like a series of pictures arranged upon the wall of an art gallery. The audience is expected to fill in the gaps between these scenes by reflecting upon how each contributes to the meaning of the others. By experimenting with this form, writers have ample opportunity to play with ideas; however, they also have the responsibility to help readers understand the nature and meaning of that play.

Because playing with ideas happens most productively when writers feel at ease, the writing that results from this activity often has a personal dimension. All of the works in this chapter employ the first person, the *I* that helps convey the sense of an individual human mind at play. The use of the first person also suggests that they have given readers their trust and expect trust in return. Notice the sense of play with which James Fallows discusses scavenging or Phyllis Rose links torture to French cuisine and beauty care. Both Fallows and Rose share their feelings and solicit yours in return. Notice, too, that Gloria Naylor, George Orwell, and Richard Selzer also share their feelings, but their moods are more serious. Playing with ideas does not necessarily make writers feel playful, but it does enable them to enjoy the pleasure that comes from discovery.

When you explore ideas, you venture into unfamiliar territory—for that is where discoveries await. Exploration thus requires a willingness to take some risks. But if there are risks, there are also rewards: originality of expression and a heightened awareness of what the world offers. Remember, however, that when you write an essay of this sort, you are expecting your readers to understand your writing, even if it involves surprising leaps and unexpected turns. You venture into unknown territories, and you hope your readers follow. It is your responsibility to at least glance back once in a while to make sure that they are still with you.

Perhaps the greatest challenge in writing to explore an idea is knowing when to stop. Because this motive allows for considerable freedom and experimentation, writers can conclude in significantly different ways. Having offered an alternative vision of how to teach science, Thomas concludes by restating the rationale for change. Fallows concludes his piece with an imaginary conflict. Naylor ends by returning to a reminiscence that she began with and that illustrates the point she has been making. Selzer achieves closure with an encapsulation, an account of his visit to a butcher shop; but that visit is open to multiple interpretations, almost as if it were the conclusion to a work of fiction.

When you are motivated to write an essay of your own along these lines, remember that you don't have to have a formal conclusion that restates your key points, but you do need to give your reader a sense of completion. The key here is to convey the sense that your journey has taken you to a point where it is convenient to rest; you have not simply broken down on an isolated stretch of highway.

Lewis Carroll's Red Queen confessed that she often entertained six contradictory ideas before breakfast. As you begin to explore ideas on your own, be aware that recognizing contradictions and incongruities can lead to new perceptions. But how you think and what you think about is ultimately up to you. No one should insist that you change ideas that you hold sacrosanct; similarly, no one should insist that you adhere to an idea you have explored thoroughly and found inadequate. Making that kind of choice for yourself is a basic human right, and writing to explore is an important tool for exercising that right. When you argue about ideas, you have the responsibility to make a well-defined position clear. But when you explore ideas, you are free to find out what you think, and that can be a great adventure—an adventure that can be satisfying to share with others.

THE ART OF TEACHING SCIENCE

Lewis Thomas

A physician and medical educator, Lewis Thomas writes about science from a point of view that nonscientists often find refreshing. In the following essay, which was first published in the New York Times, *Thomas explores why science is too important to be left to scientists. As you read, consider how Thomas tries to make science attractive to people who prefer the humanities. Think of the science classes that you have taken, and ask yourself whether you would have found more pleasure in the sort of teaching that Thomas envisions.*

Everyone seems to agree that there is something wrong with the way science is being taught these days. But no one is at all clear about when it went wrong or what is to be done about it. The term "scientific illiteracy" has become almost a cliché in educational circles. Graduate schools blame the colleges; colleges blame the secondary schools; the high schools blame the elementary schools, which, in turn, blame the family.

I suggest that the scientific community itself is partly, perhaps largely, to blame. Moreover, if there are disagreements between the world of the humanities and the scientific enterprise as to the place and importance of science in a liberal-arts education and the role of science in 20th-century culture, I believe that the scientists are themselves responsible for a general misunderstanding of what they are really up to.

During the last half-century, we have been teaching the sciences as though they were the same collection of academic subjects as always, and—here is what has really gone wrong—as though they would always be the same. Students learn today's biology, for example, the same way we learned Latin when I was in high school long ago: first, the fundamentals; then, the underlying laws; next, the essential grammar and, finally, the reading of texts. Once mastered, that was that: Latin was Latin and forever after would always be Latin. History, once learned, was history. And biology was precisely biology, a vast array of hard facts to be learned as fundamentals, followed by a reading of the texts.

Furthermore, we have been teaching science as if its facts were somehow superior to the facts in all other scholarly disciplines—more fundamental, more solid, less subject to subjectivism, immutable. English literature is not just one way of thinking; it is all sorts of ways; poetry is a moving target; the facts that underlie art, architecture and music are not really hard facts, and you can change them any way you like by arguing about them. But science, it appears, is an altogether different kind of learning: an unambiguous, unalterable and endlessly useful display of data that only needs to be packaged and installed somewhere in one's temporal lobe in order to achieve a full understanding of the natural world.

And, of course, it is not like this at all. In real life, every field of science   *5*
is incomplete, and most of them—whatever the record of accomplishment
during the last 200 years—are still in their very earliest stages. In the fields I
know best, among the life sciences, it is required that the most expert and
sophisticated minds be capable of changing course—often with a great
lurch—every few years. In some branches of biology the mind-changing is
occurring with accelerating velocity. Next week's issue of any scientific
journal can turn a whole field upside down, shaking out any number of
immutable ideas and installing new bodies of dogma. This is an almost
everyday event in physics, in chemistry, in materials research, in neurobiol-
ogy, in genetics, in immunology.

On any Tuesday morning, if asked, a good working scientist will tell
you with some self-satisfaction that the affairs of his field are nicely in order,
that things are finally looking clear and making sense, and all is well. But
come back again on another Tuesday, and the roof may have just fallen in
on his life's work. All the old ideas—last weeks' ideas in some cases—are no
longer good ideas. The hard facts have softened, melted away and vanished
under the pressure of new hard facts. Something strange has happened. And
it is this very strangeness of nature that makes science engrossing, that keeps
bright people at it, and that ought to be at the center of science teaching.

The conclusions reached in science are always, when looked at closely,
far more provisional and tentative than are most of the assumptions arrived
at by our colleagues in the humanities. But we do not talk much in public
about this, nor do we teach this side of science. We tend to say instead:
These are the facts of the matter, and this is what the facts signify. Go and
learn them, for they will be the same forever.

By doing this, we miss opportunity after opportunity to recruit young
people into science, and we turn off a good many others who would never
dream of scientific careers but who emerge from their education with the
impression that science is fundamentally boring.

Sooner or later, we will have to change this way of presenting science.
We might begin by looking more closely at the common ground that science shares with all disciplines, particularly with the humanities and with
social and behavioral science. For there is indeed such a common ground.
It is called bewilderment. There are more than seven times seven types of
ambiguity in science, all awaiting analysis. The poetry of Wallace Stevens is
crystal clear alongside the genetic code.

One of the complaints about science is that it tends to flatten every-   *10*
thing. In its deeply reductionist way, it is said, science removes one mystery
after another, leaving nothing in the place of mystery but data. I have even
heard this claim as explanation for the drift of things in modern art and
modern music: Nothing is left to contemplate except randomness and
senselessness; God is nothing but a pair of dice, loaded at that. Science is
linked somehow to the despair of the 20th-century mind. There is almost
nothing unknown and surely nothing unknowable. Blame science.

I prefer to turn things around in order to make precisely the opposite case. Science, especially 20th-century science, has provided us with a glimpse of something we never really knew before, the revelation of human ignorance. We have been accustomed to the belief, from one century to another, that except for one or two mysteries we more or less comprehend everything on earth. Every age, not just the 18th century, regarded itself as the Age of Reason, and we have never lacked for explanations of the world and its ways. Now, we are being brought up short. We do not understand much of anything, from the episode we rather dismissively (and, I think, defensively) choose to call the "big bang," all the way down to the particles in the atoms of a bacterial cell. We have a wilderness of mystery to make our way through in the centuries ahead. We will need science for this but not science alone. In its own time, science will produce the data and some of the meaning in the data, but never the full meaning. For perceiving real significance when significance is at hand, we will need all sorts of brains outside the fields of science.

It is primarily because of this need that I would press for changes in the way science is taught. Although there is a perennial need to teach the young people who will be doing the science themselves, this will always be a small minority. Even more important, we must teach science to those who will be needed for thinking about it, and that means pretty nearly everyone else—most of all, the poets, but also artists, musicians, philosophers, historians and writers. A few of these people, at least, will be able to imagine new levels of meaning which may be lost on the rest of us.

In addition, it is time to develop a new group of professional thinkers, perhaps a somewhat larger group than the working scientists and the working poets, who can create a discipline of scientific criticism. We have had good luck so far in the emergence of a few people ranking as philosophers of science and historians and journalists of science, and I hope more of these will be coming along. But we have not yet seen specialists in the fields of scientific criticism who are of the caliber of the English literary and social critics F. R. Leavis and John Ruskin or the American literary critic Edmund Wilson. Science needs critics of this sort, but the public at large needs them more urgently. ·

I suggest that the introductory courses in science, at all levels from grade school through college, be radically revised. Leave the fundamentals, the so-called basics, aside for a while, and concentrate the attention of all students on the things that are not known. You cannot possibly teach quantum mechanics without mathematics, to be sure, but you can describe the strangeness of the world opened up by quantum theory. Let it be known, early on, that there are deep mysteries and profound paradoxes revealed in distant outline by modern physics. Explain that these can be approached more closely and puzzled over, once the language of mathematics has been sufficiently mastered.

At the outset, before any of the fundamentals, teach the still impon-   *15*
derable puzzles of cosmology. Describe as clearly as possible, for the youngest minds, that there are some things going on in the universe that lie still
beyond comprehension, and make it plain how little is known.

Do not teach that biology is a useful and perhaps profitable science;
that can come later. Teach instead that there are structures squirming inside
each of our cells that provide all the energy for living. Essentially foreign
creatures, these lineal descendants of bacteria were brought in for symbiotic
living a billion or so years ago. Teach that we do not have the ghost of an
idea how they got there, where they came from, or how they evolved to
their present structure and function. The details of oxidative phosphoryla-
tion and photosynthesis can come later.

Teach ecology early on. Let it be understood that the earth's life is a
system of interdependent creatures, and that we do not understand at all
how it works. The earth's environment, from the range of atmospheric gases
to the chemical constituents of the sea, has been held in an almost unbeliev-
ably improbable state of regulated balance since life began, and the regula-
tion of stability and balance is somehow accomplished by the life itself, like
the autonomic nervous system of an immense organism. We do not know
how such a system works, much less what it means, but there are some nice
reductionist details at hand, such as the bizarre proportions of atmospheric
constituents, ideal for our sort of planetary life, and the surprising stability
of the ocean's salinity, and the fact that the average temperature of the earth
has remained quite steady in the face of at least a 25 percent increase in heat
coming in from the sun since the earth began. That kind of thing: something
to think about.

Go easy, I suggest, on the promises sometimes freely offered by science.
Technology relies and depends on science these days, more than ever before,
but technology is far from the first justification for doing research, nor is it
necessarily an essential product to be expected from science. Public decisions about the future of technology are totally different from decisions
about science, and the two enterprises should not be tangled together. The
central task of science is to arrive, stage by stage, at a clearer comprehension
of nature, but this does not at all mean, as it is sometimes claimed to mean,
a search for mastery over nature.

Science may someday provide us with a better understanding of ourselves, but never, I hope, with a set of technologies for doing something or
other to improve ourselves. I am made nervous by assertions that human
consciousness will someday be unraveled by research, laid out for close
scrutiny like the workings of a computer, and then—and *then* . . . ! I hope
with some fervor that we can learn a lot more than we now know about the
human mind, and I see no reason why this strange puzzle should remain
forever and entirely beyond us. But I would be deeply disturbed by any
prospect that we might use the new knowledge in order to begin doing
something about it—to improve it, say. This is a different matter from

searching for information to use against schizophrenia or dementia, where we are badly in need of technologies, indeed likely one day to be sunk without them. But the ordinary, everyday, more or less normal human mind is too marvelous an instrument ever to be tampered with by anyone, science or no science.

The education of humanists cannot be regarded as complete, or even *20* adequate, without exposure in some depth to where things stand in the various branches of science, particularly, as I have said, in the areas of our ignorance. Physics professors, most of them, look with revulsion on assignments to teach their subject to poets. Biologists, caught up by the enchantment of their new power, armed with flawless instruments to tell the nucleotide sequences of the entire human genome, nearly matching the physicists in the precision of their measurements of living processes, will resist the prospect of broad survey courses; each biology professor will demand that any student in his path master every fine detail within that professor's research program.

The liberal-arts faculties, for their part, will continue to view the scientists with suspicion and apprehension. "What do the scientists want?" asked a Cambridge professor in Francis Cornford's wonderful "Microcosmographia Academica." "Everything that's going," was the quick answer. That was back in 1912, and scientists haven't much changed.

But maybe, just maybe, a new set of courses dealing systematically with ignorance in science will take hold. The scientists might discover in it a new and subversive technique for catching the attention of students driven by curiosity, delighted and surprised to learn that science is exactly as the American scientist and educator Vannevar Bush described it: an "endless frontier." The humanists, for their part, might take considerable satisfaction in watching their scientific colleagues confess openly to not knowing everything about everything. And the poets, on whose shoulders the future rests, might, late nights, thinking things over, begin to see some meanings that elude the rest of us. It is worth a try.

I believe that the worst thing that has happened to science education is that the fun has gone out of it. A great many good students look at it as slogging work to be got through on the way to medical school. Others are turned off by the premedical students themselves, embattled and bleeding for grades and class standing. Very few recognize science as the high adventure it really is, the wildest of all explorations ever taken by human beings, the chance to glimpse things never seen before, the shrewdest maneuver for discovering how the world works. Instead, baffled early on, they are misled into thinking that bafflement is simply the result of not having learned all the facts. They should be told that everyone else is baffled as well—from the professor in his endowed chair down to the platoons of postdoctoral students in the laboratories all night. Every important scientific advance that has come in looking like an answer has turned, sooner or later—usually sooner—into a question. And the game is just beginning.

If more students were aware of this, I think many of them would decide to look more closely and to try and learn more about what *is* known. That is the time when mathematics will become clearly and unavoidably recognizable as an essential, indispensable instrument for engaging in the game, and that is the time for teaching it. The calamitous loss of applied mathematics from what we might otherwise be calling higher education is a loss caused, at least in part, by insufficient incentives for learning the subject. Left by itself, standing there among curriculum offerings, it is not at all clear to the student what it is to be applied to. And there is all of science, next door, looking like an almost-finished field reserved only for chaps who want to invent or apply new technologies. We have had it wrong, and presented it wrong to class after class for several generations.

An appreciation of what is happening in science today, and how great 25 a distance lies ahead for exploring, ought to be one of the rewards of a liberal-arts education. It ought to be good in itself, not something to be acquired on the way to a professional career but part of the cast of thought needed for getting into the kind of century that is now just down the road. Part of the intellectual equipment of an educated person, however his or her time is to be spent, ought to be a feel for the queernesses of nature, the inexplicable thing, the side of life for which informed bewilderment will be the best way of getting through the day.

Questions for Discussion

1. Where is the blame for "scientific illiteracy" usually put? Where does Thomas believe that at least part of the blame belongs?
2. Why does Thomas believe that science is mysterious and exciting?
3. Thomas claims that the teaching of science often leaves students feeling that science is boring. Is this true of your own education in science? How does he think science should be taught? Would you welcome the changes he proposes in this essay?
4. Why is it important for people in other fields to study science? Why not leave science to the scientists?
5. In paragraph 22 Thomas claims that the future rests upon the shoulders of poets. What do you think he means by this?
6. In exploring the nature of science and science education, Thomas has implied an argument. How would the essay probably change if Thomas wanted to emphasize that argument?

Suggestions for Writing

1. What is your least favorite subject? Write an essay exploring the reasons that have led you to feel that way.
2. Write an essay exploring what poets could contribute to science.

LAND OF PLENTY

James Fallows

> *Have you ever been tempted to retrieve something that someone else is throwing away? This is a temptation James Fallows faced when living in Japan and finding all sorts of interesting things neatly piled for trash removal. Fallows, who writes regularly about Asia for the* Atlantic *and the* Wall Street Journal, *explores what Japanese garbage says about Japan. As you read, consider what you can learn about people from what they throw away and what they decide to keep. Ask yourself how Americans and Japanese compare when it's time to put out the trash.*

On *sodai gomi* nights in Japan we learn what kind of people we are. *Sodai gomi,* which rhymes with "oh my homey," means "bulky garbage." It's sometimes used colloquially to describe husbands who have retired from the salaryman life and now spend their time around the house. That *sodai gomi* problem may be a strain on Japanese families, but *sodai gomi* in its literal sense is a more serious trial for my family.

Three nights a week the residents of our neighborhood in Yokohama deposit their household trash at specified areas on the street corners. It's wrapped in neat bundles, it looks like gifts, it disappears at dawn. For two or three nights near the end of each month they bring out the *sodai gomi*. These are articles no longer wanted around the house and too big for normal trash collection. Big garbage can really be big: I've seen sofas, refrigerators, bookcases, chairs, bed frames, vacuum cleaners, an acetylene welding tank, a motorcycle, and numerous television sets.

Sodai gomi exists for two reasons. One is the small size of the typical Japanese house, with its lack of attic, cellar, garage, or spare room. When a new TV comes in, the old one must go out. (This also applies to cars. To buy a new one, you have to prove to the government that you have a place to park it, which for most people means getting rid of the old car. I can't figure out what happens to the old cars: they're certainly not on the roads, and so far I haven't seen one in a *sodai gomi* pile.)

The other reason is the Japanese desire for freshness and purity. No one here really enjoys using something that has passed through other people's hands. My Japanese friends seem to feel about buying a second-hand radio, lamp, or table the way I'd feel about buying someone else's socks. There is a "recycle shop" in our neighborhood that sells used clothes and toys at cut rates. Presumably someone must buy there, since it's still in business, but usually shoppers seem to scoot by in embarrassment, as if it were a Frederick's of Hollywood shop. Whenever I'm listening to the Far East Network, the U.S. military's radio station, and hear an ad for a garage sale, I realize that the American soldiers are unusual not just because they have garages but also because they can sell their old possessions rather than throw them out.

Our first *sodai gomi* night came shortly after we moved into our current house. It cut into our hearts in a way none of our neighbors could have known. For one thing, we had no furniture, silverware, or other household belongings, because everything except the clothes in our suitcases was making a five-week sea journey up from our last house, in Malaysia. We had also just come from a culture with a wholly different approach to used goods. Malaysia is a land of tropical abundance, but no one throws anything away. Just before leaving we had auctioned off every spare item in the house, from frying pans and mosquito nets to half-used rolls of Scotch tape. Several customers were enthusiastically bidding for the shirts my sons had on. It was painful to go from that world to one in which we didn't have any household goods, couldn't bring ourselves to buy the overpriced new ones in the store—and then saw heaps of clean, new-looking merchandise just sitting on the street.

You can see where I am leading. It was not in us to resist. We had quickly tired of eating, sitting, relaxing, studying, and performing all other indoor activities on the floor, without tables or chairs, while waiting for our ship to come in. "Set the floor, please, boys," my wife would call at dinner time. I lay sprawled on my stomach in front of my computer keyboard, attempting to type while resting my weight on my elbows, trying to cheer myself with mental images of Abe Lincoln sprawled before the fire as a boy. Then one evening, as we trudged home at twilight from the train station, we saw two replenished-looking *sodai gomi* piles. In one was a perfectly nice plastic lawn chair, in the other an ordinary low Japanese tea table. You couldn't use both of these at the same time—if you sat in the lawn chair, you'd be too high to reach down to the table comfortably. But if we had the table we could at least eat without bending over to reach plates of food on the floor, which made me feel like a husky eating its chow.

We were in a crowd, of course, when we first saw the *sodai gomi*. We were too confused and timid to grab anything from the pile just then. But that night I sat in our kitchen, peering through our window toward the *sodai gomi* at the end of the street. The door to a *juku,* or cram school, was near the piles. The last group of teenage students left there around eleven. After midnight the trains from Tokyo become much less frequent: I could depend on intervals of fifteen or twenty minutes between clumps of salarymen teetering drunkenly from the station toward home. The street looked bare at 12:30, so I made my move. The next morning we placed our breakfast dishes on our table, and I read the morning paper while luxuriating in my full-length lawn chair.

It was two more days before the *sodai gomi* collectors came. In those two nights we laid in as many provisions as we decently could. A shiny new bell for one son's bicycle, a small but attractive wooden cupboard, a complete set of wrenches and screwdrivers in a metal toolbox, a Naugahyde-covered barstool, a lacquer serving tray. If I didn't already know English, I would probably have taken the four large boxes containing four dozen tape cassettes from the Advanced Conversational English series. My son walked in the door one day, said "Guess what?" and presented a black-and-white TV. In self-defense I should point out that everything except a few rusty wrenches looked perfectly clean, whole, and serviceable. In any other culture you'd never believe these things were being thrown out.

That was last summer; we've learned a lot since then. We realize that *sodai gomi* is part of a larger cycle, in which it's important to give as well as receive. So when our household shipment arrived, we gave the lawn chair back to the pile—and later we bought a new color TV and gave back the black-and-white one. We've learned that we're not alone in our secret practice. Last month I met an American writer who lives on the outskirts of Tokyo. I admired the leather notebook he was carrying and asked him where he got it. "You'll never believe this . . . ," he said. We've learned that some Japanese, too, overcome their squeamishness about secondhand material. When I'm up late at night, I sometimes catch a glimpse of the *sodai gomi* area—a more disinterested glimpse, now that our house is furnished—and see a van cruising back and forth, checking it out. In the morning the choicest items are gone.

And I've learned where I'll draw the line. As the only foreigners in our   10
neighborhood, we are laughably conspicuous. People must know that we're skimming the *sodai gomi,* but if we do our best to be discreet about it, operating in the dead of night, everyone can pretend not to notice and we bring no shame upon our kind. Late one night, on the way home from the train station, I saw two handsome wooden bookcases sitting by a lamppost. I thought of the books piled on our floor, I looked around me quickly, and I happily picked up one bookcase with both arms.

It was fifteen minutes before I could get back for the other—only to find that it wasn't there. Twenty yards down the street I saw a hunched, shuffling figure. An old wino in a filthy overcoat, with a crippled left leg, was laboriously dragging the bookcase away toward his lair. Within seconds I was heading home again, looking as if I'd never dream of wrestling a bum for a bookcase. But I know what first flashed through my mind when I saw my treasure disappear: "I can take this guy!"

Questions for Discussion

1. According to Fallows, *sodai gomi* means "bulky garbage," but it is also "part of a larger cycle." What does *sodai gomi* reveal about life in Japan, and what are its unwritten rules?
2. Why are the Japanese reluctant to take or purchase secondhand goods? What would the Japanese probably think of the typical American garage sale?

3. Why does Fallows wait until after midnight before making his first raid upon the *sodai gomi* pile? How would you describe his relation to neighbors at the time he wrote this essay?

4. Describing his initial response to the *sodai gomi* pile, Fallows writes, "It cut into our hearts in a way none of our neighbors could have known." Would this essay help them to understand? Or is it written only for American readers?

5. What is the purpose of this essay? Is Fallows interested in defining an aspect of life in Japan or an aspect of American character? Why does it conclude with an imaginary conflict between the author and a crippled alcoholic?

Suggestions for Writing

1. Define a foreign or ethnic custom that you have witnessed or experienced, and explore what it reveals about the culture from which it comes.

2. Are new things always better than old things? Write an essay exploring the advantages of auctions, garage sales, or thrift shops.

"MOMMY, WHAT DOES 'NIGGER' MEAN?"

Gloria Naylor

Gloria Naylor is a novelist who grew up in New York City. In the following essay Naylor draws upon a painful childhood memory to explore a complex term—whose meaning changes depending upon the rhetorical situation: who is using the word, upon what occasion, for what purpose, and to what audience. As you read, consider what the various uses of nigger *reveal about the author's heritage as a black American. And ask yourself what this essay says about the nature of language.*

Language is the subject. It is the written form with which I've managed to keep the wolf away from the door and, in diaries, to keep my sanity. In spite of this, I consider the written word inferior to the spoken, and much of the frustration experienced by novelists is the awareness that whatever we manage to capture in even the most transcendent passages falls far short of the richness of life. Dialogue achieves its power in the dynamics of a fleeting moment of sight, sound, smell and touch.

I'm not going to enter the debate here about whether it is language that shapes reality or vice versa. That battle is doomed to be waged whenever we seek intermittent reprieve from the chicken and egg dispute. I will simply take the position that the spoken word, like the written word, amounts to a nonsensical arrangement of sounds or letters without a consensus that assigns "meaning." And building from the meanings of what we hear, we order reality. Words themselves are innocuous; it is the consensus that gives them true power.

I remember the first time I heard the word "nigger." In my third-grade class, our math tests were being passed down the rows, and as I handed the papers to a little boy in back of me, I remarked that once again he had received a much lower mark than I did. He snatched his test from me and spit out that word. Had he called me a nymphomaniac or a necrophiliac, I couldn't have been more puzzled. I didn't know what a nigger was, but I knew that whatever it meant, it was something he shouldn't have called me. This was verified when I raised my hand, and in a loud voice repeated what he had said and watched the teacher scold him for using a "bad" word. I was later to go home and ask the inevitable question that every black parent must face—"Mommy, what does 'nigger' mean?"

And what exactly did it mean? Thinking back, I realize that this could not have been the first time the word was used in my presence. I was part of a large extended family that had migrated from the rural South after World War II and formed a close-knit network that gravitated around my maternal grandparents. Their ground-floor apartment in one of the buildings they owned in Harlem was a weekend mecca for my immediate family, along with countless aunts, uncles and cousins who brought along assorted friends. It was a bustling and open house with assorted neighbors and tenants popping in and out to exchange bits of gossip, pick up an old quarrel or referee the ongoing checkers game in which my grandmother cheated shamelessly. They were all there to let down their hair and put up their feet after a week of labor in the factories, laundries and shipyards of New York.

Amid the clamor, which could reach deafening proportions—two or   5
three conversations going on simultaneously, punctuated by the sound of a baby's crying somewhere in the back rooms or out on the street—there was still a rigid set of rules about what was said and how. Older children were sent out of the living room when it was time to get into the juicy details about "you-know-who" up on the third floor who had gone and gotten herself "p-r-e-g-n-a-n-t!" But my parents, knowing that I could spell well beyond my years, always demanded that I follow the others out to play. Beyond sexual misconduct and death, everything else was considered harmless for our young ears. And so among the anecdotes of the triumphs and disappointments in the various workings of their lives, the word "nigger" was used in my presence, but it was set within contexts and inflections that caused it to register in my mind as something else.

In the singular, the word was always applied to a man who had distinguished himself in some situation that brought their approval for his strength, intelligence or drive:

"Did Johnny really do that ?"

"I'm telling you, that nigger pulled in $6,000 of overtime last year. Said he got enough for a down payment on a house."

When used with a possessive adjective by a woman—"my nigger"— it became a term of endearment for husband or boyfriend. But it could be more than just a term applied to a man. In their mouths it became the pure essence of manhood—a disembodied force that channeled their past history of struggle and present survival against the odds into a victorious statement of being: "Yeah, that old foreman found out quick enough—you don't mess with a nigger."

In the plural, it became a description of some group within the com-   10
munity that had overstepped the bounds of decency as my family defined it: Parents who neglected their children, a drunken couple who fought in public, people who simply refused to look for work, those with excessively dirty mouths or unkempt households were all "trifling niggers." This particular circle could forgive hard times, unemployment, the occasional bout of depression—they had gone through all of that themselves—but the unforgivable sin was lack of self-respect.

A woman could never be a "nigger" in the singular, with its connotation of confirming worth. The noun "girl" was its closest equivalent in that sense, but only when used in direct address and regardless of the gender doing the addressing. "Girl" was a token of respect for a woman. The one-syllable word was drawn out to sound like three in recognition of the extra ounce of wit, nerve or daring that the woman had shown in the situation under discussion.

"G-i-r-l, stop. You mean you said that to his face?"

But if the word was used in a third-person reference or shortened so that it almost snapped out of the mouth, it always involved some element of communal disapproval. And age became an important factor in these exchanges. It was only between individuals of the same generation, or from an older person to a younger (but never the other way around), that "girl" would be considered a compliment.

I don't agree with the argument that use of the word nigger at this social stratum of the black community was an internalization of racism. The dynamics were the exact opposite: the people in my grandmother's living room took a word that whites used to signify worthlessness or degradation and rendered it impotent. Gathering there together, they transformed "nigger" to signify the varied and complex human beings they knew themselves to be. If the word was to disappear totally from the mouths of even the most liberal of white society, no one in that room was naïve enough to believe it would disappear from white minds. Meeting the word head-on, they proved it had absolutely nothing to do with the way they were determined to live their lives.

So there must have been dozens of times that the word "nigger" was   *15*
spoken in front of me before I reached the third grade. But I didn't "hear" it until it was said by a small pair of lips that had already learned it could be a way to humiliate me. That was the word I went home and asked my mother about. And since she knew that I had to grow up in America, she took me in her lap and explained.

Questions for Discussion

1. What two motives led Naylor to become a writer?
2. How does Naylor describe her family background? Why is it relevant to the question she is exploring in this essay?
3. How many different meanings of *nigger* does Naylor provide in this essay? Why is it that the word can only be understood by the context in which it is used and the inflection with which it is spoken? What elements of the situation described in paragraph 3 alerted Naylor to the use of a "bad word" before the teacher confirms that she had been insulted?
4. What does Naylor mean when she writes that some people consider the use of *nigger* by blacks to be "an internalization of racism"? Why does she believe that it shows the opposite?
5. Consider the final paragraph of this essay. What does the last sentence imply?

Suggestions for Writing

1. Identify another word that can be either insulting or affectionate depending upon how it is used. Explore what the varied meanings of your term reveal about the people who use it.
2. According to an expression known to many children, "Sticks and stones can break your bones, but words can never hurt you." Is this true? Write an essay exploring the extent to which words can cause injury.

TOOLS OF TORTURE

Phyllis Rose

> *In the following essay, Phyllis Rose explores the moral distinction between two acts:* soins esthétiques *(beauty treatments) and torture. Both of them involve "attention to the body"—the one for pleasure, the other for pain. As you read "Tools of Torture" consider the extent to which Rose herself seems to approve of* soins esthétiques, *and notice how she uses personal experience as she explores the distinction between these two concepts.*

In a gallery off the rue Dauphine, near the *parfumerie*° where I get my massage, I happened upon an exhibit of medieval torture instruments. It made me think that pain must be as great a challenge to the human imagination as pleasure. Otherwise there's no accounting for the number of torture instruments. One would be quite enough. The simple pincer, let's say, which rips out flesh. Or the head crusher, which breaks first your tooth sockets, then your skull. But in addition I saw tongs, thumbscrews, a rack, a ladder, ropes and pulleys, a grill, a garrote, a Spanish horse, a Judas cradle, an iron maiden, a cage, a gag, a strappado, a stretching table, a saw, a wheel, a twisting stork, an inquisitor's chair, a breast breaker, and a scourge. You don't need complicated machinery to cause incredible pain. If you want to saw your victim down the middle, for example, all you need is a slightly bigger than usual saw. If you hold the victim upside down so the blood stays in his head, hold his legs apart, and start sawing at the groin, you can get as far as the navel before he loses consciousness.

Even in the Middle Ages, before electricity, there were many things you could do to torment a person. You could tie him up in an iron belt that held the arms and legs up to the chest and left no point of rest, so that all his muscles went into spasm within minutes and he was driven mad within hours. This was the twisting stork, a benign-looking object. You could stretch him out backward over a thin piece of wood so that his whole body weight rested on his spine, which pressed against the sharp wood. Then you could stop up his nostrils and force water into his stomach through his mouth. Then, if you wanted to finish him off, you and your helper could jump on his stomach, causing internal hemorrhage. This torture was called the rack. If you wanted to burn someone to death without hearing him scream, you could use a tongue lock, a metal rod between the jaw and collarbone that prevented him from opening his mouth. You could put a person in a chair with spikes on the seat and arms, tie him down against the spikes, and beat him, so that every time he flinched from the beating he drove his own flesh deeper onto the spikes. This was the inquisitor's chair. If

---

parfumerie: French for "perfume shop."

you wanted to make it worse, you could heat the spikes. You could suspend a person over a pointed wooden pyramid and whenever he started to fall asleep, you could drop him onto the point. If you were Ippolito Marsili, the inventor of this torture, known as the Judas cradle, you could tell yourself you had invented something humane, a torture that worked without burning flesh or breaking bones. For the torture here was supposed to be sleep deprivation.

The secret of torture, like the secret of French cuisine, is that nothing is unthinkable. The human body is like a foodstuff, to be grilled, pounded, filleted. Every opening exists to be stuffed, all flesh to be carved off the bone. You take an ordinary wheel, a heavy wooden wheel with spokes. You lay the victim on the ground with blocks of wood at strategic points under his shoulders, legs, and arms. You use the wheel to break every bone in his body. Next you tie his body onto the wheel. With all its bones broken, it will be pliable. However, the victim will not be dead. If you want to kill him, you hoist the wheel aloft on the end of a pole and leave him to starve. Who would have thought to do this with a man and a wheel? But, then, who would have thought to take the disgusting snail, force it to render its ooze, stuff it in its own shell with garlic butter, bake it, and eat it?

Not long ago I had a facial—only in part because I thought I needed one. It was research into the nature and function of pleasure. In a dark booth at the back of the beauty salon the aesthetician put me on a table and applied a series of ointments to my face, some cool, some warmed. After a while she put something into my hand, cold and metallic. "Don't be afraid, madame," she said. "It is an electrode. It will not hurt you. The other end is attached to two metal cylinders, which I roll over your face. They break down the electricity barrier on your skin and allow the moisturizers to penetrate deeply." I didn't believe this hocus-pocus. I didn't believe in the electricity barrier or in the ability of these rollers to break it down. But it all felt very good. The cold metal on my face was a pleasant change from the soft warmth of the aesthetician's fingers. Still, since Algeria° it's hard to hear the word *electrode* without fear. So when she left me for a few minutes with a moist, refreshing cheesecloth over my face, I thought, What if the goal of her expertise had been pain, not moisture? What if the electrodes had been electrodes in the Algerian sense? What if the cheesecloth mask were dipped in acid?

In Paris, where the body is so pampered, torture seems particularly   5
sinister, not because it's hard to understand but because—as the dark side of sensuality—it seems so easy. Beauty care is among the glories of Paris. *Soins esthétiques* include makeup, facials, massages (both relaxing and reducing),

Algeria: The French entered Algeria in 1830 and controlled it until 1962. During the Algerian War of Independence (1954–1962), the French army used electricity to torture prisoners.

depilations (partial and complete), manicures, pedicures, and tanning, in addition to the usual run of *soins* for the hair: cutting, brushing, setting, waving, styling, blowing, coloring, and streaking. In Paris the state of your skin, hair, and nerves is taken seriously, and there is little of the puritanical thinking that tries to persuade us that beauty comes from within. Nor do the French think, as Americans do, that beauty should be offhand and low-maintenance. Spending time and money on *soins esthétiques* is appropriate and necessary, not self-indulgent. Should that loving attention to the body turn malevolent, you have torture. You have the procedure—the aesthetic, as it were—of torture, the explanation for the rich diversity of torture instruments, but you do not have the cause.

Historically torture has been a tool of legal systems, used to get information needed for a trial or, more directly, to determine guilt or innocence. In the Middle Ages confession was considered the best of all proofs, and torture was the way to produce a confession. In other words, torture didn't come into existence to give vent to human sadism. It is not always private and perverse but sometimes social and institutional, vetted by the government and, of course, the Church. (There have been few bigger fans of torture than Christianity and Islam.) Righteousness, as much as viciousness, produces torture. There aren't squads of sadists beating down the doors to the torture chambers begging for jobs. Rather, as a recent book on torture by Edward Peters says, the institution of torture creates sadists; the weight of a culture, Peters suggests, is necessary to recruit torturers. You have to convince people that they are working for a great goal in order to get them to overcome their repugnance to the task of causing physical pain to another person. Usually the great goal is the preservation of society, and the victim is presented to the torturer as being in some way out to destroy it.

From another point of view, what's horrifying is how easily you can persuade someone that he is working for the common good. Perhaps the most appalling psychological experiment of modern times, by Stanley Milgram, showed that ordinary, decent people in New Haven, Connecticut, could be brought to the point of inflicting (as they thought) severe electric shocks on other people in obedience to an authority and in pursuit of a goal, the advancement of knowledge, of which they approved. Milgram used—some would say abused—the prestige of science and the university to make his point, but his point is chilling nonetheless. We can cluck over torture, but the evidence at least suggests that with intelligent handling most of us could be brought to do it ourselves.

In the Middle Ages, Milgram's experiment would have had no point. It would have shocked no one that people were capable of cruelty in the interest of something they believed in. That was as it should be. Only recently in the history of human thought has the avoidance of cruelty moved in the forefront of ethics. "Putting cruelty first," as Judith Shklar says in *Ordinary Vices*, is comparatively new. The belief that the "pursuit of happiness" is one of man's inalienable rights, the idea that "cruel and unusual punishment" is an evil in itself, the Benthamite° notion that behavior should be guided by what will produce the greatest happiness for the greatest number—all these principles are only two centuries old. They were born with the eighteenth-century democratic revolutions. And in two hundred years they have not been universally accepted. Wherever people believe strongly in some cause, they will justify torture—not just the Nazis, but the French in Algeria.

Many people who wouldn't hurt a fly have annexed to fashion the imagery of torture—the thongs and spikes and metal studs—hence reducing it to the frivolous and transitory. Because torture has been in the mainstream and not on the margins of history, nothing could be healthier. For torture to be merely kinky would be a big advance. Exhibitions like the one I saw in Paris, which presented itself as educational, may be guilty of pandering to the tastes they deplore. Solemnity may be the wrong tone. If taking one's goals too seriously is the danger, the best discouragement of torture may be a radical hedonism that denies that any goal is worth the means, that refuses to allow the nobly abstract to seduce us from the sweetness of the concrete. Give people a good croissant and a good cup of coffee in the morning. Give them an occasional facial and a plate of escargots. Marie Antoinette picked a bad moment to say "Let them eat cake," but I've often thought she was on the right track.

All of which brings me back to Paris, for Paris exists in the imagination of much of the world as the capital of pleasure—of fun, food, art, folly, seduction, gallantry, and beauty. Paris is civilization's reminder to itself that nothing leads you less wrong than your awareness of your own pleasure and a genial desire to spread it around. In that sense the myth of Paris constitutes a moral touchstone, standing for the selfish frivolity that helps keep priorities straight.   10

Questions for Discussion

1. Rose opens her essay with a description of medieval torture instruments. Why is it useful for her to start with this information rather than with a description of beauty treatments?
2. What does Rose say is the secret of torture? How does torture differ from *soins esthétiques*?
3. Writing about the French, Rose states "Spending time and money on *soins esthétiques* is appropriate and necessary, not self-indulgent." How does she defend this statement? Do you agree with her?
4. According to Rose, what is the relationship between the procedures for and the causes of torture?

Benthamite: Jeremy Bentham (1748–1832) was an English philosopher who founded the doctrine known as utilitarianism.

5. What reason might Rose have had for describing Stanley Milgram's psychological experiment?

6. Consider the way Rose concludes her essay by discussing how people have "annexed to fashion the imagery of torture." What does this discussion illustrate?

Suggestions for Writing

1. Making reference to a psychological experiment conducted at Yale in the 1950s by Stanley Milgram, Rose comments that the ease with which it is possible to persuade people to torture their fellow beings is horrifying. Could it also be that pressure to conform, to belong, is stronger than moral beliefs? Write an essay exploring some relationships you have observed between behavior and social pressure.

2. Rose claims that Milgram's experiment "would have had no point" in the Middle Ages because people thought that it was moral to be cruel "in the interest of something they believed in." Write an essay exploring some ways people today believe cruelty is justified in the interest of things they believe in.

MARRAKECH

George Orwell

A city in North Africa, Marrakech was a popular destination for American and European tourists when Morocco was ruled by the French; and it still attracts many travelers. The following essay, first published in 1939, the year the Second World War began, provides a series of scenes of how the city looked during the colonial era. Orwell provides no transitions between these scenes, expecting his readers to see for themselves how each "snapshot" relates to another. As you read, consider what the scenes have in common.

As the corpse went past the flies left the restaurant table in a cloud and rushed after it, but they came back a few minutes later.

The little crowd of mourners—all men and boys, no women—threaded their way across the market-place between the piles of pomegranates and the taxis and the camels, wailing a short chant over and over again. What really appeals to the flies is that the corpses here are never put into coffins, they are merely wrapped in a piece of rag and carried on a rough wooden bier on the shoulders of four friends. When the friends get to the burying-ground they hack an oblong hole a foot or two deep, dump the body in it and fling over it a little of the dried-up, lumpy earth, which is like broken brick. No gravestone, no name, no identifying mark of any kind. The burying-ground is merely a huge waste of hummocky earth, like a derelict building-lot. After a month or two no one can even be certain where his own relatives are buried.

When you walk through a town like this—two hundred thousand inhabitants, of whom at least twenty thousand own literally nothing except the rags they stand up in—when you see how the people live, and still more how easily they die, it is always difficult to believe that you are walking among human beings. All colonial empires are in reality founded upon that fact. The people have brown faces—besides, there are so many of them! Are they really the same flesh as yourself? Do they even have names? Or are they merely a kind of undifferentiated brown stuff, about as individual as bees or coral insects? They rise out of the earth, they sweat and starve for a few years, and then they sink back into the nameless mounds of the grave-yard and nobody notices that they are gone. And even the graves themselves soon fade back into the soil. Sometimes, out for a walk, as you break your way through the prickly pear, you notice that it is rather bumpy underfoot, and only a certain regularity in the bumps tells you that you are walking over skeletons.

I was feeding one of the gazelles in the public gardens.

Gazelles are almost the only animals that look good to eat when they are still alive, in fact, one can hardly look at their hindquarters without thinking of mint sauce. The gazelle I was feeding seemed to know that this thought was in my mind, for though it took the piece of bread I was holding out it obviously did not like me. It nibbled rapidly at the bread, then lowered its head and tried to butt me, then took another nibble and then butted again. Probably its idea was that if it could drive me away the bread would somehow remain hanging in mid-air.

An Arab navvy° working on the path nearby lowered his heavy hoe and sidled slowly towards us. He looked from the gazelle to the bread and from the bread to the gazelle, with a sort of quiet amazement, as though he had never seen anything quite like this before. Finally he said shyly in French:

"*I* could eat some of that bread."

I tore off a piece and he stowed it gratefully in some secret place under his rags. This man is an employee of the Municipality.

When you go through the Jewish quarters you gather some idea of what the medieval ghettoes were probably like. Under their Moorish rulers the Jews were only allowed to own land in certain restricted areas, and after centuries of this kind of treatment they have ceased to bother about over-crowding. Many of the streets are a good deal less than six feet wide, the houses are completely windowless, and sore-eyed children cluster every-where in unbelievable numbers, like clouds of flies. Down the centre of the street there is generally running a little river of urine.

In the bazaar huge families of Jews, all dressed in the long black robe and little black skull-cap, are working in dark fly-infested booths that look like caves. A carpenter sits cross-legged at a prehistoric lathe, turning chair-legs at lightning speed. He works the lathe with a bow in his right hand and guides the chisel with his left foot, and thanks to a lifetime of sitting in this position his left leg is warped out of shape. At his side his grandson, aged six, is already starting on the simpler parts of the job. 10

I was just passing the coppersmiths' booths when somebody noticed that I was lighting a cigarette. Instantly, from the dark holes all round, there was a frenzied rush of Jews, many of them old grandfathers with flowing grey beards, all clamouring for a cigarette. Even a blind man somewhere at the back of one of the booths heard a rumour of cigarettes and came crawl-ing out, groping in the air with his hand. In about a minute I had used up the whole packet. None of these people, I suppose, works less than twelve hours a day, and every one of them looks on a cigarette as a more or less impossible luxury.

As the Jews live in self-contained communities they follow the same trades as the Arabs, except for agriculture. Fruit-sellers, potters, silversmiths, blacksmiths, butchers, leatherworkers, tailors, water-carriers, beggars, porters—whichever way you look you see nothing but Jews. As a matter of

---

navvy: A workman employed in excavation.

fact there are thirteen thousand of them, all living in the space of a few acres. A good job Hitler isn't here. Perhaps he is on his way, however. You hear the usual dark rumours about the Jews, not only from the Arabs but from the poorer Europeans.

"Yes, mon vieux, they took my job away from me and gave it to a Jew. The Jews! They're the real rulers of this country, you know. They've got all the money. They control the banks, finance—everything."

"But," I said, "isn't it a fact that the average Jew is a labourer working for about a penny an hour?"

"Ah, that's only for show! They're all moneylenders really. They're cunning, the Jews." 15

In just the same way, a couple of hundred years ago, poor old women used to be burned for witchcraft when they could not even work enough magic to get themselves a square meal.

All people who work with their hands are partly invisible, and the more important the work they do, the less visible they are. Still, a white skin is always fairly conspicuous. In northern Europe, when you see a labourer ploughing a field, you probably give him a second glance. In a hot country, anywhere south of Gibraltar or east of Suez, the chances are that you don't even see him. I have noticed this again and again. In a tropical landscape one's eye takes in everything except the human beings. It takes in the dried-up soil, the prickly pear, the palm tree and the distant mountain, but it always misses the peasant hoeing at his patch. He is the same colour as the earth, and a great deal less interesting to look at.

It is only because of this that the starved countries of Asia and Africa are accepted as tourist resorts. No one would think of running cheap trips to the Distressed Areas. But where the human beings have brown skins their poverty is simply not noticed. What does Morocco mean to a Frenchman? An orange-grove or a job in Government service. Or to an Englishman? Camels, castles, palm trees, Foreign Legionnaires, brass trays, and bandits. One could probably live there for years without noticing that for nine-tenths of the people the reality of life is an endless, back-breaking struggle to wring a little food out of an eroded soil.

Most of Morocco is so desolate that no wild animal bigger than a hare can live on it. Huge areas which were once covered with forest have turned into a treeless waste where the soil is exactly like broken-up brick. Nevertheless a good deal of it is cultivated, with frightful labour. Everything is done by hand. Long lines of women, bent double like inverted capital L's, work their way slowly across the fields, tearing up the prickly weeds with their hands, and the peasant gathering lucerne for fodder pulls it up stalk by stalk instead of reaping it, thus saving an inch or two on each stalk. The plough is a wretched wooden thing, so frail that one can easily carry it on one's shoulder, and fitted underneath with a rough iron spike which stirs the soil to a depth of about four inches. This is as much as the strength of the animals is equal to. It is usual to plough with a cow and a donkey yoked together. Two donkeys would not be quite strong enough, but on the other hand two cows would cost a little more to feed. The peasants possess no harrows, they merely plough the soil several times over in different directions, finally leaving it in rough furrows, after which the whole field has to be shaped with hoes into small oblong patches to conserve water. Except for a day or two after the rare rainstorms there is never enough water. Along the edges of the fields channels are hacked out to a depth of thirty or forty feet to get at the tiny trickles which run through the subsoil.

Every afternoon a file of very old women passes down the road outside   *20* my house, each carrying a load of firewood. All of them are mummified with age and the sun, and all of them are tiny. It seems to be generally the case in primitive communities that the women, when they get beyond a certain age, shrink to the size of children. One day a poor old creature who could not have been more than four feet tall crept past me under a vast load of wood. I stopped her and put a five-sou piece (a little more than a farthing)° into her hand. She answered with a shrill wail, almost a scream, which was partly gratitude but mainly surprise. I suppose that from her point of view, by taking any notice of her, I seemed almost to be violating a law of nature. She accepted her status as an old woman, that is to say as a beast of burden. When a family is travelling it is quite usual to see a father and a grown-up son riding ahead on donkeys, and an old woman following on foot, carrying the baggage.

But what is strange about these people is their invisibility. For several weeks, always at about the same time of day, the file of old women had hobbled past the house with their firewood, and though they had registered themselves on my eyeballs I cannot truly say that I had seen them. Firewood was passing—that was how I saw it. It was only that one day I happened to be walking behind them, and the curious up-and-down motion of a load of wood drew my attention to the human being beneath it. Then for the first time I noticed the poor old earth-coloured bodies, bodies reduced to bones and leathery skin, bent double under the crushing weight. Yet I suppose I had not been five minutes on Moroccan soil before I noticed the overloading of the donkeys and was infuriated by it. There is no question that the donkeys are damnably treated. The Moroccan donkey is hardly bigger than a St. Bernard dog, it carries a load which in the British Army would be considered too much for a fifteen-hands mule, and very often its pack-saddle is not taken off its back for weeks together. But what is peculiarly pitiful is that it is the most willing creature on earth, it follows its master like a dog and does not need either bridle or halter. After a dozen years of devoted work it suddenly drops dead, whereupon its master tips it into the ditch and the village dogs have torn its guts out before it is cold.

five sou . . . farthing: A sou is a former French coin; five sou equaled a centime, or a hundredth of a franc. A farthing is a former British coin worth a quarter of a penny.

This kind of thing makes one's blood boil, whereas—on the whole—the plight of the human beings does not. I am not commenting, merely pointing to a fact. People with brown skins are next door to invisible. Anyone can be sorry for the donkey with its galled back, but it is generally owing to some kind of accident if one even notices the old woman under her load of sticks.

As the storks flew northward the Negroes were marching southward—a long, dusty column, infantry, screw-gun batteries, and then more infantry, four or five thousand men in all, winding up the road with a clumping of boots and a clatter of iron wheels.

They were Senegalese, the blackest Negroes in Africa, so black that sometimes it is difficult to see whereabouts on their necks the hair begins. Their splendid bodies were hidden in reach-me-down khaki uniforms, their feet squashed into boots that looked like blocks of wood, and every tin hat seemed to be a couple of sizes too small. It was very hot and the men had marched a long way. They slumped under the weight of their packs and the curiously sensitive black faces were glistening with sweat.

As they went past a tall, very young Negro turned and caught my 25
eye. But the look he gave me was not in the least the kind of look you might expect. Not hostile, not contemptuous, not sullen, not even inquisitive. It was the shy, wide-eyed Negro look, which actually is a look of profound respect. I saw how it was. This wretched boy, who is a French citizen and has therefore been dragged from the forest to scrub floors and catch syphilis in garrison towns, actually has feelings of reverence before a white skin. He has been taught that the white race are his masters, and he still believes it.

But there is one thought which every white man (and in this connection it doesn't matter twopence if he calls himself a socialist) thinks when he sees a black army marching past. "How much longer can we go on kidding these people? How long before they turn their guns in the other direction?"

It was curious, really. Every white man there had this thought stowed somewhere or other in his mind. I had it, so had the other onlookers, so had the officers on their sweating chargers and the white N.C.O.'s marching in the ranks. It was a kind of secret which we all knew and were too clever to tell; only the Negroes didn't know it. And really it was like watching a flock of cattle to see the long column, a mile or two miles of armed men, flowing peacefully up the road, while the great white birds drifted over them in the opposite direction, glittering like scraps of paper.

Questions for Discussion

1. What is Orwell implying when he writes, in paragraph 8, "This man is an employee of the Municipality"?

2. What does Orwell accomplish by exploring aspects of Marrakech overlooked by the average tourist?
3. In paragraph 17 Orwell writes, "All people who work with their hands are partly invisible." Why are the laborers in Marrakech "partly invisible"? Are they seen by some people but overlooked by others? Are there "partly invisible" people in the United States today?
4. Orwell is well known for political novels such as *1984* and *Animal Farm*. Is there a political message in "Marrakech"?
5. Why do you think Orwell draws attention to storks and "great white birds" in paragraphs 23 and 27? How do you respond to this final scene?
6. Although the essay is divided into five sections, do the sections come together to make a whole? Is there a pattern to the arrangement of scenes Orwell describes? Are there any images that help tie the scenes together?

Suggestions for Writing

1. Choose a place that you know well, and write an essay composed of a series of scenes showing what that place is like. Without stating a specific thesis, arrange your scenes in a pattern that will help readers understand the vision you are sharing with them.
2. Write an essay exploring what a writer can accomplish by using the form Orwell has used in "Marrakech." What possibilities does it open? Does it pose any risks?

HOW TO BUILD A SLAUGHTERHOUSE

Richard Selzer

> *Richard Selzer teaches surgery at Yale, where he was invited to judge archi-*
> *tectural designs for a slaughterhouse—an invitation that led him to visit a*
> *slaughterhouse already in operation. Consider what the visit evokes for Selzer*
> *and why he chose to write about it. As you read, consider what this essay says*
> *about the nature of architecture. But be alert for other concerns. Aside from*
> *architecture, what else is Selzer exploring in this essay?*

It is May and, for whatever reason, I have been invited to serve on a
jury that is to pass judgment on the final projects of a group of candidates
for the degree of Master of Architecture at Yale University. But I am not an
architect. I am a surgeon. Nor do I know the least thing about buildings,
only that, like humans, they are testy, compliant, congenial, impertinent.
That sort of thing. When I am faced with blueprints and drawings-to-scale,
which are the lingua franca of architecture, something awful happens to the
left half of my brain. It shrinks, or dessicates, collapses, and I fall into a state
of torpor no less profound than that of the Andean hummingbird when it is
confronted with mortal danger. Sadly, my acceptance of such an invitation
by the Yale School of Architecture is just another example of the kind of
imposturage of which otherwise honest men and women are capable.

The charge that has been given the students is to design and build an
abattoir. It is understood that prior to this undertaking they have, as a class,
made a field trip to a slaughterhouse in the New Haven area. For months
afterward they have been working toward this date. It is two days before we
are all to meet for the examination in the seventh floor "pit" at the School
of Architecture. But if I cannot know what they know of buildings, at least
I can have seen what they have seen, and so I telephone the owner of the
slaughterhouse on the outskirts of New Haven, the one that the students
visited months before. "Yes," he says, "by all means." His voice is genial,
welcoming.

It will be no great shock, I think. A surgeon has grown accustomed to
primordial dramas, organic events involving flesh, blood, and violence. But
before it is done this field trip to a slaughterhouse will have become for me
a descent into Hades, a vision of life that perhaps it would have been better
never to know.

In a way, it is the last place on earth that seems appropriate to the mass
slaying of creatures. Just another grinding truck stop off Route 1 in North
Haven, Connecticut, with easy access for large vehicles and, nearby, an old
cemetery tossing in the slow upheaval of resurrection. It is 7:00 A.M. Outside, another truck rumbles into the corral.

THERMOKING is the word painted on both sides of the huge open-sided car filled with cattle. Each cow has a numbered tag punched through an ear. Outside, the enclosure is already ridiculous with lambs. What a sinister probability this truck gives out. Inside it, the cows are, for the most part, silent until one lifts its head and moos wildly. Now another joins in, and another, until the whole compound resounds with the terrible vocabulary of premonition.

The building itself is low and squat—a single story only, made of cement blocks and corrugated metal and prestressed concrete. Behind it is a huge corral. Such a building does not command but neither does it skulk. It carries out its business in secret and decides what you will see, hides from you what it chooses. If only I can come upon it—the undiscovered heart of this place that I know, must believe, is here. Does this building breathe? Has it a pulse? It must.

Now the gate at the rear of the truck is opened. The cattle mill about like bewildered children until, prodded from behind, they move sightless and will-less down the ramp and into a gated pen as if in sleep through an incurable dream. Here they come, slowly, their hooves weighted down with reluctance. The wooden floor of the entryway is scarred, packed and beaten. The hooves, staggering, thump the timbers. There is a quick lateral skid on manure. It is the sound of those skidding hooves that, months later, you will hear while waiting in line at the bank or getting a haircut.

The cowherd urges them on. They seem afraid of displeasing him. With gentle callings and whistles he inveigles them into the pen. I keep my gaze on a pair of mourning doves waddling among the droppings until, threatened by a hoof, one takes to the air with a muted small whistling of its wings. The other follows in a moment. Against a nearby fence a row of fiery tulips spurts. Into the narrow passageway the cattle go single file, crowding at the mouth of it, bumping into each other, clopping sidewise so as not to lose their place. It's as if, once having passed through that gate, they would be safe. As if what lay ahead were not extinction but respite, and there were not, just ahead, death bobbing like clover in a pasture, but life. Only the first two or three begin to suspect. One after the other these lift their heads at the sound of the stunning gun. But there is the sweet assuaging voice of the cowherd and the laughter of the men inside to draw them on.

The one at the van shies as she encounters some hard evidence. She balks, stops, the others press against her until, with a toss of her horns, she throws her new knowledge down before the herd, like an impediment. Without warning (do I imagine it?) the leaves on the trees at the periphery of the corral begin to siffle, the grass to stir. Tails rise as if in a wind. Ears and flanks shiver in a cold blast. As abruptly, all is still. But I see it has not been the wind, only death that has swept across the corral and whooshed away.

Inside, the men are waiting. All are dressed in identical uniforms—   *10*
overalls, ankle-length rubber aprons, high rubber boots and orange plastic

hard hats. The hooks, tracks, scales, tables and trays have an air of brutal metallic strength; there are no windows nor anything made of wood. The room echoes like a gymnasium. From somewhere too far off to be heard clearly, a silken radio voice announces the morning news. Something about a famine in Ethiopia . . . There is the smell of cowhide and tobacco. One of the men clicks over the multitude in the pen. " . . . six, eight, ten, four-teen . . ." he counts. "Plus one hundred sixty. Jesus! a day's work."

The Process begins. There is a muffled whump from the stunning pen, like the firing of a mortar shell. A body arches, the tail blown forward between quivering legs. She goes down, folding on all fours at once, some-thing from which the air has been let out. They drag her a foot or two to the hoist. A chain is placed about one hind leg and the winch activated. A moment later she is aloft above the Killing Oval—a kind of theater with a centrally slanting stone floor and a drain at the lowest point. As she hangs upside down, her coat seems a bit loose, shabby, with all the points and angles of her skeleton showing. The throat slitter is ready. It is clear that he is the star. Enisled in his oval space, alone there with his cattle who, one at a time, stretch out their necks to him, he shines beneath his hard hat. He is blond; his eyes blue knife blades; hefty; a side of beef himself, though not at all fat. No part of him shakes with the thrust. Still, if physiognomy is any hint of character, he has found his rightful place. The eyes boil from her head; saliva drips from her limp tongue. Up on his toes for the sticking, and oh those chicory-blue eyes. For just so long as the blade needs to burrow into the neck—one second, two—the pudgy hand of the man grasps the ear of the cow, then lets go. He is quick with the knife, like a robin beaking a worm from the ground. The slit is made just beneath the mandible, the knife moved forward and back and withdrawn. In this manner the jugular vein and carotid artery are severed. The larynx, too, is cut through. He has a kind of genius. His movements are streamlined, with no doubt about them. How different from my own surgery where no single move but is plucked at by hesitation.

In the abattoir there is gradation of rank, at the bottom of which hierarchy is the hoser, often the newest member of the group. Only after a long education to the hose will he be formally instructed in the art of stunning and hoisting. Then on to bunging, decapitation, amputation of the hooves, gutting, skinning, and, if his dream is to be realized, killing, which is at the pinnacle. In this, it is not unlike the surgical residency training program at Yale. Never mind.

The stunner turns their brains off like spigots; the slitter turns on the faucet of their blood which squirts in a forceful splash toward the stone floor. For a moment the cows are still, megaliths, then a mooing, flailing, kicking as the effect of the stunning wears off. Now and then the slitter must step out of the way of a frantic hoof. It takes so long until all movement stops! As the bleeding slackens the hose is used and the business dilutes into wateriness. The hose flogs across unblinking eyes; it is a storm of weeping. I am tempted to reach out, I am that close, and lift a velvet lip, finger a horn, but I do not. There is rebuke implicit in such acts.

"Two hundred and fifty gallons of water per second," the hoser tells me. It does not occur to me to doubt him. I peer through the scrim of blood and water to the stunning pen where the next cow has just been felled. It is in the stunning pen that the animals seem most exposed, with no tiny shield of leaves, no small tangle of brambles, such as any captured thing is entitled to hide behind. And all the while the flat mooing of the already-slit, a hollow blare pulled up and out from their cavernous insides that stops abruptly and has no echo. And the howl of the stunned. Now there is a throatful of hot vowel if ever you heard it.

Each cow is impaled at the groin on a ceiling hook and detached from *15* the hoist to make room for the next. These ceiling hooks are on tracks and can be pushed along from station to station. A second hook is used in the other groin. A light touch sends the splayed animal sliding on the rack like a coat in a factory. Already there is a second cow bleeding from the hoist, and the third has been stunned. The efficiency of the men is a glittering, wicked thing. They are synchronous as dancers and for the most part as silent. It is their knives that converse, gossip, press each other along. The smallest faltering of one would be felt at once by each of the others. There would be that slackening which the rest would have to take up. But now and then they laugh, always at each other, something one of them has said. One of them is always the butt. It does you good to hear this chaffing. I see that without laughter the thing could not be done. They are full of merriment, like boys. Or like gods, creating pain and mirth at the same time. A dozen times a day, the hoser, who is younger than the rest and a little simple, I am told, turns his hose on one of the other men who roars with outrage. Everyone else dies of laughter, then rises again, redder in the face. What are their minds like? Bright and light and shadowless, I think. Disinfected.

There is a sequence to it: stun, hoist, slit, hose, bung, behead, amputate and gut. Each step in the process is carried out by one man at his station. The cattle are slid from one to the other on the racks. What a heat! What an uproar! Already the sink and scales, all the ghastly furniture of this place retreats into far corners and I see nothing but the cattle. At one end of the room the heads are lined up on a folding rack, such as might otherwise be used to dry clothes. Tranquillity has been molded into their mouths. The once swiveling lips are still; the brown eyes opaque. Here they are axed open and the brains examined by the inspector.

"What are you looking for?" I ask him. With scissors and forceps he cuts into the base of one brain.

"Pus, spots, lumps," he says. I peer over his shoulder and see instead at the back of the cow's eyes all the black and white of her tribe puddled there. At the base of her brain a sloping pasture, green with, here and there, a savory buttercup to which all of her life she had lowered her muzzle. And in her throat, pockets of retained lowing which I think to hear escaping even as he prods the tissue with his forceps.

The beheader is not yet twenty. When he turns to see who is spying there, his smile is hesitant and shy. Around his waist a chain belt holds a bone-handled sharpener and a spare knife. He flashes his wrist and there is the quick hiss of the blade against the rasp. Later he will show me his knife, let me heft it, turn, flip, feint.

"Nice?" he asks me.   20

"Nice," I say. "Nice." Abruptly, he kneels to his work. He might be giving first aid to the victim of an accident. Not Judith at the nape of Holofernes nor Salome working her way through the gorge of John the Baptist was more avid than this youth who crouches over his meat like a lion, his blade drinking up blood.

The first slitter has been replaced by another. This one is Italian. His hair is thick and black with just a spot of russet like the flash of a fox's tail. His shoulder is jaunty, his cheek shadowed by eyelashes as he sinks the knife. It is less a stab than a gesture, delicate and powerful, the thrust of a toreador. Against the tang of his knife, the loaded artery pops, and the whole of the cow's blood chases the blade from the premises. I see the slow wavelike pulse of the slitter's jugular vein. Once he laughs out loud. The sound is sudden and unexpected. I turn to watch the mirth emerging from so much beauty of lips and teeth and throat. At eye level a posthumous hoof flexes, extends, flexes again.

All at once, a calf, thinking, I suppose, to escape, wallops through the half-open gate of the stunning pen and directly into the Killing Oval. She is struck on the flank by a bloodfall from the hoist. Her eyes are shining pits of fear. The men view this with utmost seriousness. Immediately two of them leave their tasks and go to capture the miscreant, one by the tail, the other by an always handy ear, and they wrestle the calf back into the pen to wait her turn. Now here is no Cretan bull dance with naked youths propelled by the power of horns, but an awkward graceless show, as the calf robs them of their dignity. They slide on the floor, lose their balance. At last calm is restored. Half an hour later, writhen and giving up the ghost, the calf has her turn. So, there is a predetermined schedule, an immutable order. Why?

". . . nine, ten, eleven, twelve. One dozen." Someone is counting a cluster of impaled and hanging calves. They are like black-and-white curtains ungirt, serious. The men part them with the backs of their hands in order to pass through. They are not just dead; they are more than dead, as though never alive. Beyond, trays of steaming guts; another rack of heads, all clot and teeth. Each head is tagged with the number of its carcass, just so each plastic bag of viscera. Should a beast be found diseased in any part, the inspector discards the whole of it. The men do not wear gloves but plunge boldly into the swim. Are they in a kind of stupor of blood? Oddly spellbound by the repetition of their acts? Perhaps it is the efficiency of the

Process which blinds them. I think of the wardens of Auschwitz. At the final station, barrels of pelts. For leather, for rugs.

"A guy in New Jersey buys them," the skinner tells me.   25

I see that one of the slit and hoisted continues to writhe, and all at once she gives a moo less through her clotted muzzle than from the gash in her neck. It is a soft call straight to my heart. And followed by little thirsty whispers.

"It's still mooing," I say.

"Oh, that," says the slitter.

"How can that be?" I ask. "The larynx has been severed. Hear that?" He cocks his head. There is a soft sucking sigh from the veal cluster farther on, as though someone were turning over in his sleep.

"They do that sometimes," he explains, "even that long after they've   30 been cut." There is an absolute absence of any madness in him which might explain, mollify, soften. He is entirely cool, reserved, intent.

But today they have not been able to kill them all. Some will have to wait overnight in the corral. Thirty minutes after the command has been given to stop, everything in the slaughterhouse is neat and tidy, as much as rinsing and scrubbing can make it so. The tools have been scraped clean; the planks scoured and freshly swept. When it is all done, the beheader snatches a hose from the youngest, the one who is simple, and sprays him in the crotch. Another joins in the play. How young even the older ones look now. They are eager to go home, where I should think them the gentlest of men. This slaughterhouse is a place one leaves wanting only to make love. In the courtyard my nose is feathered by the smell of fresh air. Overhead a gull blows by, beaking at the sky. From my car I see a cow swing her muzzle at a fly, lash with her tail and fall still. On the roof, along the eaves, doves mourn.

In the morning I arrive just before the men. I wait for them to come. Soon they do. One of them has brought a little dog, a terrier, who scampers along, bouncing sideways and snapping high-pitched chunks out of the silent air. The sight of the dog tickles the men, each of whom stops to pet or scratch. "You, Fritzie," they say, and growl, "little pecker." Now the building awakens, accepting clatter and water gushing into its basins. It begins again.

For two days my new colleagues and I watch and listen as the twelve students present their models, their blueprints. Never, never have there been abattoirs more clever, more ingenious than the abattoirs of Yale. For ease of access the "Plants" are unequaled. Railroad sidings, refrigerated trucks contiguous at one end, attached meat markets. It is all there. And inside, disposable plastic troughs for collecting the blood, fluorescent lighting, air purification, marvelously efficient stunning rooms. "Here," they say, pointing, "is where they are stunned." And, "I have placed the killing alcove here." The faces of the students do not change; they do not tremble at the reenactment of Purgatory. Rather, a cool, calm correctness is what they own. Like the slaughterers, the students have grown used to the awful facts; what concerns them is the efficiency of the process. When they speak of the butchers, they commend their technique. And so do I. So do I. And if ever I should wish to own an abattoir, I would be wise to choose any one of these student architects to make it for me. But there is another abattoir that concerns me now. It is the real abattoir that lies just beneath the abattoir these architects and I have seen.

In the design and building of an abattoir one must remember that once it was that the animals were the gods. Slaughtering was then no mere step in the business of meat preparation but an act charged with religious import and carried out in a temple. The altar was sprinkled with blood. The flame of animal life partook of the sacred and could be extinguished only by the sanction of religion. But, you say, what can architecture do in the face of slaughter? Beauty and spirit stop at the first splash of blood. Better to settle for efficiency. But efficiency gives way before the power of the mythic imagination. And so we shall try:

First, the location. No grinding truck stop on the highway, but a cool 35 glade at the foot of a ridge with, beyond, another ridge and another. Some place beautifully remote, I think, on a small elevation from which the sky and the sun might be consulted. Yet not so high as to be seen silhouetted against heaven from the sea. That is for temples and lighthouses. Nor ought it to be easily seen from any road but must be out of sight, like certain sanatoria, oracular pools, surgical operating rooms. A place without vista, turned in upon itself. And hidden by trees. The gods always play where there are trees that invite mist to their branches. I should build it in a grove, then, to benefit from the resident auspicious deities. And yes, trees, not so much to lend mystery and darkness as for companionship, to bear witness. Let a vivid spring leap nearby with water that is cold and delicious. To listen to its quick current is tantamount to bathing in its waters. Just so simply are ablutions performed. Hand-scooped from the stream, such water will, if drunk at certain susceptible times of the day—twilight and dawn—summon visitations, induce dreams. Pulled up into the throats of the doomed beasts, it will offer them peace, make them ready.

At this place let there be equal parts of sun and shade and at night the cold exaltation, the lambent flood of moonlight. And no nearby houses, for the shadow of this place must not fall across the dwellings of human beings. Killing of any kind has its contagious aspects. Place it thus and the abattoir becomes a god—distant, dignified, lofty, silent. Gaunt and stark until the beasts are ushered in. Only then does its blood begin to flow. Only then is the building warmed and colored, completed. Made human. Such a build-ing is a presence. I would want anyone looking at my abattoir for the first time to fall under its spell, to believe it particularly his as well—there would be that certain tilt of a roof, the phantom shadow of leaves cruising over tile.

One glance at such a site and you will say as Oedipus said at Colonus: "As for this place, it is clearly a holy one."

David, it is reported in the Bible, purchased a threshing floor from Araunah the Jebusite upon which to build the altar of his temple.° Alas, the Jebusites are no more, and neither are their threshing floors to be found in the land. Even so, I would use stone for the floor, roughhewn granite quarried nearby, granite that will wash black in the rain, turn gold in the setting sun. Granite with beveled edges cut to fit neatly, the gaps between to be filled with mortar. Brick too is permissible since the elements of earth and fire are combined to form it. Brick is earth which has gone through fire. It is sacrificial. None of this will be understood by those who see but a stone in a stone, a brick in a brick. It is in the precise placement and the relationship of these materials that their sacramental quality lies. The roofs of the inner passageway will be of slate raftered with the bisected trunks of oak trees upon which strips of bark have been left. These trees should be felled in October, for in the spring all of the power of the tree is devoted to the making of leaves. In the fall the wood is more compressed and solidified. Oak is preferred above all others, as much for its strength and resistance to water as for the news whispered by its leaves that nothing is annihilated; there is only change and the return of matter to a former state. Stone, brick and wood, then. The earth has been burnt; the stone has been cut from its place; the tree has been felled; and all three rise in the form of the abattoir. Yet their texture must survive. The memory of the original tree, clay, earth, stone, is made permanent by the form in which each is made. The builder with his hand and his eyes must do justice to the talent and potential of the material. Nor are these materials passive but offer their own obstacles and tendencies.

Centrally, there is to be a vast open atrium flanked by columns whose capitals are carved as the horned heads of beasts. Everything must reflect the cattle. They are the beating heart of the place. So let there be columns and an unroofed atrium. As nobody can live without the ample to-and-fro of air, so will the building be dead that does not permit the internal play of abundant air. Between the columns of the atrium place lustral stone basins in which water from the stream may be collected for the washing of hands. Columns too, for avenues of light that in the company of the breeze and the high fountain will rinse the air of reek.

The building faces east to receive the morning sun in which it is best for the men to work. There are to be no steps in any part of the abattoir, only timbered ramps curved like those of a ziggurat along which the animals are led up to the porch or vestibule. This antechamber measures in cubits twenty by twenty. (The cubit being the length of the forearm from elbow to fingertips.) It is the function of this room to separate the profane world from the sacred area which is the atrium. In order to enter the atrium the

---

David, . . . , temple: See the second book of Samuel 24:18–25.

cattle must pass in single file beneath an arch. It is well known that to pass through an archway is to be changed forever in some way. Who is to say that such a passage does not purify these beasts, make them ready to die? The atrium itself is vast, measuring in cubits sixty long, forty wide, and thirty high. As I have said, it is roofless in order to receive the direct rays of the sun. Nor has it any walls on either side but open colonnades. To the rear of the atrium is a third and smaller room where the men take their rest. Inside, the corridors, vestibule and resting room must be brilliant with light from wall lamps and skylights. Shadows are dangerous in an abattoir. They make you think. There is to be no rebirth here, as we know it. It is a place for endings, where residue is hosed away and no decay permitted.

Let us dwell upon the interior of the building. If a stable has the odor   40
of manure, why, that is fitting to the stable. The smell increases the stableness of the building, confirms it in its role as the dwelling place for beasts. Just so is the odor of fresh-spilled blood apt for an abattoir. You would not expect perfume. Still, I would be grateful for the sacred smell of sawdust or straw—for the sake of the cattle, to conceal it from them. Blood has no smell, you say? And it is true that there is no odor of it in the operating room. But I think that to catch the whiff of blood is a talent beyond human olfaction. Tigers smell blood and hunt it down precisely. And sharks who, having shed a single drop of their own blood, will devour themselves. Are you certain that domestication blunts the noses of these animals? No, compassion dictates that we separate the about-to-be-slain from those crossing over. Listen! The stones ring with hooves. And in a corner of the atrium, the sawdust is roiled where one of them has floundered, the cloven hoofprints brimming with red shavings. And no reek in the air.

When, as happens, they cannot all be slain in one day, the cattle are led at dusk from the clearing in front of the abattoir down to a narrow tortuous path lined by thick shrubbery. It is the same path by which they left the world at dawn. Here and there the path forks, suggesting a labyrinth. Such a serpiginous route emphasizes the immense apartness of the abattoir. They are ushered into a pasture at some remove where they spend the night in a world cast in frost and moonlight. Stay with them through these hallucinated hours white as foam and filled with heightened meaning. Be there just before dawn, waiting. Long before you see them you will hear the sound of their lips pulling at the grass of the pasture. Ah, there! Look! The first one—all white, breasting the mist, then coming clear of it, like a nymph stepping out of the woods.

Now they are led back to the slaughterhouse. I hear the soothing murmur of the herder making his sweet deceit. "Come along now, ladies. Be polite. No need to crowd. It's all the same in the end." A moo interrupts.

"Hush, now." Again the labyrinthine path must be navigated. In the early morning the climate of the place is that of a cellar—cool and cavernous. There are the pillars caught in the very act of rising. There is the sibilance of insects and a throbbing of frogs. The mist rises and soon there are drifting veils of water and sunlight, something piney in the air. Pious the feet that pace the stone floor of the atrium. The heads of the men are covered with small capulets. Prayers are recited. One of them holds the knife up to the sunlight, then turns to examine its larger shadow upon the floor. Any nick or imperfection that might cause suffering to the animal is thereby magnified and corrected before the beast is led to it. At the last moment the blade is smeared with honey for sweetness and lubrication. All the energy of the place emanates from the edge of that knife blade. It is a holy object, a radiant thing. In the dazzling sunlight it is like a silver thorn to be laid upon the willing neck of the beast.

But a cow is not much, you argue. A cow is not beautiful as a trout, say, is beautiful. A trout—made of river water, and speckled stone, and tinted by the setting sun. Nor are cows rare, as peacocks are rare, or certain blue butterflies. These cattle bring with them no paraphernalia of the past. They have none. I tell myself that. For a cow, the sun that rises each day is a brand-new sun, not the one that set the day before and rose the day before that. Humans are the only ones afflicted with a past. But then I think of the many-cattled pastures of my childhood in the milk-drenched upper counties of New York State. I close my eyes and see again a herd upon a green slope. There! One lifts her dripping muzzle to stare at a trusted human being. Nonsense, you say, to deplore this slaughter when with each footstep we erase whole histories. Besides, they do it humanely. What! Would you rescue them? Burst upon the scene with a machine gun and order the animals to be loaded on the truck and driven away? To the country, to the middle of the meadow, and set them free?

I know, I know. But to one who watches from the periphery, there   45
seems no place for this event in human experience.

Hypocrite, you say, why don't you give up meat instead of professing all this outrage?

Give up meat! Oh, no, I couldn't do that, I have eaten meat all of my life. Besides, vegetarianism seems to me a kind of national atonement, an act of asceticism like the fasting that is done during Lent or on Yom Kippur.

So. We are all meat eaters here. The desire for meat is too deeply seated in us. As deeply seated as the desire for romance. The difference between those butchers and you is that they do not come to the abattoir each day with their hearts gone fluid with emotion. They have no patience with the duplicity of sentiment.

It is the next day, and already the event is too far away for grief or pity. How quickly the horror recedes. I pass the butcher shop whose window is neatly arranged with parts of meat labeled shank, loin, T-bone. For a long time I stand gazing at the display. For one fleeting instant it occurs to me that this window full of meat is less than dead, that, at a given signal, the cut-up flesh could cast off its labels and cellophane wrappers and reassemble, seek out its head and hooves, fill with blood and *be* again. But the thought passes quickly as it came.

"Is the veal fresh?" I ask the butcher.   50

"Slaughtered yesterday," the man says. "Can't be much fresher than that."

"Let me have a pound and a half of the scallopini," I tell him. "Nice and thin, and give it a good pounding."

Questions for Discussion

1. In his third paragraph Selzer writes that his visit to the slaughterhouse was "a descent into Hades, a vision of life that perhaps it would have been better never to know." Yet in paragraph 31 he writes, "This slaughterhouse is a place one leaves wanting only to make love." Is this a contradiction? Does Selzer know how he feels about the slaughterhouse he visited?

2. Once Selzer has visited the slaughterhouse, what motivates him to return the following day?

3. This essay includes many details that do not relate directly to the design of a slaughterhouse. What is the significance of the mourning doves and tulips in paragraph 8, the radio announcement in paragraph 10, and the dog in paragraph 32?

4. What does Selzer mean when, writing about the slitter, he comments, "if physiognomy is any hint of character, he has found his rightful place"? Where else does Selzer describe the slitters? How would you describe his attitude toward them?

5. In paragraph 15 Selzer writes, "The efficiency of the men is a glittering, wicked thing." Why "glittering" and why "wicked"? How does Selzer want the work of a slaughterhouse to proceed?

6. How are the architecture students at Yale like the men who work in the slaughterhouse? What does Selzer imply about the surgical residency program at Yale?

7. What would be the effect of deleting from this essay the description Selzer provides in paragraphs 34–43 of his ideal slaughterhouse? Would anything be lost?

8. Consider the last four paragraphs of this essay. Why does Selzer buy veal slaughtered on the same day he had visited the slaughterhouse? Why does he instruct the butcher to "give it a good pounding"?

Suggestions for Writing

1. According to Richard Selzer, "We are all meat eaters here." Literally, this sentence makes no sense, since some people are vegetarians. In what sense, then, are we all meat eaters? Write an essay exploring what it means to be an eater of meat.

2. Write an imaginative description of an ideal hospital, dormitory, or shopping mall.

4

Writing to Report Information

Ask yourself whether in the course of a single week you do any of the following: ask directions, consult the telephone directory, look something up in a book, read a newspaper, check gasoline prices, or listen to a weather report. All these efforts to acquire data are things people do routinely to negotiate the pathways of their world. This task is becoming both easier and more challenging as a result of technology. Today, we have almost instant electronic access to vast reserves of data. But to keep from being overwhelmed by the data we acquire, and to avoid overwhelming others when we report to them, we need to learn how to sort, select, and arrange data—and thereby turn data into information.

By *data* we mean unorganized, unconstructed bits and pieces. Billions of them. Information is constructed out of data by a particular person or group of people with particular concerns that they wish to communicate. So information always involves a rhetorical situation. The challenge is to transform data into information by furnishing a context and a social purpose.

To understand the nature of data, you must be able to distinguish among facts, inferences, and opinions. *Facts* are independently verifiable events, statistics, and statements: The Arkansas River runs southwest from central Colorado into Kansas; Angell Memorial Hospital in Boston had a $2 million deficit in 1988; genetic engineering has recently produced a tomato that can be picked ripe. *Inferences* are reasonable suppositions drawn from facts. Naperville, Illinois, had a population of 22,600 in 1970, 42,600 in 1980, and 83,000 in 1989. We can combine these facts and infer that by the year 2000 Naperville will have a population well in excess of 100,000, because a clear pattern of population growth exists. So data also consists of inferences. Finally, *opinion* is a belief that may or may not be accurate but that nevertheless exists and must therefore be taken into account by reporters of information. You might think that Naperville would be an exciting place to move to, or you might think that it is getting too big. Whether or not an opinion is reliable matters a great deal in some rhetorical situations—in writing to evaluate, for example, or writing to persuade (which are discussed in other chapters). But right or wrong, an opinion becomes data once it is shared with others. No longer yours alone, it has become one of those random bits and pieces with which others must cope.

Our main concern in this chapter is with the way we draw upon data to transfer information from one mind to another. Although this is a very complex process—one that has been studied at length by psychologists, neurologists, and communication specialists—there is agreement that the most powerful way to transfer information from one mind to another is through language. Our concern here is specifically with written language.

GUIDELINES FOR REPORTING INFORMATION

Reading for information is very different from reading to enter imaginatively into another person's life or to reflect at length about ideas. When people read for information, they appreciate having clear signals from the author that will alert them to the most important points and give them the opportunity to skim the rest. They also appreciate having some idea of the scope of the article and why they are expected to read it.

Writing that reports information need not always have a thesis. A newspaper article, after all, rarely has a thesis, but the lack of a thesis does not mean that it consists of random pieces of data. It is still arranged in a pattern so that readers can make sense of it. Business reports, too, frequently consist simply of narratives of what has happened or of text that exists mainly to link numbers in some meaningful way. But many reports benefit from having a clearly defined thesis explicitly stated early on. For instance, because of the way Claire Sterling opens her essay, readers know that she will give us information about a little-known subject, the Russian Mafia. This direction is established by the very first sentence: "There are fifty ways of saying 'to steal' in Russian, and the Russian mafia uses them all."

Philosopher H. Paul Grice provides four rules that can guide the transfer of information so that clear communication takes place and that also can help writers decide what to tell and how to tell it when reporting information. In Grice's scheme information should observe the rules of quantity, quality, relevance, and manner.

To observe the rule of *quantity,* you need to give your readers enough information—but no more than that—so that they can understand what you want them to know, so that there are no gaps to impede their understanding, and so that they do not drown in data. An example may help. Although a biographer could write a book about Audrey Hepburn, a reporter like Caryn James writing an obituary must give enough information so that readers can understand Hepburn's accomplishments but not so much that they will be unable to take in the information quickly while scanning the morning newspaper.

The rule of *quality* dictates that you give correct, accurate information. Because reporters of information draw upon inferences and opinion as well as facts, readers must gauge the quality of the information provided. For instance, Ann Hodgman reports the factual data she reads on labels and she quotes company spokespeople, but most of her data come from actually tasting dog food. Without an independently verifiable way of judging that her reports are reliable, we must depend largely upon our trust in her as a writer. You will want your own readers to consider you reliable and your information accurate.

The rule of *relevance* means that the reader gets the information the writer promises and is not distracted with unrelated material. If you are reading an essay about the Russian mafia, you might expect to encounter information about the government and the economy in that country, but you would not expect to read several paragraphs about the Bolshoi ballet.

Finally, the rule of *manner* means that accurate information should be presented clearly and plausibly. Sam Bingham's essay is plausible because he continually distinguishes between his own impressions and the testimony he has gathered as a reporter from specific individuals, thereby encouraging our confidence in his intellectual honesty. His essay is also plausible because he presents this information clearly. Thus, the rule of manner requires a credible reporter framing information so that readers can understand it. This is not determined simply by the reporter's being personally self-confident—although that contributes to credibility—but also by the reporter's demonstrating his or her own fair-mindedness and ability to distinguish between fact and opinion.

Implicit in Grice's four rules is a point that should be emphasized: Writers transfer information most effectively when they help readers connect information to something they already know. For example, Hodgman describes the texture of Kal-Kan Pedigree dog food (with chunky chicken) by telling us that it is "like meatloaf with ground up chicken bones." And John Sedgwick relies upon what we know of hospitals and of veterinary clinics to help us understand what may be the best veterinary hospital in the country.

USING APPROPRIATE LANGUAGE

Students are often advised to couch all their information in neutral, precise, objective language, because informing is supposed to be even-handed; but that does not mean you should take all the life out of your prose. Too much scientific and informative writing sounds as if it were produced by a machine. As the clear, direct prose of Sedgwick reveals, though, you can report information and still let your own personality show through. Presenting information while conveying a human voice helps readers remain interested in the information without damaging any of its value.

Reporting information requires you to pay special attention to the interests and abilities of your audience if you are to offer the appropriate information. When you write for general readers, you should not expect them to understand specialized vocabulary and advanced concepts, and it is your responsibility to select a topic that will interest your readers and present it in an appealing way. Consider the following excerpt from a college text-book for an introductory course in astronomy.

> Based on his determination that the sun was much larger than the earth, Aristarchus proposed that the sun was at rest and the earth moved around it in a yearly orbit. This *heliocentric* (sun-centered) model was opposed to the prevailing *geocentric* (earth-centered) model. The concept of a heliocentric universe was immediately challenged. If the earth moved in an orbit, the stars would appear to shift relative to one another, depending on the position of the earth in its orbit. This phenomenon, called *parallax,* was not observed. Aristarchus' reply to this objection was that the stars must be extremely far away, making any parallax shifts too small to notice. —*Thomas Michael Corwin and Dale C. Wachowiak,* The Universe: From Chaos to Consciousness, *246*

The authors have considered their audience. They have not talked down to them, but they have recognized that vocabulary may be a problem. They have described *parallax,* a fairly difficult concept, using simple and clear language.

Compare that passage with one from Gilbert E. Satterthwaite's *Encyclopedia of Astronomy,* which also describes parallax but is directed to more sophisticated readers.

> The angle subtended at a heavenly body by a baseline of known length, usually designated P or π. It is of course directly related to the distance; the word has therefore come to be used by astronomers as synonymous with distance.
>
> The baseline used for nearer objects, such as the members of the solar system, is the equatorial radius of the earth; parallaxes determined on this basis are termed *geocentric parallaxes.* . . . For more distant objects, the baseline used is the semimajor axis of the Earth's orbit; these are termed *heliocentric parallaxes.* (305)

Satterthwaite's discussion goes on in considerable detail to discuss various kinds of parallaxes, but he can assume that his readers are highly motivated to read his discussion and have the knowledge to understand fine points—a different audience altogether from Corwin and Wachowiak's.

SUMMARIZING AND SYNTHESIZING INFORMATION

As you transform data into information, you need to know how to summarize and synthesize.

To *summarize* is to condense: Summaries report the main points—and only the main points—of something you have heard, read, or witnessed. For example, the following paragraphs appeared in the San Jose *Mercury News* for June 25, 1991.

> PCR analysis was invented and patented in 1985 by scientists at the Cetus Corp. The instrument that amplifies trace quantities of DNA is about the size of a shoe box.
>
> By cyclically changing the temperature of the contents and by supplying various building-block chemicals, the device splits apart paired strands of corkscrew-shaped DNA molecules and uses each strand as a template to create a new DNA segment.
>
> With each repetition of the procedure, the number of identical DNA segments is doubled, and trillions of copies can be manufactured rapidly. The result is that fragments of DNA formerly too small to analyze can be amplified easily for study.
>
> A feature of the system is that scientists can select any section of interest from a DNA molecule—typically a single set of genes—and amplify only that part.

Summarizing these paragraphs means understanding what they say and restating in your own words the points you consider to be important. Here is a summary of the passage.

> PCR analysis amplifies trace amounts of DNA mechanically in a boxlike device that cycles temperature as it splits all or a selected part of the characteristic DNA pairs and combines them with building-block chemicals.

The summary reduces the length of the passage to a fourth its original size. The name of the company that invented the gadget, the date it was invented, and its size are left out. So is data about the shape of DNA molecules and the data that split strands act as templates, that the segments are identical, that there can be trillions of them, and that researchers can specify which genes are amplified. Most readers will consider these details to be nonessential. However, people interested in knowing which company developed the device or the amount of reconstituted DNA it can make would not find the summary useful. Another writer having those readers in mind would summarize this passage differently. Remember that your purpose in summarizing and the audience for whom you are summarizing determine how much and which information you report.

Looking at an obituary can help you understand summarizing. In an obituary we cannot present all the information of which a life is made up. So if we wish to report the totality of a life, we must summarize its main points, as James does in her obituary for Audrey Hepburn. She mentions the important points of Hepburn's life, emphasizing her career as an actress. She gives less emphasis to Hepburn's experiences in Nazi-occupied Holland, her personal charm, her marriages, her sons, her philanthropy, and the circumstances of her death.

To *synthesize* is to put data of different kinds together in meaningful ways. Synthesis means creating information by sorting through data, identifying relationships, and presenting them in a coherent pattern. When you are summarizing, you are usually working with data that comes from a single source. When you are synthesizing, you are reaching out to draw together data that has come from many different places. For example, Bingham synthesizes data from several different sources to construct the information he gives us about water rights in Rocky Ford, Colorado. His opening description of the landscape reveals not only that he has been to Rocky Ford, but also that he has consulted maps or road signs to learn the distance from Denver and discover the route to the town. He quotes a local farmer's opinion about what has happened to the valley; and he sets that into a context by pointing out that the farmer's son is studying real estate in Denver and that in the "last twenty years, the valley of the Arkansas has lost about a quarter of its 330,000 irrigated acres to the cities," a fact Bingham may have gleaned from a local newspaper, county documents, or other such sources.

Bingham gives us historical information about the beginnings of Rocky Ford, facts about who owns what, who bought what, who sued whom, who won, and what it cost. Along the way he draws upon these facts to make inferences about what kind of future awaits the town. He closes his report by quoting an interview he had with the utilities director for the city that is buying up most of Rocky Ford's water, a man who "worries little about Rocky Ford," an opinion Bingham forms from what the man has told him. The variety of sources Bingham used to collect the data for this report and what he did with that data are apparent only in the variety of information he offers us. He has digested what he found, made it his, and given it meaning by presenting it in a pattern appropriate for his readers and his reason for writing about this subject in the first place.

OBTAINING DATA

Although writing to report information does not necessarily require you to gather more knowledge than you already possess, there may be times when you lack adequate knowledge to finish your paper. Research can provide you with additional data. There is no reason to assume, however, that research must be confined to libraries or to computers. If you have ever wondered how food is prepared in a local fast-food restaurant, you might consider doing some field research—touring the facility, asking questions of employees—and then writing an informative, behind-the-scenes report. To obtain data for his essay, Bingham went to Rocky Ford, Colorado, for instance, and Sedgwick visited Angell Memorial Hospital in Boston. Or if you are interested in writing a profile like Tim Rogers's profile of Vivian Villarreal, one of the best pool players in the world, you might interview that person and perhaps his or her associates.

When interviewing someone, always do some preliminary research so that you will be able to ask knowledgeable questions. Schedule the interview in advance, and prepare a list of questions that are specific enough to find out what you need to know but allow the person you are interviewing enough latitude to be comfortable. Try to know your questions by heart, so that you can talk naturally with the person you are interviewing without stopping to find and read a question that you wrote down. And if you want to use a tape recorder, always ask permission to do so.

For many topics, however, you will need to consult material that has already been published. There are many guides to research in print, and you will also find a chapter on how to do research in most composition handbooks. Teaching in detail the research strategies available for writers is beyond the scope of this introduction, but you should be aware of some basic principles.

- Research is not limited to long, formal papers with lengthy bibliographies, such as a ten-page "research paper" due at the end of the semester. Writers often need to consult sources when working on shorter assignments prompted by a number of different motives for writing.
- A good search strategy involves consulting different kinds of sources, including electronic databases, books and articles, and sometimes government documents and personal interviews. Don't get discouraged if you can't find a book on your topic in your local library, or if the periodicals you need have been checked out by someone else. You may be able to get the information electronically.
- Writers who use sources should be careful to remain in control of their material and not let a paper become a collection of undigested data from which the writer's own voice has disappeared.
- Information that comes from sources should be documented appropriately. (Handbooks published by the Modern Language Association and the American Psychological Association, among other groups, provide guidance. When in doubt, ask your instructor.)

The fastest, most efficient way to do research today is through electronic searching. Many colleges and universities provide students with accounts free of charge that allow them to electronically "visit" their own libraries and others around the nation, to correspond electronically with like-minded people who share similar interests, and to search on-line data depositories maintained by government and business. Not only are new information sources such as electronic databases available on-line, but also the traditional standbys such as *The Reader's Guide to Periodical Literature* are available electronically, either on-line or on CD-ROM. The most common index to periodical literature, *The Reader's Guide*, can direct you to articles on your topic in approximately five hundred general-circulation magazines, such as *Newsweek, Rolling Stone*, and *Scientific American*.

A library's main catalog will direct you to books on your subject within its collection. You can locate books electronically in your own library and also in other college and university libraries (and some municipal ones). If you do locate a book in a remote library, you can usually request it to be sent to you through interlibrary loan. However, more books are becoming available in electronic format. Consult your reference librarian for more information about what research tools are available in this rapidly changing branch of information science.

For recent information on specific topics you will often need to consult periodical literature or material, like magazines and newspapers, that is published periodically. Again, whenever possible, take advantage of electronic resources. More and more professional journals are being published electronically, and general-interest magazines such as *Newsweek* are also beginning to appear on-line. Thus, you may be able to use electronic means not only to find a citation but also to retrieve the full text of an article. For information in scholarly publications you will need to consult a specialized index. Articles about chemistry, for example, can be located by searching the *Applied Science Index*.

Whatever research strategies you use and whatever resources are available to you, remember that obtaining data is only one part of the process of reporting information. Do not allow the quest for data to become an end in itself. As we have seen, data becomes useful as it is transformed into information. To transform it, you must allow yourself plenty of time for writing and revising.

NO WONDER THEY CALL ME A BITCH

Ann Hodgman

> *Some writers believe information is equivalent to news, arguing that readers are not being informed unless they are being told something that they did not already know. In the following essay Ann Hodgman reports about dog food—a product that most people are familiar with to some extent, for we see it advertised on television and displayed in grocery stores. But unless you have experience in eating dog food, you will acquire some new information from this report. As you read, note how Hodgman engages interest in a topic that could easily be unpalatable.*

I've always wondered about dog food. Is a Gaines-burger really like a hamburger? Can you fry it? Does dog food "cheese" taste like real cheese? Does Gravy Train actually make gravy in the dog's bowl, or is that brown liquid just dissolved crumbs? And exactly what *are* by-products?

Having spent the better part of a week eating dog food, I'm sorry to say that I now know the answers to these questions. While my dachshund, Shortie, watched in agonies of yearning, I gagged my way through can after can of stinky, white-flecked mush and bag after bag of stinky, fat-drenched nuggets. And now I understand exactly why Shortie's breath is so bad.

Of course, Gaines-burgers are neither mush nor nuggets. They are, rather, a miracle of beauty and packaging—or at least that's what I thought when I was little. I used to beg my mother to get them for our dogs, but she always said they were too expensive. When I finally bought a box of cheese-flavored Gaines-burgers—after twenty years of longing—I felt deliciously wicked.

"Dogs love real beef," the back of the box proclaimed proudly. "That's why Gaines-burgers is the only beef burger for dogs with real beef and no meat by-products!" The copy was accurate: meat by-products did not appear in the list of ingredients. Poultry by-products did, though—right there next to preserved animal fat.

One Purina spokesman told me that poultry by-products consist of   5
necks, intestines, undeveloped eggs and other "carcass remnants," but not feathers, heads, or feet. When I told him I'd been eating dog food, he said, "Oh, you're kidding! Oh, *no!*" (I came to share his alarm when, weeks later, a second Purina spokesman said that Gaines-burgers *do* contain poultry heads and feet—but *not* undeveloped eggs.)

Up close my Gaines-burger didn't much resemble chopped beef. Rather, it looked—and felt—like a single long, extruded piece of redness that had been chopped into segments and formed into a patty. You could make one at home if you had a Play-Doh Fun Factory.

I turned on the skillet. While I waited for it to heat up I pulled out a shred of cheese-colored material and palpated it. Again, like Play-Doh, it was quite malleable. I made a little cheese bird out of it; then I counted to three and ate the bird.

There was a horrifying rush of cheddar taste, followed immediately by the dull tang of soybean flour—the main ingredient in Gaines-burgers. Next I tried a piece of red extrusion. The main difference beween the meat-flavored and cheese-flavored extrusions is one of texture. The "cheese" chews like fresh Play-Doh, whereas the "meat" chews like Play-Doh that's been sitting out on a rug for a couple of hours.

Frying only turned the Gaines-burger black. There was no melting, no sizzling, no warm meat smells. A cherished childhood illusion was gone. I flipped the patty into the sink, where it immediately began leaking rivulets of red dye.

As alarming as the Gaines-burgers were, their soy meal began to seem   10
like an old friend when the time came to try some *canned* dog foods. I decided to try the Cycle foods first. When I opened them, I thought about how rarely I use can openers these days, and I was suddenly visited by a long-forgotten sensation of can-opener distaste. *This* is the kind of unsavory place can openers spend their time when you're not watching! Every time you open a can of, say, Italian plum tomatoes, you infect them with invisible particles of by-product.

I had been expecting to see the usual homogeneous scrapple inside, but each can of Cycle was packed with smooth, round, oily nuggets. As if someone at Gaines had been tipped off that a human would be tasting the stuff, the four Cycles really were different from one another. Cycle-1, for puppies, is wet and soyish. Cycle-2, for adults, glistens nastily with fat, but it's passably edible—a lot like some canned Swedish meatballs I once got in a Care package at college. Cycle-3, the "lite" one, for fatties, had no specific flavor; it just tasted like dog food. But at least it didn't make me fat.

Cycle-4, for senior dogs, had the smallest nuggets. Maybe old dogs can't open their mouths as wide. This kind was far sweeter than the other three Cycles—almost liked baked beans. It was also the only one to contain "dried beef digest," a mysterious substance that the Purina spokesman defined as "enzymes" and my dictionary defined as "the products of digestion."

Next on the menu was a can of Kal Kan Pedigree with Chunky Chicken. Chunky *chicken?* There were chunks in the can, certainly—big, purplish-brown chunks. I forked one chunk out (by now I was becoming more callous) and found that while it had no discernible chicken flavor, it wasn't bad except for its texture—like meat loaf with ground-up chicken bones.

In the world of canned dog food, a smooth consistency is a sign of low quality—lots of cereal. A lumpy, frightening, bloody, stringy horror is a sign of high quality—lots of meat. Nowhere in the world of wet dog foods was this demonstrated better than in the fanciest I tried—Kal Kan's Pedigree Select Dinners. These came not in a can but in a tiny foil packet with a picture of an imperious Yorkie. When I pulled open the container, juice spurted all over my hand, and the first chunk I speared was trailing a long gray vein. I shrieked and went instead for a plain chunk, which I was able to swallow only after taking a break to read some suddenly fascinating office equipment catalogues. Once again, though, it tasted no more alarming than, say, canned hash.

Still, how pleasant it was to turn to *dry* dog food! Gravy Train was the   *15* first I tried, and I'm happy to report that it really does make a "thick, rich, real beef gravy" when you mix it with water. Thick and rich, anyway. Except for a lingering rancid-fat flavor, the gravy wasn't beefy, but since it tasted primarily like tap water, it wasn't nauseating either.

My poor dachshund just gets plain old Purina Dog Chow, but Purina also makes a dry food called Butcher's Blend that comes in Beef, Bacon & Chicken flavor. Here we see dog food's arcane semiotics at its best: a red triangle with a *T* stamped into it is supposed to suggest beef; a tan curl, chicken; and a brown *S,* a piece of bacon. Only dogs understand these messages. But Butcher's Blend does have an endearing slogan: "Great Meaty Tastes—without bothering the Butcher!" *You know, I wanted to buy some meat, but I just couldn't bring myself to bother the butcher . . .*

Purina O.N.E. ("Optimum Nutritional Effectiveness") is targeted at people who are unlikely ever to worry about bothering a tradesperson. "We chose chicken as a primary ingredient in Purina O.N.E. for several reason-ings," the long, long essay on the back of the bag announces. Chief among these reasonings, I'd guess, is the fact that chicken appeals to people who are—you know—*like us.* Although our dogs do nothing but spend eighteen-hour days alone in the apartment, we still want them to be *premium* dogs. We want them to cut down on red meat, too. We also want dog food that comes in a bag with an attractive design, a subtle typeface, and no kitschy pictures of slobbering golden retrievers.

Besides that, we want a list of the Nutritional Benefits of our dog food—and we get it on O.N.E. One thing I especially like about this list is its constant references to a dog's "hair coat," as in "Beef tallow is good for the dog's skin and hair coat." (On the other hand, beef tallow merely pro-vides palatability, while the dried beef digest in Cycle provides palatability *enhancement.*)

I hate to say it, but O.N.E. was pretty palatable. Maybe that's because it has about 100 percent more fat than, say, Butcher's Blend. Or maybe I'd been duped by the packaging; that's been known to happen before.

As with people food, dog snacks taste much better than dog meals.   *20* They're better looking too. Take Milk-Bone Flavor Snacks. The loving-hands-at-home prose describing each flavor is colorful; the writers practi-cally choke on their own exuberance. Of bacon they say, "It's so good, your dog will think it's hot off the frying pan." Of liver: "The only taste your dog wants more than liver—is even more liver!" Of poultry: "All those farm fresh flavors deliciously mixed in one biscuit. Your dog will bark with delight!" And of vegetable: "Gardens of taste! Specially blended to give your dog that vegetable flavor he wants—but can rarely get!"

Well, I may be a sucker, but advertising *this* emphatic just doesn't convince me. I lined up all seven flavors of Milk-Bone Flavor Snacks on the floor. Unless my dog's palate is a lot more sensitive than mine—and considering that she steals dirty diapers out of the trash and eats them, I'm loath to think it is—she doesn't detect any more difference in the seven flavors than I did when I tried them.

I much preferred Bonz, the hard-baked, bone-shaped snack stuffed with simulated marrow. I liked the bone part, that is; it tasted almost exactly like the cornmeal it was made of. The mock marrow inside was a bit more problematic: in addition to looking like the sludge that collects in the treads of my running shoes, it was bursting with tiny hairs.

I'm sure you have a few dog food questions of your own. To save us time, I've answered them in advance.

Q. *Are those little cans of Mighty Dog actually branded with the sizzling word* BEEF, *the way they show in the commercials?*

A. You should know by now that that kind of thing never happens. 25

Q. *Does chicken-flavored dog food taste like chicken-flavored cat food?*

A. To my surprise, chicken cat food was actually a little better—more chickeny. It tasted like inferior canned pâté.

Q. *Was there any dog food that you just couldn't bring yourself to try?*

A. Alas, it was a can of Mighty Dog called Prime Entree with Bone Marrow. The meat was dark, dark brown, and it was surrounded by gelatin that was almost black. I knew I would die if I tasted it, so I put it outside for the raccoons.

Questions for Discussion

1. Where does Hodgman include facts in this article? Where does she make inferences and offer opinions?
2. How well does Hodgman observe the rule of quantity in her report on dog food? In her conclusion she writes, "I'm sure you have a few dog food questions of your own." Do you have any additional questions? Were you satisfied by the amount of information offered here? Or did you feel you were told more about dog food than you wanted to know?
3. Does Hodgman include any data that you believe is irrelevant to a report on the taste of dog food?
4. What does Hodgman mean by "can-opener distaste"?
5. Hodgman takes the stance that she is simply reporting information that she obtained through investigation: She spent several days eating dog food to satisfy her curiosity about its taste and is now reporting what she learned. Do you think she has any other motive for writing? Do you learn anything from this piece beyond the information about dog food that it includes?

Suggestions for Writing

1. Study the data presented on the can, bottle, or package of a product that you have recently purchased. If you discover any words or phrases (like "poultry by-products") that are not clear, investigate further to discover what they mean. Then write an essay reporting what you have learned.
2. Visit a site where food is sold. Observe this site closely and, if possible, interview employees. Then write an essay reporting how food is acquired and treated at this site.

AUDREY HEPBURN

Caryn James

> *The following obituary was first published in the* New York Times *the day after Audrey Hepburn died. As you read, note how the author summarizes Hepburn's accomplishments and maintains an objective attitude toward a much-admired woman. Consider how the occasion for an obituary determines its content and arrangement.*

Audrey Hepburn, the actress who epitomized Hollywood chic in the 1950's and 60's, died yesterday at her home in Tolochenaz, near Lausanne, Switzerland. She was 63 years old and had undergone surgery for colon cancer in November.

Her death from cancer was announced by Unicef, the United Nations Children's Fund, for which she had been a special ambassador since 1988.

In recent years, she made few movies, but traveled the world raising money and awareness for the U.N. organization. Her last screen role, in 1989, was a cameo as an angel easing the hero toward death in Steven Spielberg's "Always," a role in which the character's grace and serenity echoed the image Miss Hepburn had maintained throughout a 40-year career.

AN OSCAR FOR A PRINCESS

Her first major film role made her a star. In the 1953 romance "Roman Holiday," she played a princess who runs from her duties and falls in love with a journalist played by Gregory Peck. Audiences were enchanted by her combination of grace, elegance and high spirits, and she won an Academy Award as best actress.

The same year she won her Oscar, she won a Tony for her performance   5
in the play "Ondine." Bosley Crowther, The New York Times critic, described her in words that characterized her youthful appeal. He called her "a slender, elfin and wistful beauty, alternately regal and childlike."

In a string of films that followed, she continued to play the lithe young thing with stars in her eyes and the ability to make Cinderella transformations. In "Sabrina" (1954), she was a chauffeur's daughter forced to choose between wealthy brothers, played by William Holden and Humphrey Bogart. In "Funny Face" (1957), opposite Fred Astaire, she played a bookstore clerk turned high-fashion model.

Descriptions of her beauty and appeal inevitably included the word "gamine." She was boyishly slender, with an aristocratic bearing, the trace of a European accent and a hint of mischief.

'A WILD-EYED DOE'

Billy Wilder once recalled directing her in the 1957 film "Love in the Afternoon": "You looked around and suddenly there was this dazzling creature looking like a wild-eyed doe prancing in the forest. Everybody on the set was in love within five minutes."

Among her most popular and acclaimed roles was that of Holly Golightly, the backwoods beauty turned New York sophisticate in "Breakfast at Tiffany's" (1961).

At the height of her career, she worked with such directors as William   10
Wyler and George Cukor and acted with the great male movie stars of her day, playing the younger woman opposite Gary Cooper ("Love in the Afternoon"), Cary Grant ("Charade," 1963) and Rex Harrison, in the 1964 movie version of "My Fair Lady."

There was some grumbling from the theater world when she was cast as Eliza Doolittle in "My Fair Lady," winning the role over Julie Andrews, who had originated it on Broadway. Ms. Hepburn's singing was dubbed in the film by Marni Nixon. The film won several Oscar nominations, but Miss Hepburn was not nominated.

A BLIND WOMAN TERRORIZED

Throughout her career, she also took on dramatic roles. She won an Oscar nomination for the title role of a woman questioning her vocation in "A Nun's Story" (1959). She played a woman enduring 20 years of an embattled marriage, opposite Albert Finney, in "Two for the Road" (1967). And she won her fifth Oscar nomination for her role as a blind woman terrorized in her own home in "Wait Until Dark" (1967). Other nominations were for "Sabrina" and "Breakfast at Tiffany's."

After "Wait Until Dark," she left full-time acting and lived mostly in Switzerland.

Miss Hepburn returned to the screen occasionally. In "Robin and Marian" (1976) she played the middle-aged Maid Marian to Sean Connery's Robin Hood. The role was considered the triumph of her later career and a reflection of the graceful way the actress herself had moved into middle age.

She also made some poorly received films, including "Bloodline"   15
(1979) and "They All Laughed" (1981).

Miss Hepburn, whose name originally was Edda van Heemstra Hepburn-Ruston, was born on May 4, 1929, near Brussels, to a Dutch mother and an English father, and was educated largely in London. During World War II, she and her mother were caught vacationing in Holland when the Nazis invaded and her family endured much hardship during the occupation. During the war, one of her brothers was taken to a labor camp, and an uncle and cousin were executed. She once said the family was reduced to eating tulip bulbs.

SPOTTED BY COLETTE

But when she returned to London after the war, her life took the glamorous turn she would maintain for the rest of her life. She was a ballet student and model. On the Riviera, she was spotted by the author Colette, who insisted that Miss Hepburn star in the Broadway version of "Gigi," which led to "Roman Holiday."

She attributed her work with Unicef to her childhood experience of hunger and fear during the war.

As Goodwill ambassador for Unicef she traveled extensively in Africa and Latin America. She visited Ethiopia during the drought to call attention to the plight of starving children. In 1991 she described her Unicef role as "talking my head off," and said, "I just decided to do as much as possible in the time that I'm still up to it."

Last year she visited Somalia. It was shortly after returning from that   *20* trip that her cancer was diagnosed.

WITH FREQUENT APPEARANCES

Even in her last years she remained a visible presence in the film world. She received a tribute from the Film Society of Lincoln Center in 1991. She was a frequent presenter at the Academy Awards, and the Academy of Motion Picture Arts and Sciences recently announced that she and Elizabeth Taylor would receive the Jean Hersholt Humanitarian Award this year.

In 1954, she married the actor Mel Ferrer (with whom she later co-starred in "War and Peace"). They were divorced in 1968. In 1969 she married Andrea Dotti, an Italian psychiatrist, from whom she was later divorced.

Her companion since 1980 was Robert Wolders, a Dutch actor. She is also survived by two sons, Sean, from her marriage to Mr. Ferrer, and Luca, from her marriage to Dr. Dotti.

Questions for Discussion

1. Rather than organizing this article chronologically, James begins with the announcement of Hepburn's death, and she does not report where and when Hepburn was born until paragraph 15. Why do you think she organized the obituary this way?
2. What does James accomplish by mentioning the men who starred in Hepburn's movies?
3. Consider what James reports about *My Fair Lady*. What does this information reveal about Hepburn? What does it reveal about James? Do you think it is appropriate to include negative information in an obituary?
4. James focuses this obituary upon Hepburn's career, saying relatively little about her personal life. Was this a good writing decision? Do you think more information would be appropriate for this occasion?

Suggestions for Writing

1. Newspapers and magazines frequently have drafts of obituaries on file so that when a prominent person dies suddenly, basic information on that person's life is already available for publication. Choose someone you admire and draft an obituary, including the key points of that person's life.

2. How would your own obituary read when published at some point in the distant future? Write an obituary that reports not only information already publically available about you but also information about the accomplishments you would most like to achieve in your life.

REDFELLAS

Claire Sterling

> *Dramatic political changes were readily apparent during the early 1990s after the collapse of Communist governments in Eastern Europe and the Soviet Union. What was less apparent to Western observers was how the breakdown of authority in these countries created opportunities for corruption: Political revolution became the agency for unexpected growth in organized crime. As you read the following report about the Russian Mafia, consider the implications of this information for the rest of the world.*

There are fifty ways of saying "to steal" in Russian, and the Russian mafia uses them all. It is the world's largest, busiest and possibly meanest collection of organized hoods, consisting of 5,000 gangs and 3 million people who work for or with them. Its reach extends into all fifteen of the former Soviet republics, across eleven time zones and one-sixth of the earth's land mass. It intrudes into every field of Western concern: the nascent free market, privatization, disarmament, military conversion, foreign humanitarian relief and financial aid, even state reserves of currency and gold. And it has begun to creep toward the rest of Europe and the United States— "looking at the West as a wolf looks at sheep," a Russian crime specialist told me.

The Russian mafia is a union of racketeers without equal. Unlike the mafia in Sicily, which it admires and copies as a standard of excellence, it has no home seat or central command. There are no ancestral memories or common bloodlines. Nevertheless, its proliferating clans are invading every sphere of life, usurping political power, taking over state enterprises and fleecing natural resources. They are engaged in extortion, theft, forgery, armed assault, contract killing, swindling, drug running, arms smuggling, prostitution, gambling, loan sharking, embezzling, money laundering and black marketing—all on a monumental and increasingly international scale.

Rising from the ruins of the Soviet empire, the new mafia has far outclassed the one that flourished under Leonid Brezhnev.° The mafia was Brezhnev's solution for a stifling centralized economy; it provided illicit goods and services by stealing from the state, buying protection, smuggling, cheating, bullying and bribing its way into the Kremlin. It was *korruptsiya* Communist-style, a shared monopoly of power between politicians and crooks. Liberated Russia deserved better. But the old politicians are still largely in place, yesterday's crooks are today's free entrepreneurs and *korruptsiya,* spreading uncontrollably as things fall apart, has become the curse of a

---

Leonid Brezhnev: General secretary of the Communist party and president of the U.S.S.R. from 1979 to 1982.

stricken nation. "Corruption," Boris Yeltsin exclaimed last year, "is devouring the state from top to bottom."

In 1991, the year the Communists fell, the All-Union Research Institute of the Soviet Interior Ministry estimated that half the income of an average government functionary was coming from bribes, compared with only 30 percent before 1985. During the late 1980s the Soviet prosecutor-general's office indicted 225,000 state officials for embezzlement, including eighteen who worked for the government's Department to Combat Embezzlement. By 1991, 20,000 police officers were being fired yearly for collusion with the mafia—double the rate under Brezhnev. That same year, Alexander Gurov, head of the Soviet Interior Ministry's Sixth Department to Combat Organized Crime, estimated that four out of five agents in the ministry's militia were on the take.

These were merely symptoms of a malignant growth pervading the economy, the banking system and the body politic. It is common knowledge that millions of ordinary citizens steal state property, trade on the black market, swindle each other and buy or sell protection. Obviously they aren't all tied to the mob: Russia is so chaotic and broke that few people can stay honest and survive. Yet if not all lawbreakers are mafiosi, the mafia swims among them like a great predatory shark, recruiting some, exacting payoffs from others, frightening away rivals. Insatiable and seemingly invulnerable, it swallows factories, co-ops, private enterprises, real estate, raw materials, currency and gold: one-quarter of Russia's economy in 1991, between one-third and one-half by 1992.

Between 1989 and 1991, communism's twilight years, the mafia's take shot up from less than 1 billion rubles to 130 billion—the size of the Soviet national deficit. "In the next few years, its [gross] will reach 200 billion rubles," Gurov said in 1991. "Organized crime will then control 30 to 40 percent of the country's GNP."

Meanwhile, the mafia's kill rate has climbed to a world record. Once, Soviet leaders taunted America for its sixty-odd murders per day—a mark of capitalist depravity. By 1993 murders in the Russian republic alone ran to more than eighty per day. Many of the dead were victims of drunken brawls, armed robbery and gang warfare, but contract killings were increasingly popular: there were 1,500 in 1992. In 1993 ten directors of the country's largest commercial banks were murdered, presumably for failing to extend still more outrageous loans than those they had granted already. And a disturbing number of victims were policemen: nearly 1,000 between 1989 and 1992, according to Interpol Moscow.

By the start of 1992, soon after the Soviet Union's borders opened up, all of its institutions were gone, including those for law enforcement. The Soviet-wide Sixth Department, created by Mikhail Gorbachev three years earlier to fight organized crime, was dismantled along with all other nationwide bodies. No central authority remained to coordinate police intelligence, order arrests, control 36,000 miles of border or oversee the movement of people, money and goods. The only organization fully operational in the new Commonwealth of Independent States was the mafia.

The Russian mafia is richer by far than the forces of the law and much better equipped in weapons, communications systems and transport. Members are admitted only with a sponsor, and only after proving their valor by killing somebody on order, preferably a friend or relative—exactly like their Sicilian counterparts. Once in, they risk its death penalties, communicate in private jargon and flout the tattoos marking their eternal membership: a spider web for drug traffickers, an eight-point star for robbers, a broken heart for district bosses.

The mafia is organized in something like a classic criminal pyramid. *10* First, at the base, are common street hoods, under gang leaders who run their territory like military boot camps. Moscow, for instance, is controlled by twenty criminal "brigades"—some tribal, others regional, others specialized by trade—totaling more than 6,000 armed thugs. Everybody in the city in some kind of business (restaurants, food markets, gas stations, flower stalls, newsstands, casinos, beggars' corners at the Kremlin) is "under somebody" who collects a monthly payoff. The *Dolgoprudnaya,* who drive around in Volvos with heated seats, control the best protection rackets. The *Lyubertsy* run prostitution. The *Solntsevo* run slot machines. The *Ingushy* smuggle contraband leather and skins to Italy. The Azerbaijanis control the drug trade. Then there are the Chechen, with their own army of 600 killers in Moscow. Natives of a self-proclaimed sovereign enclave in the northern Caucasus, the Chechen are the most notorious and versatile of Russia's mafiosi. They will do almost anything imaginable that is illegal.

A level up from the gangs are a "supply" group and a "security" group. The supply group serves as a conduit, ensuring that directives from above are carried out below. The security group is comprised of respectable citizens—journalists, bankers, artists, athletes, politicians—who provide intelligence, legal aid, social prestige and political cover.

On top of the pyramid are the godfathers, the indomitable *vory v zakone* (thieves-within-the-code); they preserve a "thieves' ideology," administer justice and plot strategy. There are 700 known godfathers at large or in prison. Guiding rather than governing, they provide most of the brains for their subalterns. They are not absolute rulers over violently unruly and fiercely competitive gangs. Rather, "each sphere of influence is under their control," according to I. Pavlovich, deputy chief of the Russian Interior Ministry's Sixth Department. Pavlovich says they meet periodically, settle territorial disputes, decide on operations and make policy. Their power inevitably surpasses the fragile Russian government's. Their edicts are instantly transmitted, unmistakably enforceable and almost universally obeyed.

Two stories illustrate how the mafia has of late transformed itself into a formidable force. First, in January 1991 the most powerful thieves-within-the-code gathered from all over the country to discuss a financial emergency. Valentin Pavlov, premier of the crumbling Soviet empire, had suddenly withdrawn all 50- and 100-ruble notes from circulation. His plan, he said, was to stop the illegal flow of rubles out of the country and prevent "a river of dirty money" from coming in. Everybody in the mafia kept illicit cash reserves in these notes, which at the time were the largest denominations issued.

"My operational report showed that these thieves-within-the-code— the supermen, the big-time mafiosi—got together to discuss ways of selling off or exchanging the banknotes for new ones or getting them out of the country," Gurov later said on national T.V. "The thieves-within-the-code decided where the rubles had to be exchanged or smuggled out. Then they gave permission to set aside a quarter of the entire sum for bribing the administration."

The underworld mobilized overnight. "Black-market currency sharks   15
vanished from Moscow," Gurov declared. The ruble notes were rushed to corruptible state factories and banks in remote regions to be exchanged under the counter. The Konkuret co-op, with only 1,000 rubles in its account, changed 190,000 rubles in 50s and 100s into smaller denominations at the local bank. A Novosibirsk shop taking in 10,000 rubles per day "contrived to hand in" 240,000 rubles. Hundreds of millions of rubles were washed with little trouble. Unlike the poor, who lost their lifetime savings because they had been hiding their rubles under their mattresses to dodge the tax collectors, the mafia came out very well.

Then, a few months later the godfathers met again to consider Gorbachev's 500-day program for transition to a free market. They liked it. A free market in the USSR meant not only mobility, relaxed borders and dollars from abroad, but a chance to mount the most colossal criminal buyout in history. For all the wreckage of Russia's economy, it still had the world's richest natural resources. Once privatization got under way, according to Tatjana Kurjaghina, then the Interior Ministry's top social economist, the whole country would be up for sale.

Though few realized it at the time, the Russian mafia was about to make a big strategic leap: from merely feeding off the economy to owning it. To prepare for privatization, however, the godfathers needed to stall the entire government program until January 1992, and they had to impose a new peace among Moscow's eternally warring clans. A truce that they had worked out in 1988, at Dagomys on the Black Sea, had ended in an orgy of bloodshed after barely a year. But the first stage of privatization was an imperative call to order. The logic of peace was unarguable: once inner harmony was restored, the godfathers divided zones of influence and went after the 6,000 enterprises coming up for auction in Moscow. The rules for privatization were fluid, corrupt officials were easily come by and most Russians had no money to speak of. Within weeks, the Russian news agency *Tass-Krim Press* reported that the mafia had "privatized between 50 percent and 80 percent of all shops, storehouses, depots, hotels and services in Moscow."

Today, according to Yeltsin adviser Piotr Filipov, who heads the Center for Political and Economic Analysis, Russia's mafia controls 40,000 privatized enterprises and collects protection money from 80 percent of the country's banks and private enterprises.

The mafia also controls the drug trade. Nature has endowed Russia and its fellow republics with a prodigal source of narcotics. According to Alexander Sergeev, head of the Interior Ministry's anti-narcotics unit, the ex-USSR produces twenty-five times more hashish than the rest of the world; cannabis grows wild on 7.5 million of its acres—in Kazakhstan, Siberia, the Far Eastern republics, the lower Volga River Basin, the northern Caucasus and southern Ukraine. Luxuriant poppy fields sprawl across Kazakhstan, Uzbekistan, Turkmenistan and Tajikistan.

When Soviet controls were severe, organized crime overlooked this   20 potential bonanza: the chance to create and feed a huge addict population and export for dollars. When communism fell, however, things changed. By 1992 family-sized poppy fields yielding two crops per year were under heavy armed guard. New plantations in Uzbekistan increased by 1,000 percent. Around 200,000 acres were planted in Kyrgyzstan. The number of opium growers in Kazakhstan's Chu Valley tripled. Poppies were planted over 1,000 square kilometers of empty radioactive terrain around Chernobyl. Vladimir Burlaka, St. Petersburg's anti-narcotics chief, estimated that the 1992 crop would be worth $5 billion.

Meanwhile, heroin couriers were moving up from the Golden Crescent through Tajikistan, Uzbekistan and Turkmenistan. They carried forged papers and radio telephones and had paramilitary protection as they crossed the breadth of Soviet territory bound for Odessa, Finland, the Baltic states, Poland, Western Europe and America. The drug mafia was taking over horizontally and vertically, from production and processing to transport, distribution and marketing. Free of centralized surveillance, it moved largely unhindered across the crazy quilt of internal Commonwealth borders, ignoring ethnic tensions.

Underground laboratories were also starting to produce synthetic drugs, such as "Krokodil" and "Chert" (devil), that were 1,000 times stronger than heroin and cheaper than homegrown natural drugs. The most lethal, methyl-fentanyl—diluted in proportions of 1 to 20,000—was made exclusively in Russia.

Soviet cities had always been a drug market of sorts, and it expanded as soldiers got hooked on heroin during the Afghanistan War; but galloping addiction set in only after traffickers mounted their assault around 1985. From then on the addict population doubled yearly. By 1992 Russia had at least 1.5 million addicts and occasional drug users, Sergeev says. (The figure was all the more startling for the carefully preserved fiction that Communist Russia had no addicts whatsoever. In fact, some Russian experts thought the "real" figure was "at least three to four times higher.") Also in 1992 the drug mafia's profits increased nearly fourfold, from 4 billion to 15 billion rubles—this before its first harvest of modernized, commercialized crops.

Sergeev says that Russian mafiosi have been trafficking heroin with Westerners, the Sicilian mafia especially, for nearly a decade. In 1992 they were delivering heroin to Sicilian mafiosi in New York, selling amphetamines elsewhere in the United States and moving cocaine in Vienna, Budapest and Frankfurt. They were said by Interpol Poland to have reached "precise agreements in Warsaw with big German and Dutch cocaine traffickers and Colombia's Cali cartel." That same year a shipment of pure Colombian cocaine shaped into 34,000 pairs of Peruvian-made plastic sandals was spotted in Moscow, heading for Warsaw.

Despite this, and to avoid Yeltsin's displeasure, the U.S. State Department did not list Russia among forty-eight producer or transit countries in its 1992 International Narcotics Strategy Report. No Western government publication did. In another year, though, they would. [25]

In the summer of 1992 Moscow Interpol's deputy chief, Anatoly Terechov, complained, "Less than half our joint ventures work. Only a quarter deal with their declared activities. Two or three out of five are financed with money of dubious origin. Many . . . are fictitious. Often they're one-man operations to swing hard currency deals. . . . At least 500 of our mafia groups use them to link up with international crime—in the United States, Italy, Germany, Austria, France, Canada, Poland. . . ."

Six months later Yeltsin himself adjusted this estimate upward. "At least 1,000 mafia groups have contacts with international organized crime," he said.

The American and Sicilian mafias were the first in, by way of what was to be the biggest black-market currency swap ever: a plan to trade $7.8 billion for 140 billion rubles, enabling the Westerners to buy Russia's natural resources for rubles and sell them in the West for 300 to 400 times more in dollars. (The plan was aborted in January 1991, but similar dollar-for-ruble scams followed.) With the Americans and the Sicilians entrenched, the Russians are moving out into the rest of the world—and they're heading West.

"It's wonderful that the Iron Curtain is gone," says Boris Uvarov, chief serious crimes investigator for the Russian prosecutor-general, "but it was a shield for the West. Now we've opened the gates, and this is very dangerous for the world. America is getting Russian criminals; Europe is getting Russian criminals. They'll steal everything. They'll *occupy* Europe. Nobody will have the resources to stop them. You people in the West don't know our mafia yet; you will, you will."

Questions for Discussion

1. How is the Russian Mafia structured? How does this structure differ from that of the Mafia in Sicily or the United States?
2. Why was the Mafia tolerated under communism? How has organized crime in Russia changed during the 1990s?
3. How accurate do you consider the information in this article to be? What points seem the most reliable? Are there any points where you question the numbers reported?
4. In paragraphs 13–18 Sterling narrates two stories about the Mafia. What do these stories have in common? What point are they meant to illustrate?
5. Sterling is an investigative reporter based in Europe. Judging from the report you have just read, how do you think she conducted her investigation into the Russian Mafia? What kinds of activities would she need to undertake to gather the information she reports in "Redfellas"?

Suggestions for Writing

1. Is the Mafia still powerful in the United States, or has organized crime changed in recent years because of rival gangs that are following their own rules? Research the nature of organized crime in your state or region, and report your findings.
2. As Sterling shows, organized crime is a type of social structure in which there are different levels of hierarchy. Study another kind of organization, and report on how responsibilities are divided and power is used.

A SHARE OF THE RIVER

Sam Bingham

> *Bingham sets the scene for "A Share of the River" in detail, describing the country around Rocky Ford, Colorado, and narrating the history of the town. As you read this essay, consider how the scene has changed as the result of various acts. Consider also why the information that Bingham reports could interest readers outside of Colorado.*

The Rocky Ford irrigation ditch is an unpretentious excavation, no wider than a country road, fringed by weeds and spanned by cranky creosoted bridges too low to pass under without crawling on the cracked clay bottom. It meanders south from the Arkansas River and across the largely boarded-up streets of the town of Rocky Ford, a half-dead farming community about a hundred miles southeast of Aurora, Denver's largest suburb. Aurora people don't go there, and wouldn't notice the old irrigation work if they did.

Coming down Highway 50, a traveler sees instead the wreck of the American Crystal Sugar Company's huge redbrick Victorian beet mill and the barren fields that once supplied the Foxley & Company feedlots, in Ordway, before Foxley went broke. Rocky Ford once exported ten million cantaloupes a year to New York City alone. Now it has sunk so low in the food chain of the state economy that Aurora has bought most of the water that justified the town's existence.

"They paid about $22 million for a little more than half the water rights, but we haven't seen much of that in Rocky Ford," says Ron Aschermann, the last of four generations of Aschermanns to farm along the ditch. "It's hollowed out the valley. Without the water, the land is worthless. You can't farm it, and you can't tax it. Without the farming, you've got no business on Main Street. Without the tax base, you either go without schools and services or you assess what's left so high that even those who want to stay can't afford to."

Aschermann still grows onions, wheat, and a few acres of the once famous Rocky Ford cantaloupes on his land, but he speaks as if he were the last of the Arapaho, who were driven from the area a century ago. His son is studying real estate finance in Denver.

Over the last twenty years, the valley of the Arkansas has lost about a   *5* quarter of its 330,000 irrigated acres to the cities—Pueblo, Colorado Springs, and, finally, Aurora. As Aschermann says, "They're just rolling us up."

Rocky Ford is older than Aurora. It took its name from the spot where the Santa Fe Trail crossed the Arkansas River, the place where in 1833 an enterprising merchant named William Bent built the first white outpost in the territory, which came to be called Bent's Fort. After Bent and his successors killed off the beaver and the buffalo and the Indians, Rocky Ford succeeded to cattlemen and, ultimately, farmers. Led by an Illinois immigrant named George Washington Swink, farmers dug the first irrigation ditch on the Arkansas there in 1874, two years before Colorado became a state.

By the end of the century, there were dozens of small towns thriving along the Arkansas, digging ditches and tapping off the river. Each ditch was allocated a share of the river, and anyone who could prove he would put the water to beneficial use was allocated a share of the ditch. Shareholders controlled their interests through ditch companies: the Bessemer, the Catlin, the Amity Mutual, the Fort Lyon, the Las Animas, the High Line. The oldest ditches got first rights to the water in times of drought. Shares could be sold or traded at will, and the more senior the right the more it was worth.

Few people in communities on the Arkansas questioned the buying and bartering of ditch rights. And few in Rocky Ford sensed danger when the American Crystal Sugar Company bought up a majority of shares in the local ditch. American Crystal farmed thousands of acres of sugar beets in the area, and at its height, in the sixties, the mill employed a hundred men year-round, six hundred during the fall and winter harvest. America had stopped buying Cuban sugar, there was no grain embargo, and money flowed in Rocky Ford.

Then it ebbed away. Sugar prices fluctuated wildly in the seventies, and the days of easy credit gave way to the foreclosures of the farm crisis. The mill in Rocky Ford shut down in 1979, the last of six in the valley to die.

A year later, the people of Rocky Ford learned that an outfit called the *10* Resource Investment Group had bought the whole show. For $13 million, RIG got the mill, 4,100 acres of land, and fifty-four percent of the ditch company—112 cubic feet of water per second off the top of the Arkansas River. "You could tell from the name that they weren't interested in farming," Aschermann says, "but nobody around here could raise that kind of money."

The principal partners in RIG, John and Bill Bowlen, of Calgary, Alberta, had done better than most in oil and gas speculation, and they did well in water, too. In 1983, they signed a contract selling the water rights to Aurora for a profit of nine million dollars. "We're always looking for trends," said John Bowlen of the sale not long ago. "The direction of growth was clear. It was an opportunity and we took it." A few months after that, the Bowlen family bought the Denver Bronco NFL franchise.

Aschermann and the remaining minority shareholders in the Rocky Ford ditch went to court, joined by ditch companies up and down the Arkansas. They were worried not just about insuring their share of the water but also about the fate of the American Crystal land, which RIG still owned.

The precedents were bad. In 1985, when the Foxley feedlot company sold a majority share in neighboring Colorado Canal to Colorado Springs, little was left behind on 30,000 acres but dust and weeds. Orville Tomky, a farmer who held on after Foxley left, said, "When someone sells, everyone has to jump in and spend to protect what's left. You've got to defend it 365 days of the year."

The farmers in Rocky Ford spent three years and $30,000 doing just that. In the end, they won the protection they sought, including a promise that RIG would restore natural prairie on the American Crystal land, which would no longer be irrigated; but RIG did so little to meet its requirements that three years later Aschermann et al. hauled both the company and Aurora back into court on a contempt charge. The judge fined the city and the speculators just two thousand dollars each, but he warned that further delay could cost them millions. Aurora, eager not to offend, has taken over the challenge.

Tom Griswold, utilities director for that city, is a vigorous blond man of forty-three. His office overlooks the 284 square miles of the Aurora planning area. Geographically, Aurora is arguably the largest city in the state. Denver exceeds it only because of having recently annexed a fifty-square-mile site just north of Aurora, on which it hopes to build the world's largest airport—one intended to turn the metro area into an international hub ("midway between Munich and Tokyo," say the promotional brochures). The population of Aurora grew from 74,974 to 232,800 between 1970 and 1985. "Since then, the oil bust has dropped us back a little," Griswold says, "but the new airport and completion of the beltway will set it off again. We're planning for about 430,000 by the year 2010, and the planning area, when it's built out, will support about 700,000."

He worries little about Rocky Ford. "I grew up on a hog farm in *15* Illinois myself," he said. "There's an attraction to that kind of life, but frankly if you go down to Rocky Ford you won't see any young people farming. There's no future in it anymore."

To put back the prairie, he's hired a thirty-seven-year-old former hog farmer named Gerry Knapp, whose great-grandfather broke ground along the Arkansas over a century ago. Knapp surveys his planting—grama grass, Western wheatgrass, galleta, and bluestem—with pride, and will tell visitors that the work is right on schedule. But the fact is, putting back is not as easy as plowing up. After a century of silt and salt from the river, after years of plows, fertilizers, herbicides, and pesticides, the land has changed, and nobody knows for sure whether the interplay of plants and soil life that kept the natural prairie alive can be re-created in the long term on the old fields of Rocky Ford.

When Griswold speaks of the long term, however, he speaks of Aurora. He looks at the map on his wall and then out the window at the snowy peaks beyond his densely paved landscape. "Oh, there's plenty of water out there," he says, "and it's inevitably going to flow to the cities. We have people in here every week offering us deals for water rights from one place or another. Some are more feasible than others, but one way or another we're going to get the water."

Questions for Discussion

1. How did Rocky Ford, Colorado, lose much of its water supply to a Denver suburb a hundred miles away? How has Rocky Ford changed in the last thirty years?
2. Why does Bingham take the trouble to report that Ron Aschermann's son is "studying real estate finance in Denver" and that the Bowlen family recently bought the Denver Broncos? Within the context of this article as a whole, what is the significance of this information? What does it lead you to conclude?
3. Consider the way Bingham portrays Tom Griswold. Is he good at his job? Does he have any limitations?
4. Bingham quotes Griswold three times in this article. Why do you think he chose the quotation in paragraph 17 for his conclusion?
5. Why is it that farmland cannot be easily restored to natural prairie?

Suggestions for Writing

1. Has your hometown changed since you were a child? If so, write an essay that will report how it once was and what it is like today. Pretend that you are a visiting journalist and include only those details that you could observe or learn from residents.
2. How does your town get its water supply, and how carefully is the quality of that supply maintained? Is it facing any long-term difficulties? Are there any plans for managing the water supply during a drought? Is there any danger of contamination through industrial or agricultural pollution? Interview a municipal authority and report on how the people in your community get their water and what risks, if any, they should be informed about.

TOUGH BREAK

Tim Rogers

> *Imagine writing the profile of a professional billiard player for readers who may be unable to tell a billard table from a pool table. Then as you read the following article, note how Tim Rogers attempts to engage the attention of readers and the manner in which he reports information. Consider whether his manner would be different if he were writing about a man or about a well-known athlete.*

Vivian has gone to call her mother, which seems an odd thing for a grown woman to do on a date, especially when it's a long-distance call from a bar pay phone. I hope it's not a sign the night is going badly. To be honest, I don't recall if the word *date* actually came up all that often in our phone conversations. Maybe the word I used was closer to *interview*. The dinner we just shared must have gone to my head. Vivian, truth be told, has come to San Francisco for The Connelly National Nine Ball Championship of women's pool. The twenty-nine-year-old is currently ranked the third-best woman player in the world by the Women's Professional Billiard Association. She won the championship last year, and hopes to repeat. I have come for Vivian. While I'm currently not ranked in the world standings, whenever I play my roommate, Joe, I usually win. I only hope Vivian will be my pool partner for the night, that she'll carry me for a few games. That, and I aim to find out what happens when long hair and manicured nails get mixed up with balls and sticks and other implements generally reserved for men.

Just as I begin to think Vivian's been gone too long, she walks into the room. She explains that when she's on the road for a tournament, she always calls home to let the folks in San Antonio know she's safe. She takes a seat next to me, against a wall, in a row of red vinyl chairs—the sort you'd find in a gas station. Then I relax, because I know I've got Vivian Villarreal, arguably the best woman pool player in the world, right where I want her: in a bar, where no one recognizes her, waiting to play a game of pool.

Our names sit below six others on a chalkboard, so I have time to size up this place called Paradise Lounge. A three-piece jazz band is going pretty good in the next room. Hanging lamps cast light over the pool tables; people standing back from them are only lit from the waist down, their faces hidden in the shadow and smoke above. A guy in leather pants has the table Vivian and I are waiting to play on. Between shots, he talks about motorcycles. A woman in black stretch-pants wobbles around telling anyone who will listen, "Someone just spilled my WHOLE DAMN DRINK!"

Leather Pants loses to a guy with a red beard—by the looks of it, he eats well. At some point during Red Beard's game, Vivian becomes impatient. When it ends, and there's a brief pause before the next name on the list steps up, Vivian slides out of her chair and asks the room a rhetorical question: "Who's next?"

She hands me her lipstick, strides up to the table, and has the balls   *5* racked before anyone can stop her. As she picks out a stick—before she's even taken her first shot—Red Beard turns to me: "Is she in town for the tournament?"

I quickly pocket the lipstick.

"Tournament?" I ask. "What tournament?" *That walk,* I think. *He could tell just by the way she walked to the table.*

"There's a women's professional nine-ball tournament in town."

"You don't say."

Then Red Beard breaks, doesn't sink anything, and Vivian takes over.   *10* She has a fast hard stroke. She's often ready for the next shot before the balls have stopped rolling and recovered from her last shot. She runs the table in maybe two minutes.

Red Beard doesn't look like he's accustomed to women beating him. He preempts the next name on the chalkboard and racks for Vivian, who breaks with an explosion that sends the cue ball leaping off the felt. Heads turn. While she's busy running the table again, Red Beard and I watch.

"Looks like she's ready to bet some money," he tells me over the jazz. "Does she ever bet?"

"Bet?" I ask.

Over dinner, Vivian told me about a night in a San Antonio bar a few years back. She was playing for $1,000 a game. Even after she ran nine racks in a row, the man she was playing didn't know when to give up. Vivian went home with $25,000.

"Um, no," I inform Red Beard. "As a matter of fact, I don't think she   *15* does bet."

Vivian also told me that gambling—never hustling, which involves dishonesty, misrepresenting your talent; only simple betting—is part of her past. But I wasn't entirely convinced. Neither is Red Beard—about the betting or the tournament, because he lures Vivian to an empty table, without saying a word, by setting up a diamond-shaped nine-ball rack.

Nine ball, you see, is a *contest;* whereas eight ball, what drunk men in smoky bars play, is merely an *amusement.* In eight ball, or stripes and solids, you smack your balls around in any order. Your opponent smacks his balls around. Then, whoever finishes hacking first goes for the eight.

In nine ball, both players shoot at the same balls, sinking them in numerical order, one through nine. And, so long as you strike the proper ball first, the nine ball may be sunk any time, either by a combination shot or a carom. Which means the game of nine ball requires control, strategy. It's the difference between fishing and fly-fishing, between checkers and chess.

So Red Beard trades nine-ball games with Vivian. It turns out he can handle a stick—at least on a bar table—and Vivian chats him up between shots, learning his name is Ron. She starts to draw attention to herself, the way she has of shooting hard and generally not missing much. Leather Pants and a few others have formed an audience in the shadows.

Meanwhile, I slouch a little lower in my vinyl chair and wonder if I'll *20* ever get a chance to play pool with Vivian. I'm afraid I've been relegated to the role of lipstick holder.

Just south of the Bay Bridge, a pool hall called The Great Entertainer comes to life around noon. It is here that the best women pool players from around the world have gathered for the National Championships. The place resembles a warehouse with a high ceiling and exposed concrete columns. Jazz plays over the sound system, while regulars shoot pool outside the tournament area. From behind black drapes comes periodic applause.

At the front counter, a man with a cue-stick case slung over his shoulder asks for a ticket to the tournament. "You mean to the girlie show?" the cashier behind the counter jokes, demonstrating that at least one employee has yet to get in touch with his inner, nurturing side. His term of endearment also suggests that he hasn't had a look yet behind the black curtains.

Vivian and the rest of the girlie show, sometimes known as the Women's Professional Billiard Association, have gotten two strange notions into their heads: First, physics and linear algebra can't distinguish between the sexes. Friction, inertia—all that stuff seems to work for the women. When they hit a ball, they expect it to roll.

Their second notion (and here their male counterparts really seem to disagree): Pool is just a game. In a sport still dominated by pinkie rings and testosterone, ideas like these are nothing short of radical. Maybe even a little dangerous.

For one thing, they lead to an awful lot of hugging. Before tourna- *25* ment play begins, Vivian runs into the two women in the world currently ranked above her, Loree Jon Jones and Robin Bell. Vivian knows she'll likely have to beat one or both of these women to take home first place and the $7,500 that goes with it. One expects tension, icy stares, and cold greetings; but instead, they make with the warm fuzzies. The display seems appropriate for one of those *Unsolved Mysteries* long-lost twin-sister reunion episodes, but a little surprising for professional pool players.

"The men would be kneeing each other in the groin," observes a silver-haired gentleman in a double-breasted blazer. Robert Byrne, a trick-shot legend and author of best-selling pool instruction books, says the women go about things a little differently "because the men come up from the hustling background, where it's you against the world, and you're playing for your supper, and it's a vicious world out there when you're on the road. The women don't come from that kind of background. . . . You look at the women, and then you look at the men: The women make the men look like the war in Bosnia. It's ego gone wild. It's territorial aggression. It's power-seeking. It's back-stabbing."

"The men are just interested in gambling and winning money from each other," says Vivian. "We have come together as a . . . [she struggles for the right word] family. We are all friends, and we want the sport to grow. Selfishness will only get you so far. . . . That's why we're not affiliated anymore with the men."

The women decided they'd had enough in 1992. Previously, the men and women marketed their tournaments together, but the guys always insisted on acting like, well, like *guys*. So last year, the WPBA started organizing its own events.

"When we separated from the men," Vivian says, "they never, ever thought that we could make it without them. But we're so successful now. The women never used to be close to the men as far as prize money. But now, there are about four of us who are making *more* money than them."

As recently as 1990, the women had only two events they could call *30* their own, in which only women played. In 1993, that number jumped to fourteen, one more tournament than the men played. Prize money topped $440,000, and of the top five money-winners—men and women—three were women. Excluding endorsements, this means Vivian made about $35,000 last year playing pool. And in 1994, the WPBA landed its first corporate sponsor: Gordon's gin and vodka proclaiming "the fun, refreshing mixability of Gordon's is a perfect fit."

But don't get the wrong idea. Gordon's didn't get involved with women's pool for family values. They know the women can flat-out shoot.

It's almost midnight behind the black curtains at The Great Entertainer, and Vivian is playing her fifth match of the day, tearing through the one-loss bracket. Tomorrow, ESPN shows up to tape the finals, and she wants to be there. But she's already lost one match in a double-elimination tournament. It has played out the way the seedings said it should: Across the table from Vivian, noticeably not looking for hugs, stands Robin Bell.

A guy with a Heineken in his hand watches Vivian from the bleachers. She just ran the first rack in a race to nine games, and he's lost his patience. "I don't even think she's a girl," he mutters. "Even the way she walks is like a man. It's hell on your ego."

Vivian's father taught her how to play pool at Mollie's, her grandmother's San Antonio bar. He also taught her how to walk. He would make her practice walking in heels, back and forth in the living room, while he gave pointers from the couch. "If they had such a thing as a school for walking," he would tell her, "I'd send you."

It's the same walk that Ron must have noticed at the Paradise Lounge *35* before he went to trading nine-ball games with her on that bar table. But the bar table was like a small, wet quilt compared to what Vivian has to work with now. The tournament tables are almost twice as big as most bar tables, and the cloth is so fast that the balls slide like they're on ice. Players describe good tables as "tight"; these are the tightest.

Into the fifth game, Vivian has her stroke going. It's the stroke that the other women all talk about. No matter how difficult the shot—it could be a full-table combination with a match tied at eight—Vivian always takes two practice strokes and shoots. She works so quickly that other women say they can't watch her shoot while they're playing her. It throws them off, takes them out of their own rhythm.

And then there's the break. Going into the fifteenth game, now past midnight, the match is tied at seven games each. Spectators have switched from beer to coffee. Earlier in the match, Vivian was breaking conservatively, holding back so she wouldn't send balls flying off the table. But she won the last two games and looks confident. She chalks up and lets loose.

Most players use one cue stick for breaks and another for play. They don't want to risk shattering their good shooting sticks, which often run thousands of dollars. Vivian isn't most players. She breaks with a $15,000 custom-made Omega, with nice touches like inlaid eighteen-karat gold, silver, and mastodon ivory.

It was at a tournament in Chicago that she fell in love with the stick. A rep from Omega told her she could practice with it before a match, and after she ran a few racks without missing a shot, Vivian said she wanted to finish the tournament with it. Her coach tried to stop her; it usually takes a player anywhere from six months to a year to get used to a new stick. Vivian didn't listen, and won the tournament, becoming the top-ranked woman in the world at the time. That convinced the Omega folks to sign her up for endorsements, with part of the deal being Vivian's custom-made cue.

The stick, the walk, the stroke—Vivian looks as if she's too much for Robin Bell to handle tonight. Vivian plays out the fifteenth game with precision, drawing the cue ball back for a perfect leave on the nine. With this game behind her, she'll need one more to finish the race to nine games, and then it's back to the hotel for some rest. Tomorrow, the lights and ESPN. *40*

And then she does the unthinkable. She misses. She misses the straight-in shot on the nine. It rolls, seems to trip on its own yellow stripe, and rattles around in the mouth of the corner pocket. It just stops and seems to peer over the edge. And Bell finishes it off. And goes on to win the next game after sinking the five ball in a pocket she wasn't even aiming for. But it doesn't matter. Slop counts, and Bell wins the match.

Vivian has got to be kicking herself for the fourth game, much earlier in the match, when her honesty might have cost her the tournament. She fouled on a safe, failing to drive a ball to a rail. She was nice enough to point this out to Bell, who hadn't noticed. Someone in the stands said a man would never have done that, pointed out a mistake to an opponent. With ball in hand, Bell promptly set the cue down for a two-nine combo, lined it up, and knocked it down. Vivian's mistake was Bell's game.

Vivian will return tomorrow for the finals, but she'll watch from the bleachers. For now, she gives Robin Bell a congratulatory hug, signs a few autographs, and takes her father's walk through the black curtains.

I did finally get to play pool with Vivian. We eventually left the Paradise Lounge that night and headed to a place called the Bus Stop. Ron recommended it, told us to "Tell 'em Ron sent ya." And, "Oh, boy, they're going to just looove you."

Vivian, again, got to the table a few names before her turn, and this time we played partners. At some point in our first game, one of our opponents, a guy with his short sleeves rolled up, asked if Vivian was in town for the nine-ball tournament. Vivian ran the table that game and the next.

I got my chance to shoot in game three. We had two balls left on the table, plus the eight, and the other guys had just scratched. I put the cue right where I wanted it. Lining up my shot, though, I discovered my heart literally racing, which got me to feeling a bit foolish, and I think it threw me off. Plus the table—you know, it wasn't real tight.

I sank our two balls and muffed the eight. We lost.

As we got up to leave, Vivian told me I played well. But Short Sleeves wasn't done with us. "What?" he said. "You guys lose *one game,* and you leave?"

"The tournament," I said. "She's got to get up early."

Like Vivian's father, mine taught me to shoot pool, too (obviously, he didn't do as good a job as Vivian's dad). And my father gave me this piece of pool-shooting advice, which I shared with Vivian outside the Bus Stop: "Always leave them wanting more." And I handed her the lipstick.

Questions for Discussion

1. At the beginning of his article, Rogers pretends that he is having a date with Vivian Villarreal and draws attention to her long hair and manicured nails. How would you describe his tone? Do you think it is appropriate?
2. In the world of professional billiards, what is the difference between gambling and hustling?
3. How does Rogers respond to the needs of readers who know little about billiards? Where does he include specific data about the sport?
4. How does the behavior of women professional billiard players differ from the behavior of their male counterparts?
5. Drawing upon the information reported in this article, how would you describe Vivian Villarreal?

Suggestions for Writing

1. Interview a woman athlete in a sport that interests you, and report on how she trains, what support she receives, what obstacles she has overcome, and what goals she has for the future.
2. Gather data on athletic programs at your school or in a nearby school district; then report on how well sports for men and women are funded and how those funding decisions are made.

THE DARK SIDE OF TOMATOES

Raymond Sokolov

> *You may think you already know all you need to know about tomatoes, but the following essay by food writer Raymond Sokolov contains information that may surprise you. As you read, notice how Sokolov conveys a human voice by expressing his own love for tomatoes. But be alert for information that you did not know. And as you appraise that information, try to distinguish between facts and opinion.*

In a world riven by hate, greed, and envy, everyone loves tomatoes. I have never met anyone who didn't eat tomatoes with enthusiasm. Like ice cream, the whole, perfect, vine-ripened tomato is a universal favorite. The old-fashioned kind of tomato, not the hard-walled hybrids picked green, engineered to survive long truck rides, and ripened with gas on the way to market.

Real (as I will call vine-ripened, soft-walled, acid-flavored, summer-grown) tomatoes are an article of faith, a rallying point for the morally serious, a grail. And the real tomato's acolytes are not some ragged little band of malcontents. They are us, brothers and sisters in tomatomania, converts to the first Western religion since the Stone Age to worship a plant.

Everyone I know seems to have his own story of how the scales fell from his palate as he tasted, really tasted, a real tomato for the first time. My own ecstatic rebirth as a tomatomane took place on a rail siding in some border no man's land between Yugoslavia and Greece in early August of 1960. After two days of sparse and dismal food on the old Simplon-Orient Express passing through Yugoslavia, I was able to buy a large red tomato from a boy hawking them to passengers waiting on the platform. I bit into one; juice spurted on my cheeks and tears almost mixed in. I still quiver when I recall that moment.

Such pure memories, reinforced each summer by new experiences with real tomatoes, have their dark side. They make us picky, unwilling to settle, or at least to settle happily, for false tomatoes. And so we become tomato bores, railing against square tomatoes without taste.

The Tom Paine of this rebellion is Thomas Whiteside, who attempted 5 to get to the bottom of the dark lagoon of tomato industrialization in an exhaustively reported article in *The New Yorker* in 1977. It was Whiteside who spread the word about tomatoes picked green for durability and transportability from Florida. It was Whiteside who alerted *New Yorker* sophisticates to the existence of square tomatoes, hybridized by modern plant scientists to accommodate mechanized harvesting. And it was Whiteside who raised the consciousness of upper-middle-class America about artificial ripening of tomatoes induced by ethylene gas.

Of course, there were other tomato muckrakers out there building the almost complete consensus of intelligent consumers against the supermarket tomato. But an informal survey indicates that Whiteside was the crucial figure, the tomato Jeremiah behind whom a growing throng collected. All praise to him. He pointed to a great truth: the industrial tomato is a dud. Only corporate executives of tomato companies would disagree with that.

In attempting to think clearly about this matter, it is crucial to keep in mind that the tomato we hate is the one that we buy whole and raw to be consumed whole and raw. We are not talking about tomatoes produced for canning. This means that the square tomato is a red herring. The square tomato is not a tomato you and I can normally buy. It is aimed at the commercial canning market, where delicacy of texture and taste is of far less moment than it is for fresh tomatoes. In any case, I have never laid eyes on a square tomato and I doubt most tomato radicals have. So the square tomato is an illegitimate rallying point. Yes, it exists, and Gordie C. Hanna, of the University of California at Davis, did engineer the first cultivar suitable for machine harvesting, the VF 145, in the 1950s and 1960s. But to set up the VF 145 as an outrageous example of the perversion of science in the service of agronomic pelf would be a distortion.

So is the hate campaign against artificial ripening. The gas that growers use, in storage areas and in trucks hurtling northward, to set the process of ripening in motion is the same gas that tomatoes and many other plants produce in the normal course of natural ripening. This gas is ethylene. According to *Webster's New World Dictionary,* it is "a colorless, flammable gaseous hydrocarbon of the olefin series . . . with a disagreeable odor: it is obtained from natural or coal gas, by cracking petroleum, by the action of sulfuric or phosphoric acid on alcohol, etc., and is used as a fuel and anesthetic, in hastening the ripening of fruits and to form polyethylene."

To the eye of the scientophobe, that definition settles the argument. What could be worse than to asphyxiate tomatoes with the same poison that comes from air-polluting petroleum, puts people out on operating tables, and contributes to the degradation of the environment in the form of non-biodegradable and unnecessary plastic packaging?

Yes, but ethylene per se is a benign natural organic substance. A ripe   *10* apple exudes it into the air and will hasten the ripening of other fruits, including tomatoes. Not all chemicals are bad. It is the use we put them to that counts.

Yet there must be some explanation for those pale and tooth-resistant tomatoes. My theory was that a plant geneticist/villain had messed about with the genes of "normal" garden tomatoes and concocted a sturdier hybrid fit for long interstate trips in eighteen-wheeled tractor-trailers. That mad doctor of the plant labs deserved to be the target of a campaign of vilification as a traitor to his science and to humanity. I set out to find him.

Suspect No. 1 was the man who had hybridized Florida's infamous Walter tomato. The Walter won't ripen after picking until it has been gassed. And the Walter was the ancestor of the MH-1, a grower's dream developed by the University of Florida at Homestead. According to Whiteside, you could play catch with the MH-1 at twenty paces or let it fall from more than six feet without breaking the skin. The Walter and the MH-1 are not cannery tomatoes. They are for the table. They and tomatoes like them, from south Florida and from the state of Sinaloa in Mexico, are what make tomato lovers gnash their teeth and wish for a Senate select committee to expose the whole tasteless mess.

I was one of these people until I met Charles M. Rick, a retired professor of plant genetics at the University of California, Davis, known in his field as Mr. Tomato. Ruddy, lanky, white-haired, and white-bearded, Rick is a completely unabashed enthusiast for the achievements of tomato science as he has known it since his student days, which ended in 1940 with a Harvard doctorate.

Since then, he and his colleagues all over the world have capitalized on the extraordinary genetic malleability of the tomato to increase crop yields manyfold. Rick is not, however, an ethereal lab technician. Far from it. He is famous for trekking all over Peru in search of wild tomato strains that might enrich the gene pool of cultivated plants back home. He's a home gardener, too, and talks with enthusiasm about Burpee's Better Boy and another favorite variety, Caligrande, which he grows today because of its resistance to tobacco mosaic virus.

For the past six years, Rick has been assembling a tomato germ plasm   15 bank, a collection of 2,600 to 2,700 tomato lines in the form of seeds. When I was there, two women in his lab were extracting seeds from wild green tomatoes the size of gooseberries. Andean plants like these have been the source of "virtually all tomato disease resistance since the forties," he says.

Although Rick is the epitome of the modern tomato scientist, he is also in the great tradition of untutored green thumbs who long ago hybridized the red, fist-sized tomato we think of as normal from the tiny wild fruit nature gave to our pre-Columbian ancestors. By the time Cortés reached Mexico in 1519, cultivation had already produced tomatoes we would recognize today. Hybridization continued in Europe. All the garden tomatoes we love so much are the result of centuries of human meddling. Today's commercial varieties are no more artificial than the "normal" kind. And, if Rick is right, they are not categorically worse in quality.

"I don't think it's right to attribute poor market quality to breeding," he says. "That's a bunch of nonsense. Unbiased tests have been conducted— at Michigan State, for example—blind tastings of commercial varieties that were all vine-ripened. Most of the criticism is a reaction to what's happened to these tomatoes when they're grown in the off-season. The sad fact is that you can't grow a tomato on the west coast of Mexico in January, pick it green, ship it three to four thousand miles, and expect it to be as good as a garden fruit in summer. Ethylene ripening is not the issue; it's the season, the low light in winter that hurts. And they add a greater handicap by picking them green and ripening them in transit. . . . I'm not sure the best tomato in the world would be a gem under those conditions."

He saw some possible hope in work being done on tomato ripening at a Davis biotechnology firm, Calgene Inc., which just received a patent for an alteration of tomato DNA. The change affects the function of the enzyme that causes softening of the fruit during the ripening process. By thwarting the enzyme, Calgene has created a tomato that stays firm longer, while ripening normally in other respects. In principle, the Calgene tomato could be picked mature instead of green, after it had developed flavor.

These are early reports, and the most optimistic prediction for the first retail sales of these tomatoes is two winters from now. Field tests are currently under way in Mexico. But in the meantime, the pressure of a $4 billion U. S. market for fresh tomatoes has finally convinced one bold and energetic New York family named Marcelli to take a great leap forward. This past winter, they were managing to deliver high-quality tomatoes to Manhattan restaurants and grocers. How do the Marcellis do what no one else seems able to manage? Simple. They let Florida tomatoes ripen on the vine. They truck them nonstop to New York. And they keep them cool, at 55 to 60 degrees, but don't refrigerate, which would degrade flavor.

"Real tomatoes," as the sticker on each one reads, are not up to the   *20* supreme standard of summer garden fruit. And they are certainly expensive. But they show that the real obstacle to bringing decent domestic tomatoes to U.S. tables in the off-season is human greed and laziness, not bad science or gas.

Questions for Discussion

1. Consider the first four paragraphs of this article. Why does Sokolov devote so much space to expressing his feelings about tomatoes before reporting information on tomato breeding? Do you think this was a good writing decision?
2. Is there anything wrong with using ethylene to ripen tomatoes artificially?
3. How appetizing is a tomato that you can drop "more than six feet without breaking the skin"? Why are such tomatoes like the MH-1 being grown and sold?
4. If there are already over two thousand six hundred tomato lines, why would anyone try to collect or breed new ones? What are the benefits of tomato breeding?
5. What obstacles would have to be overcome before the quality of supermarket tomatoes improved, especially during the off-season?

Suggestions for Writing

1. Investigate a commonly eaten food and report on how it is produced. Possibilities include not only the food that people buy in supermarkets but also the food products purchased in restaurants like McDonald's.
2. Interview a farmer, gardener, florist, or produce manager and report upon the problems that a person has to overcome in order to be successful in that field.

THE DOBERMAN CASE

John Sedgwick

The following essay offers an inside view of one of the country's best animal hospitals. Notice how Sedgwick develops more than one topic—telling the story of Thor the Doberman, Puppy the Labrador, and an unnamed husky, while also providing abundant information on the history, operation, and mission of Angell Memorial Hospital. As you read, think about why Sedgwick chose to write at such length. Consider how the various parts of this selection relate to one another and whether the subject is interesting enough to justify such extensive reporting.

The Doberman case begins suddenly, as emergencies always do. The veterinary ambulance—a van with "ON THE MOVE FOR ANIMALS" on its side—comes racing up with its lights flashing and horn honking to Angell Memorial Hospital's main entrance. Two attendants jump out, yank open the van's rear doors, and reach inside for a coffee-colored Doberman who lies on his side in the fetal position, his tongue drooping onto a green canvas stretcher.

With their pointed ears and fearsome reputations, Dobermans can look devilish, but this one seems almost angelic—all softness and vulnerability. According to the telephone report, he has been clubbed over the head with a hockey stick. Blood oozes out of his nostrils to form a sticky pool under his muzzle, and he is shivering.

"O.K., bud," one of the attendants says gently. "O.K."

The men lift the stretcher out of the ambulance and ease it onto a stainless-steel gurney that has been positioned on the sidewalk by two white-coated nurses. Then they briskly wheel the animal up the long cement ramp and through the sliding glass door. They hurry through the packed waiting room—where both animals and humans crane their necks to see what's coming through—and down a narrow fluorescent-lit hall and into the Intensive Care Unit, a large open room ringed with sixty cages for the hospital's sickest patients.

There the acrid smell of disinfectant mingles with the animals' musky scents. Most of the patients lie flat on their sides with I.V. tubes running into a shaved leg, their faces limp with the weary, put-upon expression common to the extremely ill of all species. At a veterinary hospital, noise is usually a good sign: the barking dog is the one who is ready to go home. The I.C.U. is pretty quiet, except for the steady blip of the heart monitors and an occasional piercing whine from a husky in the corner. But, with all this suffering, the quietness has a keen edge.

From the outside, the only hint that Boston's Angell Memorial Hospital might be an animal hospital at all, let alone one of the finest animal hospitals in the world, is the small statue of a rearing horse in front, a 1915 monument to Angell's original clientele. Otherwise, the building looks like the Catholic seminary it used to be before Angell and its parent organization, the Massachusetts Society for the Prevention of Cruelty to Animals (M.S.P.C.A.), moved in from their original quarters in Boston's medical district fifteen years ago. It's a giant brick warehouse of a building in a run-down section of Boston's Jamaica Plain that has largely been abandoned to charitable institutions—a former orphanage called the Home for Little Wanderers is just up the street—and the poor. A small chapel still stands by the main building. A security guard patrols the parking lot, and the brick wall that surrounds the property is topped in places by barbed wire.

Inside, Angell might be mistaken for a regular hospital, or, as they say in the veterinary world, a human hospital. But it's a hospital that obviously doesn't want to get wrecked. The furniture is heavy and indestructible; the floors are all covered with washable linoleum instead of wall-to-wall carpeting; and there's a peculiar configuration to the waiting room—high baffles rise up between the seats to keep the animals from seeing each other and having a fit. At least, that's the idea. Actually, the animals usually lie down on the floor and poke their noses around the corners to see who else is there. The owners are the ones who are cut off. They sit in parallel, avoiding eye contact.

Now that the Doberman has passed, a panting Rottweiler is being soothed by his owner, an environmental sculptor, while "As the World Turns" goes unwatched on the television set over their heads. There is a three-inch gash on the side of the dog's face. "But you should see the beagle," the sculptor explains. An elderly woman in white double-knits peers anxiously into a plastic Sky Kennel at her cat, Petey, who hasn't urinated in three days. A man in hiking shoes stands by a large wire cage containing a litter of Newfoundland puppies, who tumble about like clothes in a dryer as they await their first checkup. And a glassy-eyed cocker spaniel stares vacantly out from the plump lap of his suburbanite mistress, who is afraid that the dog has glaucoma.

Forty-three thousand cases came through Angell's waiting room last year. Except for a pregnant goat who appeared for an emergency delivery, all were "small animals," meaning household pets. Of these, sixty percent were dogs and thirty percent cats. It's a puzzling ratio, given that cats have recently come to outnumber dogs nationally fifty-six million to fifty-three million, and there is no evidence that the ranking runs any differently in Boston. Nor are cat owners known to be indifferent to their pets' welfare. At Angell, the tender devotion of cat people typically overwhelms that of dog people. "They'll bring in a pillow and crystal dish for Fluffy," says one nurse in Angell's I.C.U. "But for the dog, it's 'O.K., here's Fido.'" Cats, however, are less demonstrative and presumed to be self-reliant. Also, the decision to invest in medical care is ultimately financial—dogs you have to pay for, cats you usually get for free. Finally, dogs are generally far better liked. According to one prominent poll, dogs are America's favorite animal, followed by the horse and the swan. The cat comes in twelfth, just after the elephant, the owl, and the turtle, but ahead of the ladybug.

It can be a rough world for house pets, and it is Angell's responsibility *10* to repair the damage. Cats and dogs are hit by cars—cats generally taking the blow head on, dogs on the flank or rear. And they fall out of high-rises. With their nearly miraculous ability to spread their paws and stabilize themselves in mid-flight, cats land lightly. The most frequent injury is a broken jaw from smacking their mouths on the pavement. Dogs aren't as likely to fall, but when they do they drop like stones. Dogs are more prone to physical abuse. One mixed breed was hurled against a wall. (After his injuries were treated at Angell, the M.S.P.C.A. persuaded the owners to give him up, and he was adopted by Angell's chief of staff.) Another mongrel was doused with lighter fluid and set on fire. One German shepherd took four bullets in the chest to protect his owner from a burglar. And, of course, both species succumb to a range of diseases that all living creatures are prey to: tumors, cancers, infections, intestinal parasites. Cats even get a version of AIDS, the recently identified feline immuno-deficiency virus, which is transmitted to other cats by bite.

And then there are the remaining ten percent of cases, the ones that are neither dogs nor cats, which are designated "exotics," Angell's term for "other." Currently, a duck with lymphoma is swimming around a plastic bathtub in the exotics ward; a rabbit is in for hair balls; a couple of cockatiels are suffering seizures; and a box turtle is having its shell reconstructed after being pounced on by the family's black Labrador. Not too long ago, a cockfighting operation was broken up, and about fifty chickens were remanded to Angell. The nurses had never heard such clucking, but they did appreciate getting eggs from the hens in the morning. A boa constrictor came in one time after its owner discovered a gouge in its side and feared the mouse it had swallowed was trying to get out. (It wasn't.) And surgeons once removed three dollars in loose change from the stomach of a New England Aquarium seal.

To treat these problems, Angell's staff performs elaborate medical procedures that make one forget that the patient on the examining table is "just a pet." Angell does chemotherapy, open-heart surgery, radiation treatment, total hip replacement for victims of dysplasia, and cataract surgery; it even implants pacemakers, some of which the hospital obtains from undertakers to keep costs down.

There are about forty vets on Angell's staff, and they are an impressive group. Only about two thousand veterinarians graduate each year from the country's twenty-seven veterinary schools. Ten years ago, ten candidates competed for every position. That ratio fell steadily through the eighties, when potential vets were lured away by the promise of far higher incomes in business and law, and by decade's end it bottomed out at three applicants for every spot. Nevertheless, the students who do enter vet school are remarkably committed. When Tufts School of Veterinary Medicine polled its applicants to find out how long they had wanted to be vets, nearly all of them checked off the box that said "For as long as I can remember." Their interest was then usually confirmed by working with animals in a research laboratory, on a farm, or at a zoo.

While veterinarians are sometimes viewed as second-class physicians, the competition for veterinary school is actually stiffer than for medical school, whose ranks of applicants also thinned in the eighties. Because veterinary students have more than a dozen different species to master, their work load is noticeably heavier than medical students'. "We don't automatically get called Doctor, either," one Angell veterinarian grumbles, displaying a rare touch of rancor. "We don't get the M.D. plates, and we don't get our Wednesday afternoons off for golf." So why do they do it? "We're nuts," says another vet.

Actually, the individuals most likely to place vets in a separate medical 15
category are "real" doctors, but even they come away from Angell questioning their assumptions. "It's not snobbery," says Dr. Gus Thornton, Angell's former chief of staff, who is now president of the M.S.P.C.A. "It's more like amazement. I remember a physician brought his dog in and I diagnosed the animal as having diabetes. The man was *aghast*. 'That's exactly the symptoms *my* patients have!' he told me. Physicians don't seem to understand that cancer is cancer, heart disease is heart disease, and diabetes is diabetes. The only difference is the package it comes in."

The current chief of staff, Dr. Paul Gambardella, describes Angell Memorial as both the Boston City and the Massachusetts General of the veterinary world. That is, it handles the blood-soaked emergency cases, like the Doberman, that come in at all hours from the surrounding neighborhood, and the more exotic referral cases from a wider geographical range. One couple flew their dog over from Paris on the Concorde after he had gotten into some rat poison. Other pets have come from Switzerland, the Virgin Islands, and New Brunswick, Canada. General Alfred Gray, Commandant of the Marine Corps, personally escorted his teacup poodle, Cozette, from Maryland to Angell by military plane for orthopedic work. Elvis Presley flew his Chow in from Graceland for treatment of kidney failure. And the late Josephine Lilly, a daughter-in-law of the pharmaceutical magnate Eli Lilly, used to deliver her pugs, Trig and Sootchi, here from Cape Cod in the backseat of the family Rolls-Royce Silver Cloud. The dogs were accompanied only by the chauffeur, who invariably amused the vets with his report on the animals' condition. "Well, the *cook* noticed . . ." he would begin, or "The *gardener* observed . . ." Mrs. Lilly was so impressed with the hospital's care that she helped Angell raise a million dollars to modernize its I.C.U. In return, the hospital allows her pugs to use a corner of the ward as their presidential suite whenever they come to visit.

Despite all this history, it still comes as a shock to push open the heavy door of the I.C.U. and find these shaggy four-legged creatures inside, where one expects humans to be: their little bodies lying on stainless steel, their legs swathed in white bandages, their chests wired to heart monitors. And the peculiarity is only reinforced by the matter-of-fact way the staff treats the animals, as if their presence were the most natural thing in the world.

And nowadays perhaps it is. Now that darkest Africa has become a kind of theme park and every trapped whale makes the evening news, the hospital is just another meeting point in the increasingly merged worlds of humans and animals. There are now 109 million cats and dogs in American homes, one for every citizen under thirty. (Yet Americans rank second to the French in terms of pet ownership per capita, and are trailed closely by the English and the Australians.) Americans spend $7 billion a year on pet food (twice the sum spent on baby food), and another $7 billion on veterinary care of the sort provided by Angell. Apparently, the money lavished on pets is a function of affluence. The poorest countries, like China and certain African nations, rank lowest in pet ownership; they are more likely to see cats and dogs as competitors for food (if not as food itself) than as companions.

Although pets have been a feature of elite society at least since the Egyptians (whose pharaohs showed a great fondness for cats) and the Romans (whose emperors preferred caged monkeys), pet ownership didn't infiltrate the middle classes until industrialism spread and agricultural predominance receded. In that transition, animals became bound to humans more by emotion than by function. Indeed, as a recent article on the American Kennel Club (AKC) in *The Atlantic* suggested, many breeds of dogs have now lost their functional capabilities entirely after years of being bred purely for appearance. Most sheepherding dogs, like Border collies and kelpies, can no longer keep track of sheep, and once useful breeds, like Irish setters, "are now so dumb," in the words of AKC critic Michael W. Fox, "they get lost on the end of their leash."

The emotional bond may have been man's essential connection with animals all along, a connection that was obscured by the exigencies of life on the farm. One gets a different feeling about animals if one has to milk them, brand them, feed them, and ultimately slaughter them—all for one's livelihood. The ethnologist Konrad Lorenz described humans' love for animals as a spillover of our instinctual love for babies. As a result, we generally prefer those animals that look most like babies. Specifically, according to Lorenz, we like a creature with "a relatively large head, predominance of the brain capsule, large and low-lying eyes, bulging cheek region, short and thick extremities, a springy, elastic consistency, and clumsy movement." This explains why we are more drawn to puppies and kittens than to full-grown dogs and cats, but it gives a pretty good account of why we like dogs and cats, too.

It also helps explain why pet owners lavish such expensive and high-technology care on their pets when they are sick. They see their pets as members of the family. At Angell, the staff shares this view. They routinely speak of ailing pets with words usually reserved for family. They call the animals "honey" or "sweetheart," and they refer to the owner as the pet's

20

"mom" or "dad." They discuss their own pets' behavioral problems as though they were talking about Junior's troubles in kindergarten, and they put framed photographs of their animals on their desks where pictures of their children would normally go. They do this in a jokey, offhand manner, but they mean a lot by it.

Right now in the I.C.U., Dr. Deborah Cogan, a thirty-four-year-old internist on emergency duty, gives the stricken Doberman a tired, sorrowful look. It's 4:30 P.M. She has been at work since seven this morning, attending to so many sick and injured dogs and cats that she relies on a thick pack of index cards to keep them all straight. And she will be here until nine tonight, before the hour's drive to Salem, where she lives with her two cats, her shepherd-husky crossbreed, and her boyfriend, an aircraft engineer. When she arrives home, he'll probably tell her she's burning out, and she will numbly agree. But what can she do? "We're talking major love here," she says. When she was two years old, she refused to kiss a friend of the family, preferring to kiss the friend's dachshund instead. At six, she was already being asked by neighbors for veterinary advice. She started assembling a library of veterinary texts at seven, and at eleven she was subscribing to Cornell's catalog, because she knew she wanted to go to its veterinary school. Her course was set.

The Doberman's head is drooping over the edge of the stretcher, and blood from his nose is dribbling onto the floor. Cogan presses her stethoscope lightly against the dog's chest, then feels inside his rear thigh for a pulse. A Dalmation on an I.V. comes over to sniff the new patient, until he's escorted into his cage by a technician. Nearby, a blind spaniel whimpers quietly.

It is never easy to determine what is wrong with an animal who can't say where he hurts, but it is even harder when the animal is barely conscious. Lying in front of Cogan, the Doberman is darkness itself. She shines a penlight into the dog's eyes, as if to illuminate his mind. She is checking for brain damage: pupils that are jammed wide open or shut down to pinpoints are not encouraging sights. The penlight is weak and the room is bright, but Cogan is pleased to detect a flickering response to the light. Then she pries open the animal's jaws with a tongue depressor, wipes away the bloody slobber with a paper towel, and considers the dog's gums, which act as litmus paper for an animal's general condition. A rich pink is best, dull blue the worst. The dog's gums are pale pink. O.K. She can live with that. Dr. Cogan feels the animal's skull with her fingertips, trying to detect the extent of the damage. "He feels mushed over here," she tells the nurses. Under the skin, the dog's forehead is spongy with blood. "He's got some bleeding under his skull." She can feel the break with her fingertips, but the displacement—the gap between the broken bones—doesn't seem too severe. Surgical wiring probably won't be necessary. She'll need X-rays to decide the issue, however. "He's so out of it, we probably could do it without anesthesia," she says. Then she tells the nurses to put in an I.V. catheter.

"He's an attack dog, you know," Dr. Cogan reminds the nurses. "So watch your faces." At a veterinary hospital, one cannot be too careful, and   25 nearly everyone at Angell has a scar to mark an occasion of misplaced trust. One vet has a scar between her eyes where she was greeted by a pit bull. "I thought he just banged my head," she says. "Then I reached up and felt the blood."

The nurses shave one of the Doberman's forelegs and scrub it down with an antiseptic solution, then warily insert the I.V. But the dog doesn't flinch. When a nurse draws back her hand, it is dark with blood and hair. "Oh, yum," she says, reaching for a towel.

The I.V. should help the blood circulation and limit the brain damage. Now Dr. Cogan is worried about something else. The dog's pulse hasn't matched up with his heartbeat, and through her stethoscope the beat itself sounds feeble and irregular. She hooks him up to a heart monitor, and the video screen confirms her anxieties. The graph should be as regular as the teeth on a handsaw, but these waves are spaced unevenly, and the curve of one beat doesn't always duplicate that of the next. Definite arrhythmia. Dobermans, like many large dogs, are prone to cardiomyopathy, or heart disease. Does this dog have heart disease on top of all his other problems? Or could the blow to the head have damaged the dog's heart, too?

Angell came into being in large part to protect victimized animals like the Doberman. It is run by the M.S.P.C.A. as part of the society's mission to ease the suffering of animals, but its work has recently been overshadowed by the astonishing surge of the animal rights movement. Once boldly modern, the M.S.P.C.A. has started to appear rather old-fashioned in these days when animal rights activists are raiding laboratories to release captive research animals, splattering paint on those who wear furs, demanding an end to meat eating (and even an end to pet owning), and crusading so broadly—and so effectively—that Congress now receives more mail on animal rights than on any other subject. Where once the M.S.P.C.A. had the animal welfare cause virtually to itself, a hundred advocacy groups have now taken it up—most prominently the Animal Liberation Front and People for the Ethical Treatment of Animals (PETA)—with a combined membership estimated at ten million (although the hard-core activists probably number two million at most). The M.S.P.C.A. is grateful for the publicity that the movement has brought the cause, but it is careful to distance itself from the urban-guerrilla-style violence that has drawn much of that publicity. "We absolutely do not believe in any way in violent acts—the breaking and entering, the splattering of paint, the threat, all done in the name of animals," says Dr. Thornton, the M.S.P.C.A. president. "One of the biggest parts of my job is to keep telling people we don't rob and steal. We're here to protect animals." The society, he explains categorically, is "neither antivivisectionist nor vegetarian."

Angell pointedly conducts none of the animal-based research done by most teaching hospitals. While veterinarians as a group are rarely staunch animal rights advocates, since so many of them make their living performing the research the activists seek to ban, Angell veterinarians, working outside the lab, tend to be more liberal on the topic than most. Deborah Cogan is one of the few true radicals on the topic at Angell. She gave up eating meat ten years ago, eliminated fish a few months back, and is now considering an end to eggs and dairy products as well. "I just don't want that on my conscience," she says. She obtains her few makeup items from a special catalog that provides products that have not been tested on animals. She contributes to PETA, among several other like-minded organizations, and would like to see animal-based research drastically reduced if not done away with entirely. "Most research involves some really horrible experiments," she says. She cites one ballistics experiment that involved shooting cats in the head to determine the utility of giving different types of treatment after head injuries, and a sleep-deprivation test in which cats were forced to balance for hours on a tiny perch over a pool of water. "There are a million ridiculous experiments," she says. "I'd have to take each one on a case-by-case basis." She rarely proselytizes among her peers, however. "There are too many other things to do."

As part of its mission to provide care for animals, the M.S.P.C.A. *30* maintains three hospitals in the state, of which Angell is by far the largest. The society also runs eight animal shelters, publishes a bimonthly magazine called *Animals,* operates a pet cemetery, runs a law-enforcement division, and lobbies the government for the animal protection cause. Even though Angell's interests run counter in some ways to the society's formal goal of *prevention* of cruelty (since the animals are treated after the injury or illness has occurred), the hospital is by far the most illustrious of the M.S.P.C.A.'s operations, and the most expensive.

Although Angell charges market rates for its services, it runs a significant annual deficit that in 1988 came to $2 million out of a $15 million operating budget. The M.S.P.C.A. contributed a million from its $40 million endowment; the hospital made up the rest with its own fund-raising.

Angell Memorial is named for George Thorndike Angell, the founder of the M.S.P.C.A., and although he never lived to see it, the hospital is an embodiment of his vision. A prominent Boston lawyer with a stern Yankee countenance, Angell was a legal partner of the noted abolitionist and Massachusetts politician Samuel Sewall. Born in 1823, Angell had a strong, if somewhat peculiar, sense of Victorian obligation to society. He warned people about the dangers of poisonous wallpaper, leaded pottery, and adulterated food. He was so concerned about premature burial that he campaigned vigorously for what might be called death insurance, to make sure that interment did not occur until decay had actually set in. He ventured into the field of animal welfare rather impetuously in the winter of 1868, when he read a report of a race between two horses from Boston to Worcester, a distance of some forty miles, after which both horses collapsed and died of exhaustion. He fired off an indignant letter to the Boston *Daily*

Advertiser calling for fellow citizens to band together to prevent the repetition of this sort of outrage. Within hours of its publication he was the head of a new organization called the Massachusetts Society for the Prevention of Cruelty to Animals.

While drawing on the distinctively Boston style of philanthropy, the organization followed an international movement that had been started in 1824 by the Royal Society for the Prevention of Cruelty to Animals, and brought to the United States when Henry Bergh founded the American Society for the Prevention of Cruelty to Animals in New York in 1866. (All these groups predated any organizations concerned with the welfare of *children*. In fact, it was Bergh's A.S.P.C.A. that went on to found the first child advocacy group, the New York Society for the Prevention of Cruelty to Children, as an adjunct to its animal work. That occurred in 1874, when an A.S.P.C.A. agent discovered there were no laws to prevent the appalling abuse of a child known as Little Mary Ellen and argued before the court that children should at least be entitled to the same rights as animals. A Massachusetts society followed a year later.)

George Angell began by installing public drinking fountains for horses, then called for laws against blood sports—particularly dogfighting and cockfighting. But he soon realized that simple ignorance underlay most of the cruelty, and he designed an educational campaign to deepen the public's appreciation of animals. He took it upon himself to speak for the animals, largely because they couldn't speak for themselves. For this reason, he named the society's magazine *Our Dumb Animals,* and he filled it with inspiring animal stories. He got the Boston police to distribute the magazine throughout the city. Angell also brought out the first American edition of *Black Beauty,* which he termed "the *Uncle Tom's Cabin* of the horse," and, selling it at a steep discount, he made it a national best-seller. He also formed a children's humane association, something on the order of today's Cub Scouts and Brownies, called the Bands of Mercy, in which children gathered to sing the Band of Mercy hymn, recite the Band of Mercy pledge ("I will try to be kind to all living creatures and try to protect them from cruel usage"), and dedicate themselves to the animal welfare cause.

Through these acts, Angell hoped to reap a double harvest, not only 35 improving the lot of animals but also increasing mankind's sensitivity to its own species. He once noted that none of the inmates of a Boston prison had ever owned a dog or a cat as a child.

Quaint as his attitudes seem today, he left his mark on the animal world. When he died in 1909, thirty-eight cart horses, their bridles adorned with black rosettes, followed his casket to Mount Auburn Cemetery in Cambridge.

Angell Memorial Hospital was founded by George Angell's successor, Dr. Francis H. Rowley. It originally occupied a handsome brick building on Longwood Avenue, in the heart of Boston's medical district. The structure had majestic granite pillars that attested to the inherent high-mindedness of the veterinary enterprise. "The degree of civilization can be measured by the width of human sympathy," Harvard's president A. Lawrence Lowell declared at the dedication, using terms that foreshadow the animal rights movement. "In the primitive stages of civilization, as we know them, human sympathy does not extend beyond the tribe or little family. . . . Gradually, sympathy was enlarged from the tribe to the nation, from the nation to other nations, from other nations to all mankind, and from all mankind to animals. . . . This hospital is built to commemorate [the principle] that every creature capable of suffering is entitled to the sympathy of man."

Since this was still the horse-and-buggy age, the interior was designed with the needs of the city's workhorses in mind. It featured a "horse operating room," which contained a gigantic operating table, a recovery ward for horses, two stables, a covered courtyard for tying up horses outdoors, and a drinking trough out front. Some staff members feared that the popularity of the automobile in those early years might put Angell out of business. Indeed, Harvard University's School of Veterinary Medicine had closed in 1902 for precisely this reason. But the hospital was equipped with facilities for small animals as well, including a charming cat ward with wicker baskets atop each cage for the easy transportation of feline patients. And, as industrialism proceeded, companion animals replaced horses as Angell's main line of business.

In those early days, veterinary procedures had an improvised quality that seems unimaginable by the high-tech standards of today. Surgical dressings were sterilized in the oven of the gas stove in the upstairs kitchen. And the surgeons' clothes were so fragrant with ether and Lysol fumes that they sometimes caused pet owners to fall into a dead faint while their animals were being examined.

Still, Angell was quick to make use of the advances in human medicine *40* developed at the hospitals around it, establishing its own firsts as well. In 1935, Angell's Dr. C. Lawrence Blakely pioneered open-chest surgery for diaphragmatic hernia in dogs by using a bicycle pump to keep their injured lungs expanded during operations. In 1943 came the first use of aseptic surgery on small animals. In 1958, Angell researchers were the first to trace the spread of pansteatitis in cats to red-meat tuna. In 1965, they identified dangerous side effects of using medroxyprogesterone, a drug hormone, in canine birth control. And so on through 1975, when Dr. Susan Cotter, drawing on Angell's extensive pathology records, became the first person to identify the ways in which feline leukemia is transmitted.

In that year, Angell's work load had increased to the point where larger quarters were required, and the hospital moved out of its princely quarters and across the tracks, to the more forbidding part of town that one nurse calls Gotham City.

In mysteries like the Doberman case, the veterinarian often takes on the role of the detective, eagerly interviewing witnesses who might shed some light on the case. When Dr. Cogan hears that a couple of men are waiting to see her patient, she makes a point of seeing them. "I want to get everything I can," she says.

She meets them in a spare examination room painted a pleasant rose color. Standing by the stainless-steel examining table, the two men seem like rough characters. One is white and unshaven; he has on jeans with a belt buckle in the shape of a fire truck. The other is black and athletic-looking, and wears a Mets T-shirt. They work at the Always Open towing company in Dorchester, they tell her, and hand her a business card. "Wheel lift your troubles away," it says.

The Mets fan does most of the talking. He says the dog's name is Thor, he is about four years old, and he has been a guard dog at the towing company for the last few months. The dog belongs to the company's owner, Bobby Scandone. "You should see him," the Mets fan says with a laugh. "He's as big as four of us." Cogan makes a note on her clipboard. She would like to see him very much; there is a limit to how far she can go in treatment without a deposit from the owner. But she doesn't dwell on the financial considerations now.

"The dog's been in good health?" she asks, looking up. She doesn't   45
want to lead the men, but she needs to find out if there's any evidence of long-standing heart disease.

"Oh *yeah,*" says the Mets fan, plainly amazed that anyone should even wonder.

Cogan asks how Thor got hurt, and they tell her that he had been tied up by the fence and "some guy" started pestering him. They warned him to leave the dog alone for his own good. "If you mess with Thor," the Mets fan told him, "you're history." They didn't know the man had a hockey stick. The dog started to growl, and the man hit him. "He gave Thor one real good whack," the Mets fan says, "and Thor went down and that was it." The company secretary then called Angell.

The two men want to see Thor, but Dr. Cogan says it isn't possible right now. "Will he be in overnight?" the Mets fan asks.

"Definitely overnight," Dr. Cogan replies. Right now, she's figuring that he'll be lucky to be out in two weeks—if he ever recovers at all.

"You watch yourself around Thor, Doctor," says the Mets fan. "Don't   50
put your face too close." Dr. Cogan smiles weakly and says goodbye.

Back in the I.C.U., Thor has returned from radiology and is lying down in one of the five larger cages, or "runs," along the far wall. Once again, he is curled up in the fetal position, trembling. The X-rays confirm what Cogan had thought: the skull fracture isn't too bad. They place the break over the dog's left sinus, which explains the blood running out his snout.

Out of hope as much as anything, Dr. Cogan tells a nurse to add a label to his cage: "Caution—Attack Dog, Will Bite."

Thor is only one of about forty animals in peril this afternoon in Angell's I.C.U.

Down that row of runs, the husky has started to croon again. A handsome, bushy-coated dog with the mismatched irises—one brown, one pale blue—that are characteristic of his breed, he lies unhappily on the floor, his head sheathed in an Elizabethan collar, a plastic cone that keeps him from gnawing at the bandages swathed tightly around his middle. Three nights back he came in barely able to breathe.

Dr. Virginia Rentko, a cheerful second-year resident with a thick mane of dark hair, was on duty when the husky arrived. She couldn't get a stethoscope on him, the dog was in such a state of anxiety. (His coat was so thick that it would have been difficult to hear anything anyway.) X-rays, however, showed a clear case of pneumothorax: air was leaking out of his lungs, through balloonlike pockets called blebs and bullae, and getting trapped inside his chest cavity, keeping his lungs from fully expanding.

Dr. Rentko plunged a syringe into the husky's chest to drain off the trapped air. But she filled up one syringe, then another and another; air was seeping into the animal's chest faster than the syringes could tap it off.

The next step was second only to yanking molars as Dr. Rentko's least favorite veterinary activity: she drove a sharp spike between the dog's ribs to implant a valve that would release all the trapped air. The dog was now so exhausted that Dr. Rentko needed to give him only a local anesthetic. While nurses held the husky down, she thrust the spike in through his leathery skin in what she terms a "controlled push"—careful not to push too hard and puncture the dog's lungs or, more disastrously, his heart. The spike went in like a knife. ("It's a weird sensation," she says.) She wrapped a bandage around the dog's chest to hold the valve in place, and attached the Elizabethan collar so he'd leave the bandage alone.

Dr. Rentko labeled the ailment "spontaneous pneumothorax," which is a way of saying she didn't have a clue how it came about. Generally, pneumothorax is due to long-term lung disease, such as bronchitis or asthma, but the husky showed no evidence of that. It can also result from being hit by a car, but that didn't seem likely either, because the husky's toenails were all intact. In a car accident, they usually get scraped up or ripped off in the dog's sudden skid across the pavement. Abuse couldn't be ruled out, but that usually shows up as extreme skinniness. A dog who cowers in fear when a human reaches out a hand might also have been abused.

Just the opposite with this husky. Far from retreating before Dr. Rentko, the dog was coming on too strong with her. He would try to bite her every time she came in. "He was trying to dominate me," she says. So she had to bully him right back. She put him on a short leash, took him outside the hospital, and told him to sit. To her surprise, he sat. And he heeled on the way back. There have been no further problems. Now she is concerned that perhaps she went a little far. "I think I'll go in there and love him up a little bit," Dr. Rentko says. The husky perks up—his mismatched eyes brighten—as the doctor comes near. She drives her hands into his thick fur. The husky croons.

The cage diagonally across from the husky is empty. It was occupied   60
just yesterday by a black Labrador named Puppy, something of a misnomer
since the dog was actually eight years old. The owner, James Yuille, is a real
estate developer from the fishing town of Gloucester, about an hour north
of Boston. He and his wife, Nohora, had found the dog in Puerto Rico
when he was eight months old. He had been about the only constant in
their lives. "Of course," Yuille adds, "we have no children." Yuille had been
sitting in the living room on Sunday night when Puppy suddenly yelped.
Yuille looked up and saw that the dog's front leg had buckled under him as
he ran across the floor. Yuille figured that Puppy had sprained a paw. He
rushed to the dog and was reaching down to examine him when Puppy's
other front leg buckled. Yuille grabbed the dog's chest to hold him up, and
then his back legs gave way, too. "I thought, Jesus Christ," Yuille says, "the
dog is having a heart attack." He rushed Puppy to his local veterinarian,
who, completely mystified, referred him to Angell. Yuille sped to Boston
with Puppy in his wife's lap. Ten minutes from the hospital, the dog started
having seizures. Then he lost control of his muscles altogether and lay paralyzed in Nohora Yuille's lap. By the time they reached the hospital, Puppy
was no longer breathing and his heart had stopped. "For all intents and
purposes, the dog was dead," Yuille said. "There was no heartbeat, nothing."

Dr. Sheri Siegel, a quiet-spoken young intern with a Southern accent,
was on emergency duty that time. She slapped a defibrillator paddle on the
dog's chest to administer a mild electric shock and get his heart going again.
Then she put him on a respirator to restore his breathing. She ran a myelo-
gram to see if there were any lesions on his spine that would account for the
paralysis. There was one lesion, but not the kind that would explain anything. Tick paralysis was another possibility, but there were no signs of tick
infestation in Puppy's blood. "Basically," Dr. Siegel said, "what we've got is
this huge mystery."

Yuille returned the next morning. Puppy was flat on his side in his
cage, the respirator in his mouth, nearly motionless. The dog tried to perk
up for his owner, though. He flapped his tail feebly, and strained to lift his
head. Yuille opened the cage, ran a hand down Puppy's neck, and looked
quizzically at the dog. "What? What?" he asked. "Speak to me, Puppy.
Speak." Puppy opened his mouth, as if trying to answer, but no sounds came
out. "That's a good dog," Yuille said sadly, and patted him some more.

When visiting hours in the I.C.U. were over, Yuille sat by himself in
the waiting room, his head cradled in his hands.

That afternoon, Dr. Siegel saw that the dog was doing no better and
brought the owner in to see Puppy one last time. The case was hopeless, she
told him. Together, they decided to put the dog to sleep.

Into Puppy's I.V. catheter Dr. Siegel injected Fatal Plus, a lethal dose   65
of the anesthetic sodium pentobarbital, which works by anesthetizing the
brain, then stopping the heart. In seconds, Puppy went limp. Neither Yuille
nor the doctor said anything.

Since Yuille wanted to take the body with him back to Gloucester for burial, Dr. Siegel wrapped it up in brown plastic and wheeled it out on a gurney to the sidewalk. There Yuille took Puppy in his arms and placed him carefully in the back of his pickup truck. "Thanks," he said to Dr. Siegel as he turned back to her.

"Sorry," she replied. Then he drove off.

Humans haven't *always* provided care for the animals around them, but they have tried to do so for a surprisingly long time. More than 20,000 years ago, stone-age man appreciated the rudiments of animal physiognomy, even if it was only to know where to insert a spear into a tiger for the best effect. While the ancient Greeks are usually credited with the first significant advances in the treatment of animals, the Hindus of India, in keeping with their veneration of animals, were actually the first to describe the basic principles of veterinary medicine. They did so in their earliest scriptures, the Vedas of 1800 to 1200 B.C. In 250 B.C., the Indian king Asoka established hospitals for treating horses, elephants, cattle, game birds, and fish. The wardens there maintained basic hygiene and practiced fairly sophisticated surgical techniques, including the cauterization of wounds and the use of long tubes to direct medicines through the nose directly into the animal's stomach. Veterinary practice did not advance much further until the fourth century A.D., when the Byzantines described specific veterinary ailments, including fever, digestive disorders, and tetanus. Another millennium passed before the first true veterinary school was established. That occurred in Lyons, France, in 1762, after a plague wiped out half the country's cattle population. The veterinary movement swept across Europe, and in 1793 led to the foundation in London of the first modern veterinary hospital, or, as it was called, "hippiatric infirmary," after its primary patient, the horse. A decade later, a prominent London veterinarian named Delabere Blaine opened the first of Angell's historical antecedents, an Infirmary for Dogs, which offered, as he put it in an advertisement, "the most active and judicious treatment with every attention toward [the dogs'] health and comfort, on terms always moderate, but proportionate to the expense and trouble they occasion."

The Animal Medical Center in New York City was the first veterinary hospital in the United States. It was opened as the New York Women's League for Animals in 1914, a year ahead of Angell. Today it is the only other hospital in the United States that handles anything like the range of Angell's cases. The two institutions are holdovers from a time when animal hospitals provided every service necessary to healing the sick. Since then, veterinary medicine has followed the path of human medicine and split into two separate levels of care: local clinics for regular checkups and routine treatments, and teaching hospitals for major surgery. The result is that in most cities outside of Boston and New York, animals need to be driven a considerable distance—in Chicago, it's two hours—to the nearest teaching hospital for emergency care. Some animals, presumably, don't make it.

Why aren't there more Angells? One reason is cost. Paul Gambardella, Angell's chief of staff, says, "It would take one helluva pile of dough to do what we are doing." Estimates hover around the $40 million mark to found an animal hospital today. Angell is crammed with much of the same expensive equipment as human hospitals: defibrillators ($10,000 apiece), heart monitors ($4,000), oxygen chambers ($98,000). Indeed, the equipment may have come secondhand from those human hospitals, trickling down from human medicine the way much of the new clinical information does. About the only important piece of current technology that Angell does not yet possess is the CAT scan, and it has access to one at a local hospital on Saturday mornings. Angell also has to attract the personnel to cover all the major specialties: cardiology, ophthalmology, neurology, gastroenterology, anesthesiology, oncology, radiology, surgery, pathology, even psychology, in the form of a pet psychoanalyst who comes to the hospital once a week to deal with destructive behaviors. Though veterinarians routinely work for a fraction of a physician's salary, the personnel costs for so many people are substantial. Finally, any Angell must have a sufficient endowment to cover inevitable shortfalls.

But a darker factor is also at work in limiting the number of general hospitals for animals, namely the economic rivalry between the basic providers of veterinary care. Local veterinarians are understandably anxious about passing their clients along to a large hospital that can provide all the local veterinarians' services. To avoid potential conflicts, teaching hospitals have deliberately steered clear of the routine work—spayings, immunizations—that is any vet's bread and butter. How, then, is it possible for a general hospital like Angell to do everything and still get referrals? In large part because Angell has always been careful never to keep a referral case once the initial course of treatment is complete. History has its benefits.

While Angell's expenses are certainly high, they are nothing like those of human hospitals. By the standards of human medicine, its prices read like misprints: a day in its I.C.U., $150; a total hip replacement, $1,200; heart surgery, $800. Human hospitals run on the assumption that human life is of infinite value, and charge accordingly. Veterinary hospitals are forced to make a more conservative appraisal. Unlike human hospitals, animal hospitals rarely receive what are termed "third-party payments," the whatever-it-costs insurance-company payouts that have contributed to the wild escalation in the price of human medical care. (Currently, only one national insurance company, the Animal Health Insurance Agency, offers any sort of pet medical insurance. A catastrophic coverage plan costs $40 a year, has a $250 deductible, and pays up to $2,500 an incident. A comprehensive plan, for $97.50 a year, has a $50 deductible and pays a maximum of $1,000 per injury or illness. Among Angell's clients, there are few takers; pet owners would rather take their chances.) At Angell, nearly all payments are made

70

directly out of the owner's pocket, by cash, check, MasterCard, Visa, or American Express. So the owner actually puts a price on his pet, and it's usually not that high. Paul Gambardella explains the situation this way: "As soon as John Q. Public says, 'The price is too much, I can't pay it,' that's when we go out of business." Additionally, euthanasia for animals is a legal and morally respectable option, so owners have a recourse when the costs of vital treatment start to soar, disturbing as it can be to a vet to see how quickly some owners choose to put their pets to sleep. And finally, Angell bills have not been inflated by malpractice insurance, for the simple reason that pets are legally considered personal property and therefore valued only at their cost—virtually eradicating any incentive for owners to sue.

To keep care affordable, Angell goes much shorter on staff than a human hospital. White-coated doctors do not clog its halls. During a routine operation, the surgeon will often go about his work alone, without so much as a single nurse to attend him. The vets also work cheap. Even though all Angell's veterinarians have completed college, four years of veterinary school, a year's internship, and two or three years of residency, they receive an annual salary of $50,000 tops, even while working between twelve and fourteen hours a day, six days a week. The secondhand equipment offers some savings, too. And, time being money, the course of veterinary treatment runs remarkably fast. The pets get better or they don't, but either way, they do it quickly. It is rare for a patient to remain at Angell for more than a week, and almost unheard of for one to stay a month. At Angell the current titleholder is believed to be Blanca, a spaniel hit by a bus; she resided at Angell for thirty-five days. She became so well known to the entire hospital staff that whenever she returns for treatment she makes a "grand tour" of the hospital to say hello to everyone.

But another thing speeds up the action at Angell: the hardy nature of the animals themselves. Many house pets might have been bred for the purpose of undergoing major surgery, and Angell's veterinarians continue to be impressed by the speed of their convalescence. Humans who have abdominal surgery are usually bedridden for a week or more. Pets who get spayed are typically up and about the next morning, and so frisky the chief danger is they'll pop their stitches. Animals simply don't dwell on their condition the way humans do, and, at least according to Gambardella, thinking about it appears only to prolong the ordeal.

Certainly Thor is responding promptly to treatment. He came in on a 75
Wednesday afternoon. On Thursday morning, he was still pretty much dead out in an oxygen chamber, where he had been placed to make sure his brain received sufficient oxygen and because he had been suffering from seizures. That first night, Dr. Cogan had put him on a heart-stabilizing drug called digoxin for the heart arrhythmia, and by the next morning the monitor showed that his heartbeat had returned to normal. By the end of the day, he started to lift up his head and take notice of his surroundings. By Friday

morning he began to lap a bit of water out of his water bowl. Dr. Cogan was ecstatic. "He's started to drink!" she exclaimed. That afternoon he was standing, although somewhat unsteadily. And when another dog sauntered by, he brought his nose close to give him a sniff. Dr. Cogan saw that, and the sight filled her with hope.

On Saturday night, Thor took a nip out of the night nurse. Dr. Cogan offered her condolences, but it cheered her, too. The Doberman was becoming himself again. By Monday, he was stalking about his cage, although he leaned noticeably to the left. Apparently, the vestibular region of his brain, which controls balance, had been hurt by the blow. The heartbeat remained normal, which Dr. Cogan couldn't begin to explain without running a lot more tests for which there was no money. On Tuesday, Dr. Cogan pronounced herself "really happy." Thor was eating, drinking, defecating, and urinating. There might be diminished brain function, but who knew? "It's not like he has to memorize the multiplication tables," she said. Thor was ready to go home.

Thor's "parents" came in to get him that night. Both are extremely large. Bobby Scandone has a scraggly beard and dark, curly hair, and his shoes lack shoelaces. Bobby's mother, Lucille Scandone, is nearly as large, but neater. The Scandones live together in blue-collar Winthrop, just north of Boston. Cogan had been apprehensive about them: "I wasn't sure they really cared about Thor. He was a biter, you know. I figured they thought he was just a junkyard dog." Now they sit together on a heavy wooden bench outside the waiting room. They have brought in yet another Doberman, named Venus, who is slumped on the floor beside Lucille. Venus is here to see the neurologist for a few medical problems of her own. All her hair has fallen out, giving her skin an oddly porcine appearance, and she has lost control of her back legs.

Venus suddenly lets loose a flood of urine on the floor. "Now, *why* is she wetting like this?" Lucille asks.

"She's nervous, Ma," the son says. He seems nervous, too. He says it's the coffee he drank on the way over. More likely it's Thor. He hasn't seen the dog since Friday night, and he's worried about him.

"Oh, it's been awful the last few months with her," the mother goes on, referring to Venus. "God, I hope they don't put her to sleep," she says. "I'm not ready for that." She wrings her hands. "I'm very, very upset." *80*

"It'll be all right, Ma," the son says, his eyes downcast.

The neurologist, Gillian Irving, wears lipstick and speaks with an English accent. She comes up, introduces herself, and leads Venus into the examining room. After a few minutes' examination, she diagnoses the dog as having a classic case of wobbler's disease, a degenerative disease of the spinal column. Cortisone should help, plus a harness to help lift her up onto her feet. "Oh, thank God," Lucille Scandone tells her son as they retreat to the waiting room. "I was sure she was going to make me put her to sleep." She smiles for the first time.

And then Dr. Cogan appears with Thor, who is straining powerfully on his leash. His toenails clack on the linoleum, and he draws strong huffing breaths. His ears are up, and his eyes are keen. He looks sleek and athletic, ready once again to terrorize all of Dorchester. "Hey, he looks good!" Bobby shouts. He takes the dog's leash, feels the dog pulling on it. In seconds, Thor is galloping for the door, hauling his three-hundred-pound master behind him. Bouncing lightly along behind him, Bobby might be filled with helium. "My *God!*" Bobby says. "He's got his strength back. I can't hold him!" Thor drags Bobby outside, down the ramp, and past the sculpture of the rearing horse out front. "Thaw! Thaw!" Bobby yells delightedly in his Boston accent. His mother and Venus follow. Dr. Cogan trails after all of them, worried as ever, yelling after Lucille to go easy on Venus's leash, not to put more pressure on the dog's spinal cord.

Bobby bends down to Thor and rubs him all over. "That's my boy," he says. "That's my boy." Then he looks up at Dr. Cogan, who is watching proudly from the ramp, her hands stuffed in her coat pockets against the cool evening breeze. "Thanks, Doctor," he says.

"Sure thing," she says, smiling.

It is eight-fifteen. Another long day at Angell. Dr. Cogan thinks for a moment that maybe it *is* worth it after all. Then she heads back in to check on her other cases.

85

Questions for Discussion

1. Although this article is about Angell Memorial Hospital and the nature of veterinary medicine, the author chose to structure it around the story of a badly injured Doberman. What does the information about Thor contribute to the article as a whole?
2. Given the length of this article, the editors considered cutting the story of Puppy (paragraphs 60–67). Do you think that story could have been deleted? Or do you think eliminating Puppy's story could leave readers with a false impression?
3. What are the similarities between veterinary medicine and human medicine? What are the differences? How is a veterinary hospital like Angell different from a hospital for humans?
4. Although there are more cats than dogs in the United States, dogs receive veterinary care much more frequently. How does Sedgwick explain this?
5. According to this article, "surgeons once removed three dollars in loose change from the stomach of a New England Aquarium seal." How do you think it got there? What are the implications of this information?
6. Why do people have pets? Why would someone set a dog on fire?
7. Are there any conflicts between veterinarians and physicians? What does this article reveal about vets? Why would someone work more than twelve hours a day, six days a week, for a salary that is much less than most doctors earn?

8. Why are there relatively few hospitals like Angell in the United States? What kind of veterinary care would you be able to get for a seriously injured pet in your community?

Suggestions for Writing

1. Write an essay providing instructions for the care or training of an animal with which you have personal experience.
2. Visit your local humane society and report upon neglected or mistreated animals that have been brought there.

5

Writing to Interpret Information

What does it mean when you say something is "cute"? Is there a connection between gender and intelligence? Why do people disapprove of those who are different? To answer such questions requires you to interpret information so that you can help people understand what something means, what causes it to happen, and what its consequences are. In other words, you must interpret information to reveal what is not readily apparent to others. Information can legitimately be viewed in more than one way, so different writers can come to significantly different conclusions. Interpretation is an essential skill for making sense of the world around us.

When we interpret, we need to analyze or classify information, examine causes and consequences, and define concepts by distinguishing them from others that are similar. We may also need to paraphrase, which means taking someone else's words and translating them into words of our own that can be more easily understood by our audience. Any of these ways of interpreting information can be used independently or in combination with any of the others.

Suppose you are asked on a midterm exam in earth science to explain why there is a big desert between the Sierra Nevada and the Rockies. You could begin by describing what a desert is. You might then note some of the implications of that description: "Only a few very hardy plants that have adapted well to going without water can grow in deserts, and animals that require large supplies of water, such as mammals, generally avoid deserts." All you will have done to this point is report information. This step is often necessary before you can interpret information because gaps in your readers' knowledge may hinder them from understanding what you wish to convey.

But once you begin to address *why* the area became a desert, you will have moved from reporting to interpreting. Alternatively, if you explain *how* animals can adapt successfully to living in such a harsh environment, you are also offering an interpretation. You would be interpreting, too, if you defined a concept about which people can disagree. For example, although most readers would agree that "A desert is a place where there is very little annual rainfall," they may not agree about the meaning of more abstract terms such as *environmentalist*. Hence the need for definition as a kind of interpretation.

You will find examples of several interpretive strategies in the essays in this chapter. Alan Dershowitz clarifies the meaning of freedom of speech by explaining the expression "You can't shout 'Fire!' in a crowded theater." Thus, he is interpreting information by defining what something means and what it does not mean. Catharine Stimpson reports information when she notes that there are many gay and lesbian college students and a growing body of scholarship about their interests and needs; she interprets information once she begins to explain why such students are often the victims of homophobia. Her essay illustrates what is often called *cause-and-effect analysis*.

The principal difference between interpreting and reporting is the difference between knowing something and understanding something. If you were to simply describe a perfectionist named Evelyn by showing what she looks like and how she behaves, your readers would learn something about her, but they would not understand why she is the way she is. To promote an understanding of Evelyn, you would need to explain her background—considering, for example, the way she was treated by her parents as a child. You would be *reporting* if you presented information without reasons but *interpreting* if you identified the reasons underlying that information.

Consider the article on dog food by Ann Hodgman in Chapter 4. Hodgman reports much information about the appearance and taste of dog food; however, as interesting as her report is, we are not called upon to interpret—make something else out of the information she offers; we only need to know it. Her report might prompt some readers to change their dogs' diet, but it is primarily satisfying because knowledge can be an end in itself, even when it does not have practical applications. In contrast, Stephen Jay Gould, whose work appears in this chapter, reports information about nineteenth-century research on women's brains so that he can explain (among other things) how reputable scientists can come to erroneous conclusions.

When you write to interpret information, your aim is to change the way readers view the subject, not just to increase their knowledge of the subject. For instance, Witold Rybczynski not only reports when the word *weekend* originated and where the seven-day week comes from but also shows how weekends developed as a result of numerous social forces—several of which keep people from enjoying leisure time any longer. He takes the position that "for many people weekend free time has become not a chance to escape work but a chance to create work that is more meaningful . . . in order to realize the personal satisfactions that the workplace no longer offers." If his essay convinces you that weekends have become work, you may find yourself questioning how you plan to spend next Saturday afternoon. But Rybczynski does not insist upon a change in behavior—as a writer would when writing to persuade, the subject of Chapter 9. Rybczynski's emphasis is upon changing readers' understanding of his subject, not changing the way readers live. A change in understanding may eventually inspire a change in behavior, but that is the result of suggestion rather than insistence.

Occasions for interpretation abound. In an American history course, for instance, you might be asked to write about the significance of Manifest Destiny or to explain why the United States became involved in Vietnam. In a science course you might describe a Mandelbrot set or define what a *strange attractor* is in chaos theory. Alternatively, in a humanities course you might show how jazz developed from African music or discuss why one generation favors music that seems incomprehensible to another. You might compare an early painting by Monet with one of his later works to interpret his development as an artist. Or you might analyze a short story. (We discuss this kind of interpretation more fully in Chapter 10.)

Once you have identified a tentative topic, you should test your choice before proceeding. Ask yourself: "Will I be explaining something that my readers probably do not understand?" If the answer is yes, then you know that you are about to engage in meaningful communication. You are now ready to plan what you want to say about it.

One useful way to prepare for writing interpretation is to review your topic to see what its main divisions are and then list the subtopics that develop those main points. In making decisions like these, you are analyzing. *Analysis* is a systematic way of thinking about a subject so as to divide it into the elements of which it is made. This analysis must be done consistently on some logical basis.

The opposite of analysis is *classification*. Classification is a thinking process whereby you consider a number of diverse items or pieces of information, looking for ways to group this bit with that and establish some order. As with analysis, you must have some logical basis for a classification—some principle by which you decide which things go in each group. Suppose you have a bin full of plastic "jewels" to sell. You need to price them, but it is a time-consuming task to put a price tag on each piece of plastic. So you make a sign that says,

Large $3
Medium $2
Small $1

or one that says,

Red $3
Blue $2
Green $1

But you should not make a sign that says,

Red $3
Medium $2
Square $1

Using more than one basis for classification creates confusion: How much does a medium-sized, square, red piece cost?

To take another example, suppose you look at an automobile and note that it has wheels, a body, a motor, a transmission, and so on; you have analyzed the automobile by dividing it into parts. Or you can look at all those parts of an automobile lying on a garage floor and figure out that this part belongs to the motor, that one to the transmission, and so on—that is classification. Analysis involves taking things apart, and classification involves putting things together.

In the readings that follow Sissela Bok classifies different kinds of gossipy behavior according to what effect each has upon the person gossiped about. Other writers in this chapter employ different strategies for interpretation. As noted earlier, interpreting information often involves analyzing why things happen and what the results of something can be. In "Coming of Age" Stimpson identifies the causes of homophobia on college campuses. Daniel Harris also analyzes causes in his discussion of *cuteness*. He examines the social and psychological reasons why people are drawn to what they perceive as sweetly vulnerable.

We can also use *definition* to interpret information. Cause-and-effect analysis such as Harris's would be of little use if readers did not understand key terms. For instance, Harris defines *cuteness* by showing us examples of what he means by *cute,* then by explaining how the concept of *cuteness* works, and finally by discussing the reasons that people are attracted to *cute* things. Similarly, Bok defines *gossip* before analyzing its causes and effects.

To define what you mean by a word or phrase that requires interpretation, you must go beyond quoting a dictionary definition, for quoting by itself is simply reporting information already constructed by others. To compose your own definition of a problematic term, you can proceed as follows:

• Trace its origin and show how meaning has evolved.
• Contrast it with whatever it might be confused.
• Use negation to clarify what it does *not* mean.
• Provide examples.

When you read the essays in this chapter, you may identify a number of terms that require interpretation, because they could mean different things to different people. How, for example, would you define *homophobia, privacy, anger,* or *dependence?* Or consider some of the words that appear in public policy debates. Interpreting the meaning of *multicultural,* for example, can be not only a useful service in itself but also an important preliminary for other motives for writing—such as writing to evaluate or writing to persuade.

When you get ready to interpret information for others, make a realistic appraisal of who your readers are, what they know, and what they need to be told. Remember that when you write to interpret information, you are making a conscious effort to help readers make sense of information. You are assuming the role of a teacher rather than a reporter.

SHOUTING "FIRE!"

Alan M. Dershowitz

> *Americans have often been told that freedom of speech doesn't mean being able to shout "Fire!" in a crowded theater. But where does that expression come from, and what exactly does it mean? As you read this essay, notice how Alan Dershowitz, a professor of law at Harvard University, clarifies and interprets a common expression by locating it within an historical context. Note that according to Oliver Wendell Holmes, "the character of every act depends upon the circumstances in which it is done." Consider how Dershowitz himself uses the interrelationship of act and scene when making his explanation.*

When the Reverend Jerry Falwell learned that the Supreme Court had reversed his $200,000 judgment against *Hustler* magazine for the emotional distress that he had suffered from an outrageous parody, his response was typical of those who seek to censor speech: "Just as no person may scream 'Fire!' in a crowded theater when there is no fire, and find cover under the First Amendment, likewise, no sleazy merchant like Larry Flynt should be able to use the First Amendment as an excuse for maliciously and dishonestly attacking public figures, as he has so often done."

Justice Oliver Wendell Holmes's classic example of unprotected speech—falsely shouting "Fire!" in a crowded theater—has been invoked so often, by so many people, in such diverse contexts, that it has become part of our national folk language. It has even appeared—most appropriately— in the theater: in Tom Stoppard's play *Rosencrantz and Guildenstern Are Dead* a character shouts at the audience, "Fire!" He then quickly explains: "It's all right—I'm demonstrating the misuse of free speech." Shouting "Fire!" in the theater may well be the only jurisprudential analogy that has assumed the status of a folk argument. A prominent historian recently characterized it as "the most brilliantly persuasive expression that ever came from Holmes's pen." But in spite of its hallowed position in both the jurisprudence of the First Amendment and the arsenal of political discourse, it is and was an inapt analogy, even in the context in which it was originally offered. It has lately become—despite, perhaps even because of, the frequency and promiscuousness of its invocation—little more than a caricature of logical argumentation.

The case that gave rise to the "Fire!"-in-a-crowded-theater analogy— *Schenck* v. *United States*—involved the prosecution of Charles Schenck, who was the general secretary of the Socialist Party in Philadelphia, and Elizabeth Baer, who was its recording secretary. In 1917 a jury found Schenck and Baer guilty of attempting to cause insubordination among soldiers who had been drafted to fight in the First World War. They and other party members had circulated leaflets urging draftees not to "submit to intimidation" by fighting in a war being conducted on behalf of "Wall Street's chosen few." Schenck admitted, and the Court found, that the intent of the pamphlets' "impassioned language" was to "influence" draftees to resist the draft. Interestingly, however, Justice Holmes noted that nothing in the pamphlet suggested that the draftees should use unlawful or violent means to oppose conscription: "In form at least [the pamphlet] confined itself to peaceful measures, such as a petition for the repeal of the act" and an exhortation to exercise "your right to assert your opposition to the draft." Many of its most impassioned words were quoted directly from the Constitution.

Justice Holmes acknowledged that "in many places and in ordinary times the defendants, in saying all that was said in the circular, would have been within their constitutional rights." "But," he added, "the character of every act depends upon the circumstances in which it is done." And to illustrate that truism he went on to say,

> The most stringent protection of free speech would not protect a man in falsely shouting fire in a theater, and causing a panic. It does not even protect a man from an injunction against uttering words that may have all the effect of force.

Justice Holmes then upheld the convictions in the context of a war-   5
time draft, holding that the pamphlet created "a clear and present danger" of hindering the war effort while our soldiers were fighting for their lives and our liberty.

The example of shouting "Fire!" obviously bore little relationship to the facts of the Schenck case. The Schenck pamphlet contained a substantive political message. It urged its draftee readers to *think* about the message and then—if they so chose—to act on it in a lawful and nonviolent way. The man who shouts "Fire!" in a crowded theater is neither sending a political message nor inviting his listener to think about what he has said and decide what to do in a rational, calculated manner. On the contrary, the message is designed to force action *without* contemplation. The message "Fire!" is directed not to the mind and the conscience of the listener but, rather, to his adrenaline and his feet. It is a stimulus to immediate *action*, not thoughtful reflection. It is—as Justice Holmes recognized in his follow-up sentence—the functional equivalent of "uttering words that may have all the effect of force."

Indeed, in that respect the shout of "Fire!" is not even speech, in any meaningful sense of that term. It is a *clang* sound—the equivalent of setting off a nonverbal alarm. Had Justice Holmes been more honest about his example, he would have said that freedom of speech does not protect a kid who pulls a fire alarm in the absence of a fire. But that obviously would have been irrelevant to the case at hand. The proposition that pulling an alarm is not protected speech certainly leads to the conclusion that shouting the word *fire* is also not protected. But the core analogy is the nonverbal alarm, and the derivative example is the verbal shout. By cleverly substituting the derivative shout for the core alarm, Holmes made it possible to analogize one set of words to another—as he could not have done if he had begun with the self-evident proposition that setting off an alarm bell is not free speech.

The analogy is thus not only inapt but also insulting. Most Americans do not respond to political rhetoric with the same kind of automatic acceptance expected of schoolchildren responding to a fire drill. Not a single recipient of the Schenck pamphlet is known to have changed his mind after reading it. Indeed, one draftee, who appeared as a prosecution witness, was asked whether reading a pamphlet asserting that the draft law was unjust would make him "immediately decide that you must erase the law." Not surprisingly, he replied, "I do my own thinking." A theatergoer would probably not respond similarly if asked how he would react to a shout of "Fire!"

Another important reason why the analogy is inapt is that Holmes emphasizes the factual falsity of the shout "Fire!" The Schenck pamphlet, however, was not factually false. It contained political opinions and ideas about the causes of the war and about appropriate and lawful responses to the draft. As the Supreme Court recently reaffirmed (in *Fallwell* v. *Hustler*), "The First Amendment recognizes no such thing as a 'false' idea." Nor does it recognize false opinions about the causes of or cures for war.

A closer analogy to the facts of the Schenck case might have been   10
provided by a person's standing outside a theater, offering the patrons a leaflet advising them that in his opinion the theater was structurally unsafe, and urging them not to enter but to complain to the building inspectors. That analogy, however, would not have served Holmes's argument for punishing Schenck. Holmes needed an analogy that would appear relevant to Schenck's political speech but that would invite the conclusion that censorship was appropriate.

Unsurprisingly, a war-weary nation—in the throes of a know-nothing hysteria over immigrant anarchists and socialists—welcomed the comparison between what was regarded as a seditious political pamphlet and a malicious shout of "Fire!" Ironically, the "Fire!" analogy is nearly all that survives from the Schenck case; the ruling itself is almost certainly not good law. Pamphlets of the kind that resulted in Schenck's imprisonment have been circulated with impunity during subsequent wars.

Over the past several years I have assembled a collection of instances—cases, speeches, arguments—in which proponents of censorship have maintained that the expression at issue is "just like" or "equivalent to" falsely shouting "Fire!" in a crowded theater and ought to be banned, "just as" shouting "Fire!" ought to be banned. The analogy is generally invoked, often with self-satisfaction, as an absolute argument-stopper. It does, after all, claim the high authority of the great Justice Oliver Wendell Holmes. I have rarely heard it invoked in a convincing, or even particularly relevant, way. But that, too, can claim lineage from the great Holmes.

Not unlike Falwell, with his silly comparison between shouting "Fire!" and publishing an offensive parody, courts and commentators have frequently invoked "Fire!" as an analogy to expression that is not an automatic stimulus to panic. A state supreme court held that "Holmes's aphorism . . . applies with equal force to pornography"—in particular to the exhibition of the movie *Carmen Baby* in a drive-in theater in close proximity to highways and homes. Another court analogized "picketing . . . in support of a secondary boycott" to shouting "Fire!" because in both instances "speech and conduct are brigaded." In the famous Skokie case one of the judges argued that allowing Nazis to march through a city where a large number of Holocaust survivors live "just might fall into the same category as one's 'right' to cry fire in a crowded theater."

Outside court the analogies become even more badly stretched. A spokesperson for the New Jersey Sports and Exposition Authority complained that newspaper reports to the effect that a large number of football players had contracted cancer after playing in the Meadowlands—a stadium atop a landfill—were the "journalistic equivalent of shouting fire in a crowded theater." An insect researcher acknowledged that his prediction that a certain amusement park might become roach-infested "may be tantamount to shouting fire in a crowded theater." The philosopher Sidney Hook, in a letter to *The New York Times* bemoaning a Supreme Court decision that required a plaintiff in a defamation action to prove that the offending statement was actually false, argued that the First Amendment does not give the press carte blanche to accuse innocent persons "any more than the First Amendment protects the right of someone falsely to shout fire in a crowded theater."

Some close analogies to shouting "Fire!" or setting off an alarm are, of course, available: calling in a false bomb threat; dialing 911 and falsely describing an emergency; making a loud, gunlike sound in the presence of the President; setting off a voice-activated sprinkler system by falsely shouting "Fire!" In one case in which the "Fire!" analogy was directly to the point, a creative defendant tried to get around it. The case involved a man who calmly advised an airline clerk that he was "only here to hijack the plane." He was charged, in effect, with shouting "Fire!" in a crowded theater, and his rejected defense—as quoted by the court—was as follows: "If we built fire-proof theaters and let people know about this, then the shouting of 'Fire!' would not cause panic."

Here are some more-distant but still related examples: the recent incident of the police slaying in which some members of an onlooking crowd urged a mentally ill vagrant who had taken an officer's gun to shoot the officer; the screaming of racial epithets during a tense confrontation; shouting down a speaker and preventing him from continuing his speech.

Analogies are, by their nature, matters of degree. Some are closer to the core example than others. But any attempt to analogize political ideas in a pamphlet, ugly parody in a magazine, offensive movies in a theater, controversial newspaper articles, or any of the other expressions and actions catalogued above to the very different act of shouting "Fire!" in a crowded theater is either self-deceptive or self-serving.

The government does, of course, have some arguably legitimate bases for suppressing speech which bear no relationship to shouting "Fire!" It may ban the publication of nuclear-weapon codes, of information about troop movements, and of the identity of undercover agents. It may criminalize extortion threats and conspiratorial agreements. These expressions may lead directly to serious harm, but the mechanisms of causation are very different from that at work when an alarm is sounded. One may also argue—less persuasively, in my view—against protecting certain forms of public obscenity and defamatory statements. Here, too, the mechanisms of causation are very different. None of these exceptions to the First Amendment's exhortation that the government "shall make no law . . . abridging the freedom of speech, or of the press" is anything like falsely shouting "Fire!" in a crowded theater; they all must be justified on other grounds.

A comedian once told his audience, during a stand-up routine, about the time he was standing around a fire with a crowd of people and got in trouble for yelling "Theater, theater!" That, I think, is about as clever and productive a use as anyone has ever made of Holmes's flawed analogy.

Questions for Discussion

1. What was the political context that led Oliver Wendell Holmes to make his famous remark about shouting fire in a crowded theater?
2. Why does Dershowitz believe that the fire analogy was inappropriate for the Schenck case? Why does he conclude that it was "not only inapt but also insulting"?
3. How important is the word *falsely* in the quotation from Holmes in paragraph 4? Would Holmes approve of calling "Fire" when there is a fire? How would he respond to someone who calls "Fire" out of a sincere but mistaken belief that there is a fire?
4. According to Dershowitz, what types of speech might the government have legitimate reason to suppress?
5. How convincing is the alternative analogy offered by Dershowitz in paragraph 10?
6. What evidence does Dershowitz offer to support his claim that the Holmes ruling "is almost certainly not good law"?

Suggestions for Writing

1. Take a commonly used expression (such as "You can't teach an old dog new tricks," or "Don't throw the baby out with the bath water") and

explain what it means. Try to define circumstances for which the expression would be both appropriate and inappropriate.

2. Research a Supreme Court decision involving censorship, abortion, gun control, or capital punishment. Then explain why the Court reached its decision and what the implications of that decision are for the future.

WOMEN'S BRAINS

Stephen Jay Gould

> *Stephen Jay Gould is a paleontologist who teaches at Harvard University and contributes a regular column to* Natural History. *In the following essay Gould reports information about a French scientist named Paul Broca who falsely concluded that women are less intelligent than men. As you read this essay, consider Gould's purpose in reporting the story of Broca's research. Consider also what this essay reveals about the nature of information.*

In the prelude to *Middlemarch,* George Eliot° lamented the unfulfilled lives of talented women:

> Some have felt that these blundering lives are due to the inconvenient indefiniteness with which the Supreme Power has fashioned the natures of women: if there were one level of feminine incompetence as strict as the ability to count three and no more, the social lot of women might be treated with scientific certitude.

Eliot goes on to discount the idea of innate limitation, but while she wrote in 1872, the leaders of European anthropometry were trying to measure "with scientific certitude" the inferiority of women. Anthropometry, or measurement of the human body, is not so fashionable a field these days, but it dominated the human sciences for much of the nineteenth century and remained popular until intelligence testing replaced skull measurement as a favored device for making invidious comparisons among races, classes, and sexes. Craniometry, or measurement of the skull, commanded the most attention and respect. Its unquestioned leader, Paul Broca (1824–80), professor of clinical surgery at the Faculty of Medicine in Paris, gathered a school of disciples and imitators around himself. Their work, so meticulous and apparently irrefutable, exerted great influence and won high esteem as a jewel of nineteenth-century science.

Broca's work seemed particularly invulnerable to refutation. Had he not measured with the most scrupulous care and accuracy? (Indeed, he had. I have the greatest respect for Broca's meticulous procedure. His numbers are sound. But science is an inferential exercise, not a catalog of facts. Numbers, by themselves, specify nothing. All depends upon what you do with them.) Broca depicted himself as an apostle of objectivity, a man who bowed before facts and cast aside superstition and sentimentality. He declared that "there is no faith, however respectable, no interest, however legitimate, which must not accommodate itself to the progress of human knowledge and bend before truth." Women, like it or not, had smaller brains than men and, therefore, could not equal them in intelligence. This fact, Broca argued,

George Eliot: The pen name of English novelist Mary Ann Evans (1819–1880).

may reinforce a common prejudice in male society, but it is also a scientific truth. L. Manouvrier, a black sheep in Broca's fold, rejected the inferiority of women and wrote with feeling about the burden imposed upon them by Broca's numbers:

> Women displayed their talents and their diplomas. They also invoked philosophical authorities. But they were opposed by *numbers* unknown to Condorcet or to John Stuart Mill. These numbers fell upon poor women like a sledge hammer, and they were accompanied by commentaries and sarcasms more ferocious than the most misogynist imprecations of certain church fathers. The theologians had asked if women had a soul. Several centuries later, some scientists were ready to refuse them a human intelligence.

Broca's argument rested upon two sets of data: the larger brains of men in modern societies, and a supposed increase in male superiority through time. His most extensive data came from autopsies performed personally in four Parisian hospitals. For 292 male brains, he calculated an average weight of 1,325 grams; 140 female brains averaged 1,144 grams for a difference of 181 grams, or 14 percent of the male weight. Broca understood, of course, that part of this difference could be attributed to the greater height of males. Yet he made no attempt to measure the effect of size alone and actually stated that it cannot account for the entire difference because we know, a priori, that women are not as intelligent as men (a premise that the data were supposed to test, not rest upon):

> We might ask if the small size of the female brain depends exclusively upon the small size of her body. Tiedemann has proposed this explanation. But we must not forget that women are, on the average, a little less intelligent than men, a difference which we should not exaggerate but which is, nonetheless, real. We are therefore permitted to suppose that the relatively small size of the female brain depends in part upon her physical inferiority and in part upon her intellectual inferiority.

In 1873, the year after Eliot published *Middlemarch,* Broca measured the cranial capacities of prehistoric skulls from L'Homme Mort cave. Here he found a difference of only 99.5 cubic centimeters between males and females, while modern populations range from 129.5 to 220.7. Topinard, Broca's chief disciple, explained the increasing discrepancy through time as a result of differing evolutionary pressures upon dominant men and passive women:

> The man who fights for two or more in the struggle for existence, who has all the responsibility and the cares of tomorrow, who is constantly active in combating the environment and human rivals, needs more brain than the woman whom he must protect and nourish, the sedentary woman, lacking any interior occupations, whose role is to raise children, love, and be passive.

In 1879, Gustave Le Bon, chief misogynist of Broca's school, used these data to publish what must be the most vicious attack upon women in modern scientific literature (no one can top Aristotle). I do not claim his views were representative of Broca's school, but they were published in France's most respected anthropological journal. Le Bon concluded:

> In the most intelligent races, as among the Parisians, there are a large number of women whose brains are closer in size to those of gorillas than to the most developed male brains. This inferiority is so obvious that no one can contest it for a moment; only its degree is worth discussion. All psychologists who have studied the intelligence of women, as well as poets and novelists, recognize today that they represent the most inferior forms of human evolution and that they are closer to children and savages than to an adult, civilized man. They excel in fickleness, inconstancy, absence of thought and logic, and incapacity to reason. Without doubt there exist some distinguished women, very superior to the average man, but they are as exceptional as the birth of any monstrosity, as, for example, of a gorilla with two heads; consequently, we may neglect them entirely.

Nor did Le Bon shrink from the social implications of his views. He was horrified by the proposal of some American reformers to grant women higher education on the same basis as men:

> A desire to give them the same education, and, as a consequence, to propose the same goals for them, is a dangerous chimera. . . . The day when, misunderstanding the inferior occupations which nature has given her, women leave the home and take part in our battles: on this day a social revolution will begin, and everything that maintains the sacred ties of the family will disappear.

Sound familiar?*

I have reexamined Broca's data, the basis for all this derivative pronouncement, and I find his numbers sound but his interpretation ill-founded, to say the least. The data supporting his claim for increased difference through time can be easily dismissed. Broca based his contention on the samples from L'Homme Mort alone—only seven male and six female skulls in all. Never have so little data yielded such far ranging conclusions.

In 1888, Topinard published Broca's more extensive data on the Parisian hospitals. Since Broca recorded height and age as well as brain size, we may use modern statistics to remove their effect. Brain weight decreases with age, and Broca's women were, on average, considerably older than his

---

*When I wrote this essay, I assumed that Le Bon was a marginal, if colorful, figure. I have since learned that he was a leading scientist, one of the founders of social psychology, and best known for a seminal study on crowd behavior, still cited today (*La psychologie des foules*, 1895), and for his work on unconscious motivation.

men. Brain weight increases with height, and his average man was almost half a foot taller than his average woman. I used multiple regression, a technique that allowed me to assess simultaneously the influence of height and age upon brain size. In an analysis of the data for women, I found that, at average male height and age, a woman's brain would weigh 1,212 grams. Correction for height and age reduces Broca's measured difference of 181 grams by more than a third, to 113 grams.

I don't know what to make of this remaining difference because I   *10* cannot assess other factors known to influence brain size in a major way. Cause of death has an important effect: degenerative disease often entails a substantial diminution of brain size. (This effect is separate from the decrease attributed to age alone.) Eugene Schreider, also working with Broca's data, found that men killed in accidents had brains weighing, on average, 60 grams more than men dying of infectious diseases. The best modern data I can find (from American hospitals) records a full 100-gram difference between death by degenerative arteriosclerosis and by violence or accident. Since so many of Broca's subjects were elderly women, we may assume that lengthy degenerative disease was more common among them than among the men.

More importantly, modern students of brain size still have not agreed on a proper measure for eliminating the powerful effect of body size. Height is partly adequate, but men and women of the same height do not share the same body build. Weight is even worse than height, because most of its variation reflects nutrition rather than intrinsic size—fat versus skinny exerts little influence upon the brain. Manouvrier took up this subject in the 1880s and argued that muscular mass and force should be used. He tried to measure this elusive property in various ways and found a marked difference in favor of men, even in men and women of the same height. When he corrected for what he called "sexual mass," women actually came out slightly ahead in brain size.

Thus, the corrected 113-gram difference is surely too large; the true figure is probably close to zero and may as well favor women as men. And 113 grams, by the way, is exactly the average difference between a 5 foot 4 inch and a 6 foot 4 inch male in Broca's data. We would not (especially us short folks) want to ascribe greater intelligence to tall men. In short, who knows what to do with Broca's data? They certainly don't permit any confident claim that men have bigger brains than women.

To appreciate the social role of Broca and his school, we must recognize that his statements about the brains of women do not reflect an isolated prejudice toward a single disadvantaged group. They must be weighed in the context of a general theory that supported contemporary social distinctions as biologically ordained. Women, blacks, and poor people suffered the same disparagement, but women bore the brunt of Broca's argument because he had easier access to data on women's brains. Women were singularly denigrated but they also stood as surrogates for other disenfranchised groups. As one of Broca's disciples wrote in 1881: "Men of the black races have a brain scarcely heavier than that of white woman." This juxtaposition extended into many other realms of anthropological argument, particularly to claims that, anatomically and emotionally, both women and blacks were like white children—and that white children, by the theory of recapitulation, represented an ancestral (primitive) adult stage of human evolution. I do not regard as empty rhetoric the claim that women's battles are for all of us.

Maria Montessori did not confine her activities to educational reform for young children. She lectured on anthropology for several years at the University of Rome, and wrote an influential book entitled *Pedagogical Anthropology* (English edition, 1913). Montessori was no egalitarian. She supported most of Broca's work and the theory of innate criminality proposed by her compatriot Cesare Lombroso. She measured the circumferences of children's heads in her schools and inferred that the best prospects had bigger brains. But she had no use for Broca's conclusions about women. She discussed Manouvrier's work at length and made much of his tentative claim that women, after proper correction of the data, had slightly larger brains than men. Women, she concluded, were intellectually superior, but men had prevailed heretofore by dint of physical force. Since technology has abolished force as an instrument of power, the era of women may soon be upon us: "In such an epoch there will really be superior human beings, there will really be men strong in morality and in sentiment. Perhaps in this way the reign of women is approaching, when the enigma of her anthropological superiority will be deciphered. Woman was always the custodian of human sentiment, morality and honor."

This represents one possible antidote to "scientific" claims for the constitutional inferiority of certain groups. One may affirm the validity of biological distinctions but argue that the data have been misinterpreted by prejudiced men with a stake in the outcome, and that disadvantaged groups are truly superior. In recent years, Elaine Morgan has followed this strategy in her *Descent of Woman,* a speculative reconstruction of human prehistory from the woman's point of view—and as farcical as more famous tall tales by and for men.

I prefer another strategy. Montessori and Morgan followed Broca's philosophy to reach a more congenial conclusion. I would rather label the whole enterprise of setting a biological value upon groups for what it is: irrelevant and highly injurious. George Eliot well appreciated the special tragedy that biological labeling imposed upon members of disadvantaged groups. She expressed it for people like herself—women of extraordinary talent. I would apply it more widely—not only to those whose dreams are flouted but also to those who never realize that they may dream—but I cannot match her prose. In conclusion, then, the rest of Eliot's prelude to *Middlemarch:*

The limits of variation are really much wider than anyone would imagine from the sameness of women's coiffure and the favorite love stories in prose and verse. Here and there a cygnet is reared uneasily among the ducklings in the brown pond, and never finds the living stream in fellowship with its own oary-footed kind. Here and there is born a Saint Theresa, foundress of nothing, whose loving heartbeats and sobs after an unattained goodness tremble off and are dispersed among hindrances instead of centering in some long-recognizable deed.

Questions for Discussion

1. Why do you think Mary Ann Evans chose to publish under a man's name? And why do you think Gould chose to open and close his article with references to one of her books?
2. When reporting the accomplishments of the French scientist Paul Broca, Gould declares that data were carefully collected and that the numbers are reliable. But he then observes, "Numbers, by themselves, specify nothing. All depends upon what you do with them." How was Broca misled by his numbers? What did he fail to take into account?
3. What does Gould mean when he supports the claim that "women's battles are for all of us"?
4. What is the significance of Gould's footnote?
5. This article includes several long quotations. Are they all necessary? Which had the most impact upon you?

Suggestions for Writing

1. Gould's essay demonstrates, among other things, how women have been victimized by false assumptions made by men. Write a report about discrimination against women in school, in sports, or in the workplace.
2. Do research on either George Eliot or Paul Broca and interpret the data you gather to explain why she or he became a respected authority. Be sure to reveal your sources, and try to consult at least one work written by the person you are investigating.

COMING-OF-AGE

Catharine R. Stimpson

The author of numerous books and articles, Catharine R. Stimpson is University Professor at Rutgers University and a former president of the Modern Language Association, one of the country's most prestigious scholarly organizations. Her credentials would be familiar to the original audience of the following article, which first appeared in a journal read principally by college professors and administrators. As you read, consider what Stimpson achieves by writing in the first person about gays and lesbians in higher education.

On Sunday, April 25, 1993, hundreds of thousands of people marched in Washington, D.C., for gay and lesbian rights. People with AIDS who could no longer walk waved from trolleys and flat-bed trucks. Children of gay and lesbian parents sauntered down the avenue or slept in strollers. Parents of gay and lesbian children carried banners that publicized pride in their kids. Middle-aged people who had bussed into Washington in the 1960s to demonstrate against the Vietnam War applauded gays and lesbians in uniform. Adding to the good cheer were two women, professors without tenure, running down Pennsylvania Avenue, waving placards. "Emily Dickinson Scholars for Gay and Lesbian Rights," the placards read, and then, adapting a Dickinson line, "We Dwell in Possibilities."

Possibly, possibly there is an educator in America who was unaware of the march; who, on this bright Sunday, was attending only to golf bag or barbecue or church pew or briefcase full of official prose. If so, such an educator should get cracking and get with it. For the march signified the coming-of-age of the gay, lesbian, and bisexual movement, a development that carries a cargo of consequences for the United States and higher education.

For several years, higher education has taken an overt part in this development. People are coming out of the closet, although students have been far more open than faculty and administrators. Indeed, some students tell me that they have never been *in* the closet. Some institutions have published a systematic review of their treatment of sexual minorities. Two examples: *In Every Classroom* (1989), a report from Rutgers, my university, and *From Invisibility to Inclusion: Opening the Doors for Lesbians and Gay Men at the University of Michigan* (1991). The scholarship about gays and lesbians has gotten so big that it has outgrown the label of "pioneering." A major new anthology, *The Lesbian and Gay Studies Reader* (Henry Abelove, Michèle Aina Barale, and David M. Halperin, eds., Routledge, 1993), has 14 single-spaced pages of "Suggestions for Further Reading," all dated before 1993. (In the spirit of full disclosure, I should add that I have an essay about Gertrude Stein in the volume.)

All this lends credence to the argument that higher education dwells more decently with gays and lesbians than other social institutions do, especially if a college or university is secular and urbane. The campus is, however, hardly immune from pervasive homophobia and resistance to gays and lesbians. During the last few years, those who supported the ban on gays and lesbians in R.O.T.C. were forerunners of the Nunn Corps, those who now support the ban on gays and lesbians in the military at large. Some studies find that one-half to three-quarters of gay and lesbian students have been verbally harassed because of their sexuality. Committees are meeting, asking if a course about gays and lesbians should be approved, if the teacher of such a course should be hired or rehired. Bigots—some temperate, some intemperate—sit on these committees.

Inexorably, as the gay and lesbian movement has grown, so has organized opposition to it. Today, the noisiest and most vitriolic opponents are leaders of the political and religious Hard Right. To them, the queer is devil, as in let's-beat-the-devil fund-raising and vote-getting drives. "Pro-straight" is supplementing "pro-life" as a rallying cry. The dynamic tension between action and manipulative reaction is such that the struggle over gay and lesbian acceptance in civil society will be one of the great issues of this decade.

One reason why the tension is so dynamic is the ferocity and pervasiveness of the prejudice against gays and lesbians. Higher education will never exempt itself from prejudice until we dig up its roots. As I tug at them, I am amazed at their number, depth, and entanglements with each other. They burrow below gays and lesbians as well as heterosexuals. Some roots are theological, the picture of the homosexual as sinful citizen of Sodom and Gomorrah. Other roots are legal, the picture of the homosexual as criminal. Still others are medical, the picture of the homosexual as sick. Another major new anthology, *Lesbians, Gay Men, and the Law* (William B. Rubenstein, ed., New Press, 1993), reminds us that in 1967, the Supreme Court of the United States affirmed a 1952 Immigration and Nationality Act that excluded aliens if they were homosexual because homosexuals were psychopaths. Not straight? Into the straightjacket with you!

Still other roots are social, the deep belief that homosexuals, because they sometimes sleep with members of the same sex, cannot have children, do not want children, and will destroy "the family." I recollected this belief the other day with some anger and irony. Two women had dropped by the house where I was having dinner. One was a widow; one had never been married. They had met during their careers as police officers. They were both Catholic. Each planned to have one child or more, which they would raise together as a family. One woman had given birth three months before to the first child, a baby girl, now in a stroller that was a Maserati among strollers. Dressed in a sparkling white dress, socks, shoes, and bonnet, the baby blinked and smiled; cosseted, wanted, adored. The mothers were already planning her college trust fund.

Still other roots of our prejudice are psychological, a fear of gays and lesbians, an anxiety that they will contaminate and pollute the individual body and the body politic. AIDS confronted a pre-existing cultural condition. As contaminant and pollutant, the homosexual is felt to be sexually voracious and aggressive. A few years ago, before giving a lecture in a liberal arts college in upstate New York, I had lunch with the director of its honors program. He had a dilemma, he said. He was taking members of the program on a field trip to Canada, but one female student would have to stay home. Why? She had recently told another student she was a lesbian. The other student had then snitched to him. The students were going to share bedrooms on the field trip and the lesbian would try to get into bed with her roommates. He couldn't let this happen. Nothing I said could uproot his self-image as paternal protector of female virtue. The heterosexual fear of the homosexual *out there* is so wanton and so stubborn that it seems a defense mechanism against something else—perhaps homosexual desires *in here, within the self.* Given the polymorphous and shifting nature of our sexualities, it is likely that everyone, at one time or another, has felt some twinge of same-sex attraction. But what to do with forbidden desire? Repression, denial, and projection onto a villain *out there* are in our bag of tricky remedies.

All of these roots share two features. First, ignorance fertilizes them. Next, all are a consequence of the human practice of setting up two groups: me and my group; you and yours. My group is the real community; your group, The Other. My group is normal; your group abnormal. My group is good; your group bad. My group is in; your group out. My group is clean; your group dirty and in need of cleansing. This practice has its uses and its virtues, but it is also painful, useless, and literally murderous. For violence—physical, psychological, cultural, social—is the cement that holds hierarchies together. It is no accident that gay-bashing went up 31 percent between 1990 and 1991 in five major American cities.

Let us suppose, in a Utopian gesture, that we in higher education can possibly dig up the roots of our prejudice, examine them, and then throw them onto a social and cultural compost heap where they will decay and reform as new, rich soil. What then will happen to us? We will, I believe, be able to see ourselves more clearly. A body of scholarship, research, and syllabi will help us. Heterosexuals will not be members of a monolithic and normative block; homosexuals will not be members of a monolithic and hateful block. All of us will be together as individuals in history. We will share the memory of a stigma and the realities of our diversity. No gay or lesbian will be perfect. Nor will any heterosexual or bisexual. Each will have some moral and psychological work to do. Some will be racist; some greedy; some lazy; some cruel; some infantile; some fatuous; some show-offs. Everyone will be pretty ordinary.

We will, finally, dwell in kinder and more peaceable communities, that old Utopian promise. As crucially, we will have abandoned the temptations of dwelling in vicious communities. In April, I not only marched in Washington. I also went to the New York Public Library to see an extraordinary exhibit that had traveled across America, *"Degenerate Art": The Fate of the Avant-Garde in Nazi Germany.* Its subject was the Nazi hatred of modernism that led to the burning of books and pictures, among them serious books about homosexuality. The exhibit showed a nation that became a totalitarian state with a commensurate art. This art praised clarity, order, and a pure hatred of The Other, the different, the non-German. I am wary about polarities and binary oppositions, but higher education has a simple decision to make about the lesbian and gay movement. Will lesbians and gays walk cheerfully down our streets, or will higher education act like a Nazi in a tweed jacket? We have met the choice, and it is ours.

Questions for Discussion

1. Consider how the first paragraph begins with a reference to "hundreds of thousands of people," people who are then divided into smaller groups: people with AIDS, children, parents, and even "professors without tenure." Do you see a pattern governing the way Stimpson divides the crowd at the march she describes?
2. Stimpson claims that the growth of gay, lesbian, and bisexual activism "carries a cargo of consequences for the United States and higher education." Had she elaborated upon these consequences, she would have offered a cause-and-effect analysis that emphasized effects. Instead, she turns to discussing what causes prejudice. If sexual minorities continue to assert themselves, what do you think the consequences will be?
3. In paragraph 3 Stimpson reveals that she has an essay in one of the books she draws attention to. Why does she make this disclosure? How were you affected by it?
4. According to Stimpson, what are the causes of prejudice against gays, lesbians, and bisexuals? What do these causes have in common?
5. In her conclusion Stimpson comments upon the Nazi hatred of modernism and the avant-garde. How does she link these comments to her discussion of sexual minorities "coming of age"? What does she accomplish by doing so?

Suggestions for Writing

1. What happens at your school when a student or professor is openly gay or lesbian? Does that person's life become easier, become more difficult, or remain the same? Write an essay discussing the consequences of "coming out" for the individual and for the school.
2. Write an essay discussing the consequences of heterosexuality, including public displays of heterosexual affection.

WAITING FOR THE WEEKEND

Witold Rybczynski

> *In the following article Witold Rybczynski chronicles the development of an idea—the right to leisure with liberty. Using definition, Rybczynski interprets historical information to explain how and why we spend our weekends the way we do. If you have ever worried that you hadn't accomplished anything over the weekend or felt that your weekend passed too quickly, you may benefit from learning more about how leisure differs from liberty.*

The word "weekend" started life as "week-end" but lost its hyphen somewhere along the way, ceasing to be merely the end of the week and acquiring, instead, an autonomous and sovereign existence. "Have a good weekend," we say to one another—never "Have a good week." Where once the week consisted of weekdays and Sunday, it now consists of weekdays and weekend. Ask most people to name the first day of the week and they will answer, Monday, of course; fifty years ago the answer would have been Sunday. Wall calendars still show Sunday as the first day of the week, and children are taught the days of the week starting with Sunday, but how long will these conventions last? Sunday, once the day of rest, has become merely one of two days of what is often strenuous activity. Although we continue to celebrate the traditional religious and civic holidays—holy days—these now account for only a small portion of our total nonworking days, and are overshadowed by the 104 days of secular weekends.

For most of us life assumes a different rhythm on the weekend; we sleep in, cut the grass, wash the car. We also go to the movies, especially during hot weather. We travel. And of course we exercise and play games. Some of these pastimes, like tennis, have an old history and a newfound popularity; others, like whitewater canoeing, windsurfing, and hang-gliding, are more recent. Most are distinguished from nineteenth-century recreations such as croquet and golf by their relative arduousness and even riskiness.

Although the weekend is a time for sports, for shopping, and for household chores, it is foremost a manifestation of the structure of our leisure. The chief *Oxford English Dictionary* definition of leisure is "time which one can spend as one pleases." That is, "free" time. But in one of his popular columns in *The Illustrated London News*—a Saturday paper—G. K. Chesterton pointed out that leisure should not be confused with liberty. Contrary to most people's expectations, the presence of the first by no means assures the availability of the second. This confusion arose, according to Chesterton, because the term "leisure" is used to describe three different things: "The first is being allowed to do something. The second is being allowed to do anything. And the third (and perhaps most rare and precious) is being allowed to do nothing." The first, he acknowledged, was the most common form of leisure, and the one that of late—he was writing in the early 1890s—had shown the greatest quantitative increase. The second—the liberty to fashion what one willed out of one's leisure time—was more unusual and tended to be the province of artists and other creative individuals. It was the third, however, that was obviously his favorite, because it allowed idleness—in Chesterton's view, the truest form of leisure.

Perhaps only someone as portly as Chesterton (Maisie Ward, his biographer, estimated that he weighed almost 300 pounds) could rhapsodize over idleness. More likely, inactivity attracted him because he was the least lazy of men; his bibliography lists more than a hundred published books—biographies, novels, essays, poetry, and short stories. He was also a magazine editor and a lecturer and broadcaster. Although he managed to cram all this into a relatively short life (he died at sixty-two), it was, as his physique would suggest, a life replete with material enjoyments, and surprisingly unhurried. Not a life of leisure, perhaps, but one carried out at a leisurely pace.

Chesterton's observation that modern society provided many opportunities for leisure but made it "more and more easy to get some things and impossible to get others" continues to be true. Should you want to play tennis or golf, for example, courts and courses abound. Fancy a video? There are plenty of specialty stores, lending libraries, and mail-order clubs. Lepidopterists, however, will have a difficult time finding unfenced countryside in which to practice their avocation. If your pastime is laying bricks and you do not have a rural estate, as Winston Churchill had, you will not find a bricklaying franchise at your neighborhood mall. Better take up golf instead.

Chesterton argued that a man compelled by lack of choice—or by social pressure—to play golf when he would rather be attending to some solitary hobby was not so different from the slave who might have several hours of leisure while his overseer slept but had to be ready to work at a moment's notice. Neither could be said to be the master of his leisure. Both had free time but not freedom. To press this parallel further, have we become enslaved by the weekend?

At first glance it is an odd question, for surely it is our work that enslaves us, not our free time. We call people who become obsessed by their jobs workaholics, but we don't have a word for someone who is possessed by recreation. Maybe we should. I have many acquaintances for whom weekend activities seem more important than workaday existence, and who behave as if the week were merely an irritating interference in their real, extracurricular lives. I sometimes have the impression that to really know these weekend sailors, mountain climbers, and horsewomen, I would have to accompany them on their outings and excursions—see them in their natural habitat, so to speak. But would I see a different person, or merely the same one governed by different conventions of comportment, behavior, accoutrement, and dress?

I'm always charmed by old photographs of skiers which show groups of people in what appear to be street clothes, with uncomplicated pieces of bent wood strapped to sturdy walking boots. These men and women have a playful and unaffected air. Today every novice is caparisoned in skin-tight spandex, like an Olympic racer, and even cross-country skiing, a simple enough pastime, has been infected by a preoccupation with correct dress, authentic terminology, and up-to-date equipment. This reflects an attitude toward play which is different from what it was in the past. Most outdoor sports, once simply muddled through, are now undertaken with a high degree of seriousness. "Professional" used to be a word that distinguished someone who was paid for an activity from the sportsman; today the word has come to denote anyone with a high degree of proficiency; "professional-quality" equipment is available to—and desired by—all. Conversely, "amateur," a wonderful word literally meaning "lover," has been degraded to mean a rank beginner or anyone without a certain level of skill. "Just an amateur," we say; it is not, as it once was, a compliment.

The lack of carelessness in our recreation, the sense of obligation to get things right, and the emphasis on protocol and decorum do represent an enslavement of a kind. People used to "play" tennis; now they "work" on their backhand. It is not hard to imagine what Chesterton would have thought of such dedication; this is just the sort of laborious pursuit of play that he so often derided. "If a thing is worth doing," he once wrote, "it is worth doing badly."

Chesterton held the traditional view that leisure was different from the ¹⁰ type of recreation typically afforded by the modern weekend. His own leisure pastimes included an eclectic mix of the unfashionable and the bohemian—sketching, collecting weapons, and playing with the cardboard cutouts of his toy theater. Leisure was the opportunity for personal, even idiosyncratic, pursuits, not for ordered recreation; it was for private reverie rather than for public spectacles. If a sport was undertaken, it was for the love of playing—not of winning, nor even of playing well. Above all, free time was to remain that: free of the encumbrance of convention, free of the need for business, free for the "noble habit of doing nothing at all." That hardly describes the modern weekend.

WORK VERSUS LEISURE

What is the meaning of the weekday-weekend cycle? Is it yet another symptom of the standardization and bureaucratization of everyday life that social critics such as Lewis Mumford and Jacques Ellul have warned about? Is the weekend merely the cunning marketing ploy of the materialist culture, a device to increase consumption? Is it a deceptive placebo to counteract the boredom and meaninglessness of the workplace?

Or is this the heralded Leisure Society? If so, it is hardly what was anticipated. The decades leading up to the 1930s saw a continuing reduction in the number of hours in the workweek, from just under sixty to just under fifty, and during the Great Depression even below thirty-five. There was every reason to think that this trend would continue and workdays would grow shorter and shorter. This, and widespread automation, would eventually lead to universal leisure. Not everyone agreed that this would be a good thing; there was much speculation about what people would do with their newfound freedom, and some psychologists worried that universal leisure would really mean universal boredom. Hardly, argued the optimists; it would provide the opportunity for self-improvement, adult education, and a blossoming of the creative arts. Others were less sanguine about the prospects for creative ease in a society that had effectively glorified labor.

Universal leisure did not come to pass, or at least it did not arrive in the expected form. For one thing, the workday appears to have stabilized at about eight hours. Automation has reduced jobs in certain industries, as was predicted, but overall employment has increased, not decreased, although not necessarily in high-paying jobs. Women have entered the work force, with the result that more, not fewer, people are working; since housework still needs to be done, it can be argued that in many families there is really less leisure than before. On the other hand, the development of the weekend has caused a redistribution of leisure time, which for many people has effectively shortened the length of the workweek. This redistribution, coupled with more disposable income, has made it possible to undertake recreation in a variety of unexpected ways—some creative, some not—and do so throughout the year instead of at annual intervals.

All these developments have called into question the traditional relationship between leisure and work, a relationship about which our culture has always been ambivalent. Generally speaking, there are two opposing schools of thought. On the one hand is the ideal—held by thinkers as disparate as Karl Marx and the Catholic philosopher Josef Pieper—of a society increasingly emancipated from labor. This notion echoes the Aristotelian view that the goal of life is happiness, and that leisure, as distinguished from amusement and recreation, is the state necessary for its achievement. "It is commonly believed that happiness depends on leisure." Aristotle wrote in his *Ethics,* "because we occupy ourselves so that we may have leisure, just as we make war in order that we may live at peace." Or, to put it more succinctly, as did the title of Loverboy's 1981 hit song, we are "Working for the Weekend."

Opposed to this is the more modern (so-called Protestant) work ethic 15 that values labor for its own sake, and sees its reduction—or, worse, its elimination—as an unthinkable degradation of human life. "There is no substitute for work except other serious work," wrote Lewis Mumford, who considered that meaningful work was the highest form of human activity. According to this view, work should be its own reward, whether it is factory work, housework, or a workout. Leisure, equated with idleness, is suspect; leisure without toil, or disconnected from it, is altogether sinister. The weekend is not free time but break time—an intermission.

But I am getting ahead of myself. I want first to examine something that will shed light on the relation between work and leisure: how we came to adopt a rigorous division of our everyday lives into five days of work and two of play, and how the weekend became the chief temporal institution of the modern age. And how, in turn, this universally accepted structure has affected the course and nature of our leisure—whether it involves playing golf, laying bricks, or just daydreaming.

THE INVENTION OF THE WEEK

Our chief occasion for leisure—the weekend—is the direct product of the mechanical practice of measuring time. Counting days in chunks of seven now comes so naturally that it's easy to forget that this is an unusual way to mark the passage of time. Day spans the interval between the rising and the setting of the sun; the twenty-four-hour day is the duration between one dawn and the next. The month measures—or once did—the time required for the moon to wax, become full, and wane; and the year counts one full cycle of the seasons. What does the week measure? Nothing. At least, nothing visible. No natural phenomenon occurs every seven days— nothing happens to the sun, the moon, or the stars. The week is an artificial, man-made interval.

Generally speaking, our timekeeping is flexible, full of inconsistencies. The length of the day varies with the season; the duration of the month is

irregular. Adjustments need to be made: every four years we add a day to February; every 400 years we add a day to the centurial year. The week, however, is exactly seven days long, now and forever. We say that there are fifty-two weeks in a year, but that is an approximation, since the week is not a subdivision of either the month or the year. The week mocks the calendar and marches relentlessly and unbroken across time, paying no attention to the seasons. The British scholar F. H. Colson, who in 1926 wrote a fascinating monograph on the subject, described the week as an "intruder." It is an intruder that arrived relatively late. The week emerged as the final feature of what became the Western calendar sometime in the second or third century A.D., in ancient Rome. But it can be glimpsed in different guises— not always seven days long, and not always continuous—in many earlier civilizations.

Seven appeared as a magical number among the Babylonians, as early as the third millennium B.C., and played an important role in their calendar. There were seven heavenly bodies with apparent motion in the sky: the "erring" seven, the seven "wanderers"—that is, the seven planets of antiquity (including the sun and the moon). Whether they suggested the belief in the magic number or merely reinforced it is not clear. In any case, as astronomy—and astrology—spread from Babylonia to Greece, Egypt, and Rome, the seven heavenly bodies became identified with the great gods of the pantheon.

At the time that the planetary week became popular in Rome, there was already a seven-day week in place: the Judaic Sabbath observance. It is possible—although the idea is disputed by many scholars—that the Jews *20* adopted this method of timekeeping during their exile in Babylonia in the sixth century B.C., and converted the septenary fascination into their Sabbath. The adoption of a continuous seven-day period independent of the lunar cycle was unusual, and exactly why the Jews evolved this mechanism is unclear. According to the Old Testament, the Sabbath was "their" day, given to them—and them alone—by Jehovah. Unquestionably, its very singularity appealed to the exiled Jews as a way of differentiating themselves from the alien Babylonian Gentiles who surrounded them. In any case, that the Sabbath occurred on every seventh day, irrespective of the seasons, was a powerful idea, for it overrode all other existing calendars.

The origin of the planetary week is obscure as regards place and time. Dion Cassius, a Roman historian who lived in the third century A.D., thought that the planetary week was conceived in Egypt, but modern scholars dispute this claim; more likely it was a Hellenistic° practice that migrated to Rome. He also maintained that the planetary week was a relatively recent invention. There is some evidence, however, of a planetary week during the Augustan period, 200 years before, and it may have originated even earlier. What is certain is that by Dion's era the habit of measuring time in cycles of seven days was already established in private life throughout the Roman Empire.

The week was many things to many people, sometimes many things to the same people. It was magical and practical both. A superstition at first, it survived as a social convention, much as shaking hands with the right hand has endured because there is a need for a gesture to represent friendly feelings to a stranger. The week was a short unit of time around which people could organize their lives, their work, and their leisure. At the same time, the week was a simple and memorable device for relating everyday activities to supernatural concerns, whether these involved observing a commandment from Jehovah, commemorating Christ's resurrection, receiving the influence of a planetary deity, or, just to be safe, all three.

The roots of the week lie deep, too deep to understand fully. An air of mystery surrounds the week; perhaps that, too, is a part of its appeal. It is an observance that has been distilled over centuries of use, molded through common belief and ordinary usage. Above all, it is a *popular* practice that took hold without magisterial sanction. This, more than anything else, explains its durability. Less an intruder than an unofficial guest, the week was invited in through the kitchen door, and has become a friend of the family—a useful friend, for whatever else it did, the seven-day cycle provided a convenient structure for the repetitive rhythm of daily activities. It included not only a day for worship but also a day for baking bread, for washing, for cleaning house, for going to market—and for resting. Surely this over-and-over quality has always been one of the attractions of the week—and of the weekend. "Once a week" is one of the commonest measures of time. The

---

Hellenistic: Of or relating to ancient Greek culture.

planetary week is not a grand chronometer of celestial movements or a gauge of seasonal changes. It is something both simpler and more profound: a measure of ordinary, everyday life.

FROM DAY OFF TO DAYS OFF

The *Oxford English Dictionary* finds the earliest recorded use of the word "weekend" in an 1879 issue of *Notes and Queries,* an English magazine. "In Staffordshire, if a person leaves home at the end of his week's work on the Saturday afternoon to spend the evening of Saturday and the following Sunday with friends at a distance," the magazine citation goes, "he is said to be spending his *week-end* at So-and-so." This is obviously a definition, which suggests that the word had only recently come into use. It is also important to note that the "week's work" is described as ending on the Saturday afternoon. It was precisely this early ending to the week that produced a holiday period of a day and a half—the first weekend. This innovation— and it was a uniquely British one—occurred in roughly the third quarter of the nineteenth century.

Throughout the eighteenth century the workweek ended on Saturday   *25* evening; Sunday was the weekly day off. The Reformation, and later Puri- tanism, had made Sunday the weekly holy day in an attempt to displace the saints' days and religious festivals of Catholicism (the Catholic Sunday was merely one holy day among many). Although the taboo on work was more or less respected, the strictures of Sabbatarianism that prohibited merriment and levity on the Lord's Day were rejected by most Englishmen, who saw the holiday as a chance to drink, gamble, and generally have a good time.

For most people Sunday was the only official weekly holiday, but this did not necessarily mean that the life of the average British worker was one of unremitting toil. Far from it. Work was always interrupted to commem- orate the annual feasts of Christmas, New Year, and Whitsuntide (the week beginning with the seventh Sunday after Easter). These traditional holidays were universally observed, but the length of the breaks varied. Depending on local convention, work stopped for anywhere from a few days to two weeks. There were also communal holidays associated with special, occa- sional events such as prizefights, horse races, and other sporting competi- tions, and also fairs, circuses, and traveling menageries. When one of these attractions arrived in a village or town, regular work more or less stopped while people flocked to gape and marvel at the exotic animals, equestrian acrobats, and assorted human freaks and oddities.

The idea of spontaneously closing up shop or leaving the workbench for the pursuit of pleasure may strike the modern reader as irresponsible, but the eighteenth-century worker the line between work and play was blurred. Many recreational activities were directly linked to the workplace, since trade guilds often organized their own outings and had their own singing and drinking clubs and their own preferred taverns.

Eighteenth-century workers had, as Hugh Cunningham puts it in *Leisure in the Industrial Revolution,* "a high preference for leisure, and for long periods of it." This preference was hardly something new. What was new was the ability, in prosperous Georgian England,° of so many people to indulge it. For the first time in centuries many workers earned more than survival wages. Now they had choices: they could buy goods or leisure. They could work more and earn more, or they could forgo the extra wages and enjoy more free time instead. Most chose the latter course. This was especially true for the highly paid skilled workers, who had the greatest degree of economic freedom, but even general laborers, who were employed at day rates, had a choice in the matter. Many of these worked intensively, sometimes for much more than the customary ten hours a day, and then quit to enjoy themselves until their money ran out.

It was not unusual for sporting events, fairs, and other celebrations to last several days. Since Sunday was always an official holiday, usually the days following were added on. This produced a regular custom of staying away from work on Monday, frequently doing so also on Tuesday, and then working long hours at the end of the week to catch up. Among some trades the Monday holiday achieved what amounted to an official status. Weavers and miners, for example, regularly took a holiday on the Monday after payday—which occurred weekly, on Friday or Saturday. This practice became so common that it was called "keeping Saint Monday."

Saint Monday may have started as an individual preference for staying away from work—whether to relax, to recover from drunkenness, or both—but its popularity during the 1850s and 1860s was ensured by the enterprise of the leisure industry. During that period sporting events, such as horse races and cricket matches, often took place on Mondays, since their organizers knew that many working-class customers would be prepared to take the day off. And since many public events were prohibited on the Sabbath, Monday became the chief occasion for secular recreations. Attendance at botanical gardens and museums soared on Monday, which was also the day that ordinary people went to the theater and the dance hall, and the day that workingmen's social clubs held their weekly meetings.

The energy of entrepreneurs, assisted by advertising, was an important influence not only on the diffusion and persistence of Saint Monday but also on leisure in general. Hence a curious and apparently contradictory situation: not so much the commercialization of leisure as the discovery of leisure thanks to commerce. This distinction is worth bearing in mind when one considers the complaint commonly made today that contemporary leisure is being "tainted" or "corrupted" by commercialism. Beginning in the eighteenth century, with magazines, coffeehouses, and music rooms, and continuing throughout the nineteenth, with professional sports and holiday travel, the modern idea of personal leisure emerged at the same time as the business of leisure. The first could not have happened without the second.

Georgian England: The years 1714–1830, during which four Georges ruled Great Britain.

Saint Monday had many critics. Religious groups campaigned against the tradition, which they saw as linked to the drinking and dissipation that, in their eyes, dishonored the Sabbath. They were joined by middle-class social reformers and by proponents of rational recreation, who also had an interest in altering Sunday behavior. By the end of the century many shops and factories had begun closing on Saturday afternoons, leaving a half-holiday for household chores and social activities—an evening at the dance hall or the pub—and permitting Sunday to be used exclusively for prayer and sober recreations.

It's unlikely that the Saturday half-holiday would have spread as rapidly as it did if it had not been for the support of the factory owners. Factory owners had little to gain from insisting on a six-day week of workdays of up to twelve hours if on some days so few workers showed up that the factory had to be shut down anyway. The proposal for a Saturday half-holiday offered a way out, and factory owners supported it in return for a commitment to regular attendance on the part of their employees. Half Saturdays and shorter workdays became the pattern followed by all later labor negotiations, and by legislation governing the length of the workday.

In the 1870s people began to speak of "week-ending" or "spending the week-end." The country houses of the wealthy were generally located in the Home Counties, in the vicinity of London, and were now easily reached by train. It became fashionable to go to the country on Friday afternoon and return to the city on Monday, and these house parties became an important feature of upper-class social life. Weekend outings, often to the seashore, were also available to the lower classes, although their weekend was usually shorter, extending from Saturday afternoon until Sunday evening.

According to one contemporary observer, Thomas Wright, "That the   35
Saturday half-holiday movement is one of the most practically beneficial that has ever been inaugurated with a view to the social improvement of 'the masses,' no one who is acquainted with its workings will for a moment doubt." He approvingly described a variety of activities in which working people indulged on the Saturday half-holiday. The afternoon began with a leisurely midday meal at home, which was often followed by a weekly bath in the neighborhood bathhouse—an important institution at a time when few homes had running water, and one that was common in British and North American cities until well into the twentieth century. The rest of the daytime hours might be spent reading the paper, working around the house, attending a club, or strolling around town window-shopping. Saturday afternoon became a customary time for park concerts, soccer games, rowing, and bicycling—and, of course, drinking in the local pub, for despite the hopes of the reformers and Evangelicals, drinking was still the chief leisure pastime of the working classes, whether the holiday occurred on Saturday or on Monday.

Wright emphasized that the afternoon was usually brought to a close in time for tea at five o'clock, to leave plenty of time for the chief entertainment of the week. Saturday night was the time for an outing to the theater; most people brought their own food and drink into the cheap seats in the gallery. The music hall, an important influence on the spread of Saturday night's popularity, began as an adjunct to taverns but emerged as an independent entity in the 1840s, and continued to be prominent in British entertainment for the next eighty years.

This was not the elite leisure of the aristocracy and landed gentry, for whom recreations such as shooting and fox hunting had become an all-consuming way of life. Nor was it the traditional mixture of leisure and work among ordinary people. No longer were work and play interchanged at will; no longer did they occur in the same milieu. There was now a special time for leisure, as well as a special place. Being neither play as work nor work as play, middle-class leisure, which eventually infiltrated and influenced all of society, involved something new: the strict demarcation of a temporal and a physical boundary between leisure and work. These boundaries—exemplified by the weekend—more than anything else characterize modern leisure.

After it became common in the 1870s, the British half-holiday took years to expand to a full day off. The American half-holiday didn't become common until the 1920s, but its expansion was more rapid. Often the weekend arrived in a full two-day configuration. The first factory to adopt a five-day week was a New England spinning mill, in 1908, expressly to accommodate its Jewish workers. The six-day week had always made it hard for Jews to observe the Sabbath, for if they took Saturday off and worked on Sunday, they risked offending the Christian majority. Moreover, as work patterns became increasingly formalized through union agreements, many Jews did not even have a choice, a state of affairs that threatened the Sabbath tradition. The five-day week—in which both Sunday and Saturday were holidays—offered a convenient way out, and it came to be supported by Jewish workers, rabbis, and community leaders, and some Jewish employers.

At first the five-day workweek was common in only three industries: the needle trade, building construction, and printing and publishing. In a few isolated cases employers voluntarily adopted the five-day week. The earliest and most notable of these was, curiously enough, Henry Ford, a staunch anti-unionist. In 1914 Ford reduced the daily hours in his plant from nine to eight; in 1926 he announced that henceforth his factories would also be closed all day Saturday. His rationale was that an increase in leisure time would support an increase in consumer spending, not least on automobiles and automobile travel. This was a prescient view, for the weekend did indeed become associated with outings and pleasure trips. But in 1926 that was still in the future, and Ford was alone among businessmen in espousing the weekend. He was roundly criticized by U.S. Steel, Westinghouse, and the National Association of Manufacturers.

What finally consolidated the two-day weekend was not altruism or   40
activism or, paradoxically, prosperity; it was the Great Depression of 1929.

Shorter hours came to be regarded as a remedy for unemployment: each person would work less, but more people would have jobs.

Just before the Depression the workweek stood for many as close to fifty hours; later, as a result of work-sharing, it fell to thirty-five or less. Eventually the New Deal legislation embodied in the Fair Labor Standards Act of 1938 mandated a weekly maximum of forty hours to begin in 1940, although the act was mute about the length of the workday. Once the eight-hour day became customary, the five-day week arrived.

THE PROMISE OF LEISURE

Throughout the 1920s and 1930s dozens of articles and books of a general nature were published by psychiatrists, psychologists, and social scientists on the perils of what was often called the New Leisure. There was a widespread feeling that the working class would not really know what to do with its increasing free time. The underlying theme was an old one: less work meant more leisure, more leisure led to idleness, and idle hands, as everyone knew, were ripe for Satan's mischief. This was precisely the argument advanced by the supporters of Prohibition, who maintained that shorter hours provided workers with more free time, which they would only squander on drink. Whatever the merits of this argument—and undoubtedly drinking was popular—one senses that this and other such "con-

cerns" really masked an unwillingness to accept the personal freedom that was implicit in leisure. The pessimism of intellectuals about the ability of ordinary people to amuse themselves has always been profound, and never more so than when popular amusements do not accord with the intellectuals' notions of what constitutes a good time.

There were different views as to what people would do with their newfound freedom. Some economists hoped that the extra free time would spur consumption of leisure goods and stimulate the stagnant economy. Middle-class social reformers saw an opportunity for a program of national physical and intellectual self-improvement. The two goals of filling leisure time—the economic and the cultural—appeared to many to be incompatible. A 1930 article by Walter Lippmann, "Free Time and Extra Money" in *Woman's Home Companion,* articulated "the problem of leisure." Lippmann warned that leisure offered individuals difficult choices, choices for which a work-oriented society like America had not prepared them. Lippmann was concerned that if people didn't make creative use of their free time, it would be squandered on mass entertainments and commercial amusements. His views were among the most influential during a time when many books and articles of popular sociology were being published with titles such as *The Challenge of Leisure, The Threat of Leisure,* and even "The Menace of Leisure."

Much of this concern was based on the widespread assumption that the amount of available free time was greater than ever before, and that the "problem of leisure" was without precedent. Before the Depression an American working a fifty-hour week spent less than half of his 5,824 waking hours a year on the job—the rest was free time. In contrast, a hundred years earlier work had accounted for as much as two thirds of one's waking hours. But, as Hannah Arendt has observed, this reduction is misleading, because the modern period is inevitably measured against the Industrial Revolution, which represented an all-time high as far as the number of working hours was concerned. A comparison with earlier periods of history leads to a different conclusion. The fourth-century Roman, for example, with 200 annual public holidays, spent fewer than a third of his waking hours at work; in medieval Europe, religious festivals reduced the work year to well below the modern level of 2,000 hours. Indeed, until the eighteenth century, Europeans and Americans enjoyed *more* free time than they do today. The American worker of the 1930s was just catching up.

But not for long. Working hours bottomed out during the Depression and then started to rise. Job creation, not work-sharing, became the goal of the New Deal. The Fair Labor Standards Act provided for a workweek of forty hours. As Benjamin Hunnicutt, the author of *Work Without End,* observes, this marked the end of a century-long trend. On the strength of the evidence of the past fifty years it would appear that the trend has not only stopped but reversed. By 1948, 13 percent of Americans with full-time jobs worked more than forty-nine hours a week; by 1979 the figure had crept up to 18 percent. Ten years later the Bureau of Labor Statistics estimated

45

that of 88 million Americans with full-time jobs fully 24 percent worked forty-nine or more hours a week.

Surveys of leisure habits often show diverging results. Two recent surveys, by the University of Maryland and by Michigan's Survey Research Center, suggest that most Americans enjoy about thirty-nine hours of leisure time weekly. On the other hand, a 1988 survey conducted by the National Research Center of the Arts came to a very different conclusion. It found that "Americans report a median 16.6 hours of leisure time each week." The truth is probably somewhere in between. Less surprising, given the number of people working more than forty-nine hours a week, was the National Research Center's conclusion that most Americans have suffered a decline in weekly leisure of 9.6 hours over the past fifteen years. The nineteenth-century activists who struggled so hard for a shorter workweek and more free time would have been taken aback by this statistic: what happened to the "Eight Hours for What We Will"?

There are undoubtedly people who work longer hours out of personal ambition, to escape problems at home, or from compulsion. The term "workaholic" (a postwar Americanism) is recent, but addiction to work is not—Thomas Jefferson, for example, was a compulsive worker, as was G. K. Chesterton—and there is no evidence that there are more such people today than there were in the past. Of course, for many people longer hours are not voluntary—they have to work more merely to make ends meet. This was particularly true in the 1980s, when poverty in America began to increase, but because the shrinking of leisure time began during the prosperous 1960s, economic need isn't the only explanation.

Twenty years ago Staffan Linder, a Swedish economist, wrote a book whose thesis was that economic growth caused an increasing scarcity of time, and that statistics showing an increase in personal incomes did not necessarily mean growing well-being. Linder observed that with increased productivity came the possibility of shorter work hours and a wider availability of consumer goods. People had a choice: more "leisure" time or more consumption. Only the wealthy could have both. If the average person wanted to indulge in expensive recreation like skiing or sailing, or to buy expensive entertainment equipment, it would be necessary to work more— to trade free time for overtime or a second job. Whether because of the effectiveness of advertising or from simple acquisitiveness, most people chose consumption over time. According to *U.S. News & World Report,* in 1989 Americans spent more than $13 billion on sports clothing; put another way, more than a billion hours of potential leisure time were exchanged for leisure wear—for increasingly elaborate running shoes, certified hiking shorts, and monogrammed warm-up suits. In 1989, to pay for these indulgences, more workers than ever before recorded—6.2 percent—held two or more jobs.

There is no contradiction between the surveys that indicate a reversing trend, resulting in a loss of free time, and the claim that the weekend

dominates our leisure. Longer work hours and more overtime cut mainly into weekday leisure. So do longer commutes, driving the kids, and Friday-night shopping. The weekend—or what's left of it after Saturday household chores—is when we have time to relax.

But the weekend has imposed a rigid schedule on our free time, which can result in a sense of urgency ("soon it will be Monday") that is at odds with relaxation. The weekly rush to the cottage is not leisurely, nor is the compression of various recreational activities into the two-day break. The freedom to do anything has become the obligation to do something, just as Chesterton foretold, and the list of dutiful recreations includes strenuous disciplines intended for self-improvement (fitness exercises, jogging, bicycling), competitive sports (tennis, golf), and skill-testing pastimes (sailing, skiing).

Recreations like tennis and sailing are hardly new, but before the arrival of the weekend they were for most people chiefly seasonal activities. Once a year, when vacation time came around, tennis rackets were removed from the back of the cupboard, swimwear was taken out of mothballs, or skis were dusted off. The accent was less on technique than on having a good time. It was like playing Monopoly at the summer cottage: no one remembered all the rules, but everyone could still enjoy the game. Now the availability of free time every weekend had changed this casual attitude. The very frequency of weekend recreations allows continual participation and improvement, which encourages the development of proficiency and skill.

The desire to do something well, whether it is sailing a boat or building a boat, reflects a need that was previously met in the workplace. Competence was shown on the job—holidays were for messing around. Now the situation is reversed. Technology has removed craft from most occupations. This is true in assembly-line jobs, where almost no training or experience, hence no skill, is required, as well as in most service positions (store clerks, fast-food attendants), where the only talent required is to smile and say "Have a good day." But it's also true in such skill-dependent work as house construction, where the majority of parts come ready-made from the factory and the carpenter merely assembles them, or automobile repair, which consists largely in replacing one throwaway part with another. Nor is the reduction of skills limited to manual work. Memory, once the prerequisite skill of the white-collar worker, has been rendered superfluous by computers; teachers, who once needed dramatic skills, now depend on mechanical aids; in politics, oratory has been killed by the thirty-second sound bite.

Hence an unexpected development in the history of leisure: for many people weekend free time has become not a chance to escape work but a chance to create work that is more meaningful—to work at recreation—in order to realize the personal satisfactions that the workplace no longer offers.

SACRED TIME

"Leisure" is the most misunderstood word in our vocabulary. We often use the words "recreation" and "leisure" interchangeably—recreation room, rest and recreation, leisure suit, leisure industry—but they really embody two different ideas. Recreation carries with it a sense of necessity and purpose. However pleasurable this antidote to work may be, it is a form of active employment, engaged in with a specific end in mind—a refreshment of the spirit or the body or both. Implicit in this idea of renewal—usually organized renewal—is the notion that recreation is both a consequence of work and a preparation for more of it.

Leisure is different. That was what Lippmann was getting at when he   55
contrasted commercial recreation with individual leisure. Leisure is not tied to work the way that recreation is; leisure is self-contained. The root of the word is the Latin *licere,* which means "to be permitted," suggesting that leisure is about freedom. But freedom for what? When Chesterton said "doing nothing," he was describing not emptiness but an occasion for reflection and contemplation, a chance to look inward rather than outward.

Bertrand Russell° placed leisure in a larger historical context in his essay "In Praise of Idleness." "Leisure is essential to civilization," he wrote,

Bertrand Russell: English philosopher and mathematician (1872–1970).

"and in former times leisure for the few was only rendered possible by the labours of the many. But their labours were valuable, not because work is good, but because leisure is good." Russell, a member of the aristocracy, pointed out that it had been precisely the leisure classes, not the laborers, who had written books, invented philosophies, produced the sciences, and cultivated the arts. But he was not arguing for a continuation of the class system; on the contrary, he proposed extending to the many the leisure that had previously been reserved for the few. This was an explicit attack on the work ethic, which he considered a device to trick people into accepting a life without leisure. In his view, the trick hadn't succeeded; working men and women had no illusions about work—they understood that it was merely a necessary means to a livelihood.

Russell's underlying argument was that we should free ourselves from the guilt about leisure that modern society had imposed on us through the use of terms such as "idleness" and "doing nothing," which were intended as a provocation to a society that placed the highest value on "keeping busy." Both Russell and Chesterton agreed with Aristotle, who considered leisure the aim of life. "We work," he wrote, "to have leisure."

"In praise of idleness" was written in 1932, at the height of the Depression, and Russell's proposal for a four-hour workday appears hopelessly utopian now. But the weekend's later and sudden popularity in so many societies suggests that leisure is beginning to make a comeback, although not as fully as Russell desired, not in so relaxed a way as Chesterton would have wished.

I cannot shake the suspicion that something more than mere functionality accounts for the widespread popularity of the weekend. Can its universal appeal be explained by a resonance with some ancient inclination buried deep in the human psyche? Given the mythological roots of the planetary week, and the devotional nature of Sunday and the Sabbath, the answer is likely to be found in early religious attitudes.

Mircea Eliade, a historian of religion, characterized traditional pre- *60* modern societies as experiencing the world in two distinct ways corresponding to two discontinuous modes of being: the sacred and the profane. According to Eliade, the sacred manifested itself in various ways—how physical space was perceived, for example. The profane, chaotic world, full of menace, was given structure and purpose by the existence of fixed, meaningful sacred places. Not only space but also time was thus perceived. Profane time was ordinary temporal duration, but sacred time, the time of festivals and holy days, was primordial and mythical, and stood apart from everyday life. During sacred time the clock not only stopped, it was turned back. The purpose of religious rites was precisely to reintegrate the past into the present. In this way sacred time became part of a separate, repetitive continuum, an "eternal mythical present."

Is it fanciful to propose that the repetitive cycle of week and weekend is a modern paraphrase of the ancient opposition of profane and sacred time? Obviously, the weekend is not a historical remnant in any literal sense, since it didn't even exist until the nineteenth century and its emergence was in response to specific social and economic conditions. Nor am I suggesting that the secular weekend is a substitute for religious festivals, although it is obviously linked to religious observance. However, there are several striking parallels.

Weekday time, like profane time, is linear. It represents an irreversible progression of days, Monday to Friday, year after year. Past weekday time is lost time. School days are followed by workdays, the first job by the second and the third. Not only is weekday time linear but, like profane time, it encompasses the unpredictable. During the week unforeseen things happen. People get promoted or fired. Stock markets soar or crash. Politicians are elected or voted out of office. One has the impression that history occurs on weekdays.

The weekend, on the other hand, is, in the words of Plato, a time to take a breath. It is a time apart from the world of mundane problems and mundane concerns, from the world of making a living. On weekends time stands still, and not only because we take off our watches. Just as holidays at the beach are an opportunity to recreate our childhood, to build sand castles with the kids, to paddle in the surf, to lie on the sand and get a sunburn, many of the things we do on weekends correspond to the things we did on weekends past. Weekend time shares this sense of reenactment with sacred time, and just as sacred time was characterized by ritual, the weekend, despite being an opportunity for personal freedom, is governed by convention: mowing the lawn, grilling steaks on the barbecue, going to the movies, Saturday night out, reading the Sunday paper, brunch, the afternoon opera broadcast, weekend drives, garage sales, and weekend visits. The predictability of the weekend is one of its comforts.

Free time has always been partly a refuge from labor. The weekend, too, is a retreat from work, but in a different way: a retreat from the abstract and the universal to the local and the particular. In that sense leisure is likely to continue to be, a Pieper claimed, the basis of culture. Every culture chooses a different structure for its work and leisure, and in doing so it makes a profound statement about itself. It invents, adapts, and recombines new and old models. Hence the long list of leisure days: public festivals, family celebrations, market days, taboo days, evil days, holy days, feasts, Saint Mondays and Saint Tuesdays, commemorative holidays, summer vacations—and weekends.

The weekend is our own contribution, our way of dealing with the ancient duality. The institution of the weekend reflects the many unresolved contradictions in modern attitudes toward leisure. We want to have our cake and eat it too. We want the freedom to be leisurely, but we want it regularly, every week, like clockwork.

The attraction of Saint Monday was that one could "go fishing"

65

whenever one willed; the regularity of the weekend—every five days—is at odds with the ideas of personal freedom and spontaneity. There is something mechanical about this oscillation, which creates a sense of obligation that interferes with leisure. Like sacred time, the weekend is comfortingly repetitive, but the conventionality of weekend free time, which must exist side by side with private pastimes and idiosyncratic hobbies, often appears to be restrictive. "What did you do on the weekend?" "The usual," we answer, mixing dismay with relief.

We have invented the weekend, but the dark cloud of old taboos still hangs over the holiday, and the combination of the secular with the holy leaves us uneasy. This tension only compounds the guilt that many of us continue to feel about not working, and leads to the nagging feeling that our free time should be used for some purpose higher than having fun. We want leisure, but we are afraid of it too.

Do we work to have leisure, or the other way around? Unsure of the answer, we have decided to keep the two separate. If C. P. Snow° had not already used the term in another context, it would be tempting to speak of Two Cultures. We pass weekly from one to the other—from the mundane, communal, increasingly impersonal, increasingly demanding, increasingly bureaucratic world of work to the reflective, private, controllable, consoling world of leisure. The weekend: our own and not our own, it is what we wait for all week long.

Questions for Discussion

1. Writing to report information differs from writing to interpret information. Cite paragraphs and identify the kinds of information that Rybczynski reports.
2. Review your answers to question 1 and then explain how Rybczynski interprets the information that he reports. Give two examples.
3. Rybczynski refers to a number of other thinkers in this article. What advantages does he gain by citing these authorities?
4. Rybczynski defines concepts throughout the essay. What are some of these concepts, and why is it important to have defined them?
5. What is the significance of "Saint Monday"? How does the concept of *Saint Monday* differ from the concept of *weekend?*
6. What does Rybczynski say is the reason that people today work so hard at playing on their weekends?

Suggestions for Writing

1. In the last paragraph of his essay Rybczynski asks, "Do we work to have leisure, or the other way around?" Write an essay in which you answer this question.

C. P. Snow: English author, statesman, and physicist (1905–1980).

2. Reflect upon activities in which you have engaged during the previous week. Classify them as partaking of "sacred" or "profane," as Rybczynski uses the terms—that is, structured and unstructured use of time—and write an essay in which you analyze your week.

GOSSIP

Sissela Bok

Although many people like to gossip, they often wonder if they should. What would a philosopher say about gossiping? In the following article Sissela Bok interprets the meaning of gossip, shows that some gossip can be not only justifiable but useful—and then distinguishes among the various kinds of gossip that can be harmful. As you read, consider whether you have personally experienced any of the behavior she describes.

DEFINITIONS

> Round the samovar and the hostess the conversation had been meanwhile vacillating . . . between three inevitable topics: the latest piece of public news, the theater, and scandal. It, too, came finally to rest on the last topic, that is, ill-natured gossip. . . . and the conversation crackled merrily like a burning fagot-stick.

Tolstoy's group portrait from *Anna Karenina* brings to mind many a cluster of malicious gossips, delighting in every new morsel of intimate information about others, the more scandalous the better.[1] So well do we recognize this temptation, and so often do we see it indulged, that it is easy to think of all gossip as petty, ill-willed, too often unfounded—as either trivial and thus demeaning to those whose lives it rakes over, or else as outright malicious. In either case, gossip seems inherently questionable from a moral point of view.

Dictionary definitions reinforce the view of gossip as trivial. Thus the *American Heritage Dictionary* defines it as "trifling, often groundless rumor, usually of a personal, sensational, or intimate nature; idle talk."[2]

Thinkers who adopt a normative point of view often stress the more negative evaluation of gossip. Aristotle wrote of that tantalizing and yet strangely limited "great-souled man," who "claims much and deserves much," that he is no gossip *[anthropologos]*,

> for he will not talk either about himself or about another, as he neither wants to receive compliments nor to hear other people run down . . . ; and so he is not given to speaking evil himself, even of his enemies, except when he deliberately intends to give offense.[3]

Thomas Aquinas° distinguished "talebearers" from "backbiters": both speak evil of their neighbors, but a talebearer differs from a backbiter "since he intends, not to speak ill as such, but to say anything that may stir one man against another," in order to sever friendship.[4]

Thomas Aquinas: Catholic philosopher and theologian (c. 1225–1274).

Kierkegaard° abhorred gossip. He spoke out against its superficiality   5
and its false fellow-feeling. Gossip and chatter, he wrote, "obliterate the vital
distinction between what is private and what is public" and thereby trivialize
all that is inward and inherently inexpressible. He castigated his own age as
one in which the expanding press offered snide and leveling gossip to a
garrulous, news-hungry public.⁵ Heidegger° likewise, in pages echoing
those of Kierkegaard, deplored idle talk as "something which anyone can
rake up." He held that it perverts genuine efforts at understanding by making
people think they already know everything.⁶ And in their 1890 article on
the right to privacy, Samuel Warren and Louis Brandeis spoke of gossip with
similar distaste, assailing in particular its spread in the expanding yellow
press: "Gossip is no longer the resource of the idle and vicious but has
become a trade which is pursued with industry as well as effrontery."⁷

Cheap, superficial, intrusive, unfounded, even vicious: surely gossip
can be all that. Yet to define it in these ways is to overlook the whole
network of human exchanges of information, the need to inquire and to
learn from the experience of others, and the importance of not taking
everything at face value. The desire for such knowledge leads people to go
beneath the surface of what is said and shown, and to try to unravel conflict-
ing clues and seemingly false leads. In order to do so, information has to be
shared with others, obtained from them, stored in memory for future use,
tested and evaluated in discussion, and used at times to encourage, to entertain, or to warn.

Everyone has a special interest in personal information about others.
If we knew about people only what they wished to reveal, we would be
subjected to ceaseless manipulation; and we would be deprived of the pleasure and suspense that comes from trying to understand them. Gossip helps
to absorb and to evaluate intimations about other lives, as do letters, novels,
biography, and chronicles of all kinds. In order to live in both the inner and
the shared worlds, the exchange of views about each—in spite of all the
difficulties of perception and communication—is indispensable.⁸

Thanks to the illuminating studies of gossip by anthropologists and
others—in villages around the world as in offices, working teams, schools,
or conventions—we now have a livelier and clearer documentation of the
role it actually plays.⁹ These studies have disproved the traditional stereotype
of women as more garrulous and prone to gossip than men, and have shown
how such forms of communication spring up in every group, regardless of
sex.¹⁰ By tracing the intricate variations of gossip, these writings have led to
a subtler understanding of how it channels, tests, and often reinforces judgments about human nature.

Before considering the moral problems that some forms of gossip
clearly raise, we must therefore define it in a less dismissive way than those

---

Kierkegaard: Søren Kierkegaard, Danish philosopher and religious writer (1813–1855). *Heidegger:* Martin Heidegger, German philosopher (1889–1976) who was one of the founders of existentialism.

mentioned at the beginning of this chapter. We shall then be able to ask what makes it more or less problematic from a moral point of view, and weigh more carefully the dangers that Kierkegaard, Heidegger, and others have signaled.

I shall define gossip as informal personal communication about other people who are absent or treated as absent. It is informal, first of all, unlike communication in court proceedings or lectures or hospital records or biographies, in that it lacks formal rules setting forth who may speak and in what manner, and with what limitations from the point of view of accuracy and reliability. It is informal, too, in that it takes place more spontaneously and relies more on humor and guesswork, and in that it is casual with respect to who ends up receiving the information, in spite of the frequent promises not to repeat it that are ritualistically exacted along its path. (In each of these respects, gossip nevertheless has standards as well, though usually unspoken, as all who have tried to take part in gossip and been rebuffed have learned.) And the formal modes of discourse may themselves slip into more or less gossipy variations.

Secrecy is one of the factors that make gossip take the place of more formal communication about persons. Gossip increases whenever information is both scarce and desirable—whenever people want to find out more about others than they are able to. It is rampant, for instance, in speculations about the selection of prize-winners, or the marriage plans of celebrities, or the favors of a capricious boss. Gossip is more likely, too, when formal modes of discourse, though possible, have drawbacks for the participants. Thus hospital and school personnel gossip about their charges rather than entering the information on institutional records. And those who have the power to retaliate should they learn that their personal affairs are discussed are criticized in gossip rather than to their faces.

The seventeenth- and eighteenth-century New England Puritans illustrate in their writings the intensity with which human lives may be raked over, both in personal soul-searching and in talking about the lives of others. They labored with the strongest fears of not being among those who would turn out to be saved in the life to come; but they had no evidence for who was and who was not saved, and recognized no way to influence their fate, believing that it had been decided for them before birth. Might they nevertheless discern traces of such evidence in their own lives and in those of others? Might behavior and demeanor not hold some clues? Speculating about imperceptible yet all-important differences between persons took on an urgency rarely exceeded before or since. Hypocrisy naturally abounded. One of the foremost tasks of thinkers such as Thomas Shepard and Jonathan Edwards became the effort to separate the hypocrites from the sincere, and above all, to discern in self and others what they called the "inner hypocrisy" or self-deception that masked one's sins and doubts even from oneself.[11]

The second element in my definition of gossip is personal communication. The original source of what is said may be hidden or forgotten, but each time, gossip is communicated by one or more persons to others, most often in personal encounters, but also by telephone, by letter, or, in the last few centuries, in the mass media. This personal element, combined with the third—that the information is also *about* persons—makes gossip a prime vehicle for moral evaluation. Part of the universal attraction of gossip is the occasion it affords for comparing oneself with others, usually silently, while seeming to be speaking strictly about someone else. Few activities tempt so much to moralizing, through stereotyped judgments and the head-shaking, seemingly all-knowing distancing of those speaking from those spoken about. The result is hypocrisy—judging the lives of others as one would hardly wish one's own judged. As one student of the anthropology of gossip has said:

> If I suggest that gossip and scandal are socially virtuous and valuable, this does not mean that I always approve of them. Indeed, in practice I find that when I am gossiping about my friends as well as my enemies I am deeply conscious of performing a social duty; but that when I hear they gossip viciously about me, I am rightfully filled with righteous indignation.[12]

Because gossip is primarily about persons, it is not identical with the larger category of rumor; there can be rumors of war or rumors of an imminent stock-market collapse, but hardly gossip.[13] And there can be stories, but not gossip, about the foibles and escapades of animals, so long as humans are not part of the plot, or the animals taken to represent individual persons or endowed with human characteristics.

Gossip, finally, is not only about persons but about persons absent, isolated, or excluded, rather than about the participants themselves. The subjects of gossip, while usually physically absent, can also be treated as if they were absent should they be part of the group engaging in gossip. While the conversation is directed past them and around them, they are then its targets, and are meant to overhear it. Least of all can people gossip about themselves, unless they manage to treat themselves as if they were absent, and as subjects of scandal or concern. Though it is hard to gossip about oneself, one can lay oneself open to gossip, or talk about one's doings that include others in such a way as to arouse gossip. Compare, from this point of view, the rumored divorce and the announced one, or the gossip about a young girl's pregnancy and her acknowledgment of it.

These four elements of gossip—that it is (1) informal (2) personal communication (3) about persons who (4) are absent or excluded—are clearly not morally problematic in their own right. Consider the many harmless or supportive uses of gossip: the talk about who might marry, have a baby, move to another town, be in need of work or too ill to ask for help,

15

and the speculations about underlying reasons, possible new developments, and opportunities for advice or help. Some may find such talk uninteresting, even tedious, or too time-consuming, but they can hardly condemn it on moral grounds.

On the other hand, it is equally easy to conceive of occasions when the four elements do present moral problems. The informality and the speculative nature of what is said may be inappropriate, as it would be if gossip were the basis for firing people from their jobs. The communication about other persons may be of a degrading or invasive nature that renders it inappropriate, whether in gossip or in other discourse. And the talk about persons in their absence—behind their backs—is sometimes of such a nature as to require that it either be spoken to their faces or not spoken at all. Pirandello's play *Right You Are! (If You Think So)* shows how irresistibly such gossip can build up among men and women in a small town, and the havoc it can wreak.[14]

For an example of gossip that is offensive on all such grounds, and as a contrast to the many forms of harmless gossip mentioned earlier, consider the alleged leak by an FBI official to a Hollywood columnist about the private life of the actress Jean Seberg. The leak indicated that she had engaged in extramarital relations with a member of the Black Panther Party, who was said to have fathered her unborn child.[15] It was meant to cast suspicion on her support of black nationalist causes. Reprinted by *Newsweek,* it was disseminated, as intended, throughout the world. Such uses of gossip have not been rare. They injure most directly the person whose reputation they are meant to call in question. But they debilitate as well those who take part in manufacturing and spreading the rumor, and their superiors who are responsible for permitting such a scheme to go ahead; and thus they endanger still others who may be the targets of similar attacks. Such acts, with all their ramifications, overstep all bounds of discretion and of respect for persons. They are especially reprehensible and dangerous when undertaken in secrecy by a government agency in the name of the public's best interest.

In between these extremes of innocuousness and harm lie most forms of gossip: the savoring of salacious rumors, the passing on of unverified suspicions, the churning over seemingly self-inflicted burdens in the lives of acquaintances, and the consequent self-righteousness and frequent hypocrisy of those passing judgment in gossip. No testing ground for the exercise of discretion and indiscretion is more common than such everyday probing and trading of personal matters. Just as all of us play the roles of host and guest at different times, so all of us gossip and are gossiped about. Gossip brings into play intuitive responses to the tensions of insider and outsider, and forces us to choose between concealing and revealing, between inquisitiveness and restraint. Each of us develops some standards, however inarticulate, however often honored in the breach, for amounts and kinds of gossip we relish, tolerate, or reject. Can these standards be made more explicit? If so, how might we weigh them?

REPREHENSIBLE GOSSIP

> Why is gossip like a three-pronged tongue? Because it destroys three people: the person who says it, the person who listens to it, and the person about whom it is told.
>
> —THE BABYLONIAN TALMUD

Not all gossip, as I have defined it, is injurious or otherwise to be avoided. But when it is, it can harm all who take part in it, as the Babylonian Talmud warned.[16] Out of respect for oneself as much as for others, therefore, it matters to discern such cases. Three categories of gossip should be singled out as especially reprehensible: gossip in breach of confidence, gossip the speaker knows to be false, and unduly invasive gossip.

It is wrong, first of all, to reveal in gossip what one has promised to keep secret. This is why the gossip of doctors at staff meetings and cocktail parties about the intimate revelations of their patients is so inexcusable. True, pledges of confidentiality must at times be broken—to save the life of an adolescent who confides plans of suicide, for example. But such legitimate breaches could hardly be carried out through gossip, because of its lack of discrimination with respect to who ends up hearing it. Such information should, rather, be disclosed only to those who have a particular need to know, and with the utmost respect for the privacy of the individual concerned.

Must we then bar all gossip conveyed in spite of a pledge of silence? And would we then not exclude *most* gossip? After all, few pieces of information are more rapidly disseminated than those preceded by a "promise not to tell." At times such a promise is worthless, a mere empty gesture, and both parties know it; one can hardly call the subsequent repeating of the "secret" a breach of confidence. Sometimes the person who asks for the promise before sharing his bits of gossip may believe it to be more binding than it turns out to be. But, as La Rochefoucauld° asked, why should we imagine that others will keep the secret we have ourselves been unable to keep?[17] At still other times, a promise may have been sincere, but should never have been made to begin with. Many promises of secrecy are exacted with the aggressive intent of burdening someone, or of creating a gulf between that individual and others. The best policy is to be quite sparing in one's promises of secrecy about any information, but scrupulous, once having given such a promise, in respecting it.

La Rochefoucauld: François, Duc de La Rochefoucauld (1613–1680), best known for his *Maxims* (1665) in which he suggested that all human behavior is inspired by selfishness.

Second, gossip is unjustifiable whenever those who convey it know that it is false and intend to deceive their listeners (unlike someone who makes it clear that he exaggerates or speaks in jest). Whether they spread false gossip just to tell a good story, or to influence reputations, perhaps even as a weapon—as when newly separated spouses sometimes overstate each other's misdeeds and weaknesses in speaking to friends—they are exceeding the bounds of what they owe to their listeners and to those whose doings they misrepresent. The same is true of the false gossip that can spring up in the competition for favor, as in office politics or in academic backbiting, and of collective strategies for deceit. Thus in the reelection campaign of President Nixon in 1972, some individuals had been assigned the task of spreading false rumors about his opponents. Conspiratorial groups and secret police have employed such methods through the ages. Whatever the reason, there can be no excuse for such dissemination of false gossip.

Might there not be exceptional circumstances that render false gossip excusable?* I argued, in *Lying,*° that certain lies might be excusable, such as those that offer the only way to deflect someone bent on violence. But whatever lies one might tell such an assailant, false gossip about third parties would hardly provide the requisite help at such a time of crisis; and if by any chance the assailant could be stalled simply by talking about other persons, there would be no need to use falsehood in so doing.

Are there forms of false gossip that correspond to innocent white lies? 25
Gossip to please someone on his deathbed, for instance, who has always enjoyed hearing about the seedy and salacious doings of his friends, by a wife who can think of nothing truthful that is sufficiently titillating? Should she then invent stories about neighbors or friends, thinking that no harm could come thereof, since her husband would not live to spread the stories further? Such a way out would be demeaning for both, even if it injured no one else: demeaning to the dying man in the unspoken judgment about what would most please him, and in the supposition that lying to him would therefore be acceptable; and demeaning to his wife, as she reflected back on her inability to muster alternative modes of silence and speech at such a time. No matter how well meant, falsehoods about the lives of others bear little resemblance to harmless white lies.

Much of the time, of course, those who convey false gossip do not

---

*One could imagine a club dedicated to false gossip, in which members vied with one another for who could tell the most outrageous stories about fellow human beings. So long as all knew the tales were false, and the stories went no farther, the practice would not be a deceptive one, and more allied to storytelling and fiction than to the intentional misleading about the lives of others that is what renders false gossip inexcusable. Such a club, however, would be likely to have but few members; for gossip loses its interest when it is *known* to be false.

Lying: An earlier work of Bok's, *Lying: Moral Choice in Public and Private,* published by Random House in 1979.

know it to be false. It may rest on hearsay, or be unverified, or be pure speculation. Often the facts cannot easily *be* verified, or not without serious intrusion. Thus to spread rumors that a person is a secret alcoholic is made more serious because of the difficulty that listeners have in ascertaining the basis of the allegation. At times such gossip cannot be known to be true by the speakers, nor credibly denied by the subjects. This was one reason why the dissemination of the rumor about Jean Seberg's unborn baby was so insidious. She had no way before the baby's birth to demonstrate the falsity of the rumor.

In the third place, gossip may be reprehensible, even if one has given no pledge of silence and believes one's information correct, simply because it is unduly invasive. On this ground, too, planting the rumor about Jean Seberg's sexual life and the identity of the father of her unborn child was unjustifiable, regardless of whether the FBI thought the story accurate or not.

Is any gossip, then, unduly invasive whenever it concerns what is private, perhaps stigmatizing, often secret? If so, much of the gossip about the personal lives of neighbors, co-workers, and public figures would have to be judged inexcusable. But such a judgment seems unreasonable. It would dismiss many harmless or unavoidable exchanges about human foibles. To such strictures, the perspective of Mr. Bennett in Jane Austen's *Pride and Prejudice* should give pause: "For what do we live," he asked, "but to make sport for our neighbors and to laugh at them in turn?"[18]

How then might we sort out what is unduly invasive from all the gossip about private and secret lives? To begin with, there is reason to stop to consider whether gossip is thus invasive whenever those whose doings are being discussed claim to feel intruded upon. But these claims must obviously not be taken at face value: They are often claims to ownership of information about oneself. While such claims should give gossipers pause, they are not always legitimate. People cannot be said, for instance, to own aspects of their lives that are clearly evident to others and thus in fact public, such as a nasty temper or a manipulative manner, nor can they reasonably argue that others have no right to discuss them. Least of all can they suppress references to what may be an "open secret," known to all, and half-suspected even by themselves—a topic treated in innumerable comedies about marital infidelity. Similarly, more concealed aspects of their lives may be of legitimate interest to others—their mistreatment of their children, for example, or their past employment record. And the information that government leaders often try to withhold through claims to executive privilege is often such that the public has every right to acquire it. At such times, gossip may be an indispensable channel for public information.

Merely to *say* that gossip about oneself is unduly invasive, therefore, does not make it so. I would argue that additional factors must be present to render gossip unduly invasive: The information must be about matters le-

30

gitimately considered private; and it must hurt the individuals talked about.*
They may be aware of the spreading or of the harm; or else they may be
injured by invasive gossip without ever knowing why—fail to keep their
jobs, perhaps, because of rumors about their unspoken political dissent. But
the speculations in bars or sewing circles concerning even the most intimate
aspects of the married life of public figures is not intrusive so long as it does
not reach them or affect their lives in any way. Such talk may diminish the
speakers, but does not intrude on the persons spoken about.

While the three categories of represensible gossip—gossip in breach of
confidence, gossip that is known to be false, and gossip that is clearly invasive—should be avoided, each one has somewhat uncertain boundaries and
borderline regions. One cannot always be sure whether one owes someone
silence, whether one is conveying false gossip, or whether what is said of an
intimate nature about people will find its way back to them or otherwise
hurt them. In weighing such questions, discretion is required; and, given
the capacity of gossip to spread, it is best to resolve doubts in favor of silence.

Extra caution is needed under certain circumstances, when the temptation to indulge in any of the three forms may be heightened. At such
times, the borderline cases carry an even stronger presumption against taking
part in gossip. Discretion is then needed more than ever to prevent gossip
from blending with one or more of the kinds earlier ruled out. The desire
to have an effect, first of all, to impress people, perhaps to deal a blow, easily
leads to greater pressure to breach secrecy or exaggerate in gossip or to speak
intrusively about others. As soon as a speaker gains in any way from passing
on gossip, these pressures arise. Prestige, power, affection, intimacy, even
income (as for gossip columnists): Such are the gains that gossipers envisage.
It cannot be wrong to gain from gossip in its own right, since in one sense
most gossip aims at a gain of some sort—if nothing else, in closeness to the
listener, or in the status of someone who seems to be "in the know." But the
prospect of such gain increases the likelihood that promises will be broken,
unverified rumors passed on, privacy invaded. The misfortunes of another
may then be used in such a way as to traffic in them. This is in part why the
inside gossip of the former employee or the divorced spouse is more troubling when it is published for financial gain or as revenge.

A desire for gain of a different kind motivates those who take special
pleasure in passing on discreditable gossip. Maimonides, like Aquinas and

---

*For this reason, gossip should give pause whenever the speaker believes it may reach some-
one in a position to injure the person spoken of. If the listener is a judge, for instance, or an
executive having the power to make decisions over someone's employment, the gossiper must
weigh his words with care. Even when the listener is not in an official position, gossip directed
to him is problematic if he is given to injurious responses: if he is malicious, slanderous,
indiscreet, profiteering, or in any way likely to put the information to inappropriate use.
Gossip is problematic, too, if the listener is a poor intermediary: perhaps one who exaggerates
gossip in conveying it further, or who is likely to misunderstand it and spread it in false garb,
or is unable to discriminate in turn between listeners, so that he conveys the gossip to one
who is incompetent or dangerous.

many others, distinguished the talebearer from the person who speaks to denigrate: the scandalmonger, or, as Maimonides° expressed it, "the evil tongue."[19] He spoke, too, of "the dust of the evil tongue": the insinuations that sow suspicion without shedding light either on the implied offense or on the evidence concerning it. Before scandalmongers and insinuators are known as such, they can destroy trust among friends or in entire communities; in consequence they have been more distasteful to commentators than all others. And yet, all disparaging or discreditable personal information cannot be avoided. On the contrary, it must sometimes be conveyed, as when the deceitful or the aggressive or, indeed, the indiscreet are pointed out to put newcomers on their guard. Consider, as an illustration of such cautioning remarks, the following exchange in a Mexican village:

> Down the path someone spotted a young man named Xun, whose reputation as a drunkard made everyone anxious to be on his way.
>
> "If you meet him drunk on the path, he has no mercy. He won't listen to what you say, that Xun."
>
> "He doesn't understand what you say; you're right. If he's just a bit tight when you meet him on the path—puta, 'Let's go, let's go,' he'll say. You will be forced to drink."
>
> "But doesn't he get angry?"
>
> "No, no. He'll just say, 'Let's go have a little soft drink.'"
>
> "He's good-natured."
>
> "But he doesn't bother to ask if you're in a hurry to get someplace . . ."
>
> "No, he's good-hearted . . ."
>
> "If you find yourself in a hurry to get somewhere and you see him coming the best thing to do is hide . . ."
>
> ". . . or run away."
>
> And with that, the various men went on about their business.[20]

TRIVIALIZING GOSSIP

Beyond such questions of avoiding reprehensible and harmful gossip lies a larger one: that of the tone gossip can lend to discourse about human lives. It is this tone that Kierkegaard and Heidegger aimed at, in arguing that gossip streamlines and demeans what is spoken. What is utterly private and inward, Kierkegaard held, cannot be expressed; as a result, talking about it must necessarily distort and trivialize. Gossip therefore has a leveling effect, in conveying as shallow and ordinary what is unfathomable. It levels, moreover, by talking of all persons in the same terms, so that even the exceptionally gifted, the dissident, and the artist are brought down to the lowest common denominator. Finally, it erases and levels the differences between

Maimonides: Jewish rabbi and philosopher (1135–1204) who organized Jewish oral law and attempted to reconcile Jewish theology with the philosophy of Aristotle.

the different modes of talking, so that all is glossed over in the same superficial and informal chatter.

According to such a view, the informality with which we talk about   35
the weather or the latest price rises can only trivialize what we say about human beings. And this informality of gossip can combine with the special liberties taken in the absence of those spoken about so as to permit the speaker to indulge in a familiarity disrespectful of their humanity and in turn of his own. It was this reflection that gossip casts on so many who convey it that made George Eliot compare it to smoke from dirty tobacco pipes: "It proves nothing but the bad taste of the smoker."[21]

Gossip can also trivialize and demean when it substitutes personal anecdote for a careful exploration of ideas. Someone incapable of taking up political or literary questions without dwelling endlessly on personalities can do justice neither to the ideas nor to the persons under debate.

Such gossip can be an intoxicating surrogate for genuine efforts to understand. It can be the vehicle for stereotypes—of class, for instance, or race or sex. It turns easily into a habit, and for some a necessity. They may then become unable to think of other human beings in other than trivial ways. If they cannot attribute scope and depth and complexity to others, moreover, it is unlikely that they will perceive these dimensions in themselves. All news may strike them as reducible to certain trite formulas about human behavior; all riddles seem transparent.

Many do not merely gossip but are known *as* gossips. They may serve an important group function; but such a role should cause concern to the individuals thus labeled. It is far more likely to tempt to breaches of confidence, to falsehoods, to invasive gossiping—and thus to a general loss of discernment about reasons to avoid gossip and persons to shield from it. At the extreme of this spectrum is the pathological gossip, whose life revolves around prying into the personal affairs of others and talking about them.

Plutarch° wrote of the garrulous that they deny themselves the greatest benefits of silence: hearing and being heard. In their haste to speak, they listen but poorly; others, in turn, pay little heed to their words.[22] And Heidegger expounded on the strange way in which gossip and all facile discourse, so seemingly open and free-ranging, turns out instead to inhibit understanding: "By its very nature, idle talk is a closing-off, since to go back to the ground of what is talked about is something which it *leaves undone*."[23] Those whose casual talk stops at no boundaries, leaves no secret untouched, may thereby shut themselves off from the understanding they seem to seek. Gossip can be the means whereby they distance themselves from all those about whom they speak with such seeming familiarity, and they may achieve but spurious intimacy with those *with whom* they speak. In this way gossip can deny full meaning and depth to human beings, much like some forms

---

Plutarch: Greek essayist and biographer (c. 46–c. 120).

of confession: gossip, through such trivializing and distancing; confession, through molding those who confess and overcoming their independence.

These warnings go to the heart of the meaning of discernment con- *40* cerning human beings, including oneself, and of its links with the capacity to deal with openness and secrecy. Quite apart from the obvious problems with false or invasive gossip discussed earlier, all gossip can become trivializing in tone, or turn into garrulity.

Yet gossip need not deny meaning and debilitate thus. Those who warn against it often fail to consider its extraordinary variety. They ignore the attention it can bring to human complexity, and are unaware of its role in conveying information without which neither groups nor societies could function.[24] The view of all gossip as trivializing human lives is itself belittling if applied indiscriminately. When Kierkegaard and Heidegger speak out against idle talk, gossip, and chatter, and against "the public" and the "average understanding" taken in by such discourse, they erase differences and deny meaning in their own way.[25] One cannot read their strictures without sensing their need to stand aloof, to maintain distance, to hold common practices vulgar. In these passages, they stereotype social intercourse and deny it depth and diversity, just as much as gossip can deny those of individuals. When moral judgment takes such stereotyped form, it turns into moralizing: one more way in which moral language can be used to avoid a fuller understanding of human beings and of their efforts to make sense of their lives.

NOTES

1. Leo Tolstoy, *Anna Karenina,* trans. Constance Garnett (New York: Random House, Modern Library, 1950), p. 158.
2. *The American Heritage Dictionary* (Boston: Houghton Mifflin & Co., 1969).
3. Aristotle, *Nicomachean Ethics,* bk. 4, chap. 3, 31. Aristotle contrasted the "great-souled man" with the "small-souled man," on the one hand, who claims less than he deserves, and with the "vain man" on the other, who claims more than he deserves. I have used the traditional translation of Aristotle's *anthropos megalopsuchos,* as "great-souled man"; it must, needless to say, not be thought to refer to males only.
4. Thomas Aquinas, *Summa Theologica* II–II. Ques. 73–74, trans. Fathers of the English Dominican Province (New York: Benziger Brothers, 1918), pp. 290–303.
5. Søren Kierkegaard, *Two Ages* (1846), trans. Howard V. and Edna H. Hong (Princeton, N.J.: Princeton University Press, 1978). See esp. pp. 97–102.
6. Martin Heidegger, *Being and Time* (New York: Harper & Row, 1962), p. 213. See p. 212 for Heidegger's view of the role of gossip and "scribbling" in "idle talk."

7. Warren and Brandeis, "The Right to Privacy," pp. 193–220. For a discussion of this article and of the authors' distaste for gossip, see Dorothy J. Glancy, "The Invention of the Right to Privacy," *Arizona Law Review* 21 (1979): 1–39.

8. For the central role of gossip for information storage and retrieval in a society, see John M. Roberts, "The Self-Management of Cultures," in Ward H. Goodenough, *Explorations in Cultural Anthropology* (New York: McGraw-Hill Book Co., 1964), p. 441. And for an economic interpretation of information management through secrecy and gossip, see Richard A. Posner, "The Right to Privacy," *Georgia Law Review* 12 (Spring 1978): 398–422.

9. See, among others, Max Gluckman, "Gossip and Scandal," *Current Anthropology* 4 (1963): 307–16; Don Handelman, "Gossip in Encounters: The Transmission of Information in a Bounded Social Setting," *Man,* n.s. 8 (1973): 210–27; Robert Paine, "What is Gossip About? An Alternative Hypothesis," *Man,* n.s. 2(1967): 278–85; Ralph L. Rosnow and Gary A. Fine, *Rumor and Gossip: The Social Psychology of Hearsay* (New York: Elsevier, 1976); John Beard Haviland, *Gossip, Reputation, and Knowledge in Zinacantan* (Chicago: University of Chicago Press, 1977).

10. We need not go back to Aesop, Plutarch, or the eighteenth-century moralists for vivid examples of such distinctions based on sex. Carl Fullerton Sulzberger permitted himself the following tortuous speculation, put forth as self-evident fact, in "Why It Is Hard to Keep Secrets," p. 42: "As we all know, most women habitually indulge in acquiring secrets only to give them away with celebrity and obvious enjoyment. . . . When I once asked a patient why she was so eager to acquire and then spread secret rumors, her first association was 'it is like adorning myself with borrowed feathers.' . . . the greater readiness of women to disseminate secrets entrusted to them is directly related to the working of the castration complex."

11. Michael McGiffert, ed., *God's Plot: The Paradoxes of Puritan Piety, Being the Autobiography and Journal of Thomas Shepard* (Amherst: University of Massachusetts Press, 1972); Jonathan Edwards, *Religious Affections* (Edinburgh: W. Laing & J. Matthews, 1789). See also Perry Miller, *The New England Mind: The Seventeenth Century* (New York: Macmillan Co., 1939).

12. Gluckman, "Gossip and Scandal," p. 315.

13. See Gordon W. Allport and Leo Postman, *The Psychology of Rumor* (New York: Henry Holt & Co., 1947), and articles cited in note 9 above.

14. Luigi Pirandello, *Right You Are! (If You Think So),* in Montrose J. Moses, ed., *Dramas of Modernism and their Forerunners* (Boston: Little, Brown & Co., 1931), pp. 239–75.

15. "FBI Admits It Spread Lies About Actress Jean Seberg," *Los Angeles Times*, September 15, 1979, p. 1, and editorial, September 19.

16. The Babylonian Talmud, cited in Francine Klagsbrun, *Voices of Wisdom: Jewish Ideals and Ethics for Everyday Living* (New York: Pantheon Books, 1980), p. 74.

17. La Rochefoucauld, *Maximes et réflexions diverses* (1664; Paris: Gallimard, 1976), p. 143.

18. Jane Austen, *Pride and Prejudice* (New York: E. P. Dutton & Co., 1976), p. 384.

19. Maimonides, *Code*, "Laws Concerning Moral Dispositions and Ethical Conduct," chap. 7, secs. 1–4, quoted in Klagsbrun, *Voices of Wisdom*, p. 75.

20. Haviland, *Gossip, Reputation, and Knowledge in Zinacantan*, p. 15.

21. George Eliot, *Daniel Deronda*, Standard Edition, *The Works of George Eliot* (Edinburgh & London: William Blackwood & Sons, 1897), 1:207.

22. Plutarch, "Concerning Talkativeness," *Moralia*, 6:399.

23. Heidegger, *Being and Time*, p. 213.

24. See Elizabeth Drew, *The Literature of Gossip: Nine English Letter-Writers* (New York: W. W. Norton & Co., 1964), p. 26, for examples of gossipers who can "inspire the commonplace with an uncommon flavor, and transform trivialities by some original grace or sympathy or humor or affection."

25. See, for example, Kierkegaard, *Two Ages*, p. 100, and Heidegger, *Being and Time*, p. 212.

Questions for Discussion

1. Consider the first two paragraphs of this article. How does Bok signal her intention to challenge previous assumptions about the nature of gossip?

2. How does Bok establish that she has the credentials to be writing on this subject?

3. How does Bok define *gossip?* What are its essential features, and how does it differ from rumor?

4. Under what circumstances can gossip be useful and justifiable?

5. What kind of gossip is the most injurious? How can gossip injure the people who engage in it?

6. What should we do when people ask us to keep information secret? Are such requests always to be taken seriously?

Suggestions for Writing

1. Although gossip may be an activity confined to discussion about other people, there are many people who prefer to make disclosures about themselves. For example, consider the personal information that people

are willing to reveal about themselves on television talk shows. What do you think causes people to disclose intimate details about themselves to strangers?

2. Write an essay classifying the different kinds of excuses people like to give for engaging in behavior that others find questionable.

CUTENESS

Daniel Harris

> *According to an old adage, "Beauty is in the eye of the beholder." Could the same be true for what we perceive as cute? Or does cuteness, in our culture, have specific features that we are trained to respond to sympathetically? Daniel Harris offers an answer to these questions in the following essay. He shows that seeing is an act that requires more than simply opening one's eyes. He also suggests that what we see, and how we see it, can shape the way we live.*

She stands in maroon bloomers and a pink dress that flares tantalizingly above two acrylic legs that descend, unvaried in diameter, all the way down to her gout-stricken ankles crammed in her booties. Her feet, crippled and pigeon-toed, touch at their tips. A sassy tuft of a synthetic topknot sprays out of a helmet of auburn hair encircled by a polka-dot bow that sits atop her head like a windmill, dwarfing the rest of her figure. Her nose is no bigger than a button, and her astonishingly candid eyes are two moist pools framed by eyebrows penciled like quizzical circumflexes on the vast dome of her forehead. Emptied of all internal life, these mesmerizing orbs, composing at least 25 percent of a face as wide as her shoulders, stare out directly at us with a reticence exaggerated by the hectic flush of her complexion. Her name is So Shy Sherri, and she is one of toy manufacturer Galoob's nine new "Baby Faces"—a set of "superposin'" dolls with names like So Sweet Sandi, So Sorry Sarah, and So Delightful Dee Dee, each with an "adorable" expression and personality of her own.

Everywhere we turn we see cuteness, from cherubic figures batting their peepers on Charmin toilet paper to teddy bears frozen mid-embrace, the stubs of their pawless arms groping for hugs. Within their natural setting of the consumeristic landscape, such sentimental products of the modern sensibility are so commonplace that they have become the most invasive type of image possible, a form of visual clutter we respond to without really seeing. We tend to think of them not as inventions of the eighteenth or nineteenth century but as something that transcends history altogether and constitutes instead the timeless and universal appearance of purity, instinct, and spontaneity. In the eyes of most people, whose conditioned responses to this most schematic of styles prevent them from recognizing its glaring artificiality, things like calendars with droopy-eyed puppies pleading for attention or greeting cards with kitty cats in raincoats are the very embodiment of innocence and as such represent an absence of the designed and manipulated qualities characteristic of what is in fact a heavily mannered aesthetic.

For them, the foreshortened limbs and the deep wells of the sad, saucer eyes of a doll like So Shy Sherri are part of a unique and readily identifiable iconography whose distortions trigger with Pavlovian predictability a nostalgia for a mythical condition of endearing naiveté. The chilling paradox of the waxen fetishes over which we croon so irrepressibly is that the gross hokum of cuteness suggests the antithesis of what we would expect if we were to judge it on the basis of its extreme stylization alone: guilelessness, simplicity, and the refreshing lack of affectation.

Cuteness is not an aesthetic in the ordinary sense of the word at all and must by no means be mistaken for the physically appealing, the attractive. In fact, it is closely linked to the grotesque, the malformed. So Shy Sherri, for instance, is an anatomical disaster. Her legs are painfully swollen, her fingers are useless pink stumps that seem to have been lopped off at the knuckles, and her rosy cheeks are so bloated that her face is actually wider than it is long. Medieval or Renaissance images of the Christ child, those obese monstrosities whose Herculean muscularity always strikes the modern viewer as bafflingly inaccurate, make an interesting comparison. For an era like our own that prides itself on its ability to achieve effects of uncanny realism, the disfigured putti of the Baby Face series mark a decline rather than an advance in the representation of children, an eerie throwback to the slant-eyed sphinxes of Sienese altarpieces—alien, carnivorous-looking creatures who are, in many ways, as pictorially inexact as So Shy Sherri.

Far from being an accident of bad craftsmanship, the element of the   5
grotesque in cuteness is perfectly deliberate and must be viewed as the explicit intention of manufacturers of objects which elicit from us the complex emotions we feel when we encounter the fat faces and the squat, ruddy bodies of Galoob's dolls (or, to give another example, of the Trolls, a series of plastic figurines, extremely popular in the '60s, with potbellies, pug faces, and teased-up mops of brightly colored hair).

The grotesque is cute because the grotesque is pitiable, and pity is the primary emotion of this seductive and manipulative aesthetic which arouses our sympathies by creating anatomical pariahs, like the Cabbage Patch Dolls or even E.T., whose odd proportions and lack of symmetry diverge wildly from the relative balance and uniformity of ordinary bodies. The aesthetic of cuteness creates a class of outcasts and mutations, a ready-made race of lovable inferiors whom both children and adults collect, patronize, and enslave in the protective concubinage of their vast harems of homely dolls and snugglesome misfits. Something becomes cute not necessarily because of a quality it has but a quality it lacks, a certain neediness and inability to stand alone, as if it were an indigent starveling, lonely and rejected because of a hideousness we find more touching than unsightly.

The koalas, pandas, dalmatians, and lambs of the stuffed animal series "Lost 'n Founds" directly allude to this state of homeless destitution. With their "adorable 'so-sad' eyes" that shed real tears, these shameless examples of the waif or pauper syndrome seem to be begging to be rescued from their defenseless state, so tellingly emphasized by paws as cumbersome as boxing gloves—absurd appendages that lie uselessly in their laps, totally free of any of the prehensile functions hands usually serve. Because it generates enticing images like these of ugliness and dejection, cuteness has become essential in the marketplace in that advertisers have learned that consumers will "adopt" products that create, often in their packaging alone, an aura of motherlessness, ostracism, and melancholy, the silent desperation of the lost puppy dog clamoring to be befriended—namely, to be bought.

Cuteness, in short, is not something we find in our children but something we *do* to them. Because it aestheticizes unhappiness, helplessness, and deformity, it almost always involves an act of sadism on the part of its creator, who makes an unconscious attempt to maim, hobble, and embarrass the thing he seeks to idolize. The process of conveying cuteness to the viewer disempowers its objects, forcing them into ridiculous situations and making them appear more ignorant and vulnerable than they really are (as in William Wegman's hilarious photographs of his dog, the much-put-upon Man Ray, whose beseeching absurdity has made him the solemn mascot of cuteness at its most highbrow). Adorable things are often most adorable in the middle of a pratfall or a blunder: Winnie-the-Pooh with his snout stuck in the hive; the 101 dalmatians of Disney's classic collapsing in double splits and sprawling across the ice; Love-a-Lot Bear, in the movie *The Care Bears,* who stares disconsolately out at us with a paint bucket overturned on his head; or, the grimmest example of the cruelty of cuteness, the real live fainting goat which has acquired of late a perverse chic as a pet (bred with myatonia, a genetic heart defect, it coyly folds up and faints every time you scream at it). Although the gaze we turn on the cute thing seems maternal and solicitous, it is in actuality a transformative gaze that will stop at nothing to appease its hunger for expressing pity and bigheartedness, even at the expense of mutilating the object of its affections.

Turning its targets into statues and plush dolls, cuteness is ultimately dehumanizing, paralyzing its victims (who are often depicted asleep) into comatose or semiconscious things. In fact, the "thingness" of cute things is fixed firmly in our minds by means of the exaggerated textures and hues so characteristic of stuffed animals, with their shimmering satins and their luscious coats of fur, or dolls with their luxuriant profusion of hair, often of absurd length and body (as with the Cutie Kids of the Cutie Club series, a set of dolls whose psychedelic coiffures cascade down their sides in corkscrew curls that hang all of the way to their feet). "Anxiously awaiting power snuggles," F. A. O. Schwarz's huge grizzly bear is a slouching, seemingly invertebrate mammoth rippling with "serious spreads of soft spots" which are "just asking to be hauled and mauled," while their elephant, as large as a Saint Bernard, is described as "big, plump, and deliciously soft with soulful brown eyes that encourage big-time hugging and smooching." Vacant and malleable, animals like these inhabit a world of soothing tactile immediacy in which there are no sharp corners or abrasive materials but in which everything has been conveniently soft-sculpturized to yield to our importunate squeezes and hugs. If such soulless insentience is any indication, cuteness is the most scrutable and externalized of aesthetics in that it creates a world of stationary objects and tempting exteriors that deliver themselves up to us, putting themselves at our disposal and allowing themselves to be apprehended entirely through the senses. In light of the intense physicality of our response to their helpless torpor, our compulsive gropings even constitute something one might call cute sex or, in point of fact, given that one of the partners lies there groggy and catatonic, a kind of necrophilia, a neutered coupling consummated in our smothering embrace of a serenely motionless object incapable of reciprocating. Far from being content with the helplessness of our young as we find them in their natural state, we take all kinds of artificial measures to dramatize this vulnerability even further by defacing them, embarrassing them, devitalizing them, depriving them of their selfhood, and converting them, with the help of all of the visual and sartorial tricks at our disposal, into disempowered objects, furry love balls quivering in soft fabrics as they lapse into convulsive withdrawal for their daily fix of TLC.

Exaggerating the vast discrepancies of power between the sturdy adult and the enfeebled and susceptible child, the narcissism of cuteness is also very evident in the way that the aesthetic ascribes human attributes to nonhuman things. Anthropomorphism is to a large extent the rhetorical strategy of children's books, which often generate their narratives from a kind of animal transvestism in which dogs, cats, bears, and pigs have the clothing and demeanor of human beings. Calendars, another rich source of cuteness, also employ animal transvestism as a major theme—mice as prima ballerinas in toe shoes and tutus, dogs in party hats and sunglasses, or swallow-tailed hamsters in tuxes and cummerbunds rearing up on their hind legs to give each other what appears to be an affectionate peck on the cheek. Even an artist as respected as William Wegman subtly refashions, in the appropriative style of postmodernism, the lowbrow aesthetic of cuteness by decking out his lugubrious mastiff, an irresistibly funereal pooch cheerlessly resigned to his fate, in everything from Christian Dior to Calvin Klein jeans.

Examples like these reveal that the cute worldview is one of massive human chauvinism, which rewrites the universe according to an iconographic agenda dominated by the pathetic fallacy. Multiplying our image a thousandfold and reverberating like an echo chamber with the familiar sounds of our own voices, the cute vision of the natural world is a world without nature, one that annihilates "otherness," ruthlessly suppresses the nonhuman, and allows nothing, including our own children, to be separate and distinct from us.

The imitative nature of cuteness can also be seen in the aesthetic's relation to precocity. One of the things we find cutest in the behavior of our children is their persistence in mimicking us, not only in such time-honored traditions as dress-up (the anthropomorphic version of which is played out obsessively in children's literature), but in that most basic form of child's play, mothering, whether it be of a doll or of a family pet. The spectacle of toddlers rocking their babies, changing the diapers of the many incontinent toys on the market, placating anxious dolls, or thrashing disobedient teddy bears elicits some of our most gloating and unrestrained responses to cuteness. Nothing delights us more than the strange sight of a one-year-old in a stroller meeting a barely ambulatory two-year-old, who, rather than seeking to establish a kind of spontaneous esprit de corps with his peer, breaks rank and jibbers baby talk at the bewildered object of his curiously perfunctory affections.

As co-conspirators in this game of make-believe maturity, we reward children who at once feign helplessness and assume adult authority in mothering others, reinforcing simultaneously both infantilism and precocity. The child is thus taught not only to be cute in himself but to recognize and enjoy cuteness, to play the dual roles of actor and audience, cootchy-cooing as much as he is cootchy-cooed. In this way, our culture actively inculcates the aesthetic doctrines of cuteness by giving our children what amounts to a thorough education in the subject involving extensive and rigorous training in role-playing. By encouraging them to imitate the way we ourselves fawn over their own preciousness, we give them the opportunity to know cuteness from both sides of the equation, not only from the standpoint of the object receiving the attention but from the standpoint of those giving it as well, from their appreciative audience-cum-artistic directors whom they impersonate for brief and touching intervals in their own highly informative charades of child-rearing. We teach our children the nature and value of cuteness almost from the dawn of consciousness and initiate them into the esoteric rituals of its art, passing on to them the tribal legacy of its iconographic traditions, its strange, self-mutilating ceremonies, as alien in their way, at least to a culture unindoctrinated in cuteness, as many of the scarification customs of Africa or New Guinea. Because imitation allows children to observe their own behavior with the analytic detachment with which they in turn are observed by their admirers, cuteness is unique among aesthetics because it lays the foundations for its own survival by building into itself a form of proselytizing.

The association of cuteness with a delusional state of artlessness prevents us from realizing that the qualities of primitivism and droll savagery around which we have woven this all-consuming folk religion are not naturally occurring elements of the universe but cheap alloys that embody something we would *like* to see in children rather than something we actually do see there. Its conventions are the residue of unfulfilled wishes that crystallize from the heated interaction of the daily realities of children with our quixotic and unobtainable notions of what they should ideally be like. Cuteness is every parent's portable utopia, the rose-colored lenses that color and blur the profound drudgery of child-rearing with soft-focused sentimentality. We use it to allay fears of our failures as parents and to numb us to the irritations of the vigilance we must maintain over creatures who are, in many instances, despite the anesthetizing ideology of cuteness, more in control of us than we are of them.

Although it is easy to sympathize with the disquieting frustrations that underlie this aesthetic, cuteness is in fact ultimately more a source of unhappiness among parents than comfort. To superimpose the vast edifice of fetishized images and intricate rituals onto the shallow foundations of a reality that cannot withstand its weight is to invite disappointment not only for us but for our children as well. Cuteness saturates the visual landscape of consumerism with images that cause feelings of inadequacy among parents, who inevitably measure the rowdy and selfish behavior of their own children by the exacting ideals of tractability, cuddliness, and quiescence promoted by an aesthetic at loggerheads with reality. Just as the inundation of our culture with the glitzy images of recent video pornography has elevated our aesthetic standards in regard to our partners (and consequently interfered with our sexual enjoyment of ordinary bodies in all of their imperfections), so cuteness elevates our expectations in regard to our children. It prevents us from enjoying them in their natural, unindoctrinated state, oppressed as we are by our apparent failures as care givers who strive unavailingly to discern in our headstrong offspring the lineaments of the model child, that ghoulish incubus summoned forth by an aesthetic that causes so much soul-searching and self-recrimination.

The result of this psychological malaise is an entirely new aesthetic, an invention of the last few decades: the anti-cute. In an effort to counteract the lethal toxicity of the images of children we are constantly ingesting, a culture like our own naturally produces as an antidote images of the exact opposite of cuteness: the perverse. Our belief that our children are harmless little cherubs collides with their intransigence and generates in the process so much hostility that we are inclined to view them as corrupt, possessed, even satanic.

Cuteness thus coexists in a dynamic relation with the perverse. The failure of the hyperboles of one aesthetic gives rise to the hyperboles of the other, of the child as the vehicle of diabolical powers from the Great Beyond which have appropriated the tiny, disobedient bodies of our elfish changelings as instruments for their assaults on the stability of family life. The spate of films about demonic possession shows just how assiduous we have become about building up the new iconography of the anti-cute. Catering to a deep need in the popular imagination, Hollywood has begun to manufacture images that function as outrageous travesties of cuteness, like those found in *Poltergeist,* in which a young girl becomes the conduit of tormented spirits of the damned who emerge from the throbbing blue light of the television set; or in *Child's Play,* in which the spirit of a dead serial killer inhibits the body of a doll named Chuckie, who, stalking down hallways with butcher knives tucked behind its back, murders Aunt Maggie, the babysitter, by giving her such a jolt that she staggers backwards out of the kitchen window and plummets ten floors to splatter on the hood of a parked car. Similarly, in David Kronenberg's *The Brood,* the dwarfish gnomes of a protagonist's children gestate in moldy embryonic sacs hanging outside of her belly where they begin spontaneously to respond to her volatile moods, ultimately bludgeoning her mother to death with kitchen utensils in a fit of rage.

Although it is still the dominant mode of representing children, cuteness is an aesthetic under siege, the object of contempt, laughter, and skepticism. Its commercialized aura of greeting-card naiveté makes it so fragile, so vulnerable to ridicule, that it cannot withstand the frank realism with which matters of parenting, divorce, and sexuality are now, for the first time, being addressed by the public at large. In the last few decades, cuteness has been subjected to remorseless satire as we attempt to loosen the grip of its iconography on an imagination hungry for images closer to the harsh realities of the era of the latchkey kid, the two-career family, the single-parent household, the crack baby, and the less than innocent drug-running sixthgrader with a beeper in one pocket and a .44 Magnum automatic pistol in the other. Loud and chaotic, *The Simpsons* is the new anti-cute show of the '90s, the "all-American dysfunctional family," as they have been nicknamed. Their household constitutes a direct subversion of the insipidity of cuteness, with its cartoon characters' harshly contoured shapes, gaping mouths, and enormous boiled-egg eyes goggling in such a way as to suggest the mindless somnambulism of compulsive TV viewers. The anti-cute launches a frontal assault on fuzzy-wuzziness with a blitz of images of the child as the monster, the petulant and demanding brat who disdains all of the sacrosanct laws of property ownership, gleefully annihilating Cuisinarts and microwaves as he mows a broad swathe of destruction through the very heart of the household's inner sanctum.

With the rise of the anti-cute, we are witnessing what amounts to civil war in the contemporary aesthetic of the family, a battle in which the image of the child as the unnatural spawn of Satan, an impish spirit of pure malevolent mischievousness, has locked horns with that of another sort of creature altogether. Generating their plots by pitting the cute against the anti-cute, Parts 1 and 2 of *Gremlins* provide a kind of allegory of this transformation. In Part 2, the adorable Gizmo (an appropriate name for this standard-bearer of cuteness, since it emphasizes the animal's status as an inert object) purrs with a contented coo, its droopy ears and sad eyes inviting the lubricious embraces of cute sex. After it is exposed to water, however, it begins to reproduce, laying eggs that enter a larval stage in repulsive cocoons covered in viscous membranes. Whereas Gizmo is soft, dry, and relatively well behaved, the ferocious aliens that quickly hatch from their water-induced hibernation in these protoplasmic pods are, as one character calls them, "ugly, slimy, mean-spirited, and gloppy." In them, both the behavior and appearance of cute objects are at once evoked and subverted.

Gizmo's strokable fur is transformed into a wet, scaly integument, while the vacant portholes of its eyes (the most important facial feature of

20

the cute thing, giving us free access to its soul and ensuring its total scrutability, its incapacity to hold back anything in reserve) become diabolical slits hiding a lurking intelligence, just as its dainty paws metamorphose into talons and its pretty puckered lips into enormous Cheshire grimaces with full sets of sharp incisors. Whereas cute things have clean, sensuous surfaces that remain intact and unpenetrated (suggesting, in fact, that there is nothing at all inside, that what you see is what you get), the anti-cute Gremlins are constantly being squished and disemboweled, their entrails spilling out into the open, as they explode in microwaves and are run through paper shredders and blenders. With the help of food and water, they multiply exponentially and begin their devastating campaign—Hollywood's favorite plot device—against property ownership, destroying in Part 1 an entire town and, in Part 2, a skyscraper modeled on the Trump Tower. In this Manichean contrast between the precious Gizmo and its progeny, the hyperactive vandals who incarnate a new but equally stylized representation of youth and innocence, *Gremlins* neatly encapsulates the iconographic challenges to an aesthetic that is gradually relinquishing its hegemony over the popular imagination as the vapid artificialities of its conventions are burlesqued in our culture's recent attempts to purge itself of its antiquated religion of infantilism.

Questions for Discussion

1. Harris begins his essay with a description of So Shy Sherri, an example of the cuteness he then explains. What aspects of this doll illustrate Harris's definition of cuteness?
2. What causes people to be drawn to cute dolls and other manifestations of cuteness?
3. According to Harris, cute images inspire pity, but pity should not be mistaken for the "maternal and solicitous." How do you define *pity,* and how would you distinguish it from other emotions?
4. If Americans are trained to believe that children should be cute, what are the consequences for children and their parents?
5. Drawing attention to "The Simpsons," Harris notes that "cuteness is an aesthetic under siege." What factors are causing people to rebel against the cute?
6. Having begun his essay with an example of the cute, Harris concludes with a discussion of *Gremlins,* an example of the anticute. How effective is this example? Is it sufficiently developed so that it can be understood by readers who have not seen the films?

Suggestions for Writing

1. By defining terms, writers shape the discussion they have with readers; other writers may define the same terms differently. If you do not agree

with Harris's definition of *cuteness,* write a definition of your own, and illustrate it with appropriate examples.

2. Harris claims that cute products are so common in the United States that they have become "a form of visual clutter we respond to without really seeing." Write an essay identifying another kind of image that prompts consumers to buy products, and explain what causes this image to be successful.

6

Writing to Evaluate Something

When you are trying to decide whether you want to buy a wool sweater or a cotton one, when you bet your brother that your team will win the game this weekend, when you decide which dictionary to buy or make a decision to vote for a particular candidate—when you do any of these things, you are *evaluating*. Evaluating means thinking critically so that you can make intelligent choices—and when you make your evaluation public, influence others to accept your judgments.

Evaluation requires that you determine the nature or the quality of what you are judging. For instance, if you decide to consume less caffeine, that decision is probably based on a judgment that caffeine can be bad for you. Your purchase of a name brand lawn mower rather than a store brand rests upon your evaluation of the quality of the two brands to assure yourself that you will have a reliable, well-made machine; in this situation your concern is with quality. Evaluation also means determining importance, benefit, or worth. For example, importance would be the issue if you were trying to determine which in a long list of tasks you absolutely had to get done before the weekend. You are concerned with benefit if you decide that a course in art history would be more useful to you as an architecture major than a course in music history. When you buy a house or a car, you will most likely ask yourself if it is worth what you have to pay for it.

In the preceding examples you are trying to convince yourself of something. But there will be plenty of times when your evaluation must convince someone else: Which supplier should you recommend to your employer? What should you say when asked to write a letter of recommendation? Whose opinion should prevail when a couple disagree about which of two apartments to rent? Addressing situations like these means you have to define your assumptions, anticipate opposition, and draw conclusions.

When writing an evaluation, you also need to assure your readers that you have the credentials to make judgments about the subject you are addressing. Demonstrating that you know what you're talking about is essential if you want your readers to take your evaluation seriously. The more your readers think you know about your subject, the more likely they are to follow your advice. But no matter how knowledgeable you may be, try not to sound as if you have a monopoly on good advice. People can take a perverse pleasure in not following the advice of a critic who seems arrogant. Consider how Mark Twain just barely avoids the charge of arrogance in his essay on James Fenimore Cooper. Much of Twain's credibility results from his own reputation as a master of the craft of fiction; but he also disposes the reader to agree with his attack on Cooper by allowing his trademark folksy tone to show through. Thinking, "This person who seems so unpretentious couldn't possibly be an ill-tempered, arrogant boor," the reader acquits Twain and finds Cooper guilty as charged. Like Twain, you can often benefit from sounding engaging as well as knowledgeable. Although the extent to which you allow your personality to come through will depend upon your rhetorical situation, evaluations are seldom impersonal.

PLANNING YOUR ESSAY

When you are ready to choose a subject for evaluation, consider what you have some experience and knowledge of as well as what you are interested in. If you are knowledgeable about a subject, you will usually have a good idea of what criteria people use when evaluating that subject. This knowledge will help you focus on how to make your evaluation satisfy your readers' needs. For example, if you recently bought a stationary exercise bicycle for home use and think that your written evaluation of the available models will help others decide which one to buy, make sure that you don't base your evaluation only on which bicycle is cheapest. Readers also need to know what they are getting for their money. Report what you know about features such as mileage counters and tension adjustment; then discuss how well different bikes perform and how likely they are to hold up under use. Otherwise, a reader may wind up with a bicycle that was cheap because it lacked important features or because it was difficult to use.

If you have the time to do research, writing an evaluation can be an excellent way to prepare for a decision you need to make. Thus, if you are planning to buy exercise equipment but cannot decide between a stationary bicycle and a stair stepper, you can use evaluation as a way to decide what to buy. Careful shoppers go through this process routinely. They may visit a number of stores, question salespeople and friends who have experience with the product, and—if the purchase is large—go to the library and consult one or more of the magazines available for consumers. Writing an evaluation of a product you expect to purchase is a way of discovering and reporting the results of this process.

Evaluation, of course, is not limited to comparative shopping. Other situations require other strategies. But whatever your subject, you should examine what kind of information you have about it and assess whether you have to do research. Information is essential, because you must support your evaluation with specific evidence. For instance, when evaluating a novel by James Fenimore Cooper, Twain supported the claims he made with evidence from the novel. When evaluating all-season tires, *Consumer Reports* conducted extensive tests to research which are best. John Gross had to view *Schindler's List*—probably several times—before writing "Hollywood and the Holocaust." Choose evidence judiciously according to your understanding of your subject, and be sure that you have enough.

A good way to begin an evaluation is to think about your subject analytically. Here is a four-step process for using analysis to plan an evaluation.

1. Divide your subject by identifying its major components. For example, if you are evaluating a restaurant, you might address atmosphere, service, food, and prices. Or if you are evaluating an essay, you can judge it according to content, style, and organization.
2. Consider what information you have (or can obtain) to discuss the divisions you have identified.
3. Ask yourself which of these divisions are most likely to be important to readers, and consider whether you have overlooked any important part of your subject that your readers would probably want information about. Unless you are writing for your own benefit, eliminate any division that seems to be a personal interest unlikely to concern other readers.
4. Decide whether to discuss all important divisions that you have identified or to focus only upon one if you have enough information about it and feel sure that you would be focusing upon something important. An evaluation of a restaurant, for example, can be limited to a discussion of its food (although you would probably end up subdividing that subject somehow—according to appetizers, entrees, and desserts or according to selection, presentation, and taste).

When planning an evaluation, you should also consider how strongly you feel about your subject. Some people believe that you should always write about something you have a real investment in, because your enthusiasm will enhance the liveliness of your writing. Others think this policy leads to a one-sided evaluation. If you've just bought a new car and are crazy about it, you probably lack the objectivity you need to evaluate it fairly. But if you've driven the car for a year and you still love it, you probably have enough objectivity to see its flaws as well as its virtues and can execute a balanced judgment. One of the strengths of Ada Louise Huxtable's "Washington's Stillborn Behemoth" is the balance she provides: For instance, she points out that we need to look at "the best and the worst of this new building." At the other extreme, Twain finds no redeeming features in Cooper's *Deerslayer;* he uses humor to cloak the imbalance.

DEFINING YOUR CRITERIA

Effective, accurate evaluations are not the result of whim; they are based on standards that most people agree with, that the authority of the writer bolsters, or that can be independently verified. Evaluation requires you to make the criteria you use for judging absolutely clear—as Twain does when he provides a list of eighteen "rules governing literary art," or as *Consumer Reports* does to evaluate tires. Both Twain and *Consumer Reports* apply criteria that many people would agree with—and the criteria can be verified by questioning a representative sample of readers or by conducting tests. In the case of "All-Season Tires," these criteria involve tangible qualities such as size and price that anyone who cares to can verify as well as functional qualities that have been empirically tested in research laboratories. Such criteria have little or nothing to do with individual preferences. Anyone can verify the judgment that a brand X all-season tire is a better buy for $65 than the same tire for $80. And anyone would understand your choice of brand Y, considering that brand Y offers a 60,000-mile warranty. In both cases you have based your decision primarily on independently verifiable criteria—price and warranty. On the other hand, you might feel confident taking *Consumer Reports'* recommendation not only because you have read the article summarizing the results of its tests but also because you came to that article with a positive evaluation of the magazine itself—an evaluation based upon another set of criteria, which may or may not be verifiable. Your experience with the tires thus provides an opportunity for further evaluation of both the tires themselves and the magazine that recommended them.

For judging *Schindler's List,* Gross uses a criterion that the reader cannot test empirically and that he cannot state directly. He can, however, state his misgivings:

> I can't pretend, then, that I approached the movie with a completely open mind. I was apprehensive—afraid of seeing terrible events sentimentalized, afraid of sentimentality proving all the more insidious for being applied with sleek technical skill.

Stating his misgivings gives Gross a basis for implying his criteria: morality, emotional grasp, and verisimilitude. Criteria like these are subjective, internal, and a matter of the evaluator's judgment; as such, they can be risky to use. They are implicit in every piece of evidence Gross uses when criticizing the screenplay, the cinematography, the directing, and the acting. If we accept his evaluation, it is partly because we perceive Gross to be an honest evaluator—he has already told us that he didn't expect much from Spielberg. We also recognize that Gross has special expertise: He demonstrates his knowledge about the Holocaust, refers to having read the book upon which the film was based, and reveals familiarity with other Holocaust films. Gross also protects his judgment by hedging it. Although he applauds the film as "an outstanding achievement," he judges that "for all its brilliance, *Schindler's List* as a whole can't transcend the limitations of docudrama." By praising Spielberg for doing what seemed beyond his abilities and by acknowledging that the film is still a "contribution to popular culture," Gross attempts to demonstrate for readers that he is discriminating as well as fair-minded.

Criteria should also be appropriate for your audience. Suppose your criterion for evaluating a magazine for novice computer users is that each issue should include a new shortcut for software developers. Your criterion is inappropriate for your audience because someone learning how to use a computer is unlikely to develop new software. Similarly, if you base your judgment of stocks on which ones will double your money fastest, your standard is inappropriate for advising retirees, whose primary interest in stocks is a safe income. As another example, consider "Someone to Watch Over Us" by James S. Gordon, which originally appeared in the *New York Times Book Review,* a newspaper supplement read mainly by college graduates. Holding many of the same beliefs as Gordon, subscribers to the *New York Times Book Review* would probably agree that John Mack should "have done his homework better and written a far more informative and authoritative book" than *Human Encounters with Aliens* is. But readers of *National Enquirer* or other supermarket tabloids may find this evaluation based upon criteria that they do not agree with. As a final example, if you are evaluating local housing for an audience of college students who want to party, you will not want to rate housing higher because playgrounds and day-care facilities are available; whereas that information can be vital for married couples or single parents. You should set criteria you think your readers will agree with—or at least will not reject.

Examine your criteria and ask yourself if they justify the evaluation you plan to make. You may be furious at one of the local apartment complexes for charging you two months' rent as a deposit because you have a pet, but your sense of having been victimized is not necessarily a legitimate criterion for giving that complex a negative rating in your guide to local housing. You would be much better off simply stating the policy; perhaps other prospective tenants would not object to such a high deposit—may even approve of it. Base your evaluation of the apartment complex on more objective criteria. For example, what is the rent per square foot? Are the apartments furnished? What appliances are included? Is there a fireplace? What kind of storage is available? Does the rent include access to swimming pools and party facilities? Have there been complaints about how the complex is maintained? What about late-payment policies?

You also need to consider the kind of evidence that will persuade your audience to accept your evaluation. If you want the single students on campus to accept your negative evaluation of the apartment complex that has the high pet deposit, you might consider investigating management's policies about parties, whether guests can use the pool, and how management handles summer sublets. If the policies are strict in these ways, single students should be informed; and the students will probably elect to rent elsewhere, even though there is a grand party room, every unit has a fireplace, and the rent is not out of line. You should offer evidence according to what you think your readers expect to find out and how knowledgeable they are. It is rare that any subject will elicit the kind of universal agreement that will permit you to use the same criteria and information for all audiences.

Readers expect to find enough information to reconstruct the reasoning you used to arrive at your evaluation. Be sure to provide adequate information for readers unfamiliar with the subject you are evaluating. When readers are unfamiliar with a subject that is complex, a thorough evaluation can take many pages. But whatever the level of expertise your audience possesses, you are responsible for making sure that they understand the information you give them—and the criteria with which you are interpreting that information—so that the judgment you reach will be both clear and credible.

ORGANIZING YOUR ESSAY

However you choose to proceed, you should state your judgment clearly and place it prominently. It is the main point of your essay and, depending upon other decisions you have made, may appear near the beginning or the end of your writing. Generally, it is useful to put it in both places. By placing it near the beginning, you prepare readers for the conclusion you will draw; by placing it near the end, you demonstrate how specific evidence has led to that conclusion. It is also usually wise to show your readers that you have considered both the strengths and the weaknesses of your subject. To do so, you may wish to adapt the following pattern of classical oration for evaluations.

- Present your subject. (This discussion includes any background information, description, acknowledgment of weaknesses, and so forth.)
- State your criteria. (If your criteria are controversial, be sure to justify them.)

- Make your judgment. (State it as clearly and emphatically as possible.)
- Give your reasons. (Be sure to present good evidence for each reason.)
- Refute opposing evaluations. (Let your reader know you have given thoughtful consideration to opposing views, when such views exist.)
- State your conclusion. (You may restate or summarize your judgment.)

Notice that the refutation comes near the end, after the judgment is well established. An alternative strategy is to refute opposing evaluations early in the essay; this strategy can be especially effective when opposing views are already widely held and you intend to advance a new point of view. Recognizing views that your audience may already hold can, in this case, clear the way for a fresh evaluation. This is the strategy that Twain used when writing about Cooper at a time when Cooper was much praised. (For additional information on refutation, see pp. 424–426.)

Consider how you can most advantageously present your subject. Make use of appropriate techniques for developing ideas. For instance, you might make a contrastive judgment, as Huxtable does when she contrasts the new Library of Congress Building to the original library building. Comparative judgments focus on similarities, and contrastive judgments focus on differences, but the two can be (and often are) combined. In any comparison or contrast you must find a point of similarity between what you are evaluating and another item, and this similarity should be significant. For instance, *Consumer Reports* is careful to compare one brand of all-season tires with another brand of all-season tires, not with snow tires. There is little purpose in evaluating two identical tires, but a reader in need of tires will be interested in a comparison of similar tires made by different companies. Note carefully the points of similarity or difference; they will be your basis for comparison.

As you work your way through your comparison, present your evidence in an organized way. People generally find it useful to see one of two common patterns of organization: subject by subject or point by point. When two subjects are evaluated in a subject-by-subject pattern, the first subject is discussed thoroughly before the second subject is discussed. In a point-by-point pattern, both subjects are discussed throughout the article— with the discussion organized around different aspects (or points) of evaluation. In "All-Season Tires" *Consumer Reports* uses a point-by-point organization, a good choice if you have many points of comparison or more than two subjects. This kind of organization has the advantage of not requiring the reader to keep the whole subject in mind, but the frequent switches between the items compared can sometimes seem choppy. Only one switch is necessary in subject-by-subject comparison, but readers must keep a whole subject in mind, which can become difficult in a long or complicated comparison. Subject-by-subject comparison has the advantage, though, of allowing the readers to concentrate on a single item in the comparison, as Huxtable allows us to do in "Washington's Stillborn Behemoth."

Comparison and contrast are by no means limited to evaluations; elsewhere in this book you will find writers using these strategies for other motives. But comparison and contrast are especially useful for evaluation, because placing two subjects alongside each other can lead to a better understanding of each—and often help you decide whether one is superior. If offered two different jobs, both of which seem attractive, you can probably clarify which is preferable by carefully comparing them.

It would be a mistake, however, to assume that evaluation must always lead to a rating of some sort. Although criticism usually leads to a judgment regarding quality or worth, it is also concerned with improving our knowledge of what is being evaluated. In this chapter "Hollywood and the Holocaust" provides the clearest example of how evaluation can be informative. Discussing *Schindler's List,* Gross begins by offering his judgment; he calls the film "an outstanding achievement." But he then goes on to report information about the Holocaust, for his judgment makes sense only if readers can understand the knowledge that Gross brought to the film. Similarly, when Ralph de Toledano judges a new collection of Billie Holiday recordings, he devotes most of his essay to demonstrating his knowledge of Holiday's accomplishments. A critic reviewing a book or movie in a newspaper is expected to give the work an overall rating, because that is what newspaper readers most want to know: Is this work worth reading or seeing? (For information on reviewing, see pp. 478–480.) But evaluation isn't always a matter of getting people to do (or not do) something. Sometimes it's simply devoted to getting people to see something that they might otherwise miss. Judgment in this case may be implicit. Understanding that there is more to something than we had realized can lead us to reappraise our valuation of that subject.

As we have seen before, motives for writing can overlap. You will usually need to report and interpret information to show readers how you reached a particular judgment—and if you want your evaluation to be persuasive, you may need to draw upon some of the strategies discussed in the introduction to Chapter 9. The selections that follow in this chapter were chosen to give you a sense of different types of evaluation. As you read them, try to evaluate the extent to which each succeeds in accomplishing what it sets out to do.

THE GREATNESS OF BILLIE

Ralph de Toledano

> *Rooted firmly in African-American culture, jazz has become internationally recognized as an inventive and powerful contribution to the world's music. Of the women vocalists who specialized in jazz, Billie Holiday (1915–1959) was one of the very best. Rising from poverty and struggling against racism, which initially deprived her of many opportunities for singing, Holiday paid a high price for her success. In 1947 she was arrested for possessing narcotics, and her career subsequently fell into eclipse. The reissue of a number of her recordings forty years later prompted the following review by one of her original fans.*

Billie Holiday came upon us in the days when we came upon jazz—the long-dead days when each spun performance spoke to our youth, and she sang to its truths and its posturings. The generations since have forgotten her. Forgive me, then, if like the Ancient Mariner I shake my long white beard and steel my eye to talk about her.

I first heard Billie as she sang "Strange Fruit" around the eddying cigarette smoke of Café Society. It was an agitprop song about lynching—"strange fruit hanging from the poplar trees"—sung in a now long-gone Greenwich Village nightclub. But it had its power and validity in the exquisite torture of her voice and in the ungainly beauty of a dark face starkly delineated by the baby spots. John Hammond, who contributed so much to jazz by opening doors to great musicians, had been her sponsor, and we were grateful to him and to Billie.

Those were the great days for Billie and for those who loved jazz. She was recording then on the Brunswick label against the contrived rhythms of Teddy Wilson at the piano and the sidemen he assembled, and under her own name for the cheaper Vocalion label. Name any of the fine jazz musicians of the 1930s and they were on those recording dates, backing her and playing their own rich solos in the grooves between her singing. It was a Who's Who of jazz—Benny Goodman before he had been crowned King of Swing by the PR men; Artie Shaw gut-bucketing as he never did with his own orchestra; the clear, explicit tones of Bunny Berrigan's trumpet before the liquor got him; Ellington's Johnny Hodges and the arabesques of his alto saxophone; Lester Young, out of the Basie band, and Ben Webster on tenor; great trombonists like Benny Morton and Jack Teagarden, and so many more.

It was jazz, the good and the true, all the way. Later on the drugs and the hospitals and the cures took over, but Billie continued to sing even though the bell had cracked. It was jazz because Billie had it to give. Even when she was sinking into the morass, she never lost the plangency of her voice, the perfect phrasing, the instinctive feel for how far to stray from the tune before it reasserted itself, the jazz rubato sense that told her how long to hold a note before she pursued the next, the artistry that could take a banal melody and even more banal lyrics and shred them to their essentials. You can count on the fingers of one hand the singers who could do this—and after Bessie Smith, Billie led the field.

But why bother with the years when Billie sang to strings and slick   5 arrangements. The best years were those with the pick-up bands, the jazz men assembled just for this or that date to play their music and to give Billie the lift that she returned to them. Those best years have been brought together as *The Billie Holiday Story,* in six boxed LPs, by Blue Angel (1738 Allied Street, Charlottesville, Va. 22901; telephone 800-446-7964). It's all there in the interplay of singer and instrumentalists that explicates and ad-umbrates a song's inner logic, that draws out the sensibility of what is often dismissed as Tin Pan Alley.

Those who look down their noses at Tin Pan Alley should give ear to what Billie did with its product. Tin Pan Alley expressed an American idiom and an American cadence, and Billie gave us the jazz distillate. To Tin Pan Alley's sometimes saccharine voice, Billie added ironic overtones and the undertone of man's fate. Tin Pan Alley presented us with the sentimentality of "romantic" love, and Billie heightened it and gave it depth and sorrow. What American popular music offered, Billie understood and conveyed.

For those of us who sang and danced to the golden notes of the 1930s, before rock 'n' roll made it all nasal, this Blue Angel collection of Billie Holiday is so much more than a compound of nostalgia. It is a compendium of a great musical heritage—the songs that we can still hear America sing-ing. There are a few songs missing, and I regret them—"Billie's Blues," "Easy Living," "Summertime," for example. But the catalogue is complete enough.

And why cavil? Inevitably you return to Billie—the Billie Holiday we applauded in New York's boîtes, the Billie Holiday in shimmering satin who stood before the bands of the 1930s and 1940s in the caverns of now-vanished movie palaces, the Billie Holiday who could sing and mean the lyrics of one of her songs—"If you let me love you, it's for sure I'll love you all the way." She died tragically and ignominiously, but her legacy is there in *The Billie Holiday Story*—in a style and a voice that spoke of small but eternal verities.

In her lifetime, they tried to make a cult of her. They called her Lady Day, moving her into the make-believe aristocracy of jazz Counts and Dukes and Kings. But Billie Holiday was not that kind of "lady." She was a unique and tremendous talent who had escaped the Harlem pimps and risen to the small pantheon of great jazz singers. When Billie died, something of jazz died with her. But in these recordings, she is beyond life, beyond death. Even as we mourn her, Billie Holiday's singing says, *Sursum corda.*°

Sursum corda: Latin for "Lift up your hearts."

Questions for Discussion

1. Consider how de Toledano addresses this essay to his own generation, a generation that heard Billie Holiday sing in person. Did this strategy make you feel excluded from his audience, or were you willing to imagine yourself part of his "us"?

2. De Toledano claims that Billie Holiday has been forgotten by the generations after his own. Is this claim fair?

3. How would you describe the tone of this essay?

4. Why does de Toledano admire Billie Holiday? What are his criteria for a good jazz singer?

5. In addition to evaluating *The Billie Holiday Story,* what else does de Toledano evaluate in this article?

Suggestions for Writing

1. Write an evaluation of a recent recording by a singer or band of your own choice, locating that recording within the context of comparable works.

2. Since Billie Holiday's death (in 1959), many other music performers have died prematurely. Could these deaths be saying something about the American music industry? Research Holiday's career and evaluate how fairly she was treated by those who stood to profit from her work.

ALL-SEASON TIRES

Consumer Reports

Have you ever felt bewildered shopping for a product that you need but know very little about—a product important enough that you are anxious to make the right choice from among an array of similar possibilities? If so, you understand why shoppers sometimes turn to consumer magazines and other shopping guides. The following article evaluates a commonly used product that many people take for granted. As you read, note how the evaluation has been organized to show what was tested, how it was tested, and what the results were.

Tires don't get much respect. All too many motorists think of them as homely lumps of rubber rather than complex, highly engineered products that greatly affect a car's ability to stop quickly or swerve in an emergency.

Tires have improved considerably over the past decade, thanks to new rubber compounds and computer-aided design. But tire manufacturers, alas, still market their wares in the same old ways, seemingly designed to confuse rather than inform.

Hype such as "triple traction" and "ultra high performance" is singularly unhelpful in picking a safe, competent tire. Nor can you count on model names for consistency. Goodyear, for instance, created some name recognition for its high-performance *Eagle* tires—and then carried over the *Eagle* name to a wide range of tires that perform very differently.

Tire makers also commonly modify an existing tire model to meet an automaker's specifications. Take the split-personality *Firestone FR680,* for example. In a tire store, it's an all-season radial with an average expected tread life and a speed rating of S (which means the tire is certified to sustain 112 mph without failure). But when it appears as original equipment on, say, the Toyota Camry, the *FR680* has a shorter expected tread life but a higher speed rating of H (sustained speed of 130 mph).

Every tire design represents compromises. A soft rubber compound   5
that delivers good traction, for example, may wear out quickly. And a tire with low, stiff sidewalls may provide quick, accurate steering response, at the expense of ride comfort.

Carmakers typically want tires that improve fuel efficiency—lightweight tires that offer low rolling resistance. Carmakers also want tires that ride comfortably and quietly, to impress the potential car buyer during the all-important test drive. But when you replace your tires, you may be willing to give up a bit of fuel economy or ride softness for, say, better traction, longer tread life, or some other characteristic.

A TIRE FOR ALL SEASONS

Passenger-car tires fall into three loosely defined, overlapping groups: "all-season," "performance," and "touring." Within each group you'll find a wide range of prices and performance characteristics.

All-season tires are the kind that come standard on most family sedans. They try to strike a balance between reasonably high tread life and decent braking and cornering grip in both summer and winter.

Performance tires look different: They have a low sidewall profile and a wider and shallower tread. True performance tires deliver better wet and dry traction than other types, but worse traction in snow. They also tend to ride more harshly and, often, to wear more quickly.

Touring tires are a fairly new category, coined by the industry a few years ago to denote a premium all-season tire with some performance capabilities. The term has little meaning; tire makers use the term any way they choose. Dunlop, for example, calls its *Axiom* "the Touring Tire for the '90s," although we consider it an ordinary all-season tire.

10

SORTING THE CLAIMS

To sort out the manufacturers' competing claims, we tested eight brands of all-season tires. One of them was the *Dunlop Axiom,* a tire we top-rated when we reported on all-season tires in February 1992. We also included it in last February's report on supposedly higher-line "touring" tires; it finished respectably there, in the middle of the pack. The other seven all-season tires we tested are the *BF Goodrich The Advantage, Bridgestone Turanza S, Firestone FR680, General Ameri-Tech ST, Goodyear Invicta GS, Michelin XH4,* and *Sears Roadhandler Plus 70.*

We also tested two tires—the *Goodyear Aquatred* and the *General Hydro 2000*—specifically designed to grip well on wet roads. The *Aquatred* has a novel design, with a deep, wide groove running along the center of its tread. When we reported on it last year, it acquitted itself well in both wet and dry conditions, and we top-rated it. The *General Hydro* is a new competitor to the *Aquatred.*

We bought all the tires in size P185/70R14, which fits such widely sold models as the Honda Accord and Toyota Camry, and many Ford, GM, and Chrysler compact models. All the tires have a speed rating of S (sustained speeds of up to 112 mph) except the *Dunlop Axiom,* which has no speed rating. Average prices range from $58 for the *General Ameri-Tech* to $85 for the *Goodyear Aquatred* and *Michelin XH4.*

STOP AND GO

We mounted each set of tires on a 1992 Mazda 626, without letting our drivers know which tires were which. Our scoring stressed braking and cornering performance.

Braking tests included a series of severe stops, from 60 mph on dry   *15*
pavement and from 40 mph on wet pavement. We ran the wet braking tests
with the Mazda's antilock braking system engaged, and again with the ABS
disabled.

Cornering tests consisted of driving faster and faster around a "skid
pad"—an asphalt circle 200 feet in diameter—until the tires lost their grip.
We did that in both wet and dry conditions. An accelerometer in the car
recorded the lateral forces at which the tires lost their grip.

Handling tests included many laps around our snaking one-mile handling course. Our test drivers made subjective evaluations of how each set
of tires responded to the steering and how the tires felt as they began to lose
their grip. Those comments appear in the Ratings.

Rolling resistance affects fuel economy slightly. The more easily the
tires roll, the higher the mpg. We repeatedly coasted to a stop from a set
speed and measured how far the car rolled on each set of tires.

Tire noise can vary considerably from one tire model to another. We
drove at 30 mph, recorded the noise level with a digital tape recorder, and
analyzed the results in our audio lab.

We didn't check tread life, load capacity, or temperature rating. The   *20*
Government requires manufacturers to test for those characteristics and to
print the results on every tire's sidewall. . . . And we didn't judge ride, since
that's so dependent on the car's suspension. Nor did we test in snow, because
it's impossible to test accurately under all winter conditions. (The depth,
temperature, and texture of the snow would vary the test results.)

As in the past, we found significant differences between the best and
worst tires in the group, particularly in braking distance. On dry pavement,
the *Bridgestone Turanzas* came to a halt from 60 mph in about 144 feet, while
the *Goodyear Invictas* took more than 162 feet and the *General Ameri-Techs,*
nearly 170 feet.

The scores clustered closer in our wet braking tests from 40 mph. With
the antilock brakes engaged, stopping distances ranged from 71 feet to 83
feet; the *Aquatred,* the *Bridgestone Turanza,* the *General Hydro,* and the *Dunlop
Axiom* led the pack. With the ABS disengaged, stopping distances ranged
from 78 to 91 feet; the *Firestone FR680* joined the *Aquatred, General Hydro,*
and *Dunlop Axiom* as top performers in that test.

A CLOSE SHAVE

We inaugurated a new test this year to see how a tire's performance
changes as the tread wears down. Using a special lathe, we shaved off half
the tread depth on samples of every model. Then we reran our braking and
cornering tests.

In dry conditions, all the half-worn tires braked and cornered better—
some much better—than when new. That's not surprising. Half-worn tires

put more rubber on the road, which increases traction. Also, as the tread becomes shallower, it squirms less, so stability improves.

Wet performance was more surprising. With antilock brakes engaged, 25 all the tires stopped from two to eight feet shorter when worn than when new. The best performers, the *Goodyear Aquatred* and *Bridgestone Turanza,* braked shortest in both wet and dry conditions.

With the antilock feature disengaged, the shaved *General Hydra* and *BF Goodrich The Advantage* stopped shortest. The *Goodyear Aquatred* needed five more feet to stop after it was shaved, but it still finished respectably, about in the middle of the pack.

Does that mean tires improve with age? Not exactly—and certainly not indefinitely. At some point of wear, wet performance will drop dramatically. And even half-worn tires won't perform as well as new ones in snow. What it does mean, though, is that drivers generally needn't worry about performance falling off under normal driving conditions for at least the first 20,000 miles or so.

RECOMMENDATIONS

With the possible exception of the *General Ameri-Tech ST,* all the tires we tested provide satisfactory overall performance. The top four brands did even better than that in our safety-oriented tests.

Once again this year, the *Goodyear Aquatred* ($85 average price) topped our ratings by a small margin. It performed particularly well in our wet-pavement tests, in both hard stops and hard cornering. It also braked and cornered very well on dry pavement, and our testers liked the way it handled through tight turns. The *Aquatred* was noisier than average for this group, but our testers didn't find the noise all that bothersome. The *Aquatred* also has rather high rolling resistance, which means that it might reduce fuel economy slightly.

The *Bridgestone Turanza S* ($75 average) also did well on wet pavement, 30 and it stopped a little shorter than the *Aquatred* on a dry track. Without antilock brakes, however, the *Turanza's* wet-braking ability declined to average.

Two other worthy tires are the *Dunlop Axiom* and the *General Hydro 2000*. The *Axiom* turned in a good, solid overall performance. And at $66, on average, it looks like the bargain of the bunch. The *Hydro* ($78) braked very well both with and without antilock brakes. It also cornered well on dry pavement, though it scored a notch or two below the *Aquatred* in wet cornering.

Extrapolating test results from our P185/70R14-size tires to other sizes is risky. However, we've noted in previous tests a certain consistency among tires of the same profile (the "70" in our tires' size designation) and speed rating. Thus, we're reasonably confident that 15-inch, 70-series versions of these tires with a speed rating of S would perform similarly to the 14-inch tires we tested.

Questions for Discussion

1. According to *Consumer Reports,* how have tire manufacturers made shopping for tires confusing?
2. In what sense is an all-season tire a compromise? What do carmakers expect from a tire? How might your own expectations differ?
3. When testing ten different tires, how did the evaluators ensure a fair comparison? What factors remained constant?
4. How strong are the recommendations that result from this evaluation? Do the evaluators distinguish between what they are sure of and what they can only infer?

Suggestions for Writing

1. Imagine that *Consumer Reports* has hired you to test a common household product, something readily available in different brands. Design and conduct a test for evaluating this product, and report your results in a manner suitable for publication in that magazine.
2. How good is *Consumer Reports?* Try shopping for a product that has been evaluated in this magazine and report on how useful you found the advice.

SOMEONE TO WATCH OVER US

James S. Gordon

What does it mean to be abducted by aliens? It's easy to dismiss the abduction experience as fantasy, but what happens when a distinguished psychiatrist interviews a hundred different people who believe that they were abducted and seem to be in sound mind? As you read the following book review, first published in the New York Times, *note how the evaluator takes these questions seriously and attempts to praise what can be praised while nevertheless raising concerns about the quality of the science in question.*

ABDUCTION
Human Encounters with Aliens.
By John E. Mack.
432 pp. New York:
Charles Scribner's Sons. $22.

John Mack is respectfully trying to describe and explain a wildly sensational and much derided experience, one that he suggests hundreds of thousands of Americans believe they have had. For four years this noted psychiatrist, a professor at the Harvard Medical School's Cambridge Hospital and the Pulitzer Prize–winning author of a biography of T. E. Lawrence, has been recording the strange and striking stories of ordinary men and women who believe they have been abducted from their homes and cars and transported, through walls and on beams of light, to spaceships.

Nothing in Dr. Mack's conventional psychiatric and psychoanalytic training had prepared him to hear such stories from the people introduced to him by an experienced U.F.O. researcher, Budd Hopkins. These articulate, sensitive and well-educated men and women were not, it seemed to Dr. Mack, psychotic, delusional or self-promoting. They were troubled, but their experiences with U.F.O. abductions seemed to be the source, not the symptom, of their troubles. As Dr. Mack listened, he began to believe that their experiences were in some sense quite "real" and that "the abduction phenomenon has important philosophical, spiritual and social implications" for all of us.

In Dr. Mack's consulting room the abductees recalled repeated visits, often from large-eyed, short, gray beings who commanded mysterious and powerful technologies and displayed a telepathic omniscience. In isolated spots on the ground and in the curved confines of their unearthly vehicles, these visitors, sometimes under the direction of an authoritative figure—who appeared male to some, female to others—sampled the humans' semen and ova and pressed them into interspecies breeding projects.

Dr. Mack's informants said that at first they were paralyzed, terrified and recalcitrant. In time, however, they came to feel they were willing participants in the intruders' experiments. The aliens seemed to have a wider and wiser perspective than ours. They wanted to wake us all up to the ecological and political disasters that threaten our planet. They were instructing their abductees to sound a warning to the rest of us, and they were also using them to create a race of hybrid survivors.

Some of the 13 abductees whose case histories Dr. Mack presents in   5
"Abduction: Human Encounters with Aliens" (he has interviewed more than 100 people who claim to have been abducted) came to him, he says, because they consciously recalled fragments of encounters with aliens. Others were plagued by dreams of U.F.O.'s or had sensed that there were "entities" in their rooms while they slept. Several had had frequent and inexplicable nosebleeds or had found surprising scars on their bodies, while others, like Sheila, a 44-year-old social worker, had experienced fears, black moods and bodily sensations that traditional psychotherapy and pharmacotherapy had not alleviated. Some were referred to Dr. Mack by mental health professionals, but most came because they had heard through the grapevine about his work or had seen a fictionalized composite of him and Budd Hopkins in "Intruders," a 1992 television mini-series about abductions.

Dr. Mack says he found that once his patients were under hypnosis, their fragmentary memories became crystals around which complicated scenes of abduction, violation and instruction formed. Three mysterious motorcyclists whom Dave, a 38-year-old health care worker, remembered from a childhood walk turned out, under hypnosis, to be "beings" who "floated" him behind a bush and removed his shorts, "checking him out," and told him that he had been sent to earth "to do something." Some of Dr. Mack's patients said they believed they had been left with "implants," extraterrestrial devices that would "track" them as naturalists do wild animals; others, like Paul, a young businessman, felt they had been surgically "adjusted" by the aliens so they would be more open to change and less destructive.

As Dr. Mack notes, the experiences are not precisely physical—no unequivocally convincing material evidence of an implant, let alone of a spacecraft, has been produced. On the other hand, it is not certain that these are simply psychological phenomena. The frequent occurrence of U.F.O. sightings at the approximate place of the abductions, the scars and nosebleeds that self-reported abductees suffer, the hours mysteriously missing from their lives are all, according to Dr. Mack, suggestive of something beyond ordinary reality.

Dr. Mack believes that the very nature of the abduction experience eludes categorization. Whatever it actually is, he thinks, it serves as a goad to us—inviting us to dismantle our conventional notions of subjectivity and objectivity, of the real and the imaginary. For Dr. Mack, as for his subjects, this loss of certainty is the beginning of an education about higher truths. Dr. Mack, a founder of the Center for Psychology and Social Change, believes that aliens are calling us to participate in the wisdom of a larger, more generous reality. They are, it seems to him, offering us a way out of the psychological, ecological, political and social traps in which we have ensnared ourselves.

As his book reveals, the accounts of self-reported abductees led Dr. Mack to make other connections—between abductions, near-death experiences and "past-life regressions." All of these experiences are, Dr. Mack suggests, vehicles for recovering perennial wisdom about our connection to "a universe or universes that are filled with intelligences from which we have cut ourselves off." This is fascinating, suggestive and even inspiring. Unfortunately, the text on which this prophetic message is based—the abductees' accounts—lacks the weight of authority that Dr. Mack and a sympathetic reader would like to give it. It is not so much that Dr. Mack doesn't prove his case as that he doesn't offer some of the crucial data he might have collected, or present the critical and self-critical analysis that such provocative material demands.

Dr. Mack does remind us, citing the historian of religion Mircea   *10* Eliade, that "the motifs of flight and ascension" have always been part of human experience, particularly among shamans and saints, and he does nod toward the folklorists who have studied accounts of kidnappings by earth spirits in other cultures. But he does little to follow up on these historical and cross-cultural threats. Are Americans' supposed encounters with the gray beings really the modern equivalent of Irish peasants' meetings with fairies? Are these archetypal experiences of transformation or are they encounters with aliens from other galaxies?

Dr. Mack also neglects to acknowledge that the current avalanche of reported abductions is part of a larger modern phenomenon. Uninformed readers need to understand that abductions (often called "close encounters of the fourth kind") are only one aspect of the strange and confusing tapestry of modern "ufology," the study of such disparate experiences as U.F.O. sightings; supposed physical evidence of spaceship landings; gray, brown and white aliens, and theories about Government cover-ups and intergalactic alliances and conflicts.

Readers need to know as well that the experience of abduction seems to have changed in the last several years. People used to report that they felt that their germ plasm had been extracted. Now it is almost as common for them to say they are "remembering" hybrid babies that have been "presented" to them. Others, among them several who have spoken at length with Dr. Mack, have become convinced that they themselves are part or all alien, strangers left here in this strange land of Earth, sleeping prophets now awakening to alert us to the visitors and their message of transformation. Does the change in accounts of alien abduction mean the phenomenon is evolving, or that the aliens are allowing the abductees to remember more, or that the abductees are in the process, consciously or unconsciously, of elaborating a satisfying and ennobling fantasy? And how can we tell the difference?

Dr. Mack has omitted more complete consideration of these issues, partly, it appears, to focus on the abduction phenomenon and the case histories that illustrate it. And it is here, precisely on the clinical and scientific ground to which Dr. Mack has the strongest claim, that his book is most vulnerable to criticism. The case histories are often absorbing, powerful and touching, but they are not nearly comprehensive enough, particularly not for a work that gains its authority from the author's psychiatric experience and scholarship. Fewer cases, presented in greater depth and detail, would have better served his book and his readers.

The cases Dr. Mack offers don't provide some of the information that a skeptical reader or, indeed, anyone who wants to seriously examine his thesis, would need: How much did these people know about U.F.O.'s and abductions before they came to John Mack? He suggests that the youthful interest of some of his subjects was the result of actual early childhood abductions rather than the source of later memories, but we'd certainly like to know more—from their parents and their siblings, for example. And what were these people's childhoods like? We don't have enough information to accept Dr. Mack's assertions that they weren't abused (some clinicians have theorized that abduction memories are disguised memories of sexual or physical abuse). Are the people who say they have been abducted simply "histrionic" and prone to fantasizing, as some clinicians have suggested? Could these experiences be instances of sleep paralysis, a clinical condition characterized by physical immobility and disturbing images? We really should have data from psychological testing. But only one of Dr. Mack's informants seems to have been extensively tested, and we are given very little material even on that.

Equally disturbing is the dearth of material about Dr. Mack's methodology. He doesn't say exactly how he induces a hypnotic trance or how he questions his subjects under hypnosis. He mentions only in passing the "breathing" and "centering" techniques that seem to be very much a part of his work with reported abductees. His discussion of his own biases is sketchy, and there is no description of the beliefs of his clinical assistants or of their roles in his work.

These are not simply matters of academic interest. They are central to our understanding of how Dr. Mack collected his data and to our evaluation of whether the abductees' accounts may have been contaminated by the overt or unconscious cues and expectations of him and his co-workers. Dr. Mack's assertion that he was not able to influence the abductees' memories is in part contradicted by his statement that he and the abductees are "co-creating" their reality. Nor does he address more fundamental issues that are part of any interactive process and particularly of hypnotic work—the subtle shaping by the clinician of the patient's response and the possibility that the abductees use imagination rather than memory as the engine for elaboration.

My own experience in interviewing reported abductees for a 1991 article in *The Atlantic Monthly* confirmed a number of Dr. Mack's observations—and those of such earlier investigators as Jacques Vallée, the Frenchman fictionalized in Steven Spielberg's movie "Close Encounters of the Third Kind"; R. Leo Sprinkle, professor emeritus of counseling services at the University of Wyoming, and Keith Thompson, the author of "Aliens and Angels." All of us, like Dr. Mack, were impressed by the absence of gross psychopathology in people who believed they were abducted and by the elusive nature and transformative character of the abduction experience. We also noted that after their ordeal these people tended to become far more altruistic and more concerned with preserving the planet. On the other hand, my interviews also suggested that this understanding—and perhaps even some of the memories themselves—may have been shaped by interactions between abductees and those who were helping them deal with their experience. Indeed, the accounts of abductees often seemed to reflect the character and concerns of those in whom they confided. The abductees counseled by Leo Sprinkle, a deeply spiritual and optimistic man, saw their experiences as transformative. Other people whose mentors were less sanguine about the phenomenon tended to focus on their physical violation and on impending interplanetary conflict.

John Mack could have done his homework better and written a far more informative and authoritative book. Still, in giving respect to people who have been misunderstood and mocked, and visibility to a phenomenon that is ordinarily derided, he has performed a valuable and brave service, enlarging the domain and generosity of the psychiatric enterprise. Whatever future research may reveal about the abduction experience, and however much it may be alloyed with individual psychodynamics and observer bias, it is also, as Dr. Mack understands, an aspect of something bigger—an emblem of our longing for connection to the greater universe in which we live and a sign of an urgently needed individual and collective transformation.

Questions for Discussion

1. Gordon begins his evaluation by establishing Dr. Mack's credentials. Are these credentials relevant to the evaluation that follows? How does Gordon establish his own credentials as a reviewer?
2. What do people who believe they have been abducted by aliens seem to have in common?
3. How have accounts of abduction changed in recent years? What could be causing these changes?
4. What does Gordon find admirable about the book he is evaluating?
5. Consider what Gordon reports about Dr. Mack's methodology. Do you think his concerns are valid?

6. According to Gordon, "some clinicians have theorized that abduction memories are disguised memories of sexual or physical abuse." Do you think abuse and abduction have anything in common? Do the case histories quoted in this evaluation offer any reason to believe there may indeed be a connection between abuse and abduction?

Suggestions for Writing

1. Drawing upon Gordon's evaluation of Dr. Mack, write an essay defining criteria for a book review in the *New York Times.*
2. Read Gordon's 1991 article on the abduction experience and write an evaluation of it.

HOLLYWOOD AND THE HOLOCAUST: *SCHINDLER'S LIST*

John Gross

> *During the period 1933–1945, when the Nazis ruled Germany (and for four of those years most of Europe) approximately 10 million people were systematically murdered as the result of deliberate government policy—an orgy of mass killing that has come to be known as the Holocaust. At least 6 million of these victims were Jews. During these dark years, when evil seemed triumphant, some people still found the courage to risk their own lives to try to save the victims of persecution. In the early 1990s director Steven Spielberg decided to film the story of one such person: Oskar Schindler, a businessman who helped save the lives of twelve hundred Jews. The following review first appeared in the* New York Review of Books *shortly after the release of Spielberg's film.*

Suppose the Disney organization announced that it was planning a film about the Holocaust. Better still, suppose Walt Disney himself had, thirty or forty years back. In common fairness, we would have had to wait and see how it all worked out; but common sense would have suggested heavy misgivings. The gap between the Disney tradition and the demands of the material would simply have seemed too wide to be bridged.

Something of the same doubts stole into my mind when I heard that Steven Spielberg was finally making his long-deferred film of *Schindler's List.* Disney was the greatest popular entertainer of his time. Spielberg is his closest contemporary equivalent. Such words are not to be lightly spoken; they argue a kind of genius. But popular entertainment has its limits, and anything you can profitably say about the Holocaust—except, perhaps, at the level of simple lessons for children—lies well beyond them.

Spielberg's films up until now have mostly been fairy tales or adventure stories, or a mixture of both. Like other fairy tales, they have their terrors and sorrows, but terrors and sorrows that are firmly contained by the knowledge that it is all finally make-believe. And at the same time, much of his most effective work has been purely playful. This past year, reading press stories about the making of *Schindler's List,* I found myself recalling the fun-and-games Nazis in *Raiders of the Lost Ark* and *Indiana Jones and the Last Crusade.* (In *The Last Crusade* Hitler himself puts in an appearance.) Both movies are highly enjoyable hokum but one wouldn't have said that the sensibility which informs them was particularly well equipped for dealing with the realities of slave labor and genocide.

Of course, no one could have doubted that *Schindler's List* was going to be a serious film, and that it was meant to be a new departure. But here, too, the auguries were at best only mildly encouraging. The one partial precedent in Spielberg's work was *Empire of the Sun,* the adaptation of J. G. Ballard's novel about a small English boy caught up in the fighting in China in World War II; and though there are some thrilling sequences in the early parts of that film, the later Japanese prison-camp scenes struck me as superficial and melodramatic. High-level melodrama, if you like, but no more than that.

In the wrong hands, too, *Schindler's List* could easily lend itself to its 5 own forms of falsification. Schindler's courage, and the survival of those he saved, are rays of light in a dark night; but the darkness remains, undispelled, and one should be careful not to make the positive aspects of the story seem more significant in relation to the Holocaust as a whole than they were. The problem, for a film maker, is how to celebrate them adequately without being too upbeat about it—and Hollywood isn't exactly famous for resisting upbeat solutions.

I can't pretend, then, that I approached the movie with a completely open mind. I was apprehensive—afraid of seeing terrible events sentimentalized, afraid of sentimentality proving all the more insidious for being applied with sleek technical skill. In the event my fears, or the worst of them, were altogether misplaced. The skills are there, certainly, but Spielberg also shows a firm moral and emotional grasp of his material. The film is an outstanding achievement.

It is also a straightforward piece of storytelling. Whether or not its box-office takings eventually rival those of *ET* or *Jurassic Park,* it is also accessible to a mass audience. No previous American movie treatment of the Holocaust (certainly not *Sophie's Choice,* still less the dire *Holocaust* itself) comes anywhere near to it, but in its energy and confident popular approach it is still a recognizable product of Hollywood.

We open on what looks as though it is going to be a note of dark glamour. For the moment, and it's a shrewd narrative gambit, Spielberg holds the misery and viciousness of the story in reserve. We are in Cracow in the autumn of 1939, the Cracow of the conquerors. Oskar Schindler, his Nazi lapel badge pinned firmly in place, is preparing for an evening out. We follow him—tall, handsome, fur-collared—into a nightclub patronized by senior German officers and officials. The women are well-dressed, the drink flows, the dancers pose for flashbulb photographs. Memories of a hundred forgotten war movies stir. But these Nazis are the real thing. (Not a Conrad Veidt° among them.) With a succession of subtle touches, Spielberg creates a tremendous atmosphere of unease. Curiously enough, indeed, I felt Schindler was more in danger in this scene than later in the film, though in the course of it he simply ingratiates himself with the local top brass and lays the foundation of his success as a wartime industrialist, an employer of slave

---

Conrad Veidt: German-born actor who played the role of a sinister German in several Hollywood films, most notably Major Strassner in *Casablanca.*

labor. But then the scene is also *our* first introduction to the group of men who plainly intend evil. Merely to be in their presence seems dangerous, whoever you are.

They soon begin to show what they are capable of. The Jews of Cracow are deprived of their rights, herded into a ghetto, subjected to savage ill-treatment. The appalling conditions under which they live are recreated in a semi-documentary style which carries complete conviction. (No decision Spielberg took about the film was more important than deciding to shoot it in historically appropriate black and white.) And bad as things are to start with, they grow steadily worse. Deportations begin; individual Jews are killed with less concern than it takes to swat a fly. In a sense, since it is now obvious that the persecutors set no value at all on their victims' lives, we ought to be reconciled to the possibility that anything can happen, just anything. Yet nothing we have seen quite prepares us for the liquidation of the ghetto, which took place in March 1943.

If one can use such a phrase in such a context, this is the high point of   10
the movie. (It occurs about a third of the way through.) In the space of fifteen minutes Spielberg creates an impression of terror and confusion which, in my view, equals Eisenstein's Odessa Steps sequence°—no, if I am to be honest, which goes beyond it. The camera seems to be everywhere at once, amid the shooting, the shouting, the darkness, the blinding lights, the frantic scramble, the pillaged apartments, the suitcases tossed off balconies, the random murders at street corners. There are moments that seem too grotesque to be true, though one believes in them. An SS man takes time off to play an abandoned piano. Two of his colleagues argue. Is it Mozart? Is it Bach? And on every side, homes are broken into and hiding-places winkled out. Most of the earlier ghetto scenes take place in the open; here the violation is more intimate and more absolute.

Until the liquidation, or just before, there is little direct focus on the Nazis themselves. They are not so much individuals as a malign and largely anonymous force, which Schindler (no Nazi at heart, despite the badge) does his best to handle, and which the Jews have to do their best to endure. But with the arrival of Amon Goeth, oppression and persecution assume a distinctive set of features.

Goeth is the commandant of Plaszow, the dreadful labor camp near Cracow to which thousands of Jews from the city, including Schindler's workers, were dispatched. We learn a good deal less about him from the film than we do from the documentary novel by Thomas Keneally on which the film is based.* (Even the best movies can't compete with books when it comes to conveying information.) It is to Keneally that we have to go if we

Eisenstein's Odessa Steps sequence: A much praised scene in *The Battleship Potemkin* (1925), a film directed by Sergei Eisenstein (1898–1948).
***Schindler's List*. New York: Simon and Schuster, 1993.

want to find out about his early background, his education, his marriages, his cultural pretensions, the bizarre hatred he nourished for engineers—and about the full extent of his sadism, which was even more monstrous than anything we are shown on the screen. But to make up for this, the film sets the man vividly before us. Along with his savagery, the actor who plays him, Ralph Fiennes, conveys the sinister softness, and the touch of madness—though we shouldn't read too much into this last. As somebody once said of somebody else, his evil isn't a product of his insanity; on the contrary, his insanity is one of the aspects of his evil.

Fiennes is also good—as is the whole film—at bringing out the strong element of malevolent glee that so often accompanied Nazi atrocities. There is one especially revolting scene, where Goeth and his underlings shake with helpless laughter at the antics (as they suppose) of Schindler, who is trying to alleviate the agony of the sweltering victims being sent off to Auschwitz by hosing water into the cattle-trucks in which they are penned. And there are many lesser reminders of how much "humor" there was in the Holocaust, on the part of those who carried it out. You sometimes feel they saw the whole thing as a filthy joke—the filthiest (and most exciting) conceivable.

With the Jewish characters, Spielberg avoids the obvious pitfalls. He doesn't make them unnaturally noble or lovable, neither does he reduce them to a mass of undifferentiated victims. But that is putting the matter negatively. He in fact strikes an admirable balance between portraying a huge collective tragedy, and forcing us to recognize that those caught up in it suffered their fates one by one. Time and again—briefly, tellingly, and unostentatiously—he singles out a face, a gesture, a fleeting reaction, a few spoken words. Who can forget, for example, the mother desperately whispering to her child ("Look at the snow! Look at the snow!") while an old man is just about to be shot nearby?

It seems fair to assume that Spielberg is tapping something deep in   *15* himself in all this. (How else can we explain a success that couldn't have been predicted from his previous work?) And that "something" plainly includes a reservoir of specifically Jewish feeling. According to Philip Taylor's 1992 book about him, his earliest memory, a warm one, was that of being wheeled in his pram down the aisle of a synagogue in Cincinnati. Taylor adds that

> he typically describes it in cinematic terms. Out of the darkness, like a tracking shot, came a burst of red light. Bathed in it, in silhouette, were bearded men handing biscuits to him: Hassidic elders, wise old sages, bringing comfort and reassurance after the fear and wonder.

Perhaps this is more fantasy than memory, but either way it suggests the makings of the direct emotional investment that helps to give *Schindler's List* its urgency.

Not that there is anything parochial about Spielberg's approach. It is a sign of the film's breadth that the principal Jewish part, that of Itzhak Stern, should be played (and played very well) by a non-Jewish actor, Ben Kingsley. In Kingsley's performance, Stern—an accountant who managed Schindler's factories for him—is above all a study in iron self-control. His impersonality may not protect him against the Nazis (what can?), but it is a strategy for getting things done as long as circumstances permit. A strategy rather than a mask: the thoughts and feelings it conceals are fairly easy to deduce, though they are all the more eloquent for remaining unspoken.

And Schindler? It seems to me an inspired stroke to have cast Liam Neeson in the part. He has the star quality Spielberg's conception of him calls for, without being—as yet—a full-blown, over-familiar star. He may look unmistakably Irish, but he manages to look convincingly Central European as well. He gets across Schindler's expansiveness, his opportunism, his wiliness, his nerve. And in the end you are left baffled, as you are in Keneally's book. Schindler was a wheeler-dealer, a tireless womanizer, a slippery customer all round. That such a man should have risked his neck on a sudden generous impulse might have been understandable; that he should have acted as he did, systematically, over a prolonged period of time, seems inexplicable.

The mystery has been heightened by an extraordinary interview which his eighty-six-year-old widow gave to the London *Daily Mail* just before Christmas. Emilie Schindler, who lives outside Buenos Aires, is not a sweet old lady—she refers to her husband in the interview as "the asshole"—but on her own showing she has ample reason to feel bitter. Her marital troubles began on her wedding day, when Oskar was arrested on a charge brought against him by a mistress she had known nothing about; and after that they practically never stopped. Nor was it only a question of his infidelity. According to her account he was also lazy, boastful, childish, and undependable about money. After they had separated in the 1950s, for instance, he did virtually nothing to support her, even though she was living in semi-destitution: when a group of Jewish survivors gave him $1,000 to pass on to her, he pocketed half of it for himself.

On a number of points Emilie also challenges the account of Schindler's rescue work given in the book and the film. One of these is rather more than a point of detail. In October 1944, Schindler managed to get his workers sent back from Plaszow to the comparative safety of a factory in Moravia, but three hundred women prisoners were inadvertently sent to Auschwitz. According to the Keneally-Spielberg version (although Keneally leaves the matter in some doubt), Schindler rescued them by going to the camp himself and bribing SS functionaries with diamonds. According to Emilie, the job was accomplished by a friend of the family, a young woman who offered the functionaries her sexual favors.

Who can say where the truth lies? Certainly not an ordinary reader or   20 moviegoer; and at this late hour, possibly not even a historian. But even if we take some of Emilie's charges with a grain of salt, it seems likely that the real Schindler was a less congenial figure than the man we see in the film.

That only makes him more of a puzzle than ever. Emilie was closely involved with the later stages of his rescue work—she did a great deal to succor the prisoners with medicine and food once they had been moved to Moravia, where she spent the war; and though she is more than willing to query his motives, she is finally forced to admit that he was "a man of principle in some respects." They were significant respects, too; they helped to save 1,200 lives. So we are left with the same core of altruism, and same unanswerable riddle: Why did he do it? Perhaps we should stop fretting about his motives, and simply accept him, with gratitude, for what he was.

To some extent *Schindler's List* is bound to be Schindler's film, which means a film with a strong positive undertow. In all but the darkest moments he dispenses a certain cheer; having him at the center of events makes the story much more bearable than it would otherwise be, and much better adapted to popular taste.

But the film is also more than Schindler. The images which stay with one most from it are those of anguish and terror—a group of guards having a desultory technical conversation about pistols while a prisoner kneels in front of them waiting to be shot in the head; doctors arriving for a life-or-death inspection; a farmer's child glimpsed from a train speeding toward Auschwitz, drawing a finger across her throat. Most daring of all is the image of the small girl not much more than a toddler, whom we try to track through Schindler's eyes as he watches the liquidation of the ghetto from a hill overlooking the city. For the first time the film acquires, as though by magic, a dab of color: the girl is wearing a red coat. In itself, the device might seem no more than a gimmick, but in the context that Spielberg has established, it is extraordinarily effective. Focusing on a single victim, we are tempted to invest all our hopes in her; if only this one special child is spared, somehow everything else will come right. About an hour later we see her again, in the camp at Plaszow. She is still wearing her red coat, but this time she is a corpse on a pushcart.

Most of the movie's faults are minor ones, and it would seem fussy to point them out. In comparison with its enormous strengths, the brief lapses (usually into cinematic cliché) seem of small importance. But once or twice, toward the end, it does threaten to lose its way in a more serious fashion.

The episode in which the women prisoners are sent by mistake to   25
Auschwitz, for instance. In general the hellishness of the place is frighteningly well conveyed. As the prisoners stumble through the dark, as the crematorium chimney belches smoke, as an unnamed Josef Mengele° inter-

Josef Mengele: A German physician who selected among new arrivals at Auschwitz to determine who should go immediately into the gas chamber, Mengele (1911–1979) conducted horrific experiments upon inmates. After the war he escaped to South America.

rogates the older women ("How old are you, Mother?"), we feel that we have reached the ultimate verge of horror. But the central incident, in which a group of women, their heads shaved, are thrust into a "shower-bath," is at odds with the rest. The whole scene has a slightly unreal, antiseptic look, and the last-minute reprieve—the showers spray down water rather than gas—is enacted in a cliff-hanging, happy-ending style which suggests that Spielberg has momentarily wandered back to the world of adventure stories.

Again, the closing moments of the film (the penultimate ones, at least) are heavy-handed. Schindler's final address to the assembled prisoners and SS men follows Keneally's account, but it feels contrived: you can see the way Spielberg has stage-managed it. Schindler's prolonged leave-taking—breaking down, sobbing about how much more he could have done—seems positively stagey. Here there is no counterpart in Keneally; and according to Emilie, Oskar in fact sat paralyzed with fear as the two of them waited to be driven away. They were now about to become fugitives themselves.

After they have gone, we revert briefly to Keneally's scenario. A Russian horseman rides into the camp. "Don't go back east," he tells the former prisoners, "they hate you there. But don't go west either." And then, abandoning Keneally, we cut to a shot of the prisoners, in full color, marching across the horizon, singing an anthem-style Hebrew song (as far as I could make out, "Jerusalem the Golden"). This is a mistake. I've no trouble with the sentiment, but I wish it could have been presented more subtly, in a manner more consonant with the general spirit of the film.

The last scene of all, however, redeems everything. We are in the Latin Cemetery in Jerusalem where Schindler is buried. A group of mourners, mostly elderly, file past, placing stones on his grave. They are actual survivors from Cracow, men and women whose younger selves, played by actors, we have already met. It is an intensely moving scene, more moving than anything else in the film. Indeed, it derives much of its power from the contrast with the rest of the film. Here, after three hours of storytelling, is the point-blank proof that we haven't just been watching a story.

For all its brilliance, *Schindler's List* as a whole can't transcend the limitations of docudrama. We remain aware, if only at the back of our minds, of the element of artifice; and if we have read Keneally, we also realize how much has been tidied up or left out. In a sense, it is a film that falls between two stools. It can't quite match the searing authenticity of a true documentary like *Shoah* or Alain Resnais's *Night and Fog,* and it can't completely win us over with its artistry, as Louis Malle does in the lower-key *Au Revoir les Enfants.*

But what it can do, it does superlatively well. It offers as truthful a 30 picture as we are ever likely to get of regions where no documentary compilation could hope to penetrate. (The footage doesn't exist.) And it reaches out toward the mass public, the public that primarily wants to be entertained, without sacrificing its own integrity.

As a contribution to popular culture, it can only do good. Holocaust denial may or may not be a major problem in future, but Holocaust ignorance, Holocaust forgetfulness, and Holocaust indifference are bound to be, and *Schindler's List* is likely to do as much as any single work can to dispel them. One point leaves me uneasy, though. Gulag ignorance and Cultural Revolution forgetfulness are bound to be a problem too—they already are—and indifference to the fate of the Ibo and Cambodians and Eritreans and a list that is already too long for most of us to remember. Are the other genocides and mass exterminations of our century ever going to find their Spielbergs? And how many films about them can we absorb if they do?

Questions for Discussion

1. Gross begins his evaluation by linking Steven Spielberg with Walt Disney. What do these filmmakers have in common? Why does Gross compare them?
2. What are the reviewer's criteria for a film about the Holocaust? What does he mean when he writes that the filming of *Schindler's List* "could easily lend itself to its own forms of falsification"?
3. Why does Gross praise Spielberg's decision to film *Schindler's List* in black and white? Do you think Spielberg took a risk in doing so? Under what circumstances would you think it appropriate for a contemporary director to film in black and white?
4. How does Spielberg's film compare with the book upon which it was based?
5. Writing about Amon Goeth, Gross writes, "his evil isn't a product of his insanity; on the contrary, his insanity is one of the aspects of his evil." How would you explain this distinction?
6. As Gross points out in paragraphs 18–21, Schindler's widow has testified that her husband was less admirable than he is made to appear in the film. Does this trouble you? To what extent do you think Spielberg had to be historically accurate in this movie?
7. If you were writing an advertisement for *Schindler's List,* what would you quote from this review?

Suggestions for Writing

1. Watch the video of *Schindler's List* and then write your own review, emphasizing the performances and scenes that made the greatest impression on you.
2. Compare the book and film versions of the same work, evaluating the strengths and weaknesses of each and indicating which version you prefer and why.

WASHINGTON'S STILLBORN BEHEMOTH

Ada Louise Huxtable

> *What do public buildings reveal about the societies that build them? This question underlies the following review of a large federal building. The article originally appeared in the* New York Times *shortly after the building's dedication. As you read "Washington's Stillborn Behemoth," be alert not only for the criteria used to judge the building but also for the reasons why Huxtable, a prominent architecture critic, thinks readers should care about public buildings.*

After thirty-two years of planning, twenty years of design, and nine years of construction by a consortium of three architectural firms under the direction of two Librarians of Congress, two Architects of the Capitol, three chairmen of the Senate Office Building Committee, four chairmen of the House Office Building Committee, and seven chairmen of the Joint Committee on the Library, and after one abortive takeover attempt by the space-hungry House of Representatives, the James Madison Memorial Building, the new addition to the Library of Congress, was finally dedicated and turned over to the cultural and informational service of the nation in 1980.

The ceremony marking the official transfer of the completed building from the federal government to the library was held on the anniversary of the signing of the original Library of Congress legislation by President John Adams in 1800. The new Madison Memorial Library is colossal; it is the second largest building on Capitol Hill, just after the elephantine Rayburn Building. This is big even for official Washington, which specializes in Brobdingnagian scale. It is less ludicrous and more efficient than the Rayburn Building, and it is the last of the solid marble bombs in the long line willed to the nation by the late Architect of the Capitol, J. George Stewart. Stylistically, this one has not quite caught up with Moscow's Palace of Congresses, or the Soviet avant-garde of the 1960's. But any attempt to fit this born-dead behemoth into postmodern classical rethink would do a disservice to twenty-five centuries of the Western classical tradition. It is too big for camp, and lacks the leavening of corn.

Built at a cost of $130 million, it occupies the superblock bounded by Independence Avenue, C Street, and First and Second streets, just across from the main Library of Congress Building, a Beaux Arts monument of notable grandeur completed in 1897. The new building is 514 feet long and 414 feet deep, has nine stories, and contains 2.1 million square feet of space and enough computerized and mechanized library equipment to put Gutenberg into shock. Among its features are a James Madison Memorial Hall with a life-size statue of Madison surrounded by marble, travertine, and teak (the memorial was incorporated into the library in 1965 in a marriage of conspicuous political expediency), a two-story exhibition gallery that one might categorize as flashily *retardataire*,° an interior garden court that, in common with much of the staff, will never see the light of day, and 1.56 million square feet of usable working space.

Let us immediately state the best and the worst of this new building. It is both desperately needed and totally ordinary. So much ordinariness becomes almost extraordinary. The interiors that are to be devoted to the display and dissemination of the world's art and culture are pure catalogue commercial; the executive offices are unadulterated corporate cliché, from the sliding-wall conference rooms to the relentlessly overcontrived lighting. The whole is clothed in enough Georgia marble to sink a Ship of State.

But the building was long overdue for an institution bursting at every   5
seam, with personnel tucked into nooks and corners of balconies and hallways and offices carved out of corridors and triple-decked under thirty-foot ceilings. The library and its staff are grateful for every undistinguished inch. The present Architect of the Capitol, George White, who inherited the project, has managed to upgrade its execution. And the space is being very well used by the library's rather awesomely named planning unit, the Environmental Resources Office, under James Trew, to put in effect a total reorganization plan that has been conceived by the present Librarian of Congress, the historian Daniel Boorstin.

This reorganization involves the Main Building, the Thomas Jefferson Building (an extension largely for storage built in the 1930's), and the Madison Building. Collections will be shifted to form "halls of knowledge" of related artifacts and research materials devoted to Western and Eastern civilizations, the arts and sciences, language and literature, philosophy and religion, maps and geography, manuscripts, law and bibliography, and library science. The result will create a kind of "multimedia encyclopedia" for easier access and use.

The additional space that makes this rational rearrangement possible is the new building's chief virtue. But there is another conspicuous and very important benefit: the spectacular Main Building will now be released from the pressure of overuse for restoration. As the index to all of the collections, this historic structure will remain the library's centerpiece. Since this splendid building suggests a cultivated richness of mind and spirit, thank heavens for that.

It can be stated without reservation that the turn-of-the-century Library of Congress Building is one of the most magnificent works of its time in this country, representing a period and style, a quality of workmanship and material, a richness of color, detail and decoration, that will never be seen again. It is the work of a Washington architectural firm, Smithmeyer and Pelz, collaborating with sculptors, muralists, and artisans in an earnest pursuit of the muses that produced splendor at its least, and art at its best.

---

retardataire: French for "obsolete."

The interiors show a masterful use of ceremonial and symbolic public space that is still inadequately understood, and in this case, almost unequaled in American architecture. This building is one of the capital's few real gems. I am thinking, in particular, of the Great Hall with its stairs, colonnades and balconies, of an architecture so sophisticated and skilled in its manipulation of levels, planes and light, and so lavish in its use of decorative arts, that it recalls the Grand Foyer of the Paris Opéra; this is only a little less extravagantly baroque, but no less successful. The huge, domed, circular main reading room is one of the most impressive interiors in the United States.

I am thinking also of parts of the building that cannot be seen, which are increasingly visible through gaps and holes as "temporary" offices are dismantled. Four glorious corner pavilions, connected by two-block-long vaulted and coffered corridors or galleries that completely encircle the building's perimeter, have been hidden for decades by partitions, false ceilings, screen walls, and assorted interior crimes and atrocities. One could not even guess at their existence except for the presence of floating capitals and giant column segments sandwiched between wallboard and ceiling panels.

Fortunately, little was destroyed. These changes were reasonably careful acts of spatial desperation by a growing staff dealing with burgeoning collections; such incursions can be easily removed to reveal the building's original splendor. Restoration is now a top concern and priority of both the Librarian of Congress and the Architect of the Capitol. Does one need to remind the Congress that this is its library as well as the national collection? *10*

The ceremony, symbolism, and art of the older structure are the qualities most obviously lacking in the new building; there is no indication that this is a place that contains and celebrates the treasures of civilization. Nothing here suggests that architecture traditionally gives expression to such values. This is any speculative office building behind a Mussolini-modern facade. In the Madison Memorial Hall, the standard nine-foot, three-inch ceiling is pushed to two stories and the walls and columns are buttered up with wood and travertine for a result that is merely vacuous, not noble. The garden court behind the entrance is another exercise in punching up the space, three stories this time, in response to early protests about the building's lack of beauty and amenity. Because the court is topped not by sky, but by six more stories, and surrounded by standard dark glass, curtain-walled offices, a battery of artificial lights must mimic sun for ficus trees (that most durable of species) buttressed in granite. Only 6 percent of the building's surface is windowed; the set-back top floor, with a glass wall offering views from the staff dining rooms and executive offices, is like a release from limbo. There is no excuse for this at all.

One could simply file this building under the heading of the decline and fall of public architecture, but it is considerably more complex than that. The architects selected in a typical bureaucratic shotgun wedding—Roscoe DeWitt of Texas, Alfred Easton Poor and Homer Swanke of New York, and A. P. Almond and Jesse Shelton of Atlanta—were in the rear guard, rather

The Library of Congress entrance hall of 1897, above, and the Madison Memorial Hall of 1980, at right, are a study in the decline and fall of public architecture.

than the vanguard, of architecture. They produced a dated and lackluster design that embodied a program that also became obsolete as the long bureaucratic process of appropriation, approval, and construction proceeded over twenty years.

In those years, a revolution in computerized library technology took place; as recently as a year and a half before completion the power capacity of the building had to be restudied and upgraded. The flexibility that was supposed to be built into the plan has proved to be more theoretical than practical in spite of modular design; the movable partitions weigh two hundred pounds. Twenty years ago libraries and museums avoided destructive natural light like the plague. But even at that time, the new filtering and reflective glass that has created a radical and agreeable change in their architecture was being developed. Today the idea of the windowless behemoth is dead. Two of the architects who started with the project are also dead, and most of the others are retired. The Madison Library, in fact, could be called dead on arrival.

There are no easy answers to technological revolutions or congressional tastes. But even the most superficial research indicates that other countries are building national libraries in less time that relate better to the state of architecture and technology. It would be worth finding out how it is done. Washington is running out of room for these stillborn federal blockbusters, and it has long since run out of art.

Questions for Discussion

1. The first paragraph of this essay consists of a single sentence. What does Huxtable achieve by writing such a long sentence? What would be lost if an editor forced her to divide it?
2. Why does Huxtable find the Madison Memorial Library objectionable? Does she find any merit in it?
3. What does Huxtable mean when she writes that the library is "too big for camp, and lacks the leavening of corn"?
4. Why does Huxtable admire the turn-of-the-century Library of Congress Building? What does her attitude toward this building reveal about her criteria for public architecture?
5. Huxtable notes in her conclusion that other countries have built better national libraries in less time. Why do you think it took so many years to build the Madison library?

Suggestions for Writing

1. In praising the restoration of the main building, Huxtable notes that "assorted interior crimes" have been eliminated. Is there an old building in your own community that would benefit from being restored to its original state? If so, write an essay about the building, praising what you admire and calling attenion to what needs to be corrected.
2. Inspect two buildings designed to satisfy the same purpose—such as two churches, two banks, or two houses—but built in different eras. Write an essay comparing the two and determining which is the most successful.

FENIMORE COOPER'S LITERARY OFFENSES

Mark Twain

During the first half of the nineteenth century James Fenimore Cooper was regarded as a great American novelist. During the second half of that century Mark Twain emerged as a great novelist, but he was originally perceived by critics as little more than a popular humorist. As you read the following attack upon Cooper, who was dead by the time Twain wrote this essay, ask yourself what motivated this negative evaluation. Consider how it affects you. Does Twain's evaluation convince you that Cooper is not worth reading, or does it lead you to wonder whether Cooper could possibly be as bad as Twain claims?

The Pathfinder and The Deerslayer stand at the head of Cooper's novels as artistic creations. There are others of his works which contain parts as perfect as are to be found in these, and scenes even more thrilling. Not one can be compared with either of them as a finished whole.

The defects in both of these tales are comparatively slight. They were pure works of art.

— PROF. LOUNSBURY

The five tales reveal an extraordinary fulness of invention.
. . . One of the very greatest characters in fiction, Natty Bumppo. . . .

The craft of the woodsman, the tricks of the trapper, all the delicate art of the forest, were familiar to Cooper from his youth up.

— PROF. BRANDER MATTHEWS

Cooper is the greatest artist in the domain of romantic fiction yet produced by America.

— WILKIE COLLINS

It seems to me that it was far from right for the Professor of English Literature in Yale, the Professor of English Literature in Columbia, and Wilkie Collins to deliver opinions on Cooper's literature without having read some of it. It would have been much more decorous to keep silent and let persons talk who have read Cooper.

Cooper's art has some defects. In one place in *Deerslayer,* and in the restricted space of two-thirds of a page, Cooper has scored 114 offenses against literary art out of a possible 115. It breaks the record.

There are nineteen rules governing literary art in the domain of romantic fiction—some say twenty-two. In *Deerslayer* Cooper violated eighteen of them. These eighteen require:

1. That a tale shall accomplish something and arrive somewhere. But the *Deerslayer* tale accomplishes nothing and arrives in the air.

2. They require that the episodes of a tale shall be necessary parts of the tale, and shall help to develop it. But as the *Deerslayer* tale is not a tale, and accomplishes nothing and arrives nowhere, the episodes have no rightful place in the work, since there was nothing for them to develop.

3. They require that the personages in a tale shall be alive, except in the cases of corpses, and that always the reader shall be able to tell the corpses from the others. But this detail has often been overlooked in the *Deerslayer* tale.

4. They require that the personages in a tale, both dead and alive, shall exhibit a sufficient excuse for being there. But this detail also has been overlooked in the *Deerslayer* tale.

5. They require that when the personages of a tale deal in conversation, the talk shall sound like human talk, and be talk such as human beings would be likely to talk in the given circumstances, and have a discoverable meaning, also a discoverable purpose, and a show of relevancy, and remain in the neighborhood of the subject in hand, and be interesting to the reader, and help out the tale, and stop when the people cannot think of anything more to say. But this requirement has been ignored from the beginning of the *Deerslayer* tale to the end of it.

6. They require that when the author describes the character of a personage in his tale, the conduct and conversation of that personage shall justify said description. But this law gets little or no attention in the *Deerslayer* tale, as Natty Bumppo's case will amply prove.

7. They require that when a personage talks like an illustrated, gilt-edged, tree-calf, hand-tooled, seven-dollar Friendship's Offering in the beginning of a paragraph, he shall not talk like a negro minstrel in the end of it. But this rule is flung down and danced upon in the *Deerslayer* tale.

8. They require that crass stupidities shall not be played upon the reader as "the craft of the woodsman, the delicate art of the forest," by either the author or the people in the tale. But this rule is persistently violated in the *Deerslayer* tale.

9. They require that the personages of a tale shall confine themselves to possibilities and let miracles alone; or, if they venture a miracle, the author must so plausibly set it forth as to make it look possible and reasonable. But these rules are not respected in the *Deerslayer* tale.

10. They require that the author shall make the reader feel a deep interest in the personages of his tale and in their fate; and that he shall make the reader love the good people in the tale and hate the

bad ones. But the reader of the *Deerslayer* tale dislikes the good people in it, is indifferent to the others, and wishes they would all get drowned together.

11. They require that the characters in a tale shall be so clearly defined that the reader can tell beforehand what each will do in a given emergency. But in the *Deerslayer* tale this rule is vacated.

In addition to these large rules there are some little ones. These require that the author shall

12. *Say* what he is proposing to say, not merely come near it.
13. Use the right word, not its second cousin.
14. Eschew surplusage.
15. Not omit necessary details.
16. Avoid slovenliness of form.
17. Use good grammar.
18. Employ a simple and straightforward style.

Even these seven are coldly and persistently violated in the *Deerslayer* tale.

Cooper's gift in the way of invention was not a rich endowment; but such as it was he liked to work it, he was pleased with the effects, and indeed he did some quite sweet things with it. In his little box of stage-properties he kept six or eight cunning devices, tricks, artifices for his savages and woodsmen to deceive and circumvent each other with, and he was never so happy as when he was working these innocent things and seeing them go. A favorite one was to make a moccasined person tread in the tracks of the moccasined enemy, and thus hide his own trail. Cooper wore out barrels and barrels of moccasins in working that trick. Another stage-property that he pulled out of his box pretty frequently was his broken twig. He prized his broken twig above all the rest of his effects, and worked it the hardest. It is a restful chapter in any book of his when somebody doesn't step on a dry twig and alarm all the reds and whites for two hundred yards around. Every time a Cooper person is in peril, and absolute silence is worth four dollars a minute, he is sure to step on a dry twig. There may be a hundred handier things to step on, but that wouldn't satisfy Cooper. Cooper requires him to turn out and find a dry twig; and if he can't do it, go and borrow one. In fact, the Leather Stocking Series ought to have been called the Broken Twig Series.

I am sorry there is not room to put in a few dozen instances of the *5* delicate art of the forest, as practiced by Natty Bumppo and some of the other Cooperian experts. Perhaps we may venture two or three samples. Cooper was a sailor—a naval officer; yet he gravely tells us how a vessel, driving toward a lee shore in a gale, is steered for a particular spot by her skipper because he knows of an *undertow* there which will hold her back against the gale and save her. For just pure woodcraft, or sailorcraft, or whatever it is, isn't that neat? For several years Cooper was daily in the society of artillery, and he ought to have noticed that when a cannon-ball strikes the ground it either buries itself or skips a hundred feet or so; skips again a hundred feet or so—and so on, till finally it gets tired and rolls. Now in one place he loses some "females"—as he always calls women—in the edge of a wood near a plain at night in a fog, on purpose to give Bumppo a chance to show off the delicate art of the forest before the reader. These mislaid people are hunting for a fort. They hear a cannon-blast, and a cannon-ball presently comes rolling into the wood and stops at their feet. To the females this suggests nothing. The case is very different with the admirable Bumppo. I wish I may never know peace again if he doesn't strike out promptly and *follow the track* of that cannon-ball across the plain through the dense fog and find the fort. Isn't it a daisy? If Cooper had any real knowledge of Nature's ways of doing things, he had a most delicate art in concealing the fact. For instance: one of his acute Indian experts, Chingach-gook (pronounced Chicago, I think), has lost the trail of a person he is tracking through the forest. Apparently that trail is hopelessly lost. Neither you nor I could ever have guessed out the way to find it. It was very different with Chicago. Chicago was not stumped for long. He turned a running stream out of its course, and there, in the slush in its old bed, were that person's moccasin-tracks. The current did not wash them away, as it would have done in all other cases—no, even the eternal laws of Nature have to vacate when Cooper wants to put up a delicate job of woodcraft on the reader.

We must be a little wary when Brander Matthews tells us that Cooper's books "reveal an extraordinary fulness of invention." As a rule, I am quite willing to accept Brander Matthews's literary judgments and applaud his lucid and graceful phrasing of them; but that particular statement needs to be taken with a few tons of salt. Bless your heart, Cooper hadn't any more invention than a horse; and I don't mean a high-class horse, either; I mean a clothes-horse. It would be very difficult to find a really clever "situation" in Cooper's books, and still more difficult to find one of any kind which he has failed to render absurd by his handling of it. Look at the episodes of "the caves"; and at the celebrated scuffle between Maqua and those others on the table-land a few days later; and at Hurry Harry's queer water-transit from the castle to the ark; and at Deerslayer's half-hour with his first corpse; and at the quarrel between Hurry Harry and Deerslayer later; and at—but choose for yourself; you can't go amiss.

If Cooper had been an observer his inventive faculty would have worked better; not more interestingly, but more rationally, more plausibly. Cooper's proudest creations in the way of "situations" suffer noticeably from the absence of the observer's protecting gift. Cooper's eye was splendidly inaccurate. Cooper seldom saw anything correctly. He saw nearly all things as through a glass eye, darkly. Of course a man who cannot see the commonest little every-day matters accurately is working at a disadvantage when he is constructing a "situation." In the *Deerslayer* tale Cooper has a stream which is fifty feet wide where it flows out of a lake; it presently narrows to twenty as it meanders along for no given reason, and yet when a stream acts like that it ought to be required to explain itself. Fourteen pages later the width of the brook's outlet from the lake has suddenly shrunk thirty feet, and become "the narrowest part of the stream." This shrinkage is not accounted for. The stream has bends in it, a sure indication that it has alluvial banks and cuts them; yet these bends are only thirty and fifty feet long. If Cooper had been a nice and punctilious observer he would have noticed that the bends were oftener nine hundred feet long than short of it.

Cooper made the exit of that stream fifty feet wide, in the first place, for no particular reason; in the second place, he narrowed it to less than twenty to accommodate some Indians. He bends a "sapling" to the form of an arch over this narrow passage, and conceals six Indians in its foliage. They are "laying" for a settler's scow or ark which is coming up the stream on its way to the lake; it is being hauled against the stiff current by a rope whose stationary end is anchored in the lake; its rate of progress cannot be more than a mile an hour. Cooper describes the ark, but pretty obscurely. In the matter of dimensions "it was little more than a modern canal-boat." Let us guess, then, that it was about one hundred and forty feet long. It was of "greater breadth than common." Let us guess, then, that it was about sixteen feet wide. This leviathan had been prowling down bends which were but a third as long as itself, and scraping between banks where it had only two feet of space to spare on each side. We cannot too much admire this miracle. A low-roofed log dwelling occupies "two-thirds of the ark's length"—a dwelling ninety feet long and sixteen feet wide, let us say—a kind of vestibule train. The dwelling has two rooms—each forty-five feet long and sixteen feet wide, let us guess. One of them is the bedroom of the Hutter girls, Judith and Hetty; the other is the parlor in the daytime, at night it is papa's bedchamber. The ark is arriving at the stream's exit now, whose width has been reduced to less than twenty feet to accommodate the Indians—say to eighteen. There is a foot to spare on each side of the boat. Did the Indians notice that there was going to be a tight squeeze there? Did they notice that they could make money by climbing down out of that arched sapling and just stepping aboard when the ark scraped by? No, other Indians would have noticed these things, but Cooper's Indians never notice anything. Cooper thinks they are marvelous creatures for noticing, but he was almost always in error about his Indians. There was seldom a sane one among them.

The ark is one hundred and forty feet long; the dwelling is ninety feet long. The idea of the Indians is to drop softly and secretly from the arched sapling to the dwelling as the ark creeps along under it at the rate of a mile an hour, and butcher the family. It will take the ark a minute and a half to pass under. It will take the ninety-foot dwelling a minute to pass under. Now, then, what did the six Indians do? It would take you thirty years to guess, and even then you would have to give it up, I believe. Therefore, I will tell you what the Indians did. Their chief, a person of quite extraordinary intellect for a Cooper Indian, warily watched the canal-boat as it squeezed along under him, and when he had got his calculations fined down to exactly the right shade, as he judged, he let go and dropped. And *missed the house!* That is actually what he did. He missed the house, and landed in the stern of the scow. It was not much of a fall, yet it knocked him silly. He lay there unconscious. If the house had been ninety-seven feet long he would have made the trip. The fault was Cooper's, not his. The error lay in the construction of the house. Cooper was no architect.

There still remained in the roost five Indians. The boat has passed   10
under and is now out of their reach. Let me explain what the five did—you would not be able to reason it out for yourself. No. 1 jumped for the boat, but fell in the water astern of it. Then No. 2 jumped for the boat, but fell in the water still farther astern of it. Then No. 3 jumped for the boat, and fell a good way astern of it. Then No. 4 jumped for the boat, and fell in the water *away* astern. Then even No. 5 made a jump for the boat—for he was a Cooper Indian. In the matter of intellect, the difference between a Cooper Indian and the Indian that stands in front of the cigar-shop is not spacious. The scow episode is really a sublime burst of invention; but it does not thrill, because the inaccuracy of the detail throws a sort of air of fictitiousness and general improbability over it. This comes of Cooper's inadequacy as an observer.

The reader will find some examples of Cooper's high talent for inaccurate observation in the account of the shooting-match in *The Pathfinder.*

> A common wrought nail was driven lightly into the target, its head having been first touched with paint.

The color of the paint is not stated—an important omission, but Cooper deals freely in important omissions. No, after all, it was not an important omission; for this nailhead is *a hundred yards from* the marksmen, and could not be seen by them at that distance, no matter what its color might be. How far can the best eyes see a common house-fly? A hundred yards? It is quite impossible. Very well; eyes that cannot see a house-fly that is a hundred yards away cannot see an ordinary nail head at that distance, for the size of the two objects is the same. It takes a keen eye to see a fly or a nail-head at fifty yards—one hundred and fifty feet. Can the reader do it?

The nail was lightly driven, its head painted, and game called. Then the Cooper miracles begin. The bullet of the first marksman chipped an edge of the nail-head; the next man's bullet drove the nail a little way into the target—and removed all the paint. Haven't the miracles gone far enough now? Not to suit Cooper; for the purpose of this whole scheme is to show off his prodigy, Deerslayer-Hawkeye-Long-Rifle-Leather-Stocking-Pathfinder-Bumppo before the ladies.

"Be all ready to clench it, boys!" cried out Pathfinder, stepping into his friend's tracks the instant they were vacant. "Never mind a new nail; I can see that, though the paint is gone, and what I can see I can hit at a hundred yards, though it were only a mosquito's eye. Be ready to clench!"

The rifle cracked, the bullet sped its way, and the head of the nail was buried in the wood, covered by the piece of flattened lead.

There, you see, is a man who could hunt flies with a rifle, and command a ducal salary in a Wild West show today if we had him back with us.

The recorded feat is certainly surprising just as it stands; but it is not surprising enough for Cooper. Cooper adds a touch. He has made Pathfinder do this miracle with another man's rifle; and not only that, but Pathfinder did not have even the advantage of loading it himself. He had everything against him, and yet he made that impossible shot; and not only made it, but did it with absolute confidence, saying, "Be ready to clench." Now a person like that would have undertaken that same feat with a brickbat, and with Cooper to help he would have achieved it, too.

Pathfinder showed off handsomely that day before the ladies. His very first feat was a thing which no Wild West show can touch. He was standing with the group of marksmen, observing—a hundred yards from the target, mind; one Jasper raised his rifle and drove the center off the bull's-eye. Then the Quartermaster fired. The target exhibited no result this time. There was a laugh "It's a dead miss," said Major Lundie. Pathfinder waited an impressive moment or two; then said, in that calm, indifferent, know-it-all way of his, "No, Major, he has covered Jasper's bullet, as will be seen if anyone will take the trouble to examine the target."

Wasn't it remarkable! How *could* he see that little pellet fly through the air and enter that distant bullet-hole? Yet that is what he did; for nothing is impossible to a Cooper person. Did any of those people have any deep-seated doubts about this thing? No; for that would imply sanity, and these were all Cooper people.

> The respect for Pathfinder's skill and for his *quickness and accuracy of sight* [the italics are mine] was so profound and general, that the instant he made this declaration the spectators began to distrust their own opinions, and a dozen rushed to the target in order to ascertain the fact. There, sure enough, it was found that the Quartermaster's bullet had gone through the hole made by Jasper's, and that, too, so accurately as to require a minute examination to be certain of the circumstance, which, however, was soon clearly established by discovering one bullet over the other in the stump against which the target was placed.

They made a "minute" examination; but never mind, how could they know that there were two bullets in that hole without digging the latest one out? for neither probe nor eyesight could prove the presence of any more

15

than one bullet. Did they dig? No; as we shall see. It is the Pathfinder's turn now; he steps out before the ladies, takes aim, and fires.

But, alas! here is a disappointment; an incredible, an unimaginable disappointment—for the target's aspect is unchanged; there is nothing there but that same old bullet-hole!

> "If one dared to hint at such a thing," cried Major Duncan, "I should say that the Pathfinder has also missed the target!"

As nobody had missed it yet, the "also" was not necessary; but never mind about that, for the Pathfinder is going to speak. ₂₀

> "No, no, Major," said he, confidently, "that *would* be a risky decla-ration. I didn't load the piece, and can't say what was in it; but if it was lead, you will find the bullet driving down those of the Quartermaster and Jasper, else is not my name Pathfinder."

A shout from the target announced the truth of this assertion.

Is the miracle sufficient as it stands? Not for Cooper. The Pathfinder speaks again, as he "now slowly advances towards the stage occupied by the females":

> "That's not all, boys, that's not all; if you find the target touched at all, I'll own to a miss. The Quartermaster cut the wood, but you'll find no wood cut by that last messenger."

The miracle is at last complete. He knew—doubtless *saw*—at the distance of a hundred yards—that his bullet had passed into the hole *without fraying the edges*. There were now three bullets in that one hole—three bullets embedded processionally in the body of the stump back of the target. Everybody knew this—somehow or other—and yet nobody had dug any of them out to make sure. Cooper is not a close observer, but he is interest-ing. He is certainly always that, no matter what happens. And he is more interesting when he is not noticing what he is about than when he is. This is a considerable merit.

The conversations in the Cooper books have a curious sound in our modern ears. To believe that such talk really ever came out of people's mouths would be to believe that there was a time when time was of no value to a person who thought he had something to say; when it was the custom to spread a two-minute remark out to ten; when a man's mouth was a rolling-mill, and busied itself all day long in turning four-foot pigs of thought into thirty-foot bars of conversational railroad iron by attenuation; when subjects were seldom faithfully stuck to, but the talk wandered all around and arrived nowhere; when conversations consisted mainly of irrel-evancies, with here and there a relevancy, a relevancy with an embarrassed look, as not being able to explain how it got there.

Cooper was certainly not a master in the construction of dialogue. Inaccurate observation defeated him here as it defeated him in so many other enterprises of his. He even failed to notice that the man who talks corrupt English six days in the week must and will talk it on the seventh, and can't help himself. In the *Deerslayer* story he lets Deerslayer talk the showiest kind of book-talk sometimes, and at other times the basest of base dialects. For instance, when someone asks him if he has a sweetheart, and if so, where she abides, this is his majestic answer:

> "She's in the forest—hanging from the boughs of the trees, in a soft rain—in the dew on the open grass—the clouds that float about in the blue heavens—the birds that sing in the woods—the sweet springs where I slake my thirst—and in all the other glorious gifts that come from God's Providence!"

And he preceded that, a little before, with this:

> "It consarns me as all things that touches a fri'nd consarns a fri'nd."

And this is another of his remarks:

> "If I was Injin born, now, I might tell of this, or carry in the scalp and boast of the expl'ite afore the whole tribe; or if my inimy had only been a bear"

—and so on.

We cannot imagine such a thing as a veteran Scotch Commander-in- 25
Chief comporting himself in the field like a windy melodramatic actor, but Cooper could. On one occasion Alice and Cora were being chased by the French through a fog in the neighborhood of their father's fort:

> *"Point de quartier aux coquins!"* cried an eager pursuer, who seemed to direct the operations of the enemy.
> "Stand firm and be ready, my gallant 60ths!" suddenly exclaimed a voice above them; "wait to see the enemy; fire low, and sweep the glacis."
> "Father! father!" exclaimed a piercing cry from out the mist; "it is I! Alice! thy own Elsie! spare, O! save your daughters!"
> "Hold!" shouted the former speaker, in the awful tones of parental agony, the sound reaching even to the woods, and rolling back in solemn echo. "'Tis she! God has restored me my children! Throw open the sally-port; to the field, 60ths, to the field! pull not a trigger, lest ye kill my lambs! Drive off these dogs of France with your steel!"

Cooper's word-sense was singularly dull. When a person has a poor ear for music he will flat and sharp right along without knowing it. He keeps near the tune, but it is *not* the tune. When a person has a poor ear for words, the result is a literary flatting and sharping; you perceive what he is intending to say, but you also perceive that he doesn't *say* it. This is Cooper.

He was not a word-musician. His ear was satisfied with the *approximate* word. I will furnish some circumstantial evidence in support of this charge. My instances are gathered from half a dozen pages of the tale called *Deerslayer*. He uses "verbal," for "oral"; "precision," for "facility"; "phenomena," for "marvels"; "necessary," for "predetermined"; "unsophisticated," for "primitive"; "preparation," for "expectancy"; "rebuked," for "subdued"; "dependent on," for "resulting from"; "fact," for "condition"; "fact," for "conjecture"; "precaution," for "caution"; "explain," for "determine"; "mortified," for "disappointed"; "meretricious," for "factitious"; "materially," for "considerably"; "decreasing," for "deepening"; "increasing," for "disappearing"; "embedded," for "enclosed"; "treacherous," for "hostile"; "stood," for "stooped"; "softened," for "replaced"; "rejoined," for "remarked"; "situation," for "condition"; "different," for "differing"; "insensible," for "unsentient"; "brevity," for "celerity"; "distrusted," for "suspicious"; "mental imbecility," for "imbecility"; "eyes," for "sight"; "counteracting," for "opposing"; "funeral obsequies," for "obsequies."

There have been daring people in the world who claimed that Cooper could write English, but they are all dead now—all dead but Lounsbury. I don't remember that Lounsbury makes the claim in so many words, still he makes it, for he says that *Deerslayer* is a "pure work of art." Pure, in that connection, means faultless—faultless in all details—and language is a detail. If Mr. Lounsbury had only compared Cooper's English with the English which he writes himself—but it is plain that he didn't; and so it is likely that he imagines until this day that Cooper's is as clean and compact as his own. Now I feel sure, deep down in my heart, that Cooper wrote about the poorest English that exists in our language, and that the English of *Deerslayer* is the very worst that even Cooper ever wrote.

I may be mistaken, but it does seem to me that *Deerslayer* is not a work of art in any sense; it does seem to me that it is destitute of every detail that goes to the making of a work of art; in truth, it seems to me that *Deerslayer* is just simply a literary *delirium tremens*.

A work of art? It has no invention; it has no order, system, sequence, or result; it has no lifelikeness, no thrill, no stir, no seeming of reality; its characters are confusedly drawn, and by their acts and words they prove that they are not the sort of people the author claims that they are; its humor is pathetic; its pathos is funny; its conversations are—oh! indescribable; its love-scenes odious; its English a crime against the language.

Counting these out, what is left is Art. I think we must all admit that.   *30*

Questions for Discussion

1. Why does Twain preface his essay with quotes from two prominent professors and an important English novelist?
2. Consider the eighteen rules that Twain provides for "literary art." Do any of them overlap? Which seem the most important to you? Are the last

seven really "little ones"? Which of these rules is appropriate for nonfiction?

3. Why is it important for writers to be good observers? Why does Twain believe that Cooper "seldom saw anything correctly"? Does he persuade you that this is so?

4. Twain points out that Cooper always called women "females." What is the difference between these two words? Why would anyone find it objectionable to call a woman a female?

5. Consider the second sentence in paragraph 6. Do you detect a shift in diction at some point in this sentence? Do you think it was deliberate? What is its effect?

6. According to Twain, what is wrong with Cooper's dialogue? How useful are the examples he provides?

7. Cooper had been dead for forty-four years when Twain wrote this essay, and Twain later went on to write another essay attacking Cooper. What would motivate someone to make a detailed and sustained attack upon a dead writer?

Suggestions for Writing

1. Use Twain's criteria to evaluate a novel that you have recently read.

2. Read *Deerslayer* and evaluate how fairly Twain has treated Cooper. Be sure to make your evaluation criteria clear.

7

Writing to Amuse Others

Chapters 1–6 demonstrate that writing can be done for your own satisfaction or for the satisfaction of readers. In writing to evaluate, for example, you might be working toward a strictly personal decision—as when you are trying to decide which of two similar products to buy. Or you might be offering advice to others—as when you publish a book or film review. But writing to amuse (and the motives of the chapters that follow) requires that you focus upon readers—and, specifically, readers other than yourself.

THINKING ABOUT AUDIENCE

If you find pleasure in writing to amuse, it will come from knowing that you succeeded in bringing pleasure to others. Consider what happens when you tell a joke. If people laugh, you feel pleased that you told the joke—and told it well. On the other hand, if no one laughs, you'll probably feel disappointed or embarrassed but not pleased. An egotist might be so self-absorbed that he or she doesn't notice that others are not amused by his

329

or her efforts at humor, but that may explain why he is not funny: He is focusing upon himself rather than his audience.

Of course, an audience might be amused even if it is not laughing—although this is unlikely in the case of a good joke. In telling some stories and writing some essays, you may hope only to inspire a wry smile that seems to say, "I know what you mean; something like that happened to me too." It is a rare and wonderful piece of writing that can make us laugh out loud. More common, but not necessarily less valuable, is writing that makes us smile at aspects of life about which we have mixed feelings—things that we can enjoy making fun of but would hesitate to abandon altogether. Judith Rogala, for example, can make us smile at a sink full of dishes without necessarily making us feel that washing dishes is foolish. Mike Royko's essay on fitness can make us laugh without requiring us to believe that exercise is truly silly.

From this observation we can understand a basic principle about writing to amuse: Whether designed to produce belly laughs or merely to bring a twinkle of recognition to someone's eye, humor has an element of tension within it. Despite the great range of material that can be considered "comic," one constant feature is that humor always sends a double message: "Take me seriously, but don't take me seriously." People often laugh because of a sudden and surprising shift between the two parts of this message.

Laughter, however, is not always a sign of amusement, any more than amusement is always indicated by laughter. To release an excess of good spirits, you might laugh when you are having fun, even when no one has said or done anything funny. Strictly speaking, laughter is physiological—a motor and intellectual response that can be produced by many situations. And these situations are not necessarily amusing. Laughter can be inspired in ways that are essentially mean-spirited attempts to deprive other people of their humanity—as, for example, in the once common practice of laughing at dwarves. It can also signal anxiety, as in a nervous laugh, or hysteria, as when someone is emotionally overwrought and cannot stop laughing.

When writing to amuse, your primary object is to make readers enjoy themselves. You may be funny, but you should also be good-humored. This means having a sympathetic understanding of human frailty rather than a contempt for anyone or anything that seems different from what you are accustomed to. Ridicule is not genuinely amusing, and it easily lends itself to abuse. You should try to laugh *with* rather than *at,* since your purpose is to give pleasure through reconciliation. By helping readers to laugh about their failures (such as the failure to stay on a diet), you may help them to fail less frequently. But by reminding people that failure is not unique, you can make them feel part of a larger community. Humor thus reconciles people to human imperfection.

THINKING ABOUT SUBJECTS

You are probably wondering by now what types of material lend themselves most readily to humor. Answering this question is like trying to explain why a joke is funny. Part of the problem is that different people laugh at different things, and circumstances can determine whether or not something seems amusing to the same person on any given day. What seems funny in the morning could be annoying in the afternoon. Another problem is that much humor is topical, related closely to a specific cultural context; so that what amused people in the past (and inspired various theories about the comic) can provide only a general sense of what is likely to amuse people today. The humor of "Breakfast at the FDA Cafe," for example, depends upon readers being familiar with the sort of consumer warnings that are a feature of contemporary American culture. Someone from another era or culture may be altogether baffled by it and wonder how anyone could have found it funny.

Yet John Alden's work reflects one of the oldest theories of humor. In his *Poetics* Aristotle wrote that comedy—like poetry—springs from the pleasure people find in imitation. Aristotle argued that this pleasure is instinctive. Whether or not his argument is true, we can observe young children already delighting in imitation when they see someone mimic another person or when they mimic someone themselves. One way to approach "Breakfast at the FDA Cafe" is to consider how Alden mimics the language of consumer warnings. In a broader sense the other selections in this chapter also involve imitation in that their humor depends upon the portrayal of experience readers can recognize. "Farewell to Fitness," for example, does not imitate specific language, but Royko imitates a common situation: wanting to have your cake and diet too.

THE WRITER'S PERSONA

Royko also demonstrates another feature frequently found in writing to amuse. He establishes a nonthreatening *persona,* a first-person narrator who conveys a particular voice and point of view that may or may not be the authors' own. From the Latin word for the masks used in the classical theater, *persona* is usually associated today with fiction, but the creation of a literary self (that may be an imagined self) is also useful when you are writing to amuse. One way to create a persona is to make yourself seem like an average but nevertheless engaging person who is faintly bewildered by whatever you want readers to be amused by. During the 1930s Will Rogers achieved great fame by cultivating this kind of voice. More recently, Garrison Keillor and Andy Rooney have succeeded with a similar voice. Professional writers, like professional comics, choose how they want to present themselves to their audience, and they often choose to make themselves seem unthreatening. Although Judith Rogala and Andy Rooney present themselves as semicompetent, they are by no means as inept as they pretend to be—any more than Royko, a syndicated columnist for a major newspaper, sits around all day eating pork shanks and drinking beer.

In presenting themselves as flawed somehow—inept or out of shape—writers like Rogala, Rooney, and Royko also draw upon another

Aristotelian principle: that comedy concerns characters who have a "defect." According to Aristotle, "Comedy is . . . an imitation of persons inferior—not, however, in the full sense of the word bad. . . . It consists of some defect or ugliness which is not painful or destructive." Like the characters in a comedy, comic writers often seem to have some flaw we ourselves may have. But they do not truly suffer as the result of it, and this is one reason we can afford to laugh. Andy Rooney may be mildly embarrassed that his house needs painting and his lawn chairs need new webbing, but the laziness he attributes to himself seems reassuring. He is willing to drink from the jelly glass when there aren't enough wine glasses to go around, and he remains marvelously patient with some pretty dreadful house guests. We know that he is not "in the full sense of the word bad," and we find comfort in knowing that Rooney is managing to get by all right despite an exaggerated version of bad habits we ourselves may have.

By creating an engaging persona, writers can make readers laugh with them rather than against them. We may smile at the way Rogala, Royko, and Rooney present themselves, but the principal source of amusement is some problem outside themselves that they find hard to take: household chores, diet-conscious athletes, irritating house guests. This leads to another important aspect of writing to amuse: Although not didactic, it is often designed as a corrective. The assumption behind much comic writing is that if you can make people laugh, they will change their behavior. For instance, although Joseph Epstein presents his observations about language as flaws in his own character, his humor in "Your Basic Language Snob" could make people a little more careful about the language they use.

THINKING ABOUT PURPOSE

Writing to amuse can, at times, take less friendly forms. In satire, for example, the corrective aspect of writing to amuse is readily apparent. The writer of a satire has usually withdrawn from the text; we no longer have the sense of a flawed but affable persona. The satirist usually directs attention to the flaws of other people with the purpose of making people laugh at those flaws. The result can be very funny, but it can also be cruel. A basic bond between writer and audience exists even in satire, however. The satirist assumes that someone or some group has departed from behavior that is recognized as acceptable; this presumes that recognized standards exist and that the audience of a satire (if not its butt) believes in the standards that have been violated.

In keeping with its role as a social corrective, writing to amuse often reinforces traditional standards (such as marriage, which provides the happy ending that resolves so many comedies written for the stage). Beneath much humor is the message that people should grow up and stop acting silly, a conservative and responsible message made palatable through laughter.

But humor can also be subversive. As Mikhail Bakhtin, a Russian critic, has argued, comedy records "the defeat . . . of all that oppresses and restricts." The restrictions that oppress may be the very conventions that a satirist would like to restore. For example, the Marx brothers often amuse people by disrupting a very proper and pompous socialite. Or to take an example close at hand: Alden challenges government regulations even as he uses them as a source for humor. Although "Breakfast at the FDA Cafe" pokes fun at the FDA advisories about (it seems) everything we eat, the essay as a whole invites the reader to think critically about the role of government agencies in regulating our lives. While writing ostensibly about his job as a Macy's elf, David Sedaris pokes fun at the commercialization of the American Christmas season and presents himself as an agent for change.

The disruptive potential of humor may be one reason why some people are suspicious of it. Convinced that comedy inspires social rebellion, Plato proposed banning comedians from his ideal republic, and Aristotle argued that comedy is like a strong wine and, as such, unsuitable for the young. Once people have begun to laugh about authority, the credibility of that authority is undermined. Dictators do not take kindly to jokes at their expense.

It would seem, then, that humor involves a certain amount of tension, because it encourages people to laugh at what, on some level, they think is no laughing matter. Hence, humor can seem to work simultaneously toward both reconciliation and rebellion. The rebellion is against rigid and artificial authority, rules, or behavior; the reconciliation is aimed at restoring a natural sense of community. To take a simple example: Royko assumes that rules governing the way people are expected to behave have become too rigid. He is rebelling against authorities that *insist* he eat sensibly and exercise frequently. But he is also attempting to reconcile people to what, in fact, many people want to do—enjoy themselves and not worry so much about what seems socially correct.

THINKING ABOUT PATTERNS

The humor of Royko's piece depends upon people recognizing a pattern that has been frequently repeated. This essay would not seem funny if the author were the only person worried about being overweight, or the only person who had to deal with an aggressively healthy colleague. In other cases comic writers exploit the idea of a repeated pattern much more directly. According to Henri Bergson, a French theorist who wrote what critics agree is an important work on laughter, one of the principal sources of humor is a situation in which people behave mechanically, repeating the same motion or saying the same thing. Once we begin to notice this repetition, it becomes predictable—and we are inclined to laugh when our expectations are fulfilled. For example, students may laugh after noticing that their professor always says "One last thing" at least twice in every class.

Cartoons often depend heavily upon this principle of predictable repetition: We know that the Roadrunner will always outmaneuver the Coyote, and the Coyote will always be back in action no matter how many times he falls off the cliff.

Among the readings that follow, Rooney's "Old Friends" provides the clearest sense of what Bergson called "automatism": By the time we are halfway through the essay, we know that Quintin and Barbara can be counted on to always find fault with the home they are visiting. What would be annoying if it happened only once or twice becomes amusing when reduced to mechanical behavior that we can safely predict and thus, to a degree, dismiss.

WRITING TIPS

How can you go about writing an amusing essay of your own? Although there is no formula that is guaranteed to succeed, the following guidelines may help you to get started.

1. *Choose your topic.* Your own experience, or the readings that follow, may suggest a variety of topics. But if you are stuck for an idea, try to identify a flaw in the behavior of people you know. The flaw you choose should be easy to observe so that you can count upon its being recognized by your audience.

2. *Cultivate an appropriate voice.* Address your readers as members of a community who share the same values and have suffered the same problems. Be careful not to make yourself sound superior to your readers or to sound as if you would do anyone a real injury.

3. *Experiment with wordplay.* One of the great sources of humor is the pleasure people derive from unexpected combinations of words. Surprise readers with a pun or a playful variation of a cliché. (An actress of questionable virtue once described herself as being "pure as the fresh-driven slush.") Or you can invent words that are delightful simply because of the way they sound.

4. *Use repetition.* Although deliberate repetition can serve many rhetorical ends, it can be especially useful when you are trying to amuse. The repetition may take the form of someone's always saying the same thing or always reacting in a predictable way—such as Gracie Allen, who could always be counted upon to take things literally, or the houseguests who always find fault in "Old Friends."

5. *Test your choice.* A good way to measure your success in writing to amuse is to read a draft of your paper aloud to friends. But you should also ask yourself if there is anyone in whose presence you would be embarrassed to read the paper. A good-humored paper should be suitable for many audiences. It should produce a smile rather than a sneer. If you feel worried that your paper might give offense, you may be writing to ridicule rather than to amuse.

DESPERATELY SEEKING A DISHWASHER
Judith Rogala

> *To emphasize her point that washing dishes is an unpleasant task, Judith Rogala describes all the ways she avoids washing her own dishes—which include storing them anywhere they can be hidden and only "doing" them when she runs out of things to eat with. As you read "Desperately Seeking a Dishwasher," ask yourself whether Rogala's humor is directed only at a specific act or whether she has other targets as well.*

I have a love-hate relationship with my dishes. I love to eat off of them. I hate to wash them. I've been known to let dishes stack up until every inch of my kitchen counter space is precariously piled with plates, bowls, kettles, silverware, spatulas and glasses of every shape and size.

A week goes by.

Now my table and chairs are no longer for dining but rather for holding dirty dishes.

Two weeks go by.

Now the oven holds my secret stash of baked-in, caked-on pots and pans.

One day I come home from work and my cupboard is bare. Oh, there's plenty of food in there. Just nothing to eat it with or out of. You see I have an overwhelming aversion to dishpan hands. But this wasn't always the case. When I was still a toddler, I begged my mom to let me take on the task of drying dishes. As the youngest sibling, I considered this my rite of passage. When I heard the squirt of the dishwashing detergent bottle, I wanted in on the action.

I eagerly joined the dishwashing ritual every evening after supper. Most nights the chores digressed into soapsuds fights and towel snapping with my brother—and I have the dishtowel welt scars to prove it. Maybe herein lie the roots of my dread of washing and/or drying dishes.

Now you're probably thinking, "Go ahead and buy a dishwasher, already!" Not so easy. I live in an apartment with a kitchen no larger than Elvis in his lounge lizard days (although it is slightly larger than his postage stamp). There's no room to rig up a dishwasher in my kitchen even if my landlord could be convinced to invest in one.

And my nomadic life-style (I've moved 10 times in the past 10 years) doesn't particularly lend itself to owning a dishwasher, either. I'm willing to transport a closetful of clothes I'll probably never wear again, notebook after notebook from college classes I didn't comprehend when I sat through them, and assorted items including a jiffy burger appliance, a toilet paper cozy and every letter written to me since I left home at age 18. My theory is if I can pick it up and carry it, it is worth keeping. But anything that requires a dolly to move won't make it to my next change of address.

Well, then, the wise old reader with the spotless kitchen probably has   *10*
another suggestion. The answer is simple—disposable cups, paper plates,
plastic silverware, etc., etc. Bite your tongue! It's the '90s and I'd no sooner
drink out of a polystyrene cup, than, well have sex without a condom. I've
even rationalized the reason I don't do my dishes is to conserve water. So
what is an environmentally-correct girl to do?

I've studied the situation intensely and come up with my only solution: I must find someone to do my dishes for me. My mother always said,
"I don't need an automatic dishwasher, that's why I had children." Things
were much simpler back then.

I could have a baby, I suppose, but that would mean waiting several
years until my dishwasher-in-training-pants would pass that awkward stage
of throwing food, spitting up and breaking precious dinnerware and one-
of-a-kind ceramic bowls into a bazillion pieces. Then there's the fact that
I'm single. Besides, if I did have a baby, it would most likely carry my
dishwashing-loathing gene . . . surely, that's a dominant trait. What would I
do then, throw the baby out with the dishwater?

No, my only hope I fear, is to find a man who loves me and loves to
do my dishes. That's not as easy as it may seem.

Some couples can't agree on religion or politics or how to deal with
the toothpaste tube. With me, the make-or-break-up topic invariably comes
down to doing the dishes. One guy I went out with was vociferous.

"I just hate it when someone leaves dirty dishes in the sink," he ranted.   *15*
"I always wash, dry and put away my dishes immediately after use," he raved.

Perfect, I thought, while he's doing his, he can do mine as well. I
broached the subject carefully. "I sometimes let my dishes stack up for two
weeks," I replied, for if this relationship were to go any further he must be
prepared for what lurks in my kitchen. Don't let anyone tell you that oppo-
sites attract. I never heard from him again.

Another guy told me story after somebody-done somebody-wrong
story about the women in his life who had jilted him. First there was Dawn,
then Joy, then Madge. It did not bode well that this man would take kindly
to my dishwater. I could just imagine the bitterness building up in him
every time he reached for my Palmolive (you're soaking in it!).

Currently, I'm trying a new tactic. I'm developing an ongoing relationship with a man who makes his living as a real-life professional dishwasher at a restaurant. I'm hoping he's a real workaholic, a guy who likes to
do overtime work at home, a man's man who'll roll up his sleeves and plunge
right in when there's a job to be done. Heck, I'm even willing to pay
minimum wage.

But I don't think this dishwasher and gentleman is willing to make a
commitment. (Do you promise to love, honor and do her dishes every single
day, 'til death do you part?) So I'm sending out an S.O.S. (pad) to any real
man who's willing to scrub a quiche dish for the woman he loves.

I *know* you're out there, I can hear you scouring.   *20*

Questions for Discussion

1. Who do you think Rogala sees as the audience for her essay? Comment upon whether she breaks through gender stereotypes regarding domestic chores.
2. What is Rogala's purpose for writing "Desperately Seeking a Dishwasher"? Is she actively seeking a relationship with someone to wash her dishes? What is amusing about this search?
3. Comment upon how Rogala's rebuttal of solutions she expects her audience to offer helps to strengthen the essay.
4. Identify two clichés and two familiar slogans that Rogala uses. Explain what these contribute to the humor of the essay.

Suggestions for Writing

1. Identify a job that you dislike doing, and write an essay exaggerating the strategies you might use to evade the task.
2. In her last eight paragraphs Rogala plays with the idea of finding a partner who enjoys doing what she likes to avoid. Try writing an essay about a friendship or other relationship in which you have been aware of habits very unlike your own.

BREAKFAST AT THE FDA CAFE

John R. Alden

> *"Everything that's any fun," the old joke used to run, "is illegal, immoral, or fattening." In this article from the* Wall Street Journal *John R. Alden postulates that today we need to add one or two new categories. As you read "Breakfast at the FDA Cafe," notice how Alden makes a common act— ordering breakfast in a restaurant—a source of humor as well as a social critique.*

"I'll have two eggs over easy, home fries, a blueberry muffin, decaf coffee and the fresh-squeezed orange juice," I told my waiter.

"Very good, sir," he said, and hurried away.

I had just unfolded my paper as he came back with the coffee.

"Here you are," he said. "But before you can have this, our corporate legal department insists that we warn you that recent studies indicate that consumption of three or more cups of coffee a day may increase your risk of stroke and bladder cancer. This is decaffeinated, so I don't need to say that caffeine is addictive and can cause temporary but significant increases in your blood pressure and heartbeat. However, FDA regulations do require me to notify you that the decaffeination process may leave minute traces of carcinogenic solvents in the coffee beans." He poured.

I had nearly finished the front page when he returned with my breakfast.   5

"Your eggs," he said as he put my plate in front of me, "are fried in a polyunsaturated oil high in fat and calories. Eggs that are only lightly cooked may contain salmonella, an organism causing food poisoning, and the National Society for the Alleviation of Allergies warns that many Americans exhibit a mild allergic response to the ova of domestic fowl. Egg yolks contain large quantities of cholesterol, and the American Association of Cardiological Surgeons recommends that people over 40, particularly those who smoke or are more than 10 pounds overweight, limit their consumption to four eggs per week."

I sucked in my stomach.

"Potatoes," he continued, "are a member of the nightshade family, and any greenish patches on their skin may contain traces of an alkaloid poison called solanine. The Physician's Reference Manual says solanine can cause vomiting, diarrhea, and acute nausea. However, your potatoes have been carefully peeled, and our supplier has agreed to assume any liability that may arise from their consumption.

"The blueberry muffin contains enriched flour, cane sugar, eggs, butter, blueberries and low-sodium baking powder. The Institute of Alimentary Studies warns that a diet high in processed flour may add to your risk of stomach and intestinal cancer. The Center for Dietary Purity warns that processed wheat flour may be contaminated with up to two tenths of a part per billion of fungicides and rodenticides. It has been bleached and brominated and in cool wet years might also contain minute traces of ergot. Ingested in sufficient quantities, ergot can cause hallucinations and convulsions, arterial spasms, and induce abortions in pregnant women.

"Citizens Against Empty Calories, an independent research organiza- *10* tion funded in part by the American Beet Sugar Producers Association, warns that cane sugar is high in calories, low in nutritional value, and one of the principal dietary factors associated with dental cavities.

"Butter, like eggs, is high in cholesterol, a material that studies have identified as playing a potentially significant role in the development of arteriosclerosis and heart disease, particularly in genetically susceptible individuals. If any of your close relatives ever had a heart attack, the Department of Health and Human Services warns that your personal physician might advise you to limit your intake of butter, cream and other dairy products.

"Our blueberries are from Maine. They have not been fertilized or treated with pesticides. However, the U.S. Geological Survey has reported that many Maine blueberry barrens are located on granite, and granitic rock frequently contains measurable amounts of radioactive uranium, radium and radon gas.

"Finally, the baking powder used in these muffins contains sodium aluminum sulfate. Aluminum, some researchers suggest, may be a contributing factor in the development of Alzheimer's disease. The National Institute of Mental Health has not stated a position on this, but it *has* asked us to inform our customers that it will be funding a seven-year, $47 million study examining the association between aluminum consumption and senility syndromes."

He picked up a pitcher. "I have to inform you that our 'fresh-squeezed' orange juice was actually prepared before 6 this morning. It is now 8:30. The FDA and the Justice Department recently sued a restaurant in Georgia (*U.S.* v. *Mom's Home-baked Cafe*) for describing three-hour-old juice as 'fresh-squeezed.' Until that case is decided, our legal advisers have required us to get a waiver from any customer ordering a similar product."

I signed the form he handed me, and he stapled a copy to my bill. But *15* as I reached for the glass, he stopped me.

"Excuse me, please. Our salt and pepper shakers are clearly labeled, but corporate policy requires that I repeat the warnings to you verbally. On the salt it says, 'If consumed in large quantities, sodium chloride can be highly toxic, and habitual ingestion of this compound has been shown to cause life-threatening hypertension.' The other shaker says: 'Pepper. Use with extreme caution! The Center for Communicable Disease warns that sneezing associated with careless use of this powder may contribute to the transmission of rhinoviral and influenza-type diseases.' Finally, the

Department of Consumer Safety has determined that the tines of your fork are sharp, and new regulations require me to caution customers to use that utensil with extreme care."

He turned, and with a cheery "Enjoy your breakfast, sir," headed off to the next table. I picked at my meal but couldn't finish it. The food had gotten cold, and somehow I had lost my appetite.

Questions for Discussion

1. What do you think prompted Alden to write this essay? Is he making fun of the FDA's warnings? Explain.
2. Describe the setting Alden chooses for this essay, and discuss why this scene is important in this essay.
3. How does Alden use repetition for humorous effect in the essay? How does he use exaggeration?
4. Who is likely to enjoy this essay more, an audience of people who take pleasure from dining out frequently or people who are eternally on a diet? Why?
5. Alden treats the waiter much as a short story writer or a dramatist might. Describe this character, and comment upon his use of information and authority.

Suggestions for Writing

1. Have you ever been annoyed by what seems to be an endless bombardment of health messages—calorie or cholesterol consumption, fitness requirements, ridiculous warnings on appliances, signs on pillows or plastic bags? Write an essay showing how you respond to these warnings.
2. Do any of the people you know have a strict sense of what they will or will not eat? Is it ever a challenge to cook for them or to eat out with them in a restaurant? If so, write an essay showing how these people are what they eat—or will not eat, as the case may be.

FAREWELL TO FITNESS

Mike Royko

> *During the past twenty years or so it has been fashionable to be concerned about health and fitness—and almost anything that becomes fashionable is likely to attract the eye of a humorist. There is, after all, a difference between being genuinely concerned about one's health and mindlessly following the crowd headed to the nearest gym. Deciding that working out is no longer for him, Mike Royko, a columnist for the* Chicago Tribune, *declares, "pass me the cheesecake." As you read "Farewell to Fitness," consider the way Royko presents himself to readers, and be alert for signs that he may be exaggerating.*

At least once a week, the office jock will stop me in the hall, bounce on the balls of his feet, plant his hands on his hips, flex his pectoral muscles and say: "How about it? I'll reserve a racquetball court. You can start working off some of that. . . ." And he'll jab a finger deep into my midsection.

It's been going on for months, but I've always had an excuse: "Next week, I've got a cold." "Next week, my back is sore." "Next week, I've got a pulled hamstring." "Next week, after the holidays."

But this is it. No more excuses. I made one New Year's resolution, which is that I will tell him the truth. And the truth is that I don't want to play racquetball or handball or tennis, or jog, or pump Nautilus machines, or do push-ups or sit-ups or isometrics, or ride a stationary bicycle, or pull on a rowing machine, or hit a softball, or run up a flight of steps, or engage in any other form of exercise more strenuous than rolling out of bed.

This may be unpatriotic, and it is surely out of step with our muscle-flexing times, but I am renouncing the physical-fitness craze.

Oh, I was part of it. Maybe not as fanatically as some. But about 15   5
years ago, when I was 32, someone talked me into taking up handball, the most punishing court game there is.

From then on it was four or five times a week—up at 6 A.M., on the handball court at 7, run, grunt, sweat, pant until 8:30, then in the office at 9. And I'd go around bouncing on the balls of my feet, flexing my pectoral muscles, poking friends in their soft guts, saying: "How about working some of that off? I'll reserve a court," and being obnoxious.

This went on for years. And for what? I'll tell you what it led to: I stopped eating pork shanks, that's what. It was inevitable. When you join the physical-fitness craze, you have to stop eating wonderful things like pork shanks because they are full of cholesterol. And you have to give up eggs benedict, smoked liverwurst, Italian sausage, butter-pecan ice cream, Polish sausage, goose-liver pate, Sara Lee cheesecake, Twinkies, potato chips, salami-and-Swiss-cheese sandwiches, double cheeseburgers with fries, Christian Brothers brandy with a Beck's chaser, and everything else that tastes good.

Instead, I ate broiled skinless chicken, broiled whitefish, grapefruit, steamed broccoli, steamed spinach, unbuttered toast, yogurt, eggplant, an apple for dessert and Perrier water to wash it down. Blahhhhh!

You do this for years, and what is your reward for panting and sweating around a handball-racquetball court, and eating yogurt and the skinned flesh of a dead chicken?

- You can take your pulse and find that it is slow. So what? Am I a clock?
- You buy pants with a narrower wasitline. Big deal. The pants don't cost less than the ones with a big waistline.
- You get to admire yourself in the bathroom mirror for about 10 seconds a day after taking a shower. It takes five seconds to look at your flat stomach from the front, and five more seconds to look at your flat stomach from the side. If you're a real creep of a narcissist, you can add another 10 seconds for looking at your small behind with a mirror.

That's it.   10

Wait, I forgot something. You will live longer. I know that because my doctor told me so every time I took a physical. My fitness-conscious doctor was very slender—especially the last time I saw him, which was at his wake.

But I still believe him. Running around a handball court or jogging five miles a day, eating yogurt and guzzling Perrier will make you live longer.

So you live longer. Have you been in a typical nursing home lately? Have you walked around the low-rent neighborhoods where the geezers try to survive on Social Security?

If you think living longer is rough now, wait until the 1990s, when today's Me Generation potheads and coke sniffers begin taking care of the elderly (today's middle-aged joggers). It'll be: "Just take this little happy pill, gramps, and you'll wake up in heaven."

It's not worth giving up pork shanks and Sara Lee cheesecake.   15

Nor is it the way to age gracefully. Look around at all those middle-aged jogging chicken-eaters. Half of them tape hairpieces to their heads. That's what comes from having a flat stomach. You start thinking that you should also have hair. And after that comes a facelift. And that leads to jumping around a disco floor, pinching an airline stewardess and other bizarre behavior.

I prefer to age gracefully, the way men did when I was a boy. The only time a man over 40 ran was when the cops caught him burglarizing a warehouse. The idea of exercise was to walk to and from the corner tavern, mostly to. A well-rounded health-food diet included pork shanks, dumplings, Jim Beam and a beer chaser.

Anyone who was skinny was suspected of having TB or an ulcer. A fine figure of a man was one who could look down and not see his knees, his feet or anything else in that vicinity. What do you have to look for, anyway? You ought to know if anything is missing.

A few years ago I was in Bavaria, and I went to a German beer hall. It was a beautiful sight. Everybody was popping sausages and pork shanks and draining quart-sized steins of thick beer. Every so often they'd thump their magnificent bellies and smile happily at the booming sound that they made.

Compare that to the finish line of a marathon, with all those emaciated runners sprawled on the grass, tongues hanging out, wheezing, moaning, writhing, throwing up.   *20*

If that is the way to happiness and a long life, pass me the cheesecake.

May you get a hernia, Arnold Schwarzenegger. And here's to you, Orson Welles.

Questions for Discussion

1. One of the ways Royko achieves humor in this piece is to surprise the expectations of readers. What would someone normally expect to hear after "No more excuses" in a discussion of physical fitness? Where else does the essay take a surprising twist?
2. Depending upon context and purpose, exaggeration can either undermine or enhance the impact of what we write. Where does Royko exaggerate in this essay? Is he using exaggeration effectively?
3. In paragraph 5 Royko reveals that he was in his late forties when he wrote this piece. Why is that significant? Would the essay be as funny if the author were nineteen?
4. How would Royko like to age? Why does he claim to be unconcerned about living longer?
5. Does Royko have a purpose in this piece aside from being amusing? What is he making fun of besides his own appetite?

Suggestions for Writing

1. Identify a current fad and write an essay explaining why you, for one, have no intention of following the crowd.
2. Royko comments on "middle-aged jogging chicken-eaters" who try to seem younger than they are. What about people who try to seem older than they are? Write a humorous essay about teenagers who work at seeming sophisticated.

OLD FRIENDS

Andy Rooney

Andy Rooney is a writer for CBS who achieved a national following through the wry commentaries that he delivers at the end of "60 Minutes." In the following essay he invites readers to laugh at his troubles when entertaining guests who think friendship entitles them to give unsolicited advice. As you read "Old Friends," try to identify with Rooney by thinking of a time when you were tempted to trade an old friend in for a newer model.

The next time we have friends at the house over a weekend, I'm going to make sure it isn't *old* friends. I want our next house guests to be friends we don't know well enough to be perfectly at ease with—not that I didn't enjoy having Barbara and Quintin, mind you. It's just that we all know each other so well that no one holds back.

"Boy, you got a lot of work to do around this place," Quintin said.

Well I *know* I have a lot of work to do and I *know* I'm not going to do a lot of it, and I don't need a good friend telling me about it.

"I drove up to Montreal to get my paint," Quintin said, "They can still make paint with lead in it up there, and it lasts a lot longer. That's why all the paint is peeling on your house. Paint made in the U.S. isn't good anymore."

He thinks perhaps I haven't *noticed* the house needs painting?   5

"I nearly broke my neck on those stone steps out by the back porch," he said. "That slab of stone on top is rocking. Can't you jam another little stone or something under there so it doesn't rock? Someone's going to get killed."

Quintin thinks perhaps I haven't been meaning to stabilize that stone for four years now since the frost heaved it?

"That's a good aerial you've got on your television set," he said. "Of course, you're on high ground here so you get a good picture. Why don't you get yourself a decent-sized television set so you can see it?"

Saturday night we had some other friends over for a drink and dinner. Barbara and Quintin wanted to help.

"Sure," I said. "You can put the glasses and the ice and the bottles out   10
on the table on the front lawn."

"Which glasses?" Barbara said.

I told her where the glasses were and she started taking things out.

"There are only seven of these glasses and there are going to be eight of us," Barbara said.

"I know, I know," I said. "We used to have twelve of them. You have to use one jelly glass. I'll drink out of that one."

"Don't fall on that loose stone step as you go out," Quintin said to   *15*
Barbara. "What about chairs for out front?" he asked me.

I told him there were some old ones up in the garage if he wanted to
get a couple of those.

Quintin is a willing helper. He went out to the garage and he was
gone for about ten minutes before he returned carrying two aluminum
chairs with broken webbing.

"You mean *these*?" he asked incredulously.

Those were the ones I meant. I knew the webbing was broken. If the
webbing hadn't been broken they wouldn't have been in the garage in the
first place.

"Boy," he said, as he put the chairs down, "I thought my garage was a   *20*
mess. How do you ever get a car in there? You got stuff hanging all over.
You ought to have a garage sale . . . and sell the garage." He laughed. Friends
can be so cruel.

"Why don't I make the salad dressing," Barbara said to my wife. "Is
this the only vinegar you have?" she asked, holding up a bottle of supermarket house brand, El Cheapo vinegar. "I guess I'll use lemon instead of
vinegar," she said.

"Here comes the first guests," Quintin said. "There sure isn't much
space for them to park in that driveway of yours."

"I'll go greet the guests," Barbara said.

"Don't break your neck on that stone step as you go out," Quintin
yelled after her.

Questions for Discussion

1. The scene of this essay is a house in which the author has evidently lived
   for several years. How much of the dialogue depends upon the scene?
2. What is the difference between old friends and new friends? Explain
   what Rooney means by the first line in his essay.
3. Do you think Barbara and Quintin are real friends of the author's? If so,
   how would they feel upon reading this essay? If not, what are they meant
   to represent?
4. Why has Rooney relied so heavily upon dialogue in this piece?
5. Why do you think Rooney lets us know that he is willing to drink from
   a jelly glass? Does he expect readers to sympathize with him?

Suggestions for Writing

1. Has an old friend ever gotten on your nerves? Or have you ever taken a
   trip with friends only to find yourself liking them less each day? Write a
   humorous essay about a time when friendship seemed like hard work.
2. Imagine someone difficult to please taking a tour of your home. Write
   the story of that visit, using dialogue where appropriate.

SANTA'S LITTLE HELPER

David Sedaris

Set in New York during the Christmas shopping season, "Santa's Little Helper" focuses upon a time-honored business gimmick—the department store Santa—as a means for pointing out absurdities in the way people behave at Christmas time as well as the materialism that business encourages in connection with this religious holiday. Note how David Sedaris presents himself and how he characterizes other people in his "journal." As you read, ask yourself whether you recognize characters or behavior that can be found well beyond the Christmas season.

October 24

I was in a coffee shop reading the want ads when I read, "Macy's Herald Square, the largest store in the world, has big opportunities for outgoing, fun-loving people of all shapes and sizes who want more than just a holiday job! Working as an elf in Macy's SantaLand means being at the center of the excitement!"

I brought the ad home and Rusty and I were laughing about it and he dared me to call for an interview. So I did. The woman at Macy's said, "Would you be interested in full-time elf or evening-and-weekend elf?"

I said full-time elf.

I have an appointment next Wednesday at noon. I am a thirty-three-year-old man applying for a job as an elf.

October 29

I am trying to look on the bright side. I have to admit that I had high   5
hopes when I moved to New York City. In my imagination I was going to go straight from Penn Station to the offices of *One Life to Live*. In my imagination I'd go out for drinks with Cord Roberts and Victoria Buchanan, the show's biggest stars. We'd sit in a plush booth at a tony cocktail lounge and they'd lift their frosty glasses in my direction and say, "A toast to David Sedaris! The best writer this show has ever had!"

I'd say, "You guys, cut it out."

People at the surrounding tables would stare at us, whispering, "Isn't that . . . ? Isn't that . . . ?"

I might be distracted by their enthusiasm and Victoria Buchanan would lay her hand over mine and tell me that I'd better get used to being the center of attention.

But instead I am applying for a job as an elf.

Instead someone will say, "What's that shoe size again?" and hand me   10
a pair of 7½ slippers, the toes of which curl to a point.

October 31

A week ago I laughed myself silly over Macy's "Elf Wanted" ad; this afternoon I sat in the SantaLand office and was told, "Congratulations, Mr. Sedaris; you're an elf."

In order to become an elf I had to fill out ten pages of forms, take a multiple-choice personality test, undergo two interviews, and submit urine for a drug test. The first interview was general, designed to eliminate the obvious sociopaths. During the second interview we were asked why we wanted to be elves, which, when you think about it, is a fairly tough question. When the woman next to me, a former waitress in her late twenties, answered, she put question marks after everything she said. "I really want to be an elf? Because I think it's really about acting? And before this I worked in a restaurant? Which was owned by this really wonderful woman who had a dream to open a restaurant? And it made me think that it's like, really, really important? To have a dream?"

I told the interviewers that I wanted to be an elf because it was the most ridiculous thing I had ever heard of. I figured that for once in my life I would be completely honest and see how far it got me. I also failed the drug test. But they hired me anyway. Honesty had nothing to do with it. They hired me because I am five feet five inches tall.

Today we began our elf training. We learned the name of the various elf positions. You can be for example, an "Oh, My God!" elf and stand at the corner near the escalator. People arrive, see the long line around the corner, and say, "Oh, My God!"; your job is to tell them that it won't take more than an hour to see Santa.

You can be an Entrance Elf, a Watercooler Elf, a Bridge Elf, Train Elf, Maze Elf, Island Elf, Magic-Window Elf, Emergency-Exit Elf, Counter Elf, Magic-Tree Elf, Poitner Elf, Santa Elf, Photo Elf, Usher Elf, Cash-Register Elf, or Exit Elf. We were given a demonstration of the various positions, acted out by returning elves who were so "on stage" and goofy that it made me a little sick to my stomach. I don't know that I could look anyone in the eye and exclaim, "Oh, my goodness, I think I see Santa!" or, "Can you close your eyes and make a very special Christmas wish?" It makes one's mouth hurt to speak with such forced merriment. It embarrasses me to hear people talk this way. I prefer being frank with children. I'm more likely to say, "You must be exhausted" or, "I know a lot of people who would kill for that little waistline of yours."

I am afraid I won't be able to provide the enthusiasm Santa is asking for. I think I'll be a low key sort of elf.

November 21

My costume is green. I wear green velvet knickers, a yellow turtle-neck, a forest-green velvet smock, and a perky little hat decorated with spangles. This is my work uniform.

Today was elf dress rehearsal. I worked as a Santa Elf for house number two. A Santa Elf greets children at the Magic Tree and leads them to Santa's house. When you work as a Santa Elf you have to go by your elf name. My elf name is Crumpet. The other Santa elves have names like Jingle and Frosty. They take the children by the hand and squeal with forced delight. They sing and prance and behave like cartoon characters come to life. They frighten me.

November 29

Two members of the Macy's stable of Santas are black. Both are so light-skinned that, with the beard and makeup, you'd never know they weren't white. Yesterday a black woman who requested a "Santa of color" got upset after she was sent to Jerome.

"He's not black," the woman said.   20

The floor manager assured the woman that, yes, he was black. The woman said, "Well, he isn't black enough."

Jerome is a difficult Santa, moody and unpredictable. He spends a lot of time staring off into space. When a boss tells Jerome that we need to speed things up, Jerome gets defensive and says, "Listen, I'm playing a role here. Do you understand? A dramatic role that takes a great deal of preparation."

I've overheard Jerome encouraging children to enter the field of entomology. He says, "Entomology. Do you know what that is?" He tells them that the defensive spray of the stinkbug may have medicinal powers that may one day cure mankind of communicable diseases. He says, "Do you know what a communicable disease is?" That's an odd question, especially coming from Santa.

I was the Pointer Elf this afternoon. A woman approached me and whispered, "We would like a traditional Santa. I'm sure you know what I'm talking about." I sent her to Jerome.

Last Saturday Snowflake was the pointer and a woman said, "Last year   25
we had a chocolate Santa. Make sure that doesn't happen again." Snowflake sent her to Jerome.

December 9

A child came up to Santa this morning and his mother said, "All right, Jason. Tell Santa what you want."

Jason said, "I . . . want . . . Procton and . . . Gamble to . . . stop animal testing."

The mother said, "Procter, Jason, that's Procter and Gamble. And what do they do to animals? Do they torture animals, Jason? Is that what they do?"

Jason, said, yes, they torture. He was maybe six years old.

December 11

We were packed today, absolutely packed, and everyone was cranky. *30*
Once the line gets long we break it up into four different lines because no
one in their right mind would stay if they knew it would take over two
hours to see Santa. You can see a *movie* in two hours. Standing in a two-
hour line makes people worry that they're not living in a democratic nation.
They go over the edge. I was sent into the hallway to direct the second
phase of the line. The hallway was packed with people and all of them
seemed to stop me with a question: which way to the down escalator, which
way to the elevator, the Patio Restaurant, gift wrap, the women's rest room,
Trim a Tree. There was a line for Santa and a line for the women's bathroom,
and one woman, after asking me a thousand questions already, asked,
"Which is the line for the women's bathroom?" I shouted that I thought it
was the line with all the *women* in it.

She said, "I'm going to have you fired."

I had two people say that to me today: "I'm going to have you fired."
Go ahead, be my guest. I'm wearing a green velvet costume. It doesn't get
any worse than this. Who do these people think they are? I want to lean
over and say, "I'm going to have you *killed*."

December 22

This afternoon I was stuck being Photo Elf with Santa Santa. I don't
know his real name. No one does. During most days there is a slow period
when you sit around the house and talk to your Santa. Most of them are
nice guys and we sit around and laugh, but Santa Santa takes himself a bit
too seriously. I asked him where he lives and he said, "Why, I live at the
North Pole with Mrs. Claus!" I asked what he does the rest of the year and
he said, "I make toys for all of the children!"

I said, "Yes, but what do you do for money?"

"Santa doesn't need money," he said. *35*

Santa Santa sits and waves and jingles his bell sash when no one is
there. He actually recited "The Night Before Christmas" and it was just the
two of us in the house. No children, just us. What do you do with a nut
like that?

Questions for Discussion

1. What is Sedaris's opinion of department store Santa Clauses? Do you
   think his opinion is justified?
2. Sedaris presents his commentary as a series of diary entries. What advantage does this approach afford?
3. Aside from the commercialization of Christmas, what else is Sedaris
   poking fun at in this essay?
4. How do you interpret the entry for December 22? Why do you think
   Sedaris concludes with this entry?

5. Consider the scene of "Santa's Little Helper" and the scene (or circumstances) under which you have read it. Is your response to this piece influenced by the time of year when you read it? What do you think are the advantages and disadvantages of writing about material that is clearly tied to a specific time of year?

Suggestions for Writing

1. Have you ever been amused by the organization of a department store or shopping mall—or the behavior you have seen there? If so, write an essay that will humorously reveal the silly side of shopping.
2. Have you ever had a job (paid or volunteer) you wished you had not agreed to do? If you can make it seem amusing in retrospect, tell the story of the job that went wrong.

YOUR BASIC LANGUAGE SNOB

Joseph Epstein

> *Joseph Epstein is editor of* The American Scholar, *the journal of* Phi Beta Kappa. *For each issue Epstein contributes an essay under the pseudonym Aristides, the name of several philosophers of the second century. Although readers know that Epstein is Aristides, the use of a pseudonym allows him to write about what he chooses without seeming to speak officially as the editor of a prestigious journal. As you read "Your Basic Language Snob," look for evidence that Epstein is having fun in the role he has assumed here, and consider how seriously readers should take his concerns about the misuse of language.*

I don't mean to make anyone tense or otherwise edgy, but perhaps it is best you know at the outset that in me you are dealing with your basic language snob. Mention to me that when you were young your parents were very "supportive," tell me that before "finalizing" your plans you would like my "input," remark that the job in which you are "presently" employed provides you with a "nurturing environment"—say all or any of these things and you will not, I hope, see a muscle in my face move. I shall appear to show a genial interest in all you say, but beneath the geniality, make no mistake, I shall be judging you—and not altogether kindly. "Hmm," I shall be thinking, "I see that I am dealing here with someone who has a taste for psychobabble and trashy corporate and computer talk and misuses the word *presently* into the bargain." I shall, of course, say nothing about it to you; I certainly won't attempt to reform you. In fact, I rather prefer you stay the way that you are, for in using language as you do you are a source of real comfort to me. You allow me to feel that, in the realm of language at least, I am vastly superior to you; and the feeling of superiority—need I say it?— is what puts the lovely curl in the snob's smile.

As a language snob, one finds no shortage of playgrounds upon which to exercise one's snobbery. Hegel° reports that we learn from the study of history that no one learns from the study of history. So, we learn from the careful study of language that not many people have ever used language very carefully. Permit me to bring in an old adversary on this subject, that linguist of populist tendency, Professor Bernard Strawman.

"Arguably, you have a case," Strawman, trying to be polite, says.

"Wherever did you find so weak and weakly positioned an adverb as *arguably,* Bernie?" I reply.

"Perhaps," he says, "you don't allow enough leeway for societal pres-   5 sures on language use."

Hegel: Georg Wilhelm Friedrich Hegel (1770–1831), German philosopher who argued that history reveals a regular pattern of change.

"In the home of what woebegone sociologist did you ever find so ugly a word as *societal?*" I inquire.

"At this point in time," he replies, "*societal* is a very popular word. What do you have against it?"

"What I have against it, Bernie," I respond, "is that it tends to be used by so many people who also use such phrases as 'at this point in time.'"

Even Bernie Strawman, normally a model of conversational good manners, now sounds a touch petulant: "Wait a minute," he says. "Which are you against: the words or the people who use them? If the former, perhaps you are a man of principle; if the latter, it seems to me you are merely a snob."

To which I reply: "In this matter of language I view myself as a highly principled snob. May I take a moment—an essay, in fact—to explain?"   *10*

Let us look more closely at the word *supportive.* (Here you must imagine me picking up the word between my thumb and index finger, holding it as far from my body as possible, a disapproving pucker upon my lips.) At first glance, *supportive* seems harmless enough. At second glance, though, it strikes me as a fake. It is no more than the old words *supporting* or *supported* got up with a new suffix that gives it a psychological and hence high-flown air, rather like getting a letter from someone you used to know from the old neighborhood who, on his stationery, has had Ph.D. printed after his name. To use the word *supportive* is to take a sound enough old word and drag it from the solid ground of common usage into the marshlands of abstraction. The net result of this transfer, it seems to me, is not a gain in clarity but only an increase in pretension.

Richard Nixon has made it impossible ever again to say "Let me make one thing perfectly clear," so let me instead be as clear as I can be here and announce that I am not against all new words. While I have the mike, let me also announce that I am of course aware that language is almost ceaselessly changing. Some changes—such as the word "breathalyzer" to measure the drunkenness of drivers—are necessary to accommodate new inventions. Some changes I like just for their rhythm and sound. *Rip-off,* which has been in the language for roughly fifteen years now, seems to me to have earned its way. *Shuck,* a rip-off with an element of bunko to it, seems to me a fine fresh minting. I am all for invention, asking only that it be useful, describe something that really exists, and, if possible (which it often isn't), be fun. For this reason I find myself partial to the recent neologism *wimp.* It seems to me a word in the family of those fine Yiddishisms *nebbish* and *nebbekle* and their spin-off *nerd.* I think of a wimp, in fact, as a Gentile nebbish.

I trust that by now I have established myself as not your run-of-the-mill snob; I prefer, in fact, to think myself a custom-tailored snob. I like what I deem to be good new words. I like to toss in a neologism of my own every now and then, and I like what the linguistically prudish used to call Americanisms. One of the few things I have ever disagreed with Henry James about is his fear, set forth in *The American Scene,* that immigrant groups in the United States would pollute the pure stream of the English language. I think the current in this stream is stronger than James knew. It can carry a great deal before it and still remain fresh. It was, after all, the grandson of an immigrant, H. L. Mencken,° who made the English language do one-and-a-half gainers, back flips, and triple somersaults. A. J. Liebling,° another scion of the immigranti, as Mencken might have put it, for my money didn't do too shabbily either. But then I have a weakness for people who know how to play language for laughs. I have a taste for the concrete, the colorful, the comic (also, I see, for the alliterative). When the pro-basketball player Kareem Abdul-Jabbar, after dining at the home of a colleague, Julius Irving, was asked by the press if Mrs. Turquoise Irving was a good cook, Mr. Jabbar replied: "Yeah, man, Turquoise can burn." Henry James, I think, was too good-humored not to have enjoyed that.

As a snob, the people I like to lord it over are the quasi-semi-demi-ostensibly educated, B.A., M.S., Ph.D. and degrees beyond. Few things please me more, for example, than to see the novelists Norman Mailer and Joan Didion misuse the word *disinterested.* Or to hear a noted scholar, George F. Kennan, use the word *transpire* as if it were nothing more than a high-toned synonym for *happen.* Or to hear more degreed people than I care to count use *intriguing* as if it meant nothing other than *fascinating.* (Take the verb *to intrigue* away from spies and you leave these fellows practically unemployed.) To give you some notion of how far gone I am, now that it has caught on with the putatively educated classes, I have stopped using the phrase "early on"; when I hear it from others, I think "Whatsamatter, baby, *early* standing alone not good enough for a swell like you?" And of course I am death on people who use the term "bottom line."

Few things please me more than when to my language snobbery I can join my economic jealousy—I am practically ecstatic, that is, when I hear a highly paid broadcasting journalist commit an egregious error. I watch television news ready to pounce; it is good exercise, for, as a language snob, I get to pounce rather a lot. One of the local anchormen hereabouts—about a $300,000-a-year man, I would estimate—made my day not long ago when, in connection with the Libyan embassy crisis in London, he asked a visiting expert whether this might spell the possibility of a *tête à tête* for Qaddafi. "Coup d'etat, you overpaid moron," I roared, leaping from my couch, "not tête à tête." Or when, during the NCAA basketball tournament, the former coach and current announcer Billy Packer referred to "three or four Achilles' heels" that De Paul University's team had. "Ah, dear boy," I whispered to myself, "one Achilles' heel was quite enough—even for Achilles." But I don't always require major screw-ups such as these. I am satisfied when one of the truly high-priced boys—Dan Rather, Tom

15

H. L. Mencken: Henry Louis Mencken (1880–1956), American author and journalist, best known for *The American Language* (1919). *A. J. Liebling:* Abbott Joseph Liebling (1904–1963), American essayist who was much praised for his writing style.

Brokaw, or Peter Jennings—misuses *decimate,* which means to kill a tenth, or calls something "rather unique," which is akin to being rather pregnant. Do you take my point? Do you also think that what I have written thus far makes for "a good read?" If you do, please clean out your locker, for you're through—I hate the phrase "a good read."

One of the things a language snob learns early in his training is that there is probably no word or phrase that someone of stature doesn't despise. Edward Shils has kept up a running attack against the phrase "check out," as in "check it out." I know many people who hate *authored* as a verb, but I recently read that E. B. White doesn't even like the word *author.* I can never hear or see the word *workshop,* referring to a management seminar or creative writing course, without thinking of Kingsley Amis's line, from his novel *Jake's Thing,* which runs: "If there's one word that sums up everything that's gone wrong since the war, it's Workshop." Legion are the people who loathe the phrase "pick your brain," and I am among their number. Whenever anyone says to me that they would, on a particular subject, like to pick my brain, I always think, "Yes, if I may kick your butt."

"I'd like to pick your brain," is a phrase my friend Dottie uses quite often. Dottie and I go way back. She is a good soul, large-hearted in so many ways. But Dottie is one of those people who seems to absorb whatever language is in the air, and the language that has been in the air in recent years has, I fear, driven my friend Dottie a bit, well, dotty. (Perfectly lovely people sometimes use the most awful language; that they do is, alas, the pebble in the caviar of language snobbery.) Because of language, Dottie's life reminds me of a man whom Keats, in his letters, records meeting at Robert Burns's cottage, whose life, Keats notes, is "fuz, fuzzy, fuzziest."

Dottie has been going through a rough patch in recent years. Among other crises in her life, she has had a painful divorce and two job changes. She explained her divorce to me in something like the following terms. Her husband, she feels, "seemed just to want to do his thing." She no longer knew quite "where he was coming from." He used to be so steady, but, suddenly, he was so "off the wall." She supposed it was in part "a question of life-style," or maybe a "mid-life crisis." When I pressed her for greater clarity, she said: "Whatever." On her last trip to my apartment to pick my brain, her subject was a new prospective boss. She had had three interviews with him and found him rather "flakey."

"What do you mean by 'flakey'?" I asked.

"You know," she said, "he's a bit spacey."

"Spacey?" I asked.

"You know," she said, "like a real flake. I couldn't make out where exactly he was coming from."

Dottie comes ostensibly to pick my brain, but in fact she usually succeeds in scrambling it. When I left her at the door of my apartment, I suggested that she try to get a clearer picture of this man for whom she might soon be working by asking other people in her industry about him. She kissed me on the cheek and, turning to leave, announced, "Whatever."

20

Whatever!

I have never seen what I think of as the all-purpose, flying "whatever" 25
used as a transition before, as I have just used it above, but then that is what
makes it all-purpose. "I love you, I need you, whatever," or so I imagine
young men nowadays proposing to their wives-to-be. "Yes, darling, I love
you too. I want to have your children, to live out my life with you, whatever," the young woman replies, at which point they fall into each other's
arms while across the screen appears not The End but Whatever. Used in
this way, *whatever* is simply the word *etcetera* carried to the highest power.
But it can also be used in the following way: "I suppose what I really mean
is that, given society's current setup, it appears unlikely that one can find
fulfilling work as long as the structure of employment is likely to, you know,
whatever." Here *whatever* really means "Oh, the hell with it; I can't formulate
exactly what I wish to say, but you know what I mean." My problem is that
I usually don't know what the person means. What I do know is the utility
of a word such as *whatever* to a confused mind, or at any rate a mind that
chooses not to struggle with its confusions. It is a very useful word, *whatever.*
You can even end paragraphs with it. Whatever.

Whatever may also qualify for the category that the sainted H. W.
Fowler,° blessed be his named, called "meaningless words." Of meaningless
words, Fowler wrote:

> Words and phrases are often used in conversation, especially by the
> young, not as significant terms but rather, so far as they have any
> purpose at all, as aids of the same kind as are given in writing by
> punctuation, inverted commas, and underlining. It is a phenomenon
> perhaps more suitable for the psychologist than for the philologist.
> Words and phrases so employed change frequently, for they are soon
> worn out by overwork. Between the wars the most popular were DEF-
> INITELY and *sort of thing.* One may suppose that they originated in a
> subconscious feeling that there was a need in the one case to emphasize
> a right word and in the other to apologize for a possibly wrong one.
> But any meaning they ever had was soon rubbed off them, and they
> became noises automatically produced.

Fowler also mentions *actually* and *you know* among the crop of meaningless
words. (*Incidentally* is another meaningless word Fowler mentions, which,
incidentally, reminds me that, a while back, I had a long bout of beginning
most of my sentences, at least in conversation, with the phrase "By the way."
Everything, in those days, seemed to me "by the way." It takes a big-hearted
snob, don't you think, to admit to a small-gauge error.) A few years ago,
basically was having a good run. "Care for dessert?" "Basically, I don't think
I do," is a ridiculous but not unreal example. *You know* has had very long
innings, and flourishes today, particularly among athletes. Of Patrick Ewing,
the fine center for the Georgetown University basketball team, it has been

---

H. W. Fowler: English lexicographer (1858–1933), best known for *A Dictionary of Modern Usage* (1926).

said that last year he led the nation in *you knows.* It was said, obviously, by someone like me, a language snob.

A language snob's work is never done. Natural feelings of superiority being fleeting, he must maintain his vigilance, staying almost perpetually on the lookout for fresh signs of solecisms and lapsed standards, if only to maintain his desired state of self-elevation. As infantrymen are sent out on missions known as search and destroy, so the language snob is regularly on missions to search and enjoy—to find and delight in the linguistic fatuities and faux pas of his fellows. While there is no shortage of these in the contemporary world, some of course are better than others and provide more profound delight. I wasn't there to hear it, but a friend informs me that he once heard a Chicago politician claim that he "wasn't one to cast asparagus at his opponent." It is not every day that one comes upon such treasure.

Still, the language snob must take his pleasures where he finds them. In bureaucratic prose, for example. Few samples of bureaucratic prose fail to include the verb *implement,* which generally causes me to want to reach for an implement to smash the person who has used it. *Guidelines,* too, has brought many a twinkle to these crowfooted and pouchy eyes. "*Guidelines* is a bastardization," I cry out to the walls. "It comes from *guy lines,* you idiot." No question about it, bureaucratic prose writers need to prioritize, dichotomize, and finalize, at least if they are to be responsive and people-oriented. Is what I say here of any ongoing interest? If so, I shall keep on going.

A language snob must not fear descending to pedantry. I know this language snob doesn't. I have had a good deal of fun, in this regard, watching people misuse the word *whence,* turning it into a tautology by saying or writing "from whence." But I have suffered minor setbacks here. Recently I noted "from whence" in both Shakespeare and Edmund Burke. More recently still, I discovered T. S. Eliot—T. S. bloody Eliot, for God's sake—misusing *presently* to mean "now" or "currently." Shock and dismay is the language snob's lot. Believe me, I don't enjoy feeling superior to Shakespeare, Burke, and Eliot, yet what is a man of serious standards to do?

But a language snob need not confine himself to pedantry. Euphemism always yields a full crop for his scythe—and, like cauliflower, euphemism is available all year round. My very favorite euphemism over the past fifteen or so years has been, without doubt, "student unrest." It was used to refer to the attempt on the part of radical students in the late sixties and early seventies to destroy the universities. "Student unrest" implies a mild crankiness, the antidote for which was perhaps a few good afternoon naps. I like, too, "Due to mature theme viewer discretion advised," which I take to mean "simulated fornication, extreme violence, and filthy language follow—get the kids the hell out of the room." This may seem an idiosyncratic reading, but I understand the word *interdisciplinary,* used by academics, to mean "I deserve a grant." I recall reading a grant proposal for the National Endow-

30

ment for the Humanities a few years back in which the author wanted a grant for a course that would not only be "cross-curricular" but "interdisciplinary" and "interuniversity" as well. I suggested that NEH turn it down because it wasn't interplanetary. None of this parochial stuff for me.

A language snob must also be ready to outlaw words because the wrong people use them. *Charisma* is such a word. It once had a significant meaning, but no longer. "He has charisma," I not long ago heard Bucky Walters, the basketball announcer, say of a player. "He's got that smile." *Gnostic,* at least as used by literary critics, is another word I should like to ban. I have never read a sentence by a literary critic with the word *Gnostic* in it that I have ever understood (except this one). *Syndrome,* too, must go. "This is a syndrome he had foisted on him," I recently heard one politician say of another. *Structure* is another gone goose. On television the other day I heard another politician, one of the zinc-throated orators of our day, affirm: "I have invested in activities that have gone to enhance this total city's overall structure." Does everyone out there know how to enhance a structure? You add a touch of tarragon and soak it in lime juice. While we are cleaning the linguistic closet, let's toss out *learning experience,* which was never any good to begin with. Besides, I have noticed that people who say "learning experience" tend never to learn from experience.

On the subject of experience, it was Walter Pater° who invoked us to live intensely for the moment, to seek "not the fruit of experience, but experience itself." But Pater didn't live to see the word *experience* turned into a verb, lucky chap. What would he have made of recent advertisements that ask us to "Experience Yoplait Yogurt," "Experience the St. Regis," "Experience Our 9.6 Interest Rates"? Walter Pater was not notably—how to say it?—a fun person. I am not at all sure he could "wrap his mind around" what has happened to the word *experience.* Although in the passage of his I quoted above he seems to be inviting us to "get in touch with our feelings," he scarcely seems a man to whom one could say, as the people who use *experience* as a verb also tend to say, "Go for it!"

As a language snob, I judge a person less by the cut of his jib than by the grab of his gab. Where the gab has no grab I see a certain mental—not moral—flab. When a prospective buyer of *The London Observer* remarks that he intends to make that paper's editor "toe the line of viability," I make a judgment that is not charitable to him. When I read the phrase, in a book by Alvin Toffler, "decisional environment," not one but both my eyebrows fly up just beyond my receding hairline. When I read, in *The New Yorker,* about a Harvard Law School professor who refers to "a societal role not perceived as particularly helpful," to myself I exclaim, "Et tu, Harvard!" Can you identify with or relate to this? If you can—"identify," "relate"—I want

---

Walter Pater: English author and educator (1839–1894), best known for *History of the Renaissance* (1885), the work quoted here.

you to draw a final paycheck and be out of here by five o'clock this afternoon. I loathe those words and phrases. You're fired.

"I have never seen a word derive," says the heroine of Renata Adler's novel *Speedboat*. I believe I have seen a word derive, and that word is *life-style*. I recall first coming across the word *life-style* (from the German *Lebensstil*) in Max Weber's essays on social class, some of which I read as an undergraduate. I was immensely impressed with it; on Max Weber, an authentic genius, all words looked good. In those days, I used it myself, slipping it into term papers and conversation whenever possible. (Those were also the days of *ambivalence* and *love-hate*—not the condition and the relationships but the cheap phrases.) Soon I saw *life-style* taken up by advertising agencies and low-grade sociologists. College students next took the word up in the most flyblown way: "Queen Victoria lived a very different life-style than most of her subjects." The word fell into more and more common—and more and more confused—use. Today the word carries something of a philosophical freight: implicit in it is the notion, which I, for one, don't believe, that life has an almost infinite plasticity—change your life-style, change your life, it's as easy as that.

I have come to feel a fine invigorating hatred for the word. Where I could fight against it, I have done so. I have abused authors who use it when I have written about their books. My poor students always receive a slightly squinty-eyed query when the word pops up in their conversation: "*Life-style*—what do you suppose you mean when you say *life-style*?" I ask. But then a few years ago, in the course of editing a manuscript by the late Nobel-Prize-winning biologist Max Delbrück, who was a fluent and careful writer of English prose, I came across a reference to "the life-style of the cell." Over the telephone I explained to Professor Delbrück that *life-style* was a word that drove me beyond the confines of distraction and into the country of apoplexy and asked him if I couldn't persuade him to remove it from his manuscript. "I don't like it much myself," he replied, "but I am afraid that it is the word that scientists have given to the patterning of certain cellular activity and that we are stuck with it." So there you have it—living testimony of a word deriving.

Do I, I wonder, begin to seem to you—to put it ever so gently—a touch crazed? Has the cheerful snob that I advertise myself as being begun to seem the beady-eyed fanatic? There is something about caring for language that does not allow for moderation. How can you tell if you care about language? You care, I should say, if it grates upon you to hear the word *impact* used as a verb. Next you begin to care if you see *impact* used to describe anything other than ballistics, car crashes, and wisdom teeth. You care if you find yourself wishing to flee the company of anyone who uses such words as *parenting, coupling, cohabing, husbanding,* or *wiving.* You care if it turns your stomach to see or hear a reference to "the caring professions." You know for certain that you care if the last thing in the world you care to be called is "a caring person."

In recent years language snobbery has suffered a real setback by having become institutionalized. There have always been writers who worried and complained about the state of the English language. Swift, Hazlitt, and Orwell have been among their number. But of late a great many books have been published on the subject. Magazines—*The New York Times Magazine, Esquire, Gentlemen's Quarterly*—have instituted regular columns on the state of the language. Such journalists as Edwin Newman, John Simon, and William Safire—a bit of a falling off here from Swift, Hazlitt, and Orwell—have set up shop as state-of-the-language pundits. By now there are even reverse language snobs loose in the land. Thus Professor Robert Pattison, in *On Literacy,* remarks upon "the dull, pragmatic rationale of established literacy" and writes:

> The same students who resolutely remain in darkness about the niceties of correct English grammar are as capable of intelligence as any previous generation. . . . Months of exercises will not shake their nonchalance about commas, but few are likely to misspell the name Led Zeppelin.

What a shame that there isn't an antonym for the phrase "Right on!"

Mention of the state-of-the-language pundits brings to mind Lionel Trilling, who once wrote: "I find righteous denunciations of the present state of language no less dismaying than the present state of the language." Yet, I have to wonder, is what I have been doing here not also righteous? Perhaps it is, but there does remain the less than cheery state of the language. Then, too, I take some small pride in the fact that I am for the most part attacking my own class. Nearly thirty years ago, in *Noblesse Oblige* (1956), Nancy Mitford caused a great stir by pointing out the distinction in their use of language between U and non-U people—U people being those who had gone to university. This distinction, as I recall, had to do almost exclusively with social class, and spoke very little, if at all, to the quality of language used by either group. Today, though, it is people who have been to university who make the most gnawing depredations into the clarity and cleanliness of language. I cannot, for example, imagine any supposedly uneducated person using the word *supportive,* except possibly about his jockstrap. Who but a university student or graduate would refer to her mother as a "role model," or talk about "the gender gap," or say she wishes "to dialogue" with me? (I make it a rule never "to dialogue"; I find it gets in the way of serious conversation.) Who but a U person would fall back on so foggy a word as *values*? Wesleyan University, I note, has a course entitled "Touchstones of Western Values," and a current Democratic presidential candidate has said, "Values lead to values." See ya later, obfuscator.

With the possible exception of politicians, bureaucrats, professors with weak ideas, and those in other professions and trades where charlatanry is requisite, few are the people who have a real taste for obfuscatory language.

Doubtless Nietzsche° was correct when he said that "general is the need for new jingling words, which shall make life noisy and festive." Yet language is still far and away the best tool we have for deceiving ourselves. When a famous ecologist writes that, if we are to save the earth, "we must enter into a creative association with our environment," I don't think the man is a knave or even a liar; I do, though, think, perhaps unbeknownst to himself, that he is embarked on the mental equivalent of whistling Dixie. When a young mother takes an active hand in a political campaign because she wants "this country to be a positive experience for my son," I do not impugn her sincerity, only her clarity. Was Russia a positive experience for Tolstoy, Germany for Bismarck, France for Proust? Do countries supply "positive experience"? The thought makes one wonder whether this young mother isn't searching for something that is not available.

So the language snob persists, lorgnette held high. Sometimes he looks 40 quite as much at the people who use them as at the words themselves. I have never, for instance, met a professor in the humanities who called himself or herself a "humanist," without irony, whom I didn't dislike. I am extremely wary of people who go in for botanical metaphors in a big way to describe psychological states. "I feel myself growing," they will say. Or: "It has been a growthful experience." To the basic botanical metaphor of growth, further metaphors are stitched in. Abra Anderson, a Rockefeller granddaughter and a millionairess who lives in Chicago, recently told a journalist:

> Right now I don't know where I am, except that I feel everything else is finished. The apartment's finished, I've got a wonderful man, my kids are fine, the bills are paid, the charities are OK. And I'm just repotting myself.

Repotting? Hmmm. Sounds like a lot of fertilizer to me.

Certain words such as *growth* seem to have a built-in squishiness; they grow soft at the touch. But, as any language snob will be pleased to tell you, good solid words, if sedulously misused, can lose their solidity, too. The word *honest* applied to art—and for a long stretch it was the key word of praise for works of architecture—always merits suspicion. *Excellence* is nowadays all but drained of meaning, so often has it been applied to things that are scarcely mediocre. The word *complete,* when used to describe collections of one or another kind of writing, usually turns out to mean merely "quite a bit of." *Literally,* in so many current usages, doesn't mean "literally"; it's literally a scandal, so to speak. "Ballpark figure" is a nice fairly new phrase meaning "rough approximation" (such as the estimates of attendance at a ball game), but it sometimes seems, to this language snob at any rate, as if we are entering the era of ballpark language, where words are used approximately; they mean only roughly what we think they mean.

Nietzsche: Friedrich Wilhelm Nietzsche (1844–1900), German philosopher who called for a heroic morality that would affirm life.

My biases ought by now to be clear; so, too, my snobbery. But I earlier referred to myself as a principled snob. Wherein, you may about now be wondering, lie my principles? All right, turn down the houselights, boys, give me the strong spotlight and a drumroll, here they are: take out after all language that is pretentious and imprecise, under-educated and over-intellectualized. Question all language that says more than it means, that leaves the ground but does not really fly. Question authority only after you have first seriously consulted it; it isn't always as stupid as it looks. Never forget that today's hot new phrase becomes tomorrow's cold dead cliché. (What will we do, a writer in the *Chronicle of Higher Education* asks, "when the Baby Boomers get to Golden Pond?") Know in advance that the fight for careful language is probably a losing one, but at the same time don't allow this knowledge to take the edge off your appetite for battle. The war may be lost, yet the skirmishes are still worth waging. Recall the words of that grand snob, Proust's Baron de Charlus: "I have always honored the defenders of grammar and logic. We realize fifty years later that they have averted serious dangers."

Hey, you know, I guess that some of you think I'm doing a number on you. If you do, check it out. C'mon over. I'd like your input. The old lady'll put out some peanuts, pretzels maybe—you know, fun food. We'll break out a few tall cool ones. See if you think I've really gone flakey on this language thing. I think you'll find I'm pretty viable and am playing well within myself. We'll do some zero-based thinking, look at it in terms of worst-case and in terms of best-case thinking—in terms of the process itself. Maybe, when you come right down to it, it's a policy question. It's an intriguing bit. Arguably, it's worth arguing about. I haven't gone so far beyond the wall as to be above a little insightful feedback. But I'd better knock off, you know, because I've come, as they used to say in the bad old days, to the bottom line—and when I say bottom line, daddy, I mean bottom line. Out of sight. Awesome. Really.

Questions for Discussion

1. What does Epstein mean when he calls himself a "snob"? How well does he seem to understand grammar and usage? Why would careful attention to language be considered snobbish?
2. Why does Epstein object to such terms as *supportive, whatever,* and *life-style?*
3. How does Epstein create his language snob persona? Does he offer any clues indicating that the "I" in this essay should not be taken completely seriously? Comment upon how this persona affects your willingness to be amused.
4. At the end of the essay Epstein repeats some of the terms he has criticized earlier, using them in his own sentences. Why do you think he does this?

5. Are there any words that bother you when you hear them misused or used too frequently? Describe them.
6. Do you think words have fixed meanings? Or does the meaning of a word begin to change as people start using it differently? Under what circumstances is it possible to misuse language?

Suggestions for Writing

1. Identify a field of study or activity that you are knowledgeable about, and consider the misunderstandings, misuses, and mistakes that might irritate an expert in that field. Then write an essay about being a "snob" in that field.
2. Note some of the clichés you hear most frequently. Then write a comic dialogue filled with as many clichés as you can include.

8

Writing to
Move Others

The desire to move an audience has been a major motive of rhetoric since ancient times. *Ceremonial speech,* as conceived by classical rhetoric, did not need to inspire a specific decision or action; its purpose was simply to strengthen beliefs that were already held. The ancient Greeks even had contests in which speakers were judged by how successful they were in moving their audience. Such contests are rare today and are more likely to feature students than professional speakers, but it is still useful to think of "writing to move" as a type of public performance.

THINKING ABOUT AUDIENCE

You will be familiar with this kind of rhetorical situation if you have ever been addressed as part of a crowd that has something in common—the shared values that writing to move assumes. Graduation speeches, for instance, are usually written to inspire loyalty to one's old school and to exhort graduates to live productive lives. The eulogy at a funeral is usually designed to inspire admiration or respect for the dead. And churches offer sermons aimed at reinforcing beliefs that are, in theory at least, already held. In each of these cases the audience has a common bond: graduation from the same school, acquaintance with the same person, or membership in the same church. The reinforcing of common ties is one of the things that writing to move has in common with writing to amuse. In both motives writers also aim to trigger a specific response from their audience. But while writing to amuse is designed to make readers enjoy themselves, writing to move is designed to inspire strong feelings. When amused, readers are usually able to relax; when moved, they are most likely to be invigorated.

Consider, for example, the purpose of a keynote speech at a political convention. Everyone at the convention already belongs to the same party; they don't need to be persuaded to join or to be informed about what the party stands for. The speaker can usually assume that the audience will support the party's candidates in the next election and that this support will be given with varying degrees of enthusiasm. Some people at the convention probably favor candidates who were not nominated; others may be feeling hot, tired, and eager to get back home where they have other obligations to fulfill—obligations that may take precedence over helping the party win the election. The primary purpose of this keynote speech is to inspire enthusiasm—to make the delegates forget their other concerns, rise to their feet, and feel certain that they are part of a noble cause. The speaker in this case may benefit from reinforcement unavailable to writers: At key moments carefully selected video images may flash across screens surrounding the podium as red, white, and blue balloons fall from the ceiling. But this speech began as a written speech employing rhetorical strategies that specifically take advantage of communal values strategies that we can adapt for other occasions in which community is important.

PURPOSE AND STYLE

Martin Luther King's "I Have a Dream" provides an example of political exhortation at its very best. The words on the page, and the care with which they are arranged, make it a moving piece of prose without the benefit of our hearing King's voice or being present at the scene where this speech was delivered. Visualizing the situation for which this speech was designed, however, can help you understand King's purpose and the techniques he used to arouse his audience's emotions. The occasion was the hundredth anniversary of the Emancipation Proclamation; the scene was the steps of the Lincoln Memorial from which King faced an audience of more than two hundred thousand people who had marched to Washington on behalf of civil rights for African-Americans. King did not need to persuade that audience that African-Americans deserved civil rights. If they didn't already believe this, they would not have come to Washington. What King needed to do was to reinforce the beliefs his audience already shared—to vindicate whatever hardships they had endured and to help them lift up their hearts.

Although the entire speech deserves close reading, a short excerpt illustrates a number of points essential to our understanding of writing to move. Here are paragraphs 9 and 10 from the eighteen-paragraph-long speech.

> I am not unmindful that some of you have come here out of great trials and tribulations. Some of you have come fresh from narrow jail cells. Some of you have come from areas where your quest for freedom left you battered by the storms of persecution and staggered by the winds of police brutality. You have been the veterans of creative suffering. Continue to work with the faith that unearned suffering is redemptive.
>
> Go back to Mississippi, and go back to Alabama. Go back to South Carolina. Go back to Georgia. Go back to Louisiana. Go back to the slums and ghettos of our Northern cities, knowing that somehow this situation can and will be changed. Let us not wallow in the valley of despair.

When we look closely at these paragraphs, we see that King is not attempting to persuade his audience to undertake a specific action. It is true that he advises his listeners to go back home and keep on working, but the promise that "somehow this situation can and will be changed" is short on details and unlikely to satisfy someone who has not been moved by the speech as a whole.

A paraphrase focusing only upon the content of these two paragraphs might read: "I know you've all had a rough time, but go back home and cheer up. Things are going to get better." Reducing King's prose to this paraphrase is grotesque but illuminating: We have stripped these paragraphs of their beauty and their power to move—deprived them of their reason for being. What is it, then, that makes King's prose moving?

In the first place, King was a gifted stylist with a fine ear for prose rhythm; his sentences are so nicely cadenced that they can engage the attention of an audience by the quality of their music. The previous short excerpt uses two techniques that can be found in much of King's work. When he writes "trials and tribulations," he is using a simple form of *parallel construction,* which means putting similar ideas in similar form for the sake of balance. In this case a plural noun is balanced with a plural noun.

The third sentence in the first paragraph provides another example of parallelism: "battered by the storms of persecution and staggered by the winds of police brutality." "Battered" is balanced against "staggered," "storms" against "winds," and "persecution" against "police brutality"—as can be easily seen when we reformat these lines:

<u>battered</u>	<u>by the storms</u>	<u>of persecution</u>
and		
<u>staggered</u>	<u>by the winds</u>	<u>of police brutality</u>

Only "police" keeps this example from being perfectly parallel. It is being used here as an adjective describing "brutality," but there is no equivalent adjective describing "persecution." From this example we can conclude two things.

1. Parallelism does not necessarily require a word-for-word balance—although the more words that are balanced, the stronger the parallel will be.
2. A word or phrase that does not fit within a parallel will receive increased emphasis, because it interferes with the prevailing rhythm. In this case it is quite possible that King wanted "police" to have this extra emphasis. His original audience would have believed that the police were interfering with much more than parallel construction.

Although King's second paragraph also features a strong parallel structure in which patterns repeat and harmonize with one another, the first sentence of the paragraph also illustrates another rhetorical device: *anaphora*, or deliberate repetition at the beginning of sentences or clauses for the purpose of affecting the reader. King emphasizes *Go back* to such an extent here that the words no longer seem as simple as they would in another context (e.g., "Go back to your room and get a sweater."). As the *Go backs* accumulate, they become a type of song in which the words mean more than they say. Behind these *Go backs* is a meaning that can be felt even though it is unstated. *Go back* becomes "Go back and don't give up; go back and keep on fighting."

The rhetorical use of repetition for emphasis can be thought of as a more sophisticated version of how a cheerleader uses repetition ("*Go* team *go; fight* team *fight*") when trying to move a crowd. Unlike the simple chants you can hear at a pep rally, King's prose draws upon a variety of techniques and does so for a serious end. Nevertheless, one way of reading "I Have a Dream" is to read it as a type of rallying cry. King's purpose, after all, was to move the crowd to continued struggle by reaffirming the importance of their common cause.

Neither parallel construction nor deliberate repetition is limited to exhortation, and you will find examples of them in works that have other motives behind them. But because writing to move has strong links to oratory, it is especially likely to draw upon strategies like these that make sentences easy to read and easy to remember. When you read "I Have a Dream," you will find that King uses both parallelism and repetition repeatedly. You will also find that he keeps his diction simple. With the possible exception of two words ("tribulations" and "redemptive"), the words of the passage quoted previously could be understood by almost any English-speaking person. An experienced speaker, King understood that we cannot be moved by what we do not understand. On this occasion eloquence required simplicity.

Style, however, is only one of the factors that explain why King's prose is so much more effective than our paraphrase of it. Writing to move requires creating a bond between the writer and the reader. It is one thing to say "I know you've had a rough time." It is something else to show that you mean it and to leave your audience feeling personally addressed. Many of the people in King's audience would have been touched personally by the sympathetic reference to "narrow jail cells." And almost everyone in that audience would have had some experience with "persecution" and "police brutality." King then makes specific references to five southern states and a more general reference to northern cities. Anyone from Mississippi, Alabama, South Carolina, Georgia, or Louisiana would have felt as if King were addressing him or her as an individual. Furthermore, the list of five is long enough to be understood as examples representing other states that pass unmentioned. And references to different states remind the entire crowd that they are part of a nationwide struggle with friends and allies in other states.

As "I Have a Dream" suggests, writing to move requires more than eloquent phrasing. It also requires a strong sense of audience, which, in turn, ultimately depends upon understanding human nature and the types of experience that evoke different emotions.

WRITING TIPS

When analyzing "I Have a Dream" and the other readings in this chapter, you can benefit from principles laid down in the eighteenth century by Hugh Blair, a professor at the University of Edinburgh, to determine what makes language moving. He offers seven principles that can help you understand the work of other writers and to write moving essays of your own.*

1. *Choose a topic that is suitable for writing to move.* In the pages that follow King addresses the subject of social injustice, Henry Kissinger pays tribute to a former president, Dorothea Dix calls for humane treatment of the mentally ill, Alice Walker reflects upon the treatment of an animal, and both Randall Williams and Jonathan Swift write about poverty. Depending upon how a writer proceeds, topics such as these can inspire a number of emotions—including anger, indignation, pity, or grief. There are, of course, many other topics suitable for this type of writing. David James Duncan, for example, uses writing as a way to come to terms with the death of his brother—an experience that can move anyone who has suffered a serious loss. On the other hand, there are also topics (such as an explanation of how the brain functions or an evaluation of tires) that would be inappropriate for

---

*These principles are adapted from Blair's *Lectures on Rhetoric and Belles Lettres,* first published in 1783. A modern edition is available, edited by Harold E. Harding (Carbondale: Southern Illinois University Press, 1965).

writing to move. If you try to inspire an emotion that seems unrelated to the topic, your prose may seem overwrought rather than moving.

2. *Get right into the topic without warning readers of your intention.* If you begin by writing, "I am going to tell you a sad story" (or words to that effect), you are weakening your work in at least two ways. By telling readers how you want them to respond—as opposed to letting the response grow naturally out of the work—you are giving people a ready-made standard for evaluating your work; and you may find someone responding by saying, "Well, I didn't think that was so sad." Moreover, by putting readers on guard, you lose the strategic advantage of surprise. Readers alerted in advance to "a sad story" could brace themselves against feeling sad or decide to put your work aside in order to read something more cheerful. When you read "A Mickey Mantle Koan," you will find that Duncan never tells us how he wants us to feel about his brother's death. And anyone reading "A Modest Proposal" for the first time may find it shocking at first, because Swift conceals his intention for several paragraphs.

3. *Include details that can evoke the response you intend.* Although supporting detail is important in almost all types of writing, it is especially important when writing to move. And the details that you choose should have emotional appeal. For example, a specific description of a homeless person sleeping on a sidewalk is likely to be more moving than several paragraphs of statistics. Consider, in this regard, how Randall Williams makes us see his childhood through concrete detail: "I have seen my Daddy wrap copper wire through the soles of his boots to keep them together in the wintertime." His essay "Daddy Tucked the Blanket" includes many other details about growing up poor, but the copper wire is the detail with which his childhood first comes alive.

4. *Be moved yourself.* Although there are many rhetorical situations in which writers need to keep their feelings to themselves, writing to move requires that you yourself feel the emotion that you want others to share. This does not mean that you have to come out and tell how you feel; on the contrary, you should try to keep your focus on your subject rather than on yourself. It happens that all of the writers in this chapter use the first person at some point. In a piece such as Dix's "On Behalf of the Insane Poor," it's hard not to notice that Dix is angry. But even if you never mention yourself, readers should be able to tell how you feel about your subject. The main thing is to avoid insincerity. If you really don't care about poverty, but think it would be proper to sound as if you do, you are unlikely to succeed at moving others. Write about what you care about, and don't try to fake emotion.

5. *Write simply and directly.* When you feel something strongly, you are likely to use language that is simple, direct, and bold. Formal diction and long, complicated sentences will seem artful rather than direct, thus diminishing the sense that you are moved by the subject you are writing about. Here, for example, is Walker describing her response to eating meat: "I am eating misery, I thought, as I took the first bite. And spit it out." These two

sentences may be the result of several drafts, for the words that first occur to writers are not necessarily those that are the simplest and most direct. But the apparent simplicity of these sentences helps to convey emotion. The force of "And spit it out" would be lost if, afraid to use a word like *spit,* we consulted a thesaurus and tried using something like *expectorated.* Because of the directness necessary for writing to move, you should find all the selections in this chapter easy to read, with the possible exception of "A Modest Proposal." Swift's essay is the most difficult to read—in part because words written more than two hundred fifty years ago often seem less natural than those written last year, and in part because Swift deliberately violates the rule here as part of his strategy to surprise readers with a proposal that turns out to be anything but modest.

6. *Be faithful to your purpose.* When writing to move, you need to avoid any digression that would interrupt the flow of feeling you are trying to inspire. Had King paused in the middle of "I Have a Dream" to offer an analysis of congressional legislation affecting civil rights, he would have weakened the emotional power of his speech. King knew a great deal about his topic, but the occasion of "I Have a Dream" was an occasion that called for inspiration rather than information. As you revise an essay designed to move, be prepared to cut not only digressions but also any sentence that seems too fancy. As Blair put it, "Sacrifice all beauties, however bright and showy, which would divert the mind from the principal object, and which would amuse the imagination, rather than touch the heart."

7. *Know when to stop.* As a general rule, writing designed to move needs to be kept fairly short. It is difficult to sustain intensity of feeling at any great length; and if you write too much about your subject, you run the risk of readers deciding that you are making too much of a fuss. Most of the readings in this chapter are only four pages long. But "knowing when to stop" cannot be measured by word count alone. It is also a matter of understanding where you can afford to linger and where it is best to let a few carefully chosen words convey a sense of things unsaid. When your material is strong, you can often benefit from handling it with restraint, letting the imagination of your readers fill in gaps along lines that you have merely suggested. Here, for example, are two paragraphs from Williams.

> Later that night everyone was in bed and I heard Daddy get up from the couch where he was reading. I looked out from my bed across the hall into their room. He was standing right over Mama and she was already alseep. He pulled the blanket up and tucked it around her shoulders and just stood there and tears were dropping off his cheeks and I thought I could faintly hear them splashing against the linoleum rug.
>
> Now they're divorced.

What is remarkable about these paragraphs, taken from an essay describing the effects of poverty, is how they involve a combination of showing and suggesting. The first paragraph is full of detail. We know when this happened, where everyone was, what Daddy had been doing, and exactly what happened after he tucked a blanket around his wife's shoulders. The second paragraph, by contrast, confronts us with a single piece of information. But the simplicity with which that information is conveyed is more dramatic than a paragraph spelling out all the reasons that led to the divorce. Within the context of the essay we can imagine those details for ourselves. We are less likely to imagine the sound of tears upon linoleum—hence the author's decision to provide that detail. Moreover, the starkness of the second paragraph serves as a corrective to a potentially sentimental scene: One sentence about Daddy's tears is moving; a second could be maudlin. Williams wisely recognized that his material called for a mixture of intimacy and restraint.

Of course, writing to move cannot be mastered by simply memorizing a few rules. For whatever reason you may want to move people, you should not only practice the techniques outlined here but also watch and listen to other people. You may already know how to touch the hearts of people who are close to you. By reading the work of other writers and practicing the techniques of writing to move, you can ultimately learn to touch people you have not met. The ability to inspire emotion is one of the most useful achievements of rhetoric. But like any other type of writing, it takes study and practice.

I HAVE A DREAM

Martin Luther King, Jr.

"I Have a Dream" is the text of a speech King delivered in 1963 upon the hundredth anniversary of the Emancipation Proclamation. Consider how this occasion may have reinforced what King had to say, and try to imagine the scene where this speech was delivered: the Lincoln Memorial in Washington, D.C. As you read "I Have a Dream," think about why its author would be honored with the Nobel Peace Prize a year after giving this speech—and assassinated only a few years later.

I am happy to join with you today in what will go down in history as the greatest demonstration for freedom in the history of our nation.

Five score years ago, a great American, in whose symbolic shadow we stand today, signed the Emancipation Proclamation. This momentous decree came as a great beacon of light of hope to millions of Negro slaves who had been seared in the flames of withering injustice. It came as a joyous daybreak to end the long night of their captivity. But one hundred years later, the Negro still is not free. One hundred years later, the life of the Negro is still sadly crippled by the manacles of segregation and the chains of discrimination. One hundred years later, the Negro lives on a lonely island of poverty in the midst of a vast ocean of material prosperity. One hundred years later, the Negro is still anguished in the corners of American society and finds himself in exile in his own land. And so we have come here today to dramatize a shameful condition.

In a sense we have come to our nation's capital to cash a check. When the architects of our republic wrote the magnificent words of the Constitution and the Declaration of Independence, they were signing a promissory note to which every American was to fall heir. This note was the promise that all men—yes, Black men as well as white men—would be guaranteed the inalienable rights of life, liberty, and the pursuit of happiness.

It is obvious today that America has defaulted on this promissory note insofar as her citizens of color are concerned. Instead of honoring this sacred obligation, America has given the Negro people a bad check, a check which has come back marked "insufficient funds." But we refuse to believe that the bank of justice is bankrupt. We refuse to believe that there are insufficient funds in the great vaults of opportunity of this nation; and so we have come to cash this check, a check that will give us upon demand the riches of freedom and the security of justice.

We have also come to this hallowed spot to remind America of the fierce urgency of *now*. This is no time to engage in the luxury of cooling off or to take the tranquilizing drug of gradualism. *Now* is the time to make real the promises of democracy. *Now* is the time to rise from the dark and desolate valley of segregation to the sunlit path of racial justice. *Now* is the time to lift our nation from the quicksands of racial injustice to the solid rock of brotherhood. *Now* is the time to make justice a reality for all of God's children.

It would be fatal for the nation to overlook the urgency of the moment. This sweltering summer of the Negro's legitimate discontent will not pass until there is an invigorating autumn of freedom and equality. Nineteen sixty-three is not an end, but a beginning. And those who hope that the Negro needed to blow off steam and will now be content will have a rude awakening if the nation returns to business as usual. There will be neither rest nor tranquility in America until the Negro is granted his citizenship rights. The whirlwinds of revolt will continue to shake the foundations of our nation until the bright day of justice emerges.

But there is something that I must say to my people who stand on the warm threshold which leads into the palace of justice. In the process of gaining our rightful place, we must not be guilty of wrongful deeds. Let us not seek to satisfy our thirst for freedom by drinking from the cup of bitterness and hatred. We must forever conduct our struggle on the high plane of dignity and discipline. We must not allow our creative protest to degenerate into physical violence. Again and again we must rise to the majestic heights of meeting physical force with soul force. And the marvelous new militancy which has engulfed the Negro community must not lead us to a distrust of all white people; for many of our white brothers, as evidenced by their presence here today, have come to realize that their destiny is tied up with our destiny, and they have come to realize that their freedom is inextricably bound to our freedom.

We cannot walk alone. And as we walk we must make the pledge that we shall always march ahead. We cannot turn back. There are those who are asking the devotees of civil rights, "When will you be satisfied?" We can never be satisfied as long as the Negro is the victim of the unspeakable horrors of police brutality. We can never be satisfied as long as our bodies, heavy with the fatigue of travel, cannot gain lodging in the motels of the highways and the hotels of the cities. We cannot be satisfied as long as the Negro's basic mobility is from a smaller ghetto to a larger one. We can never be satisfied as long as our children are stripped of their selfhood and robbed of their dignity by signs stating "For Whites Only." We cannot be satisfied as long as the Negro in Mississippi cannot vote and a Negro in New York believes he has nothing for which to vote. No, no, we are not satisfied, and we will not be satisfied until justice rolls down like waters and righteousness like a mighty stream.

I am not unmindful that some of you have come here out of great trials and tribulations. Some of you have come fresh from narrow jail cells. Some of you have come from areas where your quest for freedom left you battered by the storms of persecution and staggered by the winds of police brutality. You have been the veterans of creative suffering. Continue to work with the faith that unearned suffering is redemptive.

Go back to Mississippi, and go back to Alabama. Go back to South Carolina. Go back to Georgia. Go back to Louisiana. Go back to the slums and ghettos of our Northern cities, knowing that somehow this situation can and will be changed. Let us not wallow in the valley of despair. *10*

I say to you today, my friends, even though we face the difficulties of today and tomorrow, I still have a dream. It is a dream deeply rooted in the American dream. I have a dream that one day this nation will rise up and live out the true meaning of its creed: "We hold these truths to be self-evident, that all men are created equal." I have a dream that one day, on the red hills of Georgia, sons of former slaves and the sons of former slave owners will be able to sit down together at the table of brotherhood. I have a dream that one day even the state of Mississippi, a state sweltering with the heat of injustice, sweltering with the heat of oppression, will be transformed into an oasis of freedom and justice. I have a dream that my four little children will one day live in a nation where they will not be judged by the color of their skin, but by the content of their character.

I have a dream today. I have a dream that one day down in Alabama— with its vicious racists, with its governor's lips dripping with the words of interposition and nullification—one day right there in Alabama, little Black boys and Black girls will be able to join hands with little white boys and white girls as sisters and brothers.

I have a dream today. I have a dream that one day every valley shall be exalted and every hill and mountain shall be made low, the rough places will be made plain and the crooked places will be made straight, and the glory of the Lord shall be revealed, and all flesh shall see it together.°

This is our hope. This is the faith that I go back to the South with. And with this faith we will be able to hew out of the mountain of despair a stone of hope. With this faith we will be able to transform the jangling discords of our nation into a beautiful symphony of brotherhood. With this faith we will be able to work together, to play together, to struggle together, to go to jail together, to stand up for freedom together, knowing that we will be free one day.

And this will be the day—this will be the day when all of God's children will be able to sing with new meaning: *15*

> My country, 'tis of thee,
> Sweet land of liberty,
>   Of thee I sing;
> Land where my fathers died,
> Land of the Pilgrims' pride,
> From every mountainside
>   Let freedom ring.

every valley shall be . . . see it together: A quotation from the Old Testament, Isaiah 40: 4–5.

And if America is to be a great nation, this must become true.

And so let freedom ring from the prodigious hilltops of New Hampshire. Let freedom ring from the mighty mountains of New York. Let freedom ring from the heightening Alleghenies of Pennsylvania. Let freedom ring from the snow-capped Rockies of Colorado. Let freedom ring from the curvaceous slopes of California.

But not only that. Let freedom ring from Stone Mountain of Georgia. Let freedom ring from Lookout Mountain of Tennessee. Let freedom ring from every hill and molehill of Mississippi. "From every mountainside let freedom ring."

And when this happens—when we allow freedom to ring, when we let it ring from every village and every hamlet, from every state and every city—we will be able to speed up that day when all of God's children, Black men and white men, Jews and Gentiles, Protestants and Catholics, will be able to join hands and sing in the words of the old Negro spiritual: "Free at last! Free at last! Thank God Almighty. We are free at last!"

Questions for Discussion

1. Why was the Lincoln Memorial an appropriate setting for this speech? Can you identify any references within the speech that link it to the setting in which it was originally presented?
2. Why does King begin paragraph 2 with "Five score years ago" instead of simply saying "one hundred years ago"?
3. *Anaphora*, as noted earlier, is a term describing the use of repetition at the beginning of sentences, clauses, or verses for rhetorical effect. Examples are the three sentences beginning "One hundred years later" in paragraph 2. Can you identify any other examples?
4. What do you think King meant by "the tranquilizing drug of gradualism" in paragraph 5?
5. Paragraph 13 concludes with a quotation from the Bible. Why was it appropriate for King to use the Bible within the context of this speech?
6. What evidence in this essay suggests that King recognized that he was speaking to an audience already committed to the importance of racial equality?

Suggestions for Writing

1. A *metaphor* is a figure of speech that makes a comparison between two unlike things without using *like* or *as*. When King writes, "we have come to our nation's capital to cash a check," he does not mean these words to be taken literally. Instead, he is making an implied comparison between an uncashed check and unfulfilled promises to African-Americans. Reread "I Have a Dream" identifying other metaphors King uses. Then

paraphrase any five successive paragraphs, eliminating all metaphors and all anaphora.

2. Using both anaphora and metaphor, write a short speech that calls attention to a current social problem that concerns you.

COURAGE IN THE FACE
OF CONTROVERSY

Henry Kissinger

> *In this eulogy Henry Kissinger, secretary of state under Richard M. Nixon and his colleague in notable foreign policy achievements, dwells upon Nixon's triumphs rather than his troubles. The only president ever forced to resign, Nixon served during what Kissinger calls times of "wrenching domestic controversy"—the cultural turmoil of the late 1960s, which produced widespread protest against the Vietnam War as well as the use of military and police power to suppress that protest.*

During the final week of Richard Nixon's life, I often imagined how he would have reacted to the tide of concern, respect, admiration and affection evoked by his last great battle. His gruff pose of never paying attention to media comment would have been contradicted by a warm glow and the ever so subtle hint that another recital of the commentary would not be unwelcome. And without saying so, he would have conveyed that it would mean a lot to him if Julie and Tricia, David and Ed were told of his friends' pride in this culmination to an astonishing life.

When I listened—when I learned the final news by then so expected, yet so hard to accept, I felt a profound void. In the words of Shakespeare, "He was a man, take him for all in all, I shall not look upon his like again."

In the conduct of foreign policy, Richard Nixon was one of the seminal Presidents. He came into office when the forces of history were moving America from a position of dominance to one of leadership. Dominance reflects strengths; leadership must be earned. And Richard Nixon earned that leadership role for his country with courage, dedication and skill.

'HE DARED CONFRONTATIONS'

When Richard Nixon took his oath of office, 550,000 Americans were engaged in combat in a place as far away from the United States as it was possible to be. America had no contacts with China, the world's most populous nation; no negotiations with the Soviet Union, the other nuclear superpower. Most Muslim countries had broken diplomatic relations with the United States, and Middle East diplomacy was stalemated. All of this in the midst of the most anguishing domestic crisis since the Civil War.

When Richard Nixon left office, an agreement to end the war in Vietnam had been concluded, and the main lines of all subsequent policy were established: permanent dialogue with China, readiness without illusion to ease tensions with the Soviet Union, a peace process in the Middle East, 5 the beginning via the European Security Conference of establishing human rights as an international issue, weakening the Soviet hold on Eastern Europe.

Richard Nixon's foreign policy goals were long-range. And he pursued them without regard to domestic political consequences. When considered our nation's interest at stake, he dared confrontations despite the imminence of elections and also in the midst of the worst crisis of his life.

And he bore, if with some pain, the disapproval of longtime friends and allies over relaxing tensions with China and the Soviet Union. He drew strength from conviction he often expressed to me: the price for doing things halfway is no less than for doing it completely, so we might as well do them properly. That's Richard Nixon's greatest accomplishment. It was as much moral as it was political.

RECONCILIATION AT JOURNEY'S END

To lead from strength at a moment of apparent weakness, to husband the nation's resilience and thus to lay the basis for victory in the cold war. Shy and withdrawn, Richard Nixon made himself succeed in the most gregarious of professions and steeled himself to conspicuous acts of extraordinary courage in the face of wrenching domestic controversy. He held fast to his basic theme that the greatest free nation in the world had a duty to lead and no right to abdicate.

Richard Nixon would be so proud that President Clinton and all living former Presidents of the United States are here, symbolizing that his long and sometimes bitter journey had concluded in reconciliation.

I wish that in his final hours I could have told him about Brian McDonald, who during the Cambodian crisis had been fasting on a bench in Lafayette Park across from the White House until, as he said, President Nixon redeemed his pledge to withdraw American forces from that anguished country in two months. A promise which was, in fact, kept.

Across the chasm of the decades Brian called me the day Richard Nixon fell ill and left a message, "When you talk to President Nixon, tell him that I'm praying for him." So let us now say goodbye to our gallant friend. He stood on pinnacles that dissolved in the precipice. He achieved greatly and he suffered deeply. But he never gave up. In his solitude he envisaged a new international order that would reduce lingering enmities, strengthen historic friendships and give new hope to mankind. A visionary dream and possibilities conjoined.

Richard Nixon ended a war. And he advanced the vision of peace of his Quaker youth. He was devoted to his family, he loved his country and he considered service his honor. It was a privilege to have been allowed to help him.

Questions for Discussion

1. What was Kissinger's primary purpose in this eulogy?
2. Kissinger never specifically identifies the audience for his eulogy. To whom is it addressed and how do you know?
3. Why does Kissinger begin the eulogy with his own reaction to Nixon's death?
4. Kissinger says that Nixon took office "when the forces of history were moving America from a position of dominance to one of leadership." What is the difference, and why is it significant?
5. Toward the end of the eulogy, Kissinger calls Nixon "our gallant friend." What evidence does Kissinger give to support this description?

Suggestions for Writing

1. Using Kissinger's eulogy as a model, write a eulogy of your own for a public figure who has died recently or for some controversial figure who "made a difference."
2. How does a eulogy differ from an obituary? Compare this eulogy with the obituary of Audrey Hepburn reprinted in Chapter 4. Drawing upon the information reported in Hepburn's obituary, write a eulogy for her. Or research the life of Richard M. Nixon and transform Kissinger's eulogy into an obituary.

A MICKEY MANTLE KOAN

David James Duncan

> *In the following essay David James Duncan defines a Zen koan as "a*
> *perfectly nonsensical statement given by an old pro . . . to a rookie" that leads*
> *to enlightenment when reflected upon at length. "A Mickey Mantle Koan"*
> *tells how the author lost the older brother he looked up to and eventually came*
> *to terms with his grief after thinking for four years about an autographed*
> *baseball. As you read, note how Duncan makes his brother come alive through*
> *words by including specific details of his attributes and behavior.*

On April 6, 1965, my brother, Nicholas John Duncan, died of what
his surgeons called "complications" after three unsuccessful open-heart operations. He was seventeen at the time—four years my elder to the very day.
He'd been the fastest sprinter in his high school class until the valve in his
heart began to close, but he was so bonkers about baseball that he'd preferred
playing a mediocre JV shortstop to starring at varsity track. As a ballplayer
he was a competent fielder, had a strong and fairly accurate arm, and stole
bases with ease—when he could reach them. But no matter how much he
practiced or what stances, grips, or self-hypnotic tricks he tried, he lacked
the hand/eye magic that consistently lays bat-fat against ball, and remained
one of the weakest hitters on his team.

John lived his entire life on the outskirts of Portland, Oregon—637
miles from the nearest major league team. In franchiseless cities in the Fifties
and early Sixties there were two types of fans: those who thought the Yankees stood for everything right with America, and those who thought they
stood for everything wrong with it. My brother was an extreme manifestation of the former type. He conducted a one-man campaign to notify the
world that Roger Maris's sixty-one homers in '61 came in three fewer at
bats than Babe Ruth's sixty in '27. He maintained—all statistical evidence to
the contrary—that Clete Boyer was a better third baseman than his brother,
Ken, simply because Clete was a Yankee. He may not have been the only
kid on the block who considered Casey Stengel the greatest sage since
Solomon, but I'm sure he was the only one who considered Yogi Berra the
second greatest. And, of course, Mickey Mantle was his absolute hero, but
his tragic hero. The Mick, my brother maintained, was the greatest raw
talent of all time. He was one to whom great gifts were given, from whom
great gifts had been ripped away; and the more scarred his knees became,
the more frequently he fanned, the more flagrant his limp and apologetic
his smile, the more John revered him. And toward this single Yankee I, too,
was able to feel a touch of reverence, if only because on the subject of scars
I considered my brother an unimpeachable authority: he'd worn one from
the time he was eight, compliments of the Mayo Clinic, that wrapped clear
around his chest in a wavy line, like stitching round a clean white baseball.

Yankees aside, John and I had more in common than a birthday. We bickered regularly with our middle brother and little sister, but almost never with each other. We were both bored, occasionally to insurrection, by schoolgoing, churchgoing, and any game or sport that didn't involve a ball. We both preferred, as a mere matter of style, Indians to cowboys, hoboes to businessmen, Buster Keaton to Charlie Chaplin, Gary Cooper to John Wayne, deadbeats to brownnosers, and even brownnosers to Elvis Presley. We shared a single cake on our joint birthday, invariably annihilating the candle flames with a tandem blowing effort, only to realize that we'd once again forgotten to make a wish. And when the parties were over or the house was stuffy, the parents cranky or the TV shows insufferably dumb, whenever we were restless, punchy, or just feeling as if there was nothing to do, catch—with a hard ball—is what John and I did.

We were not exclusive, at least not by intention: our father and middle brother and an occasional cousin or friend would join us now and then. But something in most everyone else's brain or bloodstream sent them bustling off to less contemplative endeavors before the real rhythm of the thing ever took hold. Genuine catch-playing occurs in a double limbo between busyness and idleness, and between what is imaginary and what is real. Also, as with any contemplative pursuit, it takes time, and the ability to forget time, to slip into this dual limbo and to discover (i.e., lose) oneself in the music of the game.

It helps to have a special place to play. Ours was a shaded, ninety-foot 5 corridor between one neighbor's apple orchard and the other's stand of old-growth Douglas firs, on a stretch of lawn so lush and mossy it sucked the heat out of even the hottest grounders. I always stood in the north, John in the south. We might call balls and strikes for an imaginary inning or two, or maybe count the number of errorless catches and throws we could make (300s were common, and our record was high in the 800s). But the deep shade, the 200-foot firs, the mossy footing and fragrance of apples all made it a setting more conducive to mental vacationing than to any kind of disciplined effort. During spring-training months our catch occasionally started as a drill—a grounder, then a peg; another grounder, a peg. But as our movements became fluid and the throws brisk and accurate, the pretense of practice would inevitably fade, and we'd just aim for the chest and fire, *hisssss pop! hisssss pop!* until a meal, a duty, or total darkness forced us to recall that this was the real world in which even timeless pursuits come to an end.

Our talk must have seemed strange to eavesdroppers. We lived in our bodies during catch, and our minds and mouths, though still operative, were just along for the ride. Most of the noise I made was with the four or five pieces of Bazooka I was invariably working over, though when the gum turned bland, I'd sometimes narrate our efforts in a stream-of-doggerel play-by-play. My brother's speech was less voluminous and a bit more coherent, but of no greater didactic intent: he just poured out idle litanies of Yankee worship or even idler braggadocio à la Dizzy Dean, all of it artfully spiced with spat sunflower-seed husks.

But one day when we were sixteen and twelve, respectively, my big brother surprised me out there in our corridor. Snagging a low throw, he closed his mitt round the ball, stuck it under his arm, stared off into the trees, and got serious with me for a minute. All his life, he said, he'd struggled to be a shortstop and a hitter, but he was older now, and had a clearer notion of what he could and couldn't do. It was time to get practical, he said. Time to start developing obvious strengths and evading flagrant weaknesses. "So I've decided," he concluded, "to become a junk pitcher."

I didn't believe a word of it. My brother had been a "slugger worshiper" from birth. He went on embellishing his idea, though, and even made it sound rather poetic: to foil some muscle-bound fence-buster with an off-speed piece of crap that blupped off his bat like cow custard—this, he maintained, was the pluperfect pith of an attribute he called Solid Cool.

I didn't recognize until months later just how carefully considered this new junk-pitching jag had been. That John's throwing arm was better than his batting eye had always been obvious, and it made sense to exploit that. But there were other factors he didn't mention: like the sharp pains in his chest every time he took a full swing, or the new ache that half-blinded and sickened him whenever he ran full speed. Finding the high arts of slugging and base stealing physically impossible, he'd simply lowered his sights enough to keep his baseball dreams alive. No longer able to emulate his heroes, he set out to bamboozle those who thought they could. To that end he'd learned a feeble knuckler, a roundhouse curve, a submarine fastball formidable solely for its lack of accuracy, and was trashing his arm and my patience with his attempts at a screwball, when his doctors informed our family that a valve in his heart was rapidly closing. He might live as long as five years if we let it go, they said, but immediate surgery was best, since his recuperative powers were greatest now. John said nothing about any of this. He just waited until the day he was due at the hospital, snuck down to the stable where he kept his horse, saddled her up, and galloped away. He rode about twenty miles, to the farm of a friend, and stayed there in hiding for nearly two weeks. But when he snuck home one morning for clean clothes and money, my father and a neighbor caught him, and first tried to force him but finally convinced him to have the operation and be done with it.

Once in the hospital he was cooperative, cheerful, and unrelentingly courageous. He survived second, third, and fourth operations, several stoppings of the heart, and a nineteen-day coma. He recovered enough at one point, even after the coma, to come home for a week or so. But the overriding "complication" to which his principal surgeon kept making oblique references turned out to be a heart so ravaged by scalpel wounds that an artificial valve had nothing but shreds to be sutured to. Bleeding internally, pissing blood, John was moved into an oxygen tent in an isolated room, where he remained fully conscious, and fully determined to heal, for two months after his surgeons had abandoned him. And, against all odds, his condition stabilized, then began to improve. The doctors reappeared and began to discuss, with obvious despair, the feasibility of a fifth operation.

Then came the second "complication": staph. Overnight, we were reduced from genuine hope to awkward pleas for divine intervention. We invoked no miracles. Two weeks after contracting the infection, my brother died.

At his funeral, a preacher who didn't know John from Judge Kenesaw Mountain Landis eulogized him so lavishly and inaccurately that I was moved to a state of tearlessness that lasted for four years. It's an unenviable task to try to make public sense of a private catastrophe you know little about. But had I been in that preacher's shoes, I would have mentioned one or two of my brother's actual attributes, if only to reassure late-arriving mourners that they hadn't wandered into the wrong funeral. The person we were endeavoring to miss had, for instance, been a C student all his life, had smothered everything he ate with ketchup, had diligently avoided all forms of work that didn't involve horses, and had frequently gone so far as to wear sunglasses indoors in the relentless quest for Solid Cool. He'd had the disconcerting habit of sound-testing his pleasant baritone voice by bellowing "*Beeeeeee-Ooooooooooo!*" down any alley or hallway that looked like it might contain an echo. He'd had an interesting, slangy obliviousness to proportion: any altercation, from a fistfight to a world war, was "a rack"; any authority, from our mother to the head of the U.N., was "the Brass"; any pest, from the kid next door to Khrushchev, was "a buttwipe"; and any kind of ball, from a BB to the sun, was "the orb." He was brave: whenever anybody his age harassed me, John warned them once and beat them up the second time, or got beat up trying. He was also unabashedly, majestically vain. He referred to his person, with obvious pride, as "the Bod." He was an immaculate dresser. And he loved to stare at himself, publicly or privately—in mirrors, windows, puddles, chrome car-fenders, upside-down in teaspoons—and to solemnly comb his long auburn hair over and over again, like his hero, Edd ("Kookie") Byrnes, on *77 Sunset Strip*.

His most astonishing attribute, to me at least, was his never-ending skein of girlfriends. He had a simple but apparently efficient rating system for all female acquaintances: he called it "percentage of Cool versus percentage of Crud." A steady girlfriend usually weighed in at around 95 percent Cool, 5 percent Crud, and if the Crud level reached 10 percent it was time to start quietly looking elsewhere. Only two girls ever made his "100 percent Cool List," and I was struck by the fact that neither was a girlfriend and one wasn't even pretty: whatever "100 percent Cool" was, it was not skin-deep. No girl ever came close to a "100 percent Crud" rating, by the way: my brother was chivalrous.

John was not religious. He believed in God, but passively, with nothing like the passion he had for the Yankees. He seemed a little more friendly with Jesus. "Christ is cool," he'd say, if forced to show his hand. But I don't recall him speaking of any sort of goings-on between them until he casually mentioned, a day or two before he died, a conversation they'd just had, there in the oxygen tent. And even then John was John: what impressed him even more than the fact that Christ's presence or the consoling words He spoke was the natty suit and tie He was wearing.

On the morning after his death, April 7, 1965, a small brown-paper   *15* package arrived at our house, special delivery from New York City, addressed to John. I brought it to my mother and leaned over her shoulder as she sat down to study it. Catching a whiff of antiseptic, I thought at first that it came from her hair: she'd spent the last four months of her life in a straightback chair by my brother's bed, and hospital odors had permeated her. But the smell grew stronger as she began to unwrap the brown paper, until I realized it came from the object inside.

It was a small, white, cylindrical, cardboard bandage box. "Johnson & Johnson," it said in red letters. "12 inches × 10 yards," it added in blue. Strange. Then I saw it had been split in half by a knife or a scalpel and bound back together with adhesive tape: so there was another layer, something hiding inside.

My mother smiled as she began to rip the tape away. At the same time, tears were landing in her lap. Then the tape was gone, the little cylinder fell away, and inside, nested in tissue, was a baseball. Immaculate white leather. Perfect red stitching. On one cheek, in faint green ink, the signature of American League president Joseph Cronin and the trademark REACH, THE SIGN OF QUALITY. And on the opposite cheek, with bright blue ballpoint ink, a tidy but flowing hand had written, *To John—My Best Wishes. Your Pal, Mickey Mantle. April 6, 1965.*

The ball dwelt upon our fireplace mantel—an unintentional pun on my mother's part. We used half the Johnson & Johnson box as a pedestal, and for years I saved the other half, figuring that the bandage it once contained had held Mantle's storied knee together for a game.

Even after my mother explained that the ball came not out of the blue but in response to a letter, I considered it a treasure. I told all my friends about it, and invited the closest to stop by and gawk. But gradually I began to see that the public reaction to the ball was disconcertingly predictable. The first response was usually, "Wow! Mickey Mantle!" But then they'd get the full story: "Mantle signed it the day he died? Your brother never even *saw* it?" And that made them uncomfortable. This was not at all the way an autographed baseball was supposed to behave. How could an immortal call himself your "Pal," how could you be the recipient of The Mick's "Best Wishes," and still just lie back and die?

I began to share the discomfort. Over the last three of my thirteen   *20* years I'd devoured scores of baseball books, all of which agreed that a bat, program, mitt, or ball signed by a big-league hero was a sacred relic, that we *should* expect such relics to have magical properties, and that they *would* prove pivotal in a young protagonist's life. Yet here I was, the young protagonist. Here was my relic. And all the damned thing did, before long, was depress and confuse me.

I stopped showing the ball to people, tried ignoring it, found that this was impossible, tried instead to pretend that the blue ink was an illegible scribble and that the ball was just a ball. But the ink *wasn't* illegible: it never stopped saying just what it said. So finally I picked the ball up and studied it, hoping to discover exactly why I found it so troublesome. Feigning the cool rationality I wished I'd felt, I told myself that a standard sports hero had received a letter from a standard distraught mother, had signed, packaged, and mailed off the standard ingratiatingly heroic response, had failed to think that the boy he inscribed the ball to might be dead when it arrived, and so had mailed his survivors a blackly comic non sequitur. I then told myself, "That's all there is to it"—which left me no option but to pretend that I hadn't expected or wanted any more from the ball than I got, that I'd harbored no desire for any sort of sign, any imprimatur, any flicker of recognition from an Above or a Beyond. I then began falling to pieces for lack of that sign.

Eventually, I got honest about Mantle's baseball: I picked the damned thing up, read it once more, peered as far as I could inside myself, and admitted for the first time that I was *pissed.* As is always the case with arriving baseballs, timing is the key—and this cheery little orb was inscribed on the day its recipient lay dying and arrived on the day he was being embalmed! This was *not* a harmless coincidence: it was the shabbiest, most embittering joke that Providence had ever played on me. My best friend and brother was dead, dead, dead, and Mantle's damned ball and best wishes made that loss even less tolerable, and *that,* I told myself, really was all there was to it.

I hardened my heart, quit the baseball team, went out for golf, practiced like a zealot, cheated like hell, kicked my innocuous, naive little opponents all over the course. I sold the beautiful outfielder's mitt that I'd inherited from my brother for a pittance.

But, as is usual in baseball stories, that wasn't all there was to it.

I'd never heard of Zen koans at the time, and Mickey Mantle is cer- 25 tainly no roshi. But baseball and Zen are two pastimes that Americans and Japanese have come to revere almost equally: roshis are men famous for hitting things hard with a big wooden stick; a koan is a perfectly nonsensical or nonsequacious statement given by an old pro (roshi) to a rookie (layman or monk); and the stress of living with and mediating upon a piece of mind-numbing nonsense is said to eventually prove illuminating. So I know of no better way to describe what the message on the ball became for me than to call it a koan.

In the first place, the damned thing's batteries just wouldn't run down. For weeks, months, *years,* every time I saw those nine blithely blue-inked words they knocked me off balance like a sudden shove from behind. They were an emblem of all the false assurances of surgeons, all the futile prayers

of preachers, all the hollowness of Good-Guys-Can't-Lose baseball stories
I'd ever heard or read. They were a throw I'd never catch. And yet . . .
REACH, the ball said. THE SIGN OF QUALITY.

So year after year I kept trying, kept hoping to somehow answer
the koan.

I became an adolescent, enrolling my body in the obligatory school of
pain-without-dignity called "puberty," nearly flunking, then graduating almost without noticing. I discovered in the process that some girls were
nothing like 95 percent Crud. I also discovered that there was life after
baseball, that America was not the Good Guys, that God was not a Christian, that I preferred myth to theology, and that, when it came to heroes,
the likes of Odysseus, Rama, and Finn MacCool meant incomparably more
to me than the George Washingtons, Davy Crocketts, and Babe Ruths I'd
been force-fed. I discovered (sometimes prematurely or overabundantly, but
never to my regret) metaphysics, wilderness, Europe, black tea, high lakes,
rock, Bach, tobacco, poetry, trout streams, the Orient, the novel, my life's
work, and a hundred other grown-up tools and toys. But amid these matu-
rations and transformations there was one unwanted constant: in the presence of that confounded ball, I remained thirteen years old. One peek at
the "Your Pal" koan and whatever maturity or wisdom or equanimity I
possessed was repossessed, leaving me as irked as any stumped monk or
slumping slugger.

It took four years to solve the riddle on the ball. It was autumn when
it happened—the same autumn during which I'd grown older than my
brother would ever be. As often happens with koan solutions, I wasn't even
thinking about the ball at the time. As is also the case with koans, I can't
possibly describe in words the impact of the response, the instantaneous
healing that took place, or the ensuing sense of lightness and release. But I'll
say what I can.

The solution came during a fit of restlessness brought on by a warm   *30*
Indian summer evening. I'd just finished watching the Miracle Mets blitz
the Orioles in the World Series, and was standing alone in the living room,
just staring out at the yard and the fading sunlight, feeling a little stale and
fidgety, when I realized that this was *just* the sort of fidgets I'd never had to
suffer when John was alive—because we'd always work our way through
them with a long game of catch. With that thought, and at that moment, I
simply saw my brother catch, then throw a baseball. It occurred neither in
an indoors nor an outdoors. It lasted a couple of seconds, no more. But I
saw him so clearly, and he then vanished so completely, that my eyes blurred,
my throat and chest ached, and I didn't need to see Mantle's baseball to
realize exactly what I'd wanted from it all along:

From the moment I'd first laid eyes on it, all I'd wanted was to take
that immaculate ball out to our corridor on an evening just like this one, to
take my place near the apples in the north, and to find my brother waiting

beneath the immense firs to the south. All I'd wanted was to pluck that too-perfect ball off its pedestal and proceed, without speaking, to play catch so long and hard that the grass stains and nicks and the sweat of our palms would finally obliterate every last trace of Mantel's blue ink, until all he would have given us was a grass-green, earth-brown, beat-up old baseball. Beat-up old balls were all we'd ever had anyhow. They were all we'd ever needed. The dirtier they were, and the more frayed the skin and stitching, the louder they'd hissed and the better they'd curved. And remembering this—recovering in an instant the knowledge of how little we'd needed in order to be happy—my grief for my brother became palpable, took on shape and weight, color and texture, even an odor. The measure of my loss was precisely the difference between one of the beat-up, earth-colored, grass-scented balls that had given us such happiness and this antiseptic-smelling, sad-making, icon-ball on its bandage-box pedestal. And as I felt this—as I stood there palpating my grief, shifting it around like a throwing stone in my hand—I fell through some kind of floor inside myself, landing in a deeper, brighter chamber just in time to feel something or someone tell me: *But who's to say we need even an old ball to be happy? Who's to say we couldn't do with less? Who's to say we couldn't still be happy—with no ball at all?*

And with that, the koan was solved.

I can't explain why this felt like such a complete solution. Reading the bare words, two decades later, they don't look like much of a solution. But a koan answer is not a verbal, or a literary, or even a personal experience. It's a spiritual experience. And a boy, a man, a "me," does not have spiritual experiences; only the spirit has spiritual experiences. That's why churches so soon become bandage boxes propping up antiseptic icons that lose all value the instant they are removed from the greens and browns of grass and dirt and life. It's also why a good Zen monk always states a koan solution in the barest possible terms. *"No ball at all!"* is, perhaps, all I should have written—because then no one would have an inkling of what was meant and so could form no misconceptions, and the immediacy and integrity and authority of the experience would be safely locked away.

This is getting a bit iffy for a sports story. But jocks die, and then what? The brother I played a thousand games of catch with is dead, and so will I be, and unless you're one hell of an athlete so will you be. In the face of this fact, I find it more than a little consoling to recall how clearly and deeply it was brought home to me, that October day, that there is something in us which needs absolutely *nothing*—not even a dog-eared ball—in order to be happy. From that day forward the relic on the mantel lost its irksome overtones and became a mere autographed ball—nothing more, nothing less. It lives on my desk now, beside an old beater ball my brother and I wore out, and it gives me a satisfaction I can't explain to sit back, now and then, and compare the two—though I'd still gladly trash the white one for a good game of catch.

As for the ticklish timing of its arrival, I only recently learned a couple   35
of facts that shed some light. First, I discovered—in a copy of the old letter
my mother wrote to Mantle—that she'd made it quite clear that my brother
was dying. So when The Mick wrote what he wrote, he knew perfectly
well what the situation might be when the ball arrived. And second, I found
out that my mother actually went ahead and showed the ball to my brother.
True, what was left of him was embalmed. But what was embalmed wasn't
all of him. And I've no reason to assume that the unembalmed part had
changed much. It should be remembered, then, that while he lived my
brother was more than a little vain, that he'd been compelled by his death to
leave a handsome head of auburn hair behind, and that when my mother
and the baseball arrived at the funeral parlor, that lovely hair was being
prepared for an open-casket funeral by a couple of cadaverous-looking
yahoos whose oily manners, hair, and clothes made it plain that they didn't
know Kookie from Roger Maris or Solid Cool from Kool-Aid. What if this
pair took it into their heads to spruce John up for the hereafter with a Bible
camp cut? Worse yet, what if they tried to show what sensitive, accommodating artists they were and decked him out like a damned Elvis the Pelvis
greaser? I'm not trying to be morbid here. I'm just trying to state the facts.
"The Bod" my brother had very much enjoyed inhabiting was about to be
seen for the last time by all his buddies, his family, and a girlfriend who was
only 1.5 percent Crud, and the part of the whole ensemble he'd been most
fastidious about—the coiffure—was completely out of his control! He
needed best wishes. He needed a pal. Preferably one with a comb.

Enter my stalwart mother, who took one look at what the two rouge-
and-casket wallahs were doing to the hair, said, "No, no, no!", produced a
snap-shot, told them, "He wants it *exactly* like this," sat down to critique
their efforts, and kept on critiquing until in the end you'd have thought
John had dropped in to groom himself.

Only then did she ask them to leave. Only then did she pull the
autographed ball from her purse, share it with her son, read him the
inscription.

As is always the case with arriving baseballs, timing is the key. Thanks
to the timing that has made The Mick a legend, my brother, the last time
we all saw him, looked completely himself.

I return those best wishes to my brother's pal.

Questions for Discussion

1. What did Duncan have in common with his brother? How would you
   describe their relationship?
2. Under what circumstances does a game of catch become "genuine"? Is
   there any similarity between playing catch and solving a koan?
3. After his brother's death Duncan was in "a state of tearlessness that lasted
   for four years." Why do you think he was unable to cry? What eventually
   helps him to feel and express his grief?

4. How did Duncan feel, at first, about the autographed baseball that sat on his parents' mantle? How did his feelings about the baseball change?
5. What does Duncan mean by the koan solution, "No ball at all!" Why does he think this solution preferable to a fuller answer?
6. This essay ends with an account of how John looked in his coffin. Why do you think Duncan saved this scene until the end?

Suggestions for Writing

1. If you have ever lost someone you loved, write an essay that could move others to share your feelings about that person.
2. Write an essay about an object that has inspired different feelings from one time in your life to another. Try to help readers understand these feelings and why they changed.

DADDY TUCKED THE BLANKET

Randall Williams

> *"I was ashamed of where I lived," writes Randall Williams in this essay about growing up in poverty. But although he was too ashamed as a teenager to bring friends to his house, he subsequently chose to describe it in the* New York Times, *where "Daddy Tucked the Blanket" was first published. As you read this essay, try to understand the author's purpose. What could motivate him to share such personal material with readers? The painfully embarrassing scene with which Williams concludes may provide you with a clue.*

About the time I turned 16, my folks began to wonder why I didn't stay home any more. I always had an excuse for them, but what I didn't say was that I had found my freedom and I was getting out.

I went through four years of high school in semirural Alabama and became active in clubs and sports; I made a lot of friends and became a regular guy, if you know what I mean. But one thing was irregular about me: I managed those four years without ever having a friend visit at my house.

I was ashamed of where I lived. I had been ashamed for as long as I had been conscious of class.

We had a big family. There were several of us sleeping in one room, but that's not so bad if you get along, and we always did. As you get older, though, it gets worse.

Being poor is a humiliating experience for a young person trying   5
hard to be accepted. Even now—several years removed—it is hard to talk about. And I resent the weakness of these words to make you feel what it was really like.

We lived in a lot of old houses. We moved a lot because we were always looking for something just a little better than what we had. You have to understand that my folks worked harder than most people. My mother was always at home, but for her that was a full-time job—and no fun, either. But my father worked his head off from the time I can remember in construction and shops. It was hard, physical work.

I tell you this to show that we weren't shiftless. No matter how much money Daddy made, we never made much progress up the social ladder. I got out thanks to a college scholarship and because I was a little more articulate than the average.

I have seen my Daddy wrap copper wire through the soles of his boots to keep them together in the wintertime. He couldn't buy new boots because he had used the money for food and shoes for us. We lived like hell, but we went to school well-clothed and with a full stomach.

It really is hell to live in a house that was in bad shape 10 years before you moved in. And a big family puts a lot of wear and tear on a new house, too, so you can imagine how one goes downhill if it is teetering when you move in. But we lived in houses that were sweltering in summer and freezing in winter. I woke up every morning for a year and a half with plaster on my face where it had fallen out of the ceiling during the night.

This wasn't during the Depression; this was in the late 60's and early 70's.

When we boys got old enough to learn trades in school, we would try to fix up the old houses we lived in. But have you ever tried to paint a wall that crumbled when the roller went across it? And bright paint emphasized the holes in the wall. You end up more frustrated than when you began, especially when you know that at best you might come up with only enough money to improve one of the six rooms in the house. And we might move out soon after, anyway.

The same goes for keeping a house like that clean. If you have a house full of kids and the house is deteriorating, you'll never keep it clean. Daddy used to yell at Mama about that, but she couldn't do anything. I think Daddy knew it inside, but he had to have an outlet for his rage somewhere, and at least yelling isn't as bad as hitting, which they never did to each other.

But you have a kitchen which has no counter space and no hot water, and you will have dirty dishes stacked up. That sounds like an excuse, but try it. You'll go mad from the sheer sense of futility. It's the same thing in a house with no closets. You can't keep clothes clean and rooms in order if they have to be stacked up with things.

Living in a bad house is generally worse on girls. For one thing, they traditionally help their mother with the housework. We boys could get outside and work in the field or cut wood or even play ball and forget about living conditions. The sky was still pretty.

But the girls got the pressure, and as they got older it became worse. Would they accept dates knowing they had to "receive" the young man in a dirty hallway with broken windows, peeling wallpaper and a cracked ceiling? You have to live it to understand it, but it creates a shame which drives the soul of a young person inward.

I'm thankful none of us ever blamed our parents for this, because it would have crippled our relationships. As it worked out, only the relationship between our parents was damaged. And I think the harshness which they expressed to each other was just an outlet to get rid of their anger at the trap their lives were in. It ruined their marriage because they had no one to yell at but each other. I knew other families where the kids got the abuse, but we were too much loved for that.

Once I was about 16 and Mama and Daddy had had a particularly violent argument about the washing machine, which had broken down. Daddy was on the back porch—that's where the only water faucet was— trying to fix it and Mama had a washtub out there washing school clothes for the next day and they were screaming at each other.

Later that night everyone was in bed and I heard Daddy get up from the couch where he was reading. I looked out from my bed across the hall into their room. He was standing right over Mama and she was already asleep. He pulled the blanket up and tucked it around her shoulders and just stood there and tears were dropping off his cheeks and I thought I could faintly hear them splashing against the linoleum rug.

Now they're divorced.

I had courses in college where housing was discussed, but the sociol- 20
ogists never put enough emphasis on the impact living in substandard housing has on a person's psyche. Especially children's.

Small children have a hard time understanding poverty. They want the same things children from more affluent families have. They want the same things they see advertised on television, and they don't understand why they can't have them.

Other children can be incredibly cruel. I was in elementary school in Georgia—and this is interesting because it is the only thing I remember about that particular school—when I was about eight or nine.

After Christmas vacation had ended, my teacher made each student describe all his or her Christmas presents. I became more and more uncom-
fortable as the privilege passed around the room toward me. Other children were reciting the names of the dolls they had been given, the kinds of bicycles and the grandeur of their games and toys. Some had lists which seemed to go on and on for hours.

It took me only a few seconds to tell the class that I had gotten for Christmas a belt and a pair of gloves. And then I was laughed at—because I cried—by a roomful of children and a teacher. I never forgave them, and that night I made my mother cry when I told her about it.

In retrospect, I am grateful for that moment, but I remember wanting 25
to die at the time.

Questions for Discussion

1. Describing what it was like to be poor as a child, Williams writes of the difficulty he has finding "words to make you feel what it was really like." How well does he succeed? Is it true that "you have to live it to understand it"? Or can reading lead to understanding when a writer finds the right words?
2. Trained as a journalist, Williams writes in short paragraphs, but some of his paragraphs are shorter than others. Consider paragraphs 3, 10, and 19. What is the effect of making these paragraphs unusually short?
3. What is the function of paragraphs 6–8?
4. Why does Williams believe that poverty is harder on girls than boys?
5. To what does Williams attribute his parents' divorce? Does he take a side in the dispute between his parents?
6. Consider the anecdote with which this essay concludes. Why would Williams be "grateful for that moment"?

Suggestions for Writing

1. If you have ever been upset by a fight between people you loved, describe what you witnessed, and try to show why it happened.
2. As this essay reveals, children can be cruel to one another, and teachers can be insensitive. Write an essay about betrayal on the playground or in the classroom.

AM I BLUE?

"Ain't these tears in these eyes tellin' you?"*

Alice Walker

> *Alice Walker writes about a stallion named Blue, who lives in a pasture near her home, and how his life changed when he was given a companion—a mare who is subsequently taken away from him. But as her title suggests, Walker is not interested in the horse alone. Looking at the way Blue is treated leads the author to identify with him. As you read this essay by the author of* The Color Purple, *be alert for how Walker inspires sympathy for Blue and links this sympathy to other concerns.*

For about three years my companion and I rented a small house in the country that stood on the edge of a large meadow that appeared to run from the end of our deck straight into the mountains. The mountains, however, were quite far away, and between us and them there was, in fact, a town. It was one of the many pleasant aspects of the house that you never really were aware of this.

It was a house of many windows, low, wide, nearly floor to ceiling in the living room, which faced the meadow, and it was from one of these that I first saw our closest neighbor, a large white horse, cropping grass, flipping its mane, and ambling about—not over the entire meadow, which stretched well out of sight of the house, but over the five or so fenced-in acres that were next to the twenty-odd that we had rented. I soon learned that the horse, whose name was Blue, belonged to a man who lived in another town, but was boarded by our neighbors next door. Occasionally, one of the children, usually a stocky teen-ager, but sometimes a much younger girl or boy, could be seen riding Blue. They would appear in the meadow, climb up on his back, ride furiously for ten or fifteen minutes, then get off, slap Blue on the flanks, and not be seen again for a month or more.

There were many apple trees in our yard, and one by the fence Blue could almost reach. We were soon in the habit of feeding him apples, which he relished, especially because by the middle of summer the meadow grasses—so green and succulent since January—had dried out from lack of rain, and Blue stumbled about munching the dried stalks half-heartedly. Sometimes he would stand very still just by the apple tree, and when one of us came out he would whinny, snort loudly, or stamp the ground. This meant, of course: I want an apple.

It was quite wonderful to pick a few apples, or collect those that had fallen to the ground overnight, and patiently hold them, one by one, up to his large, toothy mouth. I remained as thrilled as a child by his flexible dark lips, huge, cubelike teeth that crunched the apples, core and all, with such finality, and his high, broad-breasted *enormity;* beside which, I felt small indeed. When I was a child, I used to ride horses, and was especially friendly with one named Nan until the day I was riding and my brother deliberately spooked her and I was thrown, head first, against the trunk of a tree. When I came to, I was in bed and my mother was bending worriedly over me; we silently agreed that perhaps horseback riding was not the safest sport for me. Since then I have walked, and prefer walking to horseback riding—but I had forgotten the depth of feeling one could see in horses' eyes.

I was therefore unprepared for the expression in Blue's. Blue was   5
lonely. Blue was horribly lonely and bored. I was not shocked that this should be the case; five acres to tramp by yourself, endlessly, even in the most beautiful of meadows—and his was—cannot provide many interesting events, and once rainy season turned to dry that was about it. No, I was shocked that I had forgotten that human animals and nonhuman animals can communicate quite well; if we are brought up around animals as children we take this for granted. By the time we are adults we no longer remember. However, the animals have not changed. They are in fact *completed* creations (at least they seem to be, so much more than we) who are not likely *to* change; it is their nature to express themselves. What else are they going to express? And they do. And, generally speaking, they are ignored.

After giving Blue the apples, I would wander back to the house, aware that he was observing me. Were more apples not forthcoming then? Was that to be his sole entertainment for the day? My partner's small son had decided he wanted to learn how to piece a quilt; we worked in silence on our respective squares as I thought . . .

Well, about slavery: about white children, who were raised by black people, who knew their first all-accepting love from black women, and then, when they were twelve or so, were told they must "forget" the deep levels of communication between themselves and "mammy" that they knew. Later they would be able to relate quite calmly, "My old mammy was sold to another good family." "My old mammy was _____." Fill in the blank. Many more years later a white woman would say: "I can't understand these Negroes, these blacks. What do they want? They're so different from us."

And about the Indians, considered to be "like animals" by the "settlers" (a very benign euphemism for what they actually were), who did not understand their description as a compliment.

And about the thousands of American men who marry Japanese, Korean, Filipina, and other non-English-speaking women and of how happy they report they are, "*blissfully,*" until their brides learn to speak English, at which point the marriages tend to fall apart. What then did the men see, when they looked into the eyes of the women they married, before they could speak English? Apparently only their own reflections.

I thought of society's impatience with the young. "Why are they play-   10 ing the music so loud?" Perhaps the children have listened to much of the music of oppressed people their parents danced to before they were born, with its passionate but soft cries for acceptance and love, and they have wondered why their parents failed to hear.

I do not know how long Blue had inhabited his five beautiful, boring acres before we moved into our house; a year after we had arrived—and had also traveled to other valleys, other cities, other worlds—he was still there.

But then, in our second year at the house, something happened in Blue's life. One morning, looking out the window at the fog that lay like a ribbon over the meadow, I saw another horse, a brown one, at the other end of Blue's field. Blue appeared to be afraid of it, and for several days made no attempt to go near. We went away for a week. When we returned, Blue had decided to make friends and the two horses ambled or galloped along together, and Blue did not come nearly as often to the fence underneath the apple tree.

When he did, bringing his new friend with him, there was a different look in his eyes. A look of independence, of self-possession, of inalienable *horse*ness. His friend eventually became pregnant. For months and months there was, it seemed to me, a mutual feeling between me and the horses of justice, of peace. I fed apples to them both. The look in Blue's eyes was one of unabashed "this is *it*ness."

It did not, however, last forever. One day, after a visit to the city, I went out to give Blue some apples. He stood waiting, or so I thought, though not beneath the tree. When I shook the tree and jumped back from the shower of apples, he made no move. I carried some over to him. He managed to half-crunch one. The rest he let fall to the ground. I dreaded looking into his eyes—because I had of course noticed that Brown, his partner, had gone—but I did look. If I had been born into slavery, and my partner had been sold or killed, my eyes would have looked like that. The children next door explained that Blue's partner had been "put with him" (the same expression that old people used, I had noticed, when speaking of an ancestor during slavery who had been impregnated by her owner) so that they could mate and she conceive. Since that was accomplished, she had been taken back by her owner, who lived somewhere else.

Will she be back? I asked.

They didn't know.

15

Blue was like a crazed person. Blue *was*, to me, a crazed person. He galloped furiously, as if he were being ridden, around and around his five beautiful acres. He whinnied until he couldn't. He tore at the ground with his hooves. He butted himself against his single shade tree. He looked always and always toward the road down which his partner had gone. And then, occasionally, when he came up for apples, or I took apples to him, he looked at me. It was a look so piercing, so full of grief, a look so *human*, I almost laughed (I felt too sad to cry) to think there are people who do not know that animals suffer. People like me who have forgotten, and daily forget, all that animals try to tell us. "Everything you do to us will happen to you; we are your teachers, as you are ours. We are one lesson" is essentially it, I think. There are those who never once have even considered animals' rights: those who have been taught that animals actually want to be used and abused by us, as small children "love" to be frightened, or women "love" to be mutilated and raped. . . . They are the great-grandchildren of those who honestly thought, because someone taught them this: "Women can't think," and "niggers can't faint." But most disturbing of all, in Blue's large brown eyes was a new look, more painful than the look of despair: the look of disgust with human beings, with life; the look of hatred. And it was odd what the look of hatred did. It gave him, for the first time, the look of a beast. And what that meant was that he had put up a barrier within to protect himself from further violence; all the apples in the world wouldn't change that fact.

And so Blue remained, a beautiful part of our landscape, very peaceful to look at from the window, white against the grass. Once a friend came to visit and said, looking out on the soothing view: "And it *would* have to be a *white* horse; the very image of freedom." And I thought, yes, the animals are forced to become for us merely "images" of what they once so beautifully expressed. And we are used to drinking milk from containers showing "contented" cows, whose real lives we want to hear nothing about, eating eggs and drumsticks from "happy" hens, and munching hamburgers advertised by bulls of integrity who seem to command their fate.

As we talked of freedom and justice one day for all, we sat down to steaks. I am eating misery, I thought, as I took the first bite. And spit it out.

Questions for Discussion

1. Consider the opening paragraph of this essay, a paragraph that sets the scene but does not mention the horse that provides the focus for the paragraphs that follow. Why does Walker write that the mountains were farther away than they seemed and that an unseen town intervened?
2. Why is it significant that the horse is named Blue? How has Walker attempted to make readers sympathize with him?
3. The title of this essay, which comes from a song popular in the 1920s, can be read in more than one way. How do you interpret it?
4. Walker refers to her "companion" and "partner"; later, she refers to Blue's "friend." Why do you think she has chosen these words when there are other alternatives?
5. Walker writes that she looked into Blue's eyes and found them lonely, grief-stricken, and, eventually, filled with hatred. Do you think an animal can express these emotions? Or do you think that Walker is projecting her own feelings upon the horse?
6. Consider the transition between paragraphs 6 and 7, where Walker moves temporarily away from the story of Blue in order to reflect upon other types of oppression. How successfully has she managed this transi-

tion? How would the essay change if she kept Blue's story together and added social commentary only in her final paragraphs?

7. Explain the last paragraph of this essay. Is Walker bothered by eating meat? Or is it something else that is upsetting her?

Suggestions for Writing

1. Write about a neglected or abandoned animal so that people can begin to understand what happens to an animal that has been mistreated.

2. Write an essay comparing Walker's essay with Annie Dillard's "The Death of a Moth." Both Dillard and Walker have looked closely at a member of another species. How does their point of view differ?

ON BEHALF OF THE INSANE POOR

Dorothea Dix

> *Dorothea Dix (1802–1887) was one of the great reformers of the nine-teenth century. An educator and philanthropist, she was best known for her work on behalf of the mentally ill. She investigated the conditions under which the mentally ill were housed in several states and wrote a series of "memorials," or petitions to the legislatures of these states. The following selection is excerpted from a longer work that Dix addressed to the legislature of Massachusetts in 1843—a time when women were discouraged from taking an interest in pub-lic affairs. As you read, note how Dix uses gender expectations to stir feeling in men.*

I respectfully ask to present this Memorial, believing that the *cause,* which actuates to and sanctions so unusual a movement, presents no equiv-ocal claim to public consideration and sympathy. Surrendering to calm and deep convictions of duty my habitual views of what is womanly and becom-ing, I proceed briefly to explain what has conducted me before you unsolic-ited and unsustained, trusting, while I do so, that the memorialist will be speedily forgotten in the memorial.

About two years since leisure afforded opportunity, and duty prompted me to visit several prisons and alms-houses in the vicinity of this metropolis. I found, near Boston, in the Jails and Asylums for the poor, a numerous class brought into unsuitable connexion with criminals and the general mass of Paupers. I refer to Idiots and Insane persons, dwelling in circumstances not only adverse to their own physical and moral improvement, but productive of extreme disadvantages to all other persons brought into association with them. I applied myself diligently to trace the causes of these evils, and sought to supply remedies. As one obstacle was surmounted, fresh difficulties ap-peared. Every new investigation has given depth to the conviction that it is only by decided, prompt, and vigorous legislation the evils to which I refer, and which I shall proceed more fully to illustrate, can be remedied. I shall be obliged to speak with great plainness, and to reveal many things revolting to the taste, and from which my woman's nature shrinks with peculiar sensitiveness. But truth is the highest consideration. *I tell what I have seen—*painful and shocking as the details often are—that from them you may feel more deeply the imperative obligation which lies upon you to prevent the possibility of a repetition or continuance of such outrages upon humanity. If I inflict pain upon you, and move you to horror, it is to acquaint you with sufferings which you have the power to alleviate, and make you hasten to the relief of the victims of legalized barbarity.

I come to present the strong claims of suffering humanity. I come to place before the Legislature of Massachusetts the condition of the miserable, the desolate, the outcast. I come as the advocate of helpless, forgotten, insane and idiotic men and women; of beings, sunk to a condition from which the most unconcerned would start with real horror; of beings wretched in our Prisons, and more wretched in our Alms-Houses. And I cannot suppose it needful to employ earnest persuasion, or stubborn argument, in order to arrest and fix attention upon a subject, only the more strongly pressing in its claims, because it is revolting and disgusting in its details.

I must confine myself to few examples, but am ready to furnish other and more complete details, if required. If my pictures are displeasing, coarse, and severe, my subjects, it must be recollected, offer no tranquil, refined, or composing features. The condition of human beings, reduced to the extremest states of degradation and misery, cannot be exhibited in softened language, or adorn a polished page.

I proceed, Gentlemen, briefly to call your attention to the *present* state of Insane Persons confined within this Commonwealth, in *cages, closets, cellars, stalls, pens! Chained, naked, beaten with rods,* and *lashed* into obedience! 5

As I state cold, severe *facts,* I feel obliged to refer to persons, and definitely to indicate localities. But it is upon my subject, not upon localities or individuals, I desire to fix attention; and I would speak as kindly as possible of all Wardens, Keepers, and other responsible officers, believing that *most* of these have erred not through hardness of heart and wilful cruelty, so much as want of skill and knowledge, and want of consideration. Familiarity with suffering, it is said, blunts the sensibilities, and where neglect once finds a footing other injuries are multiplied. This is not all, for it may justly and strongly be added that, from the deficiency of adequate means to meet the wants of these cases, it has been an absolute impossibility to do justice in this matter. Prisons are not constructed in view of being converted into County Hospitals, and Alms-Houses are not founded as receptacles for the Insane. And yet, in the face of justice and common sense, Wardens are by law compelled to receive, and the Masters of Alms-Houses not to refuse, Insane and Idiotic subjects in all stages of mental disease and privation.

It is the Commonwealth, not its integral parts, that is accountable for most of the abuses which have lately, and do still exist. I repeat it, it is defective legislation which perpetuates and multiplies these abuses.

In illustration of my subject, I offer the following extracts from my Note-Book and Journal:— . . . .

Danvers. November; visited the almshouse; a large building, much out of repair; understand a new one is in contemplation. Here are from fifty-six to sixty inmates; one idiotic; three insane; one of the latter in close confinement at all times.

Long before reaching the house, wild shouts, snatches of rude songs, imprecations, and obscene language, fell upon the ear, proceeding from the occupant of a low building, rather remote from the principal building to which my course was directed. Found the mistress, and was conducted to 10 the place, which was called *'the home'* of the *forlorn* maniac, a young woman, exhibiting a condition of neglect and misery blotting out the faintest idea of comfort, and outraging every sentiment of decency. She had been, I learnt, "a respectable person; industrious and worthy; disappointments and trials shook her mind, and finally laid prostrate reason and self-control; she became a maniac for life! She had been at Worcester Hospital for a considerable time, and had been returned as incurable." The mistress told me she understood that, while there, she was "comfortable and decent." Alas! what a change was here exhibited! She had passed from one degree of violence and degradation to another, in swift progress; there she stood, clinging to, or beating upon, the bars of her caged apartment, the contracted size of which afforded space only for increasing accumulations of filth, a *foul* spectacle; there she stood with naked arms and dishevelled hair; the unwashed frame invested with fragments of unclean garments, the air so extremely offensive, though ventilation was afforded on all sides save one, that it was not possible to remain beyond a few moments without retreating for recovery to the outward air. Irritation of body, produced by utter filth and exposure, incited her to the horrid process of tearing off her skin by inches; her face, neck, and person, were thus disfigured to hideousness; she held up a fragment just rent off; to my exclamation of horror, the mistress replied, "oh, we can't help it; half the skin is off sometimes; we can do nothing with her; and it makes no difference what she eats, for she consumes her own filth as readily as the food which is brought her."

It is now January; a fortnight since, two visitors reported that most wretched outcast as "wallowing in dirty straw, in a place yet more dirty, and without clothing, without fire. Worse cared for than the brutes, and wholly lost to consciousness of decency!" Is the whole story told? What was seen, is; what is reported is not. These gross exposures are not for the pained sight of one alone; all, all, coarse, brutal men, wondering, neglected children, old and young, each and all, witness this lowest, foulest state of miserable humanity. And who protects her, that worse than Paria outcast, from other wrongs and blacker outrages? I do not *know* that such *have been*. I do know that they are to be dreaded, and that they are not guarded against.

Some may say these things cannot be remedied; these furious maniacs are not to be raised from these base conditions. I *know* they are; could give *many* examples; let *one* suffice. A young woman, a pauper, in a distant town, *Sandisfield,* was for years a raging maniac. A cage, chains, and *the whip,* were the agents for controlling her, united with harsh tones and profane language. Annually, with others (the town's poor) she was put up at auction, and bid off at the lowest price which was declared for her. One year, not long past, an old man came forward in the number of applicants for the poor wretch; he was taunted and ridiculed; "what would he and his old wife do with such a mere beast?" "My wife says yes," replied he, "and I shall take her." She was given to his charge; he conveyed her home; she was washed, neatly dressed, and placed in a decent bed-room, furnished for comfort and opening into the kitchen. How altered her condition! As yet *the chains* were not off. The first week she was somewhat restless, at times violent, but the quiet kind ways of the old people wrought a change; she received her food decently; forsook acts of violence, and no longer uttered blasphemous or indecent language; after a week, the chain was lengthened, and she was received as a companion into the kitchen. Soon she engaged in trivial employments. "After a fortnight," said the old man, "I knocked off the chains and made her a free woman." She is at times excited, but not violently; they are careful of her diet; they keep her very clean; she calls them "father" and "mother." Go there now and you will find her "clothed," and though not perfectly in her "right mind," so far restored as to be a safe and comfortable inmate.

Newburyport. Visited the almshouse in June last; eighty inmates; seven insane, one idiotic. Commodious and neat house; several of the partially insane apparently very comfortable; two very improperly situated, namely, an insane man, not considered incurable, in an out-building, whose room opened upon what was called 'the dead room,' affording in lieu of companionship with the living, a contemplation of corpses! The other subject was a woman in a *cellar.* I desired to see her; much reluctance was shown. I pressed the request; the Master of the House stated that she was *in the cellar;* that she was *dangerous to be approached;* that 'she had lately attacked his wife;' and *was often naked.* I persisted; 'if you will not go with me, give me the keys and I will go alone.' Thus importuned, the outer doors were opened. I descended the stairs from within; a strange, unnatural noise seemed to proceed from beneath our feet; at the moment I did not much regard it. My conductor proceeded to remove a padlock, while my eye explored the wide space in quest of the poor woman. All for a moment was still. But judge my horror and amazement, when a door to a closet *beneath* the *staircase* was opened, revealing in the imperfect light a female apparently wasted to a skeleton, partially wrapped in blankets, furnished for the narrow bed on which she was sitting; her countenance furrowed, not by age, but suffering, was the image of distress; in that contracted space, unlighted, unventilated, she poured forth the wailings of despair: mournfully she extended her arms and appealed to me, "why am I consigned to hell? dark—dark—I used to pray, I used to read the Bible—I have done no crime in my heart; I had friends, why have all forsaken me!—my God! my God! why hast *thou* forsaken me!" Those groans, those wailings come up daily, mingling, with how many others, a perpetual and sad memorial. When the good Lord shall require an account of our stewardship, what shall all and each answer!

Perhaps it will be inquired how long, how many days or hours was she imprisoned in these confined limits? *For years!* In another part of the cellar were other small closets, only better, because higher through the entire length, into one of which she by turns was transferred, so as to afford opportunity for fresh whitewashing, &c.

Saugus. December 24; thermometer below zero; drove to the poorhouse; was conducted to the master's family-room by himself; walls garnished with handcuffs and chains, not less than five pair of the former; did not inquire how or on whom applied; thirteen pauper inmates; one insane man; one woman insane; one idiotic man; asked to see them; the two men were shortly led in; appeared pretty decent and comfortable. Requested to see the other insane subject; was denied decidedly; urged the request, and finally secured a reluctant assent. Was led through an outer passage into a lower room, occupied by the paupers; crowded; not neat; ascended a rather low flight of stairs upon an open entry, through the floor of which was introduced a stove pipe, carried along a *few feet,* about six inches above the floor, through which it was reconveyed below. From this entry opens a room of moderate size, having a sashed-window; floor, I think, painted; apartment ENTIRELY unfurnished; no chair, table, nor bed; neither, what is seldom missing, a bundle of straw or lock of hay; cold, very cold; the first movement of my conductor was to throw open a window, a measure imperatively necessary for those who entered. *On the floor* sat a woman, her limbs immovably contracted, so that the knees were brought upward to the chin; the face was concealed; the head rested on the folded arms; for clothing she appeared to have been furnished with *fragments* of many discharged garments; these were folded about her, yet they little benefitted her, if one might judge by the constant shuddering which almost convulsed her poor crippled frame. Woful was this scene; language is feeble to record the misery she was suffering and had suffered! In reply to my inquiry if she could not change her position, I was answered by the master in the negative, and told that the contraction of limbs was occasioned by "neglect and exposure in former years," but *since she had been crazy,* and before she fell under the charge, as I inferred, of her present *guardians.* Poor wretch! she, like many others, was an example of what humanity becomes when the temple of reason falls in ruins, leaving the mortal part to injury and neglect, and showing how much can be endured of privation, exposure, and disease, without extinguishing the lamp of life.

Passing out, the man pointed to a something, revealed to more than one sense, which he called "her bed; and we throw some blankets over her at night." Possibly this is done; others, like myself, might be pardoned a doubt, if they could have seen all I saw, and heard abroad all I heard. The *bed,* so called, was about *three* feet long, and from a half to three-quarters of a yard wide; of old ticking or tow cloth was the case; the contents might have been a *full handful* of hay or straw. My attendant's exclamations on my leaving the house were emphatic, and can hardly be repeated.

The above case recalls another of equal neglect or abuse. Asking my way to the almshouse in Berkeley, which had been repeatedly spoken of as greatly neglected, I was answered as to the direction, and informed that there were "plenty of insane people and idiots there." "Well taken care of?" "Oh, well enough for such sort of creatures?" "Any violently insane?" "Yes; my sister's son in there, a real tiger. I kept him here at my house awhile, but it was too much trouble to go on; so I carried him there." "Is he comfortably provided for?" "Well enough." "Has he decent clothes?" "Good enough; wouldn't wear them if he had more." "Food?" "Good enough; good enough for him." "One more question, has he the comfort of a fire?" "Fire? fire, indeed! what does a crazy man need of fire? red-hot iron wants fire as much as he!" And such are sincerely the ideas of not a few persons in regard to the actual wants of the insane. Less regarded than the lowest brutes! no wonder they sink even lower. . . .

Violence and severity do but exasperate the Insane: the only availing influence is kindness and firmness. It is amazing what these will produce. How many examples might illustrate this position: I refer to one recently exhibited in Barre. The town Paupers are disposed of annually to some family who, for a stipulated sum agree to take charge of them. One of them, a young woman, was shown to me well clothed, neat, quiet, and employed at needle-work. Is it possible that this is the same being who, but last year, was a raving madwoman, exhibiting every degree of violence in action and speech; a very tigress wrought to fury; caged, chained, beaten, loaded with injuries, and exhibiting the passions which an iron rule might be expected to stimulate and sustain. It is the same person; another family hold her in charge who better understand human nature and human influences; she is no longer chained, caged, and beaten; but if excited, a pair of mittens drawn over the hands secures from mischief. Where will she be next year, after the annual sale?

It is not the insane subject alone who illustrates the power of the all prevailing law of kindness. A poor idiotic young man, a year or two since, used to follow me at times through the prison as I was distributing books and papers: at first he appeared totally stupid, but cheerful expressions, a smile, a trifling gift, seemed gradually to light up the void temple of the intellect, and by slow degrees some faint images of thought passed before the mental vision. He would ask for books, though he could not read. I indulged his fancy and he would appear to experience delight in examining them; and kept them with a singular care. If I read the Bible, he was reverently, wonderingly attentive; if I talked, he listened with a half-conscious aspect. One morning I passed more hurriedly than usual, and did not speak particularly to him. "Me, me, me a book." I returned; "good morning, Jemmy; so you will have a book today? well, keep it carefully." Suddenly turning aside he took the bread brought for his breakfast, and passing it with a hurried earnestness through the bars of his iron door—"Here's bread, a'nt you hungry?" Never may I forget the tone and grateful affectionate aspect of that poor idiot. How much might we do to bring back or restore the mind, if we but knew how to touch the instrument with a skilful hand! . . .

Of the dangers and mischiefs sometimes following the location of insane persons in our almhouses, I will record but one more example. In Worcester, has for several years resided a young woman, a lunatic pauper of decent life and respectable family. I have seen her as she usually appeared, listless and silent, almost or quite sunk into a state of dementia, sitting one amidst the family, 'but not of them.' A few weeks since, revisiting that almshouse, judge my horror and amazement to see her negligently bearing in her arms a young infant, of which I was told she was the unconscious parent! Who was the father, none could or would declare. Disqualified for the performance of maternal cares and duties, regarding the helpless little creature with a perplexed, or indifferent gaze, she sat a silent, but O how eloquent, a pleader for the protection of others of her neglected and out-raged sex! Details of that black story would not strengthen the cause; needs it a weightier plea, than the sight of that forlorn creature and her wailing infant? Poor little child, more than orphan from birth, in this unfriendly world! a demented Mother—a Father, on whom the sun might blush or refuse to shine!

Men of Massachusetts, I beg, I implore, I demand, pity and protection, for these of my suffering, outraged sex!—Fathers, Husbands, Brothers, I would supplicate you for this boon—but what do I say? I dishonor you, divest you at once of christianity and humanity—does this appeal imply distrust. It it comes burthened with a doubt of your righteousness in this Legislation, then blot it out; while I declare confidence in your honor, not less than your humanity. Here you will put away the cold, calculating spirit of selfishness and self-seeking; lay off the armor of local strife and political opposition; here and now, for once, forgetful of the earthly and perishable, come up to these halls and consecrate them with one heart and one mind to works of righteousness and just judgment. Become the benefactors of your race, the just guardians of the solemn rights you hold in trust. Raise up the fallen; succor the desolate; restore the outcast; defend the helpless; and for your eternal and great reward, receive the benediction. . . . "Well done, good and faithful servants, become rulers over many things!"

Questions for Discussion

1. What feelings does Dix appeal to in this essay? What assumptions has she made about her audience?
2. How does Dix use gender to inspire feeling?
3. Why was it useful for Dix to emphasize that she was reporting conditions that she had seen with her own eyes?
4. Of the abuses recorded by Dix, which made the strongest impression upon you?
5. Consider the use of italics in this essay. How do you account for the words and phrases that Dix decided to italicize?
6. How does Dix demonstrate that the insane poor would benefit from better treatment?

Suggestions for Writing

1. Many of the homeless living on our streets today are mentally ill people who might have been institutionalized in an earlier era. Research the

conditions under which such people live, and write a plea upon their behalf that would touch the hearts of men and women who believe that the poor are well provided for.

2. Visit a hospital or nursing home, and draw upon this experience to move readers to sympathize with the people you have seen. Remember that the patients you see are entitled to privacy and respect. Ask permission to visit the institution you have chosen, and ask permission of any patient you interview.

A MODEST PROPOSAL
FOR PREVENTING THE CHILDREN OF
POOR PEOPLE IN IRELAND FROM BEING
A BURDEN TO THEIR PARENTS OR
COUNTRY, AND FOR MAKING THEM
BENEFICIAL TO THE PUBLIC

Jonathan Swift

> *As you read "A Modest Proposal," you may find it useful to know that Ireland was ruled as an English colony during Swift's lifetime—and that the English enacted a number of laws that resulted in great hardship. Irish trade and industry were suppressed, and religious conflicts were intensified. Swift's parents were English colonists in Ireland, and he was a member of the Protestant ruling class, but it would be a mistake to assume that he was indifferent to the suffering he saw around him. Consider the act Swift proposes, and think about why he, a clergyman, would make such a proposal.*

It is a melancholy object to those who walk through this great town° or travel in the country, when they see the streets, the roads, and cabin doors, crowded with beggars of the female sex, followed by three, four, or six children, all in rags and importuning every passenger for an alms. These mothers, instead of being able to work for their honest livelihood, are forced to employ all their time in strolling to beg sustenance for their helpless infants: who as they grow up either turn thieves for want of work, or leave their dear native country to fight for the Pretender° in Spain, or sell themselves to the Barbadoes.°

I think it is agreed by all parties that this prodigious number of children in the arms, or on the backs, or at the heels of their mothers, and frequently of their fathers, is in the present deplorable state of the kingdom a very great additional grievance; and, therefore, whoever could find out a fair, cheap, and easy method of making these children sound, useful members of the commonwealth, would deserve so well of the public as to have his statue set up for a preserver of the nation.

But my intention is very far from being confined to provide only for the children of professed beggars; it is of a much greater extent, and shall take in the whole number of infants at a certain age who are born of parents in effect as little able to support them as those who demand our charity in the streets.

great town: Dublin.   *Pretender:* James Stuart, son of James II and a Catholic. In 1688 the throne had gone to his sister Mary, a Protestant who ruled with her husband William of Orange.   *Barbadoes:* To get out of Ireland, many people went as indentured servants to Barbados and other British colonies.

As to my own part, having turned my thoughts for many years upon this important subject, and maturely weighed the several schemes of our projectors, I have always found them grossly mistaken in their computation. It is true, a child just dropped from its dam may be supported by her milk for a solar year, with little other nourishment; at most not above the value of *2s.,* which the mother may certainly get, or the value in scraps, by her lawful occupation of begging; and it is exactly at one year old that I propose to provide for them in such a manner as instead of being a charge upon their parents or the parish, or wanting food and raiment for the rest of their lives, they shall on the contrary contribute to the feeding, and partly to the clothing, of many thousands.

There is likewise another great advantage in my scheme, that it will prevent those voluntary abortions, and that horrid practice of women murdering their bastard children, alas! too frequent among us! sacrificing the poor innocent babes I doubt more to avoid the expense than the shame, which would move tears and pity in the most savage and inhuman breast.

The number of souls in this kingdom being usually reckoned one million and a half, of these I calculate there may be about 200,000 couple whose wives are breeders; from which number I subtract 30,000 couple who are able to maintain their own children (although I apprehend there cannot be so many, under the present distress of the kingdom); but this being granted, there will remain 170,000 breeders. I again subtract 50,000 for those women who miscarry, or whose children die by accident or disease within the year. There only remain 120,000 children of poor parents annually born. The question therefore is, how this number shall be reared and provided for? which, as I have already said, under the present situation of affairs, is utterly impossible by all the methods hitherto proposed. For we can neither employ them in handicraft or agriculture; we neither build houses (I mean in the country) nor cultivate land; they can very seldom pick up a livelihood by stealing, till they arrive at six years old, except where they are of towardly parts; although I confess they learn the rudiments much earlier; during which time they can, however, be properly looked upon only as probationers; as I have been informed by a principal gentleman in the country of Cavan, who protested to me that he never knew above one or two instances under the age of six, even in a part of the kingdom so renowned for the quickest proficiency in that art.

I am assured by our merchants, that a boy or a girl before twelve years old is no saleable commodity; and even when they come to this age they will not yield above *3l.* or *3l. 2s. 6d.*° at most on the exchange; which cannot turn to account either to the parents or kingdom, the charge of nutriment and rags having been at least four times that value.

I shall now therefore humbly propose my own thoughts, which I hope will not be liable to the least objection.

3l, 2s. 6d.: Three pounds, two shillings, and six pence.

I have been assured by a very knowing American of my acquaintance in London, that a young healthy child well nursed is at a year old a most delicious, nourishing, and wholesome food, whether stewed, roasted, baked, or broiled; and I make no doubt that it will equally serve in a fricassee or a ragout.

I do therefore humbly offer it to public consideration that of the 10 120,000 children already computed, 20,000 may be reserved for breed, whereof only one-fourth part to be males; which is more than we allow to sheep, black cattle, or swine; and my reason is, that these children are seldom the fruits of marriage, a circumstance not much regarded by our savages; therefore one male will be sufficient to serve four females. That the remaining 100,000 may, at a year old, be offered in sale to the persons of quality and fortune through the kingdom; always advising the mother to let them suck plentifully in the last month, so as to render them plump and fat for a good table. A child will make two dishes at an entertainment for friends; and when the family dines alone, the fore or hind quarter will make a reasonable dish, and seasoned with a little pepper or salt will be very good boiled on the fourth day, especially in winter.

I have reckoned upon a medium that a child just born will weigh 12 pounds, and in a solar year, if tolerably nursed, will increase to 28 pounds.

I grant this food will be somewhat dear, and therefore very proper for landlords, who, as they have already devoured most of the parents, seem to have the best title to the children.

Infant's flesh will be in season throughout the year, but more plentiful in March, and a little before and after: for we are told by a grave author, an eminent French physician, that fish being a prolific diet, there are more children born in Roman Catholic countries about nine months after Lent than at any other season; therefore, reckoning a year after Lent, the markets will be more glutted than usual, because the number of popish infants is at least three to one in this kingdom: and therefore it will have one other collateral advantage, by lessening the number of papists among us.

I have already computed the charge of nursing a beggar's child (in which list I reckon all cottagers, laborers, and four-fifths of the farmers) to be about *2s.* per annum, rags included; and I believe no gentleman would repine to give *10s.* for the carcass of a good fat child, which, as I have said, will make four dishes of excellent nutritive meat, when he has only some particular friend or his own family to dine with him. Thus the squire will learn to be a good landlord, and grow popular among the tenants; the mother will have *8s.* net profit, and be fit for work till she produces another child.

Those who are more thrifty (as I must confess the times require) may 15 flay the carcass; the skin of which artificially dressed will make admirable gloves for ladies, and summer boots for fine gentlemen.

As to our city of Dublin, shambles° may be appointed for this purpose in the most convenient parts of it, and butchers we may be assured will not be wanting: although I rather recommend buying the children alive, and dressing them hot from the knife as we do roasting pigs.

A very worthy person, a true lover of his country, and whose virtues I highly esteem, was lately pleased in discoursing on this matter to offer a refinement upon my scheme. He said that many gentlemen of this kingdom, having of late destroyed their deer, he conceived that the want of venison might be well supplied by the bodies of young lads and maidens, not exceeding fourteen years of age nor under twelve; so great a number of both sexes in every country being not ready to starve for want of work and service; and these to be disposed of by their parents, if alive, or otherwise by their nearest relations. But with due deference to so excellent a friend and so deserving a patriot, I cannot be altogether in his sentiments; for as to the males, my American acquaintance assured me from frequent experience that their flesh was generally tough and lean, like that of our schoolboys by continual exercise, and their taste disagreeable; and to fatten them would not answer the charge. Then as to the females, it would, I think, with humble submission be a loss to the public, because they soon would become breeders themselves: and besides, it is not improbable that some scrupulous people might be apt to censure such a practice (although indeed very unjustly), as a little bordering upon cruelty; which, I confess, has always been with me the strongest objection against any project, how well soever intended.

But in order to justify my friend, he confessed that this expedient was put into his head by the famous Psalmanazar, a native of the island Formosa, who came from thence to London about twenty years ago: and in conversation told my friend, that in his country when any young person happened to be put to death, the executioner sold the carcass to persons of quality as a prime dainty; and that in his time the body of a plump girl of fifteen, who was crucified for an attempt to poison the emperor, was sold to his imperial majesty's prime minister of state, and other great mandarins of the court, in joints from the gibbet, at 400 crowns. Neither indeed can I deny, that if the same use were made of several plump girls in this town, who without one single groat to their fortunes cannot stir abroad without a chair, and appear at the playhouse and assemblies in foreign fineries which they never will pay for, the kingdom would not be the worse.

Some persons of a desponding spirit are in great concern about that vast number of poor people, who are aged, diseased, or maimed, and I have been desired to employ my thoughts what course may be taken to ease the nation of so grievous an encumbrance. But I am not in the least pain upon that matter, because it is very well known that they are every day dying and

---

shambles: Slaughterhouses.

rotting by cold and famine, and filth and vermin, as fast as can be reasonably expected. And as to the young laborers, they are now in as hopeful a condition: they cannot get work, and consequently pine away for want of nourishment, to a degree that if at any time they are accidentally hired to common labor, they have not strength to perform it; and thus the country and themselves are happily delivered from the evils to come.

I have too long digressed, and therefore shall return to my subject. I think the advantages by the proposal which I have made are obvious and many, as well as the highest importance.

For first, as I already observed, it would greatly lessen the number of papists, with whom we are yearly overrun, being the principal breeders of the nation as well as our most dangerous enemies; and who stay at home on purpose to deliver the kingdom to the Pretender, hoping to take their advantage by the absence of so many good Protestants, who have chosen rather to leave their country than stay at home and pay tithes against their conscience to an Episcopal curate.

Secondly, the poor tenants will have something valuable of their own, which by law may be made liable to distress and help to pay their landlord's rent, their corn and cattle being already seized, and money a thing unknown.

Thirdly, whereas the maintenance of 100,000 children from two years old and upward, cannot be computed at less than *10s.* a-piece per annum, the nation's stock will be thereby increased £50,000 per annum, beside the profit of a new dish introduced to the tables of all gentlemen of fortune in the kingdom who have any refinement in taste. And the money will circulate among ourselves, the goods being entirely of our own growth and manufacture.

Fourthly, the constant breeders, beside the gain of *8s.* sterling per annum by the sale of their children, will be rid of the charge of maintaining them after the first year.

Fifthly, this food would likewise bring great custom to taverns, where the vintners will certainly be so prudent as to procure the best receipts for dressing it to perfection, and consequently have their houses frequented by all the fine gentlemen, who justly value themselves upon their knowledge in good eating; and a skillful cook, who understands how to oblige his guests, will contrive to make it as expensive as they please.

Sixthly, this would be a great inducement to marriage, which all wise nations have either encouraged by rewards or enforced by laws and penalties. It would increase the care and tenderness of mothers toward their children, when they were sure of a settlement for life to the poor babes, provided in some sort by the public, to their annual profit instead of expense. We should see an honest emulation among the married women, which of them would bring the fattest child to the market. Men would become as fond of their wives during the time of their pregnancy as they are now of their mares in foal, their cows in calf, their sows when they are ready to farrow; nor offer to beat or kick them (as is too frequent a practice) for fear of a miscarriage.

Many other advantages might be enumerated. For instance, the addition of some thousand carcasses in our exportation of barreled beef, the propagation of swine's flesh, and improvement in the art of making good bacon, so much wanted among us by the great destruction of pigs, too frequent at our table; which are no way comparable in taste or magnificence to a well-grown, fat, yearling child, which roasted whole will make a considerable figure at a lord mayor's feast or any other public entertainment. But this and many others I omit, being studious of brevity.

Supposing that 1,000 families in this city would be constant customers for infants' flesh, besides others who might have it at merry-meetings, particularly at weddings and christenings, I compute that Dublin would take off annually about 20,000 carcasses; and the rest of the kingdom (where probably they will be sold somewhat cheaper) the remaining 80,000.

I can think of no one objection that will possibly be raised against this proposal, unless it should be urged that the number of people will be thereby much lessened in the kingdom. This I freely own, and it was indeed one principal design in offering it to the world. I desire the reader will observe, that I calculate my remedy for this one individual kingdom of Ireland and for no other that ever was, is, or I think ever can be upon earth. Therefore let no man talk to me of other expedients: of taxing our absentees at 5s. a pound: of using neither clothes nor household furniture except what is of our own growth and manufacture: of utterly rejecting the materials and instruments that promote foreign luxury: of curing the expensiveness of pride, vanity, idleness, and gaming in our women: of introducing a vein of parsimony, prudence, and temperance: of learning to love our country, in the want of which we differ even from Laplanders and the inhabitants of Topinamboo: of quitting our animosities and factions, not acting any longer like the Jews, who were murdering one another at the very moment their city was taken: of being a little cautious not to sell our country and conscience for nothing: of teaching landlords to have at least one degree of mercy toward their tenants: lastly, of putting a spirit of honesty, industry, and skill into our shopkeepers; who, if a resolution could now be taken to buy only our native goods, would immediatly unite to cheat and exact upon us in the price, the measure, and the goodness, nor could ever yet be brought to make one fair proposal of just dealing, though often and earnestly invited to it.

Therefore I repeat, let no man talk to me of these and the like expedients, till he has at least some glimpse of hope that there will be ever some hearty and sincere attempt to put them in practice. 30

But as to myself, having been wearied out for many years with offering vain, idle, visionary thoughts, and at length utterly despairing of success, I fortunately fell upon this proposal; which, as it is wholly new, so it has something solid and real, of no expense and little trouble, full in our own power, and whereby we can incur no danger of disobliging England. For this kind of commodity will not bear exportation, the flesh being of too tender a consistence to admit a long continuance in salt, although perhaps I could name a country which would be glad to eat up our whole nation without it.

After all, I am not so violently bent upon my own opinion as to reject any offer proposed by wise men, which shall be found equally innocent, cheap, easy, and effectual. But before something of that kind shall be advanced in contradiction to my scheme, and offering a better, I desire the author or authors will be pleased maturely to consider two points. First, as things now stand, how they will be able to find food and raiment for 100,000 useless mouths and backs. And secondly, there being a round million of creatures in human figure throughout this kingdom, whose subsistence put into a common stock would leave them in debt 2,000,000*l.* sterling, adding those who are beggars by profession to the bulk of farmers, cottagers, and laborers, with the wives and children who are beggars in effect; I desire those politicians who dislike my overture, and may perhaps be so bold as to attempt an answer, that they will first ask the parents of these mortals, whether they would not at this day think it a great happiness to have been sold for food at a year old in the manner I prescribe, and thereby have avoided such a perpetual scene of misfortunes as they have since gone through by the oppression of landlords, the impossibility of paying rent without money or trade, the want of common sustenance, with neither house nor clothes to cover them from the inclemencies of the weather, and the most inevitable prospect of entailing the like or greater miseries upon their breed for ever.

I profess, in the sincerity of my heart, that I have not the least personal interest in endeavoring to promote this necessary work, having no other motive than the public good of my country, by advancing our trade, providing for infants, relieving the poor, and giving some pleasure to the rich. I have no children by which I can propose to get a single penny; the youngest being nine years old, and my wife past child-bearing.

Questions for Discussion

1. At what point in this essay did you first become aware that Swift is being ironic?
2. What steps has Swift taken to make his proposal seem "modest" and his voice reasonable?
3. Why does the speaker in this essay believe that his proposal would be unsuitable for adolescents? Why isn't he worried about the problem of the elderly poor?
4. What does this essay reveal about Ireland under British domination?
5. Does Swift offer any alternative to eating the children of the poor? If there are alternatives to cannibalism, why devote so many paragraphs to a proposal that most people would quickly reject?
6. What is the function of the concluding paragraph?

7. Writers of textbooks often reprint this essay as an example of writing to persuade, and the essay does incorporate such persuasive strategies as anticipating and responding to points that might be raised by one's opponents. How would you define Swift's purpose? Is he writing to persuade readers to adopt specific proposals? Or is he writing primarily to shock people out of complacency?

Suggestions for Writing

1. Use irony to write a "modest" solution to a contemporary social problem.
2. Would you be willing to sell your child on the black market? Imagine yourself to be desperately poor, and write a response to someone who has offered to buy your child.

9

Writing to Persuade Others

As the previous chapter has shown, writers are sometimes motivated to move readers simply for the sake of producing an emotion from which some unspecified good may follow. David James Duncan, for example, does not tell his readers what they should do to cope with grief. He simply describes his own long struggle to come to terms with his brother's death. The evocation of feeling may be necessary when working for change—be it civil rights or the elimination of poverty. But when we want to argue for a specific change, we must do more than move our audience. We must persuade them to support a proposal or undertake an action.

Persuasion ranges from advertising to scholarly arguments. Between these extremes are dozens of situations in which persuasion is fundamental to everyday life. When you apply for a job, propose a marriage, try to borrow money, or ask your landlord to fix the plumbing, you are using persuasion in an attempt to get someone to do something you want. At other times you use persuasion to achieve benefits for others—as in trying to raise money for the victims of a famine or in trying to persuade the government to protect an endangered species of wildlife. And on other occasions you use persuasion when there is no question of benefits but there is a problem that needs to be resolved—as in trying to improve the functioning of a committee on which you serve when it cannot accomplish anything because of personal conflicts. What all of these examples have in common is that they presume the need to change someone's mind. We need to persuade others only when differences of opinion exist. Persuasion is unnecessary when widespread agreement already exists, and it is inappropriate when questions allow for only one correct answer.

Classical rhetoric recognized that persuasion was accomplished through three means: the credibility of the writer/speaker (*ethos*), the logic of the argument (*logos*), and the skill with which appropriate feelings are inspired (*pathos*). This threefold approach to persuasion prevailed in the West for almost two thousand years, but its practitioners vary in what they emphasize and what strategies they recommend. Aristotle, for example, believed that ethos is the most important aspect of persuasion and that we make ourselves believable by how we present ourselves in what we say and write. But Aristotle defined ethos as something created within the work (from which it would follow that a bad person could seem to be credible because of his skill in arguing). Other rhetoricians have argued that ethos cannot be created artificially and that only good people (or people who are actively trying to be good) can write arguments that are truly persuasive. Still others have emphasized the role of pathos. Cicero, one of the greatest speakers of the ancient world, argued that nothing is more important than to be able to move an audience: "For men decide far more problems by hate, or love, or lust, or rage, or sorrow, or joy, or hope, or fear, or illusion, or some other inward emotion, than by reality, or authority, or any legal standard, or judicial precedent, or statute."

In short, there has been—and there is still—no universal agreement about how to persuade others. Different opinions prevailed in the classical world, and the debate is still going on. But at this point we can offer some basic principles.

- Your strategy may vary depending upon the topic and your audience. But you should always consider the extent to which you have employed ethos, pathos, and logos. As a general rule, an argument depending upon only one of these methods probably won't be as persuasive as an argument using more than one.
- Although people sometimes make decisions upon impulse, and some forms of persuasion (like television commercials) are designed to inspire unreasoned decisions, the most persuasive arguments are those that still make sense after we have thought about them for a while. It follows that persuasion should appeal to the mind as well as to the heart.

USING LOGIC

Appealing to the mind requires at least some familiarity with logic. Classical rhetoric teaches two types of logic, inductive and deductive reasoning. Modern rhetoric has explored alternative forms of reasoning designed to complement traditional approaches. Whatever type of logic you decide best suits your needs, you should realize that you can move freely among the various options outlined in the following subsections.

Inductive Reasoning

To reason inductively means using examples to discover what seems to be true. In an inductive argument a writer presents a series of examples (or pieces of evidence) and draws a conclusion from their significance. Reaching this conclusion means going beyond the accumulated evidence and making a reasonable guess, the *inductive leap*. Induction is persuasive when the evidence is sufficient to justify the conclusion. Writers who make the inductive leap from insufficient evidence are said to be jumping to conclusions, a failure in reasoning so common that it has become a cliché.

When you use induction carefully, you will reach a conclusion that is probably true. But you should recognize that your conclusion is probable rather than absolute. It is always possible that other evidence, which you haven't considered, could lead to a conclusion different from your own. For example, suppose that it is the first week of classes and you are taking a math course from a professor you have never worked with previously. At each of the first three classes the professor arrives late and lectures in a disorganized manner that is difficult to understand. Tomorrow is the last day you can drop the class and still add a new one in its place. Concluding that your math teacher is a bad teacher, you decide to drop his course and substitute another course in its place. Within the constraints of daily life, which often require us to make decisions quickly, you have used induction to make a decision that seems reasonable under the circumstances. On the other hand, it is possible that the math professor had a bad week because he was staying up all night with sick children and that his performance will improve dramatically in the weeks that follow.

As a rule, your conclusions will be the strongest when they rest upon a foundation built of many separate pieces of evidence. When a serious conclusion is arrived at inductively, it will almost certainly have extensive information behind it. The scientific method illustrates induction at its best. Researchers conduct hundreds and sometimes thousands of experiments before arguing for a new type of medical treatment, and after publication of these results other researchers seek to verify them independently. But however solid these conclusions seem to be, they are often challenged by new studies that take a different approach. (See Lewis Thomas's essay, "The Art of Teaching Science," in Chapter 3.) So no matter how many examples support an inductively derived conclusion, you can never be certain that you have managed to discover an absolute truth.

Deductive Reasoning

To reason deductively means to identify propositions that are already believed to be true and to discover an additional truth that follows from these propositions. A deductive argument reflects the logic of a syllogism in which a major and a minor premise lead to a conclusion that is necessarily true.

Major premise: All men have hearts.
Minor premise: Bill is a man.
Conclusion: Bill has a heart.

In this case the reasoning is both valid and true. It is valid because it follows the conventions of logic: If we accept the major and the minor premise, then we must recognize that the conclusion follows logically from them. Occasionally, however, you will find syllogisms that are valid but untrue.

Major premise: All chemistry professors are boring.
Minor premise: Veronica is a chemistry professor.
Conclusion: Veronica is boring.

Although this syllogism follows the same pattern as the previous syllogism and is valid, it is untrue because it rests upon a highly questionable major premise. For a syllogism to be true as well as valid, both the major and the minor premise must be unquestionably true.

Unfortunately, there are relatively few propositions that everyone accepts as true—or "self-evident," as Thomas Jefferson declares at the beginning of "The Declaration of Independence." And the number seems to be decreasing. Consider what happens if we modify our first example.

Major premise: All men have functioning kidneys.
Minor premise: Bill is a man.
Conclusion: Bill has functioning kidneys.

A hundred years ago, this syllogism would have been both valid and true; today, it is valid but untrue, since dialysis machines allow people to live without functioning kidneys. Conceivably, the day may come when people can function without hearts. (We have already seen several attempts to support life with artificial hearts.)

Consider, also, that different readers have different responses to language and that language is dependent upon social context. To put it simply, words can (and do) change in meaning. The major premise of our first example ("All men have hearts") is already more questionable than it would have been fifty years ago. A writer beginning with this statement could face such questions as "What do you mean by *men?* Does that include women?" and "What about *hearts?* Do you mean a body organ or a capacity for feeling emotion?"

But writing an essay is not the same as writing a syllogism: You have more than three sentences to make your case. If you want to organize an essay deductively because your position derives from a fundamental principle that you are confident your audience will share, you should pace yourself according to the needs of the situation. On some topics, for some audiences, you may need to spend several paragraphs establishing your premise. At other times you may be able to take your premise for granted and offer what is called an *enthymeme,* or two-part deductive argument from which the major premise has been omitted. Abbreviating an argument in this way does not necessarily mean that it will be shorter; it just means that you have omitted one step in order to emphasize other aspects of your case.

Substantive Reasoning

Over the years deductive reasoning has been favored by philosophers because it seemed the type of logic most likely to lead to truth. But many writers find it ill suited for argumentation, and philosophers increasingly acknowledge other forms of reasoning. After spending many years analyzing arguments in practical fields such as politics and law, Chaim Perelman concluded that formal logic is seldom appropriate, since argument is more concerned with gaining the adherence of an audience than with demonstrating the truth of abstract propositions.

> What are we to think of this reduction to two forms of reasoning of all the wide variety of arguments that men use in their discussions and in pleading a cause or in justifying an action? Yet, since the time of Aristotle, logic has confined its study to deductive and inductive reasoning. . . . As a result, an argument that cannot be reduced to canonical form is regarded as logically valueless. (*The New Rhetoric and the Humanities* [Dordrecht, Holland: Reidel, 1979], 26)

Perelman showed that when we actually examine arguments that we find persuasive, we realize that many of them seem reasonable even though they do not conform strictly to the conventions of induction or deduction.

At about the same time that Perelman was conducting his research in Belgium, the British philosopher Stephen Toulmin was reaching a conclusion similar to Perelman's. Analyzing arguments made within various fields, Toulmin discovered that they had certain features in common. This discovery led him to offer a new model of argument that is easy for writers to use. *Substantive logic* was the term he preferred for his system, a working logic suitable for the needs of the diverse range of arguments identified by Perelman and other theorists.

According to Toulmin, every argument includes a claim, which is the assertion or conclusion the argument is trying to prove. The claim is supported by data, which describes the various types of evidence (such as facts, personal experience, or appeals to authority) that lead an audience to decide that the claim is reasonable. Both the claim and the data are stated explicitly in the argument. Underlying them, however, and not necessarily made explicit (although they can be) are what Toulmin called *warrants.* He described warrants as "bridges [that] authorize the sort of step to which our argument commits us." Warrants may be directly stated, but very often (especially when they are obvious), they are not.

Here is one of the examples that Toulmin used to illustrate his model.

Claim: Harry is a British subject.
Data: Harry was born in Bermuda.
Warrant: A man born in Bermuda will be a British subject.

As you can see from this example, the claim is based directly upon its data. The warrant is simply explanatory; its function is to show why the claim follows from the data. A good way to understand the warrant, especially when it has not been explicitly stated, is to imagine a statement beginning with either since or because. In the example just cited the data supports the claim, since people born in Bermuda are British subjects. If you were making this argument in Bermuda or in England, you could probably assume that your audience would understand the warrant even if you did not state it. On the other hand, if you were making this argument in Tibet, you would probably need to make sure that the warrant was clearly understood.

Behind any warrant is what Toulmin called *backing.* The backing, or grounds, for a warrant will vary from argument to argument and from field to field. For the example about Bermuda the backing consists of the specific pieces of legislation that govern the citizenship of people born in British colonies. Like the warrant, backing may be either explicit or implicit in an argument. But unlike the warrant, which is a generalization, backing consists of facts. If you use Toulmin's model for writing persuasive essays, you should always ask yourself if you could come up with backing for your warrant if someone questioned its legitimacy.

For writers, one of the advantages of Toulmin's model is that it does not require a fixed pattern of organization. You can arrange your ideas in whatever sequence seems best suited for your work, as long as you are careful to provide data for any claim you make and are able to explain why the data supports the claim when the link between them is not immediately clear. Another advantage of Toulmin's model is that it easily incorporates *qualifiers,* such as *probably* or *unless,* that protect the overall integrity of your arguments from exceptions that could be used to challenge what you are arguing. When arguing about Harry's citizenship, for example, you could point out that the data supports the claim unless Harry's parents were aliens in Bermuda or unless he has become a naturalized citizen of another country.

LOGICAL FALLACIES

Whatever type of reasoning you use, you should try to be alert for certain errors that can undermine your case. The detailed study of logic reveals many different ways arguments can break down. Dwelling upon these *logical fallacies,* as they are called, can sometimes make writers feel that writing to persuade is more difficult than it really is. Nevertheless, having some familiarity with a few of the most common fallacies can help you evaluate the arguments you read and revise those that you write.

Ad Hominem Argument

Latin for "to the man," an *ad hominem* argument is a personal attack upon someone whose view differs from that of the arguer. Writers who make *ad hominem* arguments undermine their credibility in at least two ways. To attack an opponent, rather than what an opponent has argued, is to ignore the real issues under consideration. Personal attacks also appear to be mean-spirited, which can alienate an impartial audience. When a writer arguing for gun control attacks members of the National Rifle Association as "macho men who don't understand the definition of a civilized society," she is offending the people she most needs to persuade and probably making unbiased readers sympathize with the opponents she just attacked.

There are, of course, some situations in which it can be legitimate to question the personal integrity of an opponent. In a political campaign, for example, voters might decide that a candidate who has cheated on his income tax cannot be trusted to govern, no matter how appealing his positions are on various issues. But even in politics, where personal attacks can sometimes be justified, people quickly tire of a campaign that seems to consist of nothing but *ad hominem* arguments. As a general rule, it is more honorable to focus argument upon ideas rather than personalities.

Appeal to False Authority

A good way to support an argument is to cite testimony from authorities in the field you are writing about. If you are writing about child care, for instance, you may wish to incorporate the views of a respected pediatrician. But knowledge in one field does not make someone expert in another. Citing the pediatrician in an argument on the space program is an appeal to a false authority. Advertisements offer many examples of this fallacy by attempting to persuade us to buy products that have been endorsed by well-known actors or athletes who probably know no more about the product than we do.

But appeals to false authority also occur in written arguments—in part because well-known people sometimes enjoy making public statements on anything that happens to interest them. Quote a novelist on writing novels and you will have appealed to a legitimate authority. Quote that same novelist on the conduct of American foreign policy and, unless the novelist happens to be an expert on international affairs as well, you will have appealed to a false authority.

Begging the Question

Writers beg the question when they begin an argument by assuming what they actually need to prove. At its most obvious begging the question takes the form of a statement that leads nowhere, since it goes around in a circle: "College is too expensive because it costs more than it is worth." This statement simply makes the same point two ways. An argument could be written to show that college is too expensive, but it would need to be supported with evidence rather than repetition. Begging the question can also take more subtle forms, such as introducing a word (like *unfair*) that expresses an unsupported value judgment.

Jumping to Conclusions

This fallacy, sometimes called "hasty generalization," occurs when a writer makes a conclusion based upon insufficient evidence. Consider, for example, a personnel director who decides, "I don't think we should hire any other graduates of that school; we hired Randy, and he couldn't do anything right." To judge all the graduates of a school by one person is to jump to a conclusion. People often jump to conclusions in daily life, especially when decisions are influenced by feeling: "I know you two are going out together. I saw you talking after class today!"

Writers sometimes jump to conclusions because they lack evidence or because they are anxious to complete an assignment. Rather than jumping to a conclusion your argument has not supported, you should either search for additional evidence or modify your claim in such a way that your evidence does support it.

Post Hoc, Ergo Propter Hoc

The name of this fallacy is Latin for "after this, therefore because of this." *Post hoc* arguments, as they are called for short, confuse cause with coincidence. Examples of *post hoc* reasoning are often found in discussions of large social questions: "Since MTV began broadcasting, the number of teenage pregnancies has risen sharply." This statement assumes that MTV is causing teenagers to get pregnant. Although the lyrics of rock music and the sensual imagery of rock videos may contribute to an atmosphere that encourages sexual activity, there are almost certainly many causes for the rise of teenage pregnancy during the same period that MTV happened to be broadcasting.

Superstitions can embody a type of *post hoc* reasoning: "I failed the quiz because I walked under a ladder yesterday." It is important to realize that every event is preceded by many unrelated events: The sun may come up shortly after the rooster crows, but that doesn't prove that the rooster is making the sun come up.

Slippery Slope

Although it is reasonable to consider the probable effects of any change that is being argued for, it is fallacious to base one's opposition to that change entirely upon the prediction of some future result that is, at best, a guess. Writers who use slippery slope arguments are using what is almost always a type of fear tactic: "Give them an inch, and they will take a mile." An argument like this shifts attention away from the issue at hand. Because the future is hard to predict, and one change does not necessarily have to lead to another, it is wiser to consider the immediate effects of what is being debated than to draw frightening pictures of what could happen someday.

ORGANIZING YOUR ESSAY

By using logical reasoning, you can determine the organization of your paper. When you use inductive reasoning, you will present several pieces of evidence and then draw a conclusion from that evidence. When you use deductive reasoning, you will begin by establishing a principle that you expect your readers to agree upon and then move on to show how this principle leads to a certain conclusion. And when using substantive reasoning, you can make your claim at the beginning or at the end of your essay as long as you provide sufficient evidence to support it and establish a reasonable warrant.

But while your writing can benefit from an understanding of logic, you need not confine yourself to a single method of reasoning or follow the pattern of organization called for by that method. Many writers choose to combine inductive and deductive reasoning within a single essay, and we have already seen how substantive reasoning does not demand a specific pattern of organization. Here, then, is additional advice for organizing a persuasive essay.

You may adapt a type of organization used in debates and sometimes called "presenting the stock issues." This method of arrangement calls for showing that there is a problem and then moving on to propose a solution to that problem. In the first part of your essay you would establish that a need for change exists by demonstrating how the status quo is unacceptable. In the second part you would propose a solution to the problem and demonstrate that your solution would work. Within the essays in this chapter the clearest example of this approach is provided by Louis Barbash in "Clean Up or Pay Up." After providing evidence of corruption in college sports, Barbash asks, "Well then, is there any way out of this mess?" He then goes on to offer two possible solutions and emphasize the one he thinks best.

Unfortunately, writers do not always have a solution for problems. But sometimes a writer can offer a useful service simply by persuading others that a problem exists. When this is the case—or even when it is not—you can follow the time-honored pattern recommended by classical rhetoric.

- *Introduction:* Identify your issue and capture the attention of your audience by opening with a vivid example, dramatic anecdote, memorable quotation, or appeal to common values.
- *Statement of background facts:* Report the information you think your audience needs to know before it can understand your position.
- *Exposition:* Interpret the information you have reported and define key terms.
- *Proposition:* Introduce your thesis.

- *Proof:* Provide evidence to support your thesis. These paragraphs will be the heart of your essay, for you cannot be persuasive unless you prove that your position is sound.
- *Refutation of opposing arguments:* Show why you are not convinced by the arguments of people who disagree with you.
- *Conclusion:* Summarize your most important points. Excite emotions appropriate for the occasion. And make your audience personally well-disposed toward you.

If you are using this pattern of organization for writing about a problem for which you have a solution, your solution can be offered under proposition and proof.

However you choose to proceed, refutation is an important part of persuasive writing. Unfortunately, many writers are so firmly committed to their own positions that they fail to demonstrate that they have considered the views of others. Even if they are credible sources advancing sound positions, their ethos suffers because they seem one-sided. Your own writing will benefit if you respond thoughtfully to opposition, and you do not need to wait until the end of your essay to do so. When you are taking an unpopular position, you may need to respond to prevailing views before you can gain a fair hearing for your own views.

RESPONDING TO OPPOSITION

Because persuasion assumes the existence of an audience that has views different from your own, it is essential to recognize these differences and respond to them fairly. One-sided arguments are almost never convincing. To be persuasive, writers must show that they have given consideration to views that differ from their own. After anticipating the arguments most likely to be advanced by opponents, you can respond to these arguments by either refuting them or conceding that they have merit.

Of these two strategies, refutation has been traditionally emphasized in rhetoric. By introducing an opposition argument into your own essay, and then showing why that argument is faulty, you demonstrate good credibility, or ethos, if you respond fairly to that view. You also improve the logos of your case by resolving concerns that readers may be wondering about. Many writers find that the easiest way to introduce opposition arguments without obscuring their own position is to begin a paragraph with an argument offered by opponents and then devote the rest of the paragraph to providing a counterargument. By following this method, they get the chance to have the last word.

When you consider opposition arguments, you may very well find that there is one that you cannot refute. Controversy usually exists because there is at least one good argument that can be made on different sides. If you want to be persuasive, you should be prepared to concede any point that you cannot refute. By admitting that you see merit in one of the arguments made by your opponents, you show that you are fair-minded and make it easier for opponents to recognize merit in your own case. Telling people "I am completely right, and you are completely wrong" is more likely to annoy them than to persuade them. But when you say, in effect, "I admit that you have a good point there," you create a bridge over which people can cross to your side.

Martin Luther King's "Letter from Birmingham Jail" provides examples of both refutation and concession. King responds to specific charges that had been brought against him and demonstrates why these charges were unfair. Writing at a time when the nation was badly divided over the cause he represented, King also anticipates a number of other arguments that could be raised against him and answers them eloquently. At other points, however, he reaches out to establish common ground with his opponents. In the very first paragraph, for example, he states that his critics are "men of genuine good will" who have expressed their views sincerely; later, he tells them, "You express a great deal of anxiety over our willingness to break laws. This is certainly a legitimate concern."

Strategies like these demonstrate that the purpose of "Letter from Birmingham Jail" is very different from the purpose of "I Have a Dream" (which is reprinted in Chapter 8). In "I Have a Dream" King speaks to his supporters and inspires them to hold fast to the beliefs they already hold; in "Letter from Birmingham Jail" King addresses people who disagreed with him and seeks to change their mind. Comparing these two pieces can help you to understand the difference between writing designed primarily to move others and writing designed primarily to persuade others. Like other motives for writing, these two may overlap—hence, the role of pathos within persuasion. But if you choose to inspire feelings as a strategy for persuading people to change their minds about something, remember that persuasion requires other strategies as well—such as reasoning logically, presenting evidence to support claims, and responding thoughtfully to the views of people who disagree with you.

By attempting to overcome the differences that exist between you and your opponents, you are using what Kenneth Burke called *identification*. According to Burke, identification is the necessary corrective to the divisions that exist between people. Even though individuals are distinct and may disagree strongly about a particular issue, they can be united by some principle that they share. Persuasion is achieved by identifying your cause with the interests of your audience. Responding to the clergy of Birmingham, Alabama, King emphasizes that he too is a clergyman and makes numerous theological references. But the principle of identification goes far beyond such overt statements. Once you begin to think about what you have in common with others, including your opponents, you can often detect ties that you had not previously recognized—an important discovery if you are genuinely interested in solving problems and not simply interested in chaulking up points in a debate.

Writing to persuade thus becomes a means of overcoming division and drawing people together. At its crudest levels persuasion may draw people together superficially through means that are manipulative rather than honest: A successful advertising campaign can convince thousands of people to buy a product they really don't need. But when we write about ideas and treat our opponents with respect, we open the way for long-lasting agreements built upon shared beliefs.

Persuasion should thus be conducted honorably. You should never overlook important evidence that operates against your conclusion. And you should never exaggerate or misrepresent views that differ from your own. You will find that some of the writers in this chapter follow these principles, and others seem to lose sight of them. But whatever your own views may be when you attempt to write persuasively, show that you are fair-minded, and be sure that your own position is clear and well supported.

CLEAN UP OR PAY UP

Louis Barbash

Louis Barbash believes that college sports are a "mess," and he proposes a way to clean them up. If you are a fan of college sports, you may not like his proposal, but try not to let a love for sports keep you from evaluating this essay as an argument. Look at the data Barbash provides to support his case; and if the data does not persuade you to accept his proposal, consider whether you could raise any objections that the author has not anticipated.

Tom Scates is one of the lucky ones. He has a bachelor's degree from Georgetown University, where he played basketball under the fabled John Thompson, one of the best college basketball coaches in the country, and one of the few who insist that their players go to class. Ninety percent of Thompson's players at Georgetown receive degrees, about three times the national average.

More than a decade after Tom Scates received his diploma, he has managed to parlay his Georgetown degree and education, his athletic skills, and the character he developed during his career in intercollegiate athletics, into a job as a doorman at a downtown Washington hotel.

Still, Scates *is* one of the lucky ones. He played for a good team at a good school, under a moral coach, and under a president, Father Timothy Healy, who believed that Georgetown was a school with a basketball team, not a basketball team with a school. He was not implicated in drug deals, shoplifting, violence, grade altering, point shaving, or under-the-table money scandals. He didn't have his scholarship yanked. He didn't emerge from school functionally illiterate. He got a job.

Many of the men Scates played against when he was at Georgetown, and their basketball and football counterparts at major colleges and universities, have not been so fortunate. Less than half the football and basketball scholarship athletes will graduate from college. And what education athletes do get is often so poor that it may be irrelevant whether they graduate or not.

In addition to corrupting the university's basic academic mission, big-time sports have been a lightning rod for financial corruption. College athletes are cash-poor celebrities. Although their performance on the field or court produces millions in revenue for the university, they receive in return only their scholarships—tuition, room, and board—and no spending money. They are forbidden from working part-time during the season. Athletes have been caught trying to make money by getting loans from coaches and advisers, selling the shoes and other gear they get as team members, taking allowances from agents, and getting paid for no-show summer jobs provided by jock-sniffing alumni—all violations of National Collegiate Athletic Association (NCAA) rules.

Things might be different if the NCAA would show some real inclination to clean up the college sports mess. But that organization has a well-developed instinct for the capillaries: instead of attacking the large-scale academic, financial, and criminal corruption in college sports, too often the investigators from Mission, Kansas, put their energies into busting athletes for selling their complimentary tickets and coaches for starting their practices a few weeks ahead of schedule. Meanwhile, the real problems of college athletics continue to fester.

Will the NCAA change? And if so, would that matter? Earlier this year, NCAA Executive Director Dick Schultz proposed new rules to stem college sports corruption. Schultz's reforms included "quality academic advising and career-counseling programs," restriction of recruiting, long-term contracts for coaches, reduced pressure and time demands on athletes, and the elimination of athletic dormitories to "make the athlete as indistinguishable from the rest of the student body as is humanly possible."

It's illegal to bet on sports except in Nevada, so bet on this instead: Schultz's proposals will not pass an NCAA dominated by college sports officials whose careers rest on winning games. Recall what has happened to much weaker suggestions. Even Georgetown's Coach Thompson boycotted his own team's games to protest as too severe the timid requirements of the NCAA's Proposition 48, which would have barred entering freshmen from athletic scholarships and competition if they did not have a 2.0 high school GPA and SAT scores totaling 700 points. Interested in even better odds? Take this to the bank: Even if Schultz gets every one of his proposals put in exactly as he outlined them, they—like everything else the NCAA has tried—will not work.

Well then, is there any way out of this mess? Yes. Actually, there are *two* ways out. Because the NCAA has so utterly failed, because in the present system the big-money pressures to cheat are so enormous, and because, like it or not, sports have such a widespread impact on the country's moral climate, there should be a federal law that requires schools *either* to return to the Ivy League ideal in which players are legitimate members of the student body, judged by the same standards as everybody else, *or* to let players on their teams be non-student professionals. All the trouble comes from trying to mix these two alternatives—from trying to achieve big revenues while retaining the veneer of purity.

The pure alternative doesn't have to ignore athletic ability among   10
prospective students—there were plenty of good football teams before today's double-standard disaster got firmly entrenched. You want to consider the athletic ability of college applicants for the same reason you want to consider musical or theatrical ability; a university should be a wonderfully diverse collection of talents that together stimulate people to develop in all sorts of positive ways. Athletic skill is one such talent—one that even academic purists ought to look at. But the key is that universities must consider athletic ability as only *part* of what they take into account when they accept

a student. The fundamental mistake of today's college sports system is that it supposes a student could be at a university *solely* because of his athletic skill.

While the purely amateur option is probably the more desirable of the two, the professional one isn't nearly as horrible as it might seem at first. After all, coaches were originally volunteers, and now they're paid. (Army's first head coach, Dennis Michie, received no pay. Jess Hawley coached for free at Dartmouth from 1923–28. His 1925 team went undefeated and was the national champion.) So why not players?

Sweat Equity

How much would a salaried college athlete make? If the example of minor league baseball is anything to go on—and such authorities as Roger Meiners, a Clemson University economist who specializes in the economics of college sports, and Ed Garvey, the former head of the NFL Players Association, think that it is—college salaries would be enough for a young athlete to live on, but not so much as to bust college budgets. Minor league baseball players start at around $11,000 for their first full professional season and range upward to the neighborhood of $26,000 for players on AAA teams under major league option. So it seems fair to estimate a salary of about $15,000 for an average player on an average team.

The professional option's chief virtue is honesty. The current student-athlete system requires both students and universities to pretend that the young athletes are not full-time professionals, but rather full-time students who play sports in their spare time. But does anyone suppose that high school athletes reading four and five years below grade level would be considered for college admission, much less recruited and given full scholarships, if they were not football or basketball stars? Can the abuses of NCAA rules that have been uncovered at almost half of its biggest schools have any other meaning than that giving these athletes a real education is not what universities are trying to do?

The hypocrisy begins with the fundamental relationship between the players and the university: 18- to 20-year-olds, many of them poorly educated, inner-city blacks, coerced and deceived into playing four years of football or basketball without pay so that the university can sell tickets and television rights.

The coercion comes from the colleges' control of access to professional 15
football or basketball: It is virtually impossible to go to the pros without playing college ball first. Colleges open that opportunity only to athletes who will agree to perform for the college for four years without getting a salary or even holding an outside part-time job. The athlete does receive a four-year scholarship and room and board while he is enrolled, a package the NCAA values at about $40,000. The deception lies in the fact that the inducements held out to athletes by colleges—the chance to play pro ball and getting a college education—are essentially worthless, and the schools know it.

The athlete's first priority is to play pro ball. Forty-four percent of all black scholarship athletes, and 22 percent of white athletes, entertain hopes of playing in the pros. That's why they will play four years for nothing. But in fact, the lure of sports that keeps kids in school is a false hope and a cruel hoax. "The dream in the head of so many youngsters that they will achieve fame and riches in professional sports is touching, but it is also overwhelmingly unrealistic," says Robert Atwell, president of the American Council on Education. The would-be pro faces odds as high as 400–1: of the 20,000 "students" who play college basketball, for example, only 50 will make it to the NBA. The other 19,950 won't. Many of them will wind up like Tom Scates, in minimum wages jobs, or like Reggie Ford, who lost his football scholarship to Northwest Oklahoma State after he injured his knee, and now collects unemployment compensation in South Carolina.

The scholarships and promises of education are also worthless currency. Of every 10 young men who accept scholarships to play football at major schools, according to NCAA statistics, just 4 will graduate. Only 3 of every 10 basketball players receive degrees.

Not only are these athletes being cheated out of a promised education, but they and their universities are forced to erect elaborate, meretricious curricula to satisfy the student-athlete requirement, so of those who *do* get degrees, many receive diplomas that are barely worth the parchment they're printed on. Running back Ronnie Harmon majored in computer science at the University of Iowa, but took only one computer course in his three years of college. Another Iowa football player also majored in computer science, but in his senior year took only courses in billiards, bowling, and football; he followed up by getting a D in a summer school watercolor class. Transcripts of the members of the basketball team at Ohio University list credit for something called "International Studies 69B"—a course composed of a 14-day/10-game trip to Europe.

As things stand now, athletically gifted students who genuinely want an education are often steered away by eligibility-conscious advisers. Jan Kemp, the University of Georgia academic adviser for athletes who won a lawsuit after the university fired her for insisting on the athletes' right to be educated, recalls how a Georgia athlete was always placed in "dummy" classes despite his efforts to take "real" ones. "There's nothing wrong with his mind," says Kemp. "But the situation is magnified for athletes because there is so much money involved. There is too much control over who gets in and who takes what courses."

No case illustrates the cynicism that poisons big-time college sports better than that of former Washington Redskins star defensive end Dexter Manley. Manley spent four years as a "student-athlete" at Oklahoma State University only to emerge, as he admitted years later, functionally illiterate. But OSU President John Campbell was not embarrassed: "There would be those who would argue that Dexter Manley got exactly what he wanted out

20

of OSU. He was able to develop his athletic skills and ability, he was noticed by the pros, he got a pro contract. So maybe we did him a favor by letting him go through the program."

One scarcely knows where to start in on a statement like that. It's appalling that an accredited state university would admit a functional illiterate, even recruit him, and leave him illiterate after four years as a student. It's shocking that it would do all this in order to make money from his unpaid performance as an athlete. And it is little short of grotesque that an educator, entrusted with the education of 20,000 young men and women, would argue that the cynical arrangement between an institution of higher learning and an uneducated high school boy was, after all, a fair bargain.

The infection of hypocrisy spreads from the president's office to the athletic department and coaching staff. This may be the saddest betrayal in the system. These are 17-year-olds, dreaming of a lucrative career in sports. They have placed their faith in the coaches who have visited their homes, solicited their trust, and gotten to know their parents. But those coaches, as Robert Atwell points out, "may have a vested interest in perpetuating the myth rather than pointing out its inherent fallacy." That vested interest, of course, is that if they do not produce winning teams, at whatever cost, they will lose their jobs.

So instead, to recruit highly sought-after high-school athletes, coaches promise playing time, education, and exposure to national TV audiences and professional scouts. But once the player arrives on campus, coaches are under strong pressure to treat him like what he is: an employee, whose needs must be subordinated to the needs of the enterprise, i.e., winning.

Sports without Strings

Gary Ruble, a former scholarship football player at the University of North Carolina, told a House subcommittee investigating college athletics that North Carolina "came to me and offered me, basically, the world. They came to me and said come to our school. Be a student athlete. We will guarantee that you graduate. We will promise you to be a star, et cetera, et cetera, et cetera." But once in Chapel Hill, Ruble found himself riding the bench. "You go in as an offensive lineman, which I was, at 240 pounds, and you go into a system where you have offensive linemen who are 285 and they are telling you that you are going to play. That's an impossibility," Ruble told the subcommittee. After three years, "my position coach called me into his office and stated that I should consider either transferring to another school or dropping out gracefully. I was no longer to be considered in their plans for our team," Ruble says. When he reported back to school anyway, he was told "I had no option of whether to stay or go. They were not allowing me to retain my scholarship."

A system of sports without strings—releasing college athletes and their universities from the pretense that they are students, and instead paying them   25 for their services—would cure the student-athlete system's chief vices: its duplicity and its exploitiveness.

Athletes who want to get started on careers in sports, including those whose only way out of the ghetto may be the slam dunk and the 4.4–40, would find paying jobs in their chosen field. Overnight, thousands of new jobs as professional football and basketball players would be created. Players with the ability to get to the NFL and NBA would get paid during their years of apprenticeship. For those of lesser abilities, playing for college teams would be a career in itself, a career they could start right out of high school and continue as long as skills and bodies allowed. And as they matured and their playing careers drew to a close, the prospect of a real college education might seem more inviting than it did at 17.

Releasing athletes from having to be students would, ironically, make it easier for those who want an education to get it. Even with the best intentions, today's college athletes have little hope of being serious students. Basketball practice, for instance, begins October 15, and the season does not end for the most successful teams until after the NCAA championships in early April; in other words the season starts one month after school begins and ends one month before school is out. During the season, athletes spend six or more hours a day, 30 to 40 hours a week, on practice, viewing game-films, at chalk talks, weight lifting, conditioning, and attending team meetings. The best-prepared students would have difficulty attending to their studies while working 34 hours a week—and these are not the best-prepared students.

But under no-strings sports, athletes who want educations will fare better than they do now, because the pace of their education need not be governed by their eligibility for athletic competition. A football player could play the fall semester and study in the spring. Basketball players, whose season spans the two semesters, might enroll at schools with quarter or trimester systems, or study summers and after their sports careers are over. Instead of being corralled into courses rigged to provide high grades like "Theory of Volleyball," "Recreation and Leisure," "Jogging," and "Leisure Alternatives," athletes would be in a position to take only the courses they want and need. This would be even more likely if, as part of the pro option, universities were still required to offer full scholarships to athletes, to be redeemed whenever the athletes wanted to use them.

Under these changes, those athletes who end up going to college would be doing so because they were pursuing their own educational goals. This reform would replace today's phony jock curriculum with the kind of mature academic choices that made the G.I. Bill such a success.

Such considerations make it clear that it's time for schools to choose   30 between real amateurism and real professionalism. They can't have a little of both. From now on, in college sports, it's got to be either poetry or pros.

Questions for Discussion

1. Consider the introduction to this essay. Why does Barbash begin his argument by providing information about Tom Scates? Why does he wait until the end of paragraph 2 before revealing that Scates is a hotel doorman?
2. Barbash charges that the NCAA concerns itself with only minor rules infractions while "the real problems of college athletics continue to fester." In his view, what are those real problems? How are colleges guilty of "duplicity and exploitiveness" in their dealings with student athletes?
3. Why don't gifted athletes go directly from high school to professional sports? Why are few college athletes likely to become pros?
4. How convincing is the evidence Barbash provides to support his case? How representative are his examples?
5. What would be the advantages of paying student athletes? Can you think of any disadvantages?
6. Explain the pun with which this essay concludes.

Suggestions for Writing

1. Argue for a change in the sports program at your school that would benefit either the program or the school.
2. Barbash claims that many schools have a "jock curriculum" that enables athletes to keep playing even if they are not learning anything important. Imagine a situation in which someone has asked you to identify the easiest courses at your own school. Then write an essay that would persuade that person to take more challenging courses.

THE ENVIRONMENTAL MINDSET

Rush Limbaugh III

> *Reaching an enormous audience through radio and television broadcasts, Rush H. Limbaugh has both delighted and infuriated those who listen to what he has to say. He conveys the impression of a man who is unafraid to speak his mind, especially if he is exposing the foibles of liberals, feminists, and other social activists. As you read the following essay, from his book* The Way Things Ought to Be, *consider whether or not it would persuade someone who was not already sympathetic to his views.*

I used to think that environmentalists were a bunch of political liberals who were just using a different angle to advance their cause. Some of that goes on. But it goes beyond merely advancing liberalism. There are two groups of people that have made environmentalism their new home: socialists and enviro-religious fanatics. And they have chosen two new constituencies which cannot speak or disagree and therefore cannot refuse their "help and assistance": animals and trees.

With the collapse of Marxism, environmentalism has become the new refuge of socialist thinking. The environment is a great way to advance a political agenda that favors central planning and an intrusive government. What better way to control someone's property than to subordinate one's private property rights to environmental concerns.

The second group that has latched on to the environmental movement are people who believe it is a religion; that God is the earth and that God is nothing more than the earth. Actually, it is a modern form of pantheism, where nature is divine. This group wants to preserve the earth at all costs, even if it means that much of the Third World will be forever condemned to poverty. Rather than elevate the Third World, they want to move us closer to Third World conditions. That's somehow cleaner, and purer. It's the way things were before Western white people came along and terrorized the earth by inventing things. They want to roll us back, maybe not to the Stone Age, but at least to the horse-and-buggy era.

Both of these groups are consumed with egocentricity. They behave as though they believe the world began the day they were born and that it's going to end the day they die.

Now, I've spoken about the leaders of the radical environmental move- 5 ment. The followers are also interesting. They are the people who just want to feel good; the people who want to receive accolades for their perceived care and concern for the environment. Then we have the media who willingly serve as conduits for all of these predictions, studies, prophecies, and tall tales that the environmentalist wackos disseminate.

But there are also many average Americans who consider themselves environmentalists. It is quite natural to want a clean planet, with clean water and air for ourselves and our children. It is quite commendable to not want to destroy that which enables us to live. So, if some scientist comes along and is given credibility by the media, it is not surprising that a lot of people believe him. That is how hundreds of thousands of people are mobilized for the cause and end up on the Mall in Washington and in Central Park in New York.

What these decent people have to realize is that regardless of what perspective they have—socialist, religious, or whatever—a common characteristic of those in the radical environmental movement is the belief that private property rights will have to be severely curbed in this country. That's what is behind the move to take private land out of circulation to preserve wetlands, and the efforts to save the spotted owl. If it rains in your backyard one day and you have an inch of water there, all of a sudden your yard becomes a wetland and you can't build anything there.

This hostility to private property, my friends, is based on the belief that human beings can't be trusted to own very much of the land; that we are selfish and cursed with the desire to change nature. We are 4 percent of the world's population here in America and we use 25 percent of the world's resources. How dare we be so selfish. Never mind the fact that our country feeds the world. Never mind the fact that our technology has improved life everywhere on this planet.

I believe that many environmental leaders are quite sincere, but that they all operate from a fundamentally different viewpoint than most other people. You and I and the vast majority of other people work for a living. We hold jobs in which we produce something or perform a service. We create commerce.

Most of the people running environmental groups don't work. What they do is persuade other people to donate to their cause. They live well, with a fair amount being siphoned off for expenses, conferences, and high salaries. They've become dependent on the income from donations. These people want to improve their standard of living and so they have to build up their donations. There are only so many people who will give to create bird sanctuaries in this country. That's why some environmentalists have gone into crisis mongering to increase the level of their donations. Their appeals and their scare tactics are designed to transform people into foot soldiers in the army of doomsday environmentalism.

It's interesting to note which environmental hazards these people really worry about. It is those that are caused by business or man-made things. Consider the danger of radon gas. If there is one environmental problem that is real, it is radon. Some Easterners have homes where radon seeps in from under the ground and reaches levels many times beyond what is considered safe. But there is no hysteria over radon. Why? Because it's natural, man didn't put it there. There are no dramatic calls for radon studies, nor any calls for evacuations. Everything that happens in their deified nature is somehow acceptable. Things will work themselves out. Well, man-made disasters can also work themselves out. Take the *Exxon Valdez* spill. We were told that the cleanup would take hundreds of years. Now we see that through natural processes and the incredibly resilient powers of the planet, the tide has taken care of much of the damage that man didn't clean up. And, would you believe that more fish were caught last year than ever before in Prince William Sound.

My friends, the earth is a remarkable creation and is capable of great rejuvenation. We can't destroy it. It can fix itself. We shouldn't go out of our way to do damage, but neither should we buy into the hysteria and monomania which preaches, in essence, that we don't belong here. We have a right to use the earth to make our lives better.

Questions for Discussion

1. To what social factors does Limbaugh attribute interest in preserving the environment? How fairly does he characterize environmentalists?
2. How does Limbaugh explain the interest of "average Americans" in preserving the environment?
3. In paragraph 3, Limbaugh claims that environmental preservation "means that much of the Third World will be forever condemned to poverty." What do you think he means? Is economic development dependent upon the exploitation of natural resources?
4. Why does Limbaugh believe that environmentalism threatens property rights? What does his emphasis on private property reveal about his sense of audience?
5. Consider how Limbaugh uses "my friends" when addressing his audience. How do you respond to this strategy?

Suggestions for Writing

1. Research the *Exxon Valdez* oil spill, or another major oil spill, and determine whether or not "natural processes and the incredibly resilient powers of the planet" prevented permanent environmental damage.
2. Write about an environmental problem outside the United States, and determine what steps, if any, can be taken to resolve it.

WHAT'S WRONG WITH ANIMAL RIGHTS

Vicki Hearne

Vicki Hearne is an animal trainer whose work has led her to believe, "the problem with the animal-rights advocates is not that they take it too far; it's that they've got it all wrong. Consider the extent to which she herself seems to care about animals, and notice how she uses personal experience to support her claims.

Not all happy animals are alike. A Doberman going over a hurdle after a small wooden dumbbell is sleek, all arcs of harmonious power. A basset hound cheerfully performing the same exercise exhibits harmonies of a more lugubrious nature. There are chimpanzees who love precision the way musicians or fanatical housekeepers or accomplished hypochondriacs do; others for whom happiness is a matter of invention and variation—chimp vaudevillians. There is a rhinoceros whose happiness, as near as I can make out, is in needing to be trained every morning, all over again, or else he "forgets" his circus routine, and in this you can find a clue to the slow, deep, quiet chuckle of his happiness and to the glory of the beast. Happiness for Secretariat° is in his ebullient bound, that joyful length of stride. For the draft horse or the weight-pull dog, happiness is of a different shape, most awesome and less obviously intelligent. When the pulling horse is at its more intense, the animal goes into himself, allocating all of the educated power that organizes his desire to dwell in fierce and delicate intimacy with that power, leans into the harness, and MAKES THAT SUCKER MOVE.

If we are speaking of human beings and use the phrase "animal happiness," we tend to mean something like "creature comforts." The emblems of this are the golden retriever rolling in the grass, the horse with his nose deep in the oats, the kitty by the fire. Creature comforts are important to animals—"Grub first, then ethics" is a motto that would describe many a wise Labrador retriever, and I have a pit bull named Annie whose continual quest for the perfect pillow inspires her to awesome feats. But there is something more to animals, a capacity for satisfactions that come from work in the fullest sense—what is known in philosophy and in this country's Declaration of Independence as "happiness." This is a sense of personal achievement, like the satisfaction felt by a good wood-carver or a dancer or a poet or an accomplished dressage horse. It is a happiness that, like the artist's, must come from something within the animal, something trainers call "talent." Hence, it cannot be imposed on the animal. But it is also something that does not come *ex nihilo*.° If it had not been a fairly ordinary thing, in

---

Secretariat: A very successful racehorse.   *ex nihilo:* Latin for "out of nothing."

one part of the world, to teach young children to play the pianoforte, it is doubtful that Mozart's music would exist.

Happiness is often misunderstood as a synonym for pleasure or as an antonym for suffering. But Aristotle associated happiness with ethics— codes of behavior that urge us toward the sensation of getting it right, a kind of work that yields the "click" of satisfaction upon solving a problem or surmounting an obstacle. In his *Ethics,* Aristotle wrote, "If happiness is activity in accordance with excellence, it is reasonable that it should be in accordance with the highest excellence." Thomas Jefferson identified the capacity for happiness as one of the three fundamental rights on which all others are based: "life, liberty, and the pursuit of happiness."

I bring up this idea of happiness as a form of work because I am an animal trainer, and work is the foundation of the happiness a trainer and an animal discover together. I bring up these words also because they cannot be found in the lexicon of the animal-rights movement. This absence accounts for the uneasiness toward the movement of most people, who sense that rights advocates have a point but take it too far when they liberate snails or charge that goldfish at the county fair are suffering. But the problem with the animal-rights advocates is not that they take it too far; it's that they've got it all wrong.

Animal rights are built upon a misconceived premise that rights were created to prevent us from unnecessary suffering. You can't find an animal-rights book, video, pamphlet, or rock concert in which someone doesn't mention the Great Sentence, written by Jeremy Bentham in 1789. Arguing in favor of such rights, Bentham wrote: "The question is not, Can they *reason?* nor, can they *talk?* but, can they suffer?"

The logic of the animal-rights movement places suffering at the iconographic center of a skewed value system. The thinking of its proponents— given eerie expression in a virtually sadopornographic sculpture of a tortured monkey that won a prize for its compassionate vision—has collapsed into a perverse conundrum. Today the loudest voices calling for— demanding—the destruction of animals are the humane organizations. This is an inevitable consequence of the apotheosis of the drive to relieve suffering: death is the ultimate release. To compensate for their contradictions, the humane movement has demonized, in this century and the last, those who made animal happiness their business: veterinarians, trainers, and the like. We think of Louis Pasteur as the man whose work saved you and me and your dog and cat from rabies, but antivivisectionists of the time claimed that rabies increased in areas where there were Pasteur Institutes.

An anti-rabies public relations campaign mounted in England in the 1880s by the Royal Society for the Prevention of Cruelty to Animals and other organizations led to orders being issued to club any dog found not wearing a muzzle. England still has her cruel and unnecessary law that requires an animal to spend six months in quarantine before being allowed loose in the country. Most of the recent propaganda about pit bulls—the crazy claim that they "take hold with their front teeth while they chew away with their rear teeth" (which would imply, incorrectly, that they have double jaws)—can be traced to literature published by the Humane Society of the United States during the fall of 1987 and earlier. If your neighbors want your dog or horse impounded and destroyed because he is a nuisance—say the dog barks, or the horse attracts flies—it will be the local Humane Society to whom your neighbors turn for action.

In a way, everyone has the opportunity to know that the history of the humane movement is largely a history of miseries, arrests, prosecutions, and death. The Humane Society is the pound, the place with the decompression chamber or the lethal injections. You occasionally find worried letters about this in Ann Landers's column.

Animal-rights publications are illustrated largely with photographs of two kinds of animals—"Helpless Fluff" and "Agonized Fluff," the two conditions in which some people seem to prefer their animals, because any other version of an animal is too complicated for propaganda. In the introduction to his book *Animal Liberation,* Peter Singer says somewhat smugly that he and his wife have no animals and, in fact, don't much care for them. This is offered as evidence of his objectivity and ethical probity. But it strikes me as an odd, perhaps obscene underpinning for an ethical project that encourages university and high school students to cherish their ignorance of, say, great bird dogs as proof of their devotion to animals.

I would like to leave these philosophers behind, for they are inept 10 connoisseurs of suffering who might revere my Airedale for his capacity to scream when subjected to a blowtorch but not for his wit and courage, not for his natural good manners that are a gentle rebuke to ours. I want to celebrate the moment not long ago when, at his first dog show, my Airedale, Drummer, learned that there can be a public place where his work is respected. I want to celebrate his meticulousness, his happiness upon realizing at the dog show that no one would swoop down upon him and swamp him with the goo-goo excesses known as the "teddy-bear complex" but that people actually got out of his way, gave him room to work. I want to say, "There can be a six-and-a-half-month-old puppy who can care about accuracy, who can be fastidious, and whose fastidiousness will be a foundation for courage later." I want to say, "Leave my puppy alone!"

I want to leave the philosophers behind, but I cannot, in part because the philosophical problems that plague academicians of the animal-rights movement are illuminating. They wonder, do animals have rights or do they have interests? Or, if these rightists lead particularly unexamined lives, they dismiss that question as obvious (yes, of course animals have rights, prima facie) and proceed to enumerate them, James Madison style. This leads to the issuance of bills of rights—the right to an environment, the right not to be used in medical experiments—and other forms of trivialization.

The calculus of suffering can be turned against the philosophers of festering flesh, even in the case of food animals, or exotic animals who perform in movies and circuses. It is true that it hurts to be slaughtered by man, but it doesn't hurt nearly as much as some of the cunningly cruel arrangements meted out by "Mother Nature." In Africa, 75 percent of the lions cubbed do not survive to the age of two. For those who make it to two, the average age at death is ten years. Asali, the movie and TV lioness, was still working at age twenty-one. There are fates worse than death, but twenty-one years of a close working relationship with Hubert Wells, Asali's trainer, is not one of them. Dorset sheep and polled Herefords would not exist at all were they not in a symbiotic relationship with human beings.

A human being living in the "wild"—somewhere, say, without the benefits of medicine and advanced social organization—would probably have a life expectancy of from thirty to thirty-five years. A human being living in "captivity"—in, say, a middle-class neighborhood of what the Centers for Disease Control call a Metropolitan Statistical Area—has a life expectancy of seventy or more years. For orangutans in the wild in Borneo and Malaysia, the life expectancy is thirty-five years; in captivity, fifty years. The wild is not a suffering-free zone or all that frolicsome a location.

The questions asked by animal-rights activists are flawed, because they are built on the concept that the origin of rights is in the avoidance of suffering rather than in the pursuit of happiness. The question that needs to be asked—and that will put us in closer proximity to the truth—is not, do they have rights? or, what are those rights? but rather, what is a right?

Rights originate in committed relationships and can be found, both 15 intact and violated, wherever one finds such relationships—in social compacts, within families, between animals, and between people and nonhuman animals. This is as true when the nonhuman animals in question are lions or parakeets as when they are dogs. It is my Airedale whose excellencies have my attention at the moment, so it is with reference to him that I will consider the question, what is a right?

When I imagine situations in which it naturally arises that A defends or honors or repects B's rights, I imagine situations in which the relationship between A and B can be indicated with a possessive pronoun. I might say, "Leave her alone, she's my daughter" or "That's what she wants, and she is my daughter. I think I am bound to honor her wants." Similarly, "Leave her alone, she's my mother." I am more tender of the happiness of my mother, my father, my child, than I am of other people's family members; more tender of my friends' happinesses than your friends' happinesses, unless you and I have a mutual friend.

Possession of a being by another has come into more and more disrepute, so that the common understanding of one person possessing another is slavery. But the important detail about the kind of possessive pronoun that I have in mind is reciprocity: if I have a friend, she has a friend. If I have a daughter, she has a mother. The possessive does not bind one of us while freeing the other; it cannot do that. Moreover, should the mother reject the daughter, the word that applies is "disown." The form of disowning that most often appears in the news is domestic violence. Parents abuse children; husbands batter wives.

Some cases of reciprocal possessives have built-in limitations, such as "my patient/my doctor" or "my student/my teacher" or "my agent/my client." Other possessive relations are extremely limited but still remarkably binding: "my neighbor" and "my country" and "my president."

The responsibilities and the ties signaled by reciprocal possession typically are hard to dissolve. It can be as difficult to give up an enemy as to give up a friend, and often the one becomes the other, as though the logic of the possessive pronoun outlasts the forms it chanced to take at a given moment, as though we were stuck with one another. In these bindings, nearly inextricable, are found the origin of our rights. They imply a possessiveness but also recognize an acknowledgment by each side of the other's existence.

The idea of democracy is dependent on the citizens' having knowledge   20
of the government; that is, realizing that the government exists and knowing how to claim rights against it. I know this much because I get mail from the government and see its "representatives" running about in uniforms. Whether I actually have any rights in relationship to the government is less clear, but the idea that I do is symbolized by the right to vote. I obey the government, and, in theory, it obeys me, by counting my ballot, reading the *Miranda* warning to me, agreeing to be bound by the Constitution. My friend obeys me as I obey her; the government "obeys" me to some extent, and, to a different extent, I obey it.

What kind of thing can my Airedale, Drummer, have knowledge of? He can know that I exist and through that knowledge can claim his happinesses, with varying degrees of success, both with me and against me. Drummer can also know about larger human or dog communities than the one that consists only of him and me. There is my household—the other dogs, the cats, my husband. I have had enough dogs on campuses to know that he can learn that Yale exists as a neighborhood or village. My older dog, Annie, not only knows that Yale exists but can tell Yalies from townies, as I learned while teaching there during labor troubles.

Dogs can have elaborate conceptions of human social structures, and even of something like their rights and responsibilities within them, but these conceptions are never elaborate enough to construct a rights relationship between a dog and the state, or a dog and the Humane Society. Both of these are concepts that depend on writing and memoranda, officers in uniform, plaques and seals of authority. All of these are literary constructs, and all of them are beyond a dog's ken, which is why the mail carrier who doesn't also happen to be a dog's friend is forever an intruder—this is why dogs bark at mailmen.

It is clear enough that natural rights relations can arise between people and animals. Drummer, for example, can insist, "Hey, let's go outside and do something!" if I have been at my computer several days on end. He can both refuse to accept various of my suggestions and tell me when he fears for his life—such as the time when the huge, white flapping flag appeared out of nowhere, as it seemed to him, on the town green one evening when we were working. I can (and do) say to him either, "Oh, you don't have to

worry about that" or, "Uh oh, you're right, Drum, that guy looks dangerous." Just as the government and I—two different species of organism—
have developed improvised ways of communicating, such as the vote, so
Drummer and I have worked out a number of ways to make our expressions
known. Largely through obedience, I have taught him a fair amount about
how to get responses from me. Obedience is reciprocal; you cannot get
responses from a dog to whom you do not respond accurately. I have enfran-
chised him in a relationship to me by educating him, creating the conditions
by which he can achieve a certain happiness specific to a dog, maybe even
specific to an Airedale, inasmuch as this same relationship has allowed me to
plumb the happiness of being a trainer and writing this article.

Instructions in this happiness are given terms that are alien to a culture
in which liver treats, fluffy windup toys, and miniature sweaters are confused
with respect and work. Jack Knox, a sheepdog trainer originally from Scot-
land, will shake his crook at a novice handler who makes a promiscuous
move to praise a dog, and will call out in his Scottish accent, "Eh! Eh! Get
back, get BACK! Ye'll no be abusin' the dogs like that in my clinic." America
is a nation of abused animals, Knox says, because we are always swooping at
them with praise, "no gi'ing them their freedom." I am reminded of Rainer
Maria Rilke's account in which the Prodigal Son leaves—has to leave—
because everyone loves him, even the dogs love him, and he has no path to
the delicate and fierce truth of himself. Unconditional praise and love, in
Rilke's story, disenfranchise us, distract us from what truly excites our
interest.

In the minds of some trainers and handlers, praise is dishonesty. Para-   25
doxically, it is a kind of contempt for animals that masquerades as a reverence
for helplessness and suffering. The idea of freedom means that you do not,
at least not while Jack Knox is nearby, helpfully guide your dog through the
motions of, say, herding over and over—what one trainer calls "explainy-
wainy." This is rote learning. It works tolerably well on some handlers,
because people have vast unconscious minds and can store complex prepro-
grammed behaviors. Dogs, on the other hand, have almost no unconscious
minds, so they can learn only by thinking. Many children are like this until
educated out of it.

If I tell my Airedale to sit and stay on the town green, and someone
comes up and burbles, "What a pretty thing you are," he may break his stay
to go for a caress. I pull him back and correct him for breaking. Now he
holds his stay because I have blocked his way to movement but not because
I have punished him. (A correction blocks one path as it opens another for
desire to work; punishment blocks desire and opens nothing.) He holds his
stay now, and—because the stay opens this possibility of work, new to a
heedless young dog—he watches. If the person goes on talking, and isn't
going to gush with praise, I may heel Drummer out of his stay and give him
an "Okay" to make friends. Sometimes something about the person makes
Drummer feel that reserve is in order. He responds to an insincere approach

by sitting still, going down into himself, and thinking, "This person has no business pawing me. I'll sit very still, and he will go away." If the person doesn't take the hint from Drummer, I'll give the pup a little backup by saying, "Please don't pet him, he's working," even though he was not under any command.

The pup reads this, and there is a flicker of a working trust now stirring in the dog. Is the pup grateful? When the stranger leaves, does he lick my hand, full of submissive blandishments? This one doesn't. This one says nothing at all, and I say nothing much to him. This is a working trust we are developing, not a mutual congratulation society. My backup is praise enough for him; the use he makes of my support is praise enough for me.

Listening to a dog is often praise enough. Suppose it is just after dark and we are outside. Suddenly there is a shout from the house. The pup and I both look toward the shout and then toward each other: "What do you think?" I don't so much as cock my head, because Drummer is growing up, and I want to know what he thinks. He takes a few steps toward the house, and I follow. He listens again and comprehends that it's just Holly, who at fourteen is much given to alarming cries and shouts. He shrugs at me and goes about his business. I say nothing. To praise him for this performance would make about as much sense as praising a human being for the same thing. Thus:

A. What's that?

B. I don't know. [Listens] Oh, it's just Holly.

A. What a gooooooood human being!

B. Huh?

This is one small moment in a series of like moments that will culminate in an Airedale who on a Friday will have the discrimination and confidence required to take down a man who is attacking me with a knife and on Saturday clown and play with the children at the annual Orange Empire Dog Club Christmas party.

People who claim to speak for animal rights are increasingly devoted   *30* to the idea that the very keeping of a dog or a horse or a gerbil or a lion is in and of itself an offense. The more loudly they speak, the less likely they are to be in a rights relation to any given animal, because they are spending so much time in airplanes or transmitting fax announcements of the latest Sylvester Stallone anti-fur rally. In a 1988 *Harper's* forum, for example, Ingrid Newkirk, the national director of People for the Ethical Treatment of Animals, urged that domestic pets be spayed and neutered and ultimately phased out. She prefers, it appears, wolves—and wolves someplace else—to Airedales and, by a logic whose interior structure is both emotionally and intellectually forever closed to Drummer, claims thereby to be speaking for "animal rights."

She is wrong. I am the only one who can own up to my Airedale's inalienable rights. Whether or not I do it perfectly at any given moment is no more refutation of this point than whether I am perfectly my husband's mate at any given moment refutes the fact of marriage. Only people who know Drummer, and whom he can know, are capable of this relationship. PETA and the Humane Society and the ASPCA and the Congress and NOW—as institutions—do have the power to affect my ability to grant rights to Drummer but are otherwise incapable of creating conditions or laws or rights that would increase his happiness. Only Drummer's owner has the power to obey him—to obey who he is and what he is capable of— deeply enough to grant him his rights and open up the possibility of happiness.

Questions for Discussion

1. Hearne opens her essay by stating, "Not all animals are alike." Why is it useful for her to make this point before moving on to discuss animal rights?
2. How does Hearne define *happiness?* How does it differ from *pleasure?*
3. In paragraphs 12–13 Hearne observes that both animals and human beings live longer in "captivity" than in "the wild." In doing so, she assumes that a longer life expectancy is desirable and implies that conditions that extend life expectancy are preferable to those that shorten it. Do you agree?
4. According to Hearne, how are "rights" tied to "committed relationships"?
5. What does Hearne mean by "reciprocal possessives," and what advantage does she see coming from them?
6. Consider the way Hearne concludes her essay by discussing her relationship with Drummer. What does this discussion illustrate?

Suggestions for Writing

1. Although Hearne appears to be a responsible pet owner, many people buy a dog or cat on impulse and then neglect the animal. Imagine an audience of people who leave their pets unattended and confined in poor conditions. Then write an essay persuading them to take better care of their pets.
2. Much of the public concern over animal rights has focused on the use of animals in scientific experimentation. Write an argument for or against the use of animals in medical or psychological research.

TOURIST, STAY HOME

Haunani-Kay Trask

Hawaii—or Hawai'i as it is called by native Hawaiians—was an indepen-
dent kingdom until 1893, when the monarchy was overthrown. In 1900 it
was annexed by the United States, and in 1959 it became the fiftieth state.
Native Hawaiians are now a minority, and as the following article shows, they
have serious concerns about what has happened to the land that was once theirs.
As you read Trask's argument, which is adapted from her book From a Native
Daughter: Colonialism and Sovereignty in Hawai'i, *note how she em-*
phasizes the consequences of tourism—the most common way other Americans
experience her native land.

Most Americans have come to believe that Hawai'i is as American as
hotdogs and CNN. Worse, they assume that they, too, may make the trip,
following the path of the empire into the sweet and sunny land of palm trees
and hula-hula girls.

Increasing numbers of us not only oppose this predatory view of my
native land and culture, we angrily and resolutely defy it. On January 17,
1993, thousands of Hawai'ians demonstrated against continued American
control of our homeland. Marking the 100th anniversary of the overthrow
of our native government by U.S. Marines and missionary-descended sugar
barons, Hawaiian nationalists demanded recognition of our status as native
people with claims to a land base and political self-determination.

For us, native self-government has always been preferable to American
foreign government. No matter what Americans believe, most of us in the
colonies do not feel grateful that our country was stolen along with our
citizenship, our lands, and our independent place among the family of
nations. We are not happy natives.

For us, American colonialism has been a violent process—the violence
of mass death, the violence of American missionizing, the violence of cultural destruction, the violence of the American military. Through the overthrow and annexation, American control and American citizenship replaced
Hawaiian control and Hawaiian citizenship. Our mother—our heritage and
our inheritance—was taken from us. We were orphaned in our own land.
Such brutal changes in a people's identity, its legal status, its government, its
sense of belonging to a nation, are considered among the most serious
human-rights violations by the international community today.

As we approach the Twenty-first Century, the effects of colonization   5
are obvious: outmigration of the poor amounting to a diaspora, institution-
alization in the military and prisons, continued land dispossession by the
state and Federal governments and multinational corporations, and grotesque commodification of our culture through corporate tourism.

This latest affliction has meant a particularly insidious form of cultural prostitution. Just five hours by plane from California, Hawai'i is a thousand light years away in fantasy. Mostly a state of mind, Hawai'i is the image of escape from the rawness and violence of daily American life. *Hawai'i*—the word, the image, the sound in the mind—is the fragrance and feel of soft kindness. Above all, Hawai'i is "she," the Western image of the native "female" in her magical allure. And if luck prevails, some of "her" will rub off on you, the visitor.

The predatory reality of tourism is visible everywhere: in garish "Polynesian" revues; commercial ads using Hawaiian dance and language to sell vacations and condominiums: the trampling of sacred *heiau* (temples) and burial grounds as tourist recreation sites. Thus, our world-renowned native dance, the *hula,* has been made ornamental, a form of hotel exotica for the gaping tourist. And Hawaiian women are marketed on posters from Paris to Tokyo promising an unfettered "primitive" sexuality. Far from encouraging a cultural revival, as tourist industry apologists contend, tourism has appropriated and prostituted the accomplishments of a resurgent interest in things Hawaiian (the use of replicas of Hawaiian artifacts such as fishing and food implements, capes, helmets, and other symbols of ancient power, to decorate hotels).

As the pimp for the cultural prostitution business, the state of Hawai'i pours millions into the tourist industry, even to the extent of funding a private booster club—the Hawai'i Visitors' Bureau—to the tune of $30 million a year. Radio and television propaganda tells locals "the more you give" to tourism, "the more you get."

What Hawaiians get is population densities as high as Hong Kong in some areas, a housing shortage owing to staggering numbers of migrants from Asia and the continental United States, a soaring crime rate as impoverished locals prey on ostentatiously rich tourists, and environmental crises, including water depletion, that threaten the entire archipelago. Rather than stop the flood, the state is projecting a tidal wave of twelve million tourists by the year 2010. Today, we Hawaiians exist in an occupied country. We are a hostage people, forced to witness and participate in our own collective humiliation as tourist artifacts for the First World.

Meanwhile, shiploads and planeloads of American military forces continue to pass through Hawai'i on their way to imperialist wars in Asia and elsewhere. Every major Hawaiian island has lost thousands of acres to military bases, private beaches, and housing areas. On the most populous island of O'ahu, for example, fully 30 per cent of the land is in military hands. 10

Unlike other native peoples in the United States, we have no separate legal status to control our land base. We are, by every measure, a colonized people. As a native nation, Hawaiians are no longer self-governing.

Because of these deplorable conditions, and despite the fact that we are less than 20 per cent of the million-and-a-quarter residents of Hawai'i, native Hawaiians have begun to assert our status as a people. Like the Palestinians, the Northern Irish, and the Indians of the Americas, we have started on a path of decolonization.

Beginning with the land struggles in the 1970s, and continuing with occupations, mass protests, and legislative and legal maneuvering in the 1980s and 1990s, Hawaiian resistance has matured into a full-blown nationalist struggle.

The contours of this struggle are both simple and complex. We want to control our own land base, government, and economy. We want to establish a nation-to-nation relationship with the U.S. Government, and with other native nations. We want control over water and other resources on our land base, and we want our human and civil rights acknowledged and protected.

In 1921, Congress set aside 200,000 acres of homesteading lands specifically for Hawaiians. We are fighting for control of these lands, as well as approximately 1.2 million acres of the Kingdom of Hawai'i illegally transferred by the white oligarchy to the United States in 1898. Called the "trust" lands because the Federal and state governments allegedly hold them in "trust" for the Hawaiian people, this land base is currently used for all manner of illegal activities, including airports, military reservations, public schools, parks, and county refuse sites, even private businesses and homes. Because of this long record of abuse, and because nationhood means self-determination and not wardship, Hawaiians are organized and lobbying for return of the "trust" lands to the Hawaiian people.

To this end, we have re-created our own political entity, *Ka Lāhui Hawai'i,* a native initiative for self-government. At our first Constitutional Convention in 1987, we devised a democratic form of government, with a Kai'āina or governor, a legislature and judges, elders, and chief advisory councils. We have made treaties with other native nations, and we have diplomatic representatives in many places. We want recognition as a sovereign people.

Sovereignty, as clearly defined by our citizens in 1987, is "the ability of a people who share a common culture, religion, language, value system, and land base to exercise control over their lands and lives, independent of other nations." We lay claim to the trust lands as the basis of our nation.

While we organized in Hawaiian communities, the state of Hawai'i created an Office of Hawaiian Affairs, or OHA, in 1980. Ostensibly for representation of Hawaiian rights by Hawaiians (the only group allowed to vote for its all-native trustees), OHA was powerless as a mechanism for self-government. It had no control over trust lands, and no statutory strength to prevent abuses of native culture. For the next ten years, OHA supported reparations for the overthrow and forcible annexation to the United States, rather than recognition and restoration of our nationhood.

Because OHA is a state agency beholden to the reigning Democratic Party, it has made no claims for a land base against the state. Arguing that they represented Hawaiians rather than the state, OHA trustees made an agreement with the governor—an unprincipled Hawaiian named John Waihe‘e—to settle all ceded lands claims. OHA was to receive over $100 million in 1991, then $8.5 million annually. No lands were to be transferred. They would instead be lost to Hawaiians forever.

As a result of humiliating public criticism from the Hawaiian com- 20 munity for OHA's sell-out role in this deal, OHA proposed a kind of quasi-sovereign condition which it would oversee. In direct opposition to the Ka Lāhui model of a "nation-to-nation" relationship with the Federal Government, OHA argued that the governing structure of the Hawaiian nation, landless though it might be, should come under the state of Hawai‘i.

There were several problems with this position. OHA was not representative of all Hawaiian communities and never had been, because voting procedures gave too much weight to the most populous island of O‘ahu, resulting in a skewed underrepresentation of neighbor island people. Any lands or monies transferred by the Federal Government to OHA would go to the state, not to the Hawaiian people, since OHA was a state agency; this would mean *less,* not more, control by Hawaiians over their future. Giving OHA nation status would be akin to calling the Bureau of Indian Affairs an Indian nation. And finally, state control of Hawaiians, even under an alleged "Office of Hawaiian Affairs," is still wardship, not self-determination.

While the tide of native resistance swelled, a coordinated state strategy emerged. First, Governor Waihe‘e came out in favor of a landless model of a "nation-within-a-nation." Speaking as if he invented the concept and never once mentioning Ka Lāhui's leadership, Waihe‘e publicly advocated Federal recognition of Hawaiians as a native nation. In his "state of the state" address immediately following the January 17 commemoration, Waihe‘e called for Hawaiian sovereignty to be devised by an OHA-led constitutional convention and funded by the state legislature. OHA supported the governor's efforts.

After nearly two decades of organizing, forces for and against sovereignty were clearly drawn: the state of Hawai‘i and its Bureau of Indian Affairs clone, the Office of Hawaiian Affairs, supported continued wardship of our people under the tutelage of OHA; Ka Lāhui Hawai‘i, a native initiative for self-government, supported self-determination on a definable land base with Federal recognition of our nationhood.

While OHA and the governor submitted legislation mandating the constitutional convention, Ka Lāhui's membership soared to 16,000 enrolled citizens. As the largest sovereignty organization, Ka Lāhui now poses a substantial threat to the legitimacy of OHA. Sensing this danger, and hoping to head off our own efforts in Washington, D.C., Waihe‘e traveled to the American capital to float the notion of an OHA-type nation with President Clinton and his Secretary of the Interior. As we pass the midpoint of this centennial year, the state strategy appears to be Federal recognition, but no real "nation-within-a-nation" on the order of the American Indian nations. A land base is out of the question.

For Hawaiians, the stakes are high indeed: self-determination, or the *25* yoke of perpetual wardship. In the meantime, marginalization and exploitation of Hawaiians, our culture, and our lands, continues, while corporate tourism thrives on nearly seven million visitors a year (thirty tourists for every native). In the face of Hawaiian resistance, it's still business as usual.

If OHA is successful, the Hawaiian people will be burdened with yet another agency, non-Hawaiian in design and function, set in place to prevent rather than fulfill native autonomy. Historically, the decline of Hawaiians and our culture is directly traceable to land dispossession. Therefore, any attempt to address Hawaiian sovereignty which does not return control of lands to Hawaiians is doomed to fail.

Like agencies created by the Federal government to short-circuit Indian sovereignty, OHA will be a top-down institution whose architects envision an extension of the state of Hawai'i rather than a native initiative to promote self-government.

Elsewhere in the Pacific, native peoples struggle with the same dilemma.

The Maori, like the Hawaiians a minority in their own land, have been dispossessed through conquest and occupation by a foreign white people, and have suffered psychologically from cultural suppression. They, too, have been demanding a form of sovereignty, seeking identity and cultural integrity by returning to their lands. And they have supported Hawaiian resistance, as fellow Polynesians and as fellow colonized people.

In Tahiti, a strong independence movement has captured the mayor- *30* ship of the second-largest city while uniting antinuclear, labor, and native nationalist forces to resist French colonialism. With others in the Pacific, Tahitians have spearheaded the nuclear-free and independent Pacific movements.

Aborigines, Kanaks, East Timorese, and Belauans focus world attention on genocide and military imperialism. And for each of these indigenous peoples, there is the familiar, predictable struggle for self-determination.

If Hawaiians are not alone in the Pacific Basin, our struggle for self-determination is certainly unknown across most of the North American continent, particularly to the hordes of tourists who inundate our beautiful but fragile islands. In this United Nations "Year of Indigenous People," a willful ignorance about native nationhood prevails in the dominant society. Given this, and given the collaborationist politics within colony Hawai'i, whatever successes my people do achieve will be won slowly and at great expense.

For those who might feel a twinge of solidarity with our cause, let me leave this final thought: Don't come to Hawai'i. We don't need any more tourists. If you want to help, pass this message on to your friends.

Questions for Discussion

1. Why do native Hawaiians believe that they are living in an American colony? Does the history of Hawaii justify this view?
2. In what sense is tourism "predatory"? How do mainland tourists exploit Hawaiian culture? Why does the state of Hawaii continue to promote tourism?
3. How are native Hawaiians treated differently from other native peoples in the United States?
4. What is the difference between *Ka Lāhui Hawai'i* and the Office of Hawaiian Affairs? How do their goals differ?
5. In paragraphs 28–31, Trask links the Hawaiian movement for self-determination with other movements elsewhere in the Pacific. What does she achieve by doing so?

Suggestions for Writing

1. Research the circumstances under which the United States took control of Hawaii, and then write an essay defending or criticizing this annexation.
2. If you think the economy of your state would benefit from increased tourism, write an argument that would make your state appealing to readers elsewhere in the country.

THE DECLARATION OF INDEPENDENCE

Thomas Jefferson

> *A time-honored way to organize an argument is to begin by presenting assumptions that provide a foundation for the argument that follows. Look closely at the assumptions with which Jefferson begins, and think about what they mean. Notice also Jefferson's language. Although "The Declaration of Independence" has become part of our national heritage, it began as a writing assignment that went through a number of different drafts. Before approving this document on July 4, 1776, Congress made twenty-four changes and deleted over three hundred words. As you read the final draft, ask yourself how you would respond if given the chance to edit Jefferson. Would you vote to adopt the declaration exactly as it stands, or would you recommend any changes?*

When in the course of human events, it becomes necessary for one people to dissolve the political bands which have connected them with another, and to assume among the powers of the earth, the separate and equal station to which the Laws of Nature and of Nature's God entitle them, a decent respect to the opinions of mankind requires that they should declare the causes which impel them to the separation.

We hold these truths to be self-evident, that all men are created equal, that they are endowed by their Creator with certain unalienable rights, that among these are life, liberty and the pursuit of happiness. That to secure these rights, governments are instituted among men, deriving their just powers from the consent of the governed. That whenever any form of government becomes destructive of these ends, it is the right of the people to alter or to abolish it, and to institute new government, laying its foundation on such principles and organizing its powers in such form, as to them shall seem most likely to effect their safety and happiness. Prudence, indeed, will dictate that governments long established should not be changed for light and transient causes; and accordingly all experience hath shown, that mankind are more disposed to suffer, while evils are sufferable, than to right themselves by abolishing the forms to which they are accustomed. But when a long train of abuses and usurpations, pursuing invariably the same object, evinces a design to reduce them under absolute despotism, it is their right, it is their duty, to throw off such government, and to provide new guards for their future security. Such has been the patient sufferance of these Colonies; and such is now the necessity which constrains them to alter their former systems of government. This history of the present King of Great Britain is a history of repeated injuries and usurpations, all having in direct object the establishment of an absolute tyranny over these States. To prove this, let facts be submitted to a candid world.

He has refused his assent to laws, the most wholesome and necessary for the public good.

He has forbidden his Governors to pass laws of immediate and pressing importance, unless suspended in their operation till his assent should be obtained; and when so suspended, he has utterly neglected to attend to them.

He has refused to pass other laws for the accommodation of large   5
districts of people, unless those people would relinquish the right of representation in the legislature, a right inestimable to them and formidable to tyrants only.

He has called together legislative bodies at places unusual, uncomfortable, and distant from the depository of their public records, for the sole purpose of fatiguing them into compliance with his measures.

He has dissolved representative houses repeatedly, for opposing with manly firmness his invasions on the rights of the people.

He has refused for a long time, after such dissolutions, to cause others to be elected; whereby the legislative powers, incapable of annihilation, have returned to the people at large for their exercise; the State remaining in the meantime exposed to all the dangers of invasion from without and convulsions within.

He has endeavoured to prevent the population of these states; for that purpose obstructing the laws for naturalization of foreigners; refusing to pass others to encourage their migration hither, and raising the conditions of new appropriations of lands.

He has obstructed the administration of justice, by refusing his assent   10
to laws for establishing judiciary powers.

He has made judges dependent on his will alone, for the tenure of their offices, and the amount and payment of their salaries.

He has erected a multitude of new offices, and sent hither swarms of officers to harass our people, and eat out their substance.

He has kept among us, in times of peace, standing armies without the consent of our legislatures.

He has affected to render the military independent of and superior to the civil power.

He has combined with others to subject us to a jurisdiction foreign to   15
our constitution, and unacknowledged by our laws; giving his assent to their acts of pretended legislation:

For quartering large bodies of armed troops among us:

For protecting them, by a mock trial, from punishment for any murders which they should commit on the inhabitants of these States:

For cutting off our trade with all parts of the world:

For imposing taxes on us without our consent:

For depriving us in many cases of the benefits of trial by jury: 20

For transporting us beyond seas to be tried for pretended offences:

For abolishing the free system of English laws in a neighbouring Province, establishing therein an arbitrary government, and enlarging its boundaries so as to render it at once an example and fit instrument for introducing the same absolute rule into these Colonies:

For taking away our Charters, abolishing our most valuable laws, and altering fundamentally the forms of our governments:

For suspending our own legislatures, and declaring themselves invested with power to legislate for us in all cases whatsoever.

He has abdicated government here, by declaring us out of his protec-   *25* tion and waging war against us.

He has plundered our seas, ravaged our coasts, burnt our towns, and destroyed the lives of our people.

He is at this time transporting large armies of foreign mercenaries to complete the works of death, desolation and tyranny, already begun with circumstances of cruelty and perfidy scarcely paralleled in the most barbarous ages, and totally unworthy the head of a civilized nation.

He has constrained our fellow citizens taken captive on the high seas to bear arms against their country, to become the executioners of their friends and brethren, or to fall themselves by their hands.

He has excited domestic insurrections amongst us, and has endeavoured to bring on the inhabitants of our frontiers, the merciless Indian savages, whose known rule of welfare, is an undistinguished destruction of all ages, sexes, and conditions.

In every stage of these oppressions we have petitioned for redress in   *30* the most humble terms: our repeated petitions have been answered only by repeated injury. A prince whose character is thus marked by every act which may define a tyrant is unfit to be the ruler of a free people.

Nor have we been wanting in attention to our British brethren. We have warned them from time to time of attempts by their legislature to extend an unwarrantable jurisdiction over us. We have reminded them of the circumstances of our emigration and settlement here. We have appealed to their native justice and magnanimity, and we have conjured them by the ties of our common kindred to disavow these usurpations, which would inevitably interrupt our connections and correspondence. They too have been deaf to the voice of justice and consanguinity. We must, therefore, acquiesce in the necessity, which denounces our separation, and hold them, as we hold the rest of mankind, enemies in war, in peace friends.

We, therefore, the Representatives of the United States of America, in General Congress assembled, appealing to the Supreme Judge of the world for the rectitude of our intentions, do, in the name, and by authority of the good people of these Colonies, solemnly publish and declare, That these United Colonies are, and of right ought to be, Free and Independent States; that they are absolved from all allegiance to the British Crown, and that all political connection between them and the state of Great Britain, is and ought to be totally dissolved; and that as Free and Independent States, they have full power to levy war, conclude peace, contract alliances, establish commerce, and to do all other acts and things which Independent States may of right do. And for the support of this declaration, with a firm reliance on the protection of Divine Providence, we mutually pledge to each other our lives, our fortunes, and our sacred honor.

Questions for Discussion

1. What do you think Jefferson meant by "men" in paragraph 2? What does it mean to have "unalienable rights"? And what do you think "the pursuit of happiness" means?
2. Jefferson begins his argument with truths that he declares to be "self-evident." Do any of the statements in paragraph 2 strike you as open to dispute?
3. Of the various charges Jefferson makes against King George III, which do you think are the most serious?
4. How fairly has Jefferson treated Native Americans in this document?
5. Has Jefferson taken any steps to protect his fellow colonists from the charge that they were acting rashly in declaring independence?
6. Modern conventions governing capitalization differ from those that were observed in the eighteenth century. When first published, paragraph 32 of "The Declaration of Independence" began with a reference to the "Representatives of the united States of America." Is there a difference between "united States of America" and "United States of America"?

Suggestions for Writing

1. Slavery was legal in this country for almost a hundred years after the Declaration of Independence, and women were not allowed to vote in national elections until 1920. Do you think that there are people living in this country today who still do not enjoy rights to "life, liberty, and the pursuit of happiness"? If so, write a "declaration of independence" in support of their rights.
2. According to Jefferson, George III was a tyrant guilty of "cruelty and perfidy scarcely paralleled in the most barbarous ages." Do research on George III, and then write an argument on his behalf.

HERE COMES THE GROOM

Andrew Sullivan

In recent decades gay and lesbian Americans have become a recognized political force. While they have improved their legal status in some ways, they have also encountered deep-rooted resistance and do not yet enjoy all the rights held by the heterosexual majority. The following essay argues on behalf of gay civil marriage: marriages legally entered into and recognized by the government. As you read, note how the author bases his case upon appeals to traditional family values.

Last month in New York, a court ruled that a gay lover had the right to stay in his deceased partner's rent-control apartment because the lover qualified as a member of the deceased's family. The ruling deftly annoyed almost everybody. Conservatives saw judicial activism in favor of gay rent control: three reasons to be appalled. Chastened liberals (such as the *New York Times* editorial page), while endorsing the recognition of gay relationships, also worried about the abuse of already stretched entitlements that the ruling threatened. What neither side quite contemplated is that they both might be right, and that the way to tackle the issue of unconventional relationships in conventional society is to try something both more radical and more conservative than putting courts in the business of deciding what is and is not a family. That alternative is the legalization of civil gay marriage.

The New York rent-control case did not go anywhere near that far, which is the problem. The rent-control regulations merely stipulated that a "family" member had the right to remain in the apartment. The judge ruled that to all intents and purposes a gay lover is part of his lover's family, inasmuch as a "family" merely means an interwoven social life, emotional commitment, and some level of financial interdependence.

It's a principle now well established around the country. Several cities have "domestic partnership" laws, which allow relationships that do not fit into the category of heterosexual marriage to be registered with the city and qualify for benefits that up till now have been reserved for straight married couples. San Francisco, Berkeley, Madison, and Los Angeles all have legislation, as does the politically correct Washington, D.C., suburb, Takoma Park. In these cities, a variety of interpersonal arrangements qualify for health insurance, bereavement leave, insurance, annuity and pension rights, housing rights (such as rent-control apartments), adoption and inheritance rights. Eventually, according to gay lobby groups, the aim is to include federal income tax and veterans' benefits as well. A recent case even involved the right to use a family member's accumulated frequent-flier points. Gays are not the only beneficiaries; heterosexual "live-togethers" also qualify.

There's an argument, of course, that the current legal advantages extended to married people unfairly discriminate against people who've shaped their lives in less conventional arrangements. But it doesn't take a genius to see that enshrining in the law a vague principle like "domestic partnership" is an invitation to qualify at little personal cost for a vast array of entitlements otherwise kept crudely under control.

To be sure, potential DPs have to prove financial interdependence, *5* shared living arrangements, and a commitment to mutual caring. But they don't need to have a sexual relationship or even closely mirror old-style marriage. In principle, an elderly woman and her live-in nurse could qualify. A couple of uneuphemistically confirmed bachelors could be DPs. So could two close college students, a pair of seminarians, or a couple of frat buddies. Left as it is, the concept of domestic partnership could open a Pandora's box of litigation and subjective judicial decision-making about who qualifies. You either are or are not married; it's not a complex question. Whether you are in a "domestic partnership" is not so clear.

More important, the concept of domestic partnership chips away at the prestige of traditional relationships and undermines the priority we give them. This priority is not necessarily a product of heterosexism. Consider heterosexual couples. Society has good reason to extend legal advantages to heterosexuals who choose the formal sanction of marriage over simply living together. They make a deeper commitment to one another and to society; in exchange, society extends certain benefits to them. Marriage provides an anchor, if an arbitrary and weak one, in the chaos of sex and relationships to which we are all prone. It provides a mechanism for emotional stability, economic security, and the healthy rearing of the next generation. We rig the law in its favor not because we disparage all forms of relationship other than the nuclear family, but because we recognize that not to promote marriage would be to ask too much of human virtue. In the context of the weakened family's effect upon the poor, it might also invite social disintegration. One of the worst products of the New Right's "family values" campaign is that its extremism and hatred of diversity has disguised this more measured and more convincing case for the importance of the marital bond.

The concept of domestic partnership ignores these concerns, indeed directly attacks them. This is a pity, since one of its most important objectives—providing some civil recognition for gay relationships—is a noble cause and one completely compatible with the defense of the family. But the way to go about it is not to undermine straight marriage; it is to legalize old-style marriage for gays.

The gay movement has ducked this issue primarily out of fear of division. Much of the gay leadership clings to notions of gay life as essentially outsider, anti-bourgeois, radical. Marriage, for them, is co-optation into straight society. For the Stonewall generation,° it is hard to see how this

---

Stonewall generation: the generation of gay people came of age during the 1970s. When police raided a gay bar named Stonewall in June 1969, the customers fought back. Although the struggle for gay rights had begun many years earlier, the Stonewall rebellion marked the beginning of a new era in gay activism.

vision of conflict will ever fundamentally change. But for many other gays—
my guess, a majority—while they don't deny the importance of rebellion
20 years ago and are grateful for what was done, there's now the sense of a
new opportunity. A need to rebel has quietly ceded to a desire to belong.
To be gay and to be bourgeois no longer seems such an absurd proposition.
Certainly since AIDS, to be gay and to be responsible has become a necessity.

Gay marriage squares several circles at the heart of the domestic partnership debate. Unlike domestic partnership, it allows for recognition of gay
relationships, while casting no aspersions on traditional marriage. It merely
asks that gays be allowed to join in. Unlike domestic partnership, it doesn't
open up avenues for heterosexuals to get benefits without the responsibilities of marriage, or a nightmare of definitional litigation. And unlike domestic partnership, it harnesses to an already established social convention
the yearnings for stability and acceptance among a fast-maturing gay
community.

Gay marriage also places more responsibilities upon gays: it says for   10
the first time that gay relationships are not better or worse than straight
relationships, and that the same is expected of them. And it's clear and
dignified. There's a legal benefit to a clear, common symbol of commitment. There's also a personal benefit. One of the ironies of domestic partnership is that it's not only more complicated than marriage, it's more
demanding, requiring an elaborate statement of intent to qualify. It amounts
to a substantial invasion of privacy. Why, after all, should gays be required to
prove commitment before they get married in a way we would never dream
of asking of straights?

Legalizing gay marriage would offer homosexuals the same deal society now offers heterosexuals: general social approval and specific legal advantages in exchange for a deeper and harder-to-extract-yourself-from
commitment to another human being. Like straight marriage, it would
foster social cohesion, emotional security, and economic prudence. Since
there's no reason gays should not be allowed to adopt or be foster parents, it
could also help nurture children. And its introduction would not be some
sort of radical break with social custom. As it has become more acceptable
for gay people to acknowledge their loves publicly, more and more have
committed themselves to one another for life in full view of their families
and their friends. A law institutionalizing gay marriage would merely reinforce a healthy social trend. It would also, in the wake of AIDS, qualify as a
genuine public health measure. Those conservatives who deplore promis-
cuity among some homosexuals should be among the first to support it.
Burke° could have written a powerful case for it.

The argument that gay marriage would subtly undermine the unique
legitimacy of straight marriage is based upon a fallacy. For heterosexuals,

---

Burke: Edmund Burke (1729–1797), Irish statesman and political philosopher much admired by
conservatives.

straight marriage would remain the most significant—and only legal—social bond. Gay marriage could only delegitimize straight marriage if it were a real alternative to it, and this is clearly not true. To put it bluntly, there's precious little evidence that straights could be persuaded by any law to have sex with—let alone marry—someone of their own sex. The only possible effect of this sort would be to persuade gay men and women who force themselves into heterosexual marriage (often at appalling cost to themselves and their families) to find a focus for their family instincts in a more personally positive environment. But this is clearly a plus, not a minus: gay marriage could both avoid a lot of tortured families and create the possibility for many happier ones. It is not, in short, a denial of family values. It's an extension of themselves.

Of course, some would claim that any legal recognition of homosexuality is a de facto attack upon heterosexuality. But even the most hardened conservatives recognize that gays are a permanent minority and aren't likely to go away. Since persecution is not an option in a civilized society, why not coax gays into traditional values rather than rail incoherently against them?

There's a less elaborate argument for gay marriage: it's good for gays. It provides role models for young gay people who, after the exhilaration of coming out, can easily lapse into short-term relationships and insecurity with no tangible goal in sight. My own guess is that most gays would embrace such a goal with as much (if not more) commitment as straights. Even in our society as it is, many lesbian relationships are virtual textbook cases of monogamous commitment. Legal gay marriage could also help bridge the gulf often found between gays and their parents. It could bring the essence of gay life—a gay couple—into the heart of the traditional straight family in a way the family can most understand and the gay offspring can most easily acknowledge. It could do as much to heal the gay-straight rift as any amount of gay rights legislation.

If these arguments sound socially conservative, that's no accident. It's 15 one of the richest ironies of our society's blind spot toward gays that essentially conservative social goals should have the appearance of being so radical. But gay marriage is not a radical step. It avoids the mess of domestic partnership; it is humane; it is conservative in the best sense of the word. It's also practical. Given the fact that we already allow legal gay relationships, what possible social goal is advanced by framing the law to encourage those relationships to be unfaithful, undeveloped, and insecure?

Questions for Discussion

1. Sullivan originally subtitled this essay "A (Conservative) Case for Gay Marriage." To what conservative values does he appeal? Why would conservatives be an appropriate audience for this piece? What is the implication of putting "Conservative" within parentheses?

2. Why is Sullivan opposed to domestic partnership laws? Why does he believe that marriages should be encouraged by government?
3. How would gay and lesbian Americans benefit from being allowed to enter into marriages recognized by the law?
4. In paragraph 11 Sullivan raises the possibility of gay and lesbian couples adopting children. Does this idea strengthen or weaken his case for legitimizing gay and lesbian marriages?
5. Where does Sullivan address the concerns of people opposed to providing legal recognition of homosexuality? Are there any arguments that he has overlooked?

Suggestions for Writing

1. Write an argument for or against allowing gay and lesbian couples to adopt children.
2. As the divorce rate reveals, getting married is no guarantee of staying married. Research the laws governing marriage and divorce in your state, and then write an essay defending them as they stand or advocating a change that you believe necessary.

LETTER FROM BIRMINGHAM JAIL IN RESPONSE TO PUBLIC STATEMENT BY EIGHT ALABAMA CLERGYMEN

Martin Luther King, Jr.

By 1963 the movement for civil rights for African-Americans had become a national issue, and the United States was bitterly divided between people who perceived this movement as a threat to social order and others who recognized that social justice required serious changes in our country. A few months before he delivered "I Have a Dream" from the steps of the Lincoln Memorial (see pp. 371–75), King led a nonviolent campaign to end segregation in Birmingham, Alabama. He was jailed as a result for eight days—one of fourteen times he was imprisoned because of his work for civil rights. While in jail, he read a published statement by eight prominent clergymen who condemned his work and supported the police. King began his response by writing in the margins of the newspaper in which he had been denounced, continued it on scraps of paper supplied by a prison trustee, and concluded on a pad that his attorneys were eventually allowed to give him. Here is the letter to which King responded, followed by his reply. As you read, be alert for how King defends himself from the charges brought against him.

April 12, 1963

We the undersigned clergymen are among those who, in January, is-sued "An Appeal for Law and Order and Common Sense," in dealing with racial problems in Alabama. We expressed understanding that honest con-victions in racial matters could properly be pursued in the courts, but urged that decisions of those courts should in the meantime be peacefully obeyed.

Since that time there had been some evidence of increased forbearance and a willingness to face facts. Responsible citizens have undertaken to work on various problems which cause racial friction and unrest. In Birmingham, recent public events have given indication that we all have opportunity for a new constructive and realistic approach to racial problems.

However, we are now confronted by a series of demonstrations by some of our Negro citizens, directed and led in part by outsiders. We rec-ognize the natural impatience of people who feel that their hopes are slow in being realized. But we are convinced that these demonstrations are un-wise and untimely.

We agree rather with certain local Negro leadership which has called for honest and open negotiation of racial issues in our area. And we believe this kind of facing of issues can best be accomplished by citizens of our own metropolitan area, white and Negro, meeting with their knowledge and experience of the local situation. All of us need to face that responsibility and find proper channels for its accomplishment.

Just as we formerly pointed out that "hatred and violence have no   5
sanction in our religious and political traditions," we also point out that such
actions as incite to hatred and violence, however technically peaceful those
actions may be, have not contributed to the resolution of our local problems.
We do not believe that these days of new hope are days when extreme
measures are justified in Birmingham.

We commend the community as a whole, and the local news media
and law enforcement officials in particular, on the calm manner in which
these demonstrations have been handled. We urge the public to continue to
show restraint should the demonstrations continue, and the law enforcement
officials to remain calm and continue to protect our city from violence.

We further strongly urge our own Negro community to withdraw
support from these demonstrations, and to unite locally in working peacefully for a better Birmingham. When rights are consistently denied, a cause
should be pressed in the courts and in negotiations among local leaders, and
not in the streets. We appeal to both our white and Negro citizenry to
observe the principles of law and order and common sense.

Signed by:

C. C. J. Carpenter, D.D., LL.D., *Bishop of Alabama*
Joseph A. Durick, D.D., *Auxiliary Bishop, Diocese of Mobile, Birmingham*
Rabbi Milton L. Grafman, *Temple Emanu-El, Birmingham, Alabama*
Bishop Paul Hardin, *Bishop of the Alabama-West Florida Conference of the*
    Methodist Church
Bishop Nolan B. Harmon, *Bishop of the North Alabama Conference of the*
    Methodist Church
George M. Murray, D.D., LL.D., *Bishop Coadjutor, Episcopal Diocese of*
    Alabama
Edward V. Ramage, *Moderator, Synod of the Alabama Presbyterian Church in*
    the United States
Earl Stallings, *Pastor, First Baptist Church, Birmingham, Alabama*

Following is the letter Martin Luther King, Jr., wrote in response to the
clergymen's public statement.

April 16, 1963

My Dear Fellow Clergymen:

While confined here in the Birmingham city jail, I came across your
recent statement calling my present activities "unwise and untimely." Seldom do I pause to answer criticism of my work and ideas. If I sought to
answer all the criticisms that cross my desk, my secretaries would have little
time for anything other than such correspondence in the course of the day,

and I would have no time for constructive work. But since I feel that you are men of genuine good will and that your criticisms are sincerely set forth, I want to try to answer your statement in what I hope will be patient and reasonable terms.

I think I should indicate why I am here in Birmingham, since you have been influenced by the view which argues against "outsiders coming in." I have the honor of serving as president of the Southern Christian Leadership Conference, an organization operating in every southern state, with headquarters in Atlanta, Georgia. We have some eighty-five affiliated organizations across the South, and one of them is the Alabama Christian Movement for Human Rights. Frequently we share staff, educational and financial resources with our affiliates. Several months ago the affiliate here in Birmingham asked us to be on call to engage in a nonviolent direct-action program if such were deemed necessary. We readily consented, and when the hour came we lived up to our promise. So I, along with several members of my staff, am here because I was invited here. I am here because I have organizational ties here.

But more basically, I am in Birmingham because injustice is here. Just 10 as the prophets of the eighth century B.C. left their villages and carried their "thus saith the Lord" far beyond the boundaries of their home towns, and just as the Apostle Paul left his village of Tarsus and carried the gospel of Jesus Christ to the far corners of the Greco-Roman world, so am I compelled to carry the gospel of freedom beyond my own home town. Like Paul, I must constantly respond to the Macedonian call for aid.

Moreover, I am cognizant of the interrelatedness of all communities and states. I cannot sit idly by in Atlanta and not be concerned about what happens in Birmingham. Injustice anywhere is a threat to justice everywhere. We are caught in an inescapable network of mutuality, tied in a single garment of destiny. Whatever affects one directly, affects all indirectly. Never again can we afford to live with the narrow, provincial "outside agitator" idea. Anyone who lives inside the United States can never be considered an outsider anywhere within its bounds.

You deplore the demonstrations taking place in Birmingham. But your statement, I am sorry to say, fails to express a similar concern for the conditions that brought about the demonstrations. I am sure that none of you would want to rest content with the superficial kind of social analysis that deals merely with effects and does not grapple with underlying causes. It is unfortunate that demonstrations are taking place in Birmingham, but it is even more unfortunate that the city's white power structure left the Negro community with no alternative.

In any nonviolent campaign there are four basic steps: collection of the facts to determine whether injustices exist; negotiation; self-purification; and direct action. We have gone through all these steps in Birmingham. There can be no gainsaying the fact that racial injustice engulfs this community. Birmingham is probably the most thoroughly segregated city in the

United States. Its ugly record of brutality is widely known. Negroes have experienced grossly unjust treatment in the courts. There have been more unsolved bombings of Negro homes and churches in Birmingham than in any other city in the nation. These are the hard, brutal facts of the case. On the basis of these conditions, Negro leaders sought to negotiate with the city fathers. But the latter consistently refused to engage in good-faith negotiation.

Then, last September, came the opportunity to talk with leaders of Birmingham's economic community. In the course of the negotiations, certain promises were made by the merchants—for example, to remove the stores' humiliating racial signs. On the basis of these promises, the Reverend Fred Shuttlesworth and the leaders of the Alabama Christian Movement for Human Rights agreed to a moratorium on all demonstrations. As the weeks and months went by, we realized that we were the victims of a broken promise. A few signs, briefly removed, returned; the others remained.

As in so many past experiences, our hopes had been blasted, and the   15
shadow of deep disappointment settled upon us. We had no alternative except to prepare for direct action, whereby we would present our very bodies as a means of laying our case before the conscience of the local and the national community. Mindful of the difficulties involved, we decided to undertake a process of self-purification. We began a series of workshops on nonviolence, and we repeatedly asked ourselves: "Are you able to accept blows without retaliating?" "Are you able to endure the ordeal of jail?" We decided to schedule our direct-action program for the Easter season, realizing that except for Christmas, this is the main shopping period of the year. Knowing that a strong economic-withdrawal program would be the by-product of direct action, we felt that this would be the best time to bring pressure to bear on the merchants for the needed change.

Then it occurred to us that Birmingham's mayoral election was coming up in March, and we speedily decided to postpone action until after election day. When we discovered that the Commissioner of Public Safety, Eugene "Bull" Connor,° had piled up enough votes to be in the run-off, we decided again to postpone action until the day after the run-off so that the demonstrations could not be used to cloud the issues. Like many others, we waited to see Mr. Connor defeated, and to this end we endured postponement after postponement. Having aided in this community need, we felt that our direct-action program could be delayed no longer.

You may well ask: "Why direct action? Why sit-ins, marches and so forth? Isn't negotiation a better path?" You are quite right in calling for negotiation. Indeed, this is the very purpose of direct action. Nonviolent direct action seeks to create such a crisis and foster such a tension that a

---

Eugene "Bull" Connor: Commissioner of Public Safety in Birmingham during 1937–1953 and 1957–1963. One of three commissioners responsible for governing Birmingham, and the commissioner with the most seniority, Connor (1897–1973) was a powerful opponent of integration who used the police to make war on civil rights demonstrators.

community which has constantly refused to negotiate is forced to confront the issue. It seeks so to dramatize the issue that it can no longer be ignored. My citing the creation of tension as part of the work of the nonviolent-resister may sound rather shocking. But I must confess that I am not afraid of the word "tension." I have earnestly opposed violent tension, but there is a type of constructive, nonviolent tension which is necessary for growth. Just as Socrates felt that it was necessary to create a tension in the mind so that individuals could rise from the bondage of myths and half-truths to the unfettered realm of creative analysis and objective appraisal, so must we see the need for nonviolent gadflies to create the kind of tension in society that will help men rise from the dark depths of prejudice and racism to the majestic heights of understanding and brotherhood.

The purpose of our direct-action program is to create a situation so crisis-packed that it will inevitably open the door to negotiation. I therefore concur with you in your call for negotiation. Too long has our beloved Southland been bogged down in a tragic effort to live in monologue rather than dialogue.

One of the basic points in your statement is that the action that I and my associates have taken in Birmingham is untimely. Some have asked: "Why didn't you give the new city administration time to act?" The only answer that I can give to this query is that the new Birmingham administration must be prodded about as much as the outgoing one, before it will act. We are sadly mistaken if we feel that the election of Albert Boutwell as mayor will bring the millennium to Birmingham. While Mr. Boutwell is a much more gentle person than Mr. Connor, they are both segregationists, dedicated to maintenance of the status quo. I have hope that Mr. Boutwell will be reasonable enough to see the futility of massive resistance to deseg-regation. But he will not see this without pressure from devotees of civil rights. My friends, I must say to you that we have not made a single gain in civil rights without determined legal and nonviolent pressure. Lamentably, it is an historical fact that privileged groups seldom give up their privileges voluntarily. Individuals may see the moral light and voluntarily give up their unjust posture; but, as Reinhold Niebuhr has reminded us, groups tend to be more immoral than individuals.

We know through painful experience that freedom is never voluntarily   20
given by the oppressor; it must be demanded by the oppressed. Frankly, I have yet to engage in a direct-action campaign that was "well timed" in the view of those who have not suffered unduly from the disease of segregation. For years now I have heard the word "Wait!" It rings in the ear of every Negro with piercing familiarity. This "Wait" has almost always meant "Never." We must come to see, with one of our distinguished jurists, that "justice too long delayed is justice denied."

We have waited for more than 340 years for our constitutional God-given rights. The nations of Asia and Africa are moving with jetlike speed toward gaining political independence, but we still creep at horse-and-buggy pace toward gaining a cup of coffee at a lunch counter. Perhaps it is easy for those who have never felt the stinging darts of segregation to say, "Wait." But when you have seen vicious mobs lynch your mothers and fathers at will and drown your sisters and brothers at whim; when you have seen hate-filled policemen curse, kick, and even kill your black brothers and sisters; when you see the vast majority of your twenty million Negro brothers smothering in an airtight cage of poverty in the midst of an affluent society; when you suddenly find your tongue twisted and your speech stammering as you seek to explain to your six-year-old daughter why she can't go to the public amusement park that has just been advertised on television, and see tears welling up in her eyes when she is told that Funtown is closed to colored children, and see ominous clouds of inferiority beginning to form in her little mental sky, and see her beginning to distort her personality by developing an unconscious bitterness toward white people; when you have to concoct an answer for a five-year-old son who is asking: "Daddy, who do white people treat colored people so mean?"; when you take a cross-country drive and find it necessary to sleep night after night in the uncomfortable corners of your automobile because no motel will accept you; when you are humiliated day in and day out by nagging signs reading "white" and "colored"; when your first name becomes "nigger," your middle name becomes "boy" (however old you are) and your last name becomes "John," and your wife and mother are never given the respected title "Mrs."; when you are harried by day and haunted by night by the fact that you are a Negro, living constantly at tiptoe stance, never quite knowing what to expect next, and are plagued with inner fears and outer resentments; when you are forever fighting a degenerating sense of "nobodiness"—then you will understand why we find it difficult to wait. There comes a time when a cup of endurance runs over, and men are no longer willing to be plunged into the abyss of despair. I hope, sirs, you can understand our legitimate and unavoidable impatience.

You express a great deal of anxiety over our willingness to break laws. This is certainly a legitimate concern. Since we so diligently urge people to obey the Supreme Court's decision of 1954 outlawing segregation in the public schools, at first glance it may seem rather paradoxical for us consciously to break laws. One may well ask: "How can you advocate breaking some laws and obeying others?" The answer lies in the fact that there are two types of laws: just and unjust. I would be the first to advocate obeying just laws. One has not only a legal but a moral responsibility to obey just laws. Conversely, one has a moral responsibility to disobey unjust laws. I would agree with St. Augustine that "an unjust law is no law at all."

Now, what is the difference between the two? How does one determine whether a law is just or unjust? A just law is a man-made code that squares with the moral law or the law of God. An unjust law is a code that is out of harmony with the moral law. To put it in the terms of St. Thomas Aquinas: An unjust law is a human law that is not rooted in eternal law and natural law. Any law that uplifts human personality is just. Any law that degrades human personality is unjust. All segregation statutes are unjust because segregation distorts the soul and damages the personality. It gives the segregator a false sense of superiority and the segregated a false sense of inferiority. Segregation, to use the terminology of the Jewish philosopher Martin Buber, substitutes an "I–it" relationship for an "I–thou" relationship and ends up relegating persons to the status of things. Hence, segregation is not only politically, economically and sociologically unsound, it is morally wrong and sinful. Paul Tillich has said that sin is separation. Is not segregation an existential expression of man's tragic separation, his awful estrangement, his terrible sinfulness? Thus it is that I can urge men to obey the 1954 decision of the Supreme Court, for it is morally right; and I can urge them to disobey segregation ordinances, for they are morally wrong.

Let us consider a more concrete example of just and unjust laws. An unjust law is a code that a numerical or power majority group compels a minority group to obey but does not make binding on itself. This is *difference* made legal. By the same token, a just law is a code that a majority compels a minority to follow and that it is willing to follow itself. This is *sameness* made legal.

Let me give another explanation. A law is unjust if it is inflicted on a minority that, as a result of being denied the right to vote, had no part in enacting or devising the law. Who can say that the legislature of Alabama which set up that state's segregation laws was democratically elected? Throughout Alabama all sorts of devious methods are used to prevent Negroes from becoming registered voters, and there are some counties in which, even though Negroes constitute a majority of the population, not a single Negro is registered. Can any law enacted under such circumstances be considered democratically structured?

Sometimes a law is just on its face and unjust in its application. For instance, I have been arrested on a charge of parading without a permit. Now, there is nothing wrong in having an ordinance which requires a permit for a parade. But such an ordinance becomes unjust when it is used to maintain segregation and to deny citizens the First-Admendment privilege of peaceful assembly and protest.

I hope you are able to see the distinction I am trying to point out. In no sense do I advocate evading or defying the law, as would the rabid segregationist. That would lead to anarchy. One who breaks an unjust law must do so openly, lovingly, and with a willingness to accept the penalty. I submit that an individual who breaks a law that conscience tells him is unjust, and who willingly accepts the penalty of imprisonment in order to arouse the conscience of the community over its injustice, is in reality expressing the highest respect for law.

Of course, there is nothing new about this kind of civil disobedience. It was evidenced sublimely in the refusal of Shadrach, Meshach and Abednego to obey the laws of Nebuchadnezzar, on the ground that a higher moral law was at stake. It was practiced superbly by the early Christians, who were willing to face hungry lions and the excruciating pain of chopping blocks rather than submit to certain unjust laws of the Roman Empire. To a degree, academic freedom is a reality today because Socrates practiced civil disobedience. In our own nation, the Boston Tea Party represented a massive act of civil disobedience.

We should never forget that everything Adolf Hitler did in Germany was "legal" and everything the Hungarian freedom fighters° did in Hungary was "illegal." It was "illegal" to aid and comfort a Jew in Hitler's Germany. Even so, I am sure that, had I lived in Germany at the time, I would have aided and comforted my Jewish brothers. If today I lived in a Communist country where certain principles dear to the Christian faith are suppressed I would openly advocate disobeying that country's antireligious laws.

I must make two honest confessions to you, my Christian and Jewish   30
brothers. First, I must confess that over the past few years I have been gravely disappointed with the white moderate. I have almost reached the regrettable conclusion that the Negro's great stumbling block in his stride toward freedom is not the White Citizen's Counciler or the Ku Klux Klanner, but the white moderate, who is more devoted to "order" than to justice; who prefers a negative peace which is the presence of tension to a positive peace which is the presence of justice; who constantly says: "I agree with you in the goal you seek, but I cannot agree with your methods of direct action"; who paternalistically believes he can set the timetable for another man's freedom; who lives by a mythical concept of time and who constantly advises the Negro to wait for a "more convenient season." Shallow understanding from people of good will is more frustrating than absolute misunderstanding from people of ill will. Lukewarm acceptance is much more bewildering than outright rejection.

I had hoped that the white moderate would understand that law and order exist for the purpose of establishing justice and that when they fail in this purpose they become the dangerously structured dams that block the flow of social progress. I had hoped that the white moderate would understand that the present tension in the South is a necessary phase of the transition from an obnoxious negative peace, in which the Negro passively accepted his unjust plight, to a substantive and positive peace, in which all men will respect the dignity and worth of human personality. Actually, we who engage in nonviolent direct action are not the creators of tension. We merely bring to the surface the hidden tension that is already alive. We bring it out in the open, where it can be seen and dealt with. Like a boil that can never be cured so long as it is covered up but must be opened with all its ugliness to the natural medicines of air and light, injustice must be exposed,

---

Hungarian freedom fighters: In 1956 Hungarian citizens rose up against the Communist dictatorship in their country. Their revolt was suppressed when the Soviet Union responded by sending tanks into Budapest.

with all the tension its exposure creates, to the light of human conscience and the air of national opinion before it can be cured.

In your statement you assert that our actions, even though peaceful, must be condemned because they precipitate violence. But is this a logical assertion? Isn't this like condemning a robbed man because his possession of money precipitated the evil act of robbery? Isn't this like condemning Socrates because his unswerving commitment to truth and his philosophical inquiries precipitated the act by the misguided populace in which they made him drink hemlock? Isn't this like condemning Jesus because his unique God-consciousness and never-ceasing devotion to God's will precipitated the evil act of crucifixion? We must come to see that, as the federal courts have consistently affirmed, it is wrong to urge an individual to cease his efforts to gain his basic constitutional rights because the quest may precipitate violence. Society must protect the robbed and punish the robber.

I had also hoped that the white moderate would reject the myth concerning time in relation to the struggle for freedom. I have just received a letter from a white brother in Texas. He writes: "All Christians know that the colored people will receive equal rights eventually, but it is possible that you are in too great a religious hurry. It has taken Christianity almost two thousand years to accomplish what it has. The teachings of Christ take time to come to earth." Such an attitude stems from a tragic misconception of time, from the strangely irrational notion that there is something in the very flow of time that will inevitably cure all ills. Actually, time itself is neutral; it can be used either destructively or constructively. More and more I feel that the people of ill will have used time much more effectively than have the people of good will. We will have to repent in this generation not merely for the hateful words and actions of the bad people but for the appalling silence of the good people. Human progress never rolls in on wheels of inevitability; it comes through the tireless efforts of men willing to be co-workers with God, and without this hard work, time itself becomes an ally of the forces of social stagnation. We must use time creatively, in the knowledge that the time is always ripe to do right. Now is the time to make real the promise of democracy and transform our pending national elegy into a creative psalm of brotherhood. Now is the time to lift our national policy from the quicksand of racial injustice to the solid rock of human dignity.

You speak of our activity in Birmingham as extreme. At first I was rather disappointed that fellow clergymen would see my nonviolent efforts as those of an extremist. I began thinking about the fact that I stand in the middle of two opposing forces in the Negro community. One is a force of complacency, made up in part of Negroes who, as a result of long years of oppression, are so drained of self-respect and a sense of "somebodiness" that they have adjusted to segregation; and in part of a few middle-class Negroes who, because of a degree of academic and economic security and because in some ways they profit by segregation, have become insensitive to the problems of the masses. The other force is one of bitterness and hatred, and it comes perilously close to advocating violence. It is expressed in the various black nationalists groups that are springing up across the nation, the largest and best-known being Elijah Muhammad's Muslim movement. Nourished by the Negro's frustration over the continued existence of racial discrimination, this movement is made up of people who have lost faith in America, who have absolutely repudiated Christianity, and who have concluded that the white man is an incorrigible "devil."

I have tried to stand between these two forces, saying that we need   35 emulate neither the "do-nothingism" of the complacent nor the hatred and despair of the black nationalist. For there is the more excellent way of love and nonviolent protest. I am grateful to God that, through the influence of the Negro church, the way of nonviolence became an integral part of our struggle.

If this pilosophy had not emerged, by now many streets of the South would, I am convinced, be flowing with blood. And I am further convinced that if our white brothers dismiss as "rabble-rousers" and "outside agitators" those of us who employ nonviolent direct action, and if they refuse to support our nonviolent efforts, millions of the Negroes will, out of frustration and despair, seek solace and security in black-nationalist ideologies—a development that would inevitably lead to a frightening racial nightmare.

Oppressed people cannot remain oppressed forever. The yearning for freedom eventually manifests itself, and that is what has happened to the American Negro. Something within has reminded him of his birthright of freedom, and something without has reminded him that it can be gained. Consciously or unconsciously, he has been caught up by the *Zeitgeist,°* and with his black brothers of Africa and his brown and yellow brothers of Asia, South America and the Caribbean, the United States Negro is moving with a sense of great urgency toward the promised land of racial justice. If one recognizes this vital urge that has engulfed the Negro community, one should readily understand why public demonstrations are taking place. The Negro has many pent-up resentments and latent frustrations, and he must release them. So let him march; let him make prayer pilgrimages to the city hall; let him go on freedom rides—and try to understand why he must do so. If his repressed emotions are not released in nonviolent ways, they will seek expression through violence; this is not a threat but a fact of history. So I have not said to my people: "Get rid of your discontent." Rather, I have tried to say that this normal and healthy discontent can be channeled into the creative outlet of nonviolent direct action. And now this approach is being termed extremist.

But though I was initially disappointed at being categorized as an extremist, as I continued to think about the matter I gradually gained a measure of satisfaction from the label. Was not Jesus an extremist for love: "Love your enemies, bless them that curse you, do good to them that hate

Zeitgeist: German for "spirit of the times."

you, and pray for them which despitefully use you, and persecute you." Was not Amos an extremist for justice: "Let justice roll down like waters and righteousness like an ever-flowing stream." Was not Paul an extremist for the Christian gospel: "I bear in my body the marks of the Lord Jesus." Was not Martin Luther an extremist: "Here I stand; I cannot do otherwise, so help me God." And John Bunyan: "I will stay in jail to the end of my days before I make a butchery of my conscience." And Abraham Lincoln: "This nation cannot survive half slave and half free." And Thomas Jefferson: "We hold these truths to be self-evident, that all men are created equal. . . ." So the question is not whether we will be extremists, but what kind of extremists we will be. Will we be extremists for hate or for love? Will we be extremists for the preservation of injustice or for the extension of justice? In that dramatic scene on Calvary's hill three men were crucified. We must never forget that all three were crucified for the same crime—the crime of extremism. Two were extremists for immorality, and thus fell below their environment. The other, Jesus Christ, as was an extremist for love, truth and goodness, and thereby rose above his environment. Perhaps the South, the nation and the world are in dire need of creative extremists.

I had hoped that the white moderate would see this need. Perhaps I was too optimistic; perhaps I expected too much. I suppose I should have realized that few members of the oppressor race can understand the deep groans and passionate yearnings of the oppressed race, and still fewer have the vision to see that injustice must be rooted out by strong, persistent and determined action. I am thankful, however, that some of our white brothers in the South have grasped the meaning of this social revolution and committed themselves to it. They are still all too few in quantity, but they are big in quality. Some—such as Ralph McGill, Lillian Smith, Harry Golden, James McBride Dabbs, Ann Braden and Sarah Patton Boyle—have written about our struggle in eloquent and prophetic terms. Others have marched with us down nameless streets of the South. They have languished in filthy, roach-infested jails, suffering the abuse and brutality of policemen who view them as "dirty nigger-lovers." Unlike so many of their moderate brothers and sisters, they have recognized the urgency of the moment and sensed the need for powerful "action" antidotes to combat the disease of segregation.

Let me take note of my other major disappointment. I have been so 40 greatly disappointed with the white church and its leadership. Of course, there are some notable exceptions. I am not unmindful of the fact that each of you has taken some significant stands on this issue. I commend you, Reverend Stallings, for your Christian stand on this past Sunday, in welcoming Negroes to your worship service on a nonsegregated basis. I commend the Catholic leaders of this state for integrating Spring Hill College several years ago.

But despite these notable exceptions, I must honestly reiterate that I have been disappointed with the church. I do not say this as one of those negative critics who can always find something wrong with the church. I say this as a minister of the gospel, who loves the church; who was nurtured in its bosom; who has been sustained by its spiritual blessings and who will remain true to it as long as the cord of life shall lengthen.

When I was suddenly catapulted into the leadership of the bus protest in Montgomery, Alabama, a few years ago, I felt we would be supported by the white church. I felt that the white ministers, priests and rabbis of the South would be among our strongest allies. Instead, some have been outright opponents, refusing to understand the freedom movement and misrepresenting its leaders; all too many others have been more cautious than courageous and have remained silent behind the anesthetizing security of stained-glass windows.

In spite of my shattered dreams, I came to Birmingham with the hope that the white religious leadership of this community would see the justice of our cause and, with deep moral concern, would serve as the channel through which our just grievances could reach the power structure. I had hoped that each of you would understand. But again I have been disappointed.

I have heard numerous southern religious leaders admonish their worshipers to comply with a desegregation decision because it is the law, but I have longed to hear white ministers declare: "Follow this decree because integration is morally right and because the Negro is your brother." In the midst of blatant injustices inflicted upon the Negro, I have watched white churchmen stand on the sideline and mouth pious irrelevancies and sanctimonious trivialities. In the midst of a mighty struggle to rid our nation of racial and economic injustice, I have heard many ministers say: "Those are social issues, with which the gospel has no real concern." And I have watched many churches commit themselves to a completely otherworldly religion which makes a strange, un-Biblical distinction between body and soul, between the sacred and the secular.

I have traveled the length and breadth of Alabama, Mississippi and all   45
the other southern states. On sweltering summer days and crisp autumn mornings I have looked at the South's beautiful churches with their lofty spires pointing heavenward. I have beheld the impressive outlines of her massive religious-education buildings. Over and over I have found myself asking: "What kind of people worship here? Who is their God? Where were their voices when the lips of Governor Barnett dripped with words of interposition and nullification? Where were they when Governor Wallace gave a clarion call for defiance and hatred? Where were their voices of support when bruised and weary Negro men and women decided to rise from the dark dungeons of complacency to the bright hills of creative protest?"

Yes, these questions are still in my mind. In deep disappointment I have wept over the laxity of the church. But be assured that my tears have been tears of love. There can be no deep disappointment where there is not deep love. Yes, I love the church. How could I do otherwise? I am in the rather unique position of being the son, the grandson, and the great-grandson of preachers. Yes, I see the church as the body of Christ. But, oh! How we have blemished and scarred that body through social neglect and through fear of being nonconformists.

There was a time when the church was very powerful—in the time when the early Christians rejoiced at being deemed worthy to suffer for what they believed. In those days the church was not merely a thermometer that recorded the ideas and principles of popular opinion; it was a thermostat that transformed the mores of society. Whenever the early Christians entered a town, the people in power became disturbed and immediately sought to convict the Christians for being "disturbers of the peace" and "outside agitators." But the Christians pressed on, in the conviction that they were "a colony of heaven," called to obey God rather than man. Small in number, they were big in commitment. They were too God-intoxicated to be "astronomically intimidated." By their effort and example they brought an end to such ancient evils as infanticide and gladiatorial contests.

Things are different now. So often the contemporary church is a weak, ineffectual voice with an uncertain sound. So often it is an archdefender of the status quo. Far from being disturbed by the presence of the church, the power structure of the average community is consoled by the church's silent—and often even vocal—sanction of things as they are.

But the judgment of God is upon the church as never before. If today's church does not recapture the sacrificial spirit of the early church, it will lose its authenticity, forfeit the loyalty of millions, and be dismissed as an irrelevant social club with no meaning for the twentieth century. Every day I meet young people whose disappointment with the church has turned into outright disgust.

Perhaps I have once again been too optimistic. Is organized religion   50 too inextricably bound to the status quo to save our nation and the world? Perhaps I must turn my faith to the inner spiritual church, the church within the church, as the true *ekklesia* and the hope of the world. But again I am thankful to God that some noble souls from the ranks of organized religion have broken loose from the paralyzing chains of conformity and joined us as active partners in the struggle for freedom. They have left their secure congregations and walked the streets of Albany, Georgia, with us. They have gone down the highways of the South on tortuous rides for freedom. Yes, they have gone to jail with us. Some have been dismissed from their churches, have lost the support of their bishops and fellow ministers. But they have acted in the faith that right defeated is stronger than evil triumphant. Their witness has been the spiritual salt that has preserved the true meaning of the gospel in these troubled times. They have carved a tunnel of hope through the dark mountain of disappointment.

I hope the church as a whole will meet the challenge of this decisive hour. But even if the church does not come to the aid of justice, I have no despair about the future. I have no fear about the outcome of our struggle in Birmingham, even if our motives are at present misunderstood. We will reach the goal of freedom in Birmingham and all over the nation, because the goal of America is freedom. Abused and scorned though we may be, our destiny is tied up with America's destiny. Before the pilgrims landed at Plymouth, we were here. Before the pen of Jefferson etched the majestic words of the Declaration of Independence across the pages of history, we were here. For more than two centuries our forebears labored in this country without wages; they made cotton king; they built the homes of their masters while suffering gross injustice and shameful humiliation—and yet out of a bottomless vitality they continued to thrive and develop. If the inexpressible cruelties of slavery could not stop us, the opposition we now face will surely fail. We will win our freedom because the sacred heritage of our nation and the eternal will of God are embodied in our echoing demands.

Before closing I feel impelled to mention one other point in your statement that has troubled me profoundly. You warmly commended the Birmingham police force for keeping "order" and "preventing violence." I doubt that you would have so warmly commended the police force if you had seen its dogs sinking their teeth into unarmed, nonviolent Negroes. I doubt that you would so quickly commend the policemen if you were to observe their ugly and inhumane treatment of Negroes here in the city jail; if you were to watch them push and curse old Negro women and young Negro girls; if you were to see them slap and kick old Negro men and young boys; if you were to observe them, as they did on two occasions, refuse to give us food because we wanted to sing our grace together. I cannot join you in your praise of the Birmingham police department.

It is true that police have exercised a degree of discipline in handling the demonstrators. In this sense they have conducted themselves rather "nonviolently" in public. But for what purpose? To preserve the evil system of segregation. Over the past few years I have consistently preached that nonviolence demands that the means we use must be as pure as the ends we seek. I have tried to make clear that it is wrong to use immoral means to attain moral ends. But now I must affirm that it is just as wrong, or perhaps even more so, to use moral means to preserve immoral ends. Perhaps Mr. Connor and his policemen have been rather nonviolent in public, as was Chief Pritchett in Albany, Georgia, but they have used the moral means of nonviolence to maintain the immoral end of racial injustice. As T. S. Eliot has said: "The last temptation is the greatest treason: To do the right deed for the wrong reason."

I wish you had commended the Negro sit-inners and demonstrators of Birmingham for their sublime courage, their willingness to suffer and their amazing discipline in the midst of great provocation. One day the South will recognize its real heroes. They will be the James Merediths, with the noble sense of purpose that enables them to face jeering and hostile mobs, and with the agonizing loneliness that characterizes the life of the pioneer. They will be old, oppressed, battered Negro women, symbolized in a seventy-two-year-old woman in Montgomery, Alabama, who rose up with a sense of dignity and with her people decided not to ride segregated buses, and who responded with ungrammatical profundity to one who inquired about her weariness: "My feets is tired, but my soul is at rest." They will be the young high school and college students, the young ministers of the gospel and a host of their elders, courageously and nonviolently sitting in at lunch counters and willingly going to jail for conscience' sake. One day the South will know that when these disinherited children of God sat down at lunch counters, they were in reality standing up for what is best in the American dream and for the most sacred values in our Judaeo-Christian heritage, thereby bringing our nation back to those great wells of democracy which were dug deep by the founding fathers in their formulation of the Constitution and the Declaration of Independence.

Never before have I written so long a letter. I'm afraid it is much too   55
long to take your precious time. I can assure you that it would have been much shorter if I had been writing from a comfortable desk, but what else can one do when he is alone in a narrow jail cell, other than write long letters, think long thoughts and pray long prayers?

If I have said anything in this letter that overstates the truth and indicates an unreasonable impatience, I beg you to forgive me. If I have said anything that understates the truth and indicates my having a patience that allows me to settle for anything less than brotherhood, I beg God to forgive me.

I hope this letter finds you strong in faith. I also hope that circumstances will soon make it possible for me to meet each of you, not as an integrationist or a civil-rights leader but as a fellow clergyman and a Christian brother. Let us all hope that the dark clouds of racial prejudice will soon pass away and the deep fog of misunderstanding will be lifted from our fear-drenched communities, and in some not too distant tomorrow the radiant stars of love and brotherhood will shine over our great nation with all their scintillating beauty.

> Yours for the cause of Peace and Brotherhood
> Martin Luther King, Jr.

Questions for Discussion

1. How does King present himself in this letter? Is his own character a factor in the argument he makes?
2. Where does King show that he is writing for an audience of clergymen? Is there any evidence suggesting that he may have also had a larger audience in mind as he wrote?
3. Most of paragraph 21 consists of a single sentence. How is this sentence structured, and what is its effect? If you were to divide this sentence, where would you do so? What would be the effect of breaking this sentence down into several shorter sentences?

4. Imagine that you are a white southerner in 1963 who has misgivings about the civil rights movement. Are there any points where you would feel that King was making an effort to reassure you?

5. According to King, how can we tell the difference between laws that we should obey and laws that we should break? Under what circumstances is it right to break a law?

6. How does King see the church? How does he think Christianity had changed? What does he believe the church should be like?

7. What does King's letter reveal about African-American history?

Suggestions for Writing

1. What elements of this letter make it persuasive? Write an essay explaining how King has structured his argument and identifying the rhetorical strategies that make it effective.

2. Are you concerned about social justice? Identify a social problem in the world today, and write a letter that would persuade your classmates to do something about it.

10

Writing to Understand Reading

Everyone has had the experience of trying to read something that is difficult to understand. But another type of reading experience is even more common: thinking that we understand what we have read when there are actually dozens of points we have passed right over. Although much is still unknown about reading, we do know that people read in different ways and that a dozen people reading the same text are likely to see and remember a dozen different versions. With so many words printed on any page, the eye is unlikely to give equal attention to every line. Readers may agree about what a text seems to say overall, or they may disagree strongly. But whether they agree or disagree, they will have reached their conclusions by different routes.

When reading, many people skip over words or allusions that they do not understand, and they do it so routinely that they sometimes don't realize that they are doing it. They are also likely to pause at different points—to answer the phone, take a sip of coffee, or simply rest their eyes. These pauses can influence which parts of a text are remembered most clearly. Moreover, reading triggers specific associations for each reader derived from his or her own personal experience. We all bring our own unique experiences, personality, and knowledge of the world to any text we read. To a significant degree, we *create* the meaning we derive from reading.

Most critics now agree that there is no single way to interpret a text that is the correct interpretation. This principle can yield results that are both liberating and enriching, since freeing readers to explore individual responses can add to the overall understanding of what a text can mean. Twelve people reading the same text can offer twelve different responses, all of them valuable. However, some responses to a text will be more illuminating than others if more time and care have been invested in them.

One of the best ways of testing your understanding of a text—and improving upon that understanding—is to write about what you read. Whether you are summarizing the information a work includes, evaluating the author's achievement, or exploring the ideas that have been raised, writing about reading requires you to think about the text. This usually means returning to the text and studying it carefully. To illustrate how writing can lead to a better understanding of reading, this chapter will focus upon writing about literature as it has been traditionally defined: fiction, drama, and poetry. Some critics define literature more broadly to include everything available in print. Whatever your own definition of literature, you can apply most of the techniques discussed here to almost anything you read.

RECOGNIZING WAYS TO APPROACH A TEXT

Like most types of writing, writing about literature can take a variety of different forms.

- You can *summarize* a work by briefly stating its key points.
- You can *evaluate* a work by identifying its strengths and weaknesses.
- You can *explicate* a work by providing a line-by-line explanation of what a work means and how it achieves that meaning.
- You can *analyze* a work by discussing one or more of its parts.

The approach that you take should be determined by your rhetorical situation. Your instructor may assign a specific approach, or you may need to decide for yourself which approach best suits your audience and the material you will be writing about.

As explained in Chapter 4, "Writing to Report Information," *summarizing* is useful when a work is long, tells a story, offers information, or makes an argument. When writing about literature, you may frequently find yourself needing to summarize a novel, story, or play—occasionally even a poem. Summary of a literary work can stand alone as a separate assignment, but more often it is part of a paper that then goes on to either evaluate or analyze the work summarized. As a general rule, you should write a summary only if you have been specifically asked to do so or if you believe that your audience may not be familiar with the work you want to discuss. An audience that has read the work recently might ask, "Why are you telling me this? I know it already." On the other hand, an audience unfamiliar with the work may have trouble following your discussion of it without benefit of a brief summary. For this reason a writer reviewing a new book in a newspaper will usually include some summary along with evaluation. You, too, may have occasion to summarize a work that you want to examine critically. Be cautious, however: Some writers drift into writing a summary because they find it easier to retell a story than to interpret it. When choosing to write a summary, make sure that your choice is deliberate, that your summary serves a clear purpose, that it covers the main points, and that it is as short as you can make it. (For additional information on summary, see pp. 161–62.)

Evaluating, like summarizing (which it often includes), makes the most sense when the work is unfamiliar to your audience. Both summaries and reviews attempt to provide a sense of the book as a whole; but whereas summaries limit themselves to content and try to be neutral, reviews also consider quality and offer judgments. In addition to providing a brief summary of the work, a reviewer will usually identify its theme and sometimes compare it with other works by the author that might already be known by the audience. (This is especially likely in reviews of a newly published book by a well-known author.)

At the heart of any review, however, is the reviewer's evaluation of the work's merit. Is the work original or predictable, thorough or superficial? These are among the questions a reviewer may address, offering at least one piece of evidence (such as a short quotation) that will support each opinion. Readers expect these opinions, since one of the principal reasons for reading a review is to decide whether or not you want to read the book. The extent to which readers are influenced by a review often depends upon the degree to which they trust the reviewer's judgment—either because they are already familiar with the reviewer or simply because the reviewer writes so well that he or she seems to be a credible authority. The review itself is unlikely to make an extensive argument, since it attempts to accomplish several goals within little space. Most book reviews average no more than a thousand words. That might sound like a long assignment if you are staring at a blank sheet of paper or computer screen with no idea what to write about, but it's very little space when you consider all that a reviewer is expected to cover. (For an example of a book review, see "Someone to Watch Over Us" in Chapter 6.)

An *explication* also attempts to cover an entire work, but in this case the emphasis is on interpreting the work rather than summarizing its content or appraising its quality. If you choose to explicate a work, you have the responsibility to explain the function and meaning of everything within it. Consequently, explication is usually reserved for short works, especially poems (or excerpts, such as an important speech within a longer work). If you think you might wish to offer a line-by-line explication of *War and Peace,* you had better reserve the next several years of your life. On the other hand, the explication of a poem like "Pied Beauty" may well be the best way of understanding the work's meaning.

When you are looking for topics for writing about literature, *analysis* offers the greatest range of possibilities, for it opens up room for multiple interpretations of different parts of a work. Analyzing a work requires you to recognize its parts, and many works have ready-made divisions within them. A novel, for instance, is usually divided into chapters (and sometimes groups of chapters); a play, into acts and scenes. A short story might consist of two or three separate scenes, and a poem might be divided into stanzas. For such cases you can choose to write about one of these divisions—limiting yourself, for example, to the chapter in which Huckleberry Finn pretends to be a girl or to the suicide scene in *Romeo and Juliet*. But there are many other ways of dividing a work of literature. Analytical papers may be written on the following features:

- The role of a story within the story
- The significance of a specific dialogue
- The portrayal of one of the characters
- The setting, and why it is appropriate for what happens within the work
- The theme, or central idea, that the work conveys to you
- The use of figurative language or symbolism to convey more than one meaning
- A pattern of imagery that establishes a particular mood
- The organization of the work, and why it is structured as it is

Each of these possibilities can be modified depending upon your interests, the needs of your readers, and the nature of the text. You may decide to broaden or narrow your focus. For example, you may decide to contrast two characters if you have the space to do so and if doing so will be more illuminating than analyzing a single character. Or you may focus on one of several symbols that you have identified if you have much to say about it and relatively little to say about the others. But whatever part of the whole you select for analysis, you should try to make your analysis of that part contribute to your readers' understanding of the work as a whole.

PREPARING TO WRITE

On some occasions you may feel motivated to write about something immediately after you have read it. In fact, a good way to improve both your reading and your writing is to keep a journal devoted specifically to recording responses to what you read. The entries in a reading journal will typically include brief summaries that can help you when reviewing for exams, comments evaluating the strengths and weaknesses of the material, questions that you'd like to raise during class discussion of the assignment, and reflections of your own that were inspired along the way.

Even if you do not keep a reading journal on a regular basis, you should try to honor any impulse to write about what you read. If you sometimes wish that you had more to say when people discuss their reading, you are especially likely to benefit from getting something down on paper whenever you feel stimulated by a particular assignment. Imagine yourself having the chance to talk with the author of the material you've read. What would you praise? What would you ask about? And what, if anything, would you complain about? Sometimes, it's hard to find the words to get such a conversation started; but once you've started, you've increased the likelihood of touching on something that can lead to a better understanding of the work.

When you are assigned an out-of-class paper about literature, there are a number of things you can do to make sure that you'll have something to say when you begin to write.

1. *Note your preliminary response.* The first step in writing to understand reading is defining your preliminary response. If you have the option of choosing to write about one of several works, ask yourself which inspired the strongest reaction. Which did you like best and which the least? If you are required to write about a specific work, you can modify this question by asking yourself which aspects of the work appealed to you and which did not. Discovering a text (or part of a text) that you enjoyed can help you write a good paper, since you will be writing about material that you are willing to spend time with. On the other hand, good papers can also result from writing about reading that you did *not* like if you enjoy trying to persuade others to agree with you: Consider how much fun Mark Twain must have had demolishing *The Deerslayer* in "Fenimore Cooper's Literary Offenses" (Chapter 6). In either case you are writing about material you have a clear response to, and this is usually easier than starting with material you have no particular feelings about one way or the other.

2. *Reread the work you have chosen to write about.* Once you know what work you will be writing about, the next step is to reexamine that work. Although you may not be able to reread an entire novel (or other long work), you should always be able to reread a story, poem, or play before writing an out-of-class paper about it. As you read, annotate the work by marking key passages and making marginal notations as questions and ideas occur to you. You may have already annotated the text during your initial reading, but you are almost certain to notice new dimensions of the text as you reread. Be sure to look up any words or allusions that you passed over on your initial reading, and be alert for the repetition of words or ideas. Deliberate repetition often signals a way of better understanding a text. You might ask yourself, for example, why "Abalone, Abalone, Abalone" is not simply titled "Abalone," or you might note the repeated references to Mrs. Dietrich's drinking in "Shopping." You should also note any pattern of related references, such as a number of different references to the weather or to clothing. Most importantly, you should reconsider your preliminary response to the work. If you had enjoyed reading it at first, how well does it

hold up on another reading? Can you identify specific parts that gave you pleasure? If you are writing about a text that you initially disliked, are you coming to like it better as you spend more time with it? Or are you coming to a clearer understanding of why you find the text objectionable?

3. *Ask yourself questions about the work.* You should not feel as if you must understand every dimension of the text as you are reading it. Ideas will continue to occur to you after you have reread the work if you continue to think about it. Asking yourself questions is a good way to keep these thoughts coming. For example, you can use the pentad (pp. 12–14) to ask yourself such questions as "How does the setting of this work relate to what happens within it?" Or "What act is most central to this work, and who is responsible for it?" Moving beyond the pentad, you might ask, "Why has this work been arranged in the order in which it appears? Why does it begin and end where it does?" Or "Is anything inconsistent in this work? Are there changes that are not accounted for or any departures from what seems to be the main idea?" You can ask yourself questions like these whenever you have a few minutes that you can devote to your own thoughts. Some of the best ideas in your paper may result from answering a question you were thinking about as you walked across campus, washed some dishes, or stood in line at the post office. Preparing to write a paper about literature means making yourself imaginatively and intellectually engaged by the work you are going to write about. Make your mind receptive to ideas by frequently turning your thoughts to the work during the period between receiving the assignment and writing your first draft.

4. *Test your choice.* If you think actively about a work that inspired a strong response, you will probably generate more than one possible topic for writing. At this point you should evaluate these topics for their appropriateness. For instance, some topics may be too narrow and others too broad if you have been asked to write an essay of a specified length. You should also think about your audience's potential interest in the topic. Even if you write best when imagining a broader audience, ask yourself what you know about your instructor. How would she or he respond to a paper that seemed to do nothing more than restate points that had already been made in class? On the other hand, how receptive would your instructor be to a paper that challenged the views set forth in a class lecture? These are questions that have to be settled on an individual basis. But as a general rule, good writers are willing to take chances, and most instructors welcome a paper with fresh ideas as long as those ideas have been well thought out and well supported.

5. *Define your thesis.* Once you have decided upon the topic for your paper, you will know what parts of the literary work require additional study and which parts you will not need to discuss. But having a topic is not the same as having a thesis. Your topic identifies the aspect of the text that you will be writing about; your thesis is the central idea you intend to convey about that topic. Although your thesis may occur to you immediately after

your initial reading, you will often know your topic before you feel certain about your thesis. If writing a paper about "Lullaby," for example, you may decide to write on the role of nature in that story, but you then need to decide what you believe that role to be. Your thesis may be clear to you before you begin to write, or—as is often the case—the thesis may emerge as you draft.

6. *Gather your evidence.* A thesis requires support. When interpreting or evaluating literature, think of yourself as writing a type of argument requiring evidence for whatever you claim. Although knowing something of the historical context in which a work was written can often add to your understanding of it, the data supporting your claim should usually come from the text itself. (An exception is a research paper in which evidence comes from a number of sources. But even in this case much of the evidence will still normally come from the text that generated the topic.) Think critically about the evidence you discover, and be prepared to search again for additional support, if necessary. Be careful at this stage not to ignore anything that seems to conflict with what you hope to prove. Considering apparent contradictions can prompt you to anticipate objections from your reader and thus help you strengthen your argument. Or you may decide that you need to revise your thesis so that it more accurately reflects your evidence.

WRITING THE PAPER

If you have considered your audience, chosen your topic, defined your thesis, and gathered evidence to support it, your next challenge is to decide how to organize your material.

Some papers take their pattern of organization from the work that is being written about. If you are explicating a poem, for example, you can go through it line by line in the order in which the lines appear. If you are writing a character analysis, you can trace the character's development throughout the work. And if you are discussing a theme or the use of a specific literary device, you can present your evidence in the order in which it appeared in the text. At times, however, you may wish to have more flexibility, moving around in the work from point to point. Instead of tracing a character's development from the beginning of a work to the end, you can organize your analysis in paragraphs or sections devoted to the character's various personality traits, arranging your material in whatever order best suits your purpose. Or instead of writing a line-by-line explication of a poem, you can organize an explication to focus on various dimensions such as imagery, metaphor, and rhyme, one by one.

But whatever your preliminary plan, you should be prepared to modify it if drafting generates good ideas that you didn't realize you had until you started to write. When writing about literature, you may very well find yourself arguing a position that is different from what you had originally planned—or you may find that you have much to say about what you expected to be a minor point in your paper, in which case you need to reconsider your focus. Discoveries like these are a normal part of the writing process, and they can be both illuminating and fun. Remember that you are writing to understand reading, not writing to honor an outline.

Because you cannot understand fully and exactly what you want to say until you have finished drafting a paper, revision is essential. Although there is nothing wrong with drafting a paper that ends up arguing something different from the thesis with which it begins, there is something wrong with handing it in. When revising a paper about literature, be sure to ask yourself if you wrote what you intended. You may need to revise your thesis, make serious cuts, or introduce evidence to support unsupported claims.

Here are a few additional points to keep in mind when revising a paper about literature.

- Consider how well the introduction and conclusion relate to the paper. Ask yourself if you introduced any ideas that you failed to pursue or came to a conclusion that seems unrelated to your original thesis.
- Double-check to make sure that you have supported any claims you make and that you have not overlooked anything important.
- Think about how well you have responded to the needs of your audience. Have you summarized material that didn't need to be summarized, or failed to summarize material your audience may not have read? Have you explained any unusual words or references that readers may not understand? On the other hand, have you insulted the intelligence of readers by identifying a reference they would certainly know?
- Consider how you sound. When writing a paper about literature, you are assuming the role of a teacher trying to help others to a better understanding of the work. Try not to sound apologetic by overusing phrases like "in my opinion," for they will diminish your authority as a writer. But be careful not to go to the other extreme and sound contemptuous of anyone who might disagree with you. Strive for a tone that sounds thoughtful, confident, and reasonable. You should sound as if you believe what you are writing and want others to believe it too, but you should not sound as if you believe that you alone are right.
- When considering how you sound, reexamine the number and length of any quotations within the paper. Quotations are often necessary for supporting claims, but some quotations may be longer than they have to be, and too many quotations can keep your own voice from reaching readers. Remember that you are the writer of your paper; quotations should be subordinate to what you have to say. If your own words seem to do little more than link quotations

together, you will need to become more actively involved in the paper. Keep quotations as short as possible, and be sure to weave them smoothly into what you are saying, making their significance clear.

Also, be sure to observe the conventions appropriate for writing about literature when you revise your paper.

1. Use the present tense (sometimes called "the literary present") for writing about what happens in a work of fiction, drama, or poetry.

   When Mrs. Dietrich and her daughter go shopping, they see a woman who disturbs them.

2. Identify writers initially by their full name—William Shakespeare, Joyce Carol Oates—and subsequently by their last name, regardless of gender: Shakespeare and Oates, not William or Ms. Oates.

3. Unless you are given other instructions, follow the guidelines for documentation recommended by the Modern Language Association. These are covered in full in the *MLA Handbook for Writers of Research Papers* by Joseph Gibaldi and Walter S. Achtert. Here are a few rules that are used most frequently in writing about literature.

   a. When the author of a work is clearly revealed in the paper, simply provide a page reference (without an abbreviation for page) within parentheses immediately after the second quotation mark but before the final punctuation for the sentence.

   Oates describes the morning as having "a metallic cast to the air" (496).

   b. Add the author's last name immediately before the page reference when the source of the quotation is not otherwise clear.

   According to this reasoning, wordplay "reflects real paradoxes in the nature of the world itself" (Burke 56).

   c. When quoting from a play that is divided into acts, scenes, and line numbers, identify quotations with these three numbers (separated by periods) rather than with a page reference.

   Iago warns Othello that jealousy is a "green-eyed monster" (3.3.167).

   d. When quoting from a poem, provide references to line numbers (without an abbreviation for line). Use a slash to indicate line divisions when quoting two or three lines. Leave a space blank before and after the slash. (As with a prose quotation, set off longer quotations by indenting ten spaces from the left margin.)

   One of the most difficult questions this poem raises is what the speaker means by saying, "I live between the heron and the wren, / Beasts of the hill and serpents of the den" (5–6).

After you have revised your paper, you will, of course, still need to edit it—refining your style and making any necessary changes in grammar, punctuation, and spelling. But as you make these final changes, you can feel confident about what you have written if you know that you have looked closely at a work of literature, chosen a clearly defined approach for writing about it, and supported any claims that you made. Such a paper will reveal a serious effort to understand what another writer has created.

ABALONE, ABALONE, ABALONE

Toshio Mori

Born in California, Toshio Mori writes short stories that draw upon his Japanese heritage. The following story, which is very short, has only two char-acters and a very simple plot. But like many longer stories, it has what is often called a "turning point"—a moment in the story when a character changes as the result of something that has happened. Be alert for the turning point as you read this story, and consider whether or not the change is beneficial. It may help you to know that an abalone is a type of large mollusk found in warm seas. Its flesh is eaten, and its ornamental shell is a source of mother-of-pearl.

Before Mr. Abe went away I used to see him quite often at his nursery. He was a carnation grower just as I am one today. At noontime I used to go to his front porch and look at his collection of abalone shells.

They were lined up side by side against the side of his house on the front porch. I was curious as to why he bothered to collect them. It was a lot of bother polishing them. I had often seen him sit for hours on Sundays and noon hours polishing each one of the shells with the greatest of care. Of course I knew these abalone shells were pretty. When the sun strikes the insides of these shells it is something beautiful to behold. But I could not understand why he continued collecting them when the front porch was practically full.

He used to watch for me every noon hour. When I appeared he would look out of his room and bellow, "Hello, young man!"

"Hello, Abe-*san*," I said. "I came to see the abalone shells."

Then he came out of the house and we sat on the front porch. But he did not tell me why he collected these shells. I think I have asked him dozens of times but each time he closed his mouth and refused to answer.

"Are you going to pass this collection of abalone shells on to your children?" I said.

"No," he said. "I want my children to collect for themselves. I wouldn't give it to them."

"Why?" I said. "When you die?"

Mr. Abe shook his head. "No. Not even when I die," he said. "I couldn't give the children what I see in these shells. The children must go out for themselves and find their own shells."

"Why, I thought this collecting hobby of abalone shells was a simple affair," I said.

"It is simple. Very simple," he said. But he would not tell me further.

For several years I went steadily to his front porch and looked at the beautiful shells. His collection was getting larger and larger. Mr. Abe sat and talked to me and on each occasion his hands were busy polishing shells.

"So you are still curious?" he said.

"Yes," I said.

One day while I was hauling the old soil from the benches and replacing it with new soil I found an abalone shell half buried in the dust between the benches. So I stopped working. I dropped my wheelbarrow and went to the faucet and washed the abalone shell with soap and water. I had a hard time taking the grime off the surface.

After forty minutes of cleaning and polishing the old shell it became interesting. I began polishing both the outside and the inside of the shell. I found after many minutes of polishing I could not do very much with the exterior side. It had scabs of the sea which would not come off by scrubbing and the surface itself was rough and hard. And in the crevices the grime stuck so that even with a needle it did not become clean.

But on the other side, the inside of the shell, the more I polished the more lustre I found. It had me going. There were colors which I had not seen in the abalone shells before or anywhere else. The different hues, running berserk in all directions, coming together in harmony. I guess I could say they were not unlike a rainbow which men once symbolized. As soon as I thought of this I thought of Mr. Abe.

I remember running to his place, looking for him. "Abe-*san!*" I said when I found him. "I know why you are collecting the abalone shells!"

He was watering the carnation plants in the greenhouse. He stopped watering and came over to where I stood. He looked me over closely for awhile and then his face beamed.

"All right," he said. "Do not say anything. Nothing, mind you. When you have found the reason why you must collect and preserve them, you do not have to say anything more."

"I want you to see it, Abe-*san*," I said.

"All right. Tonight," he said. "Where did you find it?"

"In my old greenhouse, half buried in the dust," I said.

He chuckled. "That is pretty far from the ocean," he said, "but pretty close to you."

At each noon hour I carried my abalone shell and went over to Mr. Abe's front porch. While I waited for his appearance I kept myself busy polishing the inside of the shell with a rag.

One day I said, "Abe-*san,* now I have three shells."

"Good!" he said. "Keep it up!"

"I have to keep them all," I said. "They are very much alike and very much different."

"Well! Well!" he said and smiled.

That was the last I saw of Abe-*san*. Before the month was over he sold his nursery and went back to Japan. He brought his collection along and thereafter I had no one to talk to at the noon hour. This was before I discovered the fourth abalone shell, and I should like to see Abe-*san* someday and watch his eyes roll as he studies me whose face is now akin to the collectors of shells or otherwise.

Questions for Discussion

1. How do you picture the narrator of this story? How old is he? What is he like at the beginning of the story? Is he the same at the end? If not, how does he change, and where does this change begin?
2. Why does Mr. Abe refuse to discuss his collection of abalone shells? Why doesn't he plan to leave his collection to his children?
3. The act of polishing an abalone shell would seem to be very simple. But is it as simple as it seems? Why is it worth doing?
4. This story begins and ends with references to Mr. Abe going away, and paragraphs 8–9 mention his eventual death. What does this sense of passing away contribute to the story?
5. How do you interpret the title of this story? Could someone understand the title without reading the story?

Suggestions for Writing

1. Describe the setting of "Abalone, Abalone, Abalone," and explain why it is appropriate for what happens in this story.
2. A symbol is something that means both what it is and something more than it is. The rainbow (mentioned in paragraph 17) has been used as a symbol for new beginnings. If you think the abalone shell stands for something else, write an essay explaining what it symbolizes and how you came to this conclusion.

WINNERS

Lon Otto

Imagine finding a way to win a contest you do not deserve to win. You know you shouldn't cheat but are tempted by the prospect of an attractive prize. You are also being encouraged to cheat by your best friend—someone a little older and more aggressive than you are. What happens then? As you read the following story about two boys trying to win a fishing contest, be alert for ways they manage to justify their behavior and eventually come to see themselves as victims.

At first we thought it was a floating plastic bleach bottle, maybe somebody's illegal minnow-trap marker tangled in the lilies. It might have been a clump of the lily pads themselves, flipped over by the wind, their pale undersides glaring in the late-morning sun. We didn't recognize what it was until we were almost on top of it, our boat nosed into the weeds that were keeping it from washing ashore. Keith and I looked at each other.

This was the summer after my parents got divorced. My father had taken me and my best friend on a fishing trip to Rhinelander, Wisconsin, where there was a contest in progress at Schramm's Sporting Goods. While Dad was paying for our licenses, Keith and I had checked out the refrigerated glass case in front of the store, with the leading bass, northern, muskie, walleye, crappie, lake trout, and sunfish lying frozen on a bed of chipped ice. The prizes for each category were displayed in the front window, from a stiff muskie rod and heavy reel with star drag and oversize handle down to a delicate fly rod and tiny reel, which some sportsmen evidently used to catch sunnies.

"What was the prize for walleye?" Keith asked now, peering over the side of the boat.

"I don't know. That Penn Silver Eagle and a Stratoflex, I think. Christ, this would have won easy."

It was the biggest walleye we'd ever seen, eight or nine pounds, we   5
guessed, floating belly up, white, and a little bloated, so it rode high in the water. The turtles hadn't gotten to it yet, as far as we could tell, but who knew what we'd find on the dorsal side. The turtles usually start on the tail, though, and that seemed still intact.

"If we'd caught this baby, we'd be set. We'd've been winners for sure."

Keith said, "Let's do. Let's catch it." And he reached for the landing net.

"We can't," I said. "We'd never get away with it. It's already dead."

"You see any live fish in Schramm's display case? That crummy little walleye in there—was it alive?"

"You got to *catch* them, man. They write up what lure you used and   10
everything."

"Okay." He lifted his rod, cast the jitterbug toward open water, and slowly retrieved it, the lure wobbling and bubbling across the surface in that fat, juicy action that is always so satisfying, even when nothing is biting. He paused, teasing it every once in a while, and led it slowly up to the walleye's mouth. He jiggled the lure against the closed bony plates and yanked hard, setting the hooks.

"Got it!" he screamed. The hooks were on the outside, but it sometimes ends up that way even with living fish. "Net him, man, before he gets away! God, what a fighter!" As Keith hauled the big stiff fish this way and that, churning the water, I reached for the net and scooped it underneath the walleye's tail. Dad had taught me always to net a fish headfirst, especially one as big as this, so that when it jumps, it just gets in deeper, but this guy wasn't going anywhere. I lifted it with effort, half the fish sticking out awkwardly, and hoisted it over the gunwale. Keith helped by pulling up on the line. We lowered it between us.

"I thought it might just fall apart," I said. "But it's still pretty good."

"Damn right," Keith said. "It's almost perfect." The dorsal fin was splayed up like a sail, chewed here and there, but nothing worse than a long and strenuous life might have done. The huge eyes were a beautiful milky color, and the scales were about five shades lighter than they should have been, except where some little black things were growing. The mouth, I saw, wasn't really closed but gaped open a little, exposing the tiger's teeth that are always a surprise in such a studious-looking fish as a walleye.

I was beginning to think it might work, we'd get away with it, we'd   *15* be winners. Then Keith gave that sickening laugh that was one of the reasons why most people at school didn't like him too much. "I was just thinking," he said. "What if the mouth opened up some more, sort of real slow, and then an enormous leech or something crawled out?"

I was used to Keith, and his sense of humor·didn't bother me, except that I started worrying again. "How long do you think it's going to last?" I asked. "Maybe we should get it back in the water, so it'll stay cool." We pried out the hooks, which hadn't sunk in past the barbs, and jammed the point of my stringer through the soft part just behind the hard lips. Then we heaved it over the side and tied the other end of the stringer to an oarlock. I cranked up the outboard (this was the first summer that Dad let me handle a motor by myself) and took us in slowly, the high-riding walleye plowing across the wake like a battleship.

Nobody was around the dock when we tied up, so we lugged the walleye up to the cabin, laid it in the shade, and went inside to get something to drink. Dad had taken the ski boat up a chain of little lakes to the Tomahawk Flowage, where he was going to cast for muskies. Fortunately Keith was thirteen, almost a year older than me, and knew how to drive a stick. We would be able to get to town and back before my father came in.

The dinky freezer compartment of the cabin's refrigerator held only a metal tray of ice, a heavily frosted box of frozen vegetables, and a couple packages of bass fillets. We emptied everything in the freezer into a garbage bag, drank some Cokes, and tossed in the rest of the soft drinks and beers from the refrigerator. It would be enough, we thought, to keep the fish cool.

When we heard some furious barking, we rushed outside and found the resort owner's German shepherd rolling around on top of our walleye. We drove him off by throwing beer cans at him and were relieved to find only minor damage. The scales were torn up along one side, but the commotion had actually squashed down some of the bloated quality, so things were about even.

We loaded the walleye into the garbage sack, arranged the ice cubes and cans and frozen food around it, and carried it up to where the car was parked. I was going to put it in the trunk, but Keith pointed out that it would be hot as an oven in there from standing in the sun all morning. The fish would explode. So we placed it on the back seat, opened all the windows, and headed for Rhinelander, about twenty miles away. *20*

Keith was not really such a good driver, tending to go off onto the shoulder when he laughed and taking turns a little too generously. We were making good time, however, when he slammed on the brakes to avoid hitting a squirrel. You could never tell about Keith: sometimes he would go out of his way to kill something, but at other times he was very considerate. I banged my head on the windshield, and it wasn't until we heard cans rolling around that we noticed the stuff on the back seat had been flung onto the floor and scattered. The walleye's tail was sticking out of the garbage bag, and the smell started to get to us. Keith stopped laughing and drove as fast as he dared, faster than the old Audi had ever been driven, trying to outdistance the odor or blow it out the windows.

When we got to the outskirts of town, a complication occurred to me. "How are we going to share the prize?" I asked.

"What do you mean, 'share'? *I* caught it."

I knew he was kidding, but still it was going to be awkward. "No, really," I said, "what are we going to do? There's only one rod and reel. We could match for it, I guess, or maybe they would give us two of something not so expensive. We don't need anything that fancy."

"I did catch it," Keith said again. *25*

"I netted it," I said, unable to believe he would betray me that way. "That was most of the work."

"You tried to talk me out of it. You said we couldn't enter a found fish in the contest. I don't want any cheap shit. I want that Penn Silver Eagle and I want that Stratoflex." He stomped on the accelerator for emphasis, and we screamed around some old farmer's truck.

"This is *my* trip!" I shouted over the roar of wind. "*My* dad paid for everything. This is *my* car. *I'm* the broken-home kid, and if anyone deserves that prize, it's me! You're just my goddamn *guest,* man."

We were passing the strip of motels, roadhouses, and fast-food joints, and Keith slowed down a little as a concession to the increased traffic, though we were still overtaking everything in sight. He started to laugh, and I hit him as hard as I could on the muscle of his arm. The car bounced up on a divider strip, then swerved back and came to a stop at the entrance of an A&W.

"Okay," Keith said, "lighten up. I was just kidding." *30*

"I knew that," I said. "So what are we going to do?"

Somebody started honking at us to get out of the way. Keith gave him the finger and drove slowly toward town, half on the road and half on the shoulder, thinking. Finally he said, "Okay, here's what we do. You get the Stratoflex, I get the Silver Eagle." I started to protest, but he slapped his hand over my mouth. "Wait. We keep them together, though. We take turns using them—me on odd days, you on even days. When we get enough money saved up, you buy a new reel and I buy a new rod." He slammed the steering wheel decisively.

I had to admit that it was a good plan. "But I want the Silver Eagle. You take the Stratoflex."

"Done."

"You take even days, and I'll take odd." *35*

He shook his head. "No way, man. I got to have odd."

"Why?"

"I just have to, is all."

I agreed to take even days, and we drove the rest of the way into town and parked right in front of Schramm's. We dumped out the cans and frozen foods that were still in the garbage sack, pushed the fish back in, and carried it into the store. When we passed the display case out front, Keith gave a thumbs-down sign to the five-pound walleye lying there on ice.

It was almost noon, and the store was pretty crowded, but people gave *40* us plenty of room. An old guy came up then—Schramm, I guessed—and asked what was going on. He was one of these really big guys who are always a little bent over, like bears. Keith dropped the sack onto the floor, pulled out the walleye, and laid it on the sack. Schramm backed off a step and swore into his hand.

"We're entering it in the contest," Keith said.

"Are you crazy? Get that damn thing out of here." The fish really didn't look as good as it had an hour or so before, but you could still tell it was a walleye.

"I know it took us a little too long to get this baby in," Keith said, "but it's got four pounds on that walleye out there, easy. Nothing's going to beat this fish."

"I can't put that piece of carrion in my display case. It looks like it's been dead in the water for a week. Where are your parents, boys?"

I said, "My dad's over at the courthouse, filing some sort of brief. He *45* said that since we caught the fish, we should collect our prize."

Schramm stared down at the fish, keeping his hand over his mouth and nose. While we were standing there, three or four people came in, sniffed, and backed out. A couple of men were looking at what was going on, but they were keeping their distance.

"God almighty," Schramm gasped at last. "Look, I'll give you five bucks for the effort. But get that thing out of here."

"Like hell!" I said. "That Silver Eagle alone is worth fifty. We want the whole deal. We're winners, man. So pay up."

Schramm looked up and saw a little group of customers and clerks gathering at the far end of the aisle, where they kept water-skis and coils of bright yellow tow rope. "Look, son," he said to me, "maybe you better leave and come back with your father."

"He said we should take care of it ourselves. He's real busy."   50

"Even if the fish was fresh," Schramm said, "the contest isn't over for another three days. Something bigger could come in."

"So we'll wait," Keith said. "Put this monster in the case, and then we'll see if anything can beat it. Nothing's going to beat it—you know that."

One of the customers gagged suddenly and ran for the back door. A couple of the men laughed, in a low, choked fashion. Schramm cursed painstakingly under his breath. He went behind the cash register, rang it open, and took out some bills. He came back and said, "I'll give you each ten dollars. That's twenty dollars for a stinking sack of garbage. Take it and get the hell out of here, or I'll throw you out."

Keith and I looked at each other and shrugged. Schramm shouted, "Eddie!" One of the clerks who had been watching from the water-ski aisle came forward, holding a handkerchief over his nose.

"Need some help, Mr. Crane?" he mumbled into the rag.   55

"Take this out back and bury it."

"Where?"

"Deep! Now!"

While Eddie, breathless, gathered up the huge fish in the garbage bag as best he could and headed for the back of the store, scattering the onlookers, the big man handed us each a ten-dollar bill. "Don't try this again," he warned us. "Now get out of here. Spend that somewhere else."

When we got out to the car, Keith started laughing. "We did it, man!   60 Twenty bucks!"

"Shit," I said. "That bastard cheated us."

"Come on."

"It wasn't even Schramm," I said. "It was 'Mr. Crane.' We *won* that contest. It's like he stole that rod and reel from us. We were winners, and that son of a bitch cheated us. And we let him do it."

Keith looked down at the ten-dollar bill in his hand as if it were dirt. We climbed into the car in silence, and while Keith drove, I twisted around and retrieved a couple cans of Coke from the mess in back. Keith steered one-handed and took a long pull of the pop. Suddenly he laughed his worst laugh, spurting Coke out of his nostrils, and yanked the car onto a side street.

"I got the perfect plan," he said when he was able to talk again. "We *65* go back right away and see where that guy buries our walleye. Then after dark we go dig it up, break open the display case, and put it in where it belongs. That fat jerk will piss in his pants."

"Forget it," I said bitterly, "just drive," knowing that we were helpless against adult treachery and betrayal. I hurled the half-empty can out the window and watched it tumble, streaming pop like smoke from a crashing jet. "Come on, Keith," I said, "floor this sucker!" The town fled from us in confusion.

Questions for Discussion

1. The boys in this story are young adolescents; one is thirteen, the other nearly a year younger. How does Otto convey a sense of their age? How does he differentiate between the two?
2. When he first sees the dead walleye, the narrator says, "If we'd caught this baby, we'd be set. We'd've been winners for sure." At the end of the story he tells the clerk in the sporting goods store, "We're winners, man. So pay up." What accounts for his change in perspective?
3. What does it mean to be a winner? In what sense are these boys "winners"?
4. Is it significant that the narrator's parents had divorced shortly before this story takes place?
5. How do you interpret the closing line of this story, "The town fled from us in confusion"?

Suggestions for Writing

1. The boys in this story are left feeling "helpless against adult treachery and betrayal." Write an essay exploring why they feel this way. Focus upon information about the boys, and how they are treated, that you find in the story itself.
2. Consider the scene of this story, when it is set as well as where it is set. Write an essay explaining what elements of the scene contribute to the act these boys commit.

SHOPPING

Joyce Carol Oates

> *Bumper stickers in recent years have featured slogans such as "Born to shop"*
> *and "When the going gets tough, the tough go shopping." For many Americans*
> *shopping has become an important ritual—and the mall a type of second home.*
> *In the following story Joyce Carol Oates uses a Saturday morning trip to the*
> *mall as a way to reveal character and conflict. The characters are an upper-*
> *middle-class woman and her seventeen-year-old daughter. As you read, try to*
> *understand why these characters conflict. The author of many novels and collec-*
> *tions of short stories, Joyce Carol Oates teaches writing at Princeton.*

An old ritual, Saturday morning shopping. Mother and daughter. Mrs.
Dietrich and Nola. Shops in the village, stores and boutiques at the splendid
Livingstone Mall on Route 12. Bloomingdale's, Saks, Lord & Taylor, Bon-
wit's, Neiman-Marcus: and the rest. Mrs. Dietrich would know her way
around the stores blindfolded but there is always the surprise of lavish seasonal displays, extraordinary holiday sales, the openings of new stores at the
Mall like Laura Ashley, Paraphernalia. On one of their Mall days Mrs. Dietrich and Nola would try to get there at midmorning, have lunch around
1 P.M. at one or another of their favorite restaurants, shop for perhaps an
hour after lunch, then come home. Sometimes the shopping trips were
more successful than at other times but you have to have faith, Mrs. Dietrich
tells herself. Her interior voice is calm, neutral, free of irony. Ever since her
divorce her interior voice has been free of irony. You have to have faith.

Tomorrow morning Nola returns to school in Maine; today will be a
day at the Mall. Mrs. Dietrich has planned it for days. At the Mall, in such
crowds of shoppers, moments of intimacy are possible as they rarely are at
home. (Seventeen-year-old Nola, home on spring break for a brief eight
days, seems always to be *busy*, always out with her *friends*—the trip to the
Mall has been postponed twice.) But Saturday, 10:30 A.M., they are in the
car at last headed south on Route 12, a bleak March morning following a
night of freezing rain, there's a metallic cast to the air and no sun anywhere
in the sky but the light hurts Mrs. Dietrich's eyes just the same. "Does it
seem as if spring will ever come?—it must be twenty degrees colder up in
Maine," she says. Driving in heavy traffic always makes Mrs. Dietrich nervous and she is overly sensitive to her daughter's silence, which seems deliberate, perverse, when they have so little time remaining together—not even
a full day.

Nola asks politely if Mrs. Dietrich would like her to drive and Mrs.
Dietrich says no, of course not, she's fine, it's only a few more miles and
maybe traffic will lighten. Nola seems about to say something more, then

thinks better of it. So much between them that is precarious, chancy—but they've been kind to each other these past seven days. Mrs. Dietrich loves Nola with a fierce unreasoned passion stronger than any she felt for the man who had been her husband for thirteen years, certainly far stronger than any she ever felt for her own mother. Sometimes in weak despondent moods, alone, lonely, self-pitying, when she has had too much to drink, Mrs. Dietrich thinks she is in love with her daughter—but this is a thought she can't contemplate for long. And how Nola would snort in amused contempt, incredulous, mocking—"Oh *Mother!*"—if she were told.

Mrs. Dietrich tries to engage her daughter in conversation of a harmless sort but Nola answers in monosyllables, Nola is rather tired from so many nights of partying with her friends, some of whom attend the local high school, some of whom are home for spring break from prep schools— Exeter, Lawrenceville, Concord, Andover, Portland. Late nights, but Mrs. Dietrich doesn't consciously lie awake waiting for Nola to come home: they've been through all that before. Now Nola sits beside her mother looking wan, subdued, rather melancholy. Thinking her private thoughts. She is wearing a bulky quilted jacket Mrs. Dietrich has never liked, the usual blue jeans, black calfskin boots zippered tightly to mid-calf. Mrs. Dietrich must resist the temptation to ask, "Why are you so quiet, Nola? What are you thinking?" They've been through all that before.

Route 12 has become a jumble of small industrial parks, high-rise office and apartment buildings, torn-up landscapes—mountains of raw earth, uprooted trees, ruts and ditches filled with muddy water. There is no natural sequence to what you see—buildings, construction work, leveled woods, the lavish grounds owned by Squibb. Though she has driven this route countless times, Mrs. Dietrich is never quite certain where the Mall is and must be prepared for a sudden exit. She remembers getting lost the first several times, remembers the excitement she and her friends felt about the grand opening of the Mall, stores worthy of serious shopping at last. Today is much the same. No, today is worse. Like Christmas when she was a small child, Mrs. Dietrich thinks. She'd hoped so badly to be happy she'd felt actual pain, a constriction in her throat like crying.

"*Are* you all right, Nola?—you've been so quiet all morning," Mrs. Dietrich asks, half-scolding. Nola stirs from her reverie, says she's fine, a just perceptible edge to her reply, and for the remainder of the drive there's some stiffness between them. Mrs. Dietrich chooses to ignore it. In any case she is fully absorbed in driving—negotiating a tricky exit across two lanes of traffic, then the hairpin curve of the ramp, the numerous looping drives of the Mall. Then the enormous parking lot, daunting to the inexperienced, but Mrs. Dietrich always heads for the area behind Lord & Taylor on the far side of the Mall, Lot D; her luck holds and she finds a space close in. "Well— we made it," she says, smiling happily at Nola. Nola laughs in reply—what does a seventeen-year-old's laughter *mean?*—but she remembers, getting out, to lock both doors on her side of the car. The smile Nola gives Mrs. Dietrich across the car's roof is careless and beautiful and takes Mrs. Dietrich's breath away.

The March morning tastes of grit with an undercurrent of something acrid, chemical; inside the Mall, beneath the first of the elegant brass-buttressed glass domes, the air is fresh and tonic, circulating from invisible vents. The Mall is crowded, rather noisy—it *is* Saturday morning—but a feast for the eyes after that long trip on Route 12. Tall slender trees grow out of the mosaic-tiled pavement, there are beds of Easter lilies, daffodils, jonquils, tulips of all colors. Mrs. Dietrich smiles with relief. She senses that Nola too is relieved, cheered. It's like coming home.

The shopping excursions began when Nola was a small child but did not acquire their special significance until she was twelve or thirteen years old and capable of serious, sustained shopping with her mother. This was about the time when Mr. Dietrich moved out of the house and back into their old apartment in the city—a separation, he'd called it initially, to give them perspective—though Mrs. Dietrich had no illusions about what "perspective" would turn out to entail—so the shopping trips were all the more significant. Not that Mrs. Dietrich and Nola spent very much money—they really didn't, *really* they didn't, when compared to friends and neighbors.

At seventeen Nola is shrewd and discerning as a shopper, not easy to please, knowledgeable as a mature woman about certain aspects of fashion, quality merchandise, good stores. Her closets, like Mrs. Dietrich's, are crammed, but she rarely buys anything that Mrs. Dietrich thinks shoddy or merely faddish. Up in Portland, at the Academy, she hasn't as much time to shop but when she is home in Livingstone it isn't unusual for her and her girlfriends to shop nearly every day. Like all her friends she has charge accounts at the better stores, her own credit cards, a reasonable allowance. At the time of their settlement Mr. Dietrich said guiltily that it was the least he could do for them—if Mrs. Dietrich wanted to work part-time, she could (she was trained, more or less, in public relations of a small-scale sort); if not, not. Mrs. Dietrich thought, It's the most you can do for us too.

Near Bloomingdale's entrance mother and daughter see a disheveled   10
woman sitting by herself on one of the benches. Without seeming to look at her, shoppers are making a discreet berth around her, a stream following a natural course. Nola, taken by surprise, stares. Mrs. Dietrich has seen the woman from time to time at the Mall, always alone, smirking and talking to herself, frizzed gray hair in a tangle, puckered mouth. Always wearing the same black wool coat, a garment of fairly good quality but shapeless, rumpled, stained, as if she sleeps in it. She might be anywhere from forty to sixty years of age. Once Mrs. Dietrich saw her make menacing gestures at children who were teasing her, another time she'd seen the woman staring

belligerently at *her*. A white paste had gathered in the corners of her mouth. . . . "My God, that poor woman," Nola says. "I didn't think there were people like her here—I mean, I didn't think they would allow it."

"She doesn't seem to cause any disturbance," Mrs. Dietrich says. "She just sits—Don't stare, Nola, she'll see you."

"You've seen her here before? Here?"

"A few times this winter."

"Is she always like that?"

"I'm sure she's harmless, Nola. She just *sits*."   15

Nola is incensed, her pale blue eyes like washed glass. "I'm sure *she's* harmless, Mother. It's the harm the poor woman has to endure that is the tragedy."

Mrs. Dietrich is surprised and a little offended by her daughter's passionate tone but she knows enough not to argue. They enter Bloomingdale's, taking their habitual route. So many shoppers!—so much merchandise! Nola speaks of the tragedy of women like that woman—the tragedy of the homeless, the mentally disturbed—bag ladies out on the street—outcasts of an affluent society—but she's soon distracted by the busyness on all sides, the attractive items for sale. They take the escalator up to the third floor, to the Juniors department where Nola often buys things. From there they will move on to Young Collector, then to New Impressions, then to Petites, then one or another boutique and designer—Liz Claiborne, Christian Dior, Calvin Klein, Carlos Falchi, and the rest. And after Bloomingdale's the other stores await, to be visited each in turn. Mrs. Dietrich checks her watch and sees with satisfaction that there's just enough time before lunch but not *too* much time. She gets ravenously hungry, shopping at the Mall.

Nola is efficient and matter-of-fact about shopping, though she acts solely upon instinct. Mrs. Dietrich likes to watch her at a short distance— holding items of clothing up to herself in the three-way mirrors, modeling things she thinks especially promising. A twill blazer with rounded shoulders and blouson jacket, a funky zippered jumpsuit in white sailcloth, a pair of straight-leg Evan-Picone pants, a green leather vest: Mrs. Dietrich watches her covertly. At such times Nola is perfectly content, fully absorbed in the task at hand; Mrs. Dietrich knows she isn't thinking about anything that would distress her. (Like Mr. Dietrich's betrayal. Like Nola's difficulties with her friends. Like her difficulties at school—as much as Mrs. Dietrich knows of them.) Once, at the Mall, perhaps in this very store in this very department, Nola saw Mrs. Dietrich watching her and walked away angrily and when Mrs. Dietrich caught up with her she said, "I can't stand it, Mother." Her voice was choked and harsh, a vein prominent in her forehead. "Let me go. For Christ's sake will you let me go." Mrs. Dietrich didn't dare touch her though she could see Nola was trembling. For a long terrible moment mother and daughter stood side by side near a display of bright brash Catalina beachwear while Nola whispered, "Let me go. *Let me go.*"

Difficult to believe that girl standing so poised and self-assured in front of the three-way mirror was once a plain, rather chunky, unhappy child. She'd been unpopular at school. Overly serious. Anxious. Quick to tears. Aged eleven she hid herself away in her room for hours at a time, reading, drawing pictures, writing little stories she could sometimes be prevailed upon to read aloud to her mother, sometimes even to her father, though she dreaded his judgment. She went through a "scientific" phase a while later—Mrs. Dietrich remembers an ambitious bas-relief map of North America, meticulous illustrations for "photosynthesis," a pastel drawing of an eerie ball of fire labeled "Red Giant" (a dying star?) which won a prize in a state competition for junior high students. Then for a season it was stray facts Nola confronted them with, often at the dinner table. Interrupting her parents' conversation to say brightly: "Did you know that Nero's favorite color was green?—he carried a giant emerald and held it up to his eye to watch Christians being devoured by lions." And once at a large family gathering: "Did you know that last week downtown a little baby's nose was chewed off by rats in his crib?—a little *black* baby?" Nola meant only to call attention to herself but you couldn't blame her listeners for being offended. They stared at her, not knowing what to say. What a strange child! What queer glassy-pale eyes! Mr. Dietrich told her curtly to leave the table—he'd had enough of the game she was playing and so had everyone else.

Nola stared at him, her eyes filling with tears. Game?   20

When they were alone Mr. Dietrich said angrily to Mrs. Dietrich: "Can't you control her in front of other people, at least?" Mrs. Dietrich was angry too, and frightened. She said "I *try*."

They sent her off aged fourteen to the Portland Academy up in Maine and without their help she matured into a girl of considerable beauty. A heart-shaped face, delicate features, glossy red-brown hair scissor-cut to her shoulders. Five feet seven inches tall, weighing less than one hundred pounds—the result of constant savage dieting. (Mrs. Dietrich, who has weight problems herself, doesn't dare to inquire as to details. They've been through that already.) Thirty days after they'd left her at the Portland Academy Nola telephoned home at 11:00 P.M. one Sunday giggly and high telling Mrs. Dietrich she adored the school she adored her suite mates she adored most of her teachers particularly her riding instructor Terri, Terri the Terrier they called the woman because she was so fierce, such a character, eyes that bore right through your skull, wore belts with the most amazing silver buckles! Nola loved Terri but she wasn't *in* love—there's a difference!

Mrs. Dietrich broke down weeping, *that* time.

Now of course Nola has boyfriends. Mrs. Dietrich has long since given up trying to keep track of their names. There is even one "boy"—or young man—who seems to be married: who seems to be, in fact, one of the junior instructors at the school. (Mrs. Dietrich does not eavesdrop on her daughter's telephone conversations but there are things she cannot help overhearing.) Is your daughter on the Pill? the women in Mrs. Dietrich's circle asked one another for a while, guiltily, surreptitiously. Now they no longer ask.

But Nola has announced recently that she loathes boys—she's fed up. 25

She's never going to get married. She'll study languages in college, French, Italian, something exotic like Arabic, go to work for the American foreign service. Unless she drops out of school altogether to become a model.

"Do you think I'm fat, Mother?" she asks frequently, worriedly, standing in front of the mirror twisted at the waist to reveal her small round belly which, it seems, can't help being round: she bloats herself on diet Cokes all day long. "Do you think it *shows?*"

When Mrs. Dietrich was pregnant with Nola she'd been twenty-nine years old and she and Mr. Dietrich had tried to have a baby for nearly five years. She'd lost hope, begun to despise herself, then suddenly it happened: like grace. Like happiness swelling so powerfully it can barely be contained. I can hear its heartbeat! her husband exclaimed. He'd been her lover then, young, vigorous, dreamy. Caressing the rock-hard belly, splendid white tight-stretched skin. Mr. Dietrich gave Mrs. Dietrich a reproduction on stiff glossy paper of Dante Gabriel Rossetti's *Beata Beatrix,* embarrassed, apologetic, knowing it was sentimental and perhaps a little silly but that was how he thought of her—so beautiful, rapturous, pregnant with their child. She told no one but she knew the baby was to be a girl. It would be herself again, reborn and this time perfect.

"Oh, Mother—isn't it *beautiful?* " Nola exclaims.

It is past noon. Past twelve-thirty. Mrs. Dietrich and Nola have made 30 the rounds of a half-dozen stores, traveled countless escalators, one clothing department has blended into the next and the chic smiling saleswomen have become indistinguishable and Mrs. Dietrich is beginning to feel the urgent need for a glass of white wine. Just a glass. "Isn't it beautiful?—it's *perfect,*" Nola says. Her eyes glow with pleasure, her smooth skin is radiant. As Nola models in the three-way mirror a queer little yellow-and-black striped sweater with a ribbed waist, punk style, mock-cheap, Mrs. Dietrich feels the motherly obligation to register a mild protest, knowing that Nola will not hear. She must have it and will have it. She'll wear it a few times, then retire it to the bottom of a drawer with so many other novelty sweaters, accumulated since sixth grade. (She's like her mother in that regard—can't bear to throw anything away.)

"*Isn't* it beautiful?" Nola demands, studying her reflection in the mirror.

Mrs. Dietrich pays for the sweater on her charge account.

Next, they buy Nola a good pair of shoes. And a handbag to go with them. In Paraphernalia, where rock music blasts overhead and Mrs. Dietrich stands to one side, rather miserable, Nola chats companionably with two girls—tall, pretty, cutely made up—she'd gone to public school in Livingstone with, says afterward with an upward rolling of her eyes, "God, I was afraid they'd latch on to us!" Mrs. Dietrich has seen women friends and acquaintances of her own in the Mall this morning but has shrunk from being noticed, not wanting to share her daughter with anyone. She has a sense of time passing ever more swiftly, cruelly.

She watches Nola preening in a mirror, watches other shoppers watching her. My daughter. Mine. But of course there is no connection between them—they don't even resemble each other. A seventeen-year-old, a forty-seven-year-old. When Nola is away she seems to forget her mother entirely—doesn't telephone, certainly doesn't write. It's the way all their daughters are, Mrs. Dietrich's friends tell her. It doesn't *mean* anything. Mrs. Dietrich thinks how when she was carrying Nola, those nine long months, they'd been completely happy—not an instant's doubt or hesitation. The singular weight of the body. A trancelike state you are tempted to mistake for happiness because the body is incapable of thinking, therefore incapable of anticipating change. Hot rhythmic blood, organs, packed tight and moist, the baby upside down in her sac in her mother's belly, always present tense, always *now*. It was a shock when the end came so abruptly but everyone told Mrs. Dietrich she was a natural mother, praised and pampered her. For a while. Then of course she'd had her baby, her Nola. Even now Mrs. Dietrich can't really comprehend the experience. *Giving birth. Had a baby. Was born.* Mere words, absurdly inadequate. She knows no more of how love ends than she knew as a child, she knows only of how love begins—in the belly, in the womb, where it is always present tense.

The morning's shopping has been quite successful but lunch at La Crêperie doesn't go well for some reason. La Crêperie is Nola's favorite Mall restaurant—always amiably crowded, bustling, a simulated sidewalk café with red-striped umbrellas, wrought-iron tables and chairs, menus in French, music piped in overhead. Mrs. Dietrich's nerves are chafed by the pretense of gaiety, the noise, the openness onto one of the Mall's busy promenades where at any minute a familiar face might emerge, but she is grateful for her glass of chilled white wine. She orders a small tossed salad and a creamed-chicken crepe and devours it hungrily—she *is* hungry. While Nola picks at her seafood crepe with a disdainful look. A familiar scene: mother watching while daughter pushes food around on her plate. Suddenly Nola is tense, moody, corners of her mouth downturned. Mrs. Dietrich wants to ask, What's wrong? She wants to ask, Why are you unhappy? She wants to smooth Nola's hair back from her forehead, check to see if her forehead is overly warm, wants to hug her close, hard. Why, why? What did I do wrong? Why do you hate me?

Calling the Portland Academy a few weeks ago Mrs. Dietrich suddenly lost control, began crying. She hadn't been drinking and she hadn't known she was upset. A girl unknown to her, one of Nola's suite mates, was saying, "Please, Mrs. Dietrich, it's all right, I'm sure Nola will call you back later tonight, or tomorrow, Mrs. Dietrich?—I'll tell her you called, all right?— Mrs. Dietrich?" as embarrassed as if Mrs. Dietrich had been her own mother.

How love begins. How love ends.

Mrs. Dietrich orders a third glass of wine. This is a celebration of sorts isn't it?—their last shopping trip for a long time. But Nola resists, Nola isn't sentimental. In casual defiance of Mrs. Dietrich she lights up a cigarette— yes, Mother, Nola has said ironically, since *you* stopped smoking *everybody* is supposed to stop—and sits with her arms crossed, watching streams of shoppers pass. Mrs. Dietrich speaks lightly of practical matters, tomorrow morning's drive to the airport, and will Nola telephone when she gets to Portland to let Mrs. Dietrich know she has arrived safely?

Then with no warning—though of course she'd been planning this all along—Nola brings up the subject of a semester in France, in Paris and Rouen, the fall semester of her senior year it would be; she has put in her application, she says, and is waiting to hear if she's been accepted. She smokes her cigarette calmly, expelling smoke from her nostrils in a way Mrs. Dietrich thinks particularly coarse. Mrs. Dietrich, who believed that particular topic was finished, takes care to speak without emotion. "I just don't think it's a very practical idea right now, Nola," she says. "We've been through it haven't we? I—"

"I'm going," Nola says.   40

"The extra expense, for one thing. Your father—"

"If I get accepted, I'm going."

"Your father—"

"The hell with him too."

Mrs. Dietrich would like to slap her daughter's face. Bring tears to   45 those steely eyes. But she sits stiff, turning her wine glass between her fingers, patient, calm, she's heard all this before; she says, "Surely this isn't the best time to discuss it, Nola."

Mrs. Dietrich is afraid her daughter will leave the restaurant, simply walk away, that has happened before and if it happens today she doesn't know what she will do. But Nola sits unmoving; her face closed, impassive. Mrs. Dietrich feels her quickened heartbeat. Once after one of their quarrels Mrs. Dietrich told a friend of hers, the mother too of a teenage daughter, "I just don't know her any longer, how can you keep living with someone you don't know?" and the woman said, "Eventually you can't."

Nola says, not looking at Mrs. Dietrich: "Why don't we talk about it, Mother?"

"Talk about what?" Mrs. Dietrich asks.

"You know."

"The semester in France? Again?"   50

"No."

"What, then?"

"You *know*."

"I don't know, really. Really!" Mrs. Dietrich smiles, baffled. She feels the corners of her eyes pucker white with strain.

Nola says, sighing, "How exhausting it is."   55

"How *what?*"

"How exhausting it is."

"What is?"

"You and me—"

"What?"   60

"Being together—"

"Being together how—?"

"The two of us, like this—"

"But we're hardly ever together, Nola," Mrs. Dietrich says.

Her expression is calm but her voice is shaking. Nola turns away,   65
covering her face with a hand, for a moment she looks years older than her age—in fact exhausted. Mrs. Dietrich sees with pity that her daughter's skin is fair and thin and dry—unlike her own, which tends to be oily—it will wear out before she's forty. Mrs. Dietrich reaches over to squeeze her hand. The fingers are limp, ungiving. "You're going back to school tomorrow, Nola," she says. "You won't come home again until June 12. And you probably will go to France—if your father consents."

Nola gets to her feet, drops her cigarette to the flagstone terrace and grinds it beneath her boot. A dirty thing to do, Mrs. Dietrich thinks, considering there's an ashtray right on the table, but she says nothing. She dislikes La Crêperie anyway.

Nola laughs, showing her lovely white teeth. "Oh, the hell with him," she says. "Fuck Daddy, right?"

They separate for an hour, Mrs. Dietrich to Neiman-Marcus to buy a birthday gift for her elderly aunt, Nola to the trendy new boutique Pour Vous. By the time Mrs. Dietrich rejoins her daughter she's quite angry, blood beating hot and hard and measured in resentment, she has had time to relive old quarrels between them, old exchanges, stray humiliating memories of her marriage as well, these last-hour disagreements are the cruelest and they are Nola's specialty. She locates Nola in the rear of the boutique amid blaring rock music, flashing neon lights, chrome-edged mirrors, her face still hard, closed, prim, pale. She stands beside another teenage girl looking in a desultory way through a rack of blouses, shoving the hangers roughly along, taking no care when a blouse falls to the floor. As Nola glances up, startled, not prepared to see her mother in front of her, their eyes lock for an instant and Mrs. Dietrich stares at her with hatred. Cold calm clear unmistakable hatred. She is thinking, Who are *you?* What have I to do with *you?* I don't know *you,* I don't love *you,* why should I?

Has Nola seen, heard?—she turns aside as if wincing, gives the blouses a final dismissive shove. Her eyes look tired, the corners of her mouth downturned. Anxious, immediately repentant, Mrs. Dietrich asks if she has found anything worth trying on. Nola says with a shrug, "Not a thing, Mother."

On their way out of the Mall Mrs. Dietrich and Nola see the disheveled woman in the black coat again, this time sitting prominently on a concrete ledge in front of Lord & Taylor's busy main entrance. Shopping bag at her feet, shabby purse on the ledge beside her. She is shaking her head in a series of annoyed twitches as if arguing with someone but her hands are loose, palms up, in her lap. Her posture is unfortunate—she sits with her knees parted, inner thighs revealed, fatty, dead white, the tops of cotton stockings rolled tight cutting into the flesh. Again, streams of shoppers are making a careful berth around her. Alone among them Nola hesitates, seems about to approach the woman—Please don't, Nola! please! Mrs. Dietrich thinks—then changes her mind and keeps on walking. Mrs. Dietrich murmurs isn't it a pity, poor thing, don't you wonder where she lives, who her family is, but Nola doesn't reply. Her pace through the first door of Lord & Taylor is so rapid that Mrs. Dietrich can barely keep up.

But Nola's upset. Strangely upset. As soon as they are in the car, packages and bags in the backseat, she begins crying.

It's childish helpless crying, as though her heart is broken. But Mrs. Dietrich knows it isn't broken, she has heard these very sobs before. Many times before. Still she comforts her daughter, embraces her, hugs her hard, hard. A sudden fierce passion. Vehemence. "Nola honey. Nola dear, what's wrong, dear, everything will be all right, dear," she says, close to weeping herself. She would embrace Nola even more tightly except for the girl's quilted jacket, that bulky L. L. Bean thing she has never liked, and Nola's stubborn lowered head. Nola has always been ashamed, crying, frantic to hide her face. Strangers are passing close by the car, curious, staring. Mrs. Dietrich wishes she had a cloak to draw over her daughter and herself, so that no one else would see.

Questions for Discussion

1. Reread the first two paragraphs of this story. Do they contain any signs of unhappiness or trouble?
2. Why are Mrs. Dietrich and her daughter silent in the car? Why do they feel they have to be careful about what they say to one another? How would you describe their relationship?
3. What is the significance of the title of this story? What are the characters shopping for? What does Mrs. Dietrich hope to experience by shopping with her daughter? What motivates Nola to go along? Why are they relieved to arrive at the mall?
4. What does the woman in the black coat represent? Why do the other shoppers try to avoid her? How do Mrs. Dietrich and Nola differ in their response to her?

5. What does the story reveal about Mr. Dietrich?
6. Why do we never learn Mrs. Dietrich's first name? What does this story suggest about her life from the glimpse of it we are allowed to see?
7. In paragraph 47 Nola abruptly asks, "Why don't we talk about it, Mother?" What is she referring to?
8. Why is Nola crying at the end of the story?

Suggestions for Writing

1. From whose point of view is "Shopping" told? Write an essay explaining how this is established and what influence it has upon your response to the story.
2. Compare Nola and Mrs. Dietrich. Despite their differences, how are they alike?

LULLABY

Leslie Marmon Silko

Born in New Mexico, Leslie Silko writes fiction that draws upon her heritage as a Native American. As you read the following story, pay particular attention to the scene. Note details about the landscape and the weather, and consider the relationship between the characters and the land. Consider what the story reveals about Native American culture, but consider also whether the story raises any concerns of universal significance.

The sun had gone down but the snow in the wind gave off its own light. It came in thick tufts like new wool—washed before the weaver spins it. Ayah reached out for it like her own babies had, and she smiled when she remembered how she had laughed at them. She was an old woman now, and her life had become memories. She sat down with her back against the wide cottonwood tree, feeling the rough bark on her back bones; she faced east and listened to the wind and snow sing a high-pitched Yeibechei° song. Out of the wind she felt warmer, and she could watch the wide fluffy snow fill in her tracks, steadily, until the direction she had come from was gone. By the light of the snow she could see the dark outline of the big arroyo a few feet away. She was sitting on the edge of Cebolleta Creek, where in the springtime the thin cows would graze on grass already chewed flat to the ground. In the wide deep creek bed where only a trickle of water flowed in the summer, the skinny cows would wander, looking for new grass along winding paths splashed with manure.

Ayah pulled the old Army blanket over her head like a shawl. Jimmie's blanket—the one he had sent to her. That was a long time ago and the green wool was faded, and it was unraveling on the edges. She did not want to think about Jimmie. So she thought about the weaving and the way her mother had done it. On the tall wooden loom set into the sand under a tamarack tree for shade. She could see it clearly. She had been only a little girl when her grandma gave her the wooden combs to pull the twigs and burrs from the raw, freshly washed wool. And while she combed the wool, her grandma sat beside her, spinning a silvery strand of yarn around the smooth cedar spindle. Her mother worked at the loom with yarns dyed bright yellow and red and gold. She watched them dye the yarn in boiling black pots full of beeweed petals, juniper berries, and sage. The blankets her mother made were soft and woven so tight that rain rolled off them like birds' feathers. Ayah remembered sleeping warm on cold windy nights, wrapped in her mother's blankets on the hogan's sandy floor.

The snow drifted now, with the northwest wind hurling it in gusts. It drifted up around her black overshoes—old ones with little metal buckles.

Yeibechei: A Navajo song of healing.

She smiled at the snow which was trying to cover her little by little. She could remember when they had no black rubber overshoes; only the high buckskin leggings that they wrapped over their elkhide moccasins. If the snow was dry or frozen, a person could walk all day and not get wet; and in the evenings the beams of the ceiling would hang with lengths of pale buckskin leggings, drying out slowly.

She felt peaceful remembering. She didn't feel cold any more. Jimmie's blanket seemed warmer than it had ever been. And she could remember the morning he was born. She could remember whispering to her mother, who was sleeping on the other side of the hogan,° to tell her it was time now. She did not want to wake the others. The second time she called to her, her mother stood up and pulled on her shoes; she knew. They walked to the old stone hogan together, Ayah walking a step behind her mother. She waited alone, learning the rhythms of the pains while her mother went to call the old woman to help them. The morning was already warm even before dawn and Ayah smelled the bee flowers blooming and the young willow growing at the springs. She could remember that so clearly, but his birth merged into the births of the other children and to her it became all the same birth. They named him for the summer morning and in English they called him Jimmie.

It wasn't like Jimmie died. He just never came back, and one day a   5 dark blue sedan with white writing on its doors pulled up in front of the boxcar shack where the rancher let the Indians live. A man in a khaki uniform trimmed in gold gave them a yellow piece of paper and told them that Jimmie was dead. He said the Army would try to get the body back and then it would be shipped to them; but it wasn't likely because the helicopter had burned after it crashed. All of this was told to Chato because he could understand English. She stood inside the doorway holding the baby while Chato listened. Chato spoke English like a white man and he spoke Spanish too. He was taller than the white man and he stood straighter too. Chato didn't explain why; he just told the military man they could keep the body if they found it. The white man looked bewildered; he nodded his head and he left. Then Chato looked at her and shook his head, and then he told her, "Jimmie isn't coming home anymore," and when he spoke, he used the words to speak of the dead. She didn't cry then, but she hurt inside with anger. And she mourned him as the years passed, when a horse fell with Chato and broke his leg, and the white rancher told them he wouldn't pay Chato until he could work again. She mourned Jimmie because he would have worked for his father then; he would have saddled the big bay horse and ridden the fence lines each day, with wire cutters and heavy gloves, fixing the breaks in the barbed wire and putting the stray cattle back inside again.

She mourned him after the white doctors came to take Danny and Ella away. She was at the shack alone that day they came. It was back in the

hogan: A traditional Navajo dwelling made of logs and mud, with a door facing east.

days before they hired Navajo women to go with them as interpreters. She recognized one of the doctors. She had seen him at the children's clinic at Cañoncito about a month ago. They were wearing khaki uniforms and they waved papers at her and a black ball-point pen, trying to make her understand their English words. She was frightened by the way they looked at the children, like the lizard watches the fly. Danny was swinging on the tire swing on the elm tree behind the rancher's house, and Ella was toddling around the front door, dragging the broomstick horse Chato made for her. Ayah could see they wanted her to sign the papers, and Chato had taught her to sign her name. It was something she was proud of. She only wanted them to go, and to take their eyes away from her children.

She took the pen from the man without looking at his face and she signed the papers in three different places he pointed to. She stared at the ground by their feet and waited for them to leave. But they stood there and began to point and gesture at the children. Danny stopped swinging. Ayah could see his fear. She moved suddenly and grabbed Ella into her arms; the child squirmed, trying to get back to her toys. Ayah ran with the baby toward Danny; she screamed for him to run and then she grabbed him around his chest and carried him too. She ran south into the foothills of juniper trees and black lava rock. Behind her she heard the doctors running, but they had been taken by surprise, and as the hills became steeper and the cholla cactus were thicker, they stopped. When she reached the top of the hill, she stopped to listen in case they were circling around her. But in a few minutes she heard a car engine start and they drove away. The children had been too surprised to cry while she ran with them. Danny was shaking and Ella's little fingers were gripping Ayah's blouse.

She stayed up in the hills for the rest of the day, sitting on a black lava boulder in the sunshine where she could see for miles all around her. The sky was light blue and cloudless, and it was warm for late April. The sun warmth relaxed her and took the fear and anger away. She lay back on the rock and watched the sky. It seemed to her that she could walk into the sky, stepping through clouds endlessly. Danny played with little pebbles and stones, pretending they were birds eggs and then little rabbits. Ella sat at her feet and dropped fistfuls of dirt into the breeze, watching the dust and particles of sand intently. Ayah watched a hawk soar high above them, dark wings gliding; hunting or only watching, she did not know. The hawk was patient and he circled all afternoon before he disappeared around the high volcanic peak the Mexicans called Guadalupe.

Late in the afternoon, Ayah looked down at the gray boxcar shack with the paint all peeled from the wood; the stove pipe on the roof was rusted and crooked. The fire she had built that morning in the oil drum stove had burned out. Ella was asleep in her lap now and Danny sat close to her, complaining that he was hungry; he asked when they would go to the house. "We will stay up here until your father comes," she told him, "because those white men were chasing us." The boy remembered then and he nodded at her silently.

If Jimmie had been there he could have read those papers and ex-   *10*
plained to her what they said. Ayah would have known then, never to sign
them. The doctors came back the next day and they brought a BIA° policeman with them. They told Chato they had her signature and that was all
they needed. Except for the kids. She listened to Chato sullenly; she hated
him when he told her it was the old woman who died in the winter, spitting
blood; it was her old grandma who had given the children this disease.
"They don't spit blood," she said coldly. "The whites lie." She held Ella and
Danny close to her, ready to run to the hills again. "I want a medicine man
first," she said to Chato, not looking at him. He shook his head. "It's too
late now. The policeman is with them. You signed the paper." His voice was
gentle.

It was worse than if they had died: to lose the children and to know
that somewhere, in a place called Colorado, in a place full of sick and dying
strangers, her children were without her. There had been babies that died
soon after they were born, and one that died before he could walk. She had
carried them herself, up to the boulders and great pieces of the cliff that
long ago crashed down from Long Mesa; she laid them in the crevices of
sandstone and buried them in fine brown sand with round quartz pebbles
that washed down the hills in the rain. She had endured it because they had
been with her. But she could not bear this pain. She did not sleep for a long
time after they took her children. She stayed on the hill where they had fled
the first time, and she slept rolled up in the blanket Jimmie had sent her. She
carried the pain in her belly and it was fed by everything she saw: the blue
sky of their last day together and the dust and pebbles they played with; the
swing in the elm tree and broomstick horse choked life from her. The pain
filled her stomach and there was no room for food or for her lungs to fill
with air. The air and the food would have been theirs.

She hated Chato, not because he let the policeman and doctors put
the screaming children in the government car, but because he had taught
her to sign her name. Because it was like the old ones always told her about
learning their language or any of their ways: it endangered you. She slept
alone on the hill until the middle of November when the first snows came.
Then she made a bed for herself where the children had slept. She did not
lie down beside Chato again until many years later, when he was sick and
shivering and only her body could keep him warm. The illness came after
the white rancher told Chato he was too old to work for him anymore, and
Chato and his old woman should be out of the shack by the next afternoon
because the rancher had hired new people to work there. That had satisfied
her. To see how the white man repaid Chato's years of loyalty and work. All
of Chato's fine-sounding English talk didn't change things.

It snowed steadily and the luminous light from the snow gradually
diminished into the darkness. Somewhere in Cebolleta a dog barked and

---

BIA: U.S. Bureau of Indian Affairs.

other village dogs joined with it. Ayah looked in the direction she had come, from the bar where Chato was buying the wine. Sometimes he told her to go on ahead and wait; and then he never came. And when she finally went back looking for him, she would find him passed out at the bottom of the wooden steps to Azzie's Bar. All the wine would be gone and most of the money too, from the pale blue check that came to them once a month in a government envelope. It was then that she would look at his face and his hands, scarred by ropes and the barbed wire of all those years, and she would think, this man is a stranger; for forty years she had smiled at him and cooked his food, but he remained a stranger. She stood up again, with the snow almost to her knees, and she walked back to find Chato.

It was hard to walk in the deep snow and she felt the air burn in her lungs. She stopped a short distance from the bar to rest and readjust the blanket. But this time he wasn't waiting for her on the bottom step with his old Stetson hat pulled down and his shoulders hunched up in his long wool overcoat.

She was careful not to slip on the wooden steps. When she pushed the door open, warm air and cigarette smoke hit her face. She looked around slowly and deliberately, in every corner, in every dark place that the old man might find to sleep. The bar owner didn't like Indians in there, especially Navajos, but he let Chato come in because he could talk Spanish like he was one of them. The men at the bar stared at her, and the bartender saw that she left the door open wide. Snowflakes were flying inside like moths and melting into a puddle on the oiled wood floor. He motioned to her to close the door, but she did not see him. She held herself straight and walked across the room slowly, searching the room with every step. The snow in her hair melted and she could feel it on her forehead. At the far corner of the room, she saw red flames at the mica window of the old stove door; she looked behind the stove just to make sure. The bar got quiet except for the Spanish polka music playing on the jukebox. She stood by the stove and shook the snow from her blanket and held it near the stove to dry. The wet wool smell reminded her of new-born goats in early March, brought inside to warm near the fire. She felt calm.

In past years they would have told her to get out. But her hair was white now and her face was wrinkled. They looked at her like she was a spider crawling slowly across the room. They were afraid; she could feel the fear. She looked at their faces steadily. They reminded her of the first time the white people brought her children back to her that winter. Danny had been shy and hid behind the thin white woman who brought them. And the baby had not known her until Ayah took her into her arms, and then Ella had nuzzled close to her as she had when she was nursing. The blonde woman was nervous and kept looking at a dainty gold watch on her wrist. She sat on the bench near the small window and watched the dark snow clouds gather around the mountains; she was worrying about the unpaved road. She was frightened by what she saw inside too: the strips of venison drying on a rope across the ceiling and the children jabbering excitedly in a

15

language she did not know. So they stayed for only a few hours. Ayah watched the government car disappear down the road and she knew they were already being weaned from these lava hills and from this sky. The last time they came was in early June, and Ella stared at her the way the men in the bar were now staring. Ayah did not try to pick her up; she smiled at her instead and spoke cheerfully to Danny. When he tried to answer her, he could not seem to remember and he spoke English words with the Navajo. But he gave her a scrap of paper that he had found somewhere and carried in his pocket; it was folded in half, and he shyly looked up at her and said it was a bird. She asked Chato if they were home for good this time. He spoke to the white woman and she shook her head. "How much longer?" he asked, and she said she didn't know; but Chato saw how she stared at the boxcar shack. Ayah turned away then. She did not say good-bye.

She felt satisfied that the men in the bar feared her. Maybe it was her face and the way she held her mouth with teeth clenched tight, like there was nothing anyone could do to her now. She walked north down the road, searching for the old man. She did this because she had the blanket, and there would be no place for him except with her and the blanket in the old adobe barn near the arroyo. They always slept there when they came to Cebolleta. If the money and the wine were gone, she would be relieved because then they could go home again; back to the old hogan with a dirt roof and rock walls where she herself had been born. And the next day the old man could go back to the few sheep they still had, to follow along behind them, guiding them, into dry sandy arroyos where sparse grass grew. She knew he did not like walking behind old ewes when for so many years he rode big quarter horses and worked with cattle. But she wasn't sorry for him; he should have known all along what would happen.

There had not been enough rain for their garden in five years; and that was when Chato finally hitched a ride into the town and brought back brown boxes of rice and sugar and big tin cans of welfare peaches. After that, at the first of the month they went to Cebolleta to ask the postmaster for the check; and then Chato would go to the bar and cash it. They did this as they planted the garden every May, not because anything would survive the summer dust, but because it was time to do this. The journey passed the days that smelled silent and dry like the caves above the canyon with yellow painted buffaloes on their walls.

He was walking along the pavement when she found him. He did not stop or turn around when he heard her behind him. She walked beside him and she noticed how slowly he moved now. He smelled strong of wood-smoke and urine. Lately he had been forgetting. Sometimes he called her by his sister's name and she had been gone for a long time. Once she had found him wandering on the road to the white man's ranch, and she asked him why he was going that way; he laughed at her and said, "You know they can't run that ranch without me," and he walked on determined, limping on the leg that had been crushed many years before. Now he looked at her curiously, as if for the first time, but he kept shuffling along, moving slowly along the side of the highway. His gray hair had grown long and spread out on the shoulders of the long overcoat. He wore the old felt hat pulled down over his ears. His boots were worn out at the toes and he had stuffed pieces of an old red shirt in the holes. The rags made his feet look like little animals up to their ears in snow. She laughed at his feet; the snow muffled the sound of her laugh. He stopped and looked at her again. The wind had quit blowing and the snow was falling straight down; the southeast sky was beginning to clear and Ayah could see a star.

"Let's rest awhile," she said to him. They walked away from the road 20 and up the slope to the giant boulders that had tumbled down from the red sandrock mesa throughout the centuries of rainstorms and earth tremors. In a place where the boulders shut out the wind, they sat down with their backs against the rock. She offered half of the blanket to him and they sat wrapped together.

The storm passed swiftly. The clouds moved east. They were massive and full, crowding together across the sky. She watched them with the feeling of horses—steely blue-gray horses startled across the sky. The powerful haunches pushed into the distances and the tail hairs streamed white mist behind them. The sky cleared. Ayah saw that there was nothing between her and the stars. The light was crystalline. There was no shimmer, no distortion through earth haze. She breathed the clarity of the night sky; she smelled the purity of the half moon and the stars. He was lying on his side with his knees pulled up near his belly for warmth. His eyes were closed now, and in the light from the stars and the moon, he looked young again.

She could see it descend out of the night sky: an icy stillness from the edge of the thin moon. She recognized the freezing. It came gradually, sinking snowflake by snowflake until the crust was heavy and deep. It had the strength of the stars in Orion, and its journey was endless. Ayah knew that with the wine he would sleep. He would not feel it. She tucked the blanket around him, remembering how it was when Ella had been with her; and she felt the rush so big inside her heart for the babies. And she sang the only song she knew to sing for babies. She could not remember if she had ever sung it to her children, but she knew that her grandmother had sung it and her mother had sung it:

> The earth is your mother,
>   she holds you.
> The sky is your father,
>   he protects you.
> Sleep,
> sleep.
> Rainbow is your sister,
>   she loves you.
> The winds are your brothers,
>   they sing to you.

Sleep,
sleep.
We are together always
We are together always
There never was a time
when this
was not so.

Questions for Discussion

1. The first four sentences of this story include references to snow, wool, babies, and memories. Why are these references important for the story that follows?
2. Why does Ayah smile at the snow in paragraph 3? How would you describe her relationship to nature?
3. How had Ayah lost her children? What loss was the hardest for her to bear? Why?
4. What is the role of Jimmie in this story? Why does Silko emphasize that Jimmie had provided the blanket that shelters his mother?
5. Why are the men in the bar afraid of Ayah when she comes looking for Chato?
6. What does this story reveal about the relationship between Native Americans and Anglo-Americans? How do Ayah and Chato differ in their expectations about how they will be treated?
7. What happens at the end of this story? If Ayah recognizes that she and Chato are freezing, why does she let it happen?

Suggestions for Writing

1. Write an essay explaining why Ayah and Chato die in the cold. Where do you put the responsibility for their death?
2. Interpret the lullaby with which this story concludes, and explain how understanding the lullaby can help readers understand the story.

POWER

Audre Lorde

Audre Lorde published her first poem when she was still in high school—a poem that her teachers didn't like but that nevertheless appealed to the editors of a national magazine. She once said that she began to write poetry "when I couldn't find the poems to express the things I was feeling." As you read "Power," ask yourself what kind of feeling it expresses.

The difference between poetry and rhetoric
is being
ready to kill
yourself
instead of your children.   5

I am trapped on a desert of raw gunshot wounds
and a dead child dragging his shattered black
face off the edge of my sleep
blood from his punctured cheeks and shoulders
is the only liquid for miles and my stomach   10
churns at the imagined taste while
my mouth splits into dry lips
without loyalty or reason
thirsting for the wetness of his blood
as it sinks into the whiteness   15
of the desert where I am lost
without imagery or magic
trying to make power out of hatred and destruction
trying to heal my dying son with kisses
only the sun will bleach his bones quicker.   20

The policeman who shot down a 10-year-old in Queens
stood over the boy with his cop shoes in childish blood
and a voice said "Die you little motherfucker" and
there are tapes to prove that. At his trial
this policeman said in his own defense   25
"I didn't notice the size or nothing else
only the color," and
there are tapes to prove that, too.

Today that 37-year-old white man with 13 years of police forcing
has been set free   30
by 11 white men who said they were satisfied
justice had been done
and one black woman who said
"They convinced me" meaning

they had dragged her 4'10" black woman's frame   *35*
over the hot coals of four centuries of white male approval
until she let go the first real power she ever had
and lined her own womb with cement
to make a graveyard for our children.

I have not been able to touch the destruction within me.   *40*
But unless I learn to use
the difference between poetry and rhetoric
my power too will run corrupt as poisonous mold
or lie limp and useless as an unconnected wire
and one day I will take my teenaged plug   *45*
and connect it to the nearest socket
raping an 85-year-old white woman
who is somebody's mother
and as I beat her senseless and set a torch to her bed
a greek chorus will be singing in 3/4 time   *50*
"Poor thing. She never hurt a soul. What beasts they are."

Questions for Discussion

1. This poem opens with a startling statement about the difference between poetry and rhetoric, and it returns to this difference in lines 41–43. How could poetry lead to killing oneself, and how could rhetoric lead to killing children?

2. Lines 6–20 describe a disturbing dream that becomes easier to understand after we read the events described in lines 21–39. Why is there a dead child in the dream? How would the poem change if the dream came after the two stanzas about the policeman?

3. What do the words quoted in the third stanza reveal? Why does the speaker twice mention that there are tapes to prove what the policeman said?

4. According to the speaker of the poem, why did a black woman serving on a jury agree to set the policeman free?

5. What lines in the poem relate to the title?

6. Does the speaker intend to rape an 85-year-old white woman? If not, how could this ever happen? Do you see any irony in line 51?

Suggestions for Writing

1. How would you describe the tone of "Power"? Write an essay in which you define the emotion conveyed by the speaker and show the language that supports your view.

2. Define in your own words the difference between poetry and rhetoric. According to your definition, is "Power" poetry or rhetoric?

OFF FROM SWING SHIFT

Garrett Hongo

A common misconception about poetry, especially among people who do not read it, is that poetry is supposed to be about a limited number of subjects— like love and nature—that are, somehow, "poetic." Another common misconception is that poetry must be beautiful and inspirational. Experienced readers recognize that poetry, like fiction and drama, is about life in all its fullness and complexity. As you read the following poem, try to understand what the speaker is saying about his father's life.

Late, just past midnight,
freeway noise from the Harbor
and San Diego leaking in
from the vent over the stove,
and he's off from swing shift at Lear's.   5
Eight hours of twisting circuitry,
charting ohms and maximum gains
while transformers hum
and helicopters swirl
on the roofs above the small factory.   10
He hails me with a head-fake,
then the bob and weave
of a weekend middleweight
learned at the Y on Kapiolani
ten years before I was born.   15

The shoes and gold London Fogger
come off first, then the easy grin
saying he's lucky as they come.
He gets into the slippers
my brother gives him every Christmas,   20
carries his Thermos over to the sink,
and slides into the one chair at the table
that's made of wood and not yellow plastic.
He pushes aside stacks
of *Sporting News* and *Outdoor Life*,   25
big round tins of Holland butter cookies,
and clears a space for his elbows, his pens,
and the *Racing Form's* Late Evening Final.

His left hand reaches out,
flicks on the Sony transistor   30

we bought for his birthday
when I was fifteen.
The right ferries in the earphone,
a small, flesh-colored star,
like a tiny miracle of hearing,   *35*
and fits it into place.
I see him plot black constellations
of figures and calculations
on the magazine's margins,
alternately squint and frown   *40*
as he fingers the knob of the tuner
searching for the one band
that will call out today's results.

There are whole cosmologies
in a single handicap,   *45*
a lifetime of two-dollar losing
in one pick of the Daily Double.

Maybe tonight is his night   *(*
for winning, his night
for beating the odds   *50*
of going deaf from a shell
at Anzio still echoing
in the cave of his inner ear,
his night for cashing in
the blue chips of shrapnel still grinding   *55*
at the thickening joints of his legs.

But no one calls
the horse's name, no one
says Shackles, Rebate, or Pouring Rain.
No one speaks a word.   *60*

Questions for Discussion

1. What is a "swing shift"? In what sense is the man in the poem "off" from swing shift?
2. The first word in this poem is "Late." What does this suggest to you? Does it have a double meaning?
3. What contrast provides the focus for the opening stanza?
4. Consider lines 44–45. What does "handicap" mean within this context? How can there be "whole cosmologies/in a single handicap"? Does line 44 relate to any other lines in the poem?
5. What is the effect of repeating "no one" in lines 57–60?

6. Why are the horses named "Shackles," "Rebate," and "Pouring Rain"?

Suggestions for Writing

1. Describe the man who is the focus of this poem. What is his life like?
2. An *image* is a detail that appeals to one of our senses; it is usually something that we can visualize (such as "big round tins of Holland butter cookies"), but it can also be something we can hear, taste, or smell. Identify the images used in this poem, and explain what they suggest.

BLACK HAIR

Gary Soto

Some readers find poetry difficult because they try to read it as quickly as they read prose. Poetry usually needs to be read more slowly—and more than once—because poets try to convey meaning through language that has been compressed. "Black Hair" comes from a collection of poems that Gary Soto wrote about his family and friends. As you read it, note the details that the speaker provides about himself. But in addition to noting what the poem states, think about what else you can learn from it. Reread the poem, and consider what individual words suggest. Then try to reconstruct the story of the speaker's life.

At eight I was brilliant with my body.
In July, that ring of heat
We all jumped through, I sat in the bleachers
Of Romain Playground, in the lengthening
Shade that rose from our dirty feet.   5
The game before us was more than baseball.
It was a figure—Hector Moreno
Quick and hard with turned muscles,
His crouch the one I assumed before an altar
Of worn baseball cards, in my room.   10

I came here because I was Mexican, a stick
Of brown light in love with those
Who could do it—the triple and hard slide,
The gloves eating balls into double plays.
What could I do with 50 pounds, my shyness,   15
My black torch of hair, about to go out?
Father was dead, his face no longer
Hanging over the table or our sleep,
And mother was the terror of mouths
Twisting hurt by butter knives.   20

In the bleachers I was brilliant with my body,
Waving players in and stomping my feet,
Growing sweaty in the presence of white shirts.
I chewed sunflower seeds. I drank water
And bit my arm through the late innings.   25
When Hector lined balls into deep
Center, in my mind I rounded the bases
With him, my face flared, my hair lifting

Beautifully, because we were coming home
To the arms of brown people.

Questions for Discussion

1. Explain the opening line of this poem. Does it conflict with lines 11 and 15?
2. Why does the speaker watch baseball?
3. What does Hector Moreno represent? Is his first name significant?
4. What does it mean to be hurt by "butter knives"? Who is being hurt in lines 19–20?

Suggestions for Writing

1. Black hair is mentioned only once in this poem, but the title suggests that it is important. Can you explain line 16? Interpret the meaning of "torch," and explain why it could be "about to go out." Then explain the reference to hair in line 28. In your opinion, what does hair represent in the poem?
2. Discuss the last two lines of this poem. What does it mean to come "home/To the arms of brown people"? Does "Black Hair" offer any insight into what it means to be Hispanic-American?

NANI

Alberto Rios

Born in Nogales, Arizona, Alberto Rios is a poet and short story writer who draws upon a heritage that includes both Spanish and English. As you read the following poem, consider the relationship between the speaker and his grandmother. Try to understand how they differ from each other and how the speaker feels about the difference between them.

Sitting at her table, she serves
the sopa de arroz° to me   *rice soup*
instinctively, and I watch her,
the absolute *mamá,* and eat words
I might have had to say more   *5*
out of embarrassment. To speak,
now-foreign words I used to speak,
too, dribble down her mouth as she serves
me albóndigas.° No more   *spiced meatballs*
than a third are easy to me.   *10*
By the stove she does something with words
and looks at me only with her
back. I am full. I tell her
I taste the mint, and watch her speak
smiles at the stove. All my words   *15*
make her smile. Nani° never serves   *granny*
herself, she only watches me
with her skin, her hair. I ask for more.
I watch the *mamá* warming more
tortillas for me. I watch her   *20*
fingers in the flame for me.
Near her mouth, I see a wrinkle speak
of a man whose body serves
the ants like she serves me, then more words
from more wrinkles about children, words   *25*
about this and that, flowing more
easily from these other mouths. Each serves
as a tremendous string around her,
holding her together. They speak
nani was this and that to me   *30*
and I wonder just how much of me
will die with her, what were the words
I could have been, was. Her insides speak
through a hundred wrinkles, now, more

than she can bear, steel around her,   *35*
shouting, then, What is this thing she serves?

She asks me if I want more.
I own no words to stop her.
Even before I speak, she serves.

Questions for Discussion

1. What is the speaker of this poem like? How does he differ from Nani?
2. Why is Spanish used in lines 2 and 9: "sopa de arroz" and "albóndigas"? Could you understand these lines without understanding Spanish? Why isn't Spanish used more extensively in the poem?
3. Why does the speaker ask for more food when he is full? Is the speaker full in more than one sense?
4. How could part of the speaker die when Nani dies?
5. Consider lines 33–36. What is it that steels around Nani? Why does Rios use such a vague word as "thing"? In your opinion, what is the "thing" that Nani serves?

Suggestions for Writing

1. What does this poem say about language? Discuss how it reveals a conflict between different cultures and different generations.
2. Four key words are repeated throughout this poem: *serves, speak, words,* and *watch.* Choose two of these and explain why they are important in the poem.

SONNET 116

William Shakespeare

> *A sonnet is a fourteen-line poem, following a fixed rhythm and rhyme scheme. Each line consists of five units, called feet, and each foot consists of an unaccented syllable followed by an accented syllable. An English or Shakespearean sonnet consists of three* quatrains *(groups of four lines); in each quatrain the first line rhymes with the third and the second with the fourth. These twelve lines are followed by a* couplet, *which is a single pair of rhymed lines. As you read the following sonnet, notice that some of the rhymes are stronger than others. Consider whether perfect rhymes are important in poetry. And ask yourself if this poem provides an accurate definition of love.*

Let me not to the marriage of true minds
Admit impediments. Love is not love
Which alters when it alteration finds,
Or bends with the remover to remove:
Oh, no! it is an ever-fixéd mark,   5
That looks on tempests and is never shaken;
It is the star to every wandering bark,
Whose worth's unknown, although his height be taken.
Love's not Time's fool, though rosy lips and cheeks
Within his bending sickle's compass come;   10
Love alters not with his brief hours and weeks,
But bears it out even to the edge of doom.
If this be error and upon me proved,
   I never writ, nor no man ever loved.

Questions for Discussion

1. According to this poem, what is the basis of true love?
2. Is there any ambiguity within the first two lines? What does it mean to admit impediments (as in the Marriage Service: "If any of you know any just cause or just impediment why these persons should not be joined together . . .")?
3. Why is "Time" associated with a "bending sickle's compass"? What effect does Time's sickle have upon "rosy lips and cheeks"? What effect does Time have upon love as it is defined by this poem?
4. Consider lines 13–14. How strongly do they affirm the definition of love offered in lines 2–12?

Suggestions for Writing

1. Paraphrase what this poem says about love, and explain why you agree or disagree with this conception of love.
2. Read more of Shakespeare's sonnets; then write an essay comparing two that are about love.

THE DRIVING RANGE

Leslie Adrienne Miller

The following poem is set on a stretch of suburban highway, lined with shopping centers, on a late summer night. Searching for "things . . . you can't get anywhere else," the woman who speaks this poem encounters a vision that reminds her of her past and the distance she has traveled from it. As you read, note what the speaker finds attractive about this vision and why she ultimately rejects it.

Even though I have something against them
I must admit they are a beautiful
spectacle, spotlit men as far as the eye
can go along this darkening reach of road.
Miniature with distance, their faces blur   5
and their tailored trousers turn in a clean
line with the body's arc, extending
and returning to itself without appearing
to have moved at all. I've come alone
out to the gleaming stretches of suburban   10
shopping centers, a thrill in the late
summer night, in the stoplights drifting
farther and farther apart, the rose glow
of the city blooming in my rearview mirror.
There are things out here you can't get   15
anywhere else: saris, leather, gold, tents,
bulk boxes of trinkets, and visions like this
embroidered with light, but it's a long way
from where I live, and there are stories
about how the clean, spacious road lures you   20
into rolling down your window, and men
who know. this and run across dark intersections
to hold a gun on you. But I roll down
my window anyway to cut the blind glare
of the stadium lights along the driving range.   25
Benign air whispers in, and the row of men
in their cage of light are as curiously
lovely as glassed insects, intricate,
designed for flight; their silver clubs
describe glinting circles around well-made   30
shoulders as they swoop toward the tiny balls.
I was expected to marry a man like that,
but something went wrong, and I have never
been near enough to one, though I might

have brushed their custom-shirted arms   35
in theaters or waiting rooms, might have
taken up their papers left on airport chairs
laced with the scent of something well-preserved.
I look at them now from a distance, dark
between us, eight lanes of highway,   40
and there is only a moment to consider
the vision, to wonder why I never came
any closer: a lawyer, a doctor,
even an insurance agent, any man
given a set of silver clubs and lessons   45
from the father in this necessary art.
Even if I chose to now, I couldn't
make it back to the country club's chintz
powder room where my mother urged me
to repair my face because a suitable boy   50
had just come into the dining room
with his suitable parents.
What I have against them is not exactly
their neatly filled, black appointment books,
their clean genitals lying in nests   55
of sweetened hair, or their pressed trousers
filed in closets by season and occasion,
but the perfection of their remoteness,
their absence, and that radiance,
always promised me, that was never   60
quite close enough to touch.

Questions for Discussion

1. In what sense are the men at the driving range "a beautiful spectacle?"
   What language in the poem conveys a sense of their beauty?
2. What does the speaker have against the men she is watching? In what
   sense are they "miniature with distance"?
3. Where is the driving range? What has drawn the speaker to its vicinity?
   What is she looking for?
4. What divides the speaker from the men she is watching? Would she like
   to overcome this division, or is she content to be alone?
5. What could the speaker mean when she describes golf as "this necessary art"? Is she being ironic? Or is golf truly a necessary art in some
   way?

Suggestions for Writing

1. Drawing upon what the poem reveals of her past and her present, write
   an essay describing the speaker of this poem.

2. Have you traveled a long distance from where you once lived? Do you ever feel separated from your past by "eight lanes of highway"? Write an essay exploring what you have in common with the speaker of this poem—or how you differ.

ULYSSES

Alfred, Lord Tennyson

A dramatic monologue is a poem in which a single speaker addresses a silent but identifiable audience, revealing his or her character. In the following poem the speaker is Ulysses—the Roman name for the hero of Homer's Odyssey. *The poem portrays Ulysses in old age, after he has returned home from the adventures described by Homer and grown restless to set sail again. As you read "Ulysses," consider the character of the speaker and what this poem says about "roaming with a hungry heart." Tennyson was poet laureate of England from 1850 to 1892.*

It little profits that an idle king,
By this still hearth, among these barren crags,
Matched with an aged wife, I mete and dole
Unequal laws unto a savage race,
That hoard, and sleep, and feed, and know not me.   5
I cannot rest from travel: I will drink
Life to the lees: all times I have enjoyed
Greatly, have suffered greatly, both with those
That loved me, and alone; on shore, and when
Thro' scudding drifts the rainy Hyades   10
Vexed the dim sea. I am become a name;
For always roaming with a hungry heart
Much have I seen and known: cities of men
And manners, climates, councils, governments,
Myself not least, but honored of them all;   15
And drunk delight of battle with my peers,
Far on the ringing plains of windy Troy.
I am a part of all that I have met;
Yet all experience is an arch wherethro'
Gleams that untravelled world, whose margin fades   20
For ever and for ever when I move.
How dull it is to pause, to make an end,
To rust unburnished, not to shine in use!
As tho' to breathe were life. Life piled on life
Were all too little, and of one to me   25
Little remains: but every hour is saved
From that eternal silence, something more,
A bringer of new things; and vile it were
For some three suns to store and hoard myself,
And this gray spirit yearning in desire   30
To follow knowledge like a sinking star,

Beyond the utmost bound of human thought.
   This is my son, mine own Telemachus,
To whom I leave the sceptre and the isle—
Well-loved of me, discerning to fulfil   *35*
This labor, by slow prudence to make mild
A rugged people, and thro' soft degrees
Subdue them to the useful and the good.
Most blameless is he, centered in the sphere
Of common duties, decent not to fail   *40*
In offices of tenderness, and pay
Meet adoration to my household gods,
When I am gone. He works his work, I mine.
   There lies the port; the vessel puffs her sail:
There gloom the dark broad seas. My mariners,   *45*
Souls that have toiled, and wrought, and thought with me—
That ever with a frolic welcome took
The thunder and the sunshine, and opposed
Free hearts, free foreheads—you and I are old;
Old age hath yet his honor and his toil;   *50*
Death closes all; but something ere the end,
Some work of noble note, may yet be done,
Not unbecoming men that strove with Gods.
The lights begin to twinkle from the rocks:
The long day wanes: the slow moon climbs: the deep   *55*
Moans round with many voices. Come, my friends,
'T is not too late to seek a newer world.
Push off, and sitting well in order smite
The sounding furrows; for my purpose holds
To sail beyond the sunset, and the baths   *60*
Of all the western stars, until I die.
It may be that the gulfs will wash us down:
It may be we shall touch the Happy Isles,
And see the great Achilles, whom we knew.
Tho' much is taken, much abides; and tho'   *65*
We are not now that strength which in old days
Moved earth and heaven, that which we are, we are:
One equal temper of heroic hearts,
Made weak by time and fate, but strong in will
To strive, to seek, to find, and not to yield.   *70*

Questions for Discussion

1. To whom is Ulysses speaking in this poem?
2. Why has Ulysses decided to abdicate? What motivates his decision to go
   back to sea?

3. Consider lines 19–21. What do they say about the nature of experience?
4. How does Ulysses characterize his son Telemachus?
5. Does Ulysses recognize that there are any risks to undertaking an adventure in old age? Does he recognize that he has any limitations?

Suggestions for Writing

1. Write a description of Ulysses as portrayed in this poem. Is he an admirable character? Consider how he sees himself, but consider also whether there is anything that he does not recognize but that is implied by his speech.
2. Drawing upon what you have learned from this poem, write an essay that would justify your decision to either stay at home or join Ulysses on his search for "a newer world."

PIED BEAUTY

Gerard Manley Hopkins

> *A Jesuit priest who was sensitive to natural beauty and the rhythm of language, Gerard Manley Hopkins wrote poems that seemed startlingly modern when first published in 1918—twenty-nine years after his death. Read this poem aloud, listening to how it sounds. Then reread it, thinking about how it is constructed and what it means. You might find it helpful to know that pied means having patches of two or more colors. Consider whether it reminds you of any other words.*

Glory be to God for dappled things—
    For skies of couple-color as a brinded cow;
      For rose-moles all in stipple upon trout that swim;
Fresh-firecoal chestnut-falls; finches' wings;
    Landscape plotted and pieced—fold, fallow and plow;   *5*
      And all trades, their gear and tackle and trim.

All things counter, original, spare, strange;
    Whatever is fickle, freckled (who knows how?)
      With swift, slow; sweet, sour; adazzle, dim;
He fathers-forth whose beauty is past change: *10*
             Praise him.

Questions for Discussion

1. What are "dappled things," and why does the poem suggest that we should be thankful for them?
2. Where is rhyme used in this poem?
3. Explain line 10. What does "fathers-forth" mean, and how can beauty be "past change"?
4. Is there anything "counter, original, spare, strange" about this poem?

Suggestions for Writing

1. *Alliteration* describes the repetition of an initial consonant sound; *assonance* describes the repetition of sound within syllables. Discuss the role of alliteration and assonance in "Pied Beauty."
2. Discuss the images in lines 2–5, and explain how they relate to the poem's title.

TRIFLES

Susan Glaspell

> *If you have ever read a story called "A Jury of Her Peers," you will recognize the plot of* Trifles. *Susan Glaspell based that story upon the following play, which she wrote in 1916. According to Glaspell, both the play and the story were inspired by an experience she had while working for a newspaper in Des Moines, Iowa. As you read the play, try to imagine how lonely and isolated a midwestern farm could be before the introduction of electricity, radio, and television. Consider how the men in the play treat the women. Be sure to read the stage instructions, and note how the women change when the men are offstage.*

Scene: *The kitchen in the now abandoned farmhouse of* JOHN WRIGHT, *a gloomy kitchen, and left without having been put in order—unwashed pans under the sink, a loaf of bread outside the bread-box, a dish-towel on the table—other signs of incompleted work. At the rear the outer door opens and the* SHERIFF *comes in followed by the* COUNTY ATTORNEY *and* HALE. *The* SHERIFF *and* HALE *are men in middle life, the* COUNTY ATTORNEY *is a young man; all are much bundled up and go at once to the stove. They are followed by the two women—the* SHERIFF'S *wife first; she is a slight wiry woman, a thin nervous face.* MRS. HALE *is larger and would ordinarily be called more comfortable looking, but she is disturbed now and looks fearfully about as she enters. The women have come in slowly, and stand close together near the door.*

COUNTY ATTORNEY: *(rubbing his hands)* This feels good. Come up to the fire, ladies.

MRS. PETERS: *(after taking a step forward)* I'm not—cold.

SHERIFF: *(unbuttoning his overcoat and stepping away from the stove as if to mark the beginning of official business)* Now, Mr. Hale, before we move things about, you explain to Mr. Henderson just what you saw when you came here yesterday morning.

COUNTY ATTORNEY: By the way, has anything been moved? Are things just as you left them yesterday?

SHERIFF: *(looking about)* It's just the same. When it dropped below zero last night I thought I'd better send Frank out this morning to make a fire for us—no use getting pneumonia with a big case on, but I told him not to touch anything except the stove—and you know Frank.

COUNTY ATTORNEY: Somebody should have been left here yesterday.

SHERIFF: Oh—yesterday. When I had to send Frank to Morris Center for that man who went crazy—I want you to know I had my hands full yesterday. I knew you could get back from Omaha by today and as long as I went over everything here myself—

COUNTY ATTORNEY: Well, Mr. Hale, tell just what happened when you came here yesterday morning.

HALE: Harry and I had started to town with a load of potatoes. We came along the road from my place and as I got here I said, "I'm going to see if I can't get John Wright to go in with me on a party telephone." I spoke to Wright about it once before and he put me off, saying folks talked too much anyway, and all he asked was peace and quiet—I guess you know about how much he talked himself; but I thought maybe if I went to the house and talked about it before his wife, though I said to Harry that I didn't know as what his wife wanted made much difference to John—

COUNTY ATTORNEY: Let's talk about that later, Mr. Hale. I do want to talk about that, but tell now just what happened when you got to the house.

HALE: I didn't hear or see anything; I knocked at the door, and still it was all quiet inside. I knew they must be up, it was past eight o'clock. So I knocked again, and I thought I heard somebody say, "Come in." I wasn't sure, I'm not sure yet, but I opened the door—this door *(indicating the door by which the two women are still standing)* and there in that rocker—*(pointing to it)* sat Mrs. Wright.

(They all look at the rocker.)

COUNTY ATTORNEY: What—was she doing?

HALE: She was rockin' back and forth. She had her apron in her hand and was kind of—pleating it.

COUNTY ATTORNEY: And how did she—look?

HALE: Well, she looked queer.

COUNTY ATTORNEY: How do you mean—queer?

HALE: Well, as if she didn't know what she was going to do next. And kind of done up.

COUNTY ATTORNEY: How did she seem to feel about your coming?

HALE: Why, I don't think she minded—one way or other. She didn't pay much attention. I said, "How do, Mrs. Wright it's cold, ain't it?" And she said, "Is it?"—and went on kind of pleating at her apron. Well, I was surprised; she didn't ask me to come up to the stove, or to set down, but just sat there, not even looking at me, so I said, "I want to see John." And then she—laughed. I guess you would call it a laugh. I thought of Harry and the team outside, so I said a little sharp: "Can't I see John?" "No," she says, kind o' dull like. "Ain't he home?" says I. "Yes," says she, "he's home." "Then why can't I see him?" I asked her, out of patience. "Cause he's dead," says she. "*Dead?*" says I. She just nodded her head, not getting a bit excited, but rockin' back and forth. "Why—where is he?" says I, not knowing what to say. She just pointed upstairs—like that *(himself pointing to the room above)*. I got up, with the idea of going up there. I walked from there to here—then I says, "Why, what did he die of?" "He died of a rope round his neck," says she, and just went on pleatin' at her apron. Well, I went out and called Harry. I thought I might—need help. We went upstairs and there he was lyin'—

COUNTY ATTORNEY: I think I'd rather have you go into that upstairs, where you can point it all out. Just go on now with the rest of the story.

HALE: Well, my first thought was to get that rope off. It looked . . . *(stops, his face twitches)* . . . but Harry, he went up to him, and he said, "No, he's dead all right, and we'd better not touch anything." So we went back down stairs. She was still sitting that same way. "Has anybody been notified?" I asked. "No," says she unconcerned. "Who did this, Mrs. Wright?" said Harry. He said it business-like—and she stopped pleatin' of her apron. "I don't know," she says. "You don't *know?*" says Harry. "No," says she. "Weren't you sleepin' in the bed with him?" says Harry. "Yes," says she, "but I was on the inside." "Somebody slipped a rope round his neck and strangled him and you didn't wake up?" says Harry. "I didn't wake up," she said after him. We must 'a looked as if we didn't see how that could be, for after a minute she said, "I sleep sound." Harry was going to ask her more questions but I said maybe we ought to let her tell her story first to the coroner, or the sheriff, so Harry went fast as he could to Rivers' place, where there's a telephone.

COUNTY ATTORNEY: And what did Mrs. Wright do when she knew that you had gone for the coroner?

HALE: She moved from that chair to this one over here *(pointing to a small chair in the corner)* and just sat there with her hands held together and looking down. I got a feeling that I ought to make some conversation, so I said I had come in to see if John wanted to put in a telephone, and at that she started to laugh, and then she stopped and looked at me— scared. *(the* COUNTY ATTORNEY, *who has had his notebook out, makes a note)* I dunno, maybe it wasn't scared. I wouldn't like to say it was. Soon Harry got back, and then Dr. Lloyd came, and you, Mr. Peters, and so I guess that's all I know that you don't.

COUNTY ATTORNEY: *(looking around)* I guess we'll go upstairs first—and then out to the barn and around there. *(to the* SHERIFF) You're convinced that there was nothing important here—nothing that would point to any motive.

SHERIFF: Nothing here but kitchen things.

(The COUNTY ATTORNEY, *after again looking around the kitchen, opens the door of a cupboard closet. He gets up on a chair and looks on a shelf. Pulls his hand away, sticky.)*

COUNTY ATTORNEY: Here's a nice mess.

(The women draw nearer.)

MRS. PETERS: *(to the other woman)* Oh, her fruit; it did freeze. *(to the* LAW-YER) She worried about that when it turned so cold. She said the fire'd go out and her jars would break.

SHERIFF: Well, can you beat the women! Held for murder and worryin' about her preserves.

COUNTY ATTORNEY: I guess before we're through she may have something more serious than preserves to worry about.

HALE: Well, women are used to worrying over trifles.

(The two women move a little closer together.)

COUNTY ATTORNEY: *(with the gallantry of a young politician)* And yet, for all their worries, what would we do without the ladies? *(the women do not unbend. He goes to the sink, takes a dipperful of water from the pail and pouring it into a basin, washes his hands. Starts to wipe them on the roller-towel, turns it for a cleaner place)* Dirty towels! *(kicks his foot against the pans under the sink)* Not much of a housekeeper, would you say, ladies?

MRS. HALE: *(stiffly)* There's a great deal of work to be done on a farm.

COUNTY ATTORNEY: To be sure. And yet *(with a little bow to her)* I know there are some Dickson county farmhouses which do not have such roller towels.

(He gives it a pull to expose its length again.)

MRS. HALE: Those towels get dirty awful quick. Men's hands aren't always as clean as they might be.

COUNTY ATTORNEY: Ah, loyal to your sex, I see. But you and Mrs. Wright were neighbors. I suppose you were friends, too.

MRS. HALE: *(shaking her head)* I've not seen much of her of late years. I've not been in this house—it's more than a year.

COUNTY ATTORNEY: And why was that? You didn't like her?

MRS. HALE: I liked her all well enough. Farmers' wives have their hands full, Mr. Henderson. And then—

COUNTY ATTORNEY: Yes—?

MRS. HALE: *(looking about)* It never seemed a very cheerful place.

COUNTY ATTORNEY: No—it's not cheerful. I shouldn't say she had the homemaking instinct.

MRS. HALE: Well, I don't know as Wright had, either.

COUNTY ATTORNEY: You mean that they didn't get on very well?

MRS. HALE: No, I don't mean anything. But I don't think a place'd be any cheerfuller for John Wright's being in it.

COUNTY ATTORNEY: I'd like to talk more of that a little later. I want to get the lay of things upstairs now.

(He goes to the left, where three steps lead to a stair door.)

SHERIFF: I suppose anything Mrs. Peters does'll be all right. She was to take in some clothes for her, you know, and a few little things. We left in such a hurry yesterday.

COUNTY ATTORNEY: Yes, but I would like to see what you take, Mrs. Peters, and keep an eye out for anything that might be of use to us.

MRS. PETERS: Yes, Mr. Henderson.

(The women listen to the men's steps on the stairs, then look about the kitchen.)

MRS. HALE: I'd hate to have men coming into my kitchen, snooping around and criticising.

(She arranges the pans under sink which the LAWYER *had shoved out of place.)*

MRS. PETERS: Of course it's no more than their duty.

MRS. HALE: Duty's all right, but I guess that deputy sheriff that came out to make the fire might have got a little of this on. *(gives the roller towel a pull)* Wish I'd thought of that sooner. Seems mean to talk about her for not having things slicked up when she had to come away in such a hurry.

MRS. PETERS: *(who has gone to a small table in the left rear corner of the room, and lifted one end of a towel that covers a pan)* She had bread set.

(Stands still.)

MRS. HALE: *(eyes fixed on a loaf of bread beside the bread-box, which is on a low shelf at the other side of the room. Moves slowly toward it)* She was going to put this in there. *(picks up loaf, then abruptly drops it. In a manner of returning to familiar things)* It's a shame about her fruit. I wonder if it's all gone. *(gets up on the chair and looks)* I think there's some here that's all right, Mrs. Peters. Yes—here; *(holding it toward the window)* this is cherries, too. *(looking again)* I declare I believe that's the only one. *(gets down, bottle in her hand. Goes to the sink and wipes it off on the outside)* She'll feel awful bad after all her hard work in the hot weather. I remember the afternoon I put up my cherries last summer.

(She puts the bottle on the big kitchen table, center of the room. With a sigh, is about to sit down in the rocking-chair. Before she is seated realizes what chair it is; with a slow look at it, steps back. The chair which she has touched rocks back and forth.)

MRS. PETERS: Well, I must get those things from the front room closet. *(she goes to the door at the right, but after looking into the other room, steps back)* You coming with me, Mrs. Hale? You could help me carry them.

(They go in the other room; reappear, MRS. PETERS *carrying a dress and skirt,* MRS. HALE *following with a pair of shoes.)*

MRS. PETERS: My, it's cold in here.

(She puts the clothes on the big table, and hurries to the stove.)

MRS. HALE: *(examining the skirt)* Wright was close. I think maybe that's why she kept so much to herself. She didn't even belong to the Ladies Aid. I suppose she felt she couldn't do her part, and then you don't enjoy things when you feel shabby. She used to wear pretty clothes and be lively, when she was Minnie Foster, one of the town girls singing in the choir. But that—oh, that was thirty years ago. This all you was to take in?

MRS. PETERS: She said she wanted an apron. Funny thing to want, for there isn't much to get you dirty in jail, goodness knows. But I suppose just to make her feel more natural. She said they was in the top drawer in this cupboard. Yes, here. And then her little shawl that always hung behind the door. *(opens stair door and looks)* Yes, here it is.

(Quickly shuts door leading upstairs.)

MRS. HALE: *(abruptly moving toward her)* Mrs. Peters?
MRS. PETERS: Yes, Mrs. Hale?
MRS. HALE: Do you think she did it?
MRS. PETERS: *(in a frightened voice)* Oh, I don't know.
MRS. HALE: Well, I don't think she did. Asking for an apron and her little shawl. Worrying about her fruit.
MRS. PETERS: *(starts to speak, glances up, where footsteps are heard in the room above. In a low voice)* Mr. Peters says it looks bad for her. Mr. Henderson is awful sarcastic in a speech and he'll make fun of her sayin' she didn't wake up.
MRS. HALE: Well, I guess John Wright didn't wake when they was slipping that rope under his neck.
MRS. PETERS: No, it's strange. It must have been done awful crafty and still. They say it was such a—funny way to kill a man, rigging it all up like that.
MRS. HALE: That's just what Mr. Hale said. There was a gun in the house. He says that's what he can't understand.
MRS. PETERS: Mr. Henderson said coming out that what was needed for the case was a motive; something to show anger, or—sudden feeling.
MRS. HALE: *(who is standing by the table)* Well, I don't see any signs of anger around here. *(she puts her hand on the dish towel which lies on the table, stands looking down at table, one half of which is clean, the other half messy)* It's wiped to here. *(makes a move as if to finish work, then turns and looks at loaf of bread outside the breadbox. Drops towel. In that voice of coming back to familiar things.)* Wonder how they are finding things upstairs. I hope she had it a little more red-up° up there. You know, it seems kind of sneaking. Locking her up in town and then coming out here and trying to get her own house to turn against her!
MRS. PETERS: But Mrs. Hale, the law is the law.
MRS. HALE: I s'pose 'tis. *(unbuttoning her coat)* Better loosen up your things, Mrs. Peters. You won't feel them when you go out.

---

red-up: Readied up; orderly.

(MRS. PETERS *takes off her fur tippet,°* *goes to hang it on hook at back of room, stands looking at the under part of the small corner table.*)

MRS. PETERS: She was piecing a quilt.

(*She brings the large sewing basket and they look at the bright pieces.*)

MRS. HALE: It's log cabin pattern. Pretty, isn't it? I wonder if she was goin' to quilt it or just knot it?

(*Footsteps have been heard coming down the stairs. The* SHERIFF *enters followed by* HALE *and the* COUNTY ATTORNEY.)

SHERIFF: They wonder if she was going to quilt it or just knot it!

(*The men laugh, the women look abashed.*)

COUNTY ATTORNEY: (*rubbing his hands over the stove*) Frank's fire didn't do much up there, did it? Well, let's go out to the barn and get that cleared up.

(*The men go outside.*)

MRS. HALE: (*resentfully*) I don't know as there's anything so strange, our takin' up our time with little things while we're waiting for them to get the evidence. (*she sits down at the big table smoothing out a block with decision*) I don't see as it's anything to laugh about.
MRS. PETERS: (*apologetically*) Of course they've got awful important things on their minds.

(*Pulls up a chair and joins* MRS. HALE *at the table.*)

MRS. HALE: (*examining another block*) Mrs. Peters, look at this one. Here, this is the one she was working on, and look at the sewing! All the rest of it has been so nice and even. And look at this! It's all over the place! Why, it looks as if she didn't know what she was about!

(*After she has said this they look at each other, then start to glance back at the door. After an instant* MRS. HALE *has pulled at a knot and ripped the sewing.*)

MRS. PETERS: Oh, what are you doing, Mrs. Hale?
MRS. HALE: (*mildly*) Just pulling out a stitch or two that's not sewed very good. (*threading a needle*) Bad sewing always made me fidgety.
MRS. PETERS: (*nervously*) I don't think we ought to touch things.
MRS. HALE: I'll just finish up this end. (*suddenly stopping and leaning forward*) Mrs. Peters?
MRS. PETERS: Yes, Mrs. Hale?

tippet: A scarf for covering the neck and sometimes the shoulders.

MRS. HALE: What do you suppose she was so nervous about?

MRS. PETERS: Oh—I don't know. I don't know as she was nervous. I sometimes sew awful queer when I'm just tired. *(MRS. HALE starts to say something, looks at MRS. PETERS, then goes on sewing)* Well I must get these things wrapped up. They may be through sooner than we think. *(putting apron and other things together)* I wonder where I can find a piece of paper, and string.

MRS. HALE: In that cupboard, maybe.

MRS. PETERS: *(looking in cupboard)* Why, here's a bird-cage. *(holds it up)* Did she have a bird, Mrs. Hale?

MRS. HALE: Why, I don't know whether she did or not—I've not been here for so long. There was a man around last year selling canaries cheap, but I don't know as she took one; maybe she did. She used to sing real pretty herself.

MRS. PETERS: *(glancing around)* Seems funny to think of a bird here. But she must have had one, or why would she have a cage? I wonder what happened to it.

MRS. HALE: I s'pose maybe the cat got it.

MRS. PETERS: No, she didn't have a cat. She's got that feeling some people have about cats—being afraid of them. My cat got in her room and she was real upset and asked me to take it out.

MRS. HALE: My sister Bessie was like that. Queer, ain't it?

MRS. PETERS: *(examining the cage)* Why, look at this door. It's broke. One hinge is pulled apart.

MRS. HALE: *(looking too)* Looks as if someone must have been rough with it.

MRS. PETERS: Why, yes.

(She brings the cage forward and puts it on the table.)

MRS. HALE: I wish if they're going to find any evidence they'd be about it. I don't like this place.

MRS. PETERS: But I'm awful glad you came with me, Mrs. Hale. It would be lonesome for me sitting here alone.

MRS. HALE: It would, wouldn't it? *(dropping her sewing)* But I tell you what I do wish, Mrs. Peters. I wish I had come over sometimes when *she* was here. I—*(looking around the room)*—wish I had.

MRS. PETERS: But of course you were awful busy, Mrs. Hale—your house and your children.

MRS. HALE: I could've come. I stayed away because it weren't cheerful—and that's why I ought to have come. I—I've never liked this place. Maybe because it's down in a hollow and you don't see the road. I dunno what it is, but it's a lonesome place and always was. I wish I had come over to see Minnie Foster sometimes. I can see now—*(shakes her head)*

MRS. PETERS: Well, you mustn't reproach yourself, Mrs. Hale. Somehow we just don't see how it is with other folks until—something comes up.

MRS. HALE: Not having children makes less work—but it makes a quiet house, and Wright out to work all day, and no company when he did come in. Did you know John Wright, Mrs. Peters?

MRS. PETERS: Not to know him; I've seen him in town. They say he was a good man.

MRS. HALE: Yes—good; he didn't drink, and kept his word as well as most, I guess, and paid his debts. But he was a hard man, Mrs. Peters. Just to pass the time of day with him—*(shivers)* Like a raw wind that gets to the bone. *(pauses, her eye falling on the cage)* I should think she would 'a wanted a bird. But what do you suppose went with it?

MRS. PETERS: I don't know, unless it got sick and died.

(She reaches over and swings the broken door, swings it again, both women watch it.)

MRS. HALE: You weren't raised round here, were you? *(MRS. PETERS shakes her head)* You didn't know—her?

MRS. PETERS: Not till they brought her yesterday.

MRS. HALE: She—come to think of it, she was kind of like a bird herself— real sweet and pretty, but kind of timid and—fluttery. How—she— did—change. *(silence; then as if struck by a happy thought and relieved to get back to everyday things)* Tell you what, Mrs. Peters, why don't you take the quilt in with you? It might take up her mind.

MRS. PETERS: Why, I think that's a real nice idea, Mrs. Hale. There couldn't possibly be any objection to it, could there? Now, just what would I take? I wonder if her patches are in here—and her things.

(They look in the sewing basket.)

MRS. HALE: Here's some red. I expect this has got sewing things in it. *(brings out a fancy box)* What a pretty box. Looks like something some-body would give you. Maybe her scissors are in here. *(Opens box. Suddenly puts her hand to her nose)* Why—*(MRS. PETERS bends nearer, then turns her face away)* There's something wrapped up in this piece of silk.

MRS. PETERS: Why, this isn't her scissors.

MRS. HALE: *(lifting the silk)* Oh, Mrs. Peters—it's—

(MRS. PETERS bends closer.)

MRS. PETERS: It's the bird.

MRS. HALE: *(jumping up)* But, Mrs. Peters—look at it! It's neck! Look at its neck! It's all—other side *to.*

MRS. PETERS: Somebody—wrung—its—neck.

(Their eyes meet. A look of growing comprehension, of horror. Steps are heard outside. MRS. HALE *slips box under quilt pieces, and sinks into her chair. Enter* SHERIFF *and* COUNTY ATTORNEY. MRS. PETERS *rises.)*

COUNTY ATTORNEY: *(as one turning from serious things to little pleasantries)* Well ladies, have you decided whether she was going to quilt it or knot it?

MRS. PETERS: We think she was going to—knot it.

COUNTY ATTORNEY: Well, that's interesting, I'm sure. *(seeing the bird-cage)* Has the bird flown?

MRS. HALE: *(putting more quilt pieces over the box)* We think the—cat got it.

COUNTY ATTORNEY: *(preoccupied)* Is there a cat?

*(*MRS. HALE *glances in a quick covert way at* MRS. PETERS.*)*

MRS. PETERS: Well, not *now*. They're superstitious, you know. They leave.

COUNTY ATTORNEY: *(to* SHERIFF PETERS, *continuing an interrupted conversation)* No sign at all of anyone having come from the outside. Their own rope. Now let's go up again and go over it piece by piece. *(they start upstairs)* It would have to have been someone who knew just the—

*(*MRS. PETERS *sits down. The two women sit there not looking at one another, but as if peering into something and at the same time holding back. When they talk now it is in the manner of feeling their way over strange ground, as if afraid of what they are saying, but as if they cannot help saying it.)*

MRS. HALE: She liked the bird. She was going to bury it in that pretty box.

MRS. PETERS: *(in a whisper)* When I was a girl—my kitten—there was a boy took a hatchet, and before my eyes—and before I could get there—*(covers her face an instant)* If they hadn't held me back I would have—*(catches herself, looks upstairs where steps are heard, falters weakly)*—hurt him.

MRS. HALE: *(with a slow look around her)* I wonder how it would seem never to have had any children around. *(pause)* No, Wright wouldn't like the bird—a thing that sang. She used to sing. He killed that, too.

MRS. PETERS: *(moving uneasily)* We don't know who killed the bird.

MRS. HALE: I knew John Wright.

MRS. PETERS: It was an awful thing was done in this house that night, Mrs. Hale. Killing a man while he slept, slipping a rope around his neck that choked the life out of him.

MRS. HALE: His neck. Choked the life out of him.

(Her hand goes out and rests on the bird-cage.)

MRS. PETERS: *(with rising voice)* We don't know who killed him. We don't know.

MRS. HALE: *(her own feeling not interrupted)* If there'd been years and years of nothing, then a bird to sing to you, it would be awful—still, after the bird was still.

MRS. PETERS: *(something within her speaking)* I know what stillness is. When we homesteaded in Dakota, and my first baby died—after he was two years old, and me with no other then—

MRS. HALE: *(moving)* How soon do you suppose they'll be through, looking for the evidence?

MRS. PETERS: I know what stillness is. *(pulling herself back)*. The law has got to punish crime, Mrs. Hale.

MRS. HALE: *(not as if answering that)* I wish you'd seen Minnie Foster when she wore a white dress with blue ribbons and stood up there in the choir and sang. *(a look around the room)* Oh, I *wish* I'd come over here once in a while! That was a crime! That was a crime! Who's going to punish that?

MRS. PETERS: *(looking upstairs)* We mustn't—take on.

MRS. HALE: I might have known she needed help! I know how things can be—for women. I tell you, it's queer, Mrs. Peters. We live close together and we live far apart. We all go through the same things—it's all just a different kind of the same thing. *(brushes her eyes, noticing the bottle of fruit, reaches out for it)* If I was you, I wouldn't tell her her fruit was gone. Tell her it *ain't.* Tell her it's all right. Take this in to prove it to her. She—she may never know whether it was broke or not.

MRS. PETERS: *(takes the bottle, looks about for something to wrap it in; takes petticoat from the clothes brought from the other room, very nervously begins winding this around the bottle. In a false voice)* My, it's a good thing the men couldn't hear us. Wouldn't they just laugh! Getting all stirred up over a little thing like a—dead canary. As if that could have anything to do with—with—wouldn't they *laugh!*

(The men are heard coming down stairs.)

MRS. HALE: *(under her breath)* Maybe they would—maybe they wouldn't.

COUNTY ATTORNEY: No, Peters, it's all perfectly clear except a reason for doing it. But you know juries when it comes to women. If there was some definite thing. Something to show—something to make a story about—a thing that would connect up with this strange way of doing it—

(The women's eyes meet for an instant. Enter HALE from outer door.)

HALE: Well, I've got the team around. Pretty cold out there.

COUNTY ATTORNEY: I'm going to stay here a while by myself. *(to the SHERIFF)* You can send Frank out for me, can't you? I want to go over everything. I'm not satisfied that we can't do better.

SHERIFF: Do you want to see what Mrs. Peters is going to take in?

(The LAWYER *goes to the table, picks up the apron, laughs.)*

COUNTY ATTORNEY: Oh, I guess they're not very dangerous things the ladies have picked out. *(Moves a few things about, disturbing the quilt pieces which cover the box. Steps back)* No, Mrs. Peters doesn't need supervising. For that matter, a sheriff's wife is married to the law. Ever think of it that way, Mrs. Peters?

MRS. PETERS: Not—just that way.

SHERIFF: *(chuckling)* Married to the law. *(moves toward the other room)* I just want you to come in here a minute, George. We ought to take a look at these windows.

COUNTY ATTORNEY: *(scoffingly)* Oh, windows!

SHERIFF: We'll be right out, Mr. Hale.

*(*HALE *goes outside. The* SHERIFF *follows the* COUNTY ATTORNEY *into the other room. Then* MRS. HALE *rises, hands tight together, looking intensely at* MRS. PETERS, *whose eyes make a slow turn, finally meeting* MRS. HALE*'s. A moment* MRS. HALE *holds her, then her own eyes point the way to where the box is concealed. Suddenly* MRS. PETERS *throws back quilt pieces and tries to put the box in the bag she is wearing. It is too big. She opens box, starts to take bird out, cannot touch it, goes to pieces, stands there helpless. Sound of a knob turning in the other room.* MRS. HALE *snatches the box and puts it in the pocket of her big coat. Enter* COUNTY ATTORNEY *and* SHERIFF.*)*

COUNTY ATTORNEY: *(facetiously)* Well, Henry, at least we found out that she was not going to quilt it. She was going to—what is it you call it, ladies?

MRS. HALE: *(her hand against her pocket)* We call it—knot it, Mr. Henderson.

(CURTAIN)

Questions for Discussion

1. Consider the kitchen in which *Trifles* takes place. Why is it a fitting scene for the play?
2. What is the most important act that takes place on stage? What important acts have taken place before the play begins?
3. Describe the marriage between the Wrights. What lines first led you to this impression?
4. What does the Sheriff reveal about himself when he says, "Nothing here but kitchen things"? And "Well, can you beat the women! Held for murder and worryin' about her preserves"?
5. According to Mrs. Hale, "women are used to worrying over trifles." Does your response to this line change as the play unfolds?

6. Why do Mrs. Hale and Mrs. Peters conceal the dead canary? What motivates them to sympathize with Mrs. Wright?

7. How do you read the final line of this play? Does it have a meaning the men do not understand?

Suggestions for Writing

1. Compare and contrast Mrs. Hale and Mrs. Peters.

2. What does *Trifles* say about women and the way they are treated by men? Look not only at what the men say and do in this play but also at how the women act.

GLOSSARY

act In Kenneth Burke's **pentad,** the event, what the **agent** does, what happened; also, one of the main divisions of a drama

agency In Kenneth Burke's **pentad,** how the **act** was performed, the means by which the event happened

agent In Kenneth Burke's **pentad,** the one who performs the **act,** the actor; usually a person, but occasionally an inanimate or abstract entity

alliteration The repetition of initial consonant sounds

allusion A reference to something or someone outside of the work, usually a literary or historical character, place, or event

analogy An extended comparison of two similar but unrelated things using the familiar to explain the unfamiliar, the simple to explain the complex

analysis Dividing a whole into its parts

anaphora A word or phrase repeated for rhetorical effect at the beginning of consecutive sentences or clauses

assonance Repetition of vowel sounds, especially of initial vowels

brainstorming A technique for generating ideas by recording thoughts for a specific period of time

causal chain Interlinked causes and effects in which what happens causes something else to happen, which in turn becomes the cause generating another effect, and so on

cause and effect A rhetorical strategy in which a writer explains why something happened or what its results were; one of the classical topics for exploring an idea

ceremonial speech Speech to move an audience generally sympathetic to the speaker's position, usually to mark an occasion such as a funeral or political gathering

claim What you are trying to prove, the idea you are arguing

classical topics Ways of thinking about a subject so as to discover what to say about it; ways to explore an idea

classification Sorting things into categories based on some specific similarity

comparison and contrast Noting similarities and/or differences between ideas or objects; two of the classical topics for exploring an idea

context All of the circumstances in which an act of writing occurs—for example, such environmental stimuli as past events, current attitudes, and so on—which influence meaning and understanding

couplet A stanza containing two lines that usually rhyme

criterion A standard for judgment (plural is *criteria*)
    internal: a personal, nonverifiable standard for judgment
    external: a standard upon which a number of people would agree

data Random pieces of fact, opinion, and inference from which information is constructed; in argument, the evidence used to support a claim

deduction A kind of reasoning that begins with a generalization, includes a related specific fact, and leads to a conclusion that fits both

definition A rhetorical strategy in which the essential nature or the meaning of a thing is explained; one of the classical topics for exploring an idea

description A rhetorical strategy that focuses on a writer's sensory experience of a subject; one of the classical topics for exploring an idea

discovery draft A written exploration of a subject in an effort to develop a thesis

division A rhetorical strategy that examines a subject by breaking it into its parts

drafting Writing words on a page to express oneself, inform others, or persuade someone of something

dramatism Kenneth Burke's theory that features the dynamic interactions of the elements of a text; see also **pentad**

enthymeme A deductive argument in which the major premise is unstated; see also **deduction**

ethos The quality in the writing that impresses the reader with the authority and sense of the writer

example A rhetorical strategy that makes its point by the use of facts or anecdotes to illustrate an idea

explication An explanation of the function and meaning of everything in a particular literary work or part of a work

figurative language The use of words in an imaginative sense
    simile: a comparison, using *like* or *as,* of two dissimilar things
    metaphor: a comparison of two dissimilar things without using a connective such as *like* or *as*
    imagery: imaginative representation using evidence perceived through the senses

foot In poetry, a single unit of meter containing a particular arrangement of accented and unaccented syllables

freewriting A way of developing ideas by writing down thoughts on a particular subject as they occur

identification Kenneth Burke's term for the means by which people overcome differences that exist between them

imagery See **figurative language**

induction Reasoning to reach a conclusion based on the significance of a series of examples or other evidence

jargon Language used by insiders as a shortcut in discussions and usually not readily understood by others; technical slang

journalist's questions Questions answered in the lead of an effective newspaper story: who, what, when, where, why, and how

logical fallacies Errors in reasoning

logic, substantive A method of reasoning that uses claims, data, warrants, and qualifiers to come to a conclusion

logos The appeal of the thought and expression in the text to the rational abilities of the reader

mapping A graphical way to discover ideas for writing by distributing topics over a sheet of paper and linking them to show relationships

memoir An account of remembered events

metaphor See **figurative language**

motive A need or desire that occasions writing; a purpose, an intention, a rationale for writing

narration A rhetorical strategy recounting events, usually in a chronological sequence; telling a story

occasion The circumstances and conditions under which writing occurs including time, place, and attitudes

paraphrase Restating a passage in different words that convey the same meaning

pathos The writer's appeal to the reader's emotions, beliefs, attitudes, and values

pentad Kenneth Burke's analysis of the dramatic component of writing; see also **act, agency, agent, purpose, scene**

persona The social, literary, psychological, or cultural "mask" or personality that a writer constructs for himself or herself; also, a character in a novel, short story, or drama

premise The underlying value or belief that one assumes as a given truth at the beginning of an argument

process The steps necessary to accomplish something, as, for instance, the *writing process;* also, a rhetorical strategy for explaining how to do something

proposition The point to be demonstrated in an argument

purpose An element of the **pentad;** why the **agent** performed the **act**

qualifiers Terms such as *probably* or *unless* that protect an argument from unforeseen exceptions

quatrain A four-line stanza, rhymed or unrhymed

ratio In Kenneth Burke's **pentad,** the dynamic interaction of elements of a text—e.g., **act** and **scene, agent** and **scene**—which enriches the reader's understanding

refutation Evidence or proof that an argument is false or erroneous

review An evaluation of an unfamiliar text that offers both a sense of the text and a judgment on quality

revision Re-seeing and reworking a draft of one's writing, noting in particular matters of audience, purpose, completeness, coherence, and unity

rhetoric The study of principles leading toward the skillful and effective use of language; the analysis of the interaction among idea, text, and language

rhyme A correspondence in the final sounds of two (or more) words

scene An element of the **pentad;** *where* and *when* the **agent** performed the **act**

sonnet A poem containing fourteen lines each of which contains five units, called feet, and each foot consists of an unaccented syllable followed by an accented syllable; the lines are rhymed in three four-line segments and a couplet, or two four-line segments and a six-line sestet, and the rhyme scheme reflects the development of the thought

subject What the writing is about; the general area addressed

substantive logic See **logic, substantive**

summary A condensation of a work presenting only the major point or points

syllogism The main scheme of deductive argument in which a major premise and a minor premise combine to form a conclusion

symbol The use of one thing to represent something else which it resembles in some way

thesis The point to be made about the **topic**

topic The specific part of the **subject** to be developed

topoi A Greek word for the strategies useful for presenting convincing arguments; see also **classical topics**

valid Follows the conventions of logic, although not necessarily true (if, for instance, the reasoner has begun with a false assumption)

warrant An explanation, based on evidence (*backing*), that shows why a claim follows from the data

ACKNOWLEDGMENTS

Text Credits

EDWARD ABBEY, "Death Valley," from *The Journey Home* by Edward Abbey. Copyright © 1977 by Edward Abbey. Used by permission of Dutton Signet, a division of Penguin Books USA Inc.

HARRY AKST, GRANT CLARKE, "Am I Blue?" © 1929 Warner Bros. Inc. (Renewed). All rights reserved. Used by permission.

JOHN R. ALDEN, "Breakfast at the FDA Cafe." Reprinted with permission of *The Wall Street Journal*. Copyright © 1991 Dow Jones & Company, Inc. All rights reserved.

JULIA ALVAREZ, "Hold the Mayonnaise" from *New York Times Magazine,* January 12, 1992. Copyright © 1992 by Julia Alvarez.

MAYA ANGELOU, "Finishing School" from *I Know Why the Caged Bird Sings* by Maya Angelou. Copyright © 1969 by Maya Angelou. Reprinted by permission of Random House, Inc.

LOUIS BARBASH, "Clean Up or Pay Up," from *The Washington Monthly,* July/August 1990. Reprinted with permission from *The Washington Monthly.* Copyright by The Washington Monthly Company, 1611 Connecticut Avenue, NW, Washington, D.C. 20009. (202) 462-0128.

STEVEN BARBOZA, "My Conversion," from *New York Times Magazine,* April 24, 1994. Copyright © 1994 by The New York Times Company. Reprinted by permission.

SAM BINGHAM, "A Share of the River." Reprinted from *Wigwag,* October 1990 by permission.

SISSELA BOK, "Gossip," from *Secrets: On the Ethics of Concealment and Revelation* by Sissela Bok. Copyright © 1982 by Sissela Bok. Reprinted by permission of Pantheon Books, a division of Random House, Inc.

CONSUMERS UNION, "Automobile Tires." Copyright 1993 by Consumers Union of U.S., Inc., Yonkers, NY 10703-1057. Reprinted by permission from *Consumer Reports,* February 1993.

ALAN DERSHOWITZ, "Shouting 'Fire!'," from *The Atlantic Monthly,* January 1989. Reprinted by permission of the author.

RALPH DE TOLEDANO, "The Greatness of Billie," from *National Review,* December 9, 1983. Copyright © 1983 by National Review, Inc., 150 East 53rd Street, New York, NY 10016. Reprinted by permission.

JOAN DIDION, "On Keeping a Notebook" from *Slouching Towards Bethlehem* by Joan Didion. Copyright © 1966, 1968 by Joan Didion. Reprinted by permission of Farrar, Straus & Giroux, Inc.

ANNIE DILLARD, "The Death of a Moth." Reprinted by permission of the author and Blanche C. Gregory, Inc. Copyright © 1976 by Annie Dillard.

MICHAEL DORRIS, "The Contest." Copyright © 1993 by Michael Dorris. Originally appeared in *The Ladies' Home Journal,* May 1993. Reprinted by permission of the author.

DAVID JAMES DUNCAN, "A Mickey Mantle Koan." Copyright © 1992 by *Harper's Magazine.* All rights reserved. Reproduced from the September issue by special permission.

JOSEPH EPSTEIN, "Your Basic Language Snob." Reprinted from *The American Scholar,* Volume 53, Number 3, Summer 1984, by permission of the publisher. Copyright © 1984 by Joseph Epstein.

JAMES FALLOWS, "Land of Plenty," from *The Atlantic,* June 1990. Reprinted by permission of the publisher.

JAMES S. GORDON, "To Watch Over Us," in *New York Times Book Review,* May 1, 1994. Copyright © 1994 by The New York Times Company. Reprinted by permission.

STEPHEN JAY GOULD, "Woman's Brains," from *The Panda's Thumb: More Reflections in Natural History* by Stephen Jay Gould with the permission of W. W. Norton & Company, Inc. Copyright © 1980 by Stephen Jay Gould.

DAVID GROFF, "Taking the Test," from *Wigwag,* June 1990. Reprinted by permission.

JOHN GROSS, "Hollywood and the Holocaust." Reprinted with permission from *The New York Review of Books.* Copyright © 1994 Nyrev, Inc.

DANIEL HARRIS, "Cuteness," from *Harper's Magazine,* July 1993. Reprinted by permission of the author.

VICKI HEARNE, "What's Wrong with Animal Rights?" Copyright © 1991 by *Harper's Magazine.* All rights reserved. Reproduced from the September issue by special permission.

ANN HODGMAN, "No Wonder They Call Me a Bitch." Reprinted with permission from *Spy Magazine.* Copyright © 1993 *Spy Magazine.*

GARRETT KAORU HONGO, "Off From Swing Shift," reprinted from *Yellow Light.* Copyright © 1982 by Garrett Kaoru Hongo, Wesleyan University Press. By permission of University Press of New England.

ADA LOUISE HUXTABLE, "Washington's Stillborn Behemoth," from *Architecture Anyone* by Ada Louise Huxtable. Copyright © 1986 by Ada Louise Huxtable. Reprinted by permission of Random House, Inc.

CARYN JAMES, "Audrey Hepburn," from *The New York Times,* January 21, 1993. Copyright © 1993 by The New York Times Company. Reprinted by permission.

MARTIN LUTHER KING, JR. "I Have a Dream," and "Letter from Birmingham Jail," reprinted by arrangement with The Heirs to the Estate of Martin Luther King, Jr., c/o Joan Daves Agency as agent for the proprietor. Copyright 1963 by Martin Luther King, Jr., copyright renewed 1991 by Coretta Scott King.

HENRY KISSINGER, "Courage in the Face of Wrenching Domestic Controversy," from *The New York Times,* April 28, 1994. Copyright © 1994 by The New York Times Company. Reprinted by permission.

RUSH H. LIMBAUGH, "The Environmental Mindset," from *The Way Things Ought to Be,* by Rush Limbaugh. Copyright © 1992 by Rush Limbaugh. Reprinted by permission of Pocket Books, a division of Simon & Schuster, Inc.

AUDRE LORDE, "Power" is reprinted from *The Black Unicorn,* Poems by Audre Lorde, by permission of W.W. Norton & Company, Inc. Copyright © 1978 by Audre Lorde.

BARBARA MELLIX, "From Outside, In" originally appeared in *The Georgia Review,* Volume XLI, No. 2 (Summer 1987), © 1987 by The University of Georgia, © 1987 by Barbara Mellix. Reprinted by permission of Barbara Mellix and *The Georgia Review.*

LESLIE ADRIENNE MILLER, "The Driving Range," reprinted from *Ungodliness* by permission of Carnegie Mellon University Press. © 1994 by Leslie Adrienne Miller.

TOSHIO MORI, "Abalone, Abalone, Abalone" from *The Chauvinist and Other Stories.* Reprinted by permission of the Estate of Toshio Mori and Asian American Studies Center, UCLA.

GLORIA NAYLOR, "Mommy, What Does 'Nigger' Mean?" from *The New York Times Magazine.* Copyright © 1986 by Gloria Naylor. Reprinted by permission of Sterling Lord Literistic, Inc.

ITABARI NJERI, "Life with Father," from *Harper's Magazine,* January 1990. Copyright © 1990 by Itabari Njeri. Reprinted by permission of Mirium Altshuler Literary Agency as agent for Itabari Njeri.

GEOFFREY NORMAN, "Gators," from *Esquire Magazine,* October, 1980.

JOYCE CAROL OATES, "Shopping," *Ms. Magazine,* March 1987. Reprinted by permission of *Ms. Magazine.* Copyright © 1987.

GEORGE ORWELL, "Marrakech" from *Such, Such Were the Joys* by George Orwell. Copyright 1953 by Sonia Brownell Orwell. Reprinted by permission of Harcourt Brace & Company.

LON OTTO, "Winners," from *Cover Me* by Lon Otto, Coffee House Press, 1988. Reprinted by permission of the publisher. Copyright © 1988 by Lon Otto.

CYNTHIA OZICK, "The Seam of the Snail," from *Ms. Magazine,* January, 1985. Reprinted by permission of *Ms. Magazine,* © 1985.

ALBERTO RIOS, "Nanti," from *Whispering to Fool the Wind,* The Sheep Meadow Press, 1982. Reprinted by permission of the author.

JUDITH ROGALA, "Desperately Seeking a Dishwasher," from *Hysteria Magazine,* Issue 5, Spring 1994. Reprinted by permission of *Hysteria Magazine: Women, Humor and Social Change,* Bridgeport, CT.

TIM ROGERS, "Tough Break." This article originally appeared in *American Way* magazine, where Tim Rogers is an assistant editor. He also writes a column for *The Met, Dallas Arts,* and *Entertainment Weekly.*

ANDREW A. ROONEY, "Old Friends." Reprinted with the permission of Atheneum Publishers, an imprint of Macmillan Publishing Company from *And More by Andy Rooney* by Andrew A. Rooney. Copyright © 1986 by Essay Productions, Inc.

PHYLLIS ROSE, "Tools of Torture," *The Atlantic,* 1986.

MIKE ROYKO, "Farewell to Fitness," *Chicago Tribune,* 1980. Reprinted by permission of Tribune Media Service.

WITOLD RYBCZYNSKI, "Waiting for the Weekend," from *The Atlantic Monthly,* August 1991. Copyright © 1991 by Witold Rybczynski.

SCOTT RUSSELL SANDERS, "Grub," from *Wigwag,* June, 1990. Reprinted by permission.

MARILYN SCHIEL, "Levi's." Copyright © 1991 by Marilyn Schiel.

DAVID SEDARIS, "Santa's Little Helper," in *Harper's Magazine.* Copyright © 1993 by *Harper's Magazine.* All rights reserved. Reprinted from the December 1993 issue by special permission.

JOHN SEDGWICK, "The Doberman Case," from *Wigwag,* June 1990. Reprinted by permission.

RICHARD SELZER, "How to Build a Slaughterhouse," from *Taking the World In for Repairs* by Richard Selzer. Copyright © 1986 by Richard Selzer. Reprinted by permission of Georges Borchardt, Inc. for the author.

LESLIE MARMON SILKO, "Lullaby." Copyright © 1981 by Leslie Marmon Silko. Reprinted from *Storyteller* by Leslie Marmon Silko, published by Seaver Books, New York, New York.

RAYMOND SOKOLOV, "The Dark Side of Tomatoes." Reprinted with permission from *Natural History,* July, 1989. Copyright the American Museum of Natural History, 1989.

GARY SOTO, "Black Hair." Reprinted from *Black Hair* by Gary Soto. © 1985 by Gary Soto.

CLAIRE STERLING, "Redfellas," adapted from Chapter 5 of *Thieves World* by Claire Sterling, as published in *The New Republic,* 4/11/94. Copyright © 1994 by Claire H. Sterling Associates, Ltd. Reprinted by permission of Simon & Schuster, Inc.

CATHARINE R. STIMPSON, "Coming-of-Age" from *Change,* July/August, 1993. Reprinted with permission of The Helen Dwight Read Educational Foundation. Published by Heldref Publications, 1319 18th Street, N.W., Washington, D.C. 20036-1802. Copyright 1993.

ANDREW SULLIVAN, "Here Comes the Groom," from *The New Republic,* August 28, 1989. Reprinted by permission of *The New Republic.* Copyright © 1989, The New Republic, Inc.

HAUNANI-KAY TRASK, "Tourist Stay Home," from *The Progressive,* July 1993. Reprinted by permission from *The Progressive,* 409 East Main Street, Madison, WI 53703.

ALICE WALKER, "Am I Blue?" from *Living by the Word: Selected Writings 1973–1987.* Copyright © 1986 by Alice Walker, reprinted by permission of Harcourt Brace & Company.

RANDALL WILLIAMS, "Daddy Tucked the Blanket," from *The New York Times,* July 10, 1975. Copyright © 1975 by The New York Times Company. Reprinted by permission.

Photography Credits

The Bettman Archive: pp. 238, 241, 247
The Granger Collection, New York: p. 250
Library of Congress: pp. 314, 315

INDEX TO THE READINGS
BY RHETORICAL STRATEGY (MODE)

INDEX OF AUTHORS AND TITLES